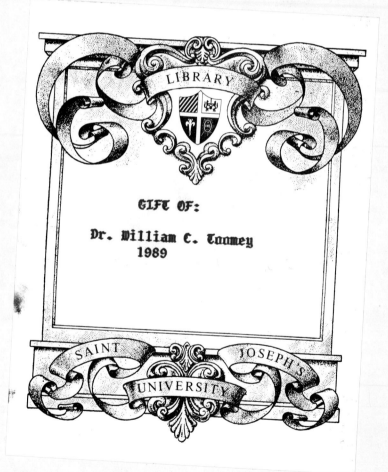

PERSPECTIVES ON
CRIME VICTIMS

Edited by

BURT GALAWAY

School of Social Development,
University of Minnesota, Duluth, Minnesota

JOE HUDSON

Office of the Auditor General of Canada,
Ottawa, Ontario, Canada

The C. V. Mosby Company

ST. LOUIS • TORONTO • LONDON   1981

The C. V. Mosby Company
11830 Westline Industrial Drive, St. Louis, Missouri 63141

Library of Congress Cataloging in Publication Data

Main entry under title:

Perspectives on crime victims.

    Includes bibliographies and index.
    1. Victims of crimes—United States—Addresses,
essays, lectures.   2. Victims of crimes—Addresses,
essays, lectures.   I. Galaway, Burt.   II. Hudson, Joe.
HV6250.3.U5P47   362.8'8'0973   80-19922
ISBN 0-8016-1733-2

GW/M/M 9 8 7 6 5 4 3 2 1   05/C/610

CONTRIBUTORS

LESTER ADELSON

Pathologist and Chief Deputy Coroner, Cuyahoga County Coroner's Office; Professor of Forensic Pathology, School of Medicine, Case Western Reserve University, Cleveland, Ohio

RANDY E. BARNETT

Assistant State's Attorney, State's Attorney's Office of Cook County, Chicago, Illinois

JOHN BENYI

Research Associate, Center for Social Analysis, State University of New York, Binghamton, New York

WARREN T. BROOKES

Economics columnist, *Boston Herald American*, Boston, Massachusetts

JAMES BROOKS

Associate Professor, New Mexico State University, Las Cruces, New Mexico

FRANK CARRINGTON

Executive Director, Americans for Effective Law Enforcement, Evanston, Illinois

STEVE CHESNEY

Research Analyst, Minnesota Department of Corrections, St. Paul, Minnesota

NILS CHRISTIE

Professor, Institute of Criminology and Criminal Law, University of Oslo, Oslo, Norway

DANIEL S. CLASTER

Associate Professor of Sociology, Brooklyn College, City University of New York, New York, New York

BERNARD COHEN

Associate Professor, Department of Sociology, Queens College, City University of New York, New York, New York

LYNN A. CURTIS

Director, Urban Initiatives Anti-Crime Program, U.S. Department of Housing and Urban Development, Washington, D.C.

DEBORAH S. DAVID

Assistant Professor, Montclair State College, Montclair, New Jersey

ROMINE R. DEMING

Associate Professor, College of Criminal Justice, Northeastern University, Boston, Massachusetts

JOHN P. J. DUSSICH

Executive Director, National Organization of Victim Assistance, Hattiesburg, Mississippi

AMASA B. FORD

Professor of Community Health and Family Medicine and Associate Professor of Medicine, School of Medicine, Case Western Reserve University, Cleveland, Ohio

ALICE P. FRANKLIN

Director of Research, Ohio Youth Commission, Columbus, Ohio

CLYDE W. FRANKLIN, II

Associate Professor of Sociology, Ohio State University, Columbus, Ohio

JANET FROHMAN

Public Safety and Criminal Justice Program, National League of Cities, Washington, D.C.

BURT GALAWAY

Assistant Professor, School of Social Development, University of Minnesota, Duluth, Minnesota

JAMES GAROFALO

Director, Research Center East, National Council on Crime and Delinquency, Hackensack, New Jersey

GILBERT GEIS

Professor, Program in Social Ecology, University of California, Irvine, California

CHARLES M. GRAY

Assistant Professor of Economics, College of St. Thomas, St. Paul, Minnesota

DONALD J. HALL

Professor of Law, Vanderbilt Law School, Vanderbilt University, Nashville, Tennessee

LEWIS F. HANES

Deputy Program Director, Westinghouse National Issues Center, Arlington, Virginia

ALAN T. HARLAND

Director, National Evaluation of Adult Restitution Programs, Criminal Justice Research Center, Albany, New York

ANNE M. HEINZ

Project Manager, Center for Urban Affairs, Northwestern University, Evanston, Illinois

CHARLES S. HIRSCH

Director of Forensic Pathology, Hamilton County Institute of Forensic Medicine, Toxicology, and Criminalistics; Clinical Professor of Pathology (Forensic), College of Medicine, University of Cincinnati, Cincinnati, Ohio

JOE HUDSON

Principal, Effectiveness Evaluations, Office of the Auditor General of Canada, Ottawa, Ontario, Canada

WAYNE A. KERSTETTER

Associate Professor, Department of Criminal Justice, University of Illinois at Chicago Circle, Chicago, Illinois

MARY S. KNUDTEN

Vice President, Evaluation/Policy Research Associates, Ltd., Milwaukee, Wisconsin

RICHARD D. KNUDTEN

Professor of Sociology, Marquette University, Milwaukee, Wisconsin

IMRE R. KOHN

Deputy Program Manager, Westinghouse National Issues Center, Arlington, Virginia

LeROY L. LAMBORN

Professor of Law, Wayne State University, Detroit, Michigan

DAVID A. LOWENBERG

Coordinator, Pima County Attorney's Victim Witness Program, Tucson, Arizona

MARC F. MADEN

Research Director, Pihas Schmidt, Westerdahl Company, Portland, Oregon

DEL MARTIN

Author and lecturer, San Francisco, California

JOHN W. McKAY

Deputy Director, Public Safety and Criminal Justice Program, National League of Cities, Washington, D.C.

DOROTHY (EDMONDS) McKNIGHT

Formerly Social Research Worker, Victim-Offender Reconciliation Project, Kitchener, Ontario, Canada

PETER B. MEYER

Associate Professor, College of Human Development, Programs in Administration of Justice and Community Development, Pennsylvania State University, University Park, Pennsylvania

SHIRLEY OBERG

Women's Advocate, Women's Coalition, Inc., Duluth, Minnesota

LYNN OLSON

Assistant Director, Public Safety and Criminal Justice Program, National League of Cities, Washington, D.C.

JOHN W. PALMER

Professor of Law, Capital University Law School, Columbus, Ohio

ELLEN PENCE

Director, Minnesota Battered Women's Program, Minnesota Department of Corrections, St. Paul, Minnesota

EDWARD J. PESCE

Consultant, Legal Management and Systems, Bowie, Maryland

JAYNE THOMAS RICH

Chief of Police and Director of Security and Safety, Montclair State College, Montclair, New Jersey

NANCY M. RUSHFORTH

Research Assistant, Case Western Reserve University, Cleveland, Ohio

NORMAN B. RUSHFORTH

Professor and Chairman, Department of Biology, and Associate Professor of Biometry, Case Western Reserve University, Cleveland, Ohio

†STEPHEN SCHAFER

Professor, College of Criminal Justice, Northeastern University, Boston, Massachusetts

ANNE LARASON SCHNEIDER

Research Scientist, Institute of Policy Analysis, Eugene, Oregon

CAROLE S. SCHNEIDER

Project Director, Crime Victim Centers, Correctional Service of Minnesota, Minneapolis, Minnesota

PETER R. SCHNEIDER

Research Scientist, Institute of Policy Analysis, Eugene, Oregon

WESLEY G. SKOGAN

Associate Professor of Political Science and Urban Affairs, Northwestern University, Evanston, Illinois

SUZANNE K. STEINMETZ

Associate Professor, Individual and Family Studies, University of Delaware, Newark, Delaware

JOHN ALAN STOOKEY

Assistant Professor of Political Science, Arizona State University, Tempe, Arizona

PAULA CHIN WEGENER

Staff Associate, Public Safety and Criminal Justice Program, National League of Cities, Washington, D.C.

LISA WELKE

Intern, Public Safety and Criminal Justice Program, National League of Cities, Washington, D.C.

MARVIN E. WOLFGANG

Professor of Sociology and Law, University of Pennsylvania, Philadelphia, Pennsylvania

---

†Deceased.

DAVID F. WRENCH

Professor of Psychology, Portland State University, Portland, Oregon

EDUARD A. ZIEGENHAGEN

Professor of Political Science and Senior Fellow, Center for Social Analysis, State University of New York, Binghamton, New York

PREFACE

During the past 10 years the field of victimology has expanded rapidly. A substantial number of publications—both books and articles—have appeared, and a variety of exciting victim service programs have been established in many areas of the United States. The published work has tended to be specialized and fragmented, and it appears in a wide range of journals. A single source from which a reader might receive an overview of the issues and questions challenging the emerging field of victimology has not been available.

This book attempts to provide that source. Articles have been selected from journals and books representing many different disciplines and have been organized to provide an overview of the field of victimology. Where published works were not readily available, original papers have been developed. This book is intended as an introduction to the field; the extensive bibliographies accompanying many of the articles, as well as the annotated selected readings at the end of each chapter, will provide a guide to persons wishing to delve deeper into some of the questions and issues considered.

This book represents the ideas of a great number of people; however, as the editors, we are solely responsible for the structure and organization of the material. We are grateful to the authors and publishers who permitted their works to be reprinted in this volume. To those who spent many hours preparing original articles we extend a special acknowledgment. Special thanks are due to the office staff at the School of Social Development, University of Minnesota, Duluth, for assisting with typing and preparation of the manuscript.

Burt Galaway
Joe Hudson

CONTENTS

INTRODUCTION

After centuries of neglect, the crime victim is being rediscovered. With rediscovery, crime victims have become the object of attention for public policy makers, social service providers, and scholar-researchers. Over the past few years, the policy makers, service providers, and academics interested in crime victims have been forging the skeleton of a new discipline—victimology, or the study of the crime victim. This book will present a series of perspectives on crime victims to introduce the study of victimology and to conceptualize issues emerging from the current focus on the crime victim.

Victimology is a very new field, with most of the published materials occurring since 1970. Two of the earliest pioneers, however, were Beniamin Mendelsohn and Hans von Hentig. Mendelsohn's published work dates to 1937; his studies focused on similarities of personality of victims and offenders and the resistance of rape victims.[1,2] Von Hentig's classic, *The Criminal and His Victim,* was published in 1948; in the final chapter, von Hentig suggests that some victims may be more susceptible to victimization than others because of demographic characteristics and that the personality characteristics of other victims may contribute to their own victimization.[3] In 1954, Henri Ellenberger, a psychiatrist, developed some of these ideas further and suggested that there may be psychological bonds between the victim and the offender, with certain types of victims needing and bringing about their own victimization.[4]

In the 1950s, Marvin Wolfgang's classic study found that in about one fifth of the homicides in the Philadelphia area the victim may have precipitated his or her own victimization.[5] Wolfgang's work offered some justification for the earlier theories advanced by Mendelsohn,

von Hentig, and Ellenberger, and also established a methodology for study of crime victim precipitation that has persisted through a series of subsequent studies. In the 1960s, several nations and states, primarily in the English-speaking world, moved to establish publicly financed programs to provide victims with financial compensation for medical costs and loss of wages because of injuries sustained as a result of violent crime. These early developments provided a groundwork for the recent proliferation of interest in the crime victim.

In the 1970s, victimology began taking on some of the formal trappings of a field of study. Scholars, policy makers, and service providers have gathered for three international victimology symposia. The papers presented at the symposia in Jerusalem (1973),[6] Boston (1976),[7] and Munster, West Germany (1979), have provided a useful exchange of materials. In addition, the Scientific Affairs Committee of the North Atlantic Treaty Organization sponsored an international study institute on victimology in Bellagio, Italy, in 1975.[8] In 1976 *Victimology: An International Journal* was first issued; it provides an international vehicle for the exchange of ideas and research. Additionally, persons in the United States involved in providing services to crime victims have banded together in the National Organization of Victim Assistance (NOVA) to advocate victim services.

Presently there is no commonly accepted framework for organizing the field of victimology. The organizational framework adopted for this volume involves four subsets of issues. An initial examination is made of the elements of the field, including the development of victimology, the cost of crime to victims, and the use of victimization surveys. The concepts of victim culpability and victim vulnerability are analyzed in a second section. The emerging interest in victims and victimology has many potential implications for the criminal justice system, which are analyzed in a third section. The fourth section presents materials regarding evolving services for crime victims.

VICTIMOLOGY AS AN EVOLVING DISCIPLINE

Several differences of view exist regarding the focus and place of the discipline. One debate centers on whether victimology should be viewed as an independent area of inquiry or as a subfield of criminology. Criminology has traditionally focused on a study of the causes of crime and the functioning of the institutions and organizations that have been created to deal with crime. The study of the crime victim might complement these two traditional foci in criminology and might logically be conceived as a subfield of the broader discipline. On the other hand, a more independent focus would permit a broader range of inquiry and more explicit emphasis on the crime victim and would reduce the likelihood that a victim focus might be eclipsed by the more established interests in criminology.

A second issue regards the breadth of crime victim–related issues to be subsumed within the field of victimology. The earliest work in the field focused on the interaction of offenders and victims with a heavy emphasis on examining conditions under which victims may have contributed to their own victimization. Understanding of this phenomenon is presently very incomplete; some scholars advocate that the discipline should limit itself to the study of victim-offender interaction and are concerned that studies in other areas will detract from this important emphasis. Others argue that the needs of crime victims, the functioning of the organizations and institutions that are developing to respond to these needs, and the emerging roles and responsibilities for crime victims within the criminal justice system are appropriate and important areas of inquiry for victimology.

A third issue is the breadth of the definition of the term *victim*. One approach is to limit the

victim concept to victims of traditional crimes (such as murder, rape, robbery, assault, and burglary). Suggestions have also been advanced, however, to include broader definitions of the concept by including prisoners,[9,10] communities (see Chapter 1, Part C), immigrants,[11] subjects of medical experimentation,[12] persons charged with crimes but not found guilty,[13] and entire cultural groups as victims of crimes.

This volume does not deal with the issue of victimology as a separate field of criminology; at these early stages in the development of the discipline little can be gained by devoting energy and space to this debate. There are, of course, clear links between victims, criminals, and the criminal justice system; in Section Three we examine some potential implications of a victim focus in the criminal justice system. We conceptualize the discipline of victimology as broader than a focus on victim-offender interaction, although this is a very important issue. Issues regarding the needs of crime victims, services for crime victims, and crime victim roles within the criminal justice system are analyzed. Finally, to a very large extent, we are maintaining a focus on victims of traditional crimes, although we do examine situations in which behaviors (such as assault) occur in contexts such as public schools, families, and correctional institutions—contexts in which such behaviors are not typically defined as crime.

Crime victims directly bear much of the cost of victimization; additional costs are borne by the taxpayers to maintain a network of criminal justice organizations and an emerging variety of crime victim service programs. Usable methodologies to estimate the cost of victimization are not presently available. To a large extent this is because there is not presently a generally accepted conceptual framework defining the categories of victimization costs. Direct pecuniary loss to the victim (such as loss of property, damage to property, medical costs, loss of wages, and reduced earning capacity because of permanent injury) are clearly costs of victimization. But what about intangible losses, such as emotional distress, pain, suffering, and fear? Should the isolation and stress of a crime victim (or even a potential victim), often an aged person, who is afraid to go out at night because of fear of victimization be considered a cost of crime? Or, more clearly, should the cost that a burglary victim experiences in moving from a neighborhood to escape the trauma of the burglary be considered a cost of victimization? An examination of victims' experiences with the criminal justice system indicates that the victim incurs additional pecuniary and intangible costs in fulfilling civic responsibilities to cooperate with the police, prosecutors, and courts. Crime victims are expected to absorb loss of wages, child care costs, and transportation costs for meeting with police and prosecutors and required court appearances. These experiences may create additional fear and stress from both the approach and attitude of the officials as well as the reliving of an upsetting event in frequently unsupportive and threatening environments. And if victims become dissatisfied with the operation of the criminal justice system and reduce their level of cooperation, will this increase the costs of law enforcement and dealing with offenders? Present efforts to assess the cost of victimization are largely limited to very rough estimates of the victim's pecuniary losses, but even these estimates are, at best, incomplete and very sketchy. Any systematic effort to assess the cost of victimization must await further conceptual work regarding categories of victimization costs.

Estimating the actual extent of victimization is also most difficult. Police data have limited usefulness because these statistics include only victimizations reported to the police and do not include information regarding victimizations for which victims choose not to make a police report; a very large number of victimizations that could be considered crimes are not reported.[15] A series of national victimization studies has been undertaken in order to attempt to provide more complete information regarding crime victimization.

The first national victimization survey was done in 1966 under the direction of Philip Ennis of the University of Chicago's National Opinion Research Center.[16] In 1973, the U.S. Law Enforcement Assistance Administration (LEAA) and the U.S. Bureau of the Census began a continuing series of victimization surveys. The LEAA surveys include national samples, as well as 26 city samples, of both households and commercial establishments. An ongoing deluge of reports is available from the surveys, including annual reports estimating the extent of victimization for selected crimes and presenting year-by-year changes, city reports, and specialized reports on topics such as public attitudes about crime and costs of victimization.[17]

The victimization surveys involve drawing a random sample of households and commercial establishments (separate national samples and city samples are drawn) and conducting interviews to determine if residents of the household or the business had been victimized during the time under study. The methodology used to conduct the surveys has been subject to sharp criticism[18]; the results of this continuing research, however, are presently the best source of data regarding crime victimization in the United States.

As an embryonic field, victimology is struggling with defining the areas of its interest and clarifying its relationships with other fields, especially criminology. Two clear areas of interest are measuring the extent of victimization and the costs of victimization. Inclusive estimates of the costs of victimization are presently not obtainable and must be preceded by further conceptual work regarding the categories of costs. Data are available for victimization surveys to permit rough estimates of the extent of victimization for specified crimes and, despite methodologic concerns, these data present the most useful material currently available.

VICTIM-OFFENDER SYSTEMS

The study of victim-offender relationships has been one of the central foci of victimology and was the initial focus for the early pioneers in the discipline. There are two fairly distinct aspects to a study of victim-offender systems—the study of victim vulnerability and the study of victim culpability. Von Hentig's early work identified both classes of victims who might be particularly vulnerable or susceptible to victimization as well as those who might be culpable in the sense that they partially precipitated their own victimization.

Victim vulnerability

Vulnerability refers to the susceptibility of certain groups of people to victimization, through no fault of their own, based on demographic or other characteristics. Are aged persons, for example, more susceptible to victimization than younger people? Are persons who live in certain neighborhoods more susceptible to victimization than those who live in other neighborhoods? Are women more susceptible than men? Are persons in some occupational groups more susceptible to victimization than persons in other occupational groups? Are persons who choose certain life styles, especially nontraditional life styles, more susceptible to victimization than persons who choose more traditional patterns of living? When studying victim vulnerability, the investigator makes an examination of the distribution of victimization in socioeconomic and demographic structures to determine if victimization is experienced more heavily by some groups of people than by others.

One aspect of vulnerability of particular interest is the study of intraracial crime contrasted with interracial crime. To what extent do victims and offenders tend to be of the same or different races? The present available evidence suggests that most victimizations are intraracial. To a very large extent, blacks tend to be victimized by black offenders and whites tend to be victimized by white offenders.[19-21]

The analysis of vulnerability serves at least two useful functions. First, identification of population groups that may be particularly susceptible to victimization may assist in directing crime prevention efforts to the most vulnerable groups. Second, such an analysis may help dispel common myths and enable a more precise focus on the nature of the crime victimization problem. For example, evidence that most assaultive crimes are intraracial should help dispel the stereotype of black offenders victimizing white victims and permit a more realistic assessment of the problems of violent crime. Furthermore, the available evidence

suggests that aged persons are actually victimized with less frequency than younger population groups, but the aged, as a group, are more fearful of crime than are other population groups.[22] The problem for the aged may be more one of fear of crime rather than actual victimization, suggesting that attention needs to be directed toward aged persons' fear.

Victim culpability

Culpability refers to actions on the part of the victim that may either invite or precipitate victimization. Under some circumstances victims may be partially responsible for their own victimization. Is the motorist who leaves keys in the ignition of an automobile partially responsible if the vehicle is stolen? Is the shopkeeper who cashes checks for strangers without proper identification partially responsible if checks are no good? Is the person who is assaulted after making derogatory comments or gestures toward another person partly responsible for the victimization? Is the husband who has chronically battered his wife only to be shot and killed by her after an attempted assault partially responsible for his own victimization? Studying victim culpability involves efforts to measure the extent to which culpability may occur for selected types of victimizations.

One of the classic studies of victim precipitation was done by Marvin Wolfgang, who used police records to make a study of homicide victims in the city of Philadelphia. Wolfgang used the following definition of victim precipitation:

The term victim-precipitated is applied to those criminal homicides in which the victim is a direct, positive precipitator in the crime. The role of the victim is characterized by his having been the first in the homicide drama to use physical force directed against his subsequent slayer. The victim-precipitated cases are those in which the victim was the first to show and use a deadly weapon, to strike a blow in an altercation—in short, the first to commence the interplay or resort to physical violence.[5]

Wolfgang then reviewed police records to determine whether victim precipitation consistent with the above definition occurred. He found that in about 20% of the homicides, victim precipitation occurred.[5] Subsequent to Wolfgang's work, several other studies have been conducted, focusing on the crimes of homicide, assault, rape, and robbery. Presently available research regarding victim precipitation has been almost totally dependent on the methodology used by Wolfgang—development of a definition and review of official records to determine if victim precipitation consistent with the definition occurred.

The concept of victim culpability in either its careless or precipitative aspects raises perplexing problems. Although there is evidence that some victims may be partially responsible for their victimization, there is also danger of fueling a widespread phenomenon of blaming the victim. Kahlil Gibran expresses this problem poetically:

One nightfall a man travelling on horseback toward the sea reached an inn by the roadside. He dismounted, and confident in man and night like all riders toward the sea, he tied his horse to a tree beside the door and entered into the inn.
At midnight when all were asleep, a thief came and stole the traveller's horse.
In the morning the man awoke, and discovered that his horse was stolen. And he grieved for his horse. . . .
Then his fellow-lodgers came and stood around him and began to talk.
And the first man said, "How foolish of you to tie your horse outside the stable."
And the second said, "Still more foolish, without even hobbling the horse!"
And the third man said, "It is stupid at best to travel to sea on horseback."
And the fourth said, "Only the indolent and the slow of foot own horses."
Then the traveller was much astonished. At last he cried, "My friends, because my horse is stolen, you have hastened one and all to tell me my faults and my shortcomings. But strange, not one word of reproach have you uttered about the man who stole my horse."[23]

Blaming the rape victim has been a common phenomenon. Recent crisis work with crime victims has indicated that many victims tend to blame themselves (many of the victims' close friends also tend to blame the victim) rather than the perpetrator for their victimization.[24] The dilemma facing the field of victimology is to be able to continue engaging in both conceptual

and empirical work regarding victim culpability but to discover ways to be sure this work is being appropriately used and to avoid widespread victim blaming.

The concept of victim culpability also illustrates the importance of clearly distinguishing between the presence of a phenomenon and its use in decision making. Establishing the presence of victim culpability does not clearly indicate how this knowledge should be used. Should knowledge of victim culpability, for example, have any bearing on determining an offender's innocence or guilt? Or should knowledge of victim culpability be considered in determining what sentence to give to a convicted offender? Should victim culpability be considered at all in determining a victim's eligibility for services or compensation? These are all public policy questions whose resolution will determine how knowledge about victim culpability will be used. But the presence of the knowledge does not *ipso facto* indicate how the policy question should be resolved.

Intrafamily crime

The concepts of victim culpability and victim vulnerability come into sharp focus in relation to crime within the family. The intense interpersonal relationships within a family may lead to an escalating pattern of conflict resulting in a victimization in which both offender and victim may have contributed to the dispute; in some families, individual family members may be particularly vulnerable to victimization.

There are several aspects of intrafamily crime, two of which are becoming fairly well developed. There is considerable literature regarding parental assaults on children (child abuse and sexual assaults including incest) but only recently has this been analyzed in the framework of crime and victimization; most typically child abuse has been considered as a social welfare rather than a criminal justice problem. Largely through the efforts of the women's movement, the problem of wife battering is being documented, called to public attention, and becoming the subject of both scholarly pursuit and human service programming. Less well understood, however, are other types of intrafamily crime, including husband battering, sibling abuse (crimes committed by one sibling against a brother or sister), granny battering (the abuse of older people by their adult children), and crimes committed against parents by their children (especially adolescent children).

Dealing with intrafamily crime presents a number of policy dilemmas. One of the most basic is the appropriate social institution to respond to these problems. Traditionally problems of intrafamily crime, especially child abuse, have been handled as social welfare problems with limited resources going to prosecution and the criminal justice system. In regard to wife battering, however, many of the advocates for battered women are strongly supporting criminal justice prosecution for batterers. To what extent should intrafamily crime be handled as a criminal justice matter, and, conversely, to what extent should these problems be diverted to other types of human service agencies?

Another issue of critical importance is the basis for intervening, especially in regard to child abuse. When is striking a child reasonable discipline and when does it become assault? In 1979, Sweden enacted legislation to make any striking of a child by the parent a crime; to many this may seem to be an extreme policy and an inappropriate intrusion by the state into family life, but it illustrates the important policy problem of defining the nature of intrafamily crime.

IMPLICATIONS FOR THE JUSTICE SYSTEM

The emerging interest in the crime victim holds intriguing potential implications for the administration of justice. These implications range from possible reduction of the focus of the justice system through development of alternative ways for dealing with victim-offender disputes to creative development of new victim roles within the criminal justice system.

The relationship of the victim to the criminal justice system is presently ill defined. But a number of interesting developments are being piloted and may lead to more widespread application. In some areas, victims and offenders are being engaged in dispute settlement processes as an alternative to criminal justice processing. Victims are traditionally the precipitator of action by the criminal justice system, and a number of efforts are underway to test expanded roles for victims, including procedures to make the criminal justice system more directly accountable to the victim, efforts to involve the victim in the disposition decision regarding the offender, and programs to include the victim as a partner in the criminal justice system, especially in relation to the use of restitution by the offender. A final area that needs considerable additional study is an examination of the impact that victim characteristics may have on decisions made by criminal justice officials. Although the present programming developments tend to be halting and limited, a few scholars are taking a giant leap forward in suggesting the possibility of restructuring the criminal justice system's purpose so that it primarily serves the interest of victims in securing a just settlement for the wrongdoing of offenders.

Dispute settlement

Practically all crimes, and thus victimizations, can be conceptualized as disputes between two persons or organizations in which one person or organization has allegedly harmed the other. These private wrongs, or torts, have become defined as crimes because the state is believed to have an interest in regulating the offender's behavior. The state's interest in the proceedings has lead largely to the exclusion of the victim. Several pilot projects have been established to develop dispute settlement mechanisms that might be used to deal with disputes between persons and/or organizations as an alternative to activation of the criminal justice system. These projects typically bring the parties involved into a mediation or arbitration proceeding whose function is to resolve the dispute in a manner acceptable to all the parties rather than to prosecute one of the parties. Presently, dispute settlement procedures are being used with intrafamily crime, private criminal complaints, and some categories of property crime, especially check offenses. Dispute settlement programs are sometimes housed within a criminal justice agency, especially the prosecutor's office, or they may be administered by an agency outside of the criminal justice system.

The use of dispute settlement as an alternative to criminal justice processing raises some interesting issues. Do such procedures reduce the work load of the criminal justice system? For what types of offenses, offenders, and victims are dispute settlement procedures appropriate? From a public policy perspective, how should a society weigh the interests of both offenders and victims in having a dispute settled and the society's interest in having punishment imposed for other purposes, such as rehabilitation of the offender, deterrence of others, or simply the doing of justice?

Victim roles in administration of justice

Actual and potential victim roles within the criminal justice system are another interest for the field of victimology. The only clearly identified role for the victim is as precipitator of action by the criminal justice system through the victim's decision to report a crime to the police. Many victims (current victimization surveys suggest that well over half for some crimes) choose not to activate this role. Why do victims choose not to report their victimization to the police? This is an ongoing area of inquiry for the field of victimology. A related public policy issue is whether efforts should be made to increase victim reporting of crime.

Beyond that of precipitating the system's action, most crime victims have no formal role within the criminal justice system other than that of a witness to be called to assist in the prosecution of the offender. A number of potential roles, however, are being suggested. Perhaps the crime victim has a role in holding the criminal justice system accountable. Should routine reports be made back to the victim regarding the successes or failures of the police, courts, and corrections agencies in dealing with the victim's offender? Or, when persons are victimized because of failures on the part of criminal justice officials to adequately perform their roles, is it possible for the victim to use litiga-

tion and sue officials who have been negligent in fulfilling public duties?

And what about the disposition decision? Once guilt has been determined, should the victim have any role in deciding what should happen to the offender? Some intriguing developments are occurring in this regard. In some jurisdictions, probation officers are routinely interviewing victims to secure both their account of the offense and their recommendations regarding sentencing of the offender; the victim's recommendations are then transmitted to the sentencing judge by way of the presentence investigation. A few pilot programs have taken this idea one step further to bring the victim and offender together as part of a team that also includes professional staff to develop a sentencing recommendation for the court.

The increasing interest in the use of monetary restitution as a sanction for offenders obviously creates additional potential roles for victims. Creative possibilities exist for integrating the victim into the criminal justice system in the processes of determining the amount, the form of restitution, and the manner in which payments are to be made. Possibilities range from the victim's performance in the passive role of recipient of the restitution payments to an active involvement with the offender to negotiate the amount of restitution and, perhaps in some cases, to receive restitution directly from the offender in the form of service rather than money.

Victim characteristics in criminal justice decision making

To what extent do the characteristics of victims impact on the decision making of criminal justice officials? Little systematic information is available regarding the extent to which victim characteristics influence the decision making of police, prosecutors, judges, juries, and corrections officials. Would the offender who robs a skid row bum be handled in the same way as the offender who robs a leading community citizen? Does information regarding alleged prior sexual behavior on the part of a rape victim impact on the decision regarding what happens to the rapist? What are the qualities of victims that may lead to vigorous prosecution of offenders and what are the qualities of victims that may be associated with case dismissal or less vigorous prosecution of the offenders? This is a rich area for study and for sorting out the possible policy and practice implications of victim characteristics impacting on decisions made by criminal justice officials.

SERVICES FOR CRIME VICTIMS

The reawakened interest in the crime victim is leading to the development of a wide variety of services for crime victims. Several service models are being developed and tested, but there is no uniform agreement regarding the needs of crime victims or the most appropriate service model to respond to these needs.

The most basic programs are those directed toward reduction of vulnerability through crime prevention and reduction of victim recidivism. Traditionally the police have been looked upon as preventers of crime, and though police can make an important contribution to crime prevention, the task requires a much larger effort. Presently there are at least three approaches being undertaken toward reduction of vulnerability. One, a neighborhood organization approach, involves efforts to help neighbors organize to take responsibility for their neighborhood. Efforts may be directed toward organizing block watches, establishing safe homes for children who need a refuge from pending trouble, and helping neighbors assist each other through activities such as watching homes in the absence of occupants, becoming alerted to suspicious strangers, and notifying police.

A second, target-hardening approach is directed toward making homes and other buildings more secure. Home security checks in which police officers review the adequacy of home locks and security to make recommendations to homeowners is an example of target hardening; additional examples include programs in which persons are encouraged to engrave identification numbers on their property to discourage theft and to aid in reclaiming stolen items and educational approaches directed toward helping the elderly reduce their vulnerability.

A third approach to crime prevention, which is gaining considerable attention, is the notion of crime prevention through environmental design. The basic idea is that environments can be designed to facilitate communication and socialization among persons who belong in particular areas, create barriers so that persons who do not belong in an area are easily identified, and permit more creative use of lighting and spatial arrangements to create a defensible space—a space in which persons who belong know and identify each other and in which intruders can be identified.

Returning home to find one's residence burglarized, experiencing a robbery or assault on the street, or in some other way being victimized may be a very emotionally upsetting experience. Another set of victim services has been evolving to help crime victims cope with the trauma of victimization. These services include activities such as crisis intervention, provision of information, referral services, and provision of immediate concrete services (such as assistance in repairing broken windows or doors to resecure a residence). Services directed toward helping crime victims deal with the trauma of victimization have typically developed in response to the needs of specific groups of victims, such as the aged, victims of sexual assault, and battered women. One of the current issues regarding these programs is the advantage of organizing them in relation to the needs of specific sets of victims contrasted with the development of a more general victim service program to serve all crime victims. These services are also confronted with major issues regarding their best home base. Are they most appropriately administered through police departments, welfare departments, or corrections organizations, or as independent organizations? Another organizational issue is whether victim crisis services should be specialized in relation to crime victims or whether these can be integrated into other crisis intervention services, such as those offered by comprehensive mental health programs.

If the victim's offender is apprehended, the crime victim will be expected, as part of his or her civic duty, to cooperate in the prosecution of the offender. The process may involve several trips to confer with prosecutors, present evidence to a grand jury, and be available for court proceedings. The victim may be thrust into the unfamiliar world of the criminal justice system and the local court house. The victim must take time off from work (frequently without compensation), resolve transportation and parking problems, and arrange for child care services.

Under the leadership of the National District Attorney's Association, a number of victim-witness assistance programs have been established to reduce the hardship of the victim's experience with the criminal justice system. These programs are usually administered by prosecutors and provide services such as orienting victims to the criminal justice system, helping interpret what is happening to them, and providing transportation services, a telephone notification service (so the victim does not unnecessarily take time off from work), private waiting rooms for victims (so they will not have to wait in crowded hallways and be confronted by the defendant and the defendant's family), child care services, and assistance with transportation and parking arrangements. Some of the programs assist victims in documenting losses and making requests for restitution; others systematically transmit the victim's thoughts regarding an appropriate disposition to the courts. Some victim-witness assistance programs have also taken on a broader function of providing crisis counseling to victims, but typically these programs limit their services to those necessary to ease the victim's experiences with the justice system.

Presumably, victim-witness services will result in increased victim satisfaction with the criminal justice system and, perhaps, a more cooperative victim-witness. One of the issues confronting these programs is whether they should be evaluated on this basis or whether they can be justified on the simple humanitarian ground of easing the victim's hardship.

In addition to psychological trauma and difficulties negotiating the criminal justice system, many crime victims may experience substantial economic loss, especially if they have sustained an injury requiring medical attention and necessitating absence from work. In response to this need, many governmental bodies have established public victim compensation programs. Victim compensation programs use tax revenues to provide financial compensation to crime victims who have sustained injuries because of their victimization. Compensation is awarded to defray the costs of medical expenses, lost wages, and out-of-pocket expenses, and, in some cases, to compensate a loss of earning power if the victim is disabled and cannot be employed at the same wage level at which he or she worked before the victimization. Victim compensation programs are a form of social insurance in which the taxing power of the state is used to distribute the cost of serious victimizations across the entire population. The first victim compensation program was established in New Zealand in 1963. The concept has spread rapidly, so that programs are now found in England, most of Australia, all of Canada, Northern Ireland, nearly half of the United States, and several western European countries.

SYNOPSIS

Victimology is a new and evolving field and one for which there is not yet a commonly accepted conceptual framework. The themes and issues introduced here will be further elaborated and analyzed in works contained in this volume. Section One further develops materials regarding the elements of the field, including discussions of the development of victimology, the victim's experience in the justice system, costs of crime, and materials regarding victimization surveys. The concepts of vulnerability, culpability, and intrafamily crime are further explored in Section Two, on victim-offender systems. Section Three, Implications for the Justice System, provides material regarding dispute settlement outside the criminal justice system, the maintenance of criminal justice system accountability to victims, potential roles for the victim in the criminal justice system, the impact of victim characteristics on criminal justice officials' decision making, and proposed models for a more victim-oriented criminal justice system. Finally, in Section Four an overview is presented of services for crime victims, including services directed toward preventing victimization, dealing with the crises of victimization, easing the victim's experience in the criminal justice system, and providing public compensation to crime victims.

A new field will likely undergo spurts of growth characterized by rapid change and development. Materials in this volume will provide a useful groundwork, however, from which to understand and assess the future development of the field of victimology.

REFERENCES

1. Mendelsohn, Beniamin. "Method to be Used by Counsel for the Defense in the Researches Made into the Personality of the Criminal," *Revue de Droit Pénal et de Criminologie,* August-October 1937, p. 877.
2. Mendelsohn, Beniamin. "The Origin of the Doctrine of Victimology," *Excerpta Criminologica,* vol. 3, no. 3, May-June 1963.
3. von Hentig, Hans. *The Criminal and His Victim* (New Haven: Yale University Press, 1948).
4. Ellenberger, Henri. "Relation Psychologiques Entre le Criminel et la Victime," *Revue Internationale de Criminologie et de Police Technique,* pp. 103-121, 1954. English translation, "Psychological Relationships Between Criminal and Victim," *Archives of Criminal Psychodynamics* 1: 257-290, 1955.
5. Wolfgang, Marvin E. *Patterns in Criminal Homicide* (Philadelphia: University of Pennsylvania Press, 1958).
6. Drapkin, Israel, and Emilio Viano, eds. *Victimology: A New Focus* (Lexington, Mass.: D. C. Heath & Co., 1975). This is a five-volume collection: vol. 1, *Theoretical Issues in Victimology;* vol. 2, *Society's Reaction to Victimization;* vol. 3, *Crimes, Victims, and Justice;* vol. 4, *Violence and Its Victims;* and vol. 5, *Exploiters and Exploited: The Dynamics of Victimization.*
7. "Second International Symposium on Victimology Abstracts," *Victimology: An International Journal* 2:51, 1977.
8. Viano, Emilio C., ed. *Victims and Society* (Washington, D.C.: Visage Press, 1976).
9. Drapkin, Israel. "The Prison Inmate as Victim," *Victimology: An International Journal* 1:98, 1976.
10. Bartollas, Clemens, Stuart J. Miller, and Simon Dinitz. "The Exploitation Matrix in a Juvenile Institution," *International Journal of Criminology and Penology,* 4:257, 1976.
11. Viano, Emilio C. "Victimization of the Immigrant: An Overlooked Area of Research and Inquiry" (Paper delivered at the Second International Symposium on Victimology, Boston, September 1976). For abstract, see *Victimology: An International Journal* 2:85, 1977.
12. Separovic, Zvonimir. "The Victim and Society: New Problems Posed by the Advancement of Medicine" (Paper delivered at the Second International Symposium on Victimology, Boston, September 1976). For abstract see *Victimology: An International Journal* 2:81, 1977.
13. Moran, Richard, and Stephen Ziedman. "Victims Without Crimes: Compensation to the Not Guilty," in Drapkin, Israel, and Emilio Viano, eds. *Victimology: A New Focus,* vol. 2 (Lexington, Mass.: D. C. Heath & Co., 1975), pp. 221-225.
14. Dadrian, Vahakn N. "The Structural-Functional Components of Genocide: A Victimological Approach to the Armenian Case," in Drapkin, Israel, and Emilio Viano, eds. *Victimology* (Lexington, Mass.: D. C. Heath & Co., 1974), pp. 123-136.
15. See, for example, U.S. Department of Justice. *Criminal Victimization in the United States: A Comparison of 1975 and 1976 Findings* (Washington, D.C.: U.S. Government Printing Office, 1977), pp. 20 and 48.
16. Ennis, Philip H. *Criminal Victimization in the United States: A Report of a National Survey* (Washington, D.C.: U.S. Government Printing Office, 1967).
17. For the most recent summary report see U.S. Department of Justice. *Criminal Victimization in the United States, 1977* (Washington, D.C.: U.S. Government Printing Office, 1979).
18. Panel for the Evaluation of Crime Surveys. *Surveying Crime* (Washington, D.C.: National Academy of Sciences, 1976).
19. Ennis, pp. 35-36.
20. U.S. Department of Justice. *Criminal Victimization in the United States, 1975* (Washington, D.C.: U.S. Government Printing Office, 1977), p. 43.
21. Silverman, Robert. "Victim-Offender Relationships in Face to Face Delinquent Acts," *Social Problems* 22:383, February 1975.
22. U.S. Department of Justice. *Criminal Victimization, 1975,* p. 20.
23. Gibran, Kahlil. *The Forerunner: His Parables and Poems* (London: Heinemann, 1963), pp. 33-34.
24. Bard, Morton, and Dawn Sangrey. *The Crime Victim's Book* (New York: Basic Books, Inc., Publishers, 1979), pp. 52-76.

SECTION ONE

Victimology as an evolving discipline

The four chapters in this section provide an introduction to the development and scope of victimology. Chapter 1 introduces the notions of victim-offender relations, victim vulnerability, and victim services. Chapter 2 deals with the crime victim's decision to report the crime to the police and, once the crime is reported, the kind of treatment the victim receives from justice system officials. Chapter 3 moves to a consideration of the various costs of crime, and Chapter 4 deals with measuring the extent of crime victimization.

The three articles in Chapter 1 present an overview of some of the major concepts of the field. The first article, by Stephen Schafer, a pioneer in the development of the victim field, introduces the notion of victim-offender relations. Schafer suggests that crime victims may play a part in being victimized and should therefore be seen as sharing responsibility for the criminal incident. This idea is elaborated upon in later chapters of the book, especially in Chapter 6. Schafer traces some of the seminal contributions to the study of victim-offender relations, from the early speculative work to more recent empirically grounded research efforts.

The idea of victim-offender relations is, however, only one of the major developments in the field of victimology, and the second article in Chapter 1, by John Dussich, deals with another major concern—providing alternative types of services to crime victims. John Dussich has been involved in both practice and research in the area of victim services, and in both roles he has played an important part in developing and implementing different types of victim programs throughout the country. In this article, Dussich traces the history of alternative types of victim service programs as well as their rationale and operations. Several of the ideas raised in his paper are addressed in greater detail in Chapters 13 and 14, where specific types of victim service programs are illustrated.

The third article in Chapter 1, by Peter Meyer, a professor of economic planning, examines actions of private corporations from a victim perspective. Meyer is concerned with defining and elaborating upon the nature of corporate criminality, especially in regard to the way in which private corporations commit crimes against communities that, if committed by individuals, would be defined as thefts. The idea that communities have particular characteristics that make them vulnerable to being victimized by private, profit-making corporations is central to Meyer's argument. This notion of victim vulnerability is elaborated upon in the second section of this book, especially in Chapter 5.

The papers in Chapter 2 deal with two general questions. First, what is the basis and extent to which victims report criminal incidents to the police? Second, once an incident is reported, what happens to crime victims in their encounters with officials of the justice system?

The first question is addressed in Wesley Skogan's paper. Skogan, a political scientist who has devoted a great deal of time and effort to studying crime victim survey data, uses information obtained from the 1973 National Crime Panel victim survey to note that a substantial number of crime victims do not report the incident to the police. Skogan examines several plausible reasons for this and finds that the characteristics of the criminal incident are most strongly and consistently related to the decision to report, so that the more serious the crime, the more likely it is to be reported. In other words, crime victims tend to filter out the less serious cases of criminal victimization by not reporting them to the police.

Once a victimization is reported, however, what happens to crime victims as they encounter the criminal justice system? Two papers in Chapter 2, one by Mary Knudten and Richard Knudten and the other by Gilbert Geis, deal with this question. Mary Knudten and Richard Knudten are sociologists who have conducted major research studies on crime victims' experiences with the justice system. Gilbert Geis, also a sociologist, has done research in many areas of victimology. Although the research procedures used in these two papers are quite different, both point to the general lack of consideration given crime victims by criminal justice officials. Furthermore, the effect of this neglect on victim attitudes toward criminal justice officials is explored and the consequent need for victim-witness and compensation programs is suggested. The operating characteristics of victim-witness programs are discussed in these papers and dealt with in further detail in papers contained in Chapter 14.

The four papers in Chapter 3 address questions about assessing the type and amount of loss associated with criminal victimization. Mel Gray, the author of the first paper in this chapter, is an economist who has combined academic research with professional experience in criminal justice planning organizations. In his paper, Gray presents some of the major concepts involved in an economic analysis of crime costs, as well as the difficulties associated with considering such costs in an economic analysis of crime incidents.

The papers by political scientists John Stookey and James Brooks illustrate and elaborate upon many of the concepts suggested by Gray. Stookey presents the results of survey research completed in Minnesota on the economic and social costs of crime victimization. He gives particular attention to assessing the extent to which alternative types of remedies are used by crime victims to help alleviate the impact of victimization. Stookey's central point is that unless effective social remedies are made available, crime victimization is likely to result in such social costs as decreased social cohesion and reduced support by the citizenry for the justice system.

James Brooks' paper complements Stookey's analysis by dealing with citizens' fear of crime. The logical extension of the public's fear of becoming crime victims is likely to be a reduced confidence in the operation of the justice system.

Reprinted from the *Boston Herald American,* the article by journalist Warren Brooks illustrates the variety of direct and indirect costs of crime in the black community of Boston. A vicious circle exists, in which unemployment leads to crime that drives business out of the community so as to cause higher levels of unemployment. At what point and how to intervene in this mutually reinforcing system then become crucial issues.

The cost of crime is directly linked to the extent of victimization, and the two articles in Chapter 4 deal with the use of victim surveys for measuring the incidence of crime. James Garofalo, the author of the first paper in this chapter, is a criminologist who has done extensive research on crime victim surveys. In this article he explains the logic of using victim surveys to obtain information about the extent of victimization and proceeds to identify some of the major methodological problems associated with such an approach. Wesley Skogan's paper describes the National Crime Panel surveys being conducted by the Bureau of the Census and summarizes the kinds of information being produced in this large-scale contemporary effort at assessing the extent of crime.

Chapter 1

OVERVIEW OF THE FIELD OF VICTIMOLOGY

A □ *The beginning of victimology*
STEPHEN SCHAFER

B □ *Evolving services for crime victims*
JOHN P. J. DUSSICH

C □ *Communities as victims of corporate crimes*
PETER B. MEYER

A □ *The beginning of victimology*

STEPHEN SCHAFER

THE FOUNDERS OF VICTIMOLOGY

The revival of the victim's importance tends to involve, among other things, the criminal-victim relationship as a partial answer to the crime problem. While compensation or restitution deals with the victim's role and the possibility of correction of the criminal in the post-crime situation, the criminal-victim relationship may point to the genesis of a crime and to a better understanding of its development and formation. "That the victim is taken as one of the determinants, and that a nefarious symbiosis is often established between doer and suf-

ferer, may seem paradoxical. The material gathered, however, indicates such a relation." If this relation can be confirmed, and if the criminal-victim interactions and personal relationships can be observed in the "functional interplay of causative elements," crime can be seen and understood in a broader perspective. Revival of the victim's role in criminal proceedings not only means participation in his own behalf, but may also indicate his share in criminal responsibility.

Hans von Hentig might not have been the first to call attention to criminal-victim relationships, but, in the postwar period, his pathfinding study made the most challenging impact on the understanding of crime in terms of doer-sufferer interactions and invited a number of contributions to this aspect of lawbreaking. He

Reprinted with permission of Reston Publishing Company, Inc., a Prentice Hall Company, 11480 Sunset Hills Road, Reston, Virginia. Excerpted from *Victimology: The Victim and His Criminal,* 1977, by Stephen Schafer, pp. 33-51.

15

seemed to be impressed by Franz Werfel's well-known novel, *The Murdered One is Guilty (Der Ermorderte ist schuld)*, and suggested that the victim himself is one of the many causes of a crime. Hentig hypothesized that, in a sense, the victim shapes and molds the criminal and his crime and that the relationship between perpetrator and victim may be much more intricate than our criminal law, with its rough and mechanical definitions and distinctions, would suggest.

Hentig suggested that a reciprocality exists between criminal and victim. He often found a mutual connection between "killer and killed, duper and dupe." "The mechanical outcome," writes Hentig, "may be profit to one party, harm to another, yet the psychological interaction, carefully observed, will not submit to this kindergarten label." A mutuality of some sort raises the question of the dependability of external criteria, because, Hentig observes, the sociological and psychological aspects of the situation may be such as to suggest that the two distinct categories of criminal and victim in fact merge; it may be the case that the criminal is victimized.

Hentig backed his hypotheses with statistical data, documented fragments of experiences, and unstructured observations; but he did not support them by empirical research. However, his highly logical and vigorous speculations aided the revival of the victim's importance in the understanding of criminal problems. The concept of the "activating sufferer," who plays a part in "the various degrees and levels of stimulation or response" and who "is scarcely taken into consideration in our legal distinctions," is not original with Hentig, but his pioneering role and its great impact cannot be denied.[1]

Beniamin Mendelsohn claims that he originated the idea.[2] He refers to his article, published a decade before Hentig's study, which, though not a study of the victim, led him to his "gradual evolution towards the conception of Victimology."[3] Mendelsohn, as a practicing attorney, had his clients answer some 300 questions. His findings from this questionnaire led him to the conclusion that a "parallelity" appears between the "biopsychological" personality of the offender and that of the victim. After

he published his first impressions,[4] he concentrated his investigation on the victim, first of all on rape victims and on the extent of their resistance.

In his basic study of criminal-victim relationships Mendelsohn proposes the term "victimology" in order to develop an independent field of study and perhaps a new discipline.[5] He views the totality of crime factors as a "criminogen-complex," in which one set of factors concerns the criminal and another the victim. He objects to "the co-existence of two parallel ways" and asks that they be separate. This divorce of the "penal-couple" (as he terms the criminal and his victim) would lead to "a new branch of science"—his victimology. Accordingly, he introduces a terminology for victimology. He proposes new terms such as "victimal" as the opposite of "criminal"; "victimity" as the opposite of "criminality"; "potential of victimal receptivity" as meaning individual unconscious aptitude for being victimized. He suggests the broadest possible acceptance and implementation of his idea. Thus he recommends the establishment of a central institute of victimology, victimological clinics, an international institute for victimological researches in the United Nations, an international society of victimology, and the publication of an international review of victimology. In Mendelsohn's view, victimology is not a branch of criminology but "a science parallel to it"; or, better, "the reverse of criminology."

EARLY VICTIM TYPOLOGIES

Both Hentig and Mendelsohn attempted to set up victim typologies, but their classifications were speculative. Their work offers useful guidelines for research, but in the absence of systematic empirical observations it should be used with caution. In any case, the possibility of a spectacular variety of victim types is indicated, particularly by Hentig in his detailed list of such types. Mendelsohn distinguished between the guilt of the criminal and his victim; Hentig used a sociological classification.

In Mendelsohn's typology the "correlation of culpability (imputability) between the victim and the delinquent" is the focal point around which he gathered his victim types.[6] In fact,

Mendelsohn's victims are classified only in accordance with the degree of their guilty contribution to the crime. They are grouped in the following categories:

1. The "completely innocent victim." Mendelsohn regards him as the "ideal" victim, and refers to children and to those who suffer a crime while they are unconscious.
2. The "victim with minor guilt" and the "victim due to his ignorance." Mentioned here as an example is the woman who "provokes" a miscarriage and as a result pays with her life.
3. The "victim as guilty as the offender" and the "voluntary victim." In explanation Mendelsohn lists the following subtypes:
   a. suicide "by throwing a coin," if punishable by law.
   b. suicide "by adhesion"
   c. euthanasia (to be killed by one's own wish because of an incurable and painful disease)
   d. suicide committed by a couple (for example, "desperate lovers," healthy husband and sick wife)
4. The "victim more guilty than the offender." There are two subtypes:
   a. the "provoker victim," who provokes someone to crime
   b. the "imprudent victim," who induces someone to commit a crime
5. The "most guilty victim" and the "victim who is guilty alone." This refers to the aggressive victim who is alone guilty of a crime (for example, the attacker who is killed by another in self-defense).
6. The "simulating victim" and the "imaginary victim." Mendelsohn refers here to those who mislead the administration of justice in order to obtain a sentence of punishment against an accused person. This type includes paranoids, hysterical persons, senile persons, and children.

Hentig's typology is more elaborate and uses psychological, social, and biological factors in the search for categories. He distinguishes born victims from society-made victims. He also sets up a victim typology in thirteen categories.[7]

1. The young
2. The female
3. The old
4. The mentally defective and other mentally deranged
5. Immigrants
6. Minorities
7. Dull normals
8. The depressed
9. The acquisitive
10. The wanton
11. The lonesome and the heartbroken
12. Tormentors
13. The blocked, exempted, and fighting

The young victim is an obvious type. Since the young are weak and inexperienced, they are likely to be victims of attacks. The young are easy victims not only because they are physically undeveloped, but because they are immature in moral personality and moral resistance. Though they are in the process of biological and cultural development, this cannot be fully complete in youth. However, the criminal's inner pressure to commit crime is normally a fully developed force against which the undeveloped resistance of the young is unable to compete on fair terms. Hentig suggested that since children do not own property, they are not usually victims of crimes for profit. However, a child may be murdered for profit if his life is insured. Kidnapping is an offense that usually involves the young. Further, children are frequently used by criminals to assist in committing crimes (mainly crimes against property).

In most countries laws are in force to protect children against involvement in moral turpitude, which indicates that they can be regarded even in this respect as victims. If the young person happens to be a girl, her victimization is well known with respect to sexual offenses. Leppmann, as cited by Hentig, pointed out that some young girls do not resist sexual assaults, and because of a mixture of curiosity, fear, physical inactivity, and intellectual challenge they do not try to escape from being victims.

The female is described by Hentig as a victim with "another form of weakness." Younger females sometimes become the victims of murder after suffering sexual assault; older women who are thought wealthy become victims of property crimes. The lesser physical strength of the female has greater significance than that of young people or children. While the criminal would find little point in committing a property crime against the propertyless young, this is not the case with regard to women. Women do have, or handle, things of financial value that may attract the criminal. Most offenders are men and therefore have the advantage of greater physical strength in crimes against women. Except in the case of rare homosexual offenses, women occupy a biologically determined victim status in sexual crimes.

The old are also likely to be victims in crimes against property. Hentig pointed out that "the elder generation holds most positions of accumulated wealth and wealth-giving power." At the same time old people are weaker physically and sometimes mentally. "In the combination of wealth and weakness lies the danger." Hentig suggests that old people are ideal victims of predatory attacks. Their comparative weakness is behind proposed measures for their special defense, which would involve greater punishment for those who commit crimes against them.

The mentally defective and other mentally deranged persons are referred to by Hentig as a large class of potential and actual victims. It seems obvious that the insane, the alcoholic, the drug addict, the psychopath, and others suffering from any form of mental deficiency are handicapped in any struggle against crime. Hentig stated that of all males killed, 66.6 percent turned out to be alcoholics. He rarely found alcoholics among murder victims, but 70 percent of manslaughter victims were found to to have been intoxicated. Often not only was the victim of manslaughter intoxicated, but the killer was also. Generally speaking, intoxicated persons are easy victims for any sort of crime, particularly property crimes. They are the targets of thieves, pickpockets, confidence men, gamblers, social criminals, and perhaps others. It has been demonstrated that crimes against persons in an intoxicated state are much greater than might be expected. As to the drug addict, Hentig refers to him as the "prototype of the doer-sufferer."

Immigrants are vulnerable because of the difficulties they experience while adjusting to a new culture. Hentig, who went through the immigration experience himself, points out that immigration is not simply a change to a new country or continent, but "it is a temporary reduction to an extreme degree of helplessness in vital human relations." Apart from linguistic and cultural difficulties, the immigrant often suffers from poverty, emotional disturbance, and rejection by certain groups in the new country. His competitive drive may evoke hostility. In these highly disturbing and conflict-producing situations, the inexperienced, poor, and credulous immigrant, who desperately clutches at every straw, is exposed to various swindles. It takes many painful years for him to adjust to a new technique of living; only then can he escape from being victimized. It is amazing that while people in general cannot fully perceive the difficulties of the immigrant, one category of the population—its criminals—understands the immigrant's disturbed situation and takes advantage of it.

The minorities' position is similar to the immigrants'. Lack of legal or real equality with the majority of the population increases the chances of victimization. Racial prejudice may increase their difficulties and can involve them in a victim situation. This may lead to violent criminal-victim relationships.

The dull normals, says Hentig, are born victims. He attributes the success of swindlers not to their brilliance but to the folly of their victims. The characteristic behavior of the dull normal is similar to that of immigrants and minorities; all three may be included in one category.

The depressed, as opposed to the previous "general" or sociological classes, are psychological victim types. Depression is an emotional attitude that is expressed by feelings of inadequacy and hopelessness, and that is accompanied by a general lowering of physical and mental activity. Sometimes it is pathological. Hentig suggests that the reciprocal operation of affinities between doer and sufferer can be measured in degrees of strength. The depressed person's attitude is apathetic and submissive, lacking fighting qualities. Resistance is reduced and he is open to victimization. Often the depressed person is weak not only in his mental resistance, but also physically, and this increases the possibility of his becoming a victim.

The acquisitive person is called "another excellent victim." Desire may not only motivate crime, but may also lead to victimization. Criminal syndicates, racketeers, gamblers, confidence men, and others exploit the victim's greed for gain. These victims can be found in almost every social strata: the poor man struggles for security, the middle-class man takes a chance in order to obtain luxuries, the rich man wants to double his money. It is well known that the latter category is the most vulnerable acquisitive victim.

The wanton is also one of Hentig's types, though he thinks of him as "obscured and dimmed by the rough generalization" of laws and social conventions.

The lonesome and the heartbroken are also seen as potential victims. Both are reminiscent of the acquisitive type, with the difference that it is not gain or profit but companionship and happiness that are desired. Hentig cites well-known mass murderers: Henri Désiré Landru, Fritz Haarmann, even Jack the Ripper; all took advantage of the loneliness and heartbroken feelings of their victims. Such credulous persons are not only victims of murder but are also, and more frequently, victims of theft, fraud, and other swindles.

The tormentor is a victim type who is found in family tragedies. Hentig gives the example of an alcoholic or psychotic father who tortured his family for a long time and who was finally killed by his son. Doubtless the latter was provoked by the father. This type of victim seems to be characterized by a lack of a normal prognostic sense. Consequently he strains a situation to such an extent that he becomes a victim of the tense atmosphere he himself creates.

The blocked, exempted, and fighting victims are Hentig's last category. By the blocked victim is meant "an individual who has been so enmeshed in a losing situation that defensive moves have become impossible or more injurious than the injury at criminal hands." Such is the case of a defaulting banker who has swindled in the hope of saving himself. Hentig refers

here also to persons who are blackmailed; they are in a situation where the assistance of the police does not seem desirable. Hentig also refers to crimes of violence in which the victim fights back. In contrast to the "easy victim," this is the "difficult victim." Actually it would be better to exclude the fighting victim from the victim categories. Fighting back indicates resistance, thus this victim is less a victim type than the one whose resistance is overcome by the superior strength of the criminal.

Barnes and Teeters mentioned another victim type, the negligent or careless victim.[8] This type was later mentioned by others in connection with the problem of victim compensation. Barnes and Teeters referred to cases in which the victim's negligent or careless attitude toward his belongings makes it easy for the criminal to commit his crime. Inadequately secured doors, windows left open, unlocked cars, careless handling of furs and jewelry—these and other instances of negligence are an invitation to the criminal. They mention the theft of jewelry valued at $750,000 from the late Aga Kahn. And they mention bank robberies in which the victims were responsible. An FBI survey reported that bank robbers were apprehended by guards in seven of the twenty-six institutions that employed guards; in two instances the guard was either at lunch or not on duty at the time of the robbery. The same survey revealed that too few employees take advantage of the protective devices that are available to them. In one instance, the teller pressed the alarm, but it did not work. It was learned afterward that the alarm system had not been checked for eighteen months.[9]

Another victim type, the *reporting or nonreporting* victim, is mentioned by Walter C. Reckless.[10] Here the victim is unwilling to report because he fears the social consequences of doing so. Reckless referred to blackmail and attempted suicide cases that remain invisible because of the nonreporting attitude of the victim. Henri Ellenberger, too, tried to classify victim types, but because his contribution is abstract, mention of it will be reserved for the section on speculative soundings about the victim.

This list of victim types could be extended

but would not serve any purpose. Personal frustration has many forms, and negligence can be split into several types. Persons who are lonesome, heartbroken, or blocked may be reacting to certain situations and may not be types of victims. These situations may, however, serve as instructive examples of the important interactions and relations between the criminal and his victim. Thus, they can enlighten social situations, can call attention to victim risks, and may assist in determining responsibility; but they may fail to develop a general victim typology.

CONTINUED EFFORTS TO DEVELOP VICTIM TYPOLOGIES

Victim typologies attempt to classify the characteristics of victims, but actually they often typify social and psychological situations rather than the constant patterns of the personal makeup of victims. The "easy" victim and the "difficult" victim appear according to the balance of forces in a given criminal drama. The lonesome are prey to the criminal only when they are lonely. The heartbroken are easy victims only when they suffer a temporary disappointment. On this basis, hundreds of victim "types" could be listed, all according to the characteristics of a situation at any given moment.

However, there are indeed biological types of victims who, compared with temporary "situational" victims, seem to be continuously and excessively prone to becoming victims of crime. To be young, to be old, or to be mentally defective are not "situations" but biological qualities that indicate a more or less lasting vulnerability to crime. Apart from them, a typology of criminal-victim relationships—along with the patterns of social situations in which they appear—might hold more promise. It might increase the defense of those who cannot compensate for their weakness through their own efforts; it might evaluate victim risks and accommodate crime control and social defense to them; it might develop a selective and universalistic rejuvenation of the responsibility concept. As the President's Commission on Law Enforcement and Administration of Justice put it, "If it could be determined with sufficient specificity that

people or businesses with certain characteristics are more likely than others to be crime victims, . . . efforts to control and prevent crime would be more productive."[11]

Nevertheless, in spite of continued efforts, no good working typology of victims has developed as yet. The President's Commission on Law Enforcement and Administration of Justice appears to have leaned toward distinguishing between reporting and nonreporting victims. In doing so, the Commission excluded willful homicide, forcible rape, and a few other crimes which had too few reported cases to be statistically useful. Among those crimes not reported to law enforcement agencies, it listed robbery, 35 percent; aggravated assault, 35 percent; simple assault, 54 percent; burglary, 42 percent; larceny over $50, 40 percent; larceny under $50, 63 percent; auto theft, 11 percent; malicious mischief, 62 percent; consumer fraud, 90 percent; other frauds, 74 percent, sex offenses (except rape), 49 percent; and family crimes (such as desertion and nonsupport), 50 percent. These nonreporting victims were revealed in a national survey of households. According to their responses, they did not notify the police because they felt it was a private matter and did not want to harm the offender; they thought that the police could not be effective and would not want to be bothered; they did not want to take time; they were too confused and did not know how to report; or they were afraid of reprisal. It is admittedly not clear whether these responses are accurate assessments of the victim's inability to help the police or merely rationalizations of their failure to report,[12] but even if we assume that they are accurate, this distinction would not serve the development of a meaningful typology of victims because it does not always reflect to the criminal-victim *relationships*, and because it does not clearly explain those *victim characteristics* that would cause the victim's negative attitude and behavior; thus, it does not lead to the solution of the problem of responsibility.

A rather complex classification of victims has been offered by Ezzat Abdel Fattah, who designed five major classes with eleven subcategories, which still did not cover all possible victim types, nor did it indicate the possible distribution of responsibilities.[13] His main types are the following:

1. Nonparticipating Victims, who feel a denial or repulsion toward the crime and the criminal, and who do not participate in the origin of the crime committed against them;
2. Latent or Predisposed Victims, who (Fattah does not explain why) have certain character predispositions for being victimized by certain kinds of offenses;
3. Provocative Victims, who precipitate the crime, or even provoke it;
4. Participating Victims, who by their passivity or other similar attitude make their own victimization possible or easier; and
5. False Victims, who are not victims at all or who victimize themselves.

In their attempt to measure delinquency, Thorsten Sellin and Marvin E. Wolfgang have offered a kind of victim typology,[14] later somewhat refined by Wolfgang.[15] They have listed:

1. Primary Victimization, which refers to personalized or individual victims;
2. Secondary Victimization, where the victim is an impersonal target of the offender (e.g. railroads, department stores, churches, and the like);
3. Tertiary Victimization, which involves the public or the administration of the society as victim;
4. Mutual Victimization, which refers to victims who themselves are offenders in a given mutually consensual act (e.g., fornication or adultery); and
5. "No Victimization" where there is no immediately recognizable victim and which refers to acts of a minor nature or of negligible significance.

This typology appears to be aimed primarily at depicting crimes, and although it describes "situations," it does not reflect the criminal-victim relationships and responsibilities. Robert A. Silverman supported this classification with slight modifications, but even so, he, in his otherwise illuminating survey, failed to be concerned with the victim's specific characteristics.[16]

While their categorization seems to fall far below what is expected from a theory-backed victim typology, the influence of the character of the victim is more clearly spelled out by David Landy and Elliot Aronson, who distinguish between "attractive victims" and "unattractive victims" as they affect decision making in the administration of criminal law.[17] Even closer to what a victim typology should really mean is Gilbert Geis's approach: he has found the key issue in the factor of "victim responsiveness."[18] It is unfortunate, however, that he has restricted his thought to only white-collar crimes.

Hans Joachim Schneider has criticized all victim typologies for the absence of an empirical-factoranalytical basis.[19] However, he also appears to have failed in proposing classes which, as he claims, should embrace all possible types, should not overlap, and should be useful for practical as well as research purposes. Actually, he refers only to victim "aptness" and victim "inclination," pointing to victims of sex offenses, marriage swindles, group rapes, child abuses, social views, and the fear of crime.

Certainly no victim typology can be perfect, and in our present state of knowledge even the best would be easily vulnerable for a critique. Since human behavior cannot be labeled and classified in clearly individual categories, all typologies and classifications necessarily exhibit a more or less arbitrary and heuristic character. This is even more obvious if the proposed typology looks as if it were forced upon a general theory of crime or a specific theory of victimology (if any such theory exists at all), or if it is not backed by a general explanation of criminal-victim relationships and the characteristics of victims. The typology that floats in a vacuum is useless except as a point of departure for other typologists. As Stephen Schafer contended, this is why so many typologies seem to be only speculative guesswork or trivial impressions supported by more or less superficial experiences.[20]

A victim typology cannot be an independent venture in the understanding of the victim, his relationship with his criminal, or his responsibility in crime. Ideally, a typology should be derived from a single plausible hypothesis or a general theory of the concept of responsibility and criminal-victim relationships (explainability); it should be the observation of general distinguishing forms common to large numbers of crimes, criminals, victims, victim characteristics, and criminal-victim relationships, which can be used as a model to which they are referrable (reality); and it should be pragmatic, permitting its application to systematic grouping of types of victims and criminal-victim relationships so that the crime participants' (the victim's and his criminal's) responsibility can be assessed accordingly (instrumentality). A victim typology remains a meaningless speculation if it is not linked to a theoretical model and if it has no responsibility-guiding application; it should not be only a set of profiles, but it should also be a directive toward assessing responsibility. Modern trends lean toward the construction of types and empirical observations that may lead only to after-the-fact theoretical formulation. To early "victimologists," such as Hentig and Mendelsohn, the refinements of the statistical *tour de force* were not known, their theories came first, and their observations afterwards.

Although one might disagree with the idea that proposes to assess *the victim's responsibility,* this concept may operationally cover the pivotal issue in the criminal-victim relationship that, after all, is the critical problem of understanding and judging crime. Based on the idea of who is responsible for what and to what extent, the following victim typology may be here tentatively proposed:

1. *Unrelated Victims,* who have no relationship whatsoever with their criminal, except that the offender has committed a crime against them. All members of society are potential victims; all by definition are exposed to be victimized, regardless of whether they had any previous personal relationship with the lawbreaker. Crime statistics indicate that a significant number of criminal offenses are purely one-sided decisions and acts of the criminal whose independent idea of violating the prohibitions of the criminal law has nothing to do with his relationship, if any, with the victim or with the victim's characteristics. The manager of the bank, for ex-

ample, is not related to the bank robber, nor is the owner of the burglarized house; these and others are selected by the criminal as victims only randomly or by situational considerations of the planned crime, thus the criminal is supposed to carry full responsibility.

2. *Provocative Victims,* who have done something against the offender who, consequently, has become roused or incited to victimize this doer-victim. In this case, the victim is the first doer. From a simple violation of a promise, through treatment with a scornful abuse, to having an affair with another's beloved, a great variety of the victim's doing against the criminal or his interest may prompt the offender to commit a crime that is directed to harm the victim. The responsibility in this case should be heavily shared.

3. *Precipitative Victims,* who have done nothing specifically against the criminal, but whose thoughtless behavior instigates, tempts, or allures the offender to commit a crime against the enticing victim. Walking alone at a dark deserted place, for example, may tempt the criminal to rob, or an overly revealing dress of a female may allure to rape. Naturally, a perfectly socialized person (if there is such a thing at all) is not supposed to be tempted or enticed to the extent of violating the rules of the criminal law, however strong or whatever the temptation or allurement might be. Yet, the characteristics of the criminal's personality are often bent by the characteristics of the victim's behavior toward committing the crime. In these cases the victim, since he ought to ponder the risk, cannot be seen as entirely blameless, and some responsibility should be carried by the victimized person.

4. *Biologically Weak Victims,* whose constitution or physical or mental characteristics develop in the offender the idea of crime against them. The child, the aged, the female, the disabled, the mentally sick or deranged, and others, though unrelated to the criminal, represent easy prey for the

offender. Although in this respect the victim actually precipitates the crime, he could not and cannot do otherwise and thus should not carry any responsibility. If any part of the criminal's responsibility is to be shared, it should be shared by the larger society or its governors, who did not provide the necessary protection for these partially or totally defenseless victims.

5. *Socially Weak Victims,* who are usually not regarded by the larger society as full-fledged members of the community. Immigrants, those affiliated with certain religions, ethnic minorities, and others who are in a socially weak position are often exploited by the criminal element. Socially weak victims are almost always blameless, and the responsibility ought to be heavily shared by both the criminal and the society that is responsible for the prejudice against them.

6. *Self-Victimizing Victims,* who victimize themselves and are thus their own criminals. Some sources tend to call their crimes "victimless" crimes, or "crimes without victims," but these terms, however spectacular, miss the point of the basic tenet that crimes, by definition, cannot exist without victims. Although most crimes involve two participants, the criminal and the victim, crimes can be immaterial acts (such as treason or espionage, for example) where only the criminal is visibly personalized and the victim may be the society as a whole or an idea. There are also crimes where the criminal and victim merge—but even in such cases, there are always victims. Drug addiction, alcoholism, homosexuality, and gambling are examples of those criminal offenses where the victim victimizes himself, or the interest of the society, and thus is a victimized criminal and plays a double role. The responsibility, therefore, need not be shared: it is to be carried by one person—the criminal-victim.

7. *Political Victims,* who suffer at the hands of their political opponents. Revolutionaries, who battle for their ideology, and

lose, do not belong in this category: according to the concept of law they are to be regarded as criminals (who may become at a later time heroes). By definition, the ruling social-political power cannot victimize the violators of its prescriptions. In a certain sense, the victim precipitates the crime by striving for a political position. The ruling power, its supporters, or actually anybody, in the course of a campaign for a powerful position, may seek out, construe or magnify any mistake or offense for the purpose of *making* a criminal of the competitor who, in the ultimate analysis, should be regarded as a political victim. Although in the formalistic-legalistic sense he is to be qualified as a criminal, looking at him from a moral angle he should be classed as a victim having no sociological responsibility.

SPECULATIVE SOUNDINGS ABOUT THE VICTIM'S ROLE

Before empirical studies started to reveal the hidden realities in criminal-victim relationships, a number of speculative soundings were made, most of them based on abstract thought.

Iturbe agreed with Mendelsohn that a science of victimology should be created,[21] but Paul Cornil suggested that this is not a new departure and the term "victim," mainly as it appears in German and Dutch translation (the German, Dutch, and French words for victim are *Opfer, Schlachtoffer,* and *Victime*), seems to have some background as a religious reference to the sacrifice of a human being or of an animal.[22]

In an early article Hentig suggested that the reality of life "presents a scale of graduated interactivities between perpetrator and victim, which elude the formal boundaries, set up by our statutes and the artificial abstractions of legal science, that should be heeded by a prevention-minded social science."[23] In his view, there is a reciprocal action between perpetrator and victim. But, as mentioned before, chronologically Hentig was not the first in the field, nor was Mendelsohn. Prior to their studies, Jules Simon, among others, discussed the consent of the victim,[24] and Jean Hemard also approached criminal-victim relationships from the same angle.[25] Kahlil Gibran was talking about victim-precipitated crimes when he called attention to the fact that "the guilty is oftentimes the victim of the injured."[26] Ernst Roesner analyzed the statistical profile of murderer-victim relationships,[27] and Boven discussed the victim's role in sexual crimes.[28] Also before Hentig and Mendelsohn, provocation of homicide has been recognized as victim-precipitated by Rollin M. Perkins[29] and by Herbert Wechlser and Jerome Michael.[30]

In the 1950s, interest in the criminal-victim relationship increased. Rhoda J. Milliken asked that the postcrime sufferings of the victim be considered. Too often, she wrote, the victim suffers not only from the crime at the time it is committed but also from a series of events that "serve to scar deeply and sometimes damage irreparably the human being for whose protection the public clamors."[31] Tahon also focused attention on the problem of the victim's consent to a crime.[32] Henri Ellenberger discussed the broader psychological aspects of the victim's relationship with his criminal,[33] and suggested that, in the common sense understanding, criminal and victim, though interrelated, are as different as black and white. In his somewhat psychoanalytic approach he emphasizes the importance of considering the doer-sufferer aspect *(le criminel-victime concept)*, the problem of the potential victim *(la victime latente),* and the special subject-object relation *(la relation spécifique criminal-victime).* He set up a list of psychological victim types, among others the murderer (criminal) of himself (victim): in other words, the person who commits suicide. Another of his types is the victim of "reflexoid" actions (discussed a half-century before by Hans Gross). Also, he called attention to the "deluded" or "fascinated" (from the German *Verblendung*) easy victims and, among others, to the "born" victim. In Ellenberger's view, special attention should be paid to "victimogen" factors and "future victims," since all individuals have the right to know the dangers to which their occupation, social class, or physical condition may expose them. He urges an investigation of the fundamental mechanisms of

the criminal-victim relationship. His message is not so much for a better understanding of crime as for more crime prevention. As a result, Ellenberger became one of the pioneers in directing attention to the practical importance of victim risks. A similar line is followed by Werner.[34]

After many attempts at understanding criminal-victim relationships through psychological investigations, Erwin O. Smigel tried to explore a segment of this field from a more or less sociological viewpoint. He was concerned with theft from organizations as related to the size of the organization.[35] Socioeconomic status, sex, religiosity, and group membership served as his variables in testing attitudes toward stealing from victim organizations of different sizes. Ehrlich analyzed fraud—its method and its victim—primarily from the preventive point of view,[36] David Reifen discussed sexual crimes and their victims,[37] and Hans Schultz[38] and Souchet[39] made general remarks on victimology and on the criminological and legal relevance of criminal-victim relationships.

The Belgian publication *Revue de Droit Pénal et de Criminologie* devoted one issue to the problems of victimology and published several articles on understanding the criminal and his victim.[40] One of the contributors, Willy Calewaert, discussed victimology in relation to cases of fraud.[41] Aimée Racine discussed the specific behavior of child victims and suggested psychiatric examination or at least social casework for young victims in certain instances.[42] De Bray distinguished three phases of victim attitudes: those before, during, and after the crime.[43] René Dellaert wrote about the dynamics of the criminal-victim relationship from a "cinéramique" view. He observed the relationship from the angles of psychotechnique, clinical psychology, social psychology, mental pathology, preventive measures, and education.[44]

Noach tried to open up a new aspect of victimology, and focused his attention on the interaction between the criminal and a collectivity as his victim.[45] It is unfortunate that his idea has not been elaborated upon: the history of mankind, even of recent times, can offer a great many illustrations. Leroy Schultz turned to an obvious and well-known example of criminal-victim relationships when, in commenting on interviews with the victims of sex offenders, he suggested that a "portion of guilt" may be attributable to the victim.[46] Edwin D. Driver investigated the victim's role in crimes in India and found that it is often possible for an affectionate or friendly relationship to end in homicide.[47] Gibbens and Joyce Prince analyzed the child victim of sex offenses. However, they seemed interested primarily in the defense and protection of children, and contributed little to the intricate relationship of the child and the criminal.[48] Albert G. Hess, some two decades before, analyzed a similar topic and offered data on the age, sex life, intelligence, and social circumstances of the victimized children.[49]

Nagel meditates on the boundaries of "criminology" and suggests that if it were redefined as "criminology of relationships," victimology would not need to be considered as a separate discipline. He calls attention to the fact that criminology is often misidentified with criminal etiology; if it could be so identified, victimology would be justified. However, Nagel proposes, the "counting, measuring, weighing, determining and comparing [of] victims"—and also the "collecting of victimological determinants, factors, associations and correlations"—will never achieve any great importance. Instead, he suggests "the removal of the conflict situation" between criminal and victim should be the goal of criminal policy.[50] Reckless does not argue about the justification of "victimology," but he does call attention to "victim proneness"; many victims are people who tend to be victimized and are in a sense responsible for provoking criminal behavior. He goes on to say that forgetfulness or absentmindedness may provoke crimes.[51] Abdel Fattah analyzed "victimological" problems from a legalistic point of view. He questions the existence of harmony between the penal codes and scientific progress. His approach to the victim's responsibility refers largely to the legal position of the crime participants.[52]

Justification of "victimology" as an independent science or discipline may indeed be a questionable objective, but only adherents of the formalistic-individualistic interpretation of crime can oppose or devalue the victim's responsibility, the measuring, weighing, and analysis of the criminal-victim relationship, and the need for special attention to victim risks. The judgment of crime *is* formalistic; and necessarily so, unless one were to advocate anarchy; and it *is* individualistic, unless the human being were to be dissolved in a collective whole. But formalism and individualism cannot be goals in themselves, and should be understood from the viewpoint of all participants in crime and from that of the societal context of criminal justice. Criminal, victim, and their society—one comprehensive concept should embrace all.

NOTES

1. Hans von Hentig, *The Criminal and His Victim, Studies in the Sociobiology of Crime* (New Haven, 1948).
2. B. Mendelsohn, "The Origin of the Doctrine of Victimology," *Excerpta Criminologica*, Vol. 3, No. 3 (May-June 1963).
3. B. Mendelsohn, "Method to Be Used by Counsel for the Defense in the Researches Made into the Personality of the Criminal," *Revue de Droit Pénal et de Criminologie* (August-October 1937), p. 877.
4. B. Mendelsohn, "Rape in Criminology," *Giustizia Penale* (1940).
5. B. Mendelsohn, "The Victimology," *Etudes Internationales de Psycho-Sociologie Criminelle* (July-September 1956), pp. 25-26 (essentially the same in French under the title "Une nouvelle branche de la science biopsychosociale, la victimologie").
6. Ibid. (French), pp. 105-07, 108.
7. Hentig, *The Criminal and His Victim,* pp. 404-38.
8. Harry Elmer Barnes and Negley K. Teeters, *New Horizons in Criminology* (3rd ed., Englewood Cliffs, 1959), pp. 595-96.
9. "Profile of a Bank Robber," *FBI Law Enforcement Bulletin,* 34 (November 1965), 22.
10. Walter C. Reckless, *The Crime Problem* (3rd ed., New York, 1961), p. 24.
11. *Task Force Report: Crime and its Impact—An Assessment,* The President's Commission on Law Enforcement and Administration of Justice (Washington, D.C., 1967), p. 80.
12. *The Challenge of Crime in a Free Society,* A Report by the President's Commission on Law Enforcement and Administration of Justice (Washington, D.C., 1967), p. 22.
13. Ezzat Abdel Fattah, "Towards a Criminological Classification of Victims," *International Criminal Police Review,* 209:162-69, 1967.
14. Thorsten Sellin and Marvin E. Wolfgang, *The Measurement of Delinquency* (New York, 1964).

15. Marvin E. Wolfgang, "Analytical Categories for Research on Victimization," in Armand Mergen-Herbert Schäfer, ed., *Kriminologische Wegzeichen, Festschrift für Hans von Hentig* (Hamburg, 1967), pp.167-85.

16. Robert A. Silverman, "Victim Typologies: Overview, Critique, and Reformation," in Israel Drapkin and Emilio Viano, eds., *Victimology* (Lexington, Mass., 1974), pp. 55-65.

17. David Landy and Elliot Aronson, "The Influence of the Character of the Criminal and His Victim on the Decisions of Simulated Jurors," in Drapkin and Viano, *Victimology*, pp. 195-204.

18. Gilbert Geis, "Victimization Patterns in White-Collar Crime," *Abstracts* of papers presented and approved by the First International Symposium on Victimology (Jerusalem, 1973), p. 24.

19. Hans Joachim Schneider, *Victimologie: Wissenschaft vom Verbrechensopfer* (Tübingen, 1975), pp. 52-85.

20. Stephen Schafer, *Theories in Criminology: Past and Present Philosophies of the Crime Problem* (New York, 1969), pp. 140-82.

21. M.O. Iturbe, "Victimologia," *Revista Penal y Penitenciario* Ministerio de Educacion y de la Republica Argentina, XXIII, No. 87-90 (1958).

22. Paul Cornil, "Contribution de la 'Victimologie' aux sciences criminologiques," *Revue de Droit Pénal et de Criminologie*, 39 (April 1959), 587-601.

23. Hans von Hentig, "Remarks on the Interaction of Perpetrator and Victim," *Journal of the American Institute of Criminal Law and Criminology*, XXXI (May-June 1940, March-April 1941), 303-9.

24. Jules Simon, "Le Consentement de la victime justifie-t-il les lésions corporelles?" *Revue de Droit Pénal et de Criminologie* (1933), pp. 457-76.

25. Jean Hemard, "Le Consentement de la victime dans le délit de coups et blessures." *Rev. crit. de législ. et jur.* (1933), pp. 292-319.

26. Kahlil Gibran, *The Prophet* (New York, 1935), p. 45.

27. Ernst Roesner, "Mörder und ihre Opfer," *Monatschrift für Kriminologie und Strafrechtsreform*, 29 (1938), 161-85, 209-28.

28. W. Boven, "Délinquants sexuels. Corrupteurs d'enfants. Coupables et victimes," *Schweizer Archiv für Neurologie und Psychiatrie*, 51 (1943), 14-25.

29. Rollin M. Perkins, "The Law of Homicide," *Journal of Criminal Law and Criminology*, 36 (March-April 1946), 412-27.

30. Herbert Wechsler and Jerome Michael, "A Rationale of the Law of Homicide," *Journal of Criminal Law and Criminology*, 36 (March-April 1946), 1280-82.

31. Rhoda J. Milliken, "The Sex Offender's Victim," *Federal Probation*, 14 (September 1950), 22-26.

32. R. Tahon, "Le Consentement de la victime," *Revue de Droit Pénal et de Criminologie* (1951-1952), pp. 323-42.

33. Henri Ellenberger, "Relation psychologiques entre le criminel et la victime," *Revue Internationale de Criminologie et de Police Technique* (1954), pp. 103-21.

34. E. Werner, "Das Opfer des Mordes," *Kriminalistik* (1956), pp. 2-5.

35. Erwin O. Smigel, "Public Attitudes toward Stealing as Related to the Size of the Victim Organization," *American Sociological Review*, 21 (February 1956), 320-27.

36. C. Ehrlich, "Der Betrüger, sein Handwerkszeung und seine Opfer," *Kriminalistik* (October 1957), pp. 365-67.

37. D. Reifen, "Le délinquant sexuel et sa victime," *Revue Internationale de L'Enfant* (1958), pp. 110-24.

38. Hans Schultz, "Kriminologische und Strafrechtliche Bemerkungen zur Beziehung zwischen Täter und Opfer," *Revue Pénale Suisse* (1958), pp. 171-91.

39. C.R. Souchet, "La Victimologie," *La Vie Judiciaire* (December 15, 1958).

40. *Revue de Droit Pénal et de Criminologie* (April 1959).

41. Willy Calewaert, "La Victimologie et l'escroquerie," Ibid., pp. 602-18.

42. Aimée Racine, "L'Enfant victime d'actes contraires aux moeurs commis sur sa personne par ascendant," Ibid., pp. 635-42.

43. L. de Bray, "Quelques Observations sur les victimes des delits de vol," Ibid., pp. 643-49.

44. René Dellaert, "Première confrontation de la psychologie criminelle et de la 'victimologie,' " Ibid., pp. 628-34.

45. W.M.E. Noach, "Het Schlachtoffer en de Strafrechtspraak," in W.P.J. Pompe and G. Th. Kempe, eds., *Strafrechtspraak, Criminologische Studiën* (Assen, 1959), pp. 29-41.

46. Leroy G. Schultz, "Interviewing the Sex Offender's Victim," *Journal of Criminal Law, Criminology and Police Science*, 50 (May-June 1959), 448-52.

47. Edwin D. Driver, "Interaction and Criminal Homicide in India," *Social Forces*, 40 (October 1961), 153-58.

48. T.C.N. Gibbens and Joyce Prince, *Child Victims of Sex Offenses* (London, 1963).

49. Albert Günter Hess, "Die Kinderschädung unter besonderer Berücksichtigung der Tatsituation," in Franz Exner, ed., *Kriminalistische Abhandlungen* (Leipzig, 1934), pp. 41-46.

50. W.H. Nagel, "The Notion of Victimology and Criminology," *Excerpta Criminologica*, Vol. 3 (May-June 1963) Similar views appear in the author's "Victimologie," *Tijdschrift voor Strafrecht* (Leiden, 1959), pp. 1-26.

51. Reckless, *The Crime Problem*, pp. 21-22.

52. Ezzat Abdel Fattah, "Quelques Problémes posés á la justice pénal par la victimologie," *International Annals of Criminology* (2nd sem., 1966). pp. 335-61.

B □ *Evolving services for crime victims*

JOHN P. J. DUSSICH

THE ORIGINS OF VICTIM SERVICES

In any discussion about crime victim services one is immediately confronted with the problem of overgeneralization. The field is rapidly becoming very specialized; therefore, to talk of services for crime victims is somewhat anachronistic. It is perhaps more accurate to focus on victim types that have been given special attention by virtue of something they have in common: the same crime, as with victims of rape, spouse abuse, or assault; the same category of crime, as with victims of personal crimes or property crimes; similarity in age, as with elderly victims and child victims; or importance to the criminal justice system, as with victim-witnesses.

The evolution of specific victim service programs originated from a small number of people with special interests. Less than a decade ago crime victims were handled primarily by hospitals, as persons with physical injuries. If emotional problems resulted from their victimization, little help was available unless the victims had the money to seek professional services. Religiously oriented groups such as the Salvation Army or local churches often rendered aid to some victims, but these were usually limited to metropolitan areas. In smaller communities, if the victim did not have strong friendship or family ties, little else was usually available.

In most communities that have established victim service programs, surprisingly little information was initially available on the actual extent of the victimization being considered, whether for child abuse, rape, or crimes against elderly victims. In such cases the establishment of the intervention effort brought about a greater awareness of the need to collect accurate data on the incidence of victimization, not only to better address the magnitude of the problem but also to measure the impact of the service delivery programs.

Most victim service programs can trace their origins to the last decade. Thus, the response to the needs of victims lacks much experience. One of the earliest organized efforts, for example, was the work done in New York State in 1964, resulting in the passage of that state's child abuse law. It set the stage for the establishment, in 1969, of the Mayor's Task Force on Child Abuse and Neglect, which was charged with the task of studying the total range of existing services within the city of New York.[1] Efforts such as this resulted in the Child Abuse Prevention and Treatment Act (P.L. 93-247), signed into law in January, 1974. This act established a National Center on Child Abuse and Neglect in the Children's Bureau, Office of Child Development, U.S. Department of Health, Education, and Welfare.[2]

Another major development in the evolution of victim service programs came about through the efforts of feminists, who brought the plight of rape victims to public attention. As a result, protest groups formed throughout the nation in response to local rape incidents and formal efforts to combat rape were formed under the name Women Against Rape (WAR). By 1972, rape crisis centers had been established in Los Angeles, Washington, D.C., and Ann Arbor; these served as the first models for the rest of the nation.[3]

The developing awareness of child victims and rape victims led to a general concern for providing services to all types of crime victims. The concept of the *victim ombudsman* was published in 1972 by the Florida Governor's Council on Criminal Justice. One of its major themes was that the *nature* and *extent of injury,* not the *type of crime,* should be the focal point of services. This represented an attempt to address all victims of crime, regardless of age, sex, race, or crime type, within a service format.[4] Under the program title of *victim advocate,* this same basic concept was implemented in Ft. Lauderdale, Florida, in April, 1974. This first victim advocate program became the model for similar victim service programs throughout the United States.

On January 14, 1974, Donald Santarelli, the administrator of the Law Enforcement Assistance Administration (LEAA), addressed the National Conference of State Criminal Justice Planning Administrators in Washington, D.C. In this speech he announced the establishment of a new unit within LEAA, called Citizens' Initiative. The unit was to have two primary functions: to get citizens involved in the war against crime and to foster greater consideration and concern for victims, witnesses, and jurors on the part of the criminal justice system.[5] This funding initiative helped the early formation of many victim witness programs that were soon to follow.

A national conference on victim services, held in Ft. Lauderdale in August, 1974, provided one of the early forums for sharing and synthesizing the incipient knowledge on victim service programs.[6] Also in October, 1974, the National District Attorneys' Commission on Victim Witness Assistance, began operations. In the first year of operation, eight district attorneys in major cities across the nation implemented the first series of prosecutor victim witness programs. Since then, over 84 such programs have been initiated; roughly the same number of nonprosecutor victim service programs have been established in a variety of agencies, including police departments, probation offices, private nonprofit agencies, corrections departments, and others.

Victim service programs designed to serve elderly persons have not kept pace with the rapid development of other victim service programs. Today, only a few programs exist, with the major response to the problem of victimization of the elderly being preventive. The first major conference to address the victimization of elderly persons was held in Washington, D.C., in June, 1975. Most of the panels, workshops, and speeches were devoted to describing the nature of the problem, with little attention given to victim services.[7] As a national effort, specific services for elderly victims have not developed significantly. However, as the propor-

tion of elderly persons increases, this type of service may increase commensurately.

The most recent area of attention has been spouse abuse. Again the feminist movement has been largely responsible for bringing this issue to national attention. One of the first program responses to the problem of spouse abuse was Refuge House, organized in Cheswick, England, in the early 1970s. Other efforts soon followed in Canada, Scotland, France, Australia, Holland, India, and Ireland.[8] In this country one of the first refuge homes for battered women was Rainbow Retreat, in Phoenix, Arizona. It started in November, 1973, with $50.00 and 11 volunteers, and was limited to families with drinking husbands. Another early program was Woman's Advocate House, started in October, 1974 in St. Paul, Minnesota. Since these early efforts, battered women shelters have developed as the best immediate solution to the problem of spouse abuse and are a far cry from the convents, charitable organizations, poor houses, hospitals, and asylums that previously were used as sanctuaries for women in distress.[8] Their central mission is to provide a safe place for women (and their children) who are in a crisis situation at home because of a battering husband or boyfriend. The refuge provides a temporary shelter for a woman and her children and permits them to meet with others in similar situations. These refuges are usually staffed by women who have themselves been battered. Thus a special empathy is offered as well as realistic counseling and guidance aimed at changing the victim's problem in some permanent way.

No discussion of the development of victim service programs would be complete without at least mentioning three additional types of victim-oriented programs established in the last half-dozen years: first, the use of arbitration and mediation services to resolve family and neighbor disputes; second, the increased use of restitution in the sentencing and correctional process so as to make offenders responsible for undoing, at least in part, the damage done; finally, recent efforts at establishing community crime control programs that stress private citizen involvement in crime prevention.[9]

PROGRAM RATIONALE AND OBJECTIVES

The dominant theme of all victim service programs has been recovery. Recovery may be short term or long term, may deal with problems that are physical, emotional, financial, or any combination of the three, and may try to help the victim either change or remove himself or herself from a damaging environment. More specifically, victim service programs can be divided into primary, secondary, and tertiary functions. Primary functions are common to most programs, are immediate in nature, and are aimed at delivering a narrow range of direct services. Secondary functions are also common to most programs but are usually of lesser importance, have long-range systems import, and are broad in scope. Tertiary functions are usually unique to specific victim categories, may either be long or short range, and have more relevance to planners, educators, and the community at large than to crime victims or agents of the criminal justice system. Some primary functions include:

- Taking immediate responsibility for the victim
- Ensuring that the victim is provided with emergency medical or social services
- Providing the victim with a temporary companion
- Addressing the client's family needs
- Ensuring that further exploitation of the victim does not occur
- Following up on the delivery of public assistance to clients

Some secondary functions include:

- Helping victims in their roles as witnesses
- Providing advice to reduce the victim's risk of revictimization
- Establishing volunteer efforts to augment victim service units
- Rendering aid to victims and their families with aftermath arrangements, such as funerals, insurance, and victim compensation
- Keeping the victim abreast of the case in which he or she is involved
- Giving relief to police officers by freeing them from crisis intervention and welfare referral tasks

- Rendering human need services and referrals to victims who have not reported their victimization to the police
- Ensuring that evidence and information from the victim is processed carefully, maintaining a balance of interests between the needs of the prosecutor and those of the victim
- Arranging with victims convenient times for court appearances
- Maintaining a victim-witness courtesy center where victims can wait for their court appearance
- Making arrangements for stolen property to be returned to victims as soon as the court's need for it as evidence is satisfied
- Providing victim-derived information for presentence investigation
- Encouraging victims to report crimes to the police

Some tertiary functions include:

- Studying individual victimizations for use in preventive planning
- Developing public awareness programs for target hardening
- Conducting periodic victimization surveys for use in planning
- Developing victim awareness throughout the community
- Gathering information from victims that could be used in community crime prevention programs
- Developing in-service training for criminal justice personnel who come in contact with the police to teach them how to deal with victim crisis and trauma
- Setting up periodic victim-awareness seminars for middle and upper management criminal justice personnel
- Developing standards to ensure that all segments of the criminal justice students take the victim's plight into account within their respective roles
- Publishing a community services directory tailored to victim needs
- Establishing a liaison with planning agencies to provide input on crime prevention and understanding the role of victims in the crime
- Assisting in developing restitution and compensation programs

TYPES OF VICTIM SERVICE PROGRAMS

Most victim service programs are described in terms of either their host agency, as with police department, prosecutor, and probation department programs, or their clientele, as with child abuse, rape, and spouse abuse programs. There are many differences in the structures of these various programs. At one extreme are loose, informal attempts at providing services on an ad hoc basis by staff who have other primary duties. Thus, when staff in the criminal justice system discover victims in need of services, they may take it upon themselves to render whatever aid seems appropriate at the moment. Somewhat more organized efforts occur where specific individuals fulfill the role of victim helper as a formal responsibility within the criminal justice or welfare system. With this type of approach some procedures are formally spelled out within the context of the organization's overall mission. Yet another level of services can be found outside the governmental realm. Many volunteer victim services have evolved in response to citizen action drives. These programs range from hot lines to very extensive counseling services. Some have been responses to severe victimizations that have aroused the community, and others have developed when civic groups recognized the plight of victims and established special forces. At the other extreme are highly organized, fully funded, formal victim service programs focusing on a comprehensive approach to victims' needs. They generally have strong support from the community and officials in the criminal justice system and most commonly have been funded with LEAA funds.

Examples of the ad hoc approach can be found where people who, in the normal course of their work, come upon victims in need of help. The most common example is the police officer, who, although not given extensive training in crisis work with victims, usually administer first aid. Often the officer's concern may prompt him or her to follow up and render additional, albeit unofficial, services. Another common example is the emergency room nurse who may be moved by a variety of motives to go beyond the medical aid required by her official role. Often a nurse will try to administer to a patient's emotional needs, whether the patient be a child recently abused, a young woman just raped, or a wife beaten by her husband. In both instances no formal training in the handling of crime victims was provided to the victim helper before his or her assumption of specific job responsibilities. The services rendered were more a function of human compassion.

As a result of the recent attention given to victims of crime, the additional-duty approach has become more prevalent. This is exemplified by the formal assignment of persons who are particularly empathetic or who have special skills to deal with victims as an added feature of their normal duties. In police agencies it may fall to the community services or community relations officers. Specialized interrogation of child victims in this and other countries (especially in larger cities) is often conducted by specially trained personnel.[10] In a prosecutor's office, one attorney is usually designated as the one who handles rape cases or child abuse cases or murder cases. Although this attorney's primary concern is the prosecution process, rather than the victim's welfare, some degree of facility is developed in dealing with victims and witnesses. In each of these cases it is clearly in the best interest of the agency to render aid to victims. The police generate goodwill, which may result in greater reporting of crimes and more cooperation in the investigative process. The prosecutor diminishes the chance of victims' withdrawing their complaints and enhances victim willingness to act as a witness at the trial. In spite of the self-serving nature of these approaches, they are institutionalized methods of rendering needed services to crime victims.

Volunteer services for victims are a unique phenomenon because of the affiliation of volunteers with the criminal justice system and its neglected client—the victim. The main difference between volunteers and others who provide victim services is that volunteers perform their tasks without remuneration. The four main national organizations that help volunteers working with victims today are the National Information Center on Volunteerism (NICOV), the Volunteers in Probation, Prison &

Parole (VIP), the National Organization for Women (NOW), and the National Organization of Victim Assistance (NOVA).

The two major advantages of these volunteer programs is their independence from financial support and control and their freedom from programmatic restrictions. Their major disadvantage is their tendency to periodic upheavals, especially when legitimacy and community acceptance are weak. Almost all volunteer programs strive toward some degree of institutionalization. When this is accomplished, a small cadre of paid staff usually ensure program continuity, with volunteers serving as auxiliary personnel.

A further program approach is the development of a comprehensive victim service program. Two examples of this approach are the victim-witness assistance programs and the witness advocate programs. Rather than serving only one victim type, both models generally provide a wide range of services to all types of victims, especially victims of serious crimes. The principal difference between the two is the host agency and the extent of crisis intervention. Victim-witness assistance programs are typically administrated as a part of prosecutors' offices. For victim advocate programs, the host agency can vary from law enforcement and local probation departments to city and county administrative offices, religious organizations, and private agencies.

The principal advantage of the victim-witness assistance model comes from the clout associated with the prosecutor's office. Cooperation with other agencies is therefore likely to be greater. The main disadvantages are: an over-emphasis on victims as "objects of proof"[11] rather than people in need of services; a screening process that restricts services primarily to victims whose offenders are being brought to trial, thereby excluding a large proportion of victims whose offenders are not arrested; and the fact that these programs deal with victims whose time of most critical need has long since passed.

The victim advocacy model, especially in the case of programs found in law enforcement agencies, offers several advantages. Services are provided closer in time to the victim's trauma, and this results in assistance at the time of greatest need. Those programs associated with law enforcement agencies are in a position to enhance reporting of crimes by responding in an immediate and positive way and are able to make contact with a larger percentage of victims than is the case with other models.[12] The disadvantage of the victim advocate model is in trying to legitimize services for a new client; the process suffers from the "new kid on the block" syndrome.

MAJOR IMPLEMENTATION PROBLEMS

Implementation is a dynamic, ongoing process that begins with the conceptualization of a project and ends only when the project is terminated. Thus a discussion of implementation problems must focus on the way each new project begins and on the difficulties encountered in operationalizing it. This perspective suggests an examination of each major stage in the evolution of a victim service project.

The conceptualization stage involves a formulation of the problem, a discussion of needs, and a general notion of what should be done to improve the plight of victims. Difficulties at this point are primarily concerned with the availability of reliable and complete information to identify the nature and extent of victimization, the resources available to help understand the nature and aftermath of victimization, and the creativity to develop a variety of methods to resolve the service needs of victims within the context of a specific community and component of the criminal justice system.

In selling the idea to decision makers, one encounters additional problem areas. The most salient of these include; identifying key decision makers (power-brokers)[13]; determining an appropriate approach to these individuals; understanding the mechanics, psychology, and politics of the planning and the funding processes; and trying to marshal a broad base of community support.[14]

During the staffing period, some of the unique problems that arise include: trying to define appropriate job specifications for a new profession; selecting personnel who can perform the tasks and who do not pose a threat to other personnel within the host agency; and withstanding informal political attempts to have friends, relatives or political supporters hired to this new and intriguing project.

Once the project passes all the hurdles of funding, it must pass the test of organizational acceptance. This means introducing a new agency to the criminal justice community, resolving "turf" disputes, and learning how to be the "new kid on the block." Victim services projects at this point in their evolution are wise to keep a very low profile until working relationships can be established with peer agencies and until basic operating procedures can be developed. Numerous programs have gone out of existence because they prematurely established immediate visibility, which led to unrealistically high community expectations that could not be met by the project at that time.

The final stage, institutionalization, is also fraught with difficulties. These include: making the transition from external grant funds to more long-term local funding sources; maintaining a high level of community awareness for the plight of victims; maintaining a high level of staff enthusiasm after the project settles into a more routine mode of operation; and ensuring continued project relevance by periodic reassessment of goals and objectives tailored to the changing needs of the victim, the community, and the criminal justice system.

SUMMARY

Because of the rich diversity of program types, functions, and objectives, a much-needed change has evolved in delivering specialized types of service to crime victims. Over 500 victim programs of all types now exist throughout the country. Continued federal funding and near-heroic efforts on the part of many in the "victim movement" will ensure the perpetuation and expansion of victim service programs. Not only is the criminal justice system humanized by these efforts, but the quality of life is enhanced in every community that hosts victim service programs. It is not important what type of structure a program takes or what agency hosts the activity. What is important is that traditional responses to victimization in many communities have been replaced with sensitive and functional substitutes that significantly reduce the suffering of victims and increase the sense of caring and justice. These pioneering ventures represent efforts to help ensure the right of all victims to be treated with dignity and respect.

REFERENCES

1. Fontana, Vincent O. *Somewhere a Child is Crying* (New York: Macmillan Publishing Co., Inc., 1973), pp. 141-142.
2. *Child Abuse and Neglect: The Problem and its Management,* vol. 3, *The Community Team: An Approach to Case Management and Prevention* (Washington, D.C.: U.S. Dept. HEW, 1976).
3. Largen, Mary Ann. "History of Women's Movement in Changing Attitudes, Laws and Treatment Toward Rape Victims," in Walker, Marcia J., and Stanley L. Brosky, eds. *Sexual Assault* (Lexington, Mass.: D.C. Heath & Co., 1976), p. 69.
4. Dussich, John. "The Victim Ombudsman, Florida: Governor's Council on Criminal Justice" (Tallahassee, Fla., 1972).
5. Santarelli, Donald. "Address to the National Conference of State Criminal Justice Planning Administrators" (Washington, D.C., LEAA, U.S. Department of Justice, August 12-14, 1974).
6. Proceedings of the First National Conference on Victim Assistance (Unpublished, Washington, D.C., LEAA, U.S. Department of Justice, August 12-14, 1974).
7. Goldsmith, Jack, and Sharon S. Goldsmith, eds. *Crime and the Elderly* (Lexington, Mass.: D.C. Heath & Co., 1976.)
8. Warrior, Betsy. *Wifebeating,* 2nd ed. (Somerville, Mass.: New England Free Press, 1976).
9. Stein, John H. *"Better Services for Crime: A Prescriptive Package,"* (Unpublished manuscript, Washington, D.C., Blackstone Institute, 1977), pp. 9-10.
10. Libai, David. "The Protection of the Child Victim of a Sexual Offense in the Criminal Justice System," *Wayne Law Review,* vol. 15, Summer 1969, pp. 986-995.
11. Lynch, Richard P. *Help for Victims and Witnesses* (an annual report from the National District Attorneys Association Commission on Victim Witness Assistance, Washington, D.C., February 1976), p. 18.
12. Dussich, John P. J. "Victim Service Models and Their Efficacy," in Viano, Emilio C., ed. *Victims and Society,* (Washington, D.C.: Visage Press, 1976), p. 473.
13. Ibid., p. 476.
14. National Advisory Commission on Criminal Justice Standards and Goals. *Community Crime Prevention* (Washington, D.C.: U.S. Government Printing Office, 1973), p. 10.

C □ *Communities as victims of corporate crimes*

PETER B. MEYER

Corporate victimizations are now readily recognized in instances of environmental degradations, collective bargaining in bad faith, consumer fraud, stock manipulations, and the like. These activities are accepted as instances in which the corporate entity is legally liable for its actions, and its actions are discernibly harmful to an identifiable aggregate or class of victims. Another group of victims of corporate behaviors that either are now or may become illegal, however, has received but minimal attention, and this aggregate is the "community" in which the corporate behavior occurs. This paper is addressed to such local communities, either as a class of local residents or as a corporate entity in its own right (as in municipal corporations). For the sake of simplicity, I will examine here only those forms of corporate behavior that could be construed as *theft,* exclusive of retail theft, in order that the victims may be clearly identified and that those characteristics of communities that render them prone to victimization may be isolated.

Corporate criminality, except insofar as negligence may be concerned, has been determined only in a limited set of economic crimes:

Apart from the civil-offense area, convictions of corporations have been largely limited to the acquisitive offenses (theft, fraud, and so forth).[1]

The types of common-law offenses which have actually resulted in corporate criminal responsibilities . . . are restricted for the most part to thefts (including frauds) and involuntary manslaughter.[2]

The actions of corporate entities deemed possible, it will be noted, exclude thefts involving intentional use of any form of coercive power. In the language of the American Law Institute's

Model Penal Code drafts, examination of corporate theft has been limited to consideration of "theft by deception," to the exclusion of consideration of "theft by intimidation."[3]

The reasons for this myopia are many, primary among which appears to be the availability of civil remedies, or remedies under other criminal statutes, for the accepted forms of intimidation (those directed at union and employee associations, shareholders, and consumers). The community as a victim has not received serious consideration in law other than that growing out of emerging environmental concerns, and little of the existing law provides coverage or protection for such victimization. It may be that the most expeditious means of providing this coverage is through extension of the theft statutes to permit consideration of coercion and intimidation by that collective person called a corporation.

This paper, then, is organized into three major sections. First, I look at what is—and what might become—corporate criminality, with an eye directed primarily at communities as victims of crime. Second, I review the types of corporate actions that parallel recognized thefts by individuals. Finally, I examine definitions of communities and the characteristics of communities that make them liable to victimization at the hands of corporations.

WHAT IS—AND WHAT MIGHT BECOME—CORPORATE CRIMINALITY?

The extension of Fourteenth Amendment protections of "life, liberty, and property" to corporations by the Supreme Court in 1886 did not include the application of an explicit set of obligations of "personhood" corresponding to the grant of citizenship in the application of the amendment's due process protections.[4] Some responsibilities and demands for actions have

An original paper prepared for the Second International Symposium on Victimology, Boston, Massachusetts, September 1976.

been imposed on corporate entities by law over time, with the imposition of environmental regulations in recent years generating a virtual explosion of such demands for action. However, none of these legal requirements has been predicated on the "personhood" of the collectivity in question. In fact, there has been a continuing pattern of discrimination in favor of the corporation-as-person, including the explicit exclusion of liability for criminal prosecution for categories of theft for which individuals are liable.[5]

The starkest instance of this exception lies in the area of so-called economic crimes. The American Law Institute explicitly excludes from its conceptions of "theft by intimidation" those "situations in which a private property economy must tolerate 'economic coercion' as an incident to free bargaining." The rationale for these exclusions is that:

Civil remedies are usually adequate to deal with abuse of the privilege. Some coercive economic bargaining may call for legal restriction by antitrust laws, labor legislation and the like; but theft penalties would be quite inappropriate.[6]

As I will demonstrate below, any remedy other than one allowing for consideration of theft from the totality of a local community fails to provide adequate restraint on the powers of economic coercion vested in multiplant, multi-location corporations.

The economic coercion considered in these phrases emanates from the real economic power of the corporate unit, vis-à-vis other economic actors. It appears that, to the drafters of the Model Penal Code at least, the exercise of such economic power is acceptable in some instances but not in others. According to the commentary just cited, the following behaviors *should* be deemed criminal:

(a) the foreman in a manufacturing plant requires the workers to pay him a percentage of their wages on pain of dismissal or other employment discrimination; (b) a close friend of the purchasing agent of a giant corporation obtains money from an important supplier by threatening to influence the purchasing agent to divert his business elsewhere; (c) a professor obtains property from a student by threatening to give him a failing grade.[7]

All three instances provided as illustrations involve the "abuse" by an *individual* of his or her unique position and its associated economic power to wrest property from other individuals. Analogous behaviors on the part of a business corporation can be briefly cited:

1. *Requiring a payoff or kickback:* A corporation, indifferent about whether to expand its existing plant in a community or build a new plant elsewhere, informs the local government of the community in which it operates that, in the absence of tax advantages for its new construction, it will move elsewhere (and cause substantial local unemployment).

2. *Influence peddling:* A corporation with a manufacturing plant in a community informs the local authorities that, should the municipality enforce environmental regulations in regard to sewage discharges, it will advise other manufacturers that the community is a poor location with inadequate services.

3. *Affecting reputation:* A commercial bank involved in floating municipal bonds informs a locality entering the bond market that, unless it deposits its funds in a stipulated local bank, its bond rating will be lowered.

It is obvious that there already exist legal remedies to address many of the impacts of such corporate behaviors. What is not so obvious is that each of these behaviors constitutes a form of theft of the property of the residents and citizens of identifiable communities. It is the fact that an act of theft occurs that makes these actions logically addressable as crimes with victims and that permits us to examine the victims of such crimes.

The business community has a strong stake in maintaining a distinction between its use of its economic power and the use of economic power on the part of "private individuals." However, the fear that treatment of business leaders' criminality may come to approach that of street people exceeds any concern over corporate liability. *Business Week* magazine has noted the "almost daily disclosures that some of the nation's most distinguished executives . . . did not care how results were obtained, even if it meant breaking the law."[8] Admission of the violation of law by businessmen, however, was not tantamount to acceptance of the criminality of those persons on the part of the magazine, which went on to observe that "getting business to own up to its sins and do something about them is a slow process."[9] However, the real issue confronting the business establishment and the nation involved not the *sins* of business (*immoral* actions) but the *crimes* of business (*illegal* actions). It appears that, for the moment at least, the first problem is one of convincing the business leadership that their actions are indeed criminal.

A recent development in regard to corporate thievery that is of some importance emerged from a case involving the efforts of a publicly held corporation to go private. The U.S. Court of Appeals, Second Circuit, ruled that:

When controlling shareholders of a publically held corporation use corporation funds to force extinction of the minority shareholders' interest for the sole purpose of feeding the pocketbooks of the controlling shareholders, such conduct goes beyond mere negligent management [and could logically be construed as fraud].[10]

This case demonstrates, as well as any could, the inherently coercive nature of the exercise of private property rights in general. The case came before the federal court because the plaintiffs could get no recourse in the Delaware courts under the law covering the corporation and its charter. The coercion, therefore, was legal, at least within one rubric; it was nevertheless the exercise of expropriative power. The protection of the federal courts was available to the class of minority shareholders, given the regulatory powers vested in the Securities and Exchange Commission. However, no protection for the class of victims who comprise the members of affected communities is provided under such legislation. Consider an extension of this case as an example.

Assume that the minority shares in a company going private, Company A, are held by a second company, Company B, and that they comprise the bulk of the reserves of Company

B. If Company A offers $150 a share to repurchase the stocks from Company B when the assets of Company A are valued at $750 a share, then Company A is coercing Company B to relinquish property worth $600 per share. Assume further that Company B, having no immediate recourse, accepts the offered price and files civil proceedings to obtain the remaining $600 per share that it claims as its due. Assume further that Company B operates a manufacturing establishment in City C that comes under an environmental protection order to clean up its emissions or close its doors shortly after Company B suffers the loss of the major portion of its reserves (through the action of Company A). As a result of its weakened reserve position and its inability to borrow further, Company B closes its plant in City C, transferring its production to another plant with idle capacity. Finally, assume that after a period of years, litigation provides that Company A must reimburse Company B for the $600 per share that it lost, along with accrued interest and compensation for other damages and costs.

The common reading of this sequence of events is that the class damaged by the inadequate tender of payment for shares repurchased by Company A, the shareholders of Company B, was adequately protected under the laws. (We have assumed here that Company B minimized the damage of Company A's action by moving out of City C.) However, there is a victim of the actions of Company A that is totally ignored in such an interpretation. This victim is City C, which lost employment, incomes, and a taxpaying enterprise as the result of the relocation of Company B's manufacturing activity. Not only have the former employees of Company B in City C lost their incomes, but their reduced spending may have generated lower incomes for the providers of goods and services in City C, and the decreased tax payments due to the closing of Company B's plant may have generated a higher tax burden for all residents of the city. City C, therefore, suffered a real loss of property and of expected income as a result of the illegal actions of Company A.

Company A caused an "involuntary transfer of property" away from City C, and to Company *B*, by which it benefitted. The liability of Company *A* should not have been limited to correcting the damage done to the profits, reserves, and stability of Company *B*, as would be required by securities regulation, but should have included the damage done inadvertently to City *C* by Company *B* in the course of its efforts to minimize the direct damage it suffered as the result of Company *A's* actions. In other words, Company *A* should have been held liable for any damage done to the shareholders of Company *B* and the *residents of all the communities in which Company B operated.* With specific reference to the closing of Company *B's* plant in City *C*, the party found guilty, Company *A*, should have been liable for all the damages to Company *B* had Company *B* remained in City *C*, paying taxes and payrolls and investing in pollution abatement equipment, in the manner in which it would have operated in the absence of the securities manipulation by Company *A*.

The use of securities regulations rather than theft statutes for correcting damage in this instance enables the perpetrator of a theft to avoid the full consequences of his actions, leaving the burden of adjustment to economic dislocation on the shoulders of the City *C* community. The regulatory legislation is inadequate, because it holds the perpetrator of a crime liable only for the damage wrought directly by his actions and ignores completely the damage wrought by second parties coerced to adjust to minimize the damaging actions of the first party. In economic terms, the regulatory mechanisms fail totally to address the issue of incidence, that is, the question of who bears the burden for any action taken in adjustment to economic coercion. The implicit assumption is that the cost of the incidence rests with the party directly injured. This assumption is rarely, if ever, warranted in the day of the multiplant, multiindustry corporation.

WHAT CORPORATE ACTIONS PARALLEL THEFTS BY INDIVIDUALS?

Before I turn to an examination of the three types of corporate behaviors that parallel the exploitations of position specifically identified as legally unacceptable by the American Law In-

stitute when done by individuals, some definitions of the crimes associated with such behaviors are in order. There are several elements of the thefts by either intimidation or deception that are engaged in by corporations. The critical components are as follows:

Coercion "Where one party is constrained by subjugation to [an]other to do what his free will would refuse. It may be actual or threatened exercise of power possessed or supposedly possessed."[11]

Extortion "Obtaining of property from another, with his consent, induced by wrongful use of force or fear. . . . To constitute 'extortion' the wrongful use of fear must be the operating cause producing consent."[12] "The natural meaning of the word 'extort' is to obtain money or other valuable thing either by compulsion, by actual force, or by the force of motives applied to the will, and often more overpowering and irresistible than physical force."[13]

Fraud "An intentional perversion of truth . . . it is something said, done, or omitted by a person with the design of perpetrating what he knows to be a cheat or deception."[14]

Fraudulent concealment "The hiding or suppression of a material fact or circumstance which the party is legally or morally bound to disclose."[15]

Fraudulent representation "A representation that is knowingly untrue, or made without belief in its truth, or made recklessly and, in any event, for the purpose of inducing action upon it."[16]

Obviously, none of these actions can be deemed to have been undertaken by a corporation without some demonstration of *mens rea*, that is, criminal intent. However, the essential objective of the corporate entity in business is the stability of its own existence and thus the maximization of such intermediate goals as profits and sales, which might contribute to stability. If corporate managers are rewarded for contributing to increased profits, sales, or other elements providing corporate stability, then the corporation will itself become liable for the actions taken by managers in pursuing corporate goals, according to Section 2.07 of the Model Penal Code.[17] Corporate guilt may be virtually assumed for criminal actions contributing to profitability and organizational stability. We can now move on toward further examination of corporate criminality, beginning with a review of the conditions of communities in general that leave them open to victimization.

Locality economic development has been a major concern of towns and states in this nation for decades.[18] Competition for the location of plants has intensified in recent years, with the federal government contributing to this development.[18,19] The tools of industrial development efforts have been varied, including tax credits and forgiveness, loan guarantees, issuance of industrial development bonds, low-interest loans, and the like, accompanied by political favors, manpower training, and extensive advertising efforts.[20] Community interest in local employment, and thus in the location of industrial enterprises, derives from a phenomenon known to economists as "the multiplier." This principle, simply stated, is that an increase in the income of one subset of the population of an area contributes to rising incomes for other residents insofar as the new spending of the first group, who pay other locals for goods and services, becomes additional income for the other groups.

The totality of the local community, therefore, is interested in the volume of employment at any local plants, as well as in the terms and conditions of wage settlements and other agreements between a corporation operating in the community and its employees. By logical extension, the community is interested in other aspects of the corporation's performance, such as the quality of the product, since the market for goods produced may affect the level of employment or pay at the factory, and the financial condition of the parent corporation, which could lead to actions and pressures with negative effects on all community members. The three examples of logically illegal corporate actions may now be elaborated.

Give me a break, or else . . .

Financial incentives for corporate relocations or plant construction are widespread in in this country, but their impact on locational decisions is questionable at best.[21] Possible fraud in corporate pursuit of tax breaks and other giveaways lies in the falsity of the claim that a locational decision would be different in the absence of such special provisions. For example:

A national mail survey conducted by the U.S. Department of Commerce, in 1972, covering 2,900 companies in high-growth industries across the country, revealed that 78 percent considered tax incentives of 'holidays' to be relevant to their locational decisions. But only 8 percent rated such incentives as 'critical'.[22]

In light of these findings, are the corporations that contribute funds to Chambers of Commerce and to campaigns directed at reducing taxes for businesses with the justification that such actions are necessary for an improved "business climate" and new industrial growth engaged in fraud? They may be if such incentives are *not* critical.

The claim that businesses will respond differently if offered a tax break is, at best, "made recklessly," and the commission of the offense, if any, is "authorized . . . by the board of directors." However, a critical aspect of the claims of industry associations and others that incentives are necessary is the *threat* (implied or made explicit) that, without special inducement, industry will flee a jurisdiction or fail to locate there. This threat may constitute extortion; it is clearly coercive, since it involves the "threatened use of power . . . supposedly possessed."

The multinational conglomerate, the epitome of the mobile, independent corporation in the latter twentieth century, invariably employs a threat of economic dislocation in forcing its will; this tool is strictly analogous to that used by the foreman extorting payments from workers in the American Law Institute commentary cited above. One such multinational firm is Litton Corporation, one of the major "go-go" conglomerates to develop during the decade of the 1960s. One study of Litton's labor relations practices observed that:

Litton uses its financial power and mobility to force the union to negotiate modest or poor contracts . . . where the union could not be dislodged, Litton subsidiary managers negotiated to impasse and then closed their plants during the ensuing strikes . . . the overall pattern proves to be aggressively anti-union and inclined toward intimidation of local bargaining units.[23]

The corporation has thus done its utmost to keep its union adversaries weak by moving its production from location to location as labor in one area becomes more militant. Eventually, of course, the threat and danger of a move (and the attendant plant shutdown) become known not only to workers in all plants but to the communities in which the plants are located as well. Thus, Litton becomes capable of implicitly threatening a plant shutdown and attendant economic dislocations in virtually all of the many communities in which it has manufacturing facilities. To the extent that communities are somewhat dependent on the employment that the corporation offers (that is, to the extent that they are "constrained by subjugation"), Litton has succeeded in coercing the citizens of all of the communities in which it operates to take its side against its workers when labor militancy appears to threaten plant shutdowns.

It may be argued that extension of theft statutes to cover corporate actions generates disincentives for corporations to take advantage of the need of small towns and depressed areas for employment and that such new laws could slow the overall economic development of the nation. However, there is a grave danger that development accomplished through such dispersion of the activities of multinational firms will generate

the same sort of dependency and unbalanced economic growth in the rich United States that it has always done in the poor Third World. New plants that are controlled by corporations headquartered elsewhere impose enormous infrastructure costs on a community. They import much of their labor (especially the "good" jobs), and they often house their highest paid labor outside the taxing jurisdiction where the plant is situated. Then—after all the effort expended to get them there in the first place—they often move to some other place when local inducements run out.[24]

Given the economic desperation of small towns with minimal income sources and high poverty levels, the corporate tendency to break promises in taking advantage of incentives offered may, under the law, be either fraud or extortion. Such actions constitute theft in the same manner as the demand for kickbacks from subordinates by a supervisory employee is theft.

Let me pollute, or else . . .

The role played by manufacturers in fouling the water and air of communities and areas abutting on their locations of operations has received growing attention in recent years. The role played by manufacturers in promoting pollution through their influence over communities was highlighted in a *Business Week* report on the aftermath of the discovery of Kepone poisoning in Hopewell, Virginia:

Officials of the Environmental Protection Agency have long suspected that cities, in their zeal to attract industry, have turned a blind eye to pollution and have allowed companies to pour toxic wastes into sewage treatment plants that were incapable of handling them. The grand jury has accused Hopewell officials of failing to notify the EPA of the alleged kepone pollution. If Hopewell is convicted, it faces a $3.9 million fine, and the EPA hopes that other cities will think twice before abetting such corporate pollution.[25]

Cities are willing to abet such pollution, according to the article, because of their zeal to attract industry. The noun *zeal* connotes a voluntary action, but the whole issue of the guilt of Hopewell and its officials centers on whether their actions were in fact voluntary.

This case involves the pollution of the James River and Chesapeake Basin, with the loss of good fishing areas and of other sources of community revenues. Thus the impact of the Kepone dumping extends beyond the effects on the employees who contracted Kepone poisoning in the plant manufacturing the insecticide. Had Hopewell insisted on closing the plant dumping Kepone into its sewage system, it would *not* have lost a *major* industry, or employer. However, the company would invariably have announced that its plant shutdown was due to the inadequacy of the sewage treatment facilities in Hopewell, which could have damaged the city's ability to attract other industry. From the point of view of efficiency as well as equity, there might be solid grounds for suggesting that manufacturers producing exceptional types of waste sludge treat by-products before dumping them in municipal sewage systems. However, few communities have the economic capacity and strength to make such demands on employers on whom they depend for payrolls and tax revenues.

The pattern of influence in pollution permissions is once again, however, not clearly either theft by fraud or by intimidation. The theft occurs if only insofar as failure to comply with environmental regulations, which saves companies money, results in additional costs to the community and its members. (Such costs may be more frequent housepainting due to particulate matter in the air, medical bills due to health hazards, or other expenses caused by the pollution; it does not matter, as the principle of theft holds.) The threat of a loss of employment, or of the emergence of a reputation that could damage future growth in employment, may be coercive, whether or not it is truthful. However, if the threat is a false claim, then the coercion based on presumed power is fraudulent as well as extortive. The capacity of the communities so victimized to resist the pressures associated with fears of employment losses is clearly a function of the locality's dependence on a single employer or industry.[26] A community need not be either small or in desperate need of jobs for it to be subject to extortion by threats to move elsewhere or to inhibit development in the area through the spreading of adverse publicity.

Handle finances as I dictate, or else . . .

Corporate-community relations are rarely manipulable in precisely the same manner as a professor can coerce students; however, a number of reputation-damaging behaviors may be manifest. The most ballyhooed cases of corporate exploitation of influence capabilities available today lie in the field of municipal finance and the relationships between governments borrowing money and commercial banks.

The power of the financiers over municipalities derives from their roles in underwriting bond issues. Any bond issue—a major means of raising funds for capital improvements in communities—is sold to underwriters who in turn offer bonds to investors. Underwriters wield power over interest rates (informing municipalities what rates they must offer to "excite

investor interest"), but may also wield more power over the operations of the community and its government by announcing that, in the absence of certain municipal reforms, "investor confidence" will not be adequate for the bonds to sell.

In the case of New York City, the exercise of power by the underwriting banks has been extensively documented. The mechanisms for the exercise of this power are devastatingly simple:

> When Morgan, Chase-Manhattan, and First National City report the lack of "investor confidence" in city bonds they are in large part talking about themselves and their clients.
>
> If enough investors refuse to lend to the city because they believe it won't have the money to pay them back, sure enough the city soon runs out of money. In this way the banks have "proved" that city bonds can be sold only at steadily increasing interest rates.[27]

This chain of events, in which the underwriting departments of the major banks advised the trust departments of the same banks not to invest in the bonds they were underwriting, assisted the financial community in raising the interest rate on bonds issued for the city of New York from 7.9% in July 1974 to as high as 11% in the summer of 1975.[27] A rationale for the claim that these actions are criminal may be based on two principles.

First, when the banks make the claim of lost investor confidence, they may be said to have a moral obligation to identify the percentage of bonds they offer for sale as underwriters that they ordinarily buy for themselves and their trust account customers. If such a moral obligation exists and the banks do not honor it, then they may be guilty of "fraudulent concealment" under the definition offered above. The second consideration is that the capacity of the underwriters to rationalize the increased interest rates depends on the threat of the city's default, and the banks may not be in a position to permit that default to occur.[28] Therefore:

> when default approaches again, another last minute emergency plan will be adopted. But the spectre of default will remain an effective weapon in the bank's at-

tempt to raise profits at the expense of government services.[28]

A fraudulently rationalized coercion can therefore be said to underlie the bank operations that place increasing pressures on the interest rates of municipal bonds and notes. This fraud may be analogous to a professor's offering grades for a fee in a computer-graded course in which no grading discretion on his part is really possible.

Beyond these financial operations, which enhance profits for banks and other actors in the nation's money markets, political power and influence are both accumulated through manipulation of bond holdings and willingness to lend. Recent experience in Massachusetts is illustrative:

> As late as 1974, the state's ratio of debt to tax revenue was only a little above the national average, and well below those of such eastern states as Connecticut, Delaware, and Pennsylvania. But with the memory of New York's problems fresh in their minds, big investors judged Massachusetts a risky place to put their loan funds, and have extracted a high price for lending to cover the state's deficit.
>
> The investors required Governor Dukakis, elected in 1974 on a campaign pledge of no new taxes, to submit a balanced budget for fiscal 1976. Dukakis went along, calling for $370 million in cutbacks and a tax hike of $700 million.[29]

Bank threats not to underwrite (and not to purchase) bonds issued by governments, therefore, can lead to financial corporations' control of budgets.

Dukakis, in submitting a balanced budget with massive tax increases, violated his campaign pledge. If Governor Dukakis, acting of his own free will, would have stood by his campaign pledge not to raise taxes, then, in submitting a budget with $700 million in proposed tax hikes, the governor may well have acted under coercion, as it was defined above. The coercion was engendered by the financial power of the banks, so the bank corporations were thus engaging in theft by intimidation, as was the hypothetical professor.

If commercial banking interests can wield such power over the political and other decisions of a state with a population of about 6 million people, what is the capacity of even a local bank in a city of under 50,000? The coercive capacity is clearly present; it is irrational to expect that the capacity will not be employed if it contributes to bank and corporate profitability and stability. Sanctions against the use of such power are clearly in order. It may be argued that the "use" of the power must be distinguished from the "abuse" of power. It may also be the case that, when the private financial interest is sufficiently large relative to the community in which it operates, *any* exercise of such power is *inherently abusive* to the community.

WHAT CHARACTERISTICS OF COMMUNITIES MAKE THEM LIABLE TO CORPORATE VICTIMIZATION?

Communities are victimized by manufacturing and financial corporations in a wide variety of manners, as has been demonstrated. Corporations engaged in retail and wholesale trade, service delivery, and transportation may similarly victimize the localities in which they operate or with which they deal. I could easily address myself to an ever-widening set of corporate behaviors that may or may not be construed to constitute forms of theft victimizing communities rather than (or in addition to) the more readily accepted classes of victims. But there is a more important task: the identification of those characteristics of communities that render them more or less likely to be victimized.

The major problem inherent in treating communities as victims of crimes is that of definition of the victim(s). A community is more than an aggregate of persons, and is thus more than just another class of victims. However, the locality or local economy affected by the actions of a corporation may include more than one community, so the victims of a corporate action may be the *class* of communities commonly affected. Any large city, for example, is one local government, but is also composed of a mass of diverse communities; actions taken by corporations affecting the city may be interpreted as damaging the city as a single victim, the communities that comprise the city taken as individuals, or the communities as a class defined by the boundaries of the city. The analysis of communities, their functions and dimensions, offered by Roland Warren in his classic work, *The Community in America*, provides the basis for a coherent approach to these definitional issues.[30]

A community may be defined in terms of four essential dimensions and five major locality-relevant functions. Taking the functions first, we have:

1. *Production, distribution, and consumption:* The traditional economic functions associated with community must be met by some structural forms.
2. *Socialization:* Processes exist that provide individuals inculcation with the mores and values of the community.
3. *Social control:* Mechanisms through which communities influence the behaviors of their members must be present.
4. *Social participation:* Institutions channeling participation in community affairs on the part of members are necessary.
5. *Mutual support:* Support must be provided by a variety of institutions and relationships directed at assisting persons in need in the community.[31]

All of these functions may be engaged in by communities that are part of local government aggregates, by larger governmental units, by units that are part of national or international organizations, and the like. There may be cross-fertilization between the institutions providing for each function, or they may operate independently. The provisions of these functions to community members, then, differs in form and content with the dimensions of the community in question. The four salient elements here are:

1. *Autonomy,* or the extent to which the community exercises its functions independent of external influence (or "vertical" ties in Warren's language)
2. *Contiguity of service areas,* or the extent to which the community's geographic boundary for one function corresponds to the boundaries for other functions
3. *Psychological identification,* or the strength of the personal ties to the community felt by its members
4. *Strength of the horizontal pattern,* or the cross-fertilization and interaction between the institutions providing the different community functions (which stands in contradistinction to the vertical ties implied by low levels of autonomy)[32]

The four dimensions may be applied to each of the five functions to get a fuller perspective on the characteristics of community ties and the relationships between communities (and their members) and extracommunity (or supracommunity) entities. Such an analysis of communities proceeds logically from Warren's definition of a community as "that combination of social units and systems which perform the major social functions having locality relevance."[33] Thus, in the production, distribution, and consumption function of communities, the extent to which the economy is dominated by national firms—that is, the degree to which the economy is *not* autonomous—affects the likelihood that the community will be victimized. Moreover, to the extent that a community is part of a one-industry or one-company town (such as Johnstown, Pennsylvania, in which 60% of the industrial work force was employed in the Bethlehem Steel Mill) that dominant employment comes to wield strong influence over the *entire* community because of its major role in socialization and in provision for social participation. The unions associated with such employers similarly come to dominate the mutual support network, and the overall dependence of the community on the one industry and employer renders it extremely vulnerable to victimization. Yet another form of potential for victimization derives from the relative size of communities and corporations, since the variety and complexity of horizontal relationships and the potential for autonomy in the small community are limited, whereas the size and diversity of multinational conglomerates render them less concerned about conditions in any of the communities in which they operate.

Perhaps the best way to summarize the various aspects of communities that affect their propensity to be victimized, all other things being equal, is through examination of the auspices under which different functions are executed. Warren distinguishes five levels that, to him, represent a shift from self-sufficiency to dependency.[34] This ranking and interpretation is subject to some modification for analysis of victimization, but the categories themselves are of value.

1. *Individuals or families as producers and providers.* This level of functioning represents the highest personal autonomy, but may not be relevant to some of the community functions, such as mutual support or socialization, and may thus generate a false sense of independence.

2. *Ad hoc informal organizations as producers and providers.* The formation of such organizations represents a low-level response to the need to assure smooth operation of community functions that require collective endeavor; such organizations are inherently localized, and a strong network of such institutions may insulate the community from some forms of corporate victimization.

3. *Formal organizations as producers and providers.* If these organizations are wholly local or are so structured that local units have virtual autonomy, then their functioning may approximate the salubrious effects of ad hoc organizations; insofar as vertical ties are dominant in such formal organizations, they may increase community vulnerability to victimization by undermining autonomy.

4. *Production and service provision for financial gain.* Insofar as any community functions are performed for financial gain (independent of the welfare of the persons employed in the activity), some vertical ties emerge that transcend local concerns, and autonomy declines; even locally owned and operated enterprises may victimize communities insofar as such business ventures are tied to national financial and product markets.

5. *Official government production and service provision.* The transfer of a function from private to public auspices does *not* necessarily imply a loss of local control or autonomy; the critical issue is the level of government that takes over the function and the extent to which it is sensitive to local conditions.

The essential question, then, is not the public or private, or formal or informal nature of the auspices under which community functions are executed but the degree to which the functions are pursued in the interests of the community, rather than of some other agency or organization. It is for this reason that the degree to which community functions are executed under profit-making auspices is critical in determining community propensity to victimization. The ever-spreading net of functions produced for profit represents a widening set of opportunities for victimization of communities, since provision of a function by a for-profit enterprise is inherently a condition in which the executor of the function (the private firm) has an interest (its own profitability) that transcends that of the community.

Corporations are one group of profit-oriented institutions that play a major role in the U.S. economy. The largest corporations in the system dominate any community in which they operate and, by their very nature, can have little interest in any one community in which they operate. (Litton Corporation, for example, maintained 1388 different plants and offices in all fifty states in 1969, and could have minimal concern for any one of the locations in which the corporation maintained facilities.[35]) Thus any vertical ties must contribute to community vulnerability, since any institution with supralocal concerns will be willing to sacrifice the interests of any one community to the "greater good"—the needs of other communities in which it has an interest. It is ironic, but some of the poorest communities in the nation, measured by annual incomes received, may be among the settings in which corporate victimizations are least likely to occur, because no major national or multinational firms operate in those communities. Some *propensity to victimization,* however, may be said to be present in *all* communities, since such impoverished localities may well be among the communities most willing to accede to corporate colonization in return for employment opportunities.

A coherent approach to the problems of corporate victimization of communities depends on recognition of the impact that corporations have on local economies as the result of their actions. Such recognition, in turn, depends on an awareness of the breadth of coercion and fraud in corporate-community dealings and an understanding of the dependence of communities on nonlocal auspices for the conduct of many critical locality-relevant functions. Corporate victimizations and white collar crimes go well beyond the forms traditionally recognized in class actions; such activities, however, remain acceptable in our socioeconomic system. David M. Reeves, President of the Industrial Development Research Council, observed recently, "If you bring industry to a community, even if you've had some bending of the law, it's hard to call that a bad thing,"[36]

Until this society admits that not all corporate actions are desirable and that a new industry may be *bad* for a community, serious discussion of corporate victimizations is virtually impossible. Moreover, no social action will be taken on victimization, especially on the coercion of communities that often accompanies corporate locational decision making, until *all* violations of law are treated as what they are—crimes, not sins.

REFERENCES

1. Perkins, R. H. *Perkins on Criminal Law,* 2nd ed. (Mineola, N.Y.: The Foundation Press, Inc., 1969), p. 640.
2. American Law Institute, *Model Penal Code, Tentative Draft No. 4* (Philadelphia: The Institute, 1955), p. 150.
3. American Law Institute, *Model Penal Code, Tentative Draft No. 2* (Philadelphia: The Institute, 1954), pp. 63, 73.
4. The appropriateness of the application of 14th Amendment protections to corporations and their property was first recognized in *Santa Clara City v. Southern Pacific R.R.,* 118 U.S. 394 (1886).
5. *Model Penal Code, Tentative Draft No. 2,* pp. 74-79.
6. Ibid., p. 75.
7. Ibid., p. 79.
8. "How Companies React to the Ethics Crisis," *Business Week* (Feb. 9, 1976), p. 78.
9. Ibid.
10. Ruling of Harold R. Medina, cited in *Business Week* (June 14, 1976), p. 44.
11. Black, H. C. *Black's Law Dictionary,* 4th ed. (St. Paul, Minn.: West Publishing Co., 1951), p. 324.
12. Ibid., p. 697.
13. Ibid., p. 696.
14. Ibid., pp. 788-789.
15. Ibid., p. 790.
16. Ballentine, J. S. *Ballentine's Law Dictionary,* 3rd ed., ed. W. S. Anderson (Rochester, N.Y.: The Lawyers Co-operative Publishing Co., 1969), p. 498.
17. *Model Penal Code, Tentative Draft No. 4,* p. 22; the clause reads as follows: "(1) A corporation may be convicted of the commission of an offense if and only if: . . . (c) the commission of the offense was authorized, requested, commanded or performed by the board of directors, or by an agent having responsibility for formation of corporate policy or by a high managerial agent having supervisory responsibility over the subject matter of the offense and acting within the scope of his employment in behalf of the corporation." Clearly, then, if promotions and pay increases are tied to performance measures, then persons acting to maximize performance have been virtually commanded, and certainly authorized and requested, to act in their capacities for the corporation by high-level management, if not by the board of directors.
18. "A Counterattack in the War Between the States," *Business Week,* June 21, 1976, pp. 71, 72, 74.
19. Harrison, B., and S. Kantor, "The Great State Robbery," *Working Papers* 4:1, Spring 1976, pp. 57-66.
20. Major financial incentives offered by different states are documented by Harrison and Kantor (ibid., p. 66).
21. Massachusetts' state tax credit of 3% of new investment, for example, would be worth only 1.6% of the investment after federal taxes, and most locational decisions are not made on such narrow margins (compare, ibid., p. 63).
22. Ibid., p. 61.
23. Craypo, C. "Workers in Common Predicament: Labor Education in an Era of Conglomerate, Multinational Enterprise," *Labor Studies Journal* 1:1, May 1976, pp. 14-15.
24. Harrison and Kantor, p. 66.
25. "How the Kepone Case Threatens the Cities," *Business Week,* May 24, 1976, p. 39.
26. One steel town, Johnstown, Pa., had fully 60% of all manufacturing jobs in primary metal production, and in one steel industry employer, Bethlehem Steel. It is no wonder that, threatened with mill closings, the *city* petitioned the EPA not to enforce pollution regulations that Bethlehem Steel's mills were violating.
27. "Banks at Core of Big Apple Crisis," *Dollars and Sense,* No. 10, October 1975, p. 13.
28. Some New York banks have 25% of their assets in municipal bonds and notes and could barely cope with a default (ibid., p. 15).
29. "Holding Housing Hostage," *Dollars and Sense,* No. 15, March 1976, p. 4.
30. Warren, R. L. *The Community in America* (Chicago: Rand McNally & Co. 1963).
31. Ibid., pp. 9-10, 167-208.
32. Ibid., pp. 12-14.
33. Ibid., p. 14.
34. Ibid., pp. 210-211.
35. Figures cited by Craypo, p. 5.
36. "A Counterattack in the War Between the States," p. 72.

Selected readings for Chapter 1

Drapkin, Israel, and Emilio Viano, eds. *Victimology* (Lexington, Mass.: D. C. Heath & Co., 1974).
    A collection of 23 readings organized in relation to the origin and scope of victimology, victim-offender relationships, the victim and society, the victim and the administration of justice, and the social reaction to victimization.

Drapkin, Israel, and Emilio Viano, eds. *Victimology: A New Focus* (Lexington, Mass.: D. C. Heath & Co., 1975).
    A five-volume collection of papers prepared for the first International Symposium on Victimology, held in Jerusalem in September 1973. The volumes are: (1) *Theoretical Issues in Victimology,* (2) *Society's Reaction to Victimization,* (3) *Crimes, Victims, and Justice,* (4) *Violence and Its Victims,* and (5) *Exploiters and Exploited: The Dynamics of Victimization.*

Mendelsohn, Beniamin. "The Origin of the Doctrine of Victimology," *Excerpta Criminologica* **3:**239-344, May-June 1963.
    Traces the early development of the field of victimology, including Mendelsohn's own contribution to the field; argues for victimology as a field separate from criminology.

Mendelsohn, Beniamin. "Victimology and Contemporary Society's Trends," *Victimology* **1:**8-28, 1976.
    Discusses the boundaries and missions of general victimology. Victimology should not be limited to the study of crime victims; this narrow approach will relegate the field to an auxiliary position in relation to criminology. The theoretical and programmatic foci of victimology should be on all victims.

"Pioneers in Victimology," *Victimology* **1:**193-228, 1976.
    Biographical sketches of Israel Drapkin, Ezzat A. Fattah, Margery Fry, Beniamin Mendelsohn, Koichi Miyazawa, Stephen Schafer, and Hans von Hentig.

Schafer, Stephen. *The Victim and His Criminal* (New York, Random House, Inc., 1968).
    Summarizes the history of victims in criminal law, analyzes material regarding victim-offender relationships, presents material regarding use of restitution and victim compensation, and develops the concept of functional responsibility, which links the victim to crime.

"Second International Symposium on Victimology," *Victimology* **2:**51-86, 1977.
    Abstracts for all papers presented at the symposium held in Boston in September 1976.

Viano, Emilio C. *Victims and Society* (Washington, D.C.: Visage Press, 1976).
    A collection of 46 papers prepared for the International Study Institute of Victimology, Bellagio, Italy, July 1975. The papers are organized in relation to conceptual issues, research methodology and findings, the victim and the justice system, treatment and prevention, and institutional victimization.

von Hentig, Hans. *The Criminal and His Victim* (New Haven: Yale University Press, 1948).
    One of the earliest works in victimology. The final chapter analyzes victim-offender relations and identifies a typology of victims that may be susceptible to victimization and a typology that may precipitate victimization.

Wolfgang, Marvin E., and Simon I. Singer. "Victim Categories of Crime," *Criminology* **69:**379-394, 1978.
    Suggests a variety of categories for victim analysis, including corporate victimization, victimless crimes, victim-offender relationships, and the criminal as victim. Provides an excellent overview of many of the recent research and program activities in the field.

Chapter 2

THE VICTIM IN THE JUSTICE SYSTEM

A □ *Citizen reporting of crime: some national panel data*
WESLEY G. SKOGAN

B □ *What happens to crime victims and witnesses in the justice system?*
MARY S. KNUDTEN and RICHARD D. KNUDTEN

C □ *Victims of crimes of violence and the criminal justice system*
GILBERT GEIS

A □ *Citizen reporting of crime*

Some national panel data

WESLEY G. SKOGAN

The decision of individuals to report criminal victimizations to the police has been the object of considerable interest. From the outset, survey studies of citizens' crime experiences and their reporting practices have identified patterns of massive nonreporting (Ennis, 1967). It is clear that large amounts of often serious crime do not come to the attention of the authorities, are not registered in our indicators of social health, and do not lead to arrests or other official deterrent action.

This nonreporting has several consequences.

First, it determines the volume and distribution of the "dark figure" of officially unknown crime. Any fluctuation in the official rate of crime (including the much-heralded "decrease in the rate of increase" registered in 1972) may simply reflect changes in citizen reporting practices and the size of this pool of unknown events. Reporting decisions determine the volume of cases facing the police and the courts and the nature of their activity. As Albert Reiss (1971) has suggested, these highly discretionary activities are perhaps the most important in the entire crime-and-justice system. Changes in citizen reporting could overload existing facilities for receiving information about crime and doing something in response. Differential nonreporting also shapes the character of the police mandate. In-

"Citizen Reporting of Crime: Some National Panel Data" by Wesley G. Skogan is reprinted from *Criminology*, Vol. 13, No. 4 (February 1976), pp. 535-549 by permission of the publisher, Sage Publications, Inc.

creases in the reporting of disputes between acquaintances, assaults within families, and the "theft" of property by people's estranged spouses, would lead the police even further into the kinds of crisis intervention roles they appear to abhor.

This report summarizes the most recent data on nonreporting produced by the National Crime Panel Study conducted by the Bureau of the Census. It examines the impact of several hypothesized determinants of reporting rates, many of which previously have been investigated only in isolated, city-specific studies. Many of those studies also conceptualized nonreporting as a social pathology, something to be explored as a problem in individual failure. This analysis indicates that nonreporting is a social process which is patterned in consistent ways; and that it reflects the experiential world of crime victims in direct and realistic fashion. People report or not for good reason.

THE PROBLEM AND
THE DATA

It is useful to think about the determinants of crime reporting in three ways. First, we can examine the extent to which behavior is a function of the characteristics of individuals. Blacks, for example, may be less willing than whites to mobilize the police, based upon their own or friends' experiences or upon accumulated group lore. Youths often face similar calculations: will their complaints be taken seriously, will they face uncomfortable demeanor problems, is it wise to become known to the police regardless of the circumstances? This mode of analysis requires that we match the attributes of individuals to their behavior vis-à-vis formal authority.

Second, we can examine the extent to which this action is a function of the relationship between the victim and the offender. It is clear from previous surveys and intensive studies of particular crimes that criminals and their victims do not come together in random fashion. Crime is an interactional process which often reflects enduring rather than discontinuous social contact. It also is often precipitated by the eventual victim's careless or aggressive be-havior (Curtis, 1974). The decision to report such events is simply one of a number of alternatives open to the "losers" in such encounters.

Finally, it is important to consider the effects of the nature of the incident itself. Crimes differ greatly in severity: the extent to which they violate the person, property, or propriety of the victim or standers-by. They also vary in the probability that any concrete return is likely to accrue to the victim in response to his mobilization of the police. Where the likelihood of the recovery of property or the arrest of an offender is slight, there is little practical incentive for shouldering the additional burden of reliving one's experiences for the police.

The data used to probe these relationships were pooled from six monthly random samples of the American population. Each month from July through December of 1973, every resident over eleven years of age in a sample of 10,000 households were interviewed by Bureau of the Census personnel and asked to recall victimization experiences during the past six months. This recall period was "bounded" by an earlier visit of an interviewer, and the interview schedule itself has been subjected in an extensive series of methodological and validity checks (see San Jose Methods Test . . . , 1972; Crimes and Victims, 1974). The respondents and the incidents have been weighted to reflect their true distribution in the population. Given the size and extent of the sample (it was drawn from 376 different primary sampling units scattered throughout the country), these population estimates have very low standard errors, and with this data it is possible to talk confidently about the distribution of relatively uncommon events (such as robbery) even within detailed subgroups of the population.

The tables which follow test a number of specific hypotheses about citizen reporting and the characteristics of victims, of victim-offender relationships, and characteristics of the incidents themselves. In each case an appropriate measure of association will be presented describing the strength of the relationship. The tables also will report national population estimates of the incidence of events and the distribution of victim characteristics for the year 1973.

NONREPORTING: THE EFFECTS OF VICTIM CHARACTERISTICS

Much of the discussion about nonreporting has focused upon victim characteristics—the social types whose crime experiences do not come to the attention of the authorities. Presumably they enjoy fewer of the ameliorative activities of the state and those who prey upon them are less likely to suffer the deterrent sting of official action in response.

One major social cleavage which has been thought to reflect this differential burden is race. Blacks have historically suffered poor relations with the police, and bad experiences continue to characterize police-community relations in the ghetto. It is commonly argued that fear of the police is so high among racial minorities that it inhibits the reporting of their crime experiences.

The data presented in Table 1 indicate that race is in fact unrelated to citizen reporting practices. In many important subcategories, blacks are if anything slightly more likely than

Table 1. Reporting and victim characteristics*

All crimes against persons: rape, assaultive robbery, assault, personal theft (non-assaultive robbery, purse snatching, pocket picked)

Race	Percent report	Percent no report	Victimizations U.S. pop. est.
White	44.2	55.8 (100%)	5,024,220
Black	45.1	54.9 (100%)	920,850
		C = .006	

All crimes against persons

Age	Percent report	Percent no report	Victimizations U.S. pop. est.
12-19	31.5	68.5 (100%)	2,161,940
20-34	49.2	50.8 (100%)	2,304,350
35-49	56.6	43.5 (100%)	797,490
50-64	53.0	47.0 (100%)	494,850
65 plus	53.6	46.4 (100%)	247,300
		$\theta = .21$	

*A small number of "don't knows" have been excluded from the calculation of these percentages, although they have been included in the estimates of the frequency of the independent variables in the population.

whites to report their experiences to the police. Grouping all crimes against persons (defined in Table 1), we observe no important racial differences in reporting; the difference is 3% among crimes involving assaultive violence and 2% among personal thefts. Given the importance of racial differences in a host of other social processes, these differences are trivial.

Sex differences in reporting practices are more consistent. Across all categories, women appear to be about 5% more likely than men to report victimizations to the authorities. Both groups fail to report the majority of most crimes, however. These differences are in accord with research on the socialization of individuals to legal norms: in general, women are more compliant and deferential to legal authority.

The effect of age differences upon reporting practices reported in Table 1 may reflect the same phenomenon. Data there make it clear that youths are largely responsible for the minority status of reported crime. Due to (1) their large numbers and high rates of victimization; and (2) their low likelihood of relaying information about them to the police, youths between the ages of 12 and 19 account for a substantial proportion of all officially unrecorded crime. Persons in this age category suffered 35% of all personal victimizations in 1973, and reported only 31% of them. This occurred despite the fact that young people suffer disproportionately from assaultive violence, which in general is highly reported. This helped keep the group's reporting rate as high as it was; the 12-19 age group reported only 22% of the nonassaultive robberies, purse snatchings, and picked pockets they suffered. The high reporting rate among oldsters probably reflects the ease of their relationship with the police and their confidence that they will not be penalized by it, for they tend to suffer fewer violent personal assaults.

Reporting rates do not vary in any consistent fashion across income levels, although members of extremely high income families ($25,000 plus per year) tend to differ from others, reporting fewer of their violent personal victimizations (only 25%) but more of their personal property losses (43%). This may be explained by differential patterns of victimization. Although patterns in the middle of the income distribution are not clear, victims at the upper end of the spectrum appear to be attacked less violently (or else they give up their money more easily) than those at the bottom: 28% of the victims of robbery making above $25,000 a year in 1973 were also physically assaulted, while 42% of those making less than $3,000 were beaten as well as robbed. Also, high income victims lost more money or goods of greater value than poor victims. As we shall see, such variations in the seriousness of a victimization greatly affect their probability of being reported to the police.

REPORTING AND VICTIM-OFFENDER RELATIONSHIPS

Victims and their offenders have a great deal in common. Studies of interpersonal crimes have revealed that they are usually of the same race, that much crime takes place between residents of the same neighborhood, and that often people in similar positions in the occupational structure prey upon one another (Schafer, 1968). One of the major interests of victimologists has been the social relationship between victims and offenders—the bonds of friendship and kinship that usually forestall violent or pecunious agression, but which occasionally break down. Studies of crimes of violence recorded in police files have suggested that homicides (Wolfgang, 1958), rapes (Amir, 1971), and assaults (Pittman and Handy, 1964) are common among neighbors, lovers, and family members.

It has been assumed that these social bonds also inhibit the initial contacting of the police, leading official files still to greatly underrepresent such cases. Criminal acts between the members of a social network often reflect the dynamics of continuing interpersonal relationships, and the decision to report such events to the police may require a much more complex calculus than anonymous violence or theft. Deciding to report may require recognizing that a family is no longer a viable social unit, or that the neighbors are too intolerable for continued coexistence; the intrusion of the police may make those ruptures permanent, while it is problematic that routine police work is capable of resolving their causes. These socially submerged crimes have been one of the major interests of victimologist-surveyors.

National Panel figures for 1973 indicate that while the incidence of crime within a web of kinship or acquaintanceship is high (about 33% of all incidents of crimes against persons), the effect of victim-offender relationships upon reporting rates is less dramatic than has been assumed. Table 2 presents reporting rates for several categories of personal crime, divided according to the nature of that relationship. "Stranger" in Table 2 encompases all offenders not known to their victims and those known "by sight only."

The effect of the relational distance between victim and offender upon the willingness of the former to mobilize the police is only about 4% in most categories. Again, the majority of incidents are not reported to the police, even when the offender is a stranger. The notable exceptions

Table 2. Reporting and victim-offender relationships

Crime	Percent incidents by strangers	Strangers percent reported	Not strangers percent reported	Incidents U.S. pop. est.
All crimes against persons	67.4	42.4	38.6	5,105,440
All assaultive violence	61.2	44.8	38.9	4,016,710
Rape	75.4	47.8	30.9	153,050
Assaultive violence with theft	83.1	64.0	48.7	359,400
Assaultive violence—no theft	59.1	41.8	38.6	3,657,310
Assault	59.8	41.4	38.8	3,517,990
Personal theft—no assault	90.1	36.9	34.8	1,088,730

occur when incidents combine assaultive violence and theft (robbery and an attack, or rape and theft). These offenses tend to be perpetrated by strangers, and they are often reported (64%) when they are. Rape also deviates from the pattern, primarily as a result of its very low reporting rate under non-stranger circumstances. This is to be expected given the com-

Table 3. Reporting and the characteristics of incidents

Personal incidents: robbery

Percent reported to the police		Incidents U.S. pop. est.
22.6	unsuccessful, no assault, no weapon	157,440
35.0	unsuccessful, no assault, with weapon	109,410
37.7	successful, no assault, no weapon	152,840
51.0	successful, minor assault, no weapon	153,160
61.6	successful, no assault, with weapon	185,410
75.0	successful, major assault, no weapon	29,680
71.6	successful, major assault, with weapon	162,830

Non-personal property crimes: burglary, larceny, auto theft

Location	Percent reported	Percent not reported	Incidents U.S. pop. est.
In or around the home	35.0	65.0 (100%)	14,196,520
Elsewhere	20.3	79.7 (100%)	19,032,600

$$C = .16$$

Non-personal property crime: larceny only

Value of item	Percent reported	Percent not reported	Incidents U.S. pop. est.
$1-9	6.6	93.4 (100%)	7,230,810
$10-24	13.4	86.6 (100%)	4,247,430
$25-49	26.4	73.6 (100%)	3,013,400
$50-99	44.2	55.8 (100%)	2,471,850
$100-249	58.7	41.3 (100%)	1,846,900
$250-999	66.8	33.2 (100%)	665,640
$1,000 plus	72.8	27.2 (100%)	118,880

$$\theta = .46$$

plicated and highly personal nature of such relationships and the likelihood that the processing of such cases by the criminal justice system will put a great deal of stress upon women who do report.

The pattern revealed in the simple assault category runs counter to most discussions of that crime, however. As Table 2 indicates, many assaults (about 40%) take place within friendship or family networks. The effect of acquaintanceship upon patterns of reporting for assault are minor. It has long been assumed that intrafamilial beatings and altercations among friends and neighbors come to the attention of the police only under very special circumstances. These data indicate that they are actually just about as likely to be reported as attacks by strangers; the difference in reporting rates is only about 2%.

The limited effect of victim-offender relationships upon reporting behavior apparent in much of this data casts some doubt upon many common assertions about crime which does not come to the attention of the authorities—that much of it reflects disputes which are resolved privately, or that the social relationship between victim and offender keeps it from being defined as "criminal" by the immediate parties. Only under limited circumstances (and, as Table 3 indicates, only among relatively infrequent crimes), does the decision to report appear to be particularly complex.

REPORTING AND THE CHARACTERISTICS OF CRIMINAL INCIDENTS

Other than the general assertion that incidents which are "serious" are more likely to be reported, little systematic attention has been focused upon the effects of the characteristics of criminal incidents themselves on the probability of their coming to the attention of the authorities (but see Richardson et al., 1972). More emphasis has been placed upon the social attributes of victims and offenders, most of which prove to be unimportant. This is curious, for while most characteristics of individuals have weak to nonexistent relationships with reporting, incident characteristics are strongly and consistently related to this action, and the process appears to reflect rational and reasonable citizen conduct.

It is important to clarify, first, the dimensions of seriousness. There appear to be at least four which accrue to the incident itself, as opposed to circumstantial contingencies such as the availability of medical care or the possession of insurance: the value of stolen or damaged property, the extent of personal injury, the use of a weapon which threatens death, and the extent to which the crime intrudes into the secure lifespace of the victim. The greater loss, harm, threat, or insecurity generated by an incident, the more likely it is to be reported to the police.

Data testing these hypotheses are reported in Table 3. First it summarizes the effect of three of the dimensions of seriousness upon reporting rates for a particularly important personal crime, robbery. Financial loss is collapsed into two categories: was the robbery attempt successful or not? Injury is classified as major, minor, or none at all. Whether or not the offender deployed a gun, knife, or other dangerous weapon (a broken bottle, ball bat, or the like) is indicated as well. The effect of each element appears to be additive—as incidents increase in seriousness, moving from unsuccessful, nonassaultive, less threatening events to more serious ones, reporting rates mount steadily. At the bottom, only 23% of the least serious robberies were reported; at the top, 72% were taken to the police. The only exception is a minor reversal at the top of the scale, which may reflect the low incidence (and large sampling error) of major assaults (leading to hospitalization) without a weapon. The cumulative effect of these dimensions of seriousness for personal crimes is clear; they are powerful predictors of the decision by victims to report their experiences to the police.

Table 3 also presents a test of the strength of the final aspect of event seriousness, the extent to which it intrudes into the private lifespace of the victim. The phrase "a man's home is his castle" reflects one of the functions which property boundaries and the walls of one's domicile perform—they provide security. Events which breach that security and threaten loss or harm within people's most personal territory should be threatening indeed, and this threat should be reflected in their willingness to mobilize the police in response.

Table 3 examines this hypothesis using national survey data on the incidence of nonpersonal property crimes: burglary, larceny, and auto theft. It compares the reporting rates of incidents which occurred on the immediate grounds or within the home of the survey respondent who recalled it with reporting rates for incidents which occurred away from home (at work, while shopping, and so on). Although the financial loss involved in most of these crimes is minor, leading to low overall reporting rates for such events, incidents which occurred in or around the home were 15% more likely to be reported to the police. The unease or insecurity generated by the occurrence of crimes in private space appears to be an important dimension of seriousness and a useful predictor of reporting rates.

Table 3 also uses data on simple larceny theft to present a more detailed breakdown of the other major dimension of seriousness for nonpersonal property crimes: the value of the loss. Larceny involves no forcible entry, no threatened victims, no personal injury; the primary consequences of larceny can be measured by the dollar value of the goods or cash stolen. As Table 3 indicates, this loss is clearly and positively related to the tendency of victims to inform the police about their experiences. Losses of small value are virtually never reported (7% of those worth less than ten dollars), while those at the top of the scale are reported almost three-fourths of the time.

REPORTING AND RATIONALITY

This essay has summarized national survey data on the correlates of one of the major discretionary acts which shape American criminal justice—the decision to report a victimization to the police. Reporting appears to be related only weakly to the characteristics of individual crime victims. The very young are less likely than everyone else to report their experiences, and persons with extremely high incomes (a numerically small group) are more likely than others to report property offenses but are less willing to call the police in response to personal victimizations. Women report more victimizations to the police than men, but the differences are small. Racial differences do not explain this form of police-community contact at all. The effects of victim-offender relationships upon reporting were strong for certain subclasses of relatively infrequent crimes, but in the main the "dark figure" of unreported crime does not differ much from that which is officially known on this dimension.

Characteristics of victims' experiences, on the other hand, were highly related to their evocation of the police. Crimes which threatened their person, violated their personal space, inflicted injury, or cost them money were reported as relatively high rates. Attributes of their experiential world rather than social or symbolic forces appear to motivate the victims of crime, suggesting that the decision to report may be a highly cognitive, reality-testing process. Far from a pathology, it may reflect people's judgment about the use of their time, and the police's time as well.

This cognitive interpretation of victim behavior is supported by a final bit of evidence, responses to the probe "Why not?" given when victims told an interviewer that a crime was not reported to the police. They indicate that victims acted on the basis of what appeared to them to be reasonable assumptions about their crimes. One common option was that the incident "wasn't important enough." Choice of this response was clearly related to the seriousness of the event. For example, fully one-third of the

nonreporting victims of larcenies under $50 chose this reason; only 13% of those losing more than $50 did so.

Victims also appear to react to their own, and reasonably accurate, estimate of the chances that anything will come of their report. Table 4 relates the proportion of nonreporters who indicated that they failed to act because "nothing could be done" to the FBI's *clearance* rate for the same offenses (Federal Bureau of Investigation, 1974). The latter is a rough measure of the solvability of an offense. In general, crimes which were solvable elicited few "nothing can be done" responses, while crimes with very low clearance rates—such as burglary—generated this reason almost one half of the time. The simplest interpretation of Table 4 is that people do not report when they think nothing will happen as a result, and that they are often right.

REFERENCES

Amir, M. (1971) Patterns in Forcible Rape. Chicago: Univ. of Chicago Press.

Crimes and Victims: A Report on the Dayton-San Jose Pilot Survey of Victimization (1974) Washington: National Criminal Justice Information and Statistics Service, Law Enforcement Assistance Administration.

Curtis, L. A. (1974) "Victim precipitation and violent crime." Social Problems 21 (April): 594-605.

Ennis, P. H. (1967) Criminal Victimization in the United States: A Report of a National Survey. Washington, D.C.: Government Printing Office.

Federal Bureau of Investigation (1974) Uniform Crime Report 1973. Washington: Government Printing Office.

Pittman, D. and W. Handy (1964) "Patterns in criminal aggravated assault." J. of Criminal Law, Criminology and Police Science 55 (December): 462-470.

Reiss, A. J., Jr. (1971) The Police and the Public. New Haven: Yale Univ. Press.

Richardson, R., O. Williams, T. Denyer, S. McGaughey, and D. Walker (1972) Perspectives on the Legal Justice System: Public Attitudes and Criminal Victimization. Chapel Hill: Institute for Research in Social Science, University of North Carolina.

San Jose Methods Test of Known Crime Victims (1972) Washington: Statistics Division, National Institute of Law Enforcement and Criminal Justice.

Schafer, S. (1968) The Victim and His Criminal. New York: Random House.

Wolfgang, M. (1958) Patterns in Criminal Homicide. Philadelphia: Univ. of Pennsylvania Press.

Table 4

Crime	Percent saying "nothing can be done"	FBI clearance rate 1973
Assault	19%	63%
Rape	23	51
Robbery	41	27
Larceny	33	19
Burglary	48	18
Auto theft	48	16

B □ *What happens to crime victims and witnesses in the justice system?*

MARY S. KNUDTEN and RICHARD D. KNUDTEN

In recent years, investigations into victim and witness concerns have gathered new momentum. The Law Enforcement Assistance Administration, working through the U.S. Bureau of the Census, has studied the scope of victimization in major American cities over a period of several years. A variety of research projects have been funded, most directed to the study of the victim as the recipient of actions by an offender. These studies have frequently focused on particular types of victims, for example, the sex or rape victim or the elderly victim.[1-7] This paper focuses on a different dimension, the experiences of victims and witnesses within the system of criminal justice.

There is evidence that victims and witnesses receive limited satisfaction when they experience a crime event and are faced with a need to participate actively within the criminal justice process.[8-11] Too often, their satisfaction tends to depend on the punishment of the offender rather than on services rendered to the victim. Often forgotten within the criminal justice system and concerned for their own manipulation by others, they have frequently expressed negative attitudes toward the existing criminal justice system. One attempt to redress this imbalance has been the passage of state victim compensation programs and consideration of similar legislation in the U.S. Congress.[12-14] A second thrust has been development of restitution programs in a number of states.[15-17] In addition, in some communities, victim and witness advocacy or service programs have developed with the support of the Law Enforcement Assistance Administration and local government sources.[18] In order to provide appropriate and adequate compensation, restitution, or services to victims and witnesses, it is necessary to know the experiences of these individuals within the criminal justice system. Therefore, this paper reports on the problems experienced by victims and nonvictim witnesses within the system, their perceptions of personnel in the system, and the implications of these findings when one is considering solutions and determining which services should be provided.

PROJECT METHODOLOGY

The data presented here were gathered by a team from Marquette University from two samples: one of victims and the other of witnesses in the criminal justice system. These groups consist of two saturation samples of citizens actually involved in the criminal justice process in the Milwaukee County, Wisconsin, court system. These persons were contacted as their cases were considered at one of four stages in the criminal justice process: the charging conference in the district attorney's office, the preliminary hearing, the misdemeanor trial, or the felony trial. The questionnaire, including both fixed-answer and open-ended items, was administered to victims and citizen witnesses over four 12-week periods between December 4, 1974, and November 4, 1975. The average interview time was 15-20 minutes. Of those contacted, the overall refusal rate was 17.8%.

Part of each sample was interviewed on-site, whereas another portion, composed of those who did not have time or were unwilling to be interviewed while on-site, was interviewed by telephone. Of the total in the two samples (3,000 interviewees), 63% were interviewed on-

The authors acknowledge the assistance of Anthony C. Meade and William G. Doerner.

Prepared under Grant No. 75-NI-99-1108 from the National Institute of Law Enforcement and Criminal Justice, Law Enforcement Assistance Administration, U.S. Department of Justice. Points of view or opinions stated in this document are those of the authors and do not necessarily represent the official position of the U.S. Department of Justice.

Table 1. Basic description of study samples

Respondent characteristic	Type of respondent	
	Victim	Nonvictim witness
Number	1,775	1,225
Age range	14-86 yr.	14-77 yr.
Mean age	34 yr.	33 yr.
Education range	0-24 yr.	1-23 yr.
Mean education	12.3 yr.	12.4 yr.
Race: White	69%	80%
Black	31%	20%
Sex: Male	54%	60%
Female	46%	40%

site and 37% by telephone. A comparison of responses given on selected items, controlling for the interviewing situation, yielded almost no variation. The characteristics of the two samples are presented in Table 1. With respect to age and education, victims and witnesses were very similar. Victims were somewhat more likely to be black (31%) than were nonvictim witnesses (20%). In terms of sex, nonvictim witnesses were somewhat more likely to be male (60%) than were victims (54%).

Comparison of the characteristics of victims and nonvictim witnesses with the population characteristics of Milwaukee County yields a finding that men, blacks, and young persons were overrepresented among Milwaukee County crime victims and nonvictim witnesses. Although 10% of the Milwaukee County population is black, 20% of the nonvictim witnesses and 31% of the victim sample was black. Similarly, though 47% of the county population is male, 54% of the victims and 60% of the nonvictim witnesses were male. Finally, although 16% of Milwaukee County's population falls between ages 18 and 24, 30% of the victim sample and 29% of the nonvictim witness sample were in this age range.

In order to monitor the extent to which the respondents in this study actually experienced what could be referred to as system-related problems, each respondent was asked whether he or she had experienced particular problems and if so how serious he or she considered the problem to be. In addition, each respondent was

asked the extent to which others close to them experienced either financial consequences, inconvenience, or mental or emotional suffering.

The attitudes of citizens toward system representatives with whom they had had contact were examined by asking for performance assessments of the three system representatives with whom they would have had experience: the police, the district attorney, and the judge. In addition to three performance criteria (effort, effectiveness, courteousness), respondents were asked two questions for which associational results are presented below. These questions were:

1. Overall, how satisfied have you been with the way the [police, district attorney, judge] handled this case? Would you say *very satisfied, satisfied, dissatisfied,* or *very dissatisfied?*

2. Based on your experience in this case, would you be willing to cooperate in the future with the [police, district attorney, court]? *Yes, no, depends on circumstances, don't know.*

FINDINGS
Problem experiences

Table 2 presents system-related problems by incidence and intensity for victims and nonvictim witnesses. As the table indicates, nonvictim witnesses were more likely than victims to indicate that time loss was a problem. Victims were, however, slightly more likely to rate such a problem as serious in nature. This finding is consistent with the fact that the average workday loss (2.1) for 1,001 victims was greater than the average time loss (1.6 work days) for 850 witnesses. In addition to time loss, a slightly higher percentage of victims than nonvictim witnesses indicated income loss as a problem, although similar percentages (85%) of both groups indicated this as a serious problem. In fact, the median victim income loss was $49.04, and 23% suffered a loss of $100 or more in income. The median nonvictim witness income loss was $36.34, with 7% suffering a loss of $100 or more.

The results presented in Table 2 underline the distinction between the experiencing of a

Table 2. Relative incidence and intensity of system-related problems among 1775 victims and 1225 nonvictim witnesses

Problem*	Respondents indicating problem				Respondents indicating problem who rated it as serious or very serious			
	Victims		Nonvictims		Victims		Nonvictims	
	Number	Percentage	Number	Percentage	Number	Percentage	Number	Percentage
Transportation and parking expenses	1360	79	849	71	501	37	332	39
Time loss	946	57	865	72	686	73	569	66
Uncomfortable conditions	491	38	371	41	303	62	218	59
Difficulty finding out what to do	291	36	151	38	187	64	94	62
Income loss	558	33	321	27	475	85	272	85
Long waiting time	929	28	694	30	667	72	483	70
Unnecessary trips	479	27	331	28	361	75	242	73
Difficulty finding parking	436	25	272	23	256	59	165	61
Exposure to threatening persons	185	23	113	20	142	77	91	81
Difficulty finding place	355	20	227	19	143	40	93	41
Difficulty arranging child care	229	14	119	11	164	69	77	64
Difficulty arranging transportation	164	10	88	7	119	73	56	64

*Property kept as evidence was not included in the table because the item was asked only of victims. The problem was experienced by 310 victims (18%), with 127 (41% of those who experienced it) rating it as a serious problem.

problem (incidence) and the perception of the seriousness (intensity) of that problem. For example, though experiences such as making unnecessary trips and suffering income loss were indicated by less than one third of the study sample, they were regarded as serious or very serious problems by about 80% of the persons who encountered them. Conversely, though transportation and parking expenses were encountered by about three fourths of the sample, they were rated as serious problems by less than 40% of the persons who experienced them.

Grouping the problems into categories and simultaneously considering incidence and intensity of system-related problems indicate that time-related and financial problems were the most prominent. Table 3 presents standard mean scores and standardized scores for system-related problem types. The standard mean score is calculated by using the following values for each item and dividing by the number of items in each category:

1 = No problem
2 = Problem, but not serious at all
3 = Problem, but not too serious
4 = Problem, and serious
5 = Problem, and very serious

The standardized score represents that percentage of the maximum possible problem-type impact actually observed for the specific type. The maximum impact would be represented by a situation in which all individuals in the sample had experienced each problem within the specific category and then rated each experience as very serious. Although there was little variation between witness groups, the results show that the time and financial problem types were considerably more likely to approach their maximum impact for both witness groups than were court or personal problem types.

Table 3. Standardized score for system-related problem types

System-related problem	Standard mean score		Standardized score	
	Victims	Nonvictims	Victims	Nonvictims
Court	1.56	1.50	31	30
1. Did you have difficulty finding parking space?				
2. Did you have difficulty finding the correct building, office, or courtroom?				
3. Did you have difficulty finding out what you were supposed to do once you got there?				
4. Were the waiting conditions uncomfortable?				
5. Were you exposed to threatening or upsetting persons?				
Time	2.37	2.53	47	51
1. Did you make unneeded or excessive trips to the police station, Courthouse or Safety Building?				
2. Did you have to spend a long time waiting?				
3. Did you lose time from work or school?				
Personal*	1.37	1.20	27	24
1. Was it difficult or necessary to find some way of taking care of your children?				
2. Was it difficult for you to get transportation?				
3. Was some of your property kept as evidence?				
Financial	2.45	2.20	49	44
1. Did you lose income?				
2. Did you have to pay for transportation or parking?				
System-related composite	1.88	1.68	38	37

*Property kept as evidence was not included for nonvictim witnesses.

To give further indication of the extent to which time and financial problem types equate to dollar losses for victims and witnesses, it is estimated (assuming 2.5 hours spent per court appearance and $6 per hour for wages plus 50¢ per hour for additional expenses) that $650,000 per year is a conservative estimate of actual income lost by citizens of Milwaukee County (population of about 1.5 million). This estimate excludes "nonproductive" work time or time for which compensation is not ordinarily given (such as housework or school time).

Examination of the statistical association between experiencing system-related problems and subgroups of witnesses (see Table 4) shows that only time loss, need for child care, and difficulty getting transportation or paying for it

were even moderately associated with some subgroups.* Better educated, white men were likely to suffer time loss. Black female victims tended to have difficulty arranging transportation and child care. Other women shared the child care difficulty. The expense of transportation and parking was more of a problem for nonwhites, whether they were victims or witnesses. In contrast to data presented elsewhere,[21-22] the elderly did not experience any of

---

*Table 4 presents a correlation matrix of ϕ or V coefficients. These statistics are equivalent to zero-order (r) values for categorical data.[19-20] The signs of the observed relationships reflect comparison with alternative rank-order statistical results and examination of percentage results within each table. Those associations that meet a minimum 0.15 criterion are emphasized.

Table 4. Statistical association between experiencing system-related problems and subgroups of witnesses (ϕ or Cramer's V)

System-related problems	Respondent variables									
	Age		Education		Sex†		Race‡		Revictimized	
	V*	NV	V	NV	V	NV	V	NV	V	NV
Income loss	.07	−.09	−.06	−.06	−.12	.04	−.07	.10	.10	.03
Exposure to threatening persons	−.08	−.08	.06	.05	.10	.13	.04	.11	.06	.11
Unnecessary trips	−.04	−.09	.06	.09	−.09	.06	−.05	.09	.04	.08
Time loss	.06	−.09	.16	.10	−.22	−.06	−.17	.13	.07	.07
Difficulty arranging transportation	−.07	−.08	−.07	−.06	.16	.12	.17	.13	.04	.05
Long waiting time	.05	−.06	.06	.08	−.07	−.08	−.06	.06	−.02	.08
Difficulty arranging child care	−.12	−.08	−.08	−.07	.26	.27	.15	.13	−.02	.04
Difficulty finding out what to do	−.09	−.10	−.04	.06	.06	.10	.05	.08	−.04	.08
Uncomfortable conditions	−.09	−.09	−.07	−.08	.04	.06	.09	.14	.04	.07
Difficulty finding parking	−.03	−.10	.05	−.05	−.10	−.07	.10	.13	−.02	.11
Difficulty finding place	−.06	−.08	−.04	−.07	.06	.02	.07	.05	−.06	.07
Transportation and parking expenses	−.04	−.07	−.07	−.07	.11	.10	.18	.17	.06	.08

*V refers to victim, NV to nonvictim witness.
†Sex coded as 1, male; 2, female.
‡Race coded as 1, white; 2, nonwhite.

these problems to a greater extent than other groups.

Secondary victimization

The extent to which the problems engendered by crime victimization and witness involvement in the criminal justice system extend beyond the individual has historically been an empirically ignored area. The present study attempted to make some headway in this area through inclusion of items concerning the financial consequences, inconvenience, and mental or emotional suffering experienced by persons close to the victim or witness of crime. Summary findings regarding these items are presented in Table 5. Certainly, these results are approximations, but they are indicative of the facts that: (1) victims and nonvictim witnesses are not the only parties significantly affected by the commission of crime and the necessity to be involved in the criminal justice system; and (2) respondents are aware of these consequences for others. These data then become meaningful as empirical verification of the wider network of costs involved in any crime victimization. As might be expected, the results in Table 5 suggest that the cost network is comparatively more extended for victims than for nonvictim witnesses. However, nonvictim witnesses themselves could be conceived as secondary victims.

Table 5. Ramification of crime victimization and witness involvement in the criminal justice process to a large network of individuals

Problem	Percent indicating that others were affected	Total number affected
Financial		
Victims	18	508
Nonvictims	11	251
Mental-emotional		
Victims	35	1690
Nonvictims	15	342
Inconvenience		
Victims	36	1266
Nonvictims	20	356

Examination of respondent characteristics and the tendency to report problems of others shows that only two associations were even minimally significant ($\phi = 0.15$ or higher). The victims and witnesses of personal crimes and females were more likely to report that others suffered from mental or emotional difficulties because of their involvement. Females were also slightly more likely to report the inconvenience of others.

Citizen assessment of system representatives and intentions of cooperation

Citizens' perceptions of criminal justice system representatives and the extent to which citizens intend to cooperate in the future may affect control efforts. Though it is difficult to know what causes a citizen's perception of system representatives and the extent to which experiencing problems affects these ratings, what people say regarding system representatives may be important for policy considerations.

Table 6 presents performance ratings of justice system personnel by victims and nonvictim witnesses. The results are remarkable in their consistency. The total picture reflects a highly positive evaluation of system representatives. For those witnesses who enter the criminal justice system, the service rendered by the official representatives of the system appears to be highly appreciated. Courteousness is the performance dimension on which all types of representatives (police, district attorneys, and judges) scored highest. Inconsequential differences between the ratings of victim and nonvictim witnesses were observed, with the exception of the slight tendency of the nonvictim witnesses to give police better ratings on effort and effectiveness than victim witnesses gave.

For each criterion (effort, effectiveness, and courteousness), however, the police were most likely to be given the highest rating, followed in order by district attorneys and judges. These results suggest the possible positive influence of increased familiarity on interpersonal relations between citizens and criminal justice personnel. It is possible that the police actually are doing a

Table 6. Percentage of respondents giving specific ratings of justice system representatives

Performance criterion	System representative					
	Police		District attorney		Judge	
	V* (1553)†	NV (1038)	V (1592)	NV (1056)	V (696)	NV (626)
Effort						
Excellent	47	49	34	33	33	32
Good	31	35	40	42	40	40
Fair	12	10	16	16	17	19
Poor	10	5	10	8	10	8
Effectiveness						
Excellent	42	44	31	29	34	31
Good	34	39	38	42	38	41
Fair	13	11	19	20	18	19
Poor	11	6	11	10	10	9
Courteousness						
Excellent	54	56	47	47	39	37
Good	32	33	39	41	44	42
Fair	10	7	10	8	12	15
Poor	4	4	4	4	4	5

*V refers to victim witnesses, NV to nonvictim witnesses.
†Figures in parentheses show total number of respondents for each category.

better job than either district attorneys or judges in regard to these criteria. However, their higher marks may simply be a function of the fact that at any stage they may have had more of an opportunity than either prosecutors or judges to interact with and become familiar with the witness. This social distance distinction is further affected by the fact that a police officer will most likely be called upon to testify as a witness. Thus not only is the police officer serving the victim in his community through his enforcement and investigatory functions, but he is also sharing the responsibility of the witness role with the citizen. These findings are in contrast to those of other studies,[23-26] which have emphasized a fairly negative perception of the police by citizens of the community.

In conjunction with the study currently being reported, a survey of Milwaukee citizens was carried out, asking them many of the same items. Although 76% to 78% of the victims who entered the criminal justice system rated police effort and effectiveness as excellent or good, only 44% to 52% of the community sample gave similar ratings. Even courteousness, which was generally highly rated among all groups, received a lower rating among the community victims (86% versus 71%). These findings strengthened the suggestion made earlier that higher ratings were given to those representatives with whom the victim has been able to interact directly. Since time order cannot be completely clarified, it is impossible to determine if negative assessments contributed to decreased reporting or if lack of extended interaction with personnel was responsible for less positive assessments among victims identified in the community at large.

The relationship of positive assessment to future cooperation intentions is clearly indicated in Table 7. The marked pattern of increased willingness to indicate intentions of future cooperation is impressive. Less than half of those who were "very dissatisfied" expected to cooperate in the future, whereas almost all of those who were "very satisfied" intended to do so. It should be noted that only victims, not nonvictim witnesses, are reported here.

Table 7. Victim's cooperation intentions by degree of performance satisfaction

Those indicating cooperation intention	Satisfaction level			
	Very dissatisfied	Dissatisfied	Satisfied	Very satisfied
With police	46* (91)†	70 (146)	90 (644)	97 (654)
With district attorney	46 (110)	59 (175)	94 (774)	98 (477)
With judge	47 (49)	66 (85)	90 (344)	97 (209)

* Refers to percentage.
† Refers to number of respondents.

SUMMARY AND IMPLICATIONS

Examination of the problems victims and nonvictim witnesses experience because of involvement in the criminal justice system shows that time loss, resulting in part from making unnecessary trips, and associated income losses are the most commonly experienced problems. They are also regarded by respondents as the most serious.

Experience of these problems is not unique to any one group. Women, as would be expected, are more likely to report child care needs. Better educated, white men are more likely to report time loss. Though each of these associations is statistically significant, the associations are at a moderately low level. Whereas others have focused on the effects of crime on the elderly, these data do not support the view that the elderly experience problems more intensely. If anything, the opposite is evident. Women are somewhat more likely to consider the problems they encounter serious, but only in the specified instance noted above.

Examination of the assessments that victims and nonvictim witnesses give of system representatives reveals very positive attitudes by citizens toward police, district attorneys, and judges. Though the reader's reaction to these findings may be that citizens of Milwaukee are much more positive in their assessment of criminal justice personnel than citizens in other communities, [23-26] McIntyre[27] and Biderman[28] have reported that over 70% of the public have respect for the police. Therefore, a finding that citizens are willing to give fairly positive assessments to the actions of police, district attorneys, and judges is not so unusual.

It is important to note that there is a distinction in assessment of the police between victims identified within the community and those who actually get involved in the criminal justice system. This latter group had seen results. An offender had been arrested and was being processed through the system. Among victims identified in the community, reporting to the police often did not result in an arrest. Although community victims reported over 1,700 incidents to the police, only about 110 actually reached the system. Therefore, most of the community respondents had not seen definite police results at the time they were interviewed. Their less positive assessments of police action, therefore, were understandable. They also support the view that positive assessments result when action occurs and that the major hurdle to a good community image of the police is lack of action by the police.

A distinct relationship between positive assessment and intention of future cooperation is also evident. Although it is logical and follows conventional wisdom that when one is dissatisfied one will be less likely to want to be involved again, the very high levels of intention to be involved (over 95%) occurring among those who were satisfied should not be assumed. Yet very strong willingness to cooperate was expressed. This suggests that citizen cooperation can be expected when action is taken in criminal cases. Cooperation, in turn, should make law enforcement officials' jobs less difficult.[25]

The findings presented here have implications for the three solutions most commonly provided for victim and witness problems. The first of these, *compensation,* is oriented entirely to the crime event. Nothing is given to cover financial losses or inconveniences caused by having to go to court. In addition, only about one third of the states have such a program. *Restitution,* which may repay a victim for property loss or damage (or partially do so), only assists victims in avoiding system-related problems if it is enacted at a pretrial level. Under such circumstances, it may enable a victim (and witnesses) to avoid court appearances. Otherwise it does virtually nothing to assist with these kinds of problems. The third solution, provision of *services* to victims and witnesses, exists only to a limited extent in most communities. Even those programs that do exist are not necessarily well known by those needing the services. Specialized victim and witness assistance programs are about the only type of program that can help with the type of problems examined here.

The findings presented here suggest that specialized victim and witness assistance programs should not focus on subgroups within the population but should be generally accessible to all. Such access should be extended to others close to the victim or witness as well. The most important problems to deal with are time and related financial losses of victims and witnesses. Thus, programs that notify witnesses when they will not be needed and that make scheduling of court cases more efficient may have the greatest effect. Other problems of lesser importance, but still requiring some attention, are transportation and parking difficulties encountered by witnesses and child care needs, particularly of women.

Within the criminal justice system, experiments should be considered that attempt to find new solutions to system-related problems of victims and witnesses. Simple modifications can greatly assist these individuals. For example, administrative reforms can save victim and witness time; waiver or other procedures can free victim property from the requirement of having to be presented as evidence at a court trial; greater police follow-through on subpoena processing can greatly assist the case flow; better allocation of manpower in a prosecutor's office can lessen witness frustration and the like.

Victims and witnesses do not expect miracles of the criminal justice system and give ready evidence of their willingness to rank law enforcement, district attorney, and court officials higher when they perceive that these system representatives have rendered effective human services. Though victim and witness opinion of criminal justice officials should improve if victim assistance programs are strengthened, this should not be the motive behind efforts to justify victim and witness services. Ultimately, such services must be grounded in the fact that they provide economic assistance, facilitate case flow, enhance the dispensation of criminal justice, and equalize the satisfactions necessary for each party in the criminal and postcriminal event. Victim and witness assistance programs and services must have their foundation within the process of system amelioration and should be conceived as one facet of needed criminal justice system improvement.

It is questionable whether providing increased aid to law enforcement, the courts, and corrections will have maximum value as long as crime victims refuse to enter the criminal justice system, decline to cooperate with the system once they enter, or are victimized further in money and time by entrance into the system proper. Unless the interests of victims and witnesses are considered and broadened within the system itself, it is highly probably that their participation in the process of justice will not increase but will remain the same or even decrease over time.

Because there is evidence that the orientation and practices of law enforcement personnel have an effect on the decision of the victim to report the crime, police and sheriffs' departments should pay greater attention to their role in effective prosecutorial and judicial activity. The law enforcement officer remains the first line of contact with persons who have been victimized and those who may serve as potential witnesses. If this encounter is unpleasant or unrewarding either to the victim or the witness, it is highly probable that the police's request to the victim to enter into the system will be either refused or accepted only half-heartedly. The data suggests that attitudes toward criminal justice representatives, though related to one's willingness to cooperate, tend to improve rather than become worse once victims and witnesses enter into the criminal justice system. If this is true, the act of making initial contact takes on added importance and has long-term implications for the criminal justice system. If persons are encouraged to report, they will be reinforced within the criminal justice system despite experiencing problems within that system. Hence, more attention should be placed on police-citizen relationships. Of utmost importance is that each police officer be his or her own public relations specialist, for the police officer has the capacity to influence the future course of the criminal justice case process. But the police are not alone in this requirement. Prosecutorial personnel must be more receptive to citizen complaints as well. In short, the system of criminal justice should be increasingly personalized and humanized, and the place of the crime victim within the criminal justice equation should be strengthened. The data suggest that there is a need to deemphasize the traditional role differences between outsiders (victims and witnesses) and insiders (policemen, district attorneys, judges, clerks, bailiffs, and other operatives). Until this is done, victims and witnesses are likely to feel that they are aliens in their own country.

Of course, the criminal justice system should not bear the entire responsibility for meeting victim and witness needs. Interagency cooperation should be encouraged in the establishment of any local victim assistance program. Because useful programs have to be multifaceted and interorganizational, efforts must be taken at the outset of program development to secure the cooperation of representative private agencies and public social control personnel.

A greater effort should be made to publicize community services that may already provide many of the services needed by victims and witnesses. Each jurisdiction should provide brochures or other documents that give potential victims and witnesses information not only about what to expect within the criminal justice system but also about where they can go for services within the local community. These brochures and other informational booklets should be made available at the entrances of public buildings, courtrooms, and other appropriate facilities, and should be supplied to designated public and private service agents. The mailing or serving of such brochures with a subpoena can do much to ease problems caused by victim and witness entrance into the criminal justice system.

The question of victim and witness assistance is one for system balance. Right now, it appears that most elements of the criminal justice system are directed to conviction of the offender and maintenance of regularized system operation. As long as the victim and witness are treated as intervening actors and not as persons in need within the system, they will respond negatively. Only when these individuals perceive that their concerns are given equal attention to those related to the offender will they recognize that the system cares about them and values their participation. Until this happens, the system of justice will not be completely whole.

REFERENCES

1. Burgess, Ann W., and Linda L. Holmstrom. "Rape: The Victim and the Criminal Justice System," in Drapkin, Israel, and Emilio Viano, eds. *Victimology: A New Focus*, vol. 3 (Lexington, Mass.: D.C. Heath & Co., 1975), pp. 21-30.
2. Chappell, Duncan. "Forcible Rape and the Criminal Justice System," *Crime and Delinquency* **22:**125-136, 1976.
3. Lamborn, LeRoy L. "Remedies for the Victims of Crime," *Southern California Law Review* **43:**26, 1970.
4. Schultz, LeRoy G. "The Child as a Sex Victim: Socio-Legal Perspectives," in Drapkin, Israel, and Emilio Viano, eds. *Victimology: A New Focus*, vol. 4 (Lexington, Mass.: D. C. Heath & Co., 1975), pp. 177-189.
5. Goldsmith, Jack, et al. "A Symposium on Crime and the Elderly," *Police Chief* **43:**18-51, 1976.
6. Gubrium, Jaber F. "Victimization in Old Age: Available Evidence and Three-Way Hypotheses," *Crime and Delinquency* **20:**145-150, 1974.
7. Pope, Carl, and William Feyerherm. "The Effects of Crime on the Elderly: A Review of Recent Trends," *Police Chief* **43,** 1976.
8. Andrew, Carolyn Jaffe. "The Reluctant Witness for the Prosecution," *Journal of Criminal Law, Criminology and Police Science* **55:**1-15, 1964.
9. Ash, Michael. "On Witnesses: A Radical Critique of Criminal Court Procedures," *Notre Dame Lawyer* **48:**380-425, 1972.

10. Bodemer, O.A. "The Expert Witness Hassle," *American Psychologist* **25**:82, 1970.

11. Cannavelle, Frank J., Jr., and William Falcon. *Witness Cooperation* (Lexington, Mass.: D. C. Heath & Co., 1976).

12. Meade, Anthony, Mary S. Knudten, William Doerner, and Richard D. Knudten. "Discovery of a Forgotten Party: Trends in Crime Victim Compensation Legislation in the United States," *Victimology: An International Journal* **1**:421-433, 1976.

13. Center for Criminal Justice and Social Policy. *Victim Compensation Laws and Programs* (Milwaukee: Marquette University, 1976).

14. Edelhertz, Herbert, and Gilbert Geis. *Public Compensation to Victims of Crime* (New York: Praeger Publishers, 1974).

15. Goldstein, Naomi. "Reparation by the Offender to the Victim as a Method of Rehabilitation for Both," in Drapkin, Israel, and Emilio Viano, eds. *Victimology: A New Focus*, vol. 2 (Lexington, Mass.: D. C. Heath & Co., 1974), pp. 193-205.

16. Jacob, Bruce R. "Reparation or Restitution by Criminal Offender to His Victim," *Journal of Criminal Law, Criminology and Police Science*, **61**:154, 1970.

17. Hudson, Joe, and Burt Galaway, eds. *Considering the Victim: Readings in Restitution and Victim Compensation* (Springfield, Ill.: Charles C Thomas, Publisher, 1975).

18. Center for Criminal Justice and Social Policy. *Victims and Witnesses: A Guide for Community Service* (Milwaukee: Marquette University, 1975).

19. Blalock, Herbert. *Social Statistics* (New York: McGraw-Hill Book Co., 1972), pp. 295-297.

20. Edwards, Allan L. *An Introduction to Linear Regression and Correlation* (San Francisco: W. H. Freeman & Co., Publishers, 1976), p. 71.

21. Pope, Carl, and William Feyerherm. "The Effects of Crime on the Elderly: A Review of Recent Trends," *Police Chief* **43**, 1976.

22. Goldsmith, Jack, and Sharon Goldsmith. *Crime and the Elderly: Challenge and Response* (Lexington, Mass.: D. C. Heath & Co., 1976).

23. Johnson, Deborah, and Robert J. Gregory. "Police-Community Relations in the United States: A Review of Recent Literature and Projects," *Journal of Criminal Law, Criminology and Police Science* **62**:94-103, 1971.

24. Jacob, Herbert. "Black and White Perceptions of Justice in the City," *Law and Society Review* **6**:69, 1971.

25. Hahn, Harlan. "Ghetto Assessment of Police Protection and Authority," *Law and Society Review* **6**:183, 1971.

26. Block, Richard L. "Police Action, Support for Police and Support for Civil Liberties" (paper delivered at the American Sociological Association Meeting, 1970).

27. McIntyre, Jennie. "Public Attitudes Toward Crime in Law Enforcement," *Annals Of American Academy of Political and Social Sciences* **374**:34-46, 1967.

28. Biderman, Albert D. et al. *Report on a Pilot Study in the District of Columbia on Victimization and Attitudes Towards Law Enforcement: Field Surveys I* Washington, D.C.: U.S. Government Printing Office, 1967).

C □ *Victims of crimes of violence and the criminal justice system*

GILBERT GEIS

Two fundamental conditions, seemingly operating at cross-purposes, bear upon the victim of criminal violence when he comes to define his response to his situation and his attitude toward the person who victimized him. On the

Reprinted by permission of the publisher, from Gilbert Geis "Victims of Crimes of Violence and the Criminal Justice System," in *Violence and Criminal Justice*, edited by Duncan Chappell and John Monahan (Lexington Mass.: Lexington Books, D. C. Heath and Company, Copyright 1975, D. C. Heath and Company).

one hand, he generally desires revenge. On the other hand, he often wishes to establish an appearance of mercifulness, to seem to possess an educated understanding of the imperatives that drove the offender to act as he did. A particularly useful catalyst for reconciling these rather contradictory feelings lies in the concept of offender "sickness,"—that is, in the setting forth of the view that there is something mentally wrong with the murderer, rapist, or mugger, and that such aberration merits compassion— or, at the least, mediation of any desire for direct retaliation. Since the offender is "sick," however, and since cure is taken as unlikely, by far the most sensible policy, the victim often suggests, would be to eliminate the offender or at least to isolate him for a very long period of "treatment." Advocacy of such a position allows the unification of what might at first have seemed to be irreconcilable impulses for vengeance and for understanding. Revenge may be had without guilt, and compassion may be indulged without compromising retributive feelings.

Numerous illustrations of such thought patterns turned up in interviews that colleagues and I conducted among victims of violent crime in California who had applied for public compensation funds. "He seemed to expect me to talk to him in the courtroom" one of the victims noted. "He looked kinda like a crazy man." A woman, who was requested to describe her assailant, called him a "sex maniac." Another victim, asked for an opinion about what she believed ought to be done to the man who had raped and savaged her, noted:

Just give him to me. I shouldn't feel this way, but I could kill him. If he did this to me, he could do it to others. He's really sick. If he can be helped, he should be. But if he can't be helped, why waste taxes on him? He should not be in society.

Similar kinds of responses—rather than those concentrating on socioeconomic factors or situational imperatives in the offender's background—were put forward in about two out of three instances, though occasionally there were refreshing variations, such as the victim of a pursesnatch assault who looked puzzled when we asked her what she thought was the cause of the offender's behavior. "How should I know?" she asked in return. 'I didn't stand there and talk with him." Equally idiosyncratic was the good-natured victim who had only sympathy for an assailant who had severely battered him during a barroom brawl. Perhaps, in this case, the important condition was the rather blithe attitude the victim himself had toward law violation. Asked if he had ever been arrested, he said: "Only once and that really wasn't nothing. They got me for 'disapposure'

in an alley downtown. The cops just got right there before I had a chance to put it back in my pants." He smiled sheepishly and ended: "But I never was so slow again . . . they never had to arrest me no more."[1]

The nature of responses of victims of criminal violence and the form in which such responses are related to elements of the criminal justice system constitute the subject matter of this chapter. Material will be drawn from the California victim compensation applicant interviews and from more recent interviews with survivors of homicide victims. This material will be supplemented with insights offered in the still-rather-sparse published literature on crime victims.[2]

It must be particularly appreciated that the crime victim rarely is able to see himself as an entirely guiltless person, an individual who has no necessity to review his actions and attitudes in order to understand what happened to him.[3] If nothing else, he must satisfactorily resolve questions relating to the lottery of human existence that resulted in injury being visited upon him rather than another. He must have at least some anodynic answer to the question of "Why me?" or thereafter must become fixed in the discomforting position that existence is hopelessly haphazard and that there is little gain to be had from rational, self-protective, planned action.

Too many alternative ways of behaving usually had been available to the crime victim (unlike, say, the cancer victim) to allow much ready surcease from soul-searching; a better door lock, more care in choosing the route to one's destination, availability of a gun or other weapon, more awareness of the danger from certain kinds of persons—these and a host of other "but ifs" nag at the victim. Almost inevitably, then, some blame attaches to one's self. Partial relief from unnerving self-doubt can be had by recourse to particular attitudes toward elements of the criminal justice system and toward the offender. We have no sophisticated data yet on the precise ingredients of such attitude linkages, but we can provide some details and offer possible interpretations of the form they often take.

PLIGHT OF THE CRIME VICTIM

Interviews indicate that no segment of the criminal justice system is altogether spared the anger and disdain of crime victims. Many victims feel that their needs have low priority in the business of the police, the courts, and the correctional system. They feel that they are, at best, tolerated and then often only with ill-humor. Their role, they say, seems much like that of the expectant father in the hospital at delivery time; necessary for things to have gotten underway in the past, but at the moment rather superfluous and mildly bothersome. Victims will sometimes note that the offenders seem to fare a good deal better than they do; the offender, at least, is regarded by criminal justice functionaries as a doer, an antagonist, someone to be wary of, a person who must be manipulated successfully if the workers in the criminal justice system—the police, the judge, the attorneys—are to have their satisfaction and rewards for a job well done.

The victim, on the other hand, is part of the background scenery—a rather drab character, in the nature of a spear-carrying supernumerary, watching from a distance the preening and posturing of the prima donna stars in the drama. There have been, on occasion, frank acknowledgements of this condition by members of the criminal justice establishment. "Railroads for some time have not done much to pleasure the customer," a defense attorney has noted. "Our system has been behaving like a railroad, because maybe it figures the victim can't just choose another court system. We've got to look at the victim like he's a customer who requires service."[4]

More often, however, even these kinds of expression of concern with the plight of crime victims are lacking, so insignificant do victims appear to those engaged in the process of dealing with the criminal offender. In this regard, the President's Commission on Law Enforcement and Administration of Justice noted that "one of the most neglected subjects in the study of crime is its victims: the persons, households, and businesses that bear the brunt of crime in the United States."[5] A law professor has echoed this observation. "Surely there will be agree-ment," Childres writes, "that some attention should be diverted from the criminal, one of the most vigorously studied animals in history, to his victim, one of the most ignored."[6]

One of the few outlets available to crime victims for expression of their concerns are the letters-to-the-editor columns of metropolitan newspapers. Some of the feelings that victims have can be gathered from a sampling of letters that appeared in *The New York Times* during 1971. It should be noted that many of the letters reproduced are from persons suffering property losses; presumably, victims of violent crimes would feel even more aggrieved.

First, there is the disillusionment with the bail system, shock at the apathy of those charged with apprehending an offender who fails to appear in court, and disgust with the role of appointed counsel for the defendant in thwarting what are seen as fundamental principles of justice:

On October 19, I encountered a thief who had broken into my parked car and who was in the process of removing the FM radio tuner. I followed him for eight blocks and was fortunate enough to spot a police prowl car. The man was duly arrested and charged. In his possession was the FM tuner.

That evening, playing the role of "good citizen," I spent three hours in night court waiting my chance to see justice administered. Taken before Judge Hyman Skolniker, the defendant pleaded "not guilty." . . . Because of a legal complication, the prisoner, to my great shock, was released without bail despite the fact that he admitted to being a heroin addict with a previous arrest record. . . . The entire court appearance lasted between sixty and ninety seconds.

On October 28, the defendant failed to appear in court. As one who took the trouble to follow, to apprehend, and to appear in court, I am totally disillusioned with the results. I am informed by the Appearance Control Project people at the District Attorney's office that no one will attempt to locate the defendant. I was told that his failure to appear in court will merely be recorded and that should he ever be re-arrested, he will then face the music.

Basically what has happened is that this man has been given license to commit more crimes. This has been effected by sixty-second justice administered with the help of Legal Aid Society lawyers.

From my point of view, I deeply regret being involved and having wasted my time in the interest of justice. Should this situation recur (and I have no doubt that it will), I will not participate. Should I witness a crime, I will turn my back. It is obvious that under our present court system the victim gets no redress, and the petty criminal, when caught, goes free.[7]

A second writer complains that he met with "bureaucratic obstructionism" when he tried to obtain a weapon with which to protect himself against crime, while offenders readily obtain guns through extralegal channels, he claims. This person adds a lament against what he believes to be the press' insensitivity to crime victims:

. . . It is the law-abiding citizen who is most often the victim and it is for them that no protection exists under law. While the criminals' rights are zealously guarded by ever-watchful libertarians, the victims writhe in suffering and pain, suffer permanent harm and disfigurement or death, and great newspapers talk of the rule of law.[8]

I do not advocate unlimited access to guns or to weapons of any type, but until the law of the jungle is repealed in this city and across America, surely, who can criticize the man able and willing to defend his life through use of a legally registered weapon.

Further, as the witness who can identify the assassins who attacked him, the press places the victim once again in jeopardy of his life by publishing his home address, tempting the killers to murder him or members of his family in their home. Again we see that there is no protection under law for the victim but only the law of the jungle.[9]

Another writer contrasts the care and concern afforded the offender when he is incarcerated in contrast to the neglect of the crime victim:

Your July 26 news story about the Rikers Island Reformatory again reveals the city administration's perversion of justice and retribution. The story deals extensively with . . . the alleged denial of adequate training and rehabilitation to youthful offenders, and their subjection to "empty days and useless work."

But what of their victims? Are their days, in many cases, not tragically empty? . . . When will the Legal Aid Society, the city's public defender organization, bring suit to require that our elected officials protect the victims and not the muggers, murderers, the rapists, the thieves?

It would seem proper to assume that the offenders are in jail not because of virtuous behavior but rather because of explicit and, at times, recidivistic acts of violence, acts that cannot be tolerated. More sympathetic attention must be paid to the victims (whose numbers grow daily) and less cajolery—or none—given to the criminal element.[10]

A businessman, owner of eleven stores in Manhattan, reports that they had been broken into on 49 occasions during a two-year period. Every store had been victimized at least once. Finally, an arrest was made. The owner details the events that followed:

Our friendly neighborhood burglar . . . broke the locks in three [display] windows—looting the contents. When the fourth window resisted his best efforts, he broke the glass. A nearby guard phoned the police, who found a 41-year-old man up to his armpits in shirts and ties. It turned out that the man had a record of 51 arrests and was on the wanted list for having jumped bail three times.

What happens when a criminal is finally caught? This happened:

—All our window display merchandise was tied up by the court as evidence.
—Our manager spent one entire day in court, and because the case was not reached, he lost half the next day.
—Ditto for the policeman.
—Despite the defendant's history, the District Attorney bargained with him to plead guilty to a lesser crime.
—Despite the fact that the man had jumped bail three times, the judge granted him bail again—making him free to conduct business as usual.
Is it possible that we can fly to the moon but can't cope with crime in the streets?[11]

Finally, mention might be made of a terse three-line communication to the paper that, in its way, summarizes all the foregoing letters: "Crime," it notes, "will not decrease until being a criminal becomes more dangerous than being a victim."[12]

These letters, of course, are by no means representative. They come from New York City where citizens have a defined and, perhaps, real crime problem, which is more aggravated than in most cities and which may add a certain acerbity to the tone of the letters. That they appear in the paper at all indicates their origin with persons accustomed to making strong opinions known at large. The *Times* itself probably intruded some bias; there was a sharp upsurge in letters such as these during 1971 and then an obvious diminution thereafter. Perhaps the paper began to receive fewer such letters, though, more likely, it merely ceased to broadcast the same refrain. It seems worth marking, however, the manner in which the writers sometimes agitate against offenders not out of patently retributive impulses, but because they feel that the victim's position has been derogated vis-à-vis the criminal's. It would be worth knowing, among other things, how better attention to the cares and needs of the crime victim might bring about more compassionate concern with the welfare of the offender.

THE CRIME VICTIM AND THE POLICE

It is possible to discover some relatively clear patterns of responses by crime victims to most functionaries in the criminal justice system. The foregoing letters, for instance, indicate a hostility to court processes and personnel that is found among virtually all crime victims. There is a very wide range of opinion in regard to the police, however, among victims. Most generally, persons who suffer property losses tend to complain that the police act in an apathetic, perfunctory manner toward them. The police appear to be regarded much more sympathetically by victims of violence, especially by women (except, of course, for rape victims, whose true victimization the police notoriously tend to regard as unlikely[13]). Apart from emotional distinctions between reactions to personal and property victimization, it is probable that the police find in the much higher prospect of solving personal offenses considerable encouragement for rapport, since officers and victim can link up in a successful endeavor to get the offender, and later can join forces in collaborative scorn for the "indulgence" of the criminal by other segments of the criminal justice mechanism.

An illustration of victim disenchantment with the police appears in a newspaper interview with a Washington, D.C., man who had been forced into an alley at knife point and then robbed of his watch, credit cards, $1200 ring,

and $80 in cash. He reported the police performance this way:

They were useless. All they did was to take down my story and ask me questions about it, like I was the robber or something. They wouldn't even go back to where it happened to get the guy's fingerprints, which were all over my wallet and the cellophane. In the end one of them said, "Why were you carrying so much money?" and that was the end of it. He didn't even say goodnight. It happened two weeks ago, and I haven't seen them since.[14]

Considerable insight into the dynamics of victim-police interaction is offered by a Los Angeles man, who was scared out of his wits by robbers who pushed their way into his house and trussed him at gunpoint and then left with his stereo and other valuables:

Police, being used to hearing lots of horror tales, are rarely impressed. They also feel the quite reasonable need to inject some calm into the situation. The details that make the story real merely slow down the average cop who wants to get his job done and his report written, or possibly, get some relevant information out on the radio, usually information like the description you cannot provide.[15]

The remarks of an apartment owner in New York are quite different, as she identifies the police as her protectors and castigates those who she believes are handcuffing them from doing the kind of job she presumes they are interested in. She had been mugged three times during the previous three years, once by a 17-year-old girl and twice by boys no more than 12-years old:

. . . the police is not allowed to do nothing! This mayor of ours, he stopped the police from doing anything to the Negroes and the Spanish. The president, what did he do yet to let the police go? I tell you something—if the cops would take their sticks and give a good beating to these lousy kids the first time they do something wrong, they wouldn't do it a second time. But nobody does nothing for the white folks— only they do for the others.[16]

This recourse to "racial" explanations of crime victim-system interaction, incidentally, is something that took us rather by surprise in our own interviews, because it occurred so often. Perhaps our startlement merely indicates our own encapsulation from persons and circles among whom criminal behavior is commonplace, though it may point to a need to resolve more satisfactorily victim difficulties as an important step toward ameliorating in some way broader racial problems in our society. Apparently, smoldering resentments and bigotry are given full rein when a victim feels thwarted by the criminal justice process. A San Francisco truck driver, for instance, who was stabbed 17 times by a black man he said he never saw before (our best guess is that they earlier had exchanged words in a liquor store and that the assailant followed the victim to the parking lot of a supermarket to which he was making a delivery) ranted about the fact that courts are disinterested in "bringing people to justice" and insisted that the assailant's witnesses were given priority over his because "niggers are running the country now." As long as the person who stabbed him was "a nigger," he said, "nothing will be done."

A 66-year-old woman, beaten into unconsciousness and raped in her bedroom by an intruder, thought that her problem in part was associated with the fact that "the colored race is trying to get that 'black power' going." "They should have equal rights," she said, "but they are going about it wrong." Along the way, she also threw in the idea that one of the things causing trouble was that "Mexicans can get a liscense to drive without reading or writing." This victim illustrated, at the same time, the fact that a simplistic view about the relationship between injury from crime and what can be called anti-liberal impulses do not always prevail. Thus, though she went on at some length about the need for "whipping posts so that people can see who the criminals are," this woman was even more insistent that laws against prostitution had to be repealed in order to protect persons like herself. This latter view, she insisted firmly, was a total reversal of the attitude that she had held before the victimization episode.

CRIME VICTIMS AND THE COURTS

The shuffling about of the crime victim during court processes is notorious. Astute defense attorneys devote a good deal of time and ingenuity to disconcerting, hazing, and otherwise making the victim of crime miserable. Clearly, this latter is a fundamental element of the adversary system of criminal justice, and perhaps it is part of the slag that is unfortunately essential in order to produce a reasonably pure product. Such philosophical speculations, however, do little to alleviate the malaise of the crime victim. Consider, for example, the position of a victim of a mugging—a person who has already run up a drawerful of hospital bills and missed days or weeks of work because of the criminal incident—who is cross-examined by a defense attorney operating in accord with the following advise offered in a standard book on trial tactics:

When you have forced the witness into giving you a direct answer to your question you really have him under control; he is off-balance, and usually rather scared. This advantage should be followed up with a few simple questions, such as, "You did not want to answer that question, did you?" If the witness says that he wanted to answer it, ask him in a resounding voice, "Well, why did you not answer it when I first asked you!" Whatever his answer is, you then ask him, "Did you think that you were smart enough to evade answering the question?" Again, whatever the answer is you ask him, "Well, I would like for the jurors to know what you have behind all this dodging and ducking you have done!" . . . This battering and legal-style "kicking the witness around" not only humiliates but subdues him.[17]

The position of the crime victim in court has been examined by Richard H. Kuh, newly appointed district attorney in Manhattan, on the basis of a decade of experience as a prosecutor. "What is nearest and dearest to the heart of the victim of crime?" Kuh asks rhetorically and goes on to answer.

. . . equal standing in the criminal courts to the standing of the defendant in a criminal case, and by that I mean something very simple, and that is the right of the complainant, when it comes to such things as adjournments, appearances in court, to be entitled to some consideration.

I have seen complainants scolded and harassed by judges, and I will say by prosecutors, including myself, and when they have said to us, "I will not come down again, I have been here twelve times and every time I am here there is some reason for an adjournment, and I cannot miss any more days of work. I just will not come again."

And I as a prosecutor have had—and I might say it is the most hateful thing I have done in my years of prosecution—I have had the problem of telling these complainants we have no alternative but to hold you in contempt if you don't come down again.[18]

When he was appointed to succeed Frank S. Hogan as district attorney early in 1974, one of Kuh's first moves was to establish regional offices throughout the borough so that crime victims could more easily register their complaints.[19] Whether Kuh will institute further changes in order to be responsive to his own awareness of the plight of the crime victim will be worth watching.

Attitudes of crime victims toward the courts are typified, though in slightly stronger form, in an interview we had with a Lamont, California, victim who had been shot in the back when he was leaving the scene where he had been involved in a drinking dispute:

His lawyers and the D.A. were in court. The D.A. dropped the charges from shooting with attempt to commit murder to assault and battery. When I heard this I left the courtroom. He was given only 150 days . . . I don't think it was right and neither does the police. The chief wrote an article for the newspaper about it.

Both the court situation and the earlier problem of crime victims with the police have also been noted by Donald E. Santarelli, director of the Law Enforcement Assistance Administration. A newspaper report on a speech by Santarelli to state and city officials sums up his concerns:

The policeman says, "You be down at the stationhouse at 9 o'clock tomorrow night for the lineup." The victim wonders: Where's the stationhouse? Where's the lineup? How do I get there? Is it in the ghetto? Is it at night when I don't want to go out?

You take it to the courthouse, where it really becomes a hassle. The typical witness room looks like the waiting room in a mental hospital.

A prosecution witness may find himself next to the defendant's mother-in-law with her big umbrella . . . . and every kook and nut and friend of the addict, junkie, and arrestee.

More often than not, you find a clash occurring and the witness is just scared to death and that's the end of the case. The testimony suddenly becomes very unclear.[20]

SURVIVORS OF HOMICIDE VICTIMS

The foregoing materials can be supplemented with the results of a survey of survivors of homicide victims in regard to their attitudes toward criminal justice processes conducted by Shirley Blumberg with ten persons in southern California during 1972 as a class project.[21] She came to the following conclusions:

1. In cases in which there has been a final court disposition, all survivors except one reported some dissatisfaction with the courts. The exception was a case in which the offender is permanently paralyzed from a policeman's bullet in his spine. Statements such as, "The courts were too lenient," "He didn't get what he deserved; he deserved the death penalty," and "They should spend the rest of their lives in prison" were common. Plea bargaining was uniformly condemned on the ground that it resulted in undeservedly light sentences. Laziness of prosecutors and crowded court calendars were blamed for the reductions in charges.

2. In response to questions about causes of crime or attitudes toward the killer, eight of ten respondents adhered to a medical model of explanation. They repeatedly said, "He was obviously sick," "I know it had to be a sick mind," and "They were sick; they had to be." Early identification of deviant behavior with subsequent mental treatment was suggested by several persons as the best cure for crime. "In school, when they see behavior like that develop, they should catch it. They should refer him to an analyst or something," one person said. Another stated: "Families who become cognizant that one of their children deviates from the normal should seek help. They shouldn't be ashamed of it or try to hide it. They should seek help right away."

3. In all cases, general attitudes toward the police depended upon the amount and kind of attention given by the law enforcement officer

to the survivor. When the police called on a family member and kept him informed of progress in the case, attitudes were invariably friendly. When the police did not make or keep friendly contact, the survivor harbored bitter feelings. In one case, the police did not inform the parents of their son's death; rather, a witness to the crime told them about it a day later. In another instance, the survivor is angry with the police, understandably enough, because they suspected him at first of having killed his wife. Still another respondent has always enjoyed good, cooperative relations with the police, but he says he is now disturbed because they appear to be "dragging their feet."

4. In response to the inquiry, "Do you think politicians care about crime, or can control it?" the respondents uniformly exhibited a combination of goodwill and skepticism toward politicians. Answers included the cynical observation of a 23-year-old Mexican-American: "They don't want crime to go on, but when it doesn't happen to them, it's just all statistics." A 63-year-old widow said: "If they cared enough, they could do something. There's just too many things they care about more." A 62-year-old widower thought that "They could do something, but won't unless it helps keep them in power."

Several case vignettes flesh out the above conclusions:

• The respondent was the mother of a 17-year-old girl who had been dumped in an alley after being given enough barbiturates to kill her. Evidence was not conclusive as to whether she had been alive at the time she was abandoned. Following a plea bargain, two young men pled guilty to voluntary manslaughter. A third received a lesser sentence for agreeing to testify for the state. The mother is extremely bitter toward the offenders, the courts, and society in general. She believes that the case constituted first-degree murder and that sentences of 1 to 15 years are totally inadequate. She reports that her family has disintegrated since the incident. Her oldest child, a 19-year-old daughter, no longer speaks to her. A 10-year-old son has been sent to Colorado to attend private school. The mother says she is fearful for her 3-year-old son. She believes that the city environment could turn him toward drugs. She would like to leave, but feels that she can't afford it. Her

grief, she says, is still acute; she reports that she "bleeds all the time. It gets worse and worse."

• The survivor, a realtor came home one evening and discovered that his wife had been strangled, beaten, and shot in the back of the head. There was no sign of a struggle and nothing was missing except some coins from a piggy bank. There has not been an arrest. The husband was under suspicion at first but was cleared after taking a lie detector test. The initial police suspicion plus what the survivor believes is a lack of interest in the case on the part of the police has led this politically conservative man to a feeling of bitterness toward the police. He blames general permissiveness and lack of discipline in today's society for crime. His wife's sister has become convinced that he killed the wife, and this had led to a rift between the families. Because the police suspect that his wife was killed by someone she knew, the husband finds himself looking at his acquaintances with suspicion.

• The body of a 59-year-old psychiatric nurse who died of asphyxiation during a rape attempt was discovered by the respondent, her daughter. Her mother's hands were bound and a pillowcase was over her head. She had a nasal obstruction from a previous injury, and was unable to breathe with a gag stuffed into her mouth. The daughter believes the man did not intend to murder. The suspect, believed to have committed at least 24 rapes, was captured following another rape attempt. He escaped from jail and fled to Illinois. Two years later, while breaking into a house, he was shot in the spine by police and is now permanently paralyzed. Following extradition, he was convicted of rape and of breaking and entering. The daughter is satisfied; she believes that a lifetime paralysis is worse than life imprisonment and "he got what's coming to him." She would like to see him brought to trial for her mother's death, though, so that the case "can be closed." She feels that the offender is sick and should have had treatment when he was younger.

• A 21-year-old Chicano was visiting some friends. In the apartment with him were two women, a baby, and another man. There was an intrusion by two other men who were high on pills. During a squabble, one of the intruders slipped or was pushed down the stairs. He reported this to his 30-year-old brother who returned to the scene with an automatic rifle and began firing into the room from the doorway. One injured man staggered outside, was taken to a hospital, and survived. The other died 15 minutes after being hit. The respondent, the decedent's 23-year-old brother, thinks quicker action could have saved his brother's life. He reports that the police did not inform his parents of the murder, although they arrested the killer immediately. He is particularly bitter toward the courts. In spite of several eyewitnesses, the District Attorney reduced the charge to second-degree murder, and the offender was sentenced to 5 years to life. The brother asks: "If this isn't cold-blooded murder, what is?" He has purchased a gun so that he will not, he says, be unprepared like his brother was. He believes that the murderer, whom he knew only slightly, was always "mean" and "goofy." He reports that his mother has changed; she's now very quiet and sad.

Perhaps it needs to be indicated, in summary, that the purpose here is not to adjudicate the fairness of the treatment accorded the offenders in these cases. Justice may indeed have been served in all instances. The interviews show, however, a seething and deep discontent in many of the survivors of victims of violent crime. To the extent that these feelings exist, some part of the criminal justice system seems to have failed to do as much as could have been done to see to it that the victimized were comforted and dealt with more satisfactorily in their distress.

CONCLUSIONS

Two conclusions emerge from our materials: First, it is fortunate for the functionaries in the adjudication stage in the criminal justice system that they have a monopoly on the administration of justice. Rarely has a group been so uniformly regarded with so little respect, much less admiration, by those with whom they do business. That there are important consequences of this low esteem seems undeniable: it is probably reflected in crime reporting rates, in local and national elections, in patriotism quotients, and in similar significant ways.

Second, it is fortunate for the same functionaries that those who they offend tend, as crime victims, to be among the most powerless and least articulate persons within the society. Insulated on high, judges are grandly protected from the disparagement that so routinely was divulged to us by the crime victims whose cases the courts handled. Blumberg clearly portrays the in-group camaraderie and clubbiness that marks the work of officials in the criminal jus-

tice system and excludes the participants in the process from access to or retaliation against wrongs they feel they have suffered.[22] In their private lives, the officials generally mingle to a large extent with persons who never have reason to experience the indifference that the lower class, who constitute the vast number of crime victims, maintain that they receive.

Given these conclusions, what can be done? The following are but a few of the remedial steps that ought to be considered:

1. Somebody has to be designated to see that victims get a fairer shake, if only in the name of public relations. A letter informing them of the disposition of their case, thanking them for their cooperation, explaining to them what will go on or what has gone on would be a minimum fulfillment of the dictates of courtesy and consideration.

2. Somebody has to attend to scheduling that takes into account inconveniences to the victim and sees to it that adequate compensation, at a minimum, is accorded to citizens who suffer losses through court appearances and postponements.

3. System of victim compensation[23] that include not only medical and loss-of-earning reparations, but also social service assistance, vocational advice, and encouragement—not as charity, but as the right of a citizen in need— should be mounted and expanded.

4. Scholars must turn further attention to the plight of the crime victim. We need more information on what it means to be a criminal victim. What are the costs and other consequences? How about the "labeling" of the victim, by physical injury or psychological trauma from criminal activity directed against him or her? On the basis of such research and much more careful thought than has been given to the subject until now, new programs bringing justice and decency to crime victims must be inaugurated.

NOTES

1. The interview was conducted by Dorothy Zietz, professor of social work, California State University, Sacramento.

2. For an overview of the field see Israel Drapkin and

Emilio Viano, editors, *Victimology* (Lexington, Mass.: D. C. Heath. 1974).

3. See, generally, Robert Lejeune and Nicholas Alex, "On Being Mugged: The Event and Its Aftermath," *Urban Life and Culture* 2 (1973):259-287. See also Carl Bernstein, "Fear Haunts Holdup Victims: Mental Stress May Overshadow Physical Harm" *Washington Post,* September 5, 1970.

4. David Epstein, quoted in Ivan G. Goldman, "Crime is Just the Start of Victims' Difficulties," *Washington Post,* June 6, 1971.

5. President's Commission on Law Enforcement and Administration of Justice, *Task Force Report–Assessment of Crime* (Washington: Government Printing Office, 1967), p. 80.

6. Robert D. Childres, "Compensation for Criminally Inflicted Personal Injury," *New York University Law Review* 39 (1964):471.

7. Joseph A. Silverman, Letter to the Editor, *The New York Times,* November 15, 1971. Reprinted by permission of Dr. Silverman.

8. For a particularly sophisticated statement on this subject, see Sidney Hook, "The Rights of the Victim: Thoughts on Crime and Compassion," *Encounter* 38 (1972):11-15.

9. William A. Conway, Letter to the Editor, *The New York Times,* November 2, 1971. Reprinted by permission of Mr. Conway.

10. A. G. Hanau, Letter to the Editor, *The New York Times,* August 2, 1971. Reprinted by permission of Mr. Hanau.

11. Mortimer Levitt, Letter to the Editor, *The New York Times,* December 18, 1971. Reprinted by permission of Mr. Levitt.

12. Donald A. Windsor, Letter to the Editor, *The New York Times,* December 8, 1971. Reprinted by permission of Mr. Windsor.

13. Susan Griffin, "Rape: The All-American Crime," *Ramparts* 10 (1971):26-36, is a good representative of a considerable literature to this point.

14. Quoted in Tom Wolff, "Pain, Terror Concealed in Reports of Muggings," *Los Angeles Times,* December 14, 1972.

15. Charles T. Powers, " 'Say One Word and I'll Cut Your Throat,' " *Los Angeles Times,* January 13, 1974.

16. Morton Hunt, *The Mugging* (New York: New American Library, 1973), p. 394. I have put Hunt's attempt to capture phonetically the landlady's German-English back into plain English.

17. Lewis W. Lake, *How to Win Lawsuits Before Juries* (New York: Prentice-Hall, 1954), pp. 164-65.

18. New York, Meeting of the Governor's Committee on the Compensation of Victims of Violent Crime, January 14, 1966, pp. 37-38.

19. "Kuh is Sworn In: Plans Neighborhood D.A. Offices," *The New York Times,* February 14, 1974.

20. "Aid Sought for Crime Victims," *Los Angeles Times* (AP), January 14, 1974.

21. Shirley Blumberg, "The Survivors: Attitudes of Families of Homicide Victims," unpublished seminar paper, Program in Social Ecology, University of California, Irvine, December 8, 1972.

22. Abraham S. Blumberg, *Criminal Justice* (Chicago: Quadrangle, 1967).

23. See, generally, Herbert Edelhertz and Gilbert Geis, *Public Compensation to Victims of Crime* (New York: Praeger, 1974).

Selected readings for Chapter 2

Ash, Michael. "On Witnesses: A Radical Critique of Criminal Court Procedures," *Notre Dame Lawyer* **48:**386-425, 1972.

> Describes the problems, interests, and rights of witnesses, who are characterized as experiencing a "dreary, time-wasting, depressing, exhausting, confusing, frustrating, numbing, and seemingly endless" process.

Garofalo, James. *The Police and Public Opinion: An Analysis of Victimization and Attitude Data from 13 American Cities* (Washington, D.C.: U.S. Government Printing Office, 1977).

> This report is based on the results of the National Crime Survey from thirteen major American cities in 1975 and deals with the relationship between attitudes toward the police and such factors as respondent characteristics, experiences with victimization, other attitudes, and whether victimizations were reported to the police.

Hawkins, Richard O. "Who Called the Cops?: Decisions to Report Victimizations," *Law and Society Review* **7:**427-444, 1973.

> Analysis of data from a victimization survey conducted in Seattle in 1968. Among 1,411 interviews from a random selection of households, 744 victimizations were reported to have occurred in the year before the interview, but only about 45% of the victimizations

became known to the police. The research was directed toward discovering why some victims report crimes to the police and others do not. Threat of victimization was associated with reporting; persons who felt the threat of crime were likely to report victimizations if they were victimized. Attitudes toward the police did not appear to influence the decision to report.

Hindelang, Michael J. "Decisions of Shoplifting Victims to Invoke the Criminal Justice Process," *Social Problems* **21**:580-593, 1974.

A report of a study examining factors affecting the decisions of shoplifting victims to refer shoplifters to the police. The author concludes that the decisions of victims to make police referrals were found to be more closely related to the value of the goods stolen, what was stolen, and how it was stolen, than to the characteristics of the offender.

Holstrom, Linda Lytle, and Ann Wolbert Burgress. *The Victim of Rape: Institutional Reactions* (New York: John Wiley & Sons, Inc., 1978).

An examination of how three major institutions—police, hospital, and court—respond to the rape victim and the impact of this response on the victim. This book is based on research that involved following a group of victims from the time they arrived at the emergency ward until the end of the legal process. It shows clearly the devastating effect of this official processing on the victims.

Knudten, Richard D., Anthony C. Meade, Mary S. Knudten, William G. Doerner. *Victims and Witnesses: Their Experiences with Crime and the Criminal Justice System* (Washington, D.C.: U.S. Government Printing Office, 1977).

An executive summary of a major research project to determine the experiences of victims and witnesses in the criminal courts in Milwaukee, Wisconsin. Interviews were conducted with 2,000 victims and witnesses at various points in the criminal processing of a case as well as with a group of victims previously identified through the national victimization surveys. Data were collected regarding the victims' and witnesses' experiences with the criminal justice system, the costs of their participation, and their satisfaction with criminal justice officials.

McDonald, William. *Criminal Justice and the Victim* (Beverly Hills, Calif.: Sage Publications, Inc., 1976).

A collection of twelve original articles analyzing victims' experiences in the criminal justice system, from the decision to report a crime to the police to possible victim involvement in securing restitution from the offender.

Chapter 3

THE COSTS OF CRIME

A □ *The assessment of costs in criminal justice*
CHARLES M. GRAY

B □ *A cost theory of victim justice*
JOHN ALAN STOOKEY

C □ *The fear of crime in the United States*
JAMES BROOKS

D □ *Crime: economic scourge of the ghetto*
WARREN T. BROOKES

A □ *The assessment of costs in criminal justice*

CHARLES M. GRAY

During most of the last two decades, crime has been a social problem of unquestionable significance. Various levels of government—federal, state, and local—have allocated substantial funds to criminal justice budgets in an attempt to stanch what has been perceived as a highly disruptive social phenomenon: "The existence of crime, the talk about crime, the reports of crime, and the fear of crime have eroded the basic quality of life of many Americans."[1] Private individuals and business firms have invested heavily in self-protection and have otherwise changed their behavior to decrease the likelihood of their own victimization.

Fig. 1 reflects trends in criminal justice expenditures by all levels of government. Like reported crime rates, these expenditures have climbed incessantly, resulting in the contention that increased spending has been ineffective in reducing crime. Of course, these two trends alone are insufficient for making such a determination; this is an issue that will be discussed throughout this chapter, and it is one that requires careful analysis.

Table 1 depicts the functional allocation of public spending for several recent years, as well as the proportion of the gross national product (GNP) that criminal justice expenditures repre-

This chapter was completed while the author was on the staff of the Minnesota Crime Control Planning Board and was supported in part by grant number 78-NI-AX-0002 from the National Institute of Law Enforcement and Criminal Justice. Views expressed are those of the author and do not represent the official position of any public or private agency.

73

sent. Clearly, criminal justice system (CJS) spending is increasing relative to total output.

The wise allocation of resources of this magnitude dictates the employment of efficiency criteria, a primary contribution of economic analysis. Yet economists have not, for a variety of reasons, been consulted often, nor have they taken the initiative in exploring the problems of resource allocation in crime and criminal justice until the decade of the 1960s.

THE ECONOMIC APPROACH

The Task Force on Assessment of the President's Commission on Law Enforcement and Administration of Justice attempted to measure the economic impact of crime, noting that crime "costs all Americans money."[2]

Crime in the United States today imposes a very heavy economic burden upon both the community as a whole and individual members of it. Risks and responses cannot be judged with maximum effectiveness until the full extent of economic loss has been ascertained. Researchers, policy-makers, and operating agencies should know which crimes cause the greatest economic loss, which the least; on whom the costs of crime fall, and what the costs are to prevent or protect against it; whether a particular or general crime situation warrants further expenditures for control or prevention and, if so, what expenditures are likely to have the greatest impact.

The Task Force further stated, "In view of the importance . . . it is surprising that the cost information . . . is as fragmentary as it is." It is

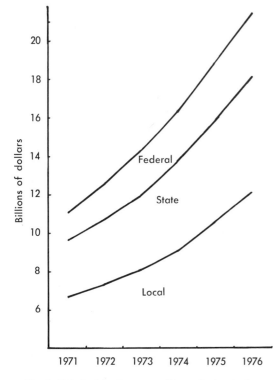

Fig. 1. Criminal justice expenditures by level of government.

Table 1. Criminal justice expenditures, all governments: 1971-1976

Category of expenditure	1971	1972	1973	1974	1975	1976
Total expenditures	$10,513,854	$11,731,802	$13,006,721	$14,842,053	$17,248,860	$19,681,409
(Percentage of GNP)	(0.99)	(1.00)	(1.00)	(1.06)		
Police protection	6,164,918	6,903,304	7,624,178	8,511,676	9,786,162	11,028,244
Judicial	1,358,282	1,490,649	1,579,457	1,798,153	2,067,664	2,428,472
Legal services, prosecution	491,326	580,381	663,810	770,762	933,126	1,047,929
Indigent defense	128,547	167,508	206,705	244,593	280,270	331,102
Corrections	2,291,073	2,422,330	2,740,208	3,240,208	3,843,313	4,385,512
Other	82,937	167,508	192,363	276,473	338,325	460,150

Source: U.S. Department of Justice, Law Enforcement Assistance Administration, and Bureau of the Census. *Trends in Expenditure and Employment Data For the Criminal Justice System: 1971-1976* (Washington, D.C.: U.S. Government Printing Office, 1978).

perhaps even more surprising that we have made so little additional progress in the ensuing decade. The reasons seem numerous and complicated; in essence, we lack a general guide to the measures of costs and the potential uses of cost data.

Economics is widely viewed as a difficult subject; crime is regarded as a complicated phenomenon. It may then seem paradoxical to assert that the economic approach can greatly simplify analyses of crime and the CJS. Yet that appears to be precisely the case.

Furthermore, economic considerations are of increasing importance as the taxpaying public becomes ever more aware of the size of the public budget and perceives public expenditures as a burden to be minimized. Although criminal justice expenditures are much smaller than some categories of public spending, efficiency still is a prime consideration.

From time to time some more-or-less-prominent figure will make such a pronouncement as: "We must reduce (or eliminate) crime at any cost." Of course this is absurd; total elimination would be virtually impossible regardless of the size of expenditures. Yet the message is clear. The citizenry wants safety *and* economy.

DEFINITIONS

A few preliminary definitions are in order. Reference will often be made to the *demand* for various aspects of criminal justice. To the economist, this has a very precise meaning. Demand for a good or a service means the willingness and ability to pay for it. Demand does *not* necessarily mean *need, want, desire,* or *insistence.*

The *supply* of a good or service reflects the willingness and ability of a seller to make a quantity available at a given price. In the case of a public service, the quantity supplied is determined by available revenues and input prices.

The interaction of demand for criminal justice with the supply yields an equilibrium price and quantity, that is, the price per unit and the number of units of criminal justice. Fig. 2 reflects this phenomenon. The amount of criminal justice secured is Q, and the price per unit is P. Unfortunately, we have no concrete measures of "criminal justice" that can be divided into denumerable units for the determination of P and Q. We can, however, obtain an approximate measure of $P \times Q$, that is, total criminal justice expenditures used to secure resources that "produce" criminal justice. Clearly these expen-

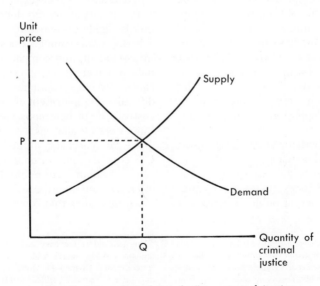

Fig. 2. A hypothetical "market" in criminal justice.

ditures represent a cost to society incurred as a direct result of the existence of crime. But these are far from the only such costs incurred.

Crime and costs

Crime is a term that seems to have defied precise definition (compare Sutherland and Cressey,[3] Schafer,[4] and Glaser[5]). Hann[6] has provided a definition, "A crime simply [is] any activity that causes uncompensated external diseconomies."* A subset of these criminal activities can be designated as "socially bad" crimes, which should be restricted in order to achieve optimum community welfare. Hann says, "A criminal activity is a 'socially bad' activity if, by restricting its level, the government could achieve a Pareto better level of welfare for the community."† This serves quite clearly to beg additional questions of definition.

Opportunity costs. Economists agree that the actual costs of the use of resources in some fashion are the foregone opportunities of using these resources in some other fashion. These costs are incurred even in the absence of any market transaction. For example, an individual who chooses to spend an evening watching television programs foregoes other uses of that time; the opportunity cost incurred by that person is, perhaps, completion of a good book or the writing of a letter to friends. A cost more closely related to the subject at hand might be a moonlight stroll through a park or, even more extreme, attendance at a concert or play, a visit with friends, or any of a number of alternative uses of time. If these decisions are dictated by a fear of crime, then one could reasonably argue that these foregone opportunities are, in fact, costs of crime.

Rottenberg[7] and Clotfelter[8] both have argued that such behavior alterations may be the largest single component of the cost of crime. Indeed, such costs are very difficult to measure, but intelligent allocation of public resources to crime control may require some attempt at such measurement.

External costs. Any human activity is resource-using and, hence, generates opportunity costs. Many activities involve the expenditure of resources by individuals who were not parties to the decision to undertake the activity, that is, who are "external" to the activity. The opportunity costs incurred by these individuals are termed "external costs," sometimes also called external diseconomies. One very familiar example is air pollution, where a firm's use of the atmosphere as a "free" repository of industrial wastes may impose medical or property costs on residents of the surrounding area. The polluter gains at the expense of other users of the air.

In like manner, and somewhat in the extreme, a robber or burglar who expropriates the property of others gains at the expense of the victims. Though there are clear differences between pollution and robbery, they are differences of timing, visibility, and degree. What these actions have in common is the concept of uncompensated external harm or costs.

Social costs. Any resource-using activity that reduces aggregate well-being or welfare in a society is said to generate "social costs." The magnitude of such costs, is, then, the valuation of the aggregate welfare foregone. This definition is highly deceptive in its simplicity, for it actually entails complex questions of definition, measurement, and comparison among individuals, which are topics of a subfield of economics called "welfare economics."* Despite these difficulties, employment of the concept of social cost can be of enormous value in providing a framework for analysis.

We can reasonably argue that the goal of the CJS is to allocate criminal justice resources in such a fashion as to minimize the social costs of crime. Rottenberg speaks to the same issue when he argues that "optimization of harm" is

---

*A diseconomy, or external cost, is defined below.

†According to the Pareto criterion, resources should be reallocated if, by so doing, *someone* is made better off, while *no one else* is made worse off. This is deemed an unequivocally better or preferred allocation.

*This subfield is not easy going for the uninitiated. The ambitious reader might find a useful, albeit challenging, introduction in Chapter 4 of Quirk, J., and R. Saposnik, *Introduction to General Equilibrium Theory and Welfare Economics* (New York, McGraw-Hill Book Co., 1968).

the appropriate goal: "A rational, calculating society would prefer to experience harm to the point where the last unit of harm prevented has a value just equal to the value of the resources employed in preventing that unit of harm."[7] That is, the CJS seeks *not* to eradicate crime but to minimize the sum total of the damage caused.

A very useful formulation of this concept has been provided by Phillips and Votey.[9] They assert quite unequivocally "that the question of defining actions as crime depends upon the concept of social cost." In their view, the social costs of crime consist of two components: the costs of criminal behavior and expenditures for protection and deterrence. The cost of criminal behavior is a rising function of the level of crime, whereas crime itself is deemed to be a decreasing function of expenditures. This is depicted in Fig. 3, where *E* is the expenditures function, *C* is the crime cost function, and their vertical sum is *SC*, the social cost of crime. As depicted, social cost declines over some range of crime, reaches a minimum value, then begins to rise. The level of crime associated with minimum social cost, *OA*, is the optimal level of crime. Criminal justice expenditures would be *OB*, and the costs of criminal behavior *OD*. It may well be that *OD* exceeds *OB* at the point

of optimality, but it does *not* follow that CJS expenditures should be increased.

The Phillips-Votey approach bears strong resemblance to the somewhat broader analysis of Schwartz and Tullock.[10] The cost categories proposed by the latter include costs of breach (that is, the harm from anticipated violation, similar to Phillips' and Votey's cost expenditures for protection) and costs of error (that is, wrongfully imposed sanctions). Clearly, the last can contribute to social costs; the true perpetrator escapes the socially desired consequence, whereas another party suffers from the imposition of a sanction with no clear relationship to his or her behavior. As a misallocation of resources, this creates social costs.

THE INCIDENCE OF COSTS

The previous section divided the social costs of crime into two components: expenditures and crime costs. Here, that division is discussed further.

Public costs of protection

We as a society undertake to supplement private efforts to control crime. The reason for the existence of the CJS is twofold and is firmly grounded in the theory of public finance. The first reason is the likelihood that the free market

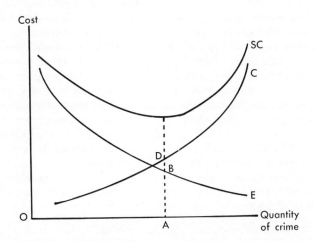

Fig. 3. The social costs of crime.

will not provide sufficient protection, adjudication, and correction (if indeed any of the latter two). Thus the CJS produces a "merit good."

Further, the CJS is financed for the most part by public tax revenues rather than a user charge, because the "exclusion principle" does not apply. If, for example, private police replaced local law enforcement agencies, it is quite likely that one individual's "private cop" would deter crime that otherwise would be committed against the purchaser, but he or she may also happen to discourage crime in an entire neighborhood. Since the neighbors have received protection without paying for it, the market has failed; thus, public provision is proper.

Private costs of protection

To protect themselves from crime, many, even most, citizens do not rely entirely on protection provided by public expenditures. Rather, most take additional measures, some perhaps so commonplace as to be almost automatic. Yet these measures do represent costs attributable to criminal behavior. Measures ranging from simple door locks to sophisticated security systems, from leaving houselights and radios operating in the inhabitant's absence to installing window bars and security screens, represent costs. So also do theft insurance, private security guards, and lack of evening access to public parks.

Although the magnitude of some of these costs is obvious, that of others is far more difficult to quantify. These latter costs include fear, inconvenience, and other subjective aspects of crime proximity, which have no direct market valuation. It will be shown, however, that even these factors manifest themselves in behaviors that do yield a market valuation.

Costs of victimization

Victims of criminal acts bear the most obvious costs attributable to crime. Victims lose items of value because of theft or robbery. They incur medical costs because of assault or rape and replacement or repair costs because of vandalism and other property destruction. They sometimes lose life itself. Direct but far less obvious costs of victimization include fear, loss of faith or trust, and, again, precautionary behavior and evasive action.

DISTRIBUTION OF CRIME AND JUSTICE

An especially troublesome question is that of equity: who should get how much criminal justice? Shoup poses these questions: "Shall a certain service, say police protection, be distributed equally among the residents of a city? What does 'equally' imply? If a service is not distributed equally, what other standards, perhaps implicit, are employed?"[11]

Shoup explores the trade-off between efficiency (crime minimization) and equity (equal risk) and notes that the goals may be both mutually exclusive and inconsistent with community preference. The Pareto criterion cannot be considered especially useful; it fails to indicate which among the possible states of the economy is equitable or just. A "social welfare function" may provide some guidance, but the nature of the values underlying such a function is at best subject to disagreement.* Economists emphasize efficient use of productive factors but this is not a theory of distributive justice. The concern of distributive justice is with distribution among individuals (or families), not among groups of factors.

Musgrave and Musgrave distinguished three aspects of the distribution problem:

1. Even where distributional objectives are not the primary policy target, the distributional implications of various policies must be taken into account in setting the overall policy package.
2. If distributional changes are to be made, they should be done so as to be least costly in terms of efficiency loss.
3. To decide what distributional changes, if any, should be made, or to evaluate the distributional implications of other policies, there must be a basis for choosing among alternative distributions, that is, a

---

*A social welfare function is a largely hypothetical index of aggregate satisfaction.

standard of distributive justice or fairness must be applied.[12]

Even though we may conclude that the public sector should provide criminal justice, it does not follow that the production should be public as well. For example, some correctional services may be produced in the private sector under contract to the public sector; most prisons, however, are governmentally owned and operated.

The CJS competes with other public goods and services for budgetary allocation. Furthermore, CJS components frequently compete among themselves for portions of the public pie. There must be some set of criteria to permit public sector decision makers to make rational choices among the budgetary possibilities.

Some aspects of the CJS smack more of private goods. For example, one person's consumption of judicial services reduces the quantity available to others. The mixed nature of the CJS renders it somewhat more difficult to analyze than, say, national defense. Nonetheless, a thorough understanding of the underlying principles will enable even the beginning student to cut through apparent difficulties and reach the analytical core.

A major problem is deciding how much criminal justice to provide and how much to charge various consumers. Should the individual pay for benefits received? There is no unique and effective method to determine how each individual values a unit of criminal justice. The criminal may place a low value on it; the victim may value it highly. We typically rely on the political process to supplant the market mechanism in this case. Yet both nonincarcerated offenders and victims can vote. The outcome of a voting process, under optimal conditions, will approximate the community's preference.

SUMMARY AND CONCLUSIONS

The occurrence of crime entails substantial resource allocation effects, including public expenditures for the CJS. Intelligent public policy decisions regarding such expenditures require knowledge of the costs generated by crime as well as potential benefits to be derived from CJS expenditures.

Before the concept "cost of crime" can be dealt with effectively, some precise definitions are required. Crime is defined as an activity that generates an uncompensated external cost. This cost, defined as that incurred by a party not a consensual participant to an activity, is a component of the "social costs" of crime (that is, the reduction in societal well-being generated by crime). These definitions now permit a statement of purpose for the CJS: to minimize the social costs of crime.

Concern with the economic impact of illegal activity is not a recent concern, the first "major" study having been published near the turn of the century.[13] Although ensuing studies (such as the Wickersham Commission, in 1931,[14] and several articles in *U.S. News and World Report* [15-17]) have improved upon the very early efforts, they have generally been hamstrung by the divergence between prevailing concepts of crime and definitions amenable to cost consideration. Thus, dollar magnitudes of estimates remain suspect, and much additional work remains to be done.

REFERENCES

1. President's Commission on Law Enforcement and Administration of Justice. *The Challenge of Crime in a Free Society* (Washington, D.C.: U.S. Government Printing Office, 1967), p. v.
2. President's Commission on Law Enforcement and Administration of Justice, Task Force on Assessment. *Crime and Its Impact: An Assessment* (Washington, D.C.: U.S. Government Printing Office, 1967), p. 42.
3. Sutherland, E. H., and D. R. Cressey. *Criminology,* ed. 9 (Philadelphia: J. B. Lippincott Co., 1974), p. 4.
4. Schafer, S. *Introduction to Criminology* (Reston, Va: Reston Publishing Co., Inc., 1976), p. 6.
5. Glaser, D., ed. *Handbook of Criminology* (Chicago: Rand McNally & Co., 1974), p. 46.
6. Hann, R. G. "Crime and the Cost of Crime: An Economic Approach," *Journal of Research in Crime and Delinquency,* January 1973, pp. 22-25.
7. Rottenberg, S. "The Social Cost of Crime and Crime Prevention," in McLennan, B., ed. *Crime in Urban Society* (New York: Dunellen Publishing Co., 1970), p. 58.
8. Clotfelter, C. T. "Urban Crime and Household Protective Measures," *Review of Economics and Statistics* **59**(4):499-503, 1977.
9. Phillips, L., and H. L. Votey, Jr. "An Economic Basis for the Definition and Control of Crime," in Nagel, S., *Modeling the Criminal Justice System* (Beverly Hills, Calif.: Sage Publications, Inc., 1977), pp. 89-109.

10. Schwartz, W. F., and G. Tullock. "The Costs of a Legal System," *J. Legal Studies* **4**(1):75-82, 1975.
11. Shoup, C. S. "Standards for Distributing a Free Governmental Service: Crime Prevention," *Public Finance* **19**:383-392, 1964.
12. Musgrave, R. A., and P. B. Musgrave. *Public Finance in Theory and Practice,* ed. 2 (New York: McGraw-Hill Book Co., 1976), p. 4.
13. Smith, E. The Cost of Crime (Report prepared for the International Prison Commission) (Washington, D.C.: Government Printing Office, 1901).

14. Wickersham Commission (National Commission on Law Observance and Enforcement). *Report on the Cost of Crime* (Montclair, N.J.: Patterson Smith Publishing Corp., 1968).
15. U.S. News and World Report. "Crime Expense Now Up to 51 Billions a Year," October 26, 1970, p. 30.
16. U.S. News and World Report. "Crime: A High Price Tag that Everybody Pays," December 16, 1974, p. 32.
17. U.S. News and World Report. "Crime's Big Payoff," Feburary 9, 1976, p. 50.

B □ *A cost theory of victim justice*

JOHN ALAN STOOKEY

The cost of criminal victimization has been of increasing concern to the American public and the scholarly community. This concern has primarily focused on the individual psychological and economic costs associated with victimization. This paper will make the argument that this concern for the cost of victimization has not gone far enough and that greater concern is mandated not only by humanitarian motivations, but also by such societal needs as social cohesion and support for the criminal justice system.

COST THEORY AND SOCIETY'S RESPONSIBILITY TO THE CRIME VICTIM

Clearly, the most desirable piece of victimization public policy would be the elimination of the crime problem. However, it is doubtful that any advanced industrial society such as the United States will ever completely eradicate crime problems. Thus, taking the rather pessimistic view of the inevitability of a certain level of crime, the question remains as to the amount of social responsibility the polity has to the individual victim. Traditionally, society has provided one type of service to the victim, controlled retribution. In other words, according to the existing paradigm, the only responsibility the polity has to the victim is to appre-

hend, convict, and punish the offender.[1] The contention here is that this retributive theory of criminal justice is not sufficient to ensure victim justice. The cost theory postulates that in addition to controlled retribution, the social system is responsible for making the victim whole again; in other words, returning him to his original economic, psychological, and physical state, if possible.

The key element in the justification of this contention is the meaning of "responsible." Why is the polity "responsible" for making the victim whole again? Several answers can be offered to this question. The first argues that the cost theory is implicit in the retribution approach. More specifically, because the society has taken away the individual's right to retribution and to making himself whole again, it is the responsibility of the polity to provide this forfeited service.

A second justification would be a simple social welfare view. In other words, it is the responsibility of the society to assist any person who suffers at the hands of society. Therefore, just as the unemployed, the disabled, or the poor are assisted by government, so should the victim be.

According to the third perspective, the polity is responsible to the victim because such concern is necessary to prevent other negative social consequences. That is, the society is responsible for the costs of victimization because if it does not meet those costs, there will be social consequences that are within the responsibility of the polity to prevent.

The negative consequences that may be associated with the lack of a cost theory of victim justice include decreased social cohesion and a reduction in the level of needed support for the criminal justice system. This linkage is hypothesized on the basis of an intermediating theoretical concept, alienation. More specifically, the failure of society to meet the cost of victimization will lead to alienation, which will in turn lead to the posited negative consequences. In order to support this contention it is necessary to confront three issues: (1) the definition of alienation, (2) the factors that produce alienation, and (3) the consequences of alienation.

Definition of alienation

Philosophers and social scientists have historically been concerned with a mental state called alienation. The thinking about this phenomenon involves complex and varied theories, but some central themes prevail. Man, according to all of the theories, when alienated sees himself dwarfed, powerless, and subject to forces beyond his control. To support the contention that the failure to make the victim whole again will lead to such feeling in society, it is necessary to understand the genesis of alienation.

Causes of alienation

There are as many theories of the causes of alienation as there are writers about the subject.[2] Among the most recent attempts to look at alienation from a political perspective are those of Easton[3] and Easton and Dennis.[4,5] According to these authors, alienation is manifest in the lack of support for the political system, based upon a feeling that the society is not concerned with one's feelings and is not worthy of one's support or participation. However, Easton and Dennis also conclude that such feelings are not likely to occur in a stable democracy, because regimes have a number of

mechanisms at their disposal that may restrain alienation. Paramount among these is political socialization.[4,5] Socialization is the inculcation of values toward the society primarily through childhood training in the family, school, and media.[6] Easton and Dennis hypothesize that this socialization will normally result in the child's adopting positive views toward the existing political system and its components. Thus, socialization results in "a reservoir of favorable attitudes . . . that help members to accept or tolerate outputs (policy—societal treatment) which they see as damaging to their wants."[7]

An important implication of their theory is that the attitudes of support (lack of alienation), once established in early socialization, are relatively independent of subsequent life experiences. If this is true, the assumption stated earlier about the alienating consequences of the sole use of the retributive theory of criminal justice is false.

It should be noted, however, that all of the assumptions of Easton and Dennis are simply that, assumptions. None of them is supported by empirical data. Wright, in his analysis of the threads of alienation in America, has come to the conclusion that Easton and Dennis are wrong and that alienation is a product of the particular life situations of a certain era.[8] In other words, such events as the Vietnam War or Watergate lead to increased alienation, according to Wright, as do other failures and anomalies of the system.

The thesis of this argument is that the post-victimization treatment of an individual falls into the category of life experiences that would lead to such alienation. These hypothesized alienating effects of the status quo in the criminal justice system can be seen in the following scenario. The victim is unable to control his victimization. He is made to suffer economic loss, fear, or bodily harm from sources that are "supposed" to be controlled by the criminal justice system. Because of societal norms the victim is unable to take any action to determine who the offender is or to regain his lost property or money. This is the domain of the criminal justice system. However, statistics show that the system will fail in this task and the crime will probably never be solved. If the offender is caught, he is usually released with little penalty and no requirement to repay the victim. If the case goes to court, the victim must suffer the pain and expense of being a witness and hearing primarily about the offender's rights, not his. Finally, the victim normally will never recover his property or be compensated for his loss. Thus, the victim is left with psychological and economic costs for which he must bear the entire burden.

Many of the alienating facts in this scenario are not within the direct control of the criminal justice system to solve. For example, it is not possible to simply remove the risk of crime. Likewise, most crimes could not be solved no matter how efficient the criminal justice system were. Similarly, we cannot deprive the offender of his rights or punish him too severely just to meet the needs of the victim. Thus, we are left with a problem. We are aware of the alienating conditions, but are unable to alter most of them.

We are not, however, unable to alter the effects of the process, and this is the essence of the cost theory of victim justice. It says that the polity has the responsibility to control these effects by using all means possible to make the victim economically and psychologically whole again. In this way it is hypothesized that a degree of concern will be demonstrated to the victim, thereby forestalling the feelings of alienation. Herein lies the societal mandate for implementation of a cost theory.

One final point is important to this theory of the genesis of alienation: the alienating impact of victimization may go beyond the direct victim, thereby making the hypothesized consequences even more important. For each victim there are a number of indirect and peripheral victims. These are the relatives and friends of the victim. Skogan has found that being a member of the family of a victim significantly affects the feelings of safety of all members of that family.[9] Additionally, LeJeune and Alex indicate that victims of a robbery spend a great deal of time communicating their experience to their friends and acquaintances.[10] Although there is no direct evidence that such

communication affects attitudes, it seems plausible to hypothesize that many of the attitudinal results of victimization will be shared by the victim's family, friends, and acquaintances. Thus, the alienating impact of failure to make the victim whole again is spread to a large portion of the population, thereby increasing the level of alienation in society.

Impact of alienation on society

If what has been theorized to this point is accepted, it is then necessary to ask what the consequences of such alienation would be. Alienation theory posits several consequences. The most commonly mentioned is withdrawal from active participation in the system—a feeling that it does not make any difference whether one participates.[11] Such withdrawal would likely include an unwillingness to become involved in aiding a policeman, being a witness or juror, or any other lay activities that are necessary to the maintenance of the criminal justice system.

Finally, it has been argued here that alienation would lead to lessened social cohesion and greater class cleavages. This claim is based on two factors: (1) victims of crime are disproportionately from the lower socioeconomic class, and (2) of those individuals who are victimized, those that are made whole again presently are disproportionately from the upper class. The combination of these two factors would lead to increased support and positive feelings for society on the part of the upper class groups, while at the same time decreasing the support for society and heightening the alienation of the lower class. When the indirect and peripheral victims are included, it can be seen how such a process would contribute greatly to exacerbated class cleavages and a growing feeling of resentment on the part of the lower class groups. This is not to say that the actual continuance of the American polity is at stake, but merely that such a decrease in social cohesion could not help but be damaging to the fabric of American society.

Although the argument just presented, postulating a relationship between the failure to make the victim whole again and the negative social consequences of reduced support for the criminal justice system and reduced social cohesion, has not been empirically verified, its plausibility at the common sense and scholarly level mandates its further consideration. A complete testing of this theory would require a longitudinal study of individuals to determine the impact that victimization has on them and the differential impact of being made whole again as opposed to not being assisted. Such a project is beyond the scope of this study. However, the two most important assumptions of the entire theory can be and are tested here:

1. There is a substantial net cost of criminal victimization. This means that there is a large percentage of victims who suffer substantial economic and psychological costs of crime for which they are not compensated.
2. Of the individuals who are victimized, those who are made whole again are disproportionately from the upper class.

If these two assumptions are not correct, the remainder of the theory is irrelevant. Thus, the final portions of this paper address the validity of these assumptions.

EMPIRICAL ANALYSIS

To determine the net psychological and economic costs of crime it is necessary to interview the victims. This is because police records are inadequate in terms of documenting psychological costs and the percentage of gross loss that was repaid by various remedies such as insurance.

Sampling method

The data upon which this study is based were gathered in a statewide victimization study in Minnesota. Seven hundred victims representative of the entire population of victims were selected at random from police departments throughout the state. A cluster sampling procedure was used to select the police departments. Within each of these departments, the victims were stratified according to crime, so as to ensure that the sample was reflective of the population. When dealing with property crimes, the study reflects only those with a dollar value

of over $100. The victims were sampled from records for the period July 1, 1974, to January 1, 1975.

Remedies available

To determine net cost it is necessary to determine all remedies, or sources of reducing cost, and subtract these from the gross effect of the victimization. Thus, as a first step each of the potential remedies is discussed in general terms and then as it operates in Minnesota.

Private insurance. Private insurance is one of the most common and well-understood remedies available in the state of Minnesota. It involves the payment of victim-related losses by a private firm that has been contracted to insure the victim. In most instances a $100 deductible is applied, meaning that the insurance firm will not pay the first $100 of loss.

Civil suit. A civil suit can be brought by a victim against the offender to obtain the losses incurred as a result of victimization.

Restitution. Restitution is defined as payment by the offender to the victim in full or part compensation for the victimization loss. Restitution has been commonly used as a condition of probation in Minnesota, although no law permitting or prescribing its use for adult offenders exists. In 1976, research on the use of restitution in the state of Minnesota demonstrated that restitution existed as a condition of probation in approximately one fourth (24.2%) of all adult felony probation cases and in about one fifth (19.95%) of all juvenile probation cases.[12] In addition to its use as a condition of probation, restitution was also used as a condition of parole in a pilot program in Minneapolis. Although this program has now been terminated as a residential program and incorporated as a nonresidential program into Minnesota's new "Victims Program," it was in existence during the time of this study and therefore will be included in this analysis.

The Restitution Center was a residential facility where offenders stayed during their parole from state corrections institutions. To be released from the state institution into this program the offender had to sign a contract whereby he agreed to pay all or part of the loss suffered by the person he victimized. Minnesota has taken a leading position among the states in the expanded use of restitution.

Compensation. Compensation schemes provide for the state to pay for all or a portion of the victimization loss, thus eliminating the need for the apprehension, conviction, and solvency of the offender as conditions of victim repayment, as is the case with restitution.

Minnesota established the Crime Victims Reparation Board in July 1974 to pay for the treatment of injuries sustained as a direct result of a crime committed against a person. Only out-of-pocket medical costs are covered. Out-of-pocket loss means reasonable medical care or other services necessary as a result of the victimization injury. No payments are made for pain and suffering or for loss of property. In order to be eligible, the victim must file a claim with the Board within 1 year of the crime and be willing to cooperate in any way the police and the Board request. The maximum amount that can be received is $10,000. There is a $100 deductible, and further deductions are made for amounts received or available from insurance or other public agencies.

Local medical facilities. The Twin Cities area and other cities and counties in the state have local facilities that will attend to the medical needs of those who are not able to pay. These facilities could be used by victims of violent crime who could not afford private medical help.

Psychological help. Numerous areas in the state have programs set up to help those victims with resultant psychological problems. Minnesota has, for example, active programs for providing psychological help for victims of rape.

Analysis of data

Victims of burglary. In this section the cost to and the remedies used by victims of burglary are examined. Burglary is by far the most common crime in the state of Minnesota, constituting 70% of all crime. In the Minnesota study, 558 burglary victims were interviewed. This group lost a total of $400,099.76, or an average loss of $717.02 per victim.

Table 1. Insured victims of burglary: size of loss and insurance payment*

Total before insurance loss	$306,672.76
Mean before insurance loss	$802.81
Total insurance paid	$190,629.46
Mean insurance paid	$499.03
Total after-insurance loss	$116,031.80
Mean after-insurance loss	$303.78

*The total number of insured burglary victims was 382.

In regard to these victims, the only remedy that provided any substantial relief was private insurance. Because compensation is limited to violent offenses in the state of Minnesota, the Crime Victims Reparation Board is not a potential source of reimbursement for victims of burglary. Though civil suits and restitution are potential remedies, their lack of use makes them almost meaningless as a source of victim help. In the survey one victim employed a civil suit to obtain repayment from the offender. The resulting payment was only $75 of the total loss of $586. There were four victims who received restitution at an average of $70 per victim.

Of the sampled 558 burglary victims, 382 (or 68.4%) received insurance payments for their losses. Table 1 shows the losses incurred and the amount of insurance received by this subsample of victims. The data in the table also indicate that although a majority of the loss suffered by burglary victims with insurance is paid by the insurance company, there is still a very substantial after-insurance loss of $303.78 per victim. If one further analyzes the burglary victims who had insurance, one finds that it was the higher income groups who suffered the highest average after-insurance loss (Table 2). Though initially this was surprising, because it was expected that lower income groups would have the least ability to deal with insurance companies, additional thought suggested the likely cause of this phenomenon: higher income groups tend to have more expensive items stolen. These expensive items are also the most susceptible to great depreciation. Less expensive items, stolen more often from the low income groups,

Table 2. Victims of burglary who received insurance: loss by income level

Income	No.	Total before-insurance loss	Mean before-insurance loss	Mean insurance payment	Total after-insurance loss	Mean after-insurance loss
0 to $7,499	58	$46,009.66	$793.27	$544.17	$14,447.80	$249.10
$7,500 to $14,999	112	$64,856.94	$579.08	$397.66	$20,319.04	$181.42
$15,000 up	212	$195,806.16	$923.61	$540.29	$81,264.96	$383.32
TOTAL	382	$306,672.76	$802.81	$499.03	$116,031.80	$303.78

Table 3. Burglary victims without insurance: loss by income level

Income	No.	Mean loss	Total loss
0 to $7,499	40	$593.10	$23,724.00
$7,500 to $14,999	84	$440.88	$37,033.92
$15,000 up	52	$628.27	$32,669.84
TOTAL	176	$530.84	$93,427.76

Table 4. Percentage of burglary victims in each income category who did not have insurance

Income	Percentage who did not have insurance
0 to $7,499	41%
$7,500 to $14,999	43%
$15,000 up	20%

do not depreciate as fast. Therefore, the higher income groups with insurance tend to have higher after-insurance losses than lower income groups with insurance. However, as Table 2 clearly shows, after-insurance loss is quite substantial for all groups. This can be explained by the fact that insurance companies pay merely depreciated values rather than replacement costs, and these two amounts are often very different. This results in the conclusion that even insurance cannot protect the burglary victim from substantial out-of-pocket loss.

To this point I have limited my analysis to burglary victims who had insurance. However, 176 (or 31.5%) of our sample did not receive any insurance payment for their losses. This group

suffered an average loss of $530.84. This compares unfavorably with the after-insurance loss of those with insurance of $303.78. Thus, insurance is effective in mitigating some of the loss of burglary. Table 3 shows the losses of noninsured victims, controlling for income level. As with burglary victims who have insurance, those with higher income tend to have the highest loss. The organization of data, as I have presented it thus far, appears to indicate that the high income groups suffer the largest monetary losses as a result of burglary. However, when one compares within each income group the percentage of victims who have insurance, keeping in mind that victims with insurance suffer much lower net losses than those without insurance, the picture of which income groups are coming out the worst is reversed. As can be seen in Table 4, whereas only 20% of the upper income groups do not have insurance, over 40% of the lower income groups do not have such coverage. Therefore, it would appear that there is a bias against lower income groups in the private insurance system.

Though the burden of burglary tends to weigh heavier on certain groups, it is substantial for all. Clearly, insurance as a sole mechanism for victim compensation is not effective. One may ask what other remedies would have been used. The only two that may have some potential utility are civil suits and restitution. Because the civil suit is so cumbersome, I doubt that it will ever become a viable source of compensation. Though restitution might appear to be a solution, there are numerous problems with using it as a source of victim compensation. First is the fact that only a small fraction of offenders are ever captured and convicted. Thus, in the pres-

Table 5. Victims of violent crime: amount and type of loss

Type of loss	Mean amount of loss	No.
Property	$174.67	76
Monetary loss due to loss of work	$65.68	76
Monetary loss due to medical expenses	$102.78	76
TOTAL	$343.13	76

ent sample only an additional 50 victims could have potentially reduced their losses through restitution, because this is the number of captured offenders who were not ordered to pay restitution. However, I have no data on the ability of these offenders to pay the victim. It is likely that a large percentage would not have been able to do so. Furthermore, as Chesney has shown, it is primarily the upper income group of offenders who are ordered to pay restitution, because they can afford it.[12] Previous evidence indicates that there tends to be a correlation between the income of the offender and that of the victim. Thus, even if restitution is expanded, it is likely that it will increase the already existing gulf between the net loss of low income groups and that of high income groups, by disproportionately giving additional repayment to the latter group.

Crimes of violence. In this section the monetary losses suffered and remedies used by victims of violent crime are examined. For the purposes of this report, crimes of violence are defined as aggravated assault and robbery. Simple assault has been excluded, because in most instances these crimes involve no appreciable monetary loss for which a remedy could be employed.

Of the interviewed victims, 108 (15.1%) were victims of violent crime. Of these, 32 victims did not suffer any monetary loss. The remaining 76 suffered an average loss of $343.13 per victim. This loss can be further broken down according to the type of loss indicated in Table 5.

All of the remedies I have identified (civil suits, insurance, restitution, and compensation) are potential sources of repayment for victims of violent crime. However, in the sample of 76 who actually suffered losses, none of the victims received restitution or used civil action to gain repayment. Similarly, only one of the victims received money from the compensation board. As with burglary, the only remedy of significant importance was private insurance. Insurance payments were made to 24 of the 76 victims who had monetary loss. This group had an average total loss of $593.37. The average insurance payment to those insured was $255.88. Therefore, the average victim of violent crime with insurance suffered a $337.52 net loss.

The question now is whether this rather sizable after-insurance loss could have been reduced through the use of other remedies. Restitution is primarily used for property crimes, and therefore is not likely to be employed in this category of offense. However, if one assumes for the moment that restitution is a viable alternative, one needs to examine whether restitution was possible. The prime requisite for restitution is the identity and apprehension of the offender. However, only 2 of 24 victims under analysis here indicated that they knew their offender was arrested. Therefore, even if restitution were to be broadened in scope to include crimes of violence, its utility would be almost totally negated by the lack of apprehension of the offender.

To determine if the compensation board could be of use in reducing this after-insurance cost, one must further analyze the loss according to the type. This is necessary because the compensation board will only pay medical or work-loss payments. Table 6 reviews the breakdown of loss by category. As can be seen, though insurance covers medical costs, it does not cover lost income, and as in the case of burglaries, insurance fails to cover property loss completely. As was observed in the case of burglaries, this disparity in property loss is due primarily to the fact that victims identify as the monetary loss the actual replacement cost of the item, whereas insurance companies determine payoff by depreciating the original cost of the item. The breakdown in Table 6 reveals that the compensation board would not be a very effective way of further reducing the cost of crime to this sub-

Table 6. Victims of violent crime who received insurance: loss by type before and after insurance payment

Type of loss	Mean loss before insurance	Mean loss after insurance	No.
Property loss	$325.63	$233.36	24
Monetary loss due to loss of work	$104.16	$104.16	24
Medical loss	$163.58	$0	24
TOTAL	$593.37	$337.52	24

group of victims of violent crime. This is because of the $100 deductible that the compensation board employs. As can be seen in the table, most of the after-insurance medical and work costs are at or below this minimum.

Thus, it appears that although insurance covers some of the cost of crime for victims of violent crimes who have insurance, there is still a sizable loss involved that is not subject to reduction by any existing remedy.

To this point I have limited my consideration to violent crime victims who had insurance. However, 52 of our 76 victims who suffered monetary loss did not receive insurance. Table 7 reveals the size of the monetary loss suffered by this group according to type.

Of the 53 victims in Table 7 who did not receive insurance payments, 20 did not receive such payments because the amount lost was either too small to claim or too small to bother with. However, the remaining 32 victims indicated that they did not have insurance. This group was clearly from a comparatively low socioeconomic level, with a mean income of $5,230, compared with the overall mean income of $9,450 for all victims of violent crime. Thus, it appears that the viability of insurance as a remedy for victims of violent crime is related to economic status. This is further exemplified by the fact that 90% of the violent crime victims in the survey who had an income less than $7,500 did not have insurance, whereas only 33% of the victims with an income over $15,000 did not have such insurance. However, in the case of violent crime one finds that even if low income groups did have insurance, it is doubtful that it would be of much utility, because the amount lost is usually quite small. In short, it seems that although lower income victims of

Table 7. Victims of violent crime who did not receive insurance: loss by type and amount

Type of loss	Mean amount	No.
Property loss	$105.00	52
Monetary loss due to loss of work	$48.00	52
Medical loss	$75.00	52
TOTAL	$228.00	52

violent crime are less likely to have insurance coverage, the fact that they experience relatively small losses also would detract from the potential benefits of such coverage. Thus, there is a paradox: victims of violent crime who do not have insurance have an average total loss of $228.00, whereas victims of violent crime who do have insurance have an average after-insurance loss of $337.52. In absolute terms, the noninsured victim comes out better in the end. However, given that the victim with no insurance also tends to be the one with the lower income, the loss in proportionate terms (loss as a percentage of income) is about equal for victims of violent crime with insurance and those without.

As is clear, although there is some variation in loss, depending on the income level and insurance coverage of its victims, victims of violent crime as a whole are suffering substantial unrepaid losses.

Auto theft. In this section the loss resulting from and the remedies used by victims of auto theft are examined. Fifty such victims were interviewed. This crime, unlike all others, has an extremely high clearance rate. Of the 50 autos that were stolen, 41 (or 82%) were recovered. However, of these 41, 25 suffered some type of damage. The average damage was $1,442.48. Insurance covered, on the average, $305.20 of this loss. Thus, those victims whose cars were recovered but were damaged during the theft suffered a substantial after-insurance loss of $1,137.28. None of these victims received any other form of remedy. This appears to be fertile ground for the increased use of restitution, in that of the 25 victims whose cars were recovered in damaged condition, 12 indicated that the offender was captured. Thus, it appears that restitution could be increasingly used (assuming the solvency of the offender) to reimburse the victim whose car is stolen, damaged, and then recovered.

Nine of the 50 stolen autos were not recovered. Six of these owners had insurance. The average loss was $2,956, and the average insurance payment was $1,858, resulting in an average after-insurance loss of $1,098. Three additional cars, which were not covered by insurance, were taken. However, these three cars were of low monetary value (less than $200) and would not have been covered by most insurance policies in any case.

With the exception of auto theft victims whose cars were recovered undamaged, the victim of motor vehicle theft suffers substantial loss.

Psychological costs. To this point only the monetary cost of crime has been examined. However, in addition, there is another cost: the psychological cost, or "pain and suffering." Clearly, this cost is less easily identified than the monetary costs. For example, how does one measure lost sleep, fear of going out on the street at night, or anxiety about entering one's home at night? Though no direct cost analysis of these factors can be made, the victims were asked if they felt that they had suffered fear or pain and suffering as a result of the victimization. A majority of the victims indicated that some degree of fear or anxiety resulted from their experience. Of this group, 32 of the victims indicated that they had experienced significant pain and suffering. Half of these victims, though reporting significant pain and suffering, did not feel that their psychological trauma was intense enough to warrant any

type of professional help. Of the remaining 16, 4 used existing local mental health agencies to assist in their victimization-related problems and found such treatment helpful.

The victims of most concern were those remaining 12 who suffered significant psychological problems and felt that they needed some psychological help, but did not know that any such help existed. Thus, the major problem here is the actual knowledge of the victims concerning the availability of remedies. Obviously, some type of publicity program must be undertaken to ensure that all remedies that are available for the psychological counseling of crime victims are known by those victims.

CONCLUSION

In summary, it may again be noted that victims of burglary, violent crimes, and auto theft all suffer substantial net losses. Thus, the assumption behind the cost theory that there are such costs appears correct, at least in this particular situation. Also apparently valid is the assumption that the greater weight of crime falls upon the lower income groups. This appears to be true because of the insurance system. Insurance is the only remedy that has a significant impact in reducing these costs. As lower income groups are less likely to carry insurance, victims with lower incomes tend to suffer a proportionately higher cost of victimization than upper income groups.

Given the validity of these basic assumptions and the posited theory of negative social consequences of such conditions, it seems a logical conclusion to argue that methods of implementing the cost theory of victim justice must be explored. Two primary methods of doing this are currently available: restitution and compensation. Restitution, as has been noted, is offender repayment to the victim; compensation is societal repayment.

Although the data indicate that there is some potential for increased use of victim restitution, such a method is clearly not the ultimate answer. This is because such factors as failure to capture the offender, failure to convict the offender, or the offender's insolvency prevent victim payment under a restitution model in most instances. Given this failure, the most apparent alternative is a state-sponsored compensation program such as that used in Minnesota. Such a system does not rely on the capture and solvancy of the offender and therefore has the potential for full implementation of the cost theory. The Crime Victims Reparation Board in Minnesota does not appear to meet this overall need because of its limited objective: the repayment of net medical costs above $100. To fully implement the cost theory, this jurisdiction would have to be expanded greatly or some other form of compensation substituted, such as subsidized private insurance.

Many methods of implementing the cost theory can be suggested. The one that appears to be the most satisfactory to me would be a combined restitution–subsidized private insurance model. This would call for restitution to be required in *all* instances possible, with this potential pool increased by expanded jobs for probationers and parolees and wages for inmates. Whenever restitution is not possible, the victim would be repaid by a private insurance company, which would insure each person with the help of a subsidy from the government, the size of which would depend on the income of the individual.

Whatever the methods used, I believe that the data and theory presented here mandate serious consideration of a cost theory of victim justice.

NOTES

1. For a discussion of the current criminal justice "paradigm," see Barnett, Randy. "Restitution," *Ethics,* vol. 4, July 1977.
2. Some of the more important recent analyses of alienation, include: Feuer, Lewis. "What is Alienation? The Career of a Concept," *New Politics* **1:**116-134, Spring 1962; Johnson, Frank, ed. *Alienation: Concept, Term, and Meaning* (New York: Academic Press, Inc., 1973); Horowitz, Irving. "On Alienation and the Social Order," *Philosophy and Phenomenological Research* **27:**230-237, 1966.
3. Easton, David. *A Systems Analysis of Political Life* (New York: John Wiley & Sons, Inc., 1965).
4. Easton, David, and Jack Dennis. "The Child's Acquisition of Regime Norms: Political Efficacy," *American Political Science Review* **61:**25-38, March 1967.
5. Easton, David, and Jack Dennis. *Children in the Political System* (New York: McGraw-Hill Book Co., 1969).
6. Easton. *A Systems Analysis of Political Life,* p. 272.
7. Ibid., p. 273.
8. Wright, James D. *The Dissent of the Governed: Alienation and Democracy in America* (New York: Academic Press, Inc., 1976).
9. Skogan, Wesley G. "Public Policy and the Fear of Crime in Large American Cities" (Paper presented at the Annual Meeting of the Midwest Political Science Association, Chicago, May 1976), p. 12.
10. LeJeune, Robert, and Nicholas Alex. "On Being Mugged," *Urban Life and Culture* **3:**259-387, October 1973.
11. For a discussion of the "withdrawal" effects of alienation, see: Horton, J. E. and W. E. Thompson. "Powerlessness and Political Negativism," *American Journal of Sociology* **67:**485-493, March 1962; Mason, Gene, and Dean Jaros. "Alienation and the Support of Demagogues," *Polity* **1:**477-498, Summer 1969.
12. Chesney, Steven. *The Assessment of Restitution in Minnesota Probation Services* (St. Paul: Minnesota Department of Corrections, 1976).

C □ *The fear of crime in the United States*

JAMES BROOKS

The fear of crime has recently become more pervasive. To an objective investigator of this phenomenon, much of it is irrational. But the fear exists. Regardless of the reasons for being fearful, fear itself is a reality that policy-makers must consider. The lessening of fear thus becomes an important step in a comprehensive effort to combat crime and the effects of crime.

Certain kinds of crime—the "personal" crimes—produce more intense alarm than others. "The crimes that concern Americans the most are those that affect their personal safety—at home, at work, or in the streets. The most frequent and serious of these crimes of violence against the person are willful homicide, forcible rape, aggravated assault, and robbery."[1] How does it come about that "offenses involving physical assaults against the person are the most feared crimes" and that "the greatest concern is expressed about those in which a weapon is used"?[2] One explanation finds an answer in xenophobia:

The fear of crimes of violence is not a simple fear of injury or death or even of all crimes of violence, but, at bottom, a fear of strangers. The personal injury that Americans risk daily from sources other than crime are enormously greater. The annual rate of all Index offenses involving either violence or the threat of violence is 1.8 per 1,000 Americans. This is minute relative to the total accidental injuries calling for medical attention or restricted activity of 1 day or more, as reported by the Public Health Service. A recent study of emergency medical care found the quality, numbers, and distribution of ambulances and other emergency services severely deficient, and estimated that as many as 20,000 Americans die unnecessarily each year as a result of improper emergency care. The means necessary for correcting this situation are very clear and would probably yield greater immediate return in reducing death than would expenditures for reducing the incidence of crimes of violence. But a different personal significance is attached to deaths due to the willful acts of felons as compared to the incompetence or poor equipment of emergency medical personnel.[3]

It would appear, then, to be more logical for Americans to direct their worry and fear toward inadequate or too few ambulances. But these deficiencies do not seem to concern the general public. The man in the street is most afraid of being victimized by a criminal stranger. A disproportionate amount of the thought given to crime in general is concentrated on crimes of violence. One of the stimulants that nourish this fear is the mass media's lurid portrayal of the victim of crime. "The available data indicate that for most people, attitudes about serious crimes and crime trends come largely from vicarious sources."[4] So, while most people are not themselves victims of crime and do not know anyone who has been the victim of crime, they feel threatened because they have seen on television or heard on the radio or read in newspapers and magazines case histories and depictions of violent crime. Their emotions and anxieties become aroused and fed with each day's reports of new victims of crime. Although the chances of one's becoming a victim of crime might be statistically remote, the prevailing reaction seems to be, "It could have been me" or "Next time it might be me." Since this at-

Reprinted, with permission of the National Council on Crime and Delinquency, from James Brooks, "The Fear of Crime in the United States," *Crime and Delinquency*, July 1974, pp. 241-244.
1. President's Commission on Law Enforcement and Administration of Justice, *The Challenge of Crime in a Free Society* (Washington, D.C.: U.S. Government Printing Office, 1967), p. 18.
2. President's Commission on Law Enforcement and Administration of Justice, *Task Force Report: Crime and Its Impact —An Assessment* (Washington, D.C.: U.S. Government Printing Office, 1967), p. 87.

3. *Id.,* p. 88.
4. *Id.,* p. 86.

titude is not completely rational, it cannot be neutralized completely by rational rebuttals. It remains a force to contend with.

Aside from the undeniable realities of crime itself, the manner of reporting them actually contributes to an unjustified fear of crime. The fashion in America seems to require dramatic flair even in the preparation and presentation of crime statistics.

Considering the current public sensitivity about crime and violence, the following comparison to European countries is significant:

"The publication of criminal statistics [in England and Scandinavia] is not regarded as a dramatic act to mobilize public awareness against the danger of rape, murder and other kinds of crimes, but it is regarded as a regular kind of source of information, bringing to the knowledge of those who are interested—unfortunately very few—what is going on in this vast amount of crime.

"Our [England's] criminal statistics in comparison to your publications differ as much as—if I may bluntly say so—an old English cup of tea compares with a dry Martini on the rocks. They [British statistics] are very prosaic, very quiet. And this in some ways makes them less attractive to read. But it does produce them for the public."[5]

There are other deficiencies as well in the reporting of crime in the United States that possibly contribute to the widespread belief in a much greater incidence of crime than is actually the case. This is not to say that crime is not a very serious problem in the United States but rather to suggest that generally held perceptions of reality can be at least as important as reality itself in the way they influence a person assessing his own well-being. It may be doubly important when the realities of crime are not determined.

The consequences of fear of criminal attack seem to be exclusively detrimental for the individual and for society; the ways in which this fear is externalized can be viewed only as

damaging. It is not an exaggeration to suggest that the feeling of well-being among the citizenry is in danger of being perhaps fatally eroded by this fear. Already, there are indications that preferred life styles are being modified to preserve some feeling of safety.

This fear leads many people to give up activities they would normally undertake particularly when it may involve going out on the streets or into the parks and other public places at night. The costs of this fear are not only economic, though a burdensome price may be paid by many poor people in high crime rate areas who feel compelled to purchase protective locks, bars, and alarms, who reject an attractive night job because of fear of traversing the streets or who pay the expense of taxi transportation under the same circumstances. In the long run more damaging than costs are the loss of opportunities for pleasure and cultural enrichment, the reduction of the level of sociability and mutual trust, and perhaps even more important, the possibility that people will come to lose faith in the trustworthiness and stability of the social and moral order of the society.[6]

This is as fundamental an impact as one can imagine; its significance should not be understated. Because of this fear, a most unhealthy state of affairs has arisen and promises to worsen. "Watch the people," advises a policeman in Washington, D.C.; "see how they walk quickly and with a purpose. There's no casual strolling. People don't come into this town at night unless they have a specific destination in mind. They go straight to it and then go home as fast as possible."[7] It is not only the nighttime visitor who is deterred; more and more, the daytime visitor also tends to avoid the downtown area. A survey undertaken by the Metropolitan Washington Council of Governments showed that "65 per cent of the city's largely white suburban residents visit the downtown area less than once a month, and 15 per cent come downtown less than once a year. Asked their chief worry, the large majority of those surveyed responded: 'Crime.' "[8] Such is the condition of society. The manifestations of fear are beginning to per-

5. National Commission on the Causes and Prevention of Violence, *Crimes of Violence*, vol. 11, Staff Report, by Donald J. Mulvihill and Melvin M. Tumin with Lynn A. Curtis (Washington, D.C.: U.S. Government Printing Office, 1969), p. 35, quoting statement of Leon Radzinowicz, Hearings before the Commission, Sept. 26, 1968, p. 642.

6. *Task Force Report, op. cit. supra* note 2, p. 94.
7. *Wall Street Journal*, Feb. 11, 1970, p. 1, col. 1.
8. *Ibid.*

meate our existence. They take the form of "the locked doors, the empty streets, the growing number of guns bought for self-protection, the signs on public buses that say: 'Driver does not carry cash.' "[9]

With increasing crime rates and the accompanying perceptions of what this increase means to the individual, we are experiencing also an increase in societal costs other than those that are the direct result of victimization. "What economists label opportunity costs for feeling safe probably are far greater economic burdens of crime for these citizens than the direct costs of victimization. With these precautions go . . . the psychic costs of living in an atmosphere of anxiety."[10]

Insofar as crimes against individual citizens are concerned, then, it is suspected that "the immediate consequences are of much less moment than are people's intense reactions to the perceived crime situation."[11] It is important for public policy-makers to be aware of this distinction and to make reduction of the fear of crime an object of attention, just as reducing the incidence of crime is an object of attention. If they do not act appropriately on this knowledge, the result may be an extraordinary anomaly: the fear of crime will increase at the same time that the incidence of crime may decline. A reduction in the incidence of crime will not automatically be accompanied by a corresponding reduction in the fear of crime.

So little attention has been paid to this aspect of crime and its effects that we do not know just what tactics might be most effective in combating the fear of crime. But it should be emphasized that this aspect of the general problem of crime will require its own special attention and solutions. Because of its irrational qualities, it may be more difficult to combat than criminality itself.

9. *Daily Congressional Record,* 92d Cong., 1st Sess., 1971, CXVII, No. 17, S1419.
10. Albert D. Biderman, Louise A. Johnson, Jennie McIntyre, and Adrianne W. Weir, *Report on a Pilot Study in the District of Columbia on Victimization and Attitudes toward Law Enforcement,* Bureau of Social Science Research, Inc. (Washington, D.C.: U.S. Government Printing Office, 1967), p. 159.

11. *Id.,* p. 160.

D □ *Crime: economic scourge of the ghetto*

WARREN T. BROOKES

George B. is unemployed and black. Until six months ago he worked in a small factory in Roxbury. The factory was vandalized and burned out for the fourth time in three years. The owner could not get either the bank or the insurance company to renew. So the business shut down—and George and nine others are out of work.

Fred L. is in a nursing home. Until last year he and his wife ran a small gorcery store in Dorchester. He had to close the store after seven robberies in three years—in the last of which he was brutally beaten. Fred L. is also black.

Zelma C. is on welfare. Until March she worked in a small dry-cleaning plant in Mattapan. The plant closed down because its theft insurance premium had risen to more than $7000 a year—and the plant had been burglarized four times. Zelma, too, is black.

Robert C. is a mechanic. He, too, is unemployed and black. The service station he worked

This article originally appeared in the September 5, 1976, edition of the *Boston Herald American.* Reprinted by permission of the *Boston Herald American.*

in for four years was forced to close because the owner had been robbed four times, had lost money the last three years, and had to abandon the station.

These four cases, in which the names and locations have purposely been scrambled, illustrate the growing economic impact of high crime and violence on the black community—a tragedy of alarming and growing proportions.

They also demonstrate a stark fact of life in the modern city ghetto—while high unemployment undoubtedly contributes to crime, crime is also becoming one of the main causes of unemployment.

Unquestionably, one of the most serious and explosive problems facing the nation today is the fact that between 40 and 50 percent of inner city black teenagers are now unemployed—and from this large block of young people with too much time on their hands, and too little to do, are coming elements that are destroying the economic and social fabric of their own communities through excessive crime.

In short, crime, bred in part by unemployment, is resulting in even more unemployment and economic hardship for the entire inner city.

As Mayor Thomas Bradley of Los Angeles put it at the recent Urban League Conference in Boston:

A community already suffering from blight and high unemployment, loses jobs, services, and hope. The process is like a cycle from which there seems to be no escape.

Thousands turn to crime because they have no jobs. Many can't find jobs because the companies fled to escape the crime. . . . High crime drives away reputable businesses and developers—it raises the cost of housing, and goods and services. On the other hand, low incomes, and a high cost of living coupled with poor housing inevitably lead to crime.

In speaking frankly about this subject to the Urban League, Mayor Bradley joined a number of other distinguished black leaders who, while demanding national action against high unemployment, are also "talking tough" to the black community about the need to deal with excessive crime as an essential condition for economic recovery.

They are recognizing that in order to attract industry and jobs to the ghetto, or to its borders, something must be done to make it economically and physically safe for this industry to operate.

They are also recognizing that in order to keep inner city jobs from moving out, inner-city business men and women—the majority of whom are black—must be protected from the economic devastation of the crime that threatens to engulf them—the untenable situation of trying to operate in "an armed camp."

As Mayor Bradley described it:

Businesses and homes must now install iron bars and gates on their windows to be sure their belongings will not be ripped off during the night. Gang fights are daily. Gang killings number almost 100 in one city alone. Such neighborhoods become like war-time "no man's lands," places of terror and fear for old and young alike.

The figures tell the stark story. While blacks comprise 11.5 percent of the U.S. population, they account for 51.3 percent of all the arrests for violent crime in the U.S., and 56 percent of all violent crime arrests in U.S. cities.

In Boston, where blacks make up 16.3 percent of the population, the picture is even more striking.

	ARRESTS BY RACE— BOSTON 1974		
			Other
	White	**Black**	**minorities**
Murder	34%	63%	3%
Rape	33%	58%	9%
Armed robbery	27%	69%	4%
Aggravated assault	38%	55%	7%
Burglary (breaking and entering)	55%	40%	5%
Larceny	41%	54%	5%
Auto theft	57%	35%	8%
Total violent crime	33%	61%	6%

(Source: FBI Uniform Crime Reports)

Altogether, blacks accounted for 52 percent of all serious crime in the city, and 61 percent of all violent crime (murder, rape, armed robbery and aggravated assault). When you add in the other minorities, you find that less than 20 percent of the city's population accounts for 67 percent of the total violent crime.

The tragedy is that, contrary to some popular myths, the chief victims of this high crime rate are not whites, but other blacks and minorities.

The FBI Uniform Statistics show that in 1973, 89 percent of the violent crimes (rape, murder, etc.) committed by blacks, were committed against other blacks. More than 80 percent of the robberies committed by blacks are committed against businesses within the black community. Similarly, most crime by whites is against whites.

Thus, while it is accurate to say that an average member of the black community is six to eight times more likely to be involved in crime than the average member of the white community, it is more to the point to say that the average member of the black community is six to eight times more likely to become the victim of crime than the average white person.

Even more to the point is the fact that a business located within the black community or on its fringe is six to eight times more likely to be the target of armed robbery, vandalism, breaking and entering, and larceny than a business located anywhere else in Boston.

This stark statistic is reflected in the fact that it now costs a businessman in Roxbury $670 for every $1000 in theft insurance—compared with $170 per thousand anywhere else in the city.

Facts like these show once again that while unemployment problems in the black community are contributing to high crime, the sheer level of violence within the ghetto itself is driving out businesses and jobs because it is making it too costly for them to operate.

That is why it is not possible to drive through large areas of Roxbury, Dorchester and Mattapan without seeing closed-up stores and abandoned small businesses and factories—the industrial and commercial "blight" that hangs like a pall over the entire area.

A prime example of this "blight" is the now vacant Bayside Shopping Center in the Columbia Point area, which until six years ago provided a comprehensive array of retail services for a very large community—a community that must now pay for tax costs to reach distant shopping areas outside the community.

One by one, stores like Almy's, Zayre's and Stop & Shop were forced to close because of the skyrocketing costs of vandalism, robbery and employe theft.

In nearly every case, the Bayside center stores closed long before their leases expired. They found it cheaper to pay rent on boarded-up stores than to suffer excessive economic loses from crime and vandalism.

One black businessman told this columnist that his store had been robbed more than 37 times in three years, and that it was only a matter of time before he, too, would have to close.

But Boston is not alone in this.

As Mayor Bradley described the situation in his own city of Los Angeles:

The flight to the suburbs of some businesses and industries has left blocks of abandoned buildings with broken windows and gutted interiors.

As these firms left, they took thousands of jobs— often too far away for black employes to follow.

These abandoned buildings become attractive nuisances and encouraged more vandalism and destruction. These added to a process of blight and deterioration that had an effect upon the businesses which remained. The blight swept through entire neighborhoods like a destructive cyclone.

Store after store, shop after shop, business after business—large and small—closed or moved.

Sears Roebuck closed what had been one of its busiest stores after five years of steadily rising losses. These losses were the result of theft and vandalism at their store and a steady erosion of the nearby commercial and residential neighborhood.

The economic loss, direct and indirect was devastating. Many large supermarkets have closed or moved out because of staggering losses from shoplifting, bad checks, or employe thefts.

Clearly, what Mayor Bradley is saying is that unemployment is contributing to crime—it is more true than ever before that high crime is driving out the very jobs that the inner city needs, and keeping away businesses and industries that it must have to solve its unemployment problems.

The reality is that these unemployment problems are probably not going to be solved unless there is a serious attack not only on the unemployment problem, but on the crime rate itself.

As Mayor Bradley put it, "We cannot attack these problems separately, we must coordinate our approach."

What Bradley is saying is that any effort to deal with black unemployment, particularly among teenagers, must also come to grips with high crime at the same time—or it is probably not going to work.

This fact was demonstrated convincingly by the wholly apathetic response of many urban politicians and business leaders when Jimmy Carter called recently for solving black unemployment problems by "moving more industry into the ghetto where the people are."

Aside from the obvious problems of transportation, taxes and congestion, urban politicians and business leaders are only too well aware of the hazards and the costs of locating plants within urban ghettos. Many experiments of this kind have been tried, only to fail.

We have talked with several business executives in this area about the idea of locating branch plants in the inner city and Roxbury areas as a method of dealing with the explosive problem of teenage unemployment, particularly among blacks.

Again and again, the same problems were cited:

- Prohibitive costs of insurance for vandalism, crime and theft. Most say such insurance can no longer be purchased.
- Prohibitive costs of personnel turnover. Job turnover among inner city black youths under 20 is nearly 64 percent, according to the BLS [Bureau of Labor Statistics]—a figure six times greater than that of adult whites and nearly three times that of white teenagers.
- Excessive costs for unemployment compensation caused by this low "job attachment" and high turnover of black youths.
- The enormously high costs of plant security, running almost four times greater within the ghetto areas than elsewhere in the city.

- The extraordinary problems of providing for personal safety of plant personnel, particularly women and white collar and executive workers.

Several of these business executives cited the experience of a number of companies during the ABCD programs of the late 1960s in which these companies were simply not able to handle the extraordinary costs of training and retraining youths whose job attachment was so slight. Some plants reported turnover rates in these situations of as much as 75 to 80 percent.

But underlying all of their comments was the recurring theme and stark fear of high crime —the inability to cope with excessive violence and losses to theft, vandalism, and robbery.

Thus, while black leaders are undoubtedly right in calling for some national action to deal with high teenage unemployment in particular, and unemployment among blacks generally, they are also right in demanding their own inner cities follow a "get-tough" policy on crime.

As Mayor Maynard Jackson of Atlanta said in an interview on CBS recently, "We have got to stop excusing hoodlums as 'brothers' and start dealing with them as crooks. A crook is not a 'brother,' a crook is a crook, is a crook, is a crook."

Unfortunately, there is very little evidence that this kind of "get tough" message is having much impact on the courts, where statistics continue to show the ratio of incarcerations to arrests is 62 percent lower now than it was 15 years ago—and where even the repeat offender today is five to six times more likely to go free than he was 15 years ago. Indeed, studies show that less than 1 percent of all serious crimes result in punishment and less than 10 percent of all arrests result in incarceration.

This is even more true of youth crime, where courts in recent years have increasingly shied away from sending the youthful offender to prison. Today less than 3 percent of all juvenile arrests (under 18) result in some kind of punishment or restraint.

Unfortunately today youth is almost synonymous with crime. Since 1960 crime among teenagers under 18 has increased nearly four times faster than among those above 18.

And, since 1960, total crimes committed by youths under age 25 have increased from 38 percent of the total to this year's figures of more than 80 percent of all crimes or offenses committed, and 75 percent of all serious crimes.

What this means is that the main reason for rising crime in this country is not adult crime at all (which actually is declining) but an explosion of crime among youth:

| | PERCENT OF TOTAL ARRESTS BY YOUTH—1974 | |
	Boston— under age 25	Nationwide— under age 25
Murder	57%	45%
Rape	54%	61%
Robbery	84%	76%
Assault	48%	48%
Burglary (B&E)	81%	84%
Larceny	72%	77%
Auto theft	89%	86%
Total	73%	75%

(Source: FBI Uniform Crime Reports)

The figures show that while the crime rate among mature adults over 25 is actually on the decrease in Boston and has been for nearly 15 years, crime among both teenagers and the 18-25 group has been soaring—and now accounts for nearly three-quarters of all the crime committed in the city of Boston.

More important is the fact that 85 to 90 percent of the property crimes against business both in and out of the ghetto are now being committed by youths under the age of 25.

And, in Boston, more than half of the crimes committed against inner city businesses are being committed by black teenagers between the ages of 14 and 19.

What this suggests is that today's extraordinary crime and violence problem in Boston in general, and in the ghetto areas in particular, could be cut in half if we could find a satisfactory way to deal with the 40 to 60 percent unemployment problems among black teenagers, and the 20 to 30 percent unemployment problem among white inner city teenagers.

The question is how?

How do you get jobs into an area which is so riddled with crime that businesses are afraid to come and established businesses are now leaving?

How do you employ young people whose job skills and job attachment are so low that even government public service jobs fail to hold them for any significant length of time?

How do you find work for individuals who do not yet have the social and employment skills that will enable them to take and hold work even when economic conditions improve?

These are the questions that puzzle and trouble many politicians and social scientists today. Increasingly they are becoming convinced that there are no simplistic answers. Even public service jobs programs have proved more valuable to inner city adults than to teenagers.

However, two simultaneous approaches do seem to commend themselves. One is a concerted effort on the part of the courts and the police to deal more harshly with criminal offenders—of all ages, and, in particular, the repeat offender, who needs to be removed from the community so that he does it less economic damage.

Studies in both Philadelphia and Los Angeles show that more than 80 percent of all serious crime is committed not by first offenders, but by repeat offenders—and that more than half the crime is committed by individuals who have been involved in four or more previous offenses.

A significant reduction in crime in Boston and in the ghetto could be achieved just by tougher and firmer removal of the repeat offender from the scene through incarceration.

Such a policy could have a highly salutary effect on "de-victimizing" a whole community that is now beset by "repeat marauders" who are "brothers" in skin color only, but who are now actively destroying the economy on which law abiding citizens depend.

Coupled with this could well be a national plan such as that proposed by John Connally which, though it offends the sensibilities of both liberals and conservatives, might well be the only realistic short-term answer to the whole teenage unemployment problem.

That plan: a national compulsory job-service corps in which those who were not able to find and hold full-time work or to sustain full-time education opportunities, would be required to join a government-operated youth training program. The corps would be similar to the Army, but emphasize vocational training and public service for a mandatory period of one to three years.

Such a program might well be required as a temporary method to deal with the intense twin problems of high crime and high unemployment among the nation's inner city youth, problems that will be alleviated somewhat in the 1980s, as the present teenage "population bulge" disappears.

Such a plan would take some of the economic and social pressure off the inner cities today,

reduce their crime, stabilize their economic environment, and help "normalize" their societies.

These are harsh solutions, but if the inner cities cannot deal with their crime problems, they probably cannot deal with their unemployment problems—and they are, therefore, doomed to an even harsher future.

One thing seems clear. We are not likely to solve the unemployment problems in the inner city unless we deal with excessive crime —and we are also not likely to deal with crime effectively unless we forcefully and quickly reduce inner city unemployment. The one is feeding the other.

Selected readings for Chapter 3

Conklin, John E. *The Impact of Crime* (New York, Macmillan, Inc., 1975).
>   The first chapter of this book deals extensively with the direct and indirect costs of crime.
Normandeau, A., and A. Rizkall, "Economic and Social Consequence of Crime: New Challenges for Research and Planning in Canada," *Canadian Journal of Criminology and Corrections* **19**:206-229, 1977.
>   Reviews research regarding the economic impact of crime and the cost of administration of justice, and considers the economic consequences of crime on overall criminal and social policy.
President's Commission on Law Enforcement and Administration of Justice, Task Force on Assessment. *Crime and Its Impact: An Assessment* (Washington, D.C.: U.S. Government Printing Office, 1967).
>   Chapter 3 provides an assessment of the economic impact of crime, including estimates of the costs of individual crime, crimes against persons and property, public expenditures for law enforcement and criminal justice, and private costs, including those of prevention, dealing with the impact of crime, insurance, and those associated with being a witness.
U.S. Congress, Joint Economic Committee, *The Cost of Crime in 1976* (Washington, D.C.: U.S. Government Printing Office, 1976).
>   Estimates that crime cost the nation $125 billion in 1976, including costs of maintaining the criminal justice system. White collar crime, estimated at $44 billion, was the most expensive crime.
Victimology **3**:Nos. 3-4, 1978.
>   A special issue devoted to analysis of the fear of crime.

Chapter 4

VICTIM SURVEYS

A □ *Victimization surveys: an overview*
JAMES GAROFALO

B □ *Sample surveys of the victims of crime*
WESLEY G. SKOGAN

A □ *Victimization surveys*

An overview

JAMES GAROFALO

Information about the victims of crime is not easily obtained. The criminal justice system created to deal with crime in the United States focuses on the offender. When the police talk to victims and witnesses, they gather information, such as how the crime was committed and what the offender looked like, that will be helpful in their primary mission, the apprehension of offenders. Similarly, arrest, court, probation, parole, and prison records contain an enormous amount of information about offenders who have become enmeshed in the nets of the criminal justice system. But the system gathers information about victims only incidentally. For example, victims' names and addresses are recorded so that they can be called upon to testify in court if needed, and the amount of property loss suffered by a victim might be recorded so

that the crime can be classified under the proper statute (grand versus petty larceny, for example). Perhaps this focus on offenders in official records is one reason that criminologists, who have traditionally relied on official records for their data, have concentrated their studies on offenders and have neglected the study of victims, at least until recently.

However, even if the existing criminal justice data system were reformed so that extensive victim information was routinely recorded, a major problem would remain: not all crimes come to the attention of the police, and data at later stages of the criminal justice system (for example, from the courts and corrections institutions) reflect an even smaller subset of crimes. Researchers interested in studying *offender* characteristics have been aware for some time that offenders who have been arrested or incarcerated may not be representative of all persons who commit crimes.[1] In fact, recent criticisms of theories that purport to explain

The author would like to thank Professor Michael J. Hindelang for his helpful comments on an earlier version of this work.

criminality have been based on the contention that the theories were derived from information about arrested or incarcerated offenders who are not representative of all offenders.[2] To overcome the suspected bias stemming from the use of police and other agency data about offenders, attempts have been made to select representative samples of people from the general population and to ask people in the samples about criminal acts they might have committed. Because of the sensitive nature of such questioning and because of the expense of selecting and locating representative samples of the adult population, most studies of self-reported offending behavior have dealt with juveniles and have not concentrated on serious criminality.[3]

Efforts to obtain information about *victims,* then, face twin problems: (1) information about victims is not routinely collected by the criminal justice system, and (2) the information that does exist in agency files pertains only to those criminal events that come to the attention of and are recorded by agency personnel. One solution to these problems is the victimization survey. Basically, the notion of a victimization survey is parallel to the notion of a self-report study of offending behavior that was mentioned above: a representative sample of persons is selected from the general population, and people in the sample are interviewed about victimizations they may have suffered. During the interview, respondents can be asked whether particular victimizations have occurred during any specific length of time preceding the interview (such as a week, a month, a year, or 2 years). This length of time is called a reference period. For reasons that will be discussed later, the most common practice is to use a reference period of 6 months or 1 year. In its basic concept, the victimization survey has striking simplicity: if you want to find out about victims, ask people who have been victimized! But when the technique is put into operation, some very difficult problems become apparent.

Victimization surveys are faced with the same problems that confront all types of survey research: selecting a sample that will be representative of the population from which it is drawn, designing a questionnaire, deciding whether to interview in person or by telephone, hiring and training personnel, and so forth. However, there are some problems that are more applicable to a victimization survey than to, for example, an election year presidential preference poll. General survey research issues are treated in most survey research textbooks, so I will deal only with the issues that are particularly germane to victimization surveying.

SAMPLE SIZE

Perhaps the major impediment to the use of victimization surveys is the rather large sample size required. The more rare the phenomenon being studied is, the larger the sample size necessary to obtain reliable information about the phenomenon; and the serious crimes studied in most major victimization surveys—rape, robbery, assault, burglary, vehicle theft—are relatively rare. For example, if a researcher were interested in studying robbery victimizations during the past year in a city, and (unbeknown to the researcher) 3% of the residents have been victims of personal robbery during that time,[4] he or she would locate only about 60 robbery victims in a sample of 2,000 persons. For the analyst who is interested in subdividing the robbery victimizations according to criteria such as the age of the victim, when the incident occurred, whether a weapon was used, how much property was stolen, and so forth, 60 cases are a very small number with which to work.[5]

An even larger sample would be required if a purpose of the research were to use the sample data to make an estimate of the total number of robbery victimizations that occurred in the city. Whenever population estimates are derived from a sample of the population, there exists the potential for a certain amount of error, which is measured by a statistic called the standard error of the estimate. The rarer the phenomenon being estimated (such as robbery victimization) is, the larger the sample size needed to obtain a standard error that is reasonably small.[6]

Of course, the need for large samples in victimization surveys would not be a major problem if unlimited funds were available to the researcher, so the sample size issue usually reduces to a cost issue. Therefore, consideration has been given to ways of reducing the cost of victimization surveying by reducing the sample size needed.[7] Basically, this can be accomplished by decreasing the proportion of nonvictims among interviewees so that the same number of interviews uncovers a larger number of victims. In the hypothetical robbery study discussed earlier, for example, only about 3% of the interviewees had suffered a robbery during the reference period; thus, 97% of the interviews were wasted (at least for the purpose of locating robbery victims). Three ways of reducing the proportion of nonvictims among interviewees are now discussed.

First, individuals known to have been victimized can be included in the sample. To do so, however, requires victimization information about individuals that can be obtained before those individuals are interviewed, and the most obvious source of such information is police files. Thus, the researcher might select, from police files, the names of persons known to have been victimized during the time period under study; then those known victims would be located and interviewed. But this procedure defeats one of the main purposes of the victimization survey—namely, to obtain victimization and victim information that does not depend on whether the victim decided to report the crime to the police and whether the police decided to officially classify and record the event as a crime. Research has indicated that the characteristics of crimes reported to the police differ systematically from the characteristics of crimes that victims do not report to the police; reported crimes have higher average dollar losses, higher injury rates, proportionately more weapon use by offenders, and so forth, than do unreported crimes.[8,9] So, a sample of known victims selected from police files probably would not be representative of all victims in the jurisdiction.

A second way to decrease the proportion of nonvictims among interviewees is to conduct the survey in geographic areas known to have a high incidence of victimization. Naturally, surveying in *only* the high-crime areas of a city will not yield results that are representative

of the whole city, but it is possible to oversample high-crime areas as part of a research design that would otherwise produce a representative sample. For example, a sample could be selected so that it is representative of a city, but then additional cases could be selected from high-crime areas of the city to supplement the initial sample. Results from the sample would have to be reweighed to account for this oversampling if the researcher wanted to use the sample data to estimate the extent and nature of victimization in the entire city. For example, suppose one high-crime area of a city had been oversampled so that persons from the high-crime area constituted 20% of the sample but only 10% of the city's population. The sample data for people in the high-crime area would have to be multiplied by 0.5 to make the sample representative of the general population of the city.[10] Oversampling, however, does not completely solve the sample size problem. Even in high-crime areas, it is likely that *most* of the residents do not suffer a serious criminal victimization during any one year. In addition, the identification of areas as high- or low-crime areas must rely on some data source in existence before the survey itself, such as police records, which may not reflect the geographic distribution of victimizations in a completely accurate manner.

The third method that can be used to ensure that a smaller proportion of nonvictims exists in the sample is to extend the length of the reference period. Theoretically, twice as many victimizations will be recorded in a survey that asks respondents about their victimization experiences during the 2 years preceding the interview than in a survey that asks the same number of respondents about their victimization experiences during the past 1 year. Extending the reference period, however, introduces another important set of problems—namely, memory effects.

MEMORY EFFECTS

Analyses of victimization survey results have indicated that: (1) people tend to forget victimizations that they have suffered, and (2) victimizations that are remembered are not always placed accurately in time by respondents.[11] Forgetting events is an easy problem to comprehend: as one asks people to recall events that occurred further and further back in the past, the chances that the events will have been forgotten increase. A more complex phenomenon occurs when respondents do recall events but inaccurately place them in time. The complexity arises because there are several types of such misplacement.

For victimization surveys, the most important type of temporal misplacement is the tendency to recall events as occurring more recently than they actually did occur; this is generally referred to as forward telescoping, and it can affect victimization surveys in two different ways. First, an event that actually occurred before the start of the reference period can be remembered as occurring within the reference period. For example, in a survey with a 1 year reference period, a respondent might recall a victimization as having occurred 11 months before the interview when it actually occurred 14 months before. If the event had not been misplaced in time, it would not have been counted in the survey, because it actually occurred before the start of the reference period. Thus, this form of forward telescoping operates in a manner that is the opposite of forgetting: forgetting results in the failure to uncover victimizations that should be counted in the survey, whereas the telescoping of prereference-period victimizations forward into the reference period results in the counting of victimizations that should not be counted.[12]

The second form of forward telescoping occurs within the reference period itself. For example, in a survey using a 1-year reference period, a victimization that occurred 10 months before the interview might be recalled as having occurred only 8 months before. The victimization would have been counted in the survey even if it had been placed properly in time by the respondent, because it did, in fact, occur within the reference period. Thus, forward telescoping within the reference period only creates problems if the research requires that information about when the victimization occurred be more specific than simply whether it occurred during the reference period. Of course, the same comment applies to the memory effect that causes the respondent to recall a victimization as occurring at a more distant time in the reference period than when it actually occurred (reverse telescoping within the reference period).

Because memory effects become more acute as the length of the reference period is extended, there is a major trade-off that must be made in victimization surveying: longer reference periods allow the use of smaller samples (and thus, lower costs), although they simultaneously jeopardize the accuracy of respondent recall. Thus, there is a need to strike some sort of balance between these two considerations. The results of a survey using a reference period of, for example, 5 years will obviously be contaminated by memory effects. On the other hand, most organizations could not afford the methods used in the National Crime Survey (NCS), which the U.S. Bureau of the Census has been conducting since 1972 for the U.S. Department of Justice. In those surveys, a 6-month reference period is used, but national samples of about 60,000 households (containing about 136,000 eligible individual respondents) and 50,000 businesses are used every 6 months.[13]

TYPES OF CRIME

There are a host of other methodological issues confronting victimizations surveys, but only one other is discussed here: What types of crime can and cannot be studied with the victimization survey technique? Some apparent restrictions can be noted.

First, if the victim is to be interviewed personally, homicide is excluded. Second, victims cannot be interviewed about victimizations of which they are not aware. This limitation applies to all types of crime to some extent, but its effect is greater for some than for others. For example, some forms of consumer fraud (such as an automobile repair shop's charging for parts that were not used) may never be noticed by the victims, but a purse snatching or a burglary is much less likely to go unnoticed. Third, even when survey respondents are aware that a crime has occurred, they must define themselves as victims. Thus, consensual illegal acts (such as gambling, prostitution, and drug sales) do not fit well into the notion of a victimization survey. Fourth, there must be some identifiable victim (or spokesman for the victim) who can be interviewed. This problem is especially acute in any attempt to study victimizations of large organizations, such as employee theft and shoplifting against large businesses or tax evasion against a government. To communicate such information, a representative of the organization must generally rely on the organization's records, and this defeats one of the aims of the victimization survey, namely, to gather information that is independent of record-keeping processes.

Because of such technical limitations, in addition to the preferences of the agencies funding victimization survey projects, most victimization surveys have focused on rape, robbery, assault, burglary, vehicle theft, and larceny (from persons and households). However, the exact nature of the limitations on the types of crime amenable to being studied by means of victimization surveying has not been thoroughly investigated. One piece of research indicated that the technique may have difficulty in trying to elicit reports of victimizations that were committed by persons known to the victims (especially relatives);[14] another found that businesses generally do not maintain records that allow them to differentiate the amounts of "inventory shrinkage" attributable to factors such as employee theft, shoplifting, and accidental loss.[16] But there is still a great need for creative research that will push against the limits of the technique to determine whether victimization surveys, using either traditional methodologies or variants of those methodologies, can be applied to the study of a wider range of victimizations than is currently the case.

THE VICTIM PERSPECTIVE

The data gathered in victimization surveys can help answer a number of important questions: How much injury and financial loss do victims suffer, and how are injury and loss dis-

tributed among subgroups of the population? How do subgroups of the population differ in their likelihood of being victimized? How do people react to victimization? Questions such as these are already being addressed with existing victimization survey data. But perhaps more important than any single question that can be answered with the data collected, an emphasis on the victimization survey as a primary data collection technique in criminal justice tends to support a reorientation of interest in the field. One can describe this reorientation as the emergence of a victim perspective in criminal justice.

The victim perspective implies a renewed concern with and interest in the victim—putting the victim on at least an equal footing with the offender in terms of resource expenditure and research attention. The victimization survey is a key component of the victim perspective. The defining characteristic of the victimization survey, going directly to the public to obtain information about victims, exemplifies the new perspective.

Information about victims could be collected by police departments; offense-reporting forms could be revised so that police officers would record the relevant data when they respond to a crime. However, this is not a substitute for the victimization survey once commitment is given to a victim perspective. No matter how well police offense reports are devised, they cannot be used to collect information about victimizations that victims decide not to report to the police. Dependence on police offense reports for information that will be used to develop policy and programs to benefit victims (or potential victims) implicitly states that people's experiences as victims of crime will not count in policymaking and planning unless they first report their victimizations to the police. Such a passive stance by the criminal justice system does not enhance its claim to be developing a victim perspective. The more active role of the victimization survey in seeking out and eliciting information about victims, regardless of whether those victims reported their victimizations to the police, would seem to be more consistent with the victim perspective.

The victimization survey can be used as a vehicle for extending the victim perspective. Currently, the technique is used to answer predefined questions and to gather data about crimes that the initiators of the surveys believe are important. But a strong victim perspective in a democratic society should provide a means for the public to define what constitutes victimization and what should be done about it. Methodological obstacles to using the victimization survey as a means to that end can be overcome. The major obstacles are more political than methodological, but perhaps the growth of the victim perspective in criminal justice, reinforced by external demands on the system to give more priority to that perspective, will eventually overcome those obstacles.

We have progressed from noting the logic of the victimization survey as a means of obtaining information about victims, through some of the methodological problems of the technique itself, and to a discussion of the promise that the technique has for strengthening and extending a victim perspective within the criminal justice system. It has been only about a decade since victimization surveys were first seriously used in the United States. During the past decade, we have begun to accumulate more and more data from the surveys that have been (and are being) conducted. Equally important, many of the complex methodological problems associated with the technique have received a great deal of attention; some have even been resolved, at least to the point where the surveys can proceed with some degree of confidence in the quality of the data collected. Most important, however, has been the influence that victimization surveys have had in reorienting the criminal justice system toward a victim perspective. In the future, the challenge will be to creatively adapt the victimization survey to act as a channel for bringing the public's view to bear on criminal justice policy.

NOTES

1. One of the first to allude to the problem was the Belgian statistician and astronomer, Quetelet, in *A Treatise on Man and the Development of His Faculties*, published in English in 1842 and reproduced by Scholars' Facsimiles & Reprints; Delmar, N.Y., 1969. Also see Cohen, Albert K. *Delinquent Boys* (New York: The Free Press, 1955), pp. 169-171.

2. See, for example: Phillipson, Michael. *Understanding Crime and Delinquency* (Chicago: Aldine Publishing Co., 1974), pp. 11-12.

3. For reviews of self-report methods and results, see: Hood, Roger, and Richard Sparks. *Key Issues in Criminology* (New York: McGraw-Hill Book Co., 1970), Chs. 1-2; Doleschal, Eugene. "Hidden Crime," *Crime and Delinquency Literature* **2:**546-572, 1970; Nettler, Gwynn. *Explaining Crime* (New York: McGraw-Hill Book Co., 1974), Ch. 4.

4. Three percent is not an unreasonable figure. A victimization survey in New York City found that, in 1974, there were 2.4 personal robbery victimizations for every 100 persons 12 years or older. Law Enforcement Assistance Administration. *Criminal Victimization Surveys in Chicago, Detroit, Los Angeles, New York, and Philadelphia: A Comparison of 1972 and 1974 Findings,* National Criminal Justice Information and Statistics Service Report No. SD-NCS-C-6 (Washington, D.C.: U.S. Government Printing Office, 1976), p. 63.

5. Actually, there would probably be more than 60 robbery *victimizations* among the 60 robbery victims because some persons would have suffered more than one robbery during the 12-month reference period. However, the number of these repetitive victims would be relatively small. See: Hindelang, Michael J., Michael R. Gottfredson, and James Garofalo. *Victims of Personal Crimes: An Empirical Foundation for a Theory of Personal Victimization* (Cambridge, Mass.: Ballinger Publishing Co., 1978), Ch. 6.

6. For a more complete discussion of sampling, sample size, and standard errors in victimization surveys, see: Garofalo, James. *Local Victim Surveys: A Review of the Issues,* Law Enforcement Assistance Administration, National Criminal Justice Information and Statistics Service, Analytic Report SD-VAD-2 (Washington, D.C.: U.S. Government Printing Office, 1977), pp. 13-20.

7. Other cost reduction ideas have been explored, the most notable being the possibility of using random-digit-dialing telephone interviews as a substitute for face-to-face interviewing, See: Tuchfarber, Alfred J., and William R. Klecka. *Random Digit Dialing: Lowering the Cost of Victimization Surveys* (Washington, D.C.: Police Foundation, 1976).

8. Hindelang, Michael J., and Michael R. Gottfredson. "The Victim's Decision Not to Invoke the Criminal Process," in McDonald, William, ed., *The Victim and the Criminal Justice System* (Beverly Hills, Calif.: Sage Publications, Inc., 1976).

9. Skogan, Wesley G. "Dimensions of the Dark Figure of Unreported Crime," *Crime and Delinquency* **23:**41-50, 1977.

10. For an introductory discussion of oversampling and reweighting, see: Babbie, Earl R. *Survey Research Methods* (Belmont, Calif.: Wadsworth Publishing Co., Inc., 1973), pp. 102-106.

11. The following works deal with various aspects of memory effects in victimization surveys: Biderman, Albert D.,

Louise A. Johnson, Jennie McIntyre, and Adrianne W. Weir. *Report on a Pilot Study in the District of Columbia on Victimization and Attitudes Toward Law Enforcement,* Field Surveys I, President's Commission on Law Enforcement and Administration of Justice (Washington, D.C.: U.S. Government Printing Office, 1967); Ennis, Philip H. *Criminal Victimization in the United States: A Report of a National Survey,* Field Surveys II, President's Commission on Law Enforcement and Administration of Justice (Washington, D.C.: U.S. Government Printing Office, 1967); Law Enforcement Assistance Administration, *San Jose Methods Test of Known Crime Victims,* Statistics Technical Report No. 1 (Washington, D.C.: U.S. Government Printing Office, 1972); Hindelang, Michael J. *Criminal Victimization in Eight American Cities: A Descriptive Analysis of Common Theft and Assault* (Cambridge, Mass.: Ballinger Publishing Co., 1976); Gottfredson, Michael R., and Michael J. Hindelang. "A Consideration of Memory Decay and Telescoping Biases in Victimization Surveys," *Journal of Criminal Justice* **5:**205-216, 1977.

12. Reverse telescoping can also occur; that is, events can be remembered as having occurred further back in the past than when they actually occurred. If reverse telescoping results in a respondent's recalling a victimization as occurring before the start of the reference period when, in fact, it occurred during the reference period, the practical effect on the survey is the same as the effect of forgetting—a victimization that should be counted is not counted. However, evidence indicates that forward telescoping is more important than reverse telescoping in victimization surveys.

13. The NCS is a panel survey in which addresses are revisited by interviewers at 6-month intervals. Apart from the enormous sample size used, costs of the NCS are increased by other features of the survey, such as the use of a "bounding" procedure, which generally results in the initial interviews with respondents not being treated as usable data for the survey. For more detail, see: Garofalo, James, and Michael J. Hindelang. *An Introduction to the National Crime Survey,* Law Enforcement Assistance Administration, National Criminal Justice Information and Statistics Service, Analytic Report SD-VAD-4 (Washington, D.C.: U.S. Government Printing Office, 1978).

14. Law Enforcement Assistance Administration. *San Jose Methods Test of Known Crime Victims,* Statistics Technical Report No. 1 (Washington, D.C.: U.S. Government Printing Office, 1972).

15. Joerg, Karen. "The Cleveland-Akron Commercial Victimization Feasibility Test," Law Enforcement Assistance Administration, Statistics Division Technical Series, Report No. 2 (mimeographed), 1971.

B □ *Sample surveys of the victims of crime*

WESLEY G. SKOGAN

In July 1972, the Census Bureau began one of the largest interview programs ever conducted: the crime victimization surveys of the Law Enforcement Assistance Administration. The national survey is designed to generate estimates of quarterly and yearly victimization rates for individuals, households and commercial establishments. In addition, special surveys have been conducted in twenty-six communities, producing victimization rates and other crime data for many of the nation's major central cities. While the city surveys are "one shot" cross-sectional studies of the experiences of their citizens during a particular year, the national program is on-going; the residents of 10,000 households are interviewed each month in a rotating panel design, producing continuous reports of the crime experiences of ordinary citizens. The individual and household interview schedules are designed to elicit detailed accounts of six categories of offenses: rape, robbery, assault, burglary, larceny, and auto theft. The commercial survey instrument focuses upon only two crimes, burglary and robbery. In addition to the personal or organizational characteristics of the victims of these offenses, the data include self-reports of the value of stolen property, the extent of personal injuries, medical costs, insurance claims and collections, the restitution of lost property, the attributes of offenders, the reporting of incidents to the police, and self-defensive measures

Excerpted from Volume 4, Number 1 of the *Review of Public Data Use,* Copyright, Data Use and Access Laboratories, 1976.

taken by victims. Attitude questionnaires were administered to one-half of the respondents over sixteen years of age in the city survey; these question probe perceptions of crime, the fear of crime, and the effect of crime upon personal mobility. Because these studies are intended to gather information about relatively rare events —serious crimes—the samples are very large. Tapes containing the data are now being prepared by the Bureau of the Census, and soon will enter the public domain.

This report describes these samples, and advances a few ideas about the data and their organization. It also summarizes key methodological problems about which users should be aware, and lists several publications which refer to the survey.

THE NATIONAL HOUSEHOLD SAMPLE

The household sample focuses upon the victimization experiences of persons as individuals and as collective units. The households in the sample were chosen through a multi-stage stratified cluster procedure. In addition to standard dwelling units and mobile homes, the sample may include group quarters such as flop houses, communes, and dormitories. The households are divided into panels of approximately 10,000 units, one of which is interviewed each month. All household members twelve years of age and over are questioned about their experiences during the preceding six months. Reinterviews are conducted with each panel for up to three years, then the panel is dropped from the sample and replaced by a new group of respondents.

The heart of the interview schedule is the "incident screen," a list of questions probing the experiences of each respondent. Individuals are asked eleven questions, including:
- (During the last six months) Did you have your pocket picked, or purse snatched?
- Did anyone beat you up, attack you, or hit you with something such as a rock or a bottle?

In addition, a household informant is quizzed about burglaries, auto thefts, and other incidents which are treated as victimizations of the group as a whole. Each affirmative response to a screen item is followed up by a series of detailed questions which elicit reports about the incident, perceptions of the offender, and consequent financial losses and physical disabilities. The resulting information is used to catalogue the event: the data to be released by the Census Bureau are coded in one of thirty-six categories, which can be recombined to produce analytic typologies or to create classifications compatible with those employed by the F.B.I. in *Uniform Crime Report*.

THE NATIONAL COMMERCIAL SAMPLE

The commercial study focuses upon burglary and robbery. The national sample was selected by a stratified, multi-stage cluster procedure conducted by the Business Division of the Bureau of the Census. The sample potentially includes a broad range of organizations. In addition to retail establishments, it may include wholesale suppliers, manufacturing establishments, museums and theatres, medical centers, coal mines. In principle, the 1972 break-in of the Democratic National Committee's headquarters could have been included in the data. However, these establishments were chosen from a sampling frame developed in 1948. Although it was somewhat updated in 1964 (primarily in large cities), the age of the sampling frame is a major weakness of this phase of the victim study.

The selection procedure yielded an initial sample of 14,000 interviewed commercial units. In each place, owners or managers are questioned about events which victimized the organization during the preceding six months; robberies of employees or customers are treated as individual rather than commerical crimes, although injuries to the former "in the line of duty" are recorded. The commercial respondents are divided into six panels, but unlike the household sample, the commercial group is not rotated.

THE CITY HOUSEHOLD SAMPLES

In addition to the national household and commercial surveys, interviews were also con-

Table 1. Victim survey cities

Cities interviewed July-September, 1972

Atlanta	Denver
Baltimore	Newark
Cleveland	Portland, Oregon
Dallas	St. Louis

Cities interviewed January-March, 1973

Chicago	New York
Detroit	Philadelphia
Los Angeles	

Cities interviewed January-March, 1974

Boston	New Orleans
Buffalo	Oakland
Cincinnati	Pittsburgh
Houston	San Diego
Miami	San Francisco
Milwaukee	Washington, D.C.
Minneapolis	

ducted in twenty-six major cities. These communities were selected for a variety of reasons: some because they were the focus of special federal crime-reduction programs, some because they are large and have an extraordinary impact upon the crime rate of the nation as a whole, and others because they gave the collection a good geographical and demographic spread. A list of these cities and the dates during which interviews were conducted in them is presented in Table 1.

Households in each of the cities were selected from 1970 Census computer tapes which contained information about the units which entered the sample. They were chosen at random in predetermined proportions to fill 100 strata defined by the race and income of their heads, whether they owned or rented their quarters, and the size of the family group. This sample was updated by the inclusion of a randomly-selected group of units chosen from lists of building permits issued since the 1970 Census. Again, the range of households eligible for inclusion was wide, primarily excluding residents of jails and households already selected for the national survey. Response rates for the city samples were quite high, averaging about 95 percent of all households which could

have been questioned. Each city sample numbers about 10,000 interviewed households and 21,000 individual respondents. Each respondent was quizzed about his or her victimization experiences during the preceding twelve months. It is important to note that data from the city studies refer to the experiences of city residents, not to crimes which took place in those cities. Incidents reported in the surveys include many which took place elsewhere, while crimes which victimize commuters, tourists, and others who do not live within the boundaries of the central city are necessarily excluded by the nature of the sampling frame. Among other things, this makes it perilous to compare survey victimization figures with official police statistics.

THE CITY COMMERCIAL SAMPLE

Commercial establishments were selected in each city using the Census of Business sampling frame that was employed in the national sample. Interviewers were sent to selected areas of each community to compile lists of all visible establishments. Samples of these units were chosen, taking care to avoid establishments which belonged to the national commercial sample. Areas which had been annexed to the central cities since 1948 were examined for commercial areas, which were also sampled. Interviews were conducted with owners or managers, gathering information about burglaries or robberies which had affected their operations during the previous twelve months. The refusal rate was low, averaging less than four percent. In the end, representatives of about 2,500 commercial establishments were interviewed in each of the twenty-six cities.

DATA ORGANIZATION

There are several ways to organize data collected in the victim surveys, some of which are necessary for answering certain questions, but are inefficient for probing others. The largest files will contain information on all interviewed units, including those which were victimized and those which were not. Household files of this type will be hierarchial: each record will contain data describing the household and its head, which will be followed by descriptions of a varying number of individuals in the household, each of whose attributes will in turn be followed by a varying number of data characters describing their victimization experiences, if any. Files of this sort may be utilized to examine differences between victims and non-victims of various offenses. Smaller and more efficient files may be constructed to explore the characteristics of victims or incidents only. For example, an Incident File would link the attributes of each incident with those of its victim; an individual or household would be in the file as often as they were the target of a crime, and there would be one record for each incident. Such a file could be used to explore the characteristics of incidents (Were they reported to the police, or not?) and the relationship between the attributes of incidents and the attributes of their victims (Were the victimizations of whites more likely to be reported than the victimizations of blacks?).

Incident Files as well as "full files" containing information on all respondents will be released by the Bureau of the Census. In every case the records will include weights which must be used to adjust them to their proper proportion in the population. The weights reflect the probability of a unit being selected and they provide estimates for similar units which were not interviewed. In addition, incidents are weighted by the inverse of the number of victims they involved. Because crimes with two victims, for example, are twice as likely to be uncovered in a random sample of the popula-

tion as those with only one victim, it is necessary to adjust for their differential chance of appearing in the data. The weights calculated by the Bureau of the Census also will provide population estimates of the frequency of each incident or victimization.

Also crucial to the organization of any data set from the national crime survey is the *time frame* to which it refers. Two concepts are important: the "collection period" and the "reference period" for a set of data. Because the interviews gather retrospective reports, information collected at one point refers to some prior period of time, always six months in length in the national study. Data for a particular calendar reference period—say, 1974—would be gathered from persons interviewed between February 1974 and June 1975. Those reports may be organized in Incident Files containing information about events which occurred within the reference period of interest. Files organized around persons or households, on the other hand, may contain incidents from variously overlapping reference periods, for reports gathered from respondents in more than one collection period will refer to different calendar months. Unless only respondents from a single monthly panel are used in an analysis, the incidents in the file will have occurred during different parts of a year. This has serious implications if crime patterns are highly seasonal, or if there is a strong secular trend in the data. Reports gathered in each city study, on the other hand, share virtually identical collection and reference periods.

Selected readings for Chapter 4

Ennis, Philip H. *Criminal Victimization in the United States: A Report of a National Survey* (Washington, D.C.: U.S. Government Printing Office, 1967).

> Report of a national victimization survey conducted in 1966. The sample was 10,000 households randomly selected to be representative of the nation. The methodology is described and estimates are secured regarding the extent, costs, and distribution of crime in the United States. Victims' decisions to report victimizations to the police and victim attitudes toward police and individual security are studied.

Garofalo, James, and Michael J. Hindelang. *An Introduction to the National Crime Survey* (Washington, D.C.: U.S. Government Printing Office, 1977).

> A guide designed to acquaint the reader with the background, methods, limits, and current status of the National Crime Survey of victimization in the country.

Levine, James P. "The Potential for Crime Overreporting in Criminal Victimization Surveys," *Criminology* **14:**307-330, 1976.

> Several reasons are offered, including mistaking incidents as crimes, faulty memory, lying, and interviewer-coder bias to suggest that victimization surveys may overestimate crime; caution is urged regarding use of the findings.

Penick, Bettye K. Edison, ed. *Surveying Crime* (Washington, D.C.: National Academy of Sciences, 1976).

> A report of The Panel for the Evaluation of Crime Surveys of the National Academy of Sciences that evaluates the National Crime Surveys. The first part of the report focuses on substantive issues, such as the completeness, accuracy, reliability, analysis, and dissemination of the National Crime Survey, and the second part evaluates the utility of the survey results and offers suggestions on modifications in the survey approach.

St. Louis, Alfred. "Measuring Crime by Mail Surveys: The Texas Crime Trend Survey," *Victimology* **3:**124-135, 1978.

> Describes methodology and reports initial findings for a Texas victimization survey using questionnaires mailed to the general public; comparisons are made with official police crime data.

Skogan, Wesley G., ed. *Sample Surveys of the Victims of Crime* (Cambridge, Mass.: Ballinger Publishing Co., 1976).

> This collection of articles presents information on patterns of victimization, the costs of crime, and the relationship between victims and police, as well as material on methodological questions about the use of victim surveys.

United States Department of Justice, Law Enforcement Assistance Administration.

> Since 1973 the Law Enforcement Assistance Administration in cooperation with the United States Bureau of the Census has been conducting a series of victimization studies. The following reports, all published by the U.S. Government Printing Office, are available:
>
> > *Criminal Victimization in the United States* (annual):
> >> *A Comparison of 1975 and 1976 Findings*
> >> *A Comparison of 1974 and 1975 Findings*
> >> *A Comparison of 1973 and 1974 Findings*
> >> *1975* (final report)
> >> *1974* (final report)
> >> *1973* (final report)

Criminal Victimization Surveys in Boston, Buffalo, Cincinnati, Houston, Miami, Milwaukee, Minneapolis, New Orleans, Oakland, Pittsburgh, San Diego, San Francisco, and Washington, D.C. (final report, 13 vols.)

Criminal Victimization Surveys in 13 American Cities (summary report, 1 vol.)

Criminal Victimization Surveys in Chicago, Detroit, Los Angeles, New York, and Philadelphia: A Comparison of 1972 and 1974 Findings

Criminal Victimization Surveys in the Nation's Five Largest Cities: National Crime Panel Survey in Chicago, Detroit, Los Angeles, New York, and Philadelphia, 1972

Criminal Victimization Surveys in Eight American Cities: A Comparison of 1971/ 72 and 1974/75 Findings—National Crime Surveys in Atlanta, Baltimore, Cleveland, Dallas, Denver, Newark, Portland, and St. Louis.

Crime in Eight American Cities: National Crime Panel Surveys in Atlanta, Baltimore, Cleveland, Dallas, Denver, Newark, Portland, and St. Louis—Advance Report, 1971/72.

Crimes and Victims: A Report on the Dayton–San Jose Pilot Survey of Victimization.

Public Opinion about Crime: The Attitudes of Victims and Nonvictims in Selected Cities

Local Victim Surveys: A Review of the Issues

The Police and Public Opinion: An Analysis of Victimization and Attitude Data from 13 American Cities

An Introduction to the National Crime Survey, Compensating Victims of Violent Crime: Potential Costs and Coverage of a National Program

SECTION TWO

Victim-offender systems

The concepts of vulnerability and culpability are introduced and illustrated in this section. Papers in Chapter 5 deal with the vulnerability to crime victimization of such groups as the aged, ethnic minorities, and school children. The papers in Chapter 6 consider the concept of culpability and in doing so pick up on the theme of victim-offender relations introduced in Chapter 1. Chapter 7 addresses issues of vulnerability and culpability in relation to victimization within the family in the form of spouse beating and child abuse.

Victim vulnerability refers to the idea that people differ in their probability of being victimized. The first article in Chapter 5, by professor of law LeRoy Lamborn, provides an overview of the idea of vulnerability and notes that the probability of being victimized is related to a disadvantaged status and an ease of access by the criminal perpetrator. Family members are particularly vulnerable to being victimized, as are the aged, the young, and minorities. The article by Norman Rushforth and his medical colleagues and the article by sociologists Marvin Wolfgang and Bernard Cohen give convincing evidence of the differential vulnerability of blacks to becoming crime victims. More recent National Crime Panel data confirms this point in showing that blacks have higher victimization rates than whites for the personal crimes of violence, rape, robbery, and assault, as well as for the property crimes of auto theft and burglary.

The vulnerability of the elderly to being victimized is dealt with here in a selection from a report by the House of Representatives Select Committee on Aging. Arguing against the notion that the elderly have low victimization rates, this report points out that the elderly are particularly vulnerable to crimes of larceny with contact and robbery with injury and that economic, physical, social, and environmental factors act to increase the vulnerability of the aged to criminal victimization.

Chapter 6 returns to a consideration of the idea of victim culpability, victim responsibility, victim precipitation, or, as Schafer referred to it in Chapter 1, victim-offender relations. The selection by LeRoy Lamborn suggests six levels of victim responsibility, ranging from such lesser degrees of responsibility as direct invitation, facilitation, provocation, and perpetration, to cooperation and instigation. Lamborn is concerned with the policy implications of each of these levels of victim responsibility for punishing the offender and compensating the victim. However, no empirical evidence is offered in support of this classification, and the extent to which it actually accords with particular types of criminal incidents is an open question. The important point, however, is that the notion of victim responsibility for the genesis of the criminal act may take a variety of different forms that result in different degrees of culpability.

The paper by sociologist Lynn Curtis uses several of the levels of responsibility suggested by Lamborn in attempting to arrive at estimates of the incidence of victim responsibility in the crimes of criminal homicide, aggravated assault, robbery, and rape. A sample of police offenses and arrest reports from 17 major American cities in 1967 provides the basis for the estimates that victims not uncommonly share in responsibility for criminal homicides and aggravated assaults, less frequently share responsibility for robbery, and least commonly share responsibility for forceable rape. Finally, Curtis raises the question about the extent to which the failure of the government to bring about social change may itself be seen as precipitating violent criminal acts on the part of those subjected to institutional racism. From this type of perspective, the concept of victim responsibility begins to take on some interesting implications about who is the victim and who the offender.

A critical assessment of the central assumptions underlying the notion of victim responsibility is provided in the paper by sociologists Clyde Franklin and Alice Franklin. These authors examine several assumptions they see as basic to the notion of victim precipitation or victim responsibility and suggest that these assumptions are illogical, based on an inadequate model of human behavior, and not supported by empirical evidence. They offer an alternative perspective on victim precipitation, one that emphasizes the active role of humans in interpreting and defining interactions with others, as these interactions may culminate in the criminal act. Clearly, the Franklins do not argue against the potential utility of the concept of victim precipitation but do suggest that the way the concept has been used is open to major question and needs to be reconceptualized in order to serve as a useful explanatory formulation in victimology.

The final paper in Chapter 6, by sociologists Daniel Claster and Deborah David, looks at the idea of victim responsibility from a different perspective. Rather than taking the traditional view of the victim's responsibility for precipitating a criminal act, Claster and David consider the responsibility of the victim for resisting and interfering with the completion of a criminal act. Though it is acknowledged that victim resistance may provoke, promote, or minimize victimization, the central question addressed in this paper is the basis upon which certain classes of victims actively resist the criminal perpetrator. Using a small sample of elderly crime victims, the authors assess the extent to which victim involvement with significant social relationships was associated with resistance or compliance. They find no clear relationship between victim resistance and social disengagement.

Chapter 7 contains three articles dealing with victims of family violence—battered women, battered men, and battered children. The first article, by Del Martin, draws on her experience as a pioneer in the field of spouse battering to discuss the scope of the policy issues involved. What is a battered woman, and how many are there? What are the common responses made by police, prosecutors, judges, and social welfare agencies and programs to battered women? What kinds of public policies are required so as to better address the needs of battered women? These are among the major questions addressed in Martin's paper. Several of these questions are also addressed in Chapter 13, particularly in the paper by Ellen Pence in which she provides a case illustration of the kinds of policies, programs, and services being provided battered women in Minnesota.

Complementing Martin's paper is the discussion of battered husbands by sociologist Suzanne Steinmetz. Using both historical and contemporary data, Steinmetz argues that although not uncommon, husband beating is frequently ignored or dismissed as a social problem. The various reasons that men fail to report their victimization and that they stay in a battering situation are examined, and some stereotyped notions about the relationship of men to their families are critically addressed. Clearly, Steinmetz is not suggesting that the developing concern about the problem of battered wives be minimized; instead, she argues for a comprehensive approach to studying and dealing with family violence in its varied forms.

The final article in Chapter 7 deals with the nature and extent of child abuse within the family setting. Marc Maden and David Wrench present a comprehensive review of the research done on child abuse. They assess evidence in such key areas as incidence and characteristics of victims and perpetrators, and the research, theory, and practice implications of this evidence are identified and discussed. Quite clearly, a comprehensive approach to studying and dealing with family violence in all of its different manifestations is called for. Difficult questions of public policy and programs are, however, raised by issues of family violence. For example, what is the appropriate role of the criminal justice system in preventing and controlling violent and abusive behavior within the home setting? The privacy of marriage and the family are well guarded in American law and policy. The courts are reluctant to interfere in an ongoing marriage and will generally uphold the authority of parents over their children. Nevertheless, legislators in many of the states have seen fit to make exceptions to this policy in order to protect children from abuse and neglect by their parents. At the same time, legislators have given relatively little attention to adults being abused within the home. Although the extent and nature of adult abuse within the family has only recently begun to be documented, the evidence seems to indicate that the problem is extensive and that adults, as with children, may need outside intervention to protect them from further injury. The ethical and legal issues surrounding government intervention in the home and in the marriage relationship become especially difficult.

Chapter 5

VICTIM VULNERABILITY

A □ *The vulnerability of the victim*

LeROY LAMBORN

In the discussion of what was termed the relationship of the victim to the crime, the nature of the contacts between the victim and the criminal at the time of the crime and with direct regard to the nature of the offense was considered. Also of interest are the common characteristics of the victims of crime, including the relationship between the victim and the

Excerpted by permission of the publisher from *The Rutgers Law Review* **22**:757-760, 1968. Footnotes have been renumbered from the original for this excerpt.

criminal prior to the commission of and without regard to the crime. Knowledge of the characteristics of victims may be helpful in the prevention and detection of crime and is surely pertinent to any program of compensation of the victims. Criminologists have long theorized over the causes of crime, some even to the extent of predicting an individual's chances of becoming a criminal. Although there is a dearth of empirical research in the comparable area of victimology, it is possible, on the basis of reasoned conjecture and the result of the research that has been conducted, to construct a vulnerability index that will indicate the relative probability of an individual's becoming the victim of crime.[1] Broadly speaking, it is those factors that tend to disadvantage a person in general that makes him more vulnerable to crime. It is quite true that crimes of all types are perpetrated against persons representing all segments of society; it is also true that members of certain groups are more vulnerable than others. The persons most vulnerable to crime are the less intelligent, the very young, the very old, the female, the nonwhite, the poor, the foreign born, and the urban dweller.

Victim vulnerability may be classified according to the nature of the weakness. For example, such characteristics of the individual as the physical, the geographical, and even the psychological[2] might be listed. Reason would dictate that the female, because of their generally lesser physical strength; the very young and the very old, because of their lesser physical strength and inferior mental powers; the

nonwhite, the immigrant, and those of low income, because of their generally inferior education and the crowded, deprived areas of the country in which they are forced to live; and for example, the unstable, the depressed, and the ambitious, because of the risks that they might be willing to assume, would be most vulnerable to crime. Differences in weaknesses result in the variation of crimes to which a person is most vulnerable. The physically weak are prey to assaults and robberies. The mentally deficient and uneducated are apt to be defrauded. The poor are often unable to afford protection against the theft or damage of their property. Those forced to live in criminogenic conditions are readily accessible to all types of criminals.

Although not all criminals act rationally, certainly the reasonable criminal, upon contemplation, chooses the weaker of two otherwise equal victims. However, the ease of access to a potential victim is important in the evaluation of the desirability of attacking him rather than another person. The probability of two persons entering into the victim-criminal relationship is a function of those factors that tend to bring persons into contact or to separate them; the closer the contact, the greater the probability of crimes of passion than nonpassionate crimes and vice versa. However, even the victim of the nonpassionate crime must have some contact with the criminal. Although the opportunity for the commission of crime must not be so obvious as to point directly from the victim to the criminal, the opportunity must be sufficiently obvious to come to the attention of the criminal and to facilitate his taking advantage of it. Because criminals generally reside in the same area as their victims, the same factors that are conducive to crime are conducive to victimization. The factors that characterize areas of high crime rates are low socio-economic status of the inhabitants, high population density, substandard housing, and reliance upon social welfare agencies. Significant correlations are found between the extent of victimization and the nature of the prior relationship of the victim to the criminal, the geographical proximity of their residences, their race, and their

---

1. See, e.g., Bensing & Schroeder, *Homicide in an Urban Community* (1960); Biderman, Johnson, McIntyre & Weir, *Report on a Pilot Study in the District of Columbia on Victimization and Attitudes Toward Law Enforcement* (1967); Criminal Injuries Compensation Board, *Third Report*, Cmd. No. 3427 (1967); Ennis, *Criminal Victimization in the United States* (1967); Federal Bureau of Investigation, *District of Columbia Offenders* (Nov. 26, 1965); Federal Bureau of Investigation, *Uniform Crime Reports—1967* (1968); Gebhard, Gagnon, Pomeroy & Christenson, *Sex Offenders* (1965); McClintock, *Crimes of Violence* (1963); McClintock & Gibson, *Robbery in London* (1961); President's Commission on Law Enforcement and Administration of Justice, Task Force Report, *Crime and Its Impact—An Assessment* 80 (1967); Wolfgang, *Patterns in Criminal Homicide* (1958); Amir, *Victim Precipitated Forcible Rape,* 58 J. Crim. L.C. & P.S. 493 (1967); Bullock, *Urban Homicide in Theory and Fact,* 45 J. Crim. L.C. & P.S. 565 (1955); Morris & Blom-Cooper, *The Victim's Contribution,* in Wolfgang, *Studies in Homicide* 66 (1967); Pittman & Handy, *Patterns in Criminal Aggravated Assault,* 55 J. Crim. L.C. & P.S. 455 (1964); Pokorny, *A Comparison of Homicides in Two Cities,* 56 J. Crim. L.C. & P.S. 476 (1965); Reiss, *Measurement of the Nature and Amount of Crime,* in Reiss, *Studies in Crime and Law Enforcement in Major Metropolitan Areas* (1967).

2. See, e.g., Ellenberger, *Psychological Relationships Between Criminal and Victim,* 1 *Archives of Crim. Psychodynamics* 257 (1965); von Hentig, *The Criminal and His Victim* (1948).

economic status. The correlations are strong because of the tendencies of persons of similar backgrounds to live near one another. The correlations are not perfect because of the mixed nature of most communities, the increasingly easy means of transportation for both victims and criminals, the preference for injuring outsiders, if someone is to be injured, and the fact that persons of low economic status are not apt to have resources that are attractive to others of the same class, while persons of the highest economic status are not as apt to resort to the same types of crime. Thus it is that the male and the mature, because of their greater engagement in the processes of society, are more apt to be the victims of crimes against the person than the female, the very young, and the very old. The white, the native, and the middle class, because of their greater ownership of property, are as apt to be the victims of fraud or of theft as the nonwhite, the immigrant, and the poor.

The victim may be any of the following to the criminal: member of the family, lover, friend, acquaintance, stranger, rival, or enemy. One of the closest potential relationships between victim and criminal is membership in the same family. The crime of incest, of course, can be committed only within prescribed family limits; and rape, absent accessorial liability, cannot be committed by a husband upon his wife. But most other crimes can be committed either within or without the family unit. "Family" is an ambiguous term, potentially encompassing all persons related by blood, marriage, or adoption, present and past, and all other persons living within the household; or equally reasonably restricted to include only those persons who are presently lawful spouses and their natural, legitimate children, all presently residing in the same dwelling. Whether the broader, the narrower, or some other definition of the family is selected, the relative incidence of crime between spouses, siblings, parents and children, and other members of the family as compared to unrelated persons is of interest on three grounds. Prevention of crime is facilitated if potential victims are made aware of potential criminals and are thus able to take steps to rectify a dangerous situation or to elude the criminal. The detection of the criminal is made simpler the more that is known about the interrelationships between criminal and victim, in that the scope of the investigation is narrowed. Moreover, the extent of compensation of the victim of the crime may be dependent upon society's feelings toward making payments to one person with the knowledge that the member of that person's family who caused the injury is likely to benefit from the payment as an indirect victim of crime.

Certain crimes, those commonly called "crimes of passion," are most likely to be committed within the family unit or among persons with close personal contacts. Such crimes are the unpremeditated physical attacks. That crimes of passion are of relatively high incidence within the family should not, after reflection, be surprising. Despite the bonds of affection that bring husband and wife together, and that naturally develop between parent and child, it is the opportunity for friction that leads to crimes of passion, and the opportunity for friction is the greatest among those who have the greatest amount of contact, the members of a family. In contrast, those crimes that are not crimes of passion are less likely to be committed by one member of a family against another because of the ties of affection and the relatively great chances of detection, which are realized by the potential criminal upon reflection. The same factors that act upon family members in their relations with one another also are active, to a lesser extent, in the relationships between friends, acquaintances, and co-workers.

B □ *Violent death in a metropolitan county*

NORMAN B. RUSHFORTH, AMASA B. FORD, CHARLES S. HIRSCH,
NANCY M. RUSHFORTH and LESTER ADELSON

During the decade from 1960 to 1970, for the first time since the Great Depression, a sizable segment of the United States population experienced an increased death rate. Among men 25 to 34 years old, the overall mortality rate rose 16 per cent. The increase was 39 per cent for nonwhite men in this age range living in central-city metropolitan counties. Roughly half the increased death rate is attributable to rapidly rising homicide rates.[1] In fact, homicide has now surpassed accidents as the leading cause of death for nonwhite men 25 to 34 years old. The national increase in homicide mortality in this population group was 80 per cent (from 81.4 to 146.3 per 100,000 population); simultaneously, the rate attributable to assault by firearms and explosives jumped 135 per cent (from 45.5 to 106.7 per 100,000 population).

In a previous study,[2] we evaluated long-term trends in homicide and suicide rates in Cuyahoga County, Ohio (metropolitan Cleveland), stressing a recent marked increase in homicide frequency. The annual homicide rate had been stable from 1940 to 1960: 5.5 to 6.6 victims per 100,000 of county population. In the mid-sixties the homicide rate reached 9.4, and then escalated to 18.4 by 1970. Most of the increase occurred in the centrally located City of Cleveland. The majority of victims were black men who had been shot to death with handguns.

This study focuses on details of the homicide pattern from 1958 through 1974. To investigate changing variables, we have subdivided the 17-year interval into three periods: 1958-1962, a base-line period with a relatively low and stable homicide rate (average, 5.6); 1963-1968, an intermediate period during which the initial increase in homicide rate occurred (average, 9.2); and 1969-1974, a third period with high and slightly increasing rates (average, 19.2). This time span is longer than those evaluated in most studies of homicide and permits an analysis of changes in age, sex and race-specific homicide rates and their relation to the lethal instrument. In addition, we have analyzed patterns of justifiable and nonjustifiable homicide, felony and nonfelony homicide and intra-racial and inter-racial homicide.

METHODS

Cuyahoga County ("county") consists of the City of Cleveland ("city") and an adjacent aggregate of 36 cities, 20 villages and four townships ("suburbs"). All known or suspected violent ("unnatural") deaths in the county must be investigated by the Coroner, regardless of the fashion in which the violence arose. Only the Coroner can sign a valid death certificate when injury causes or contributes to death. Criteria for the verdicts of homicide have been consistent throughout the study period because one man (Samuel R. Gerber, M.D., L.L.B.) has been County Coroner since 1936. Data from police reports, eyewitness accounts and hospital records supplement the anatomic, toxicologic and other objective findings of the Coroner's staff.

We calculated annual homicide rates using data from the Coroner's records to determine the number of victims and from Census Bureau publications for population figures. The latter include a 1965 special census for the City of Cleveland as well as the decennial censuses of 1960 and 1970. Suburban and county populations for 1965 were estimated by linear interpolation of the decennial census figures. Average annual homicide rates for the three previously defined periods are based on population estimates for 1960, 1965 and 1970.

Printed by permission from the New England Journal of Medicine. Vol. 297, pages 531-538, September 8, 1977.

Justifiable homicide is a legally excusable killing in which the decedent was killed while perpetrating (or attempting to perpetrate) a felony or fleeing after its commission. Felony-homicides are those in which the assailant kills while committing some other serious crime such as robbery, burglary, rape, kidnapping, or arson. Traffic manslaughters are not included in our homicide data. Fatalities are tabulated according to the location of the homicidal incident (city vs. suburbs) rather than the place of death or residence of the victim.

This study analyzes homicide rates for age, race, and sex of the victim; location of the incident (city vs. suburbs); type of homicide (justifiable vs. nonjustifiable and felony vs. nonfelony); method of lethal violence; and race and sex of assailant. Race is designated as white or nonwhite; the nonwhite county population was 98.7 per cent black in 1960 and 97.3 per cent in 1970.

RESULTS
Sex and race of homicide victims

The number of homicide victims and homicide rates (unadjusted and age-adjusted) for the total county population as well as those based on race and sex are shown in Table 1. Homicide rates adjusted for changes in the age composition of the county population over the period of the study were similar to corresponding unadjusted rates, indicating that shifts in the age composition of the population had little effect. Hereafter, we report unadjusted rates, expressed as the number of victims per 100,000.

Over the 17-year interval, the total county homicide rate rose from 5.6 in the base-line period to 19.2 in the third period, a 243 per cent increase. The rise during the third period (from 18.4 in 1970 to 22.0 in 1974) was far more gradual than that in the preceding intermediate period. (The overall homicide rate in 1975 was 21.6 and in 1976 was 19.1, suggesting that for the county, the homicide rate probably has plateaued.)

In several studies of urban populations,[3-8] homicide has been reported to be disproportionately frequent among nonwhite men. The difference in homicide rates between this group and other sex and race categories increased markedly during the past decade in Cuyahoga County (Table 1). Although the greatest rise in absolute rates occurred among nonwhite men, the greatest percentage increase in homicide rate was that for white men. The relative increase from the base-line to the third period for nonwhite men was 224 per cent as compared with a corresponding rise of 289 per cent for white males. Women were killed less frequently than men of the same race, and white women had the lowest homicide rate. Nevertheless, female homicide rates for both races are now approximately double those of the initial period.

Table 1. Homicide rates in Cuyahoga County according to race and sex (1958-1974), showing number, annual rate and age-adjusted annual rate*

Group	1958-1962			1963-1968			1969-1974		
	No.	Rate	Adj. rate	No.	Rate	Adj. rate	No.	Rate	Adj. rate
	Victims/100,000 population†								
White males	91	2.7	2.6	199	5.0	5.1	418	10.5	10.5
Nonwhite males	247	39.6	39.2	520	61.2	64.8	1,220	128.3	135.7
White females	46	1.3	1.2	81	1.9	1.8	115	2.6	2.6
Nonwhite females	75	11.2	10.4	125	13.3	12.8	234	21.8	21.2
COUNTY TOTALS	459	5.6	5.3	925	9.2	9.1	1,987	19.2	19.1

*Age adjusted (Adj) with US population in 1970 as standard population.
†Census figures for county population: 1960—1,647,895; 1970—1,721,300.

Table 2. Homicide rates in the city of Cleveland and suburbs according to race and sex (1958-1974), showing number and annual rate

Group & location	1958-1962		1963-1968		1969-1974	
	No.	Rate	No.	Rate	No.	Rate
	Victims/100,000 population					
City						
White males	75	4.9	170	11.0	357	27.2
Nonwhite males	242	39.6	512	64.6	1,169	142.1
White females	32	2.0	58	3.5	75	5.2
Nonwhite females	72	11.0	121	13.7	213	22.8
CITY TOTALS	421	9.6	861	17.7	1,814	40.3
Suburbs						
White males	16	0.9	29	1.2	61	2.3
Nonwhite males	5	16.0*	8	16.0*	51	39.7
White females	14	0.7	23	0.9	40	1.4
Nonwhite females	3	8.0*	4	8.0*	21	15.0
SUBURB TOTALS	38	1.0	64	1.2	173	3.0

* Estimated rate for period 1958-1968 since there were too few nonwhites in the suburbs to calculate meaningful rates for period 1958-1962.

Homicide rates for the city of Cleveland and suburbs

In the suburbs, both races and both sexes have lower homicide rates than their counterparts in the city (Table 2). The difference is greatest for white men, since in the third period, the suburban rate is only 8.5 per cent of the city rate, whereas rates for suburban nonwhite men, white women and nonwhite women are 27.9 per cent, 26.9 per cent and 65.8 per cent of the corresponding city rates. Nevertheless, the increased number of killings is not confined to the city: homicide rates for suburbanites doubled over the base-line level.

In the city, nonwhite men had the highest homicide rate in all three periods of the study, and the rate also increased 259 per cent over the base-line value. However, the greatest relative increase occurred in white city men (455 per cent). Their rate now surpasses that of nonwhite women, altering the traditional ranking of race-sex homicide mortality found in Cleveland[3] and other urban communities.[4-6]

Age of homicide victims

A striking illustration of the changing homicide pattern in the city is provided by the age-sex-race specific rates (Table 3). During the base-line period, the highest homicide rates for white men were in the group 55 to 64 years old and for nonwhite men in the range of 35 to 44. In subsequent periods, however, the modal age shifted to 25 to 34 for all men. The rate for white women killed in the city shows a similar decreasing modal age, from 55 to 64 in the base-line period to the group 25 to 34 years old in the third period. The rate for nonwhite women in the city is highest in the group 35 to 44 years of age throughout the 17 years of the study.

City teen-agers and men in their early twenties have experienced the greatest increases in homicide rates. With use of five-year age groupings, nonwhite males, age 15 to 19, had a base-line rate of 34.5, whereas in the third period, the rate was 132.3, representing a 283 per cent increase. For white males 15 to 19 years old in the city, the increase from the intermediate to the third period was 1.1 to 20.3, a 1745 per cent jump. Increases from base-line values for corresponding groups 20 to 24 years of age were also astonishing: nonwhite males, 54.2 to 345.1 (537 per cent); and white males 4.1 to 57.7 (1307 per cent). The rise in the city white teen-age male homicide rate constituted the largest pro-

Table 3. Age-race-sex-specific annual homicide rates in the city of Cleveland (1958-74)

Age	White males			Nonwhite males			White females			Nonwhite females		
	'58-'62	'63-'68	'69-'74	'58-'62	'63-'68	'69-'74	'58-'62	'63-'68	'69-'74	'58-'62	'63-'68	'69-'74
	Victims/100,000 population			Victims/100,000 population			Victims/100,000 population			Victims/100,000 population		
15-24	2.6	14.7	39.3	44.1	92.4	214.6	0.9	4.3	3.8	14.1	19.1	35.7
25-34	8.4	23.0	51.4	82.1	167.0	344.0	3.1	5.8	9.3	18.1	25.7	34.0
35-44	6.9	18.6	43.6	83.0	126.2	253.0	3.7	8.0	6.8	24.3	26.3	41.3
45-54	6.8	12.8	32.6	57.1	89.3	193.8	2.0	2.3	5.0	12.7	18.1	31.0
55-64	10.7	7.2	29.3	37.1	43.7	113.2	4.3	0.6	5.8	4.7	10.4	13.6
65+	5.9	10.6	19.3	13.8	29.5	74.4	1.0	3.5	5.5	3.0	4.0	7.8

Table 4. Nonfelony and felony homicides in the city of Cleveland and Cuyahoga County, annual rate

Group & area	1958-1962		1963-1968		1969-1974	
	Nonfelony	Felony	Nonfelony	Felony	Nonfelony	Felony
	Victims/100,000		Victims/100,000		Victims/100,000	
City						
White males	4.1	0.8 (16.3)*	9.3	1.7 (15.5)	20.7	6.5 (23.9)
Nonwhite males	36.5	3.1 (7.8)	60.2	4.4 (6.8)	122.2	19.9 (14.0)
White females	2.0	0.0 (0.0)	3.4	0.1 (2.9)	4.6	0.6 (11.5)
Nonwhite females	11.0	0.0 (0.0)	13.7	0.0 (0.0)	21.6	1.2 (5.3)
Total county	5.2	0.4 (7.1)	8.5	0.7 (7.6)	16.3	2.9 (15.1)

*Figures in parentheses denote % felony homicides.

portionate increase for any age group. However, the largest absolute increase in homicide rate has been for city nonwhite males 25 to 29 years of age, rising from a base-line value 93.9 to 391.4 victims per 100,000 population.

Justifiable and nonjustifiable homicide

Legally excusable killings as a proportion of all homicides have remained constant, accounting for roughly 13 per cent of the total homicide rate in each study period. Approximately 75 per cent of these incidents involve civilians rather than police officers. Victims of justifiable homicide were almost exclusively male, and the rate for nonwhite males was almost eight times that of white males. In general, the rates of justifiable and nonjustifiable homicides have increased in a parallel manner in Cuyahoga County.

Felony and nonfelony homicides

Most homicide victims are killed by relatives, friends or acquaintances during or after a quarrel.[6] Although most such killings are per se felonies, they are designated as nonfelony homicides to indicate that they occurred independently of some other crime.

Killing by a stranger is almost exclusively of the felony type (that is, associated with another crime). The rising crime rates experienced in most metropolitan areas led to the prediction that more homicides would occur in conjunction with other crimes. We investigated this hypothesis using the data of the present study.

During the base-line and intermediate periods 7.1 to 7.6 per cent of all homicides in the county were committed in conjunction with another felony (Table 4). In the third period there was a doubling of the proportion of felony homicides.

Table 5. Homicides according to mode of lethal violence

Group & area	Firearms			Cutting & piercing instruments			Other modes		
	Victims/100,000			Victims/100,000			Victims/100,000		
	'58-'62	'63-'68	'69-'74	'58-'62	'63-'68	'69-'74	'58-'62	'63-'68	'69-'74
City									
White males	2.4 (48.0)*	7.5 (67.6)	20.7 (76.4)	0.8 (16.0)	1.1 (10.0)	2.5 (9.2)	1.7 (36.0)	2.4 (22.4)	3.9 (14.5)
Nonwhite males	20.4 (55.6)	45.6 (72.2)	122.0 (85.9)	12.9 (32.6)	13.8 (21.3)	10.6 (7.5)	4.3 (10.8)	5.1 (6.5)	9.4 (6.6)
White females	1.1 (53.1)	1.3 (37.9)	2.6 (50.7)	0.3 (15.6)	0.8 (22.4)	0.5 (9.3)	0.6 (31.3)	1.4 (39.7)	2.1 (40.0)
Nonwhite females	6.1 (55.6)	7.1 (52.1)	15.2 (66.7)	2.0 (18.1)	3.1 (22.3)	1.9 (8.3)	2.9 (26.3)	3.5 (25.6)	5.7 (25.0)
Total county	3.0 (54.0)	6.1 (66.8)	15.6 (81.0)	1.4 (24.8)	1.7 (18.6)	1.6 (8.2)	1.2 (21.2)	1.4 (14.6)	2.0 (10.8)

*Figures in parentheses denote % according to mode of homicide, calculated before rounding rates to 1 decimal.

Over the period of the study the total homicide rate for the county increased 243 per cent, non-felony homicides rose 213 per cent, and felony homicides jumped 625 per cent. Although the relative increase was much greater for felony than for nonfelony homicides, in terms of absolute rates nonfelony homicides still claim the great majority of victims.

Mode of lethal violence

In a previous study[2] of long-term trends in homicide rates in the county, we noted a disproportionate increase in firearm killings. The sustained increase in felony homicides and homicides among younger victims in the third period of this study prompted us to investigate the role of firearms as a mode of lethal violence. We predicted that there would be greater use of firearms in killing of younger victims and in commission of felony homicide.

In the base-line period, firearms claimed more than twice as many victims in the county as either cutting and piercing instruments or all other methods combined (Table 5). The last category consisted primarily of assaults (including fists, feet, and blunt instruments) and strangulation. In subsequent periods, firearms were used more frequently, and by the third period, they accounted for four fifths of all county homicides. Firearm homicide rates increased in all race-sex groups in the city, with the greatest relative increase (762 per cent) in white male victims. However, firearms were used in the greatest proportion of nonwhite city male homicides within each interval, accounting for 85.9 per cent of the victims in the third period.

Deaths from the use of cutting and piercing instruments became proportionately less frequent as a mode of lethal violence in the third period for all race-sex groups in the city. The decline was most dramatic in nonwhite city men, among whom there was not only a relative reduction in homicides by means of these weapons but also a decrease in the absolute homicide rates for this mode. Cutting and piercing instruments were used in 32.6 per cent of the nonwhite city male homicides during the base-line period. However, by the third period

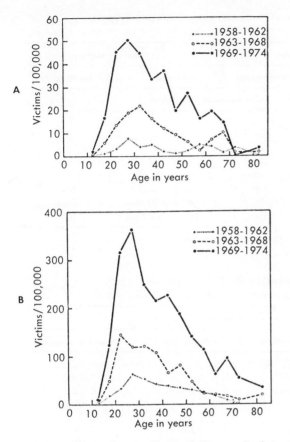

Fig. 1. Age-race-sex specific homicide rates for firearm victims in the city of Cleveland among white (A) and nonwhite (B) males.

"other modes" increased. Thus, the general increase in homicide rates does not result exclusively from a rise in deaths by firearms.

The age distribution of firearm homicides for the three periods shows that young adult men have experienced the greatest increase (Fig. 1). The pattern of increase for whites and nonwhites has been similar, with the peak in the third period at 25 to 29 years of age, but the magnitude of rates is far greater among nonwhites. Clearly, the general escalation of homicide rates among young men has been mainly an increase in firearm homicides.

The use of firearms in felony and nonfelony male homicides in the city is compared for the time periods in Table 6. The proportion of white male felony homicide victims killed by firearms remained constant at a level of roughly 76 per cent during the 17-year study interval, although the rate of these killings increased by 600 per cent. For this group, the increase in firearm deaths was more conspicuous in nonfelony homicides, in addition to which the rate jumped 829 per cent. Nonwhite men, starting with high firearm rates, experienced substantial relative and absolute increases of firearm deaths in both felony and nonfelony homicides. Almost all felony homicides in this group are now committed with guns, and the felony and nonfelony firearm homicide rates rose by 631 per cent and by 421 per cent, respectively. The preponderant increase in the use of guns in nonfelony deaths suggests that increasing availability of firearms is converting more quarrels into fatalities.[9]

Race and sex of assailant

Earlier studies,[4-7] including one in Cleveland,[3] demonstrated that most homicides were intra-racial. However, in 1973 Block and Zimring[8] reported an increasing proportion of white men slain by nonwhite men in Chicago. We evaluated our data to determine whether interracial homicide had increased in Cuyahoga County.

Table 7 shows homicide rates for each sex-race group in the city, matching assailant with victim for incidents having a known single assailant and victim. Victims with known single

deaths by this mode had decreased to only 7.5 per cent.

A surprising finding was that, among white women living in the city, there was a greater relative increase in homicide by modes other than firearms or cutting and piercing instruments. In this group, for whom homicide rates are relatively low in all periods, the rate of victimization with firearms more than doubled, and rates of homicide with piercing and cutting instruments increased by two thirds, whereas the rates for other modes more than tripled. Firearm homicides dropped slightly in this group as a proportion of all homicides between the initial and third periods, whereas rates for

Table 6. Mode of lethal violence for felony and nonfelony city male homicides, annual rate

	White males		Nonwhite males	
	Firearms	Nonfirearms	Firearms	Nonfirearms
Period & type of homicide	Victims/100,000 population			
Felony homicides				
1958-62	0.7 (76.9)*	0.2	2.6 (84.2)	0.5
1963-68	1.3 (74.1)	0.5	4.4 (100.0)	0.0
1969-74	4.9 (76.5)	1.5	19.0 (95.5)	0.9
Nonfelony homicides				
1958-62	1.7 (41.9)	2.4	19.8 (54.3)	16.7
1963-68	6.2 (66.4)	3.1	42.2 (70.1)	18.0
1969-74	15.8 (76.0)	5.0	103.1 (84.6)	18.8

*Figures in parentheses denote % firearms, calculated before rounding rates to 1 decimal.

Table 7. Race and sex of victim and known assailant in the city of Cleveland (1958-74) (ratio of victims per 100,000 victim population to victims per 100,000 assailant population)

	Assailants			
Victims & period	White males	White females	Nonwhite males	Nonwhite females
White males				
1958-62	2.6/2.6	0.5/0.5	1.0/2.5	0.0/0.0
1963-68	6.0/6.0	0.8/0.8	2.1/4.2	0.1/0.1
1969-74	12.0/12.0	1.1/1.0	5.6/9.2	0.8/1.0
White females				
1958-62	1.4/1.5	0.0/0.0	0.1/0.3	0.1/0.2
1963-68	2.1/2.1	0.3/0.3	0.4/5.3	0.1/0.1
1969-74	2.8/3.0	0.3/0.3	0.6/1.1	0.0/0.0
Nonwhite males				
1958-62	3.1/1.2	0.3/0.1	24.6/24.6	9.8/9.2
1963-68	3.7/1.9	0.4/0.2	38.1/38.1	15.9/14.3
1969-74	6.3/3.9	0.5/0.3	81.8/81.8	23.2/20.8
Nonwhite females				
1958-62	0.0/0.0	0.2/0.1	9.0/9.7	0.6/0.6
1963-68	0.2/0.1	0.0/0.0	9.6/10.7	1.8/1.8
1969-74	0.2/0.2	0.0/0.0	15.4/17.8	1.7/1.7

assailants constituted between 70 and 95 per cent of all victims in the four race-sex groups for the three periods. Inter-racial attacks increased in both directions for males in the city. To avoid distortion, however, these data must be viewed in the light of trends in the population's changing racial composition. Two rates are calculated: victims per 100,000 of victim population and victims per 100,000 of assailant population. For example, the homicide rate for white male victims in the city slain by other white men increased from 2.6 to 12.0 (362 per cent) during the study interval, and their death rate at the hands of nonwhite men increased from 1.0 to 5.6 (460 per cent). However, calculation of the city white male inter-racial homicide rate in terms of the nonwhite male assailant population shows a smaller proportionate increase from 2.5 to 9.2 (268 per cent). This difference is explained by a relative increase in the city nonwhite as compared to white male population over the 17-year period. Thus, if one considers the changing racial composition of the city, there is no disproportionate increase in the frequency with which black men kill white men. The homicide rate for nonwhite men in the city killed by other nonwhite men increased from 24.6 to 81.8 (233 per cent) whereas their homicide rate by white men rose from 3.1 to 6.3 (103 per cent). However, calculation of the city nonwhite male homicide rate in terms of the white male assailant population shows a greater relative increase, from 1.2 to 3.9 (225 per cent).

Analysis of the percentage of homicide victims according to type of assailant shows that the majority of victims are killed by male assailants of the same race (62 to 92 per cent). Taking population changes into account, there has been no consistent change in this pattern over the 17 years covered by the study. Thus, our data support those of previous studies showing that homicide remains primarily an intra-racial crime committed by men.[3-7]

DISCUSSION

The homicide trends reported in this study shock us. What has happened in Cleveland reflects, in a magnified way, national trends during the same period. Total and age-adjusted homicide rates for the United States also showed a relatively low base line in 1958-1962, a sharp increase from 1963 through 1968, and a continued rise from 1969 through 1973.[1]

Nationally, as in Cuyahoga County, rates have increased dramatically for both sexes and among whites and nonwhites, with the greatest absolute increase occurring in nonwhite men and the greatest relative increase among white men. The proportion of homicide victims slain by firearms, which was slightly over 50 per cent in both the United States and Cuyahoga County in 1960, rose steeply by 1973 to 67 and 81 per cent, respectively. The proportion of felony homicides also increased both nationally and lo-

cally, but the local figure of 15 per cent based on Coroner's reports was lower than the national figure of 29 per cent (felony and suspected felony) estimated by the Federal Bureau of Investigation on the basis of police reports.[10]

In other respects, however, the picture of homicide in Cuyahoga County is even more somber than in the nation as a whole and worse than that of many comparable cities. In 1970, Cleveland and Detroit had identical homicide rates of 34.5 per 100,000 population, second only to St. Louis (with a rate of 39.9).

The increase in homicide rates between 1960 and 1970 in the most severely affected group —namely, young men—has been twice as great in our county as the average for other metropolitan counties containing central cities. These, in turn, have experienced greater increases than the country as a whole (Table 8).

The impact of this change has been so great that, during the 1960's among United States men 25 to 34 years of age, half again as many were killed in domestic homicides as in Vietnam. For these young men, mortality from all causes, excluding war casualties, rose 15 per cent during the decade.[11] Four of the six leading causes of death showed increases during this time, ranging from 18 per cent for accidents to 85 per cent for homicides. Young nonwhite men (85 per cent black) suffered the most. They started with higher mortality rates from accidents, homicides and cirrhosis than those experienced by white men and experienced greater absolute increases in all three categories by 1970. Homicide rates for young nonwhite men have increased to the point that they now surpass accidents as the leading cause of death in these age groups. Nonwhite suicide rates, which were lower in 1960 than those for their white contemporaries, rose to become virtually equal to white rates by 1970.

Since 1930, the expectation of life at all ages has been rising in the United States. The estimated length of life for all Americans increased from 59.7 years in 1930 to 70.9 years in 1970, with gains of 9.0 years for males, 13.2 years for females, 10.3 years for whites and 17.2 years for nonwhites. In the 1960-1970 decade, however, the pattern for young nonwhite males was

Table 8. Average annual homicide death rates per 100,000 men, 25 to 34 years of age, 1959-61 and 1969-71, United States and Cuyahoga County

Period & area	White males			All other males			Total males		
		Decade change			Decade change			Decade change	
	Death rate	Rate	%	Death rate	Rate	%	Death rate	Rate	%
1959-61									
US	5.9			81.4			14.3		
Metropolitan counties with central cities	6.2			80.5			16.3		
Cuyahoga County	5.2			98.3			22.3		
1969-71									
US	12.9	7.0	119	146.3	64.9	80	28.3	14.0	98
Metropolitan counties with central cities	15.3	9.1	147	155.9	75.4	94	36.1	19.8	121
Cuyahoga County	17.7	12.5	240	278.4	180.1	183	67.0	44.7	200

broken. During these 10 years, the average life expectancy for nonwhite males between one and 20 dropped by more than a year. For example, a nonwhite male aged 20 could expect to live 45.8 more years in 1960 but only 44.7 more years in 1970. In contrast, the expected survival of a 20-year-old white male remained stable (50.2 years in 1960 and 50.3 in 1970).[11] The major factor in the increasing mortality rate and resultant decreased life expectancy among young nonwhite males during the past decade was the increase in homicides.

The marked rise in firearm killings in Cuyahoga County documented in this study is also evident in the national pattern of homicide. The homicide rate among young American adults killed by firearms and explosives increased from 4.6 in 1960 to 11.6 in 1973.[12] The percentage of all United States homicides committed by these means rose from 54.7 to 67.2 during this period,[1] as compared to an increase from 54.0 to 81.0 per cent in Cuyahoga County.

Several studies suggest that an important factor contributing to increased homicide rates in the United States over the past decade is the more ready availability of firearms, especially handguns.[13] During this period, increases in production, importation and ownership of firearms were accompanied by increases in both the national firearm homicide rate and the proportion of homicides caused by firearms. Moreover, rates of accidental firearm deaths and the proportion of homicides and aggravated assault with firearms have been found to be positively associated with gun ownership in various geographic regions of the United States.[14] In Cuyahoga County, a threefold increase in accidental firearm fatalities has paralleled the dramatic increase in homicides with firearms documented here.[15]

The President's Commission on Law Enforcement and Administration of Justice noted that gun use and crime are associated with handgun availability,[16] suggesting that the relatively low rates of gun use in crimes committed in New York City result in part from the strict screening of would-be purchasers and the use of permit procedures for firearms. On the basis of their study of foreign crime statistics, Etzioni and Remp conclude that the availability of handguns significantly increases rates of homicide and armed robbery.[17] Thus, there is a positive correlation between gun availability and homicide rates.

Guns are so numerous in the United States that about half of all American homes harbor at least one firearm. In 1968, a time of rapid acceleration in homicide rates, it was estimated that 90 million firearms, of which 24 million were handguns, were in civilian hands.[14] Fear of crime, violence and civil disorders apparently stimulated the sales of handguns in the nation's cities.

Roughly two thirds of respondents in a 1968 survey cited "protection" as the reason for owning a handgun. Unfortunately, this goal of security through gun possession is illusory. A handgun in the home is more likely to be used in a domestic homicide or to cause serious injury, intentional or accidental, than to deter a robber or burglar.[13] In Cuyahoga County, firearms in the home are six times as likely to cause accidental deaths as to kill an intruder.[15]

It is alleged that a gun is merely a passive instrument in the hand of a person intent on killing someone. Implicit in this belief is the assumption that assailants would use knives or other weapons with equally lethal efficiency if guns were not available. However, evidence indicates that this belief is erroneous. Homicide is usually not the result of a coldly calculated, premeditated intent to kill. The majority of these deaths occur during attacks precipitated by enraged quarrels. Most killings involve persons acquainted with each other "where spontaneous violence is generated and the weapon is used to win a fight or wreak vengeance or injury, whether or not this means that a death will result."[18]

There is a striking similarity between many fatal attacks and those that do not result in death. (The latter constitute aggravated assault.) Both involve the same kinds of victims and assailants, occur in similar circumstances and have their highest frequencies at the same hours of the day and the same days of the week. However, assaults in which a gun is used are five times more likely to result in death than assaults involving a knife, the next most lethal weapon.[14]

When guns are used in the commission of other crimes, they increase the probability of a fatal outcome. Armed robberies, in which a gun is the "arm," are four times more likely than other kinds of robberies to end in the death of the victim.[18] Firearms are the most destructive of readily available weapons in modern society. They permit an attack at a greater distance by persons who are unable to overpower their victims by other means. However, in most homicides the choice of a gun in preference to other modes of assault does not depend on the circumstances precipitating the incident. Data from a Chicago study indicate that the motive for an attack does not determine the weapon used. Comparable situations exist in firearm and knife homicides.[14] Evidence suggests that assailants using firearms are no more intent on killing their victims than those who use knives or other methods of assault.

The foregoing evidence leads to the conclusion that homicide rates would fall if the availability of firearms, particularly handguns, were decreased, an opinion with which the Staff Report on Firearms and Violence in American Life concurs.[14]

Although greater availability (and consequent misuse) of handguns in prominently involved in the increased homicide rate observed in the past decade, other factors have also played an important part. Somers,[19] in calling attention to the alarming increases in homicide rates among children and teen-agers, implicates a "culture of violence," which has become a way of life for large segments of the nation's youth. She maintains that television's daily diet of synthetic crime and violence is a contributory factor.

Although our data show a disproportionate increase in firearm killings for most groups in the city of Cleveland, an exception is the greater relative increase in city white female homicides by modes other than firearms. This finding suggests an increase in homicides not attributable solely to the greater availability and abuse of handguns.

Elements contributing to increased homicide rates are numerous and complex. They are unlikely to act as single causal agents, functioning rather as a meshwork of interacting factors. Although we have emphasized the role of firearms, other contributory components deserve detailed study. Alcohol as a catalyst for violence, for example, has been implicated in the events frequently leading to homicide.[3,6]

In addition to further description of overall trends, epidemiologic investigations of homicide that analyze additional component elements are needed. New approaches to the problem call for methods using specific homicide types, as suggested by Bourdois.[7] Future studies should relate the interactions of physical, psychologic, socioeconomic, political and cultural factors in the etiology of homicide. Similar studies of suicide and fatal accidents may ultimately define constellations of factors that are responsible for the increase in violent death in our urban communities and may point the way to effective prevention.

REFERENCES

1. Klebba AJ: Homicide trends in the United States, 1900-74. Public Health Rep 90:195-204, 1975
2. Hirsch CS, Rushforth NB, Ford AB, et al: Homicide and suicide in a metropolitan county. I. Long-term trends. JAMA 223:900-905, 1973
3. Bensing RC, Schroeder O Jr: Homicide in an Urban Community. Springfield, Illinois, CC Thomas, 1960
4. Bullock HA: Urban homicide in theory and fact. J Crim Law Crim Pol Sci 45: 565-575, 1955
5. Harlan H: Five hundred homicides. J Crim Law Crim Pol Sci 49:736-752, 1950
6. Wolfgang ME: Patterns in Criminal Homicide. Philadelphia, University of Pennsylvania Press, 1958
7. Bourdois J: Trends in Homicide, Detroit: 1926-1968. Dissertation, Wayne State University, 1970
8. Block B, Zimring RE: Homicide in Chicago, 1965-1970. J Res Crime Delinquency 10:1-12, 1973
9. Goldstein JH: Aggression and Crimes of Violence. New York, Oxford University Press, 1975
10. United States Department of Justice, Federal Bureau of Investigation: Crime in the United States, 1973. Washington, DC, Federal Bureau of Investigation, September, 1974
11. Department of Health, Education, and Welfare: Vital Statistics of the United States. Vol 2, Section 5, (Life tables). 1970 and 1973
12. Weiss NS: Recent trends in violent deaths among young adults in the United States. Am J. Epidemiol 103:416-422, 1976
13. Alviani JD, Drake WF: Handgun control: Issues and alternatives. Presented at the United States Conference of Mayors, Washington, DC, 1975
14. Newton GD Jr, Zimring FE: Firearms and Violence in American Life: A staff report submitted to the National Commission on the Causes and Prevention of Violence. Washington, DC, Government Printing Office, 1969
15. Rushforth NB, Hirsch CS, Ford AB, et al: Accidental firearm fatalities in a metropolitan county (1958-1973). Am J Epidemiol 100:499-505, 1974
16. President's Commission on Law Enforcement and Administration of Justice: The Challenge of Crime in a Free Society. Washington, DC, Government Printing Office, 1967
17. Etzioni A, Remp R: Technological "shortcuts" to social change. Science 175:31-38, 1972
18. Zimring FE: Getting serious about guns. Nation, April 10, 1972
19. Somers AR: Violence, television and the health of American youth. N Engl J Med 294:811-817, 1976

C □ *Crime and race*

The victims of crime

MARVIN E. WOLFGANG and BERNARD COHEN

We have thus far raised questions about systematic errors in available information about known crimes and persons arrested, and have pointed out that there has been little research either about the extent to which police practice discrimination in making arrests, or how much lower Negro crime rates would be if there were no differential treatment at the police level.

However, there are several questions on which research does cast some light: (1) Who are the victims of crime or who suffer most from criminality? (2) Is the oft-expressed fear among whites of being victimized by non-white criminals justifiable?

Until recently, there was virtually no information on the victims of crime in the United States, except for some useful and consistent local data on homicide and forcible rape. For the past few years, however, the UCR has been publishing data on homicides for the entire

Reprinted by permission of the American Jewish Committee, Institute of Human Relations, from Marvin Wolfgang and Bernard Cohen, *Crime and Race: Conceptions and Misconceptions* (New York: American Jewish Committee, 1970), pp. 40-56. Table has been renumbered for internal consistency.

nation. The President's Crime Commission also presented the results of several studies based upon national samples of victims of property and violent crimes.

The UCR reveals that throughout the nation during 1967 Negroes were the most likely victims of homicide. Even in absolute numbers more blacks than whites were slain—5,990 blacks compared with 5,011 whites. Thus, while blacks comprise approximately 10 per cent of the population, they constituted 54 per cent of the homicide victims. Most of these victims were males between 15 and 44; few were women, children or elderly people.[1]

Information about the victims of a wider range of offenses was obtained through the special survey conducted by the National Opinion Research Center (NORC) for the President's Crime Commission,[2] covering a probability sample of 10,000 households and providing intensive interviews with each victim of a crime. The information sought included the type of crime, its location, the extent of injury, theft or damage, whether police were notified, and if not, the reasons for failing to report the incident.

The NORC data provide a great deal of new

Table 1. Victims of serious personal and property crimes per 100,000 population—by race and income level (1966)

Type of crime	Incomes under $6,000		Incomes $6,000 or more	
	Whites	Negroes	Whites	Negroes
Against person	402	738	244	262
Against property	1,829	1,927	1,765	3,024
(Number of interviews)	(10,008)	(3,462)	(15,452)	(1,827)

Source *Field Surveys II, Criminal Victimization in the United States: A Report of a National Survey,* by P. H. Ennis, The President's Commission on Law Enforcement and Administration of Justice, 1967, p. 32.

information on a national scale for index crimes other than homicide. A major finding is that non-whites are victimized more often than whites, not only by homicide, but also by robbery, rape, aggravated assault, burglary and auto theft. Only in crimes involving larceny $50 and over are whites more often the victims, most likely because fewer blacks possess large sums of money and expensive items. Black victim rates also are relatively low for such minor crimes as simple assault, malicious mischief and fraud.

Although blacks are consistently more often victimized than whites, the NORC findings show, there are differences according to economic levels (Table 1). In serious crimes against persons, blacks with incomes below $6,000 are almost twice as likely to be victims as whites in the same income group; in the income category above $6,000 the discrepancy is much smaller. With respect to property crimes the opposite pattern prevails.

Blacks with incomes below $6,000 are only slightly more likely to be victims than are their white counterparts, but more affluent blacks are a great deal more likely to be victimized than are more affluent whites. Presumably, residential segregation increases the more affluent Negro's risk of being burglarized, because he lacks the protection provided in sheltered middle-class neighborhoods.

Another special field survey conducted for the President's Crime Commission examined victim data secured from the Chicago Police Department for the period September 1965 to March 1966.[3] When the race and sex of offenders and their victims in cases of rape, robbery and assault were analyzed, the patterns that emerged were similar to those of the NORC study. For all major offenses against the person, black males were most often the victims. As many as four out of 100 Negro men are victims of a robbery or assault and battery each year, and black women run the second highest risk of suffering such offenses. Thus, three out of every 100 Negro women are the victims of rape, robbery or assault and battery in Chicago each year.

White men and women have much less reason to fear attack than blacks. Fewer than one out of 100 white men is likely to be attacked in any given year; the probability rate for white women is much lower (35 out of 100,000).

The fear of being raped or assaulted is most real for Negro women. According to available statistics, Negro women are 18 times more likely to be victims of rape than are white women; and black women, like black men, stand a much greater chance of suffering armed or strong-armed robbery.

The data on assault with a dangerous weapon revealed that black males run the greatest risk of being shot, cut or stabbed (20 times greater than for white males), and black females run the next highest risk. The risks are lowest for white men and white women in that order. A Negro woman is four times more likely to be shot than a white man, and eight times more likely to be stabbed.

In summary, the Chicago study showed that the danger of being a victim of rape, robbery or assault and battery is six times greater for Negro men than for white men. The likelihood of a Negro woman being victimized is about eight times greater than that of a white woman and even four times higher than that of a white man. Regardless of sex, blacks are much more likely than whites to be victims of serious crimes against the person. These statistics suggest that blacks have an equal if not greater stake in reducing crime than do whites.

VICTIM AND OFFENDER: HOMICIDE, RAPE, ROBBERY AND ASSAULT

Since the statistics indicate that blacks attack, rob, and assault others more often than whites, most people, white or black, tend to anticipate and fear attacks by blacks.

It has been difficult to determine the validity of this assumption, because there are few data about the race of the victim related to the race of the offender. Even among the relatively small sample of property offenses which result in arrest, no systematic nationwide collection of criminal statistics is published about this kind of victim-offender relationship. However, for two particular types of crimes, homicide and rape, there are some useful and consistent data. Also, during the last three years a number of studies on victim-offender relationships for robbery as well as other assaultive crimes have been published.[4]

Enough research has been conducted to permit the definite statement that criminal homicide, like most other assaultive offenses, is predominately an intragroup, intraracial act. In a detailed five-year study of homicides in Philadelphia (1948-1952), it was noted that in 516, or 94 per cent, of the 550 identified relationships, the victim and offender were members of the same race.[5] Hence, in only 34, or 6 per cent, of these homicides did an offender cross the race line: 14 were Negro victims slain by whites, and 20 were whites slain by Negroes. The ratio of same-race (intraracial) to different-race (interracial) homicide was as high as 15 to 1. In terms of rates per 100,000 population it is interesting to note that while Negro offenders (1.0) crossed the race line more often than did whites (.2), Negroes were victims (.7) of white offenders approximately three times more frequently than were whites (.2) of Negro offenders. These are criminal homicides as recorded in police reports. If justifiable homicides (14 during the five years in Philadelphia) were included, the total of interracial homicides would be somewhat larger, for 12 persons slain by white police officers were Negroes while two were whites.

Summarizing other research, Sutherland noted that "in crimes of personal violence the victims and the offenders are generally of the same racial group, and have residence not far apart. Negroes murder Negroes, Italians murder Italians, and Chinese murder Chinese."[6]

The amount of interracial homicide and the relative frequency with which whites and Negroes cross the race line vary slightly in different parts of the country; but most data indicate that more whites slay Negroes than vice versa. Speaking primarily about the South, Porterfield says that "whites kill many more nonwhite men than vice versa, probably five times as many. A Negro does not dare to kill a white man as a rule. The consequences are too painful; but probably four-fifths of Negro homicide victims are struck down by members of their own race."[7]

Harrington C. Brearley refers to the fact that mortality data from the Office of Vital Statistics on causes of death give no information regarding interracial slayings: "If, obviously, the Negro is more often slain by whites than he, himself, slays a white victim, his homicide death rate is not an accurate index of his tendency to commit deeds of violence. Little evidence upon this point is available, for the death certificates upon which all homicide rates are based give information concerning the slain only."[8]

A few studies do report on the race of victims and offenders. In Memphis, Tennessee, during 1923, Frederick L. Hoffman found seven Negroes killed by whites, and only two whites by Negroes.[9] A.A. Bruce and P. S. Fitzgerald, referring to the same city between 1920 and 1925, during which time there were 379 known cases, said that 3 per cent were whites slain by Negroes, in contrast to 13 per cent Negroes killed by whites.[10] In New York City during 1925, Brearley points out, 68 Negroes were feloniously killed, of whom 20 were not slain by Negroes; and in South Carolina, of a total of 89 interracial homicides, 32 whites were killed by Negroes, and 57 Negroes by whites.[11] In Chicago, a survey for 1926-1927 showed that white males killed 14 per cent of all Negro male victims, and Negro males were responsible for 12 per cent of all white male victims.[12]

Harold Garfinkel, who studied 821 cases of homicide which occurred in 10 North Carolina counties from 1930 to 1940, found that 9 per cent of the homicides were interracial, of which the victims were 6 per cent Negro and 3 per cent white.[13] In a report by Arthur C. Meyers on 212 criminal homicides in St. Louis from 1949 to 1951, only six cases, or less than 3 per cent, were interracial.[14] And in a study of aggravated assaults, David J. Pittman and William Handy found that of the 238 cases which represented a one-quarter sample in St. Louis in 1961, only 10 cases, or 4 per cent, were interracial.[15]

Howard Harlan found that of the 500 consecutive criminal homicides committed in Birmingham, Alabama, during the period from January 1937 to December 1944, less than 3 per cent crossed race lines.[16] This is considerably less than the 6 per cent in the Philadelphia study. But in Birmingham as in Philadelphia, female offenders never crossed race lines when killing females. Furthermore, in Birmingham, all interracial offenses were among males, but in Philadelphia, females were involved both as victims and offenders.

More recent research shows similar patterns. A Chicago replication of the Philadelphia study, involving all cases of criminal homicide filed in Chicago from January 1, 1965 through December 31, 1965, revealed that the overwhelming majority of homicides were intraracial.[17] Of the 394 homicides for which the race of the victim and offender were known, 93 per cent involved offenders and victims of the same race. Only in 6.6 per cent of the cases were racial lines crossed. A study of homicide in Queens County, New York, showed that, in 1967, out of 52 cases in which the race of offender and victim were known, only four (or 8 per cent) involved interracial slayings.[18]

These findings leave no doubt that criminal homicide, like rape and aggravated assault, is overwhelmingly an intraracial phenomenon, mostly among inmates and acquaintances, as the National Violence Commission reaffirmed in its 17-city survey in 1969. From these studies it should be clear that if whites are afraid that Negroes are likely to attack and slay them, the fear is not supported by what we know about interracial crime. Most of the evidence suggests the contrary, that Negroes are more likely to be killed by whites. And certainly any fear among white women of being slain by Negro men should be dispelled by examining the real world. Not only does the evidence we have from Philadelphia show that the number of Negro women slain by white men equals that of white women slain by Negro men, but of the three white victims, two were prostitutes and had long criminal records, while of the three Negro victims, none had a criminal record. Moreover, only three cases of each type occurred in this community of two million population over a five-year period. It also may be of interest that all three of the Negro offenders were convicted of first degree murder, one being sentenced to death and the others to life imprisonment. Of the three white offenders, one was sent to a mental hospital and had no trial, one was still

awaiting trial at the time of the study, and the third received a two-year county prison sentence for voluntary manslaughter.[19]

It is clear from many reports and research over the years that the non-white population has a rate of committing homicide that sometimes and in some places exceeds the white rate by three, four and even 10 times.[20] What is often overlooked by the non-research community is that these crime rates vary considerably within each racial group by community and region. Referring to general homicide death rates, Sutherland pointed out that "the high crime rates in the Southern states are generally interpreted as due to the large number of Negroes, but it is evident that homicides, at least, cannot be explained so simply, for the death rate by homicide for white persons in the South is approximately five times as high as in New England."[21]

This same generalization seems borne out when the Philadelphia data are compared with material collected by Harlan[22] in Birmingham, where the white offender rate (5.8) was over three times higher than the white offender rate in Philadelphia (1.8).

In a concise analysis of homicide death rates by racial and regional groups, George Vold said that the homicide rates for the New England States are generally low partly because the black population there is very small.[23] But Vold also cautioned:

Lest anyone conclude . . . that regional differences in homicide are equivalent to, or due only to, differences in the proportions of the total population classed as other than white, attention is invited to the similar consistent and large differences in the rates as between regions for the white group alone.

When comparisons are made between the state of Massachusetts and Georgia, the following will be found to obtain: The homicide rate of the white group in Georgia (5.6) is almost exactly four times as high as that of the white group in Massachusetts (1.4); the Georgia "other than white rate" (47.1) is likewise almost exactly four times the "other than white" rate (11.8) for Massachusetts. This basic regional or sectional difference must be recognized and taken account of, independent of, and in spite of, the obviously important differences between the several major racial groups.[24]

Although no exhaustive attempt has been made in this present analysis to examine regional differences in the racial complexion of homicide, a few additional comments may be pertinent.

Returning to Birmingham and Philadelphia as examples of segregated and relatively unsegregated communities, Harlan found that 85 per cent of the 492 offenders were Negro, and that this race comprised 40 per cent of the Birmingham population.[25] In sum, the proportion of Negro offenders in criminal homicide was twice the proportion of blacks in the general population. But in Philadelphia, 75 per cent of the offenders were Negro, although this race made up only 18 percent of the population. Thus, in Philadelphia, blacks contributed four times their expected "share" of offenders. In this type of comparative analysis, which describes Negro killings within the context of a Northern city on the one hand, and a Southern city on the other, it appears at first that in their total settings blacks are twice as homicidal in the North as in the South.

But when rates per 100,000 population are used in the comparison, both Negroes and whites in Birmingham appear to have committed criminal homicide more often than the respective races in Philadelphia. The general criminal homicide rate in Birmingham (23.4) was over four times higher than that for Philadelphia (5.7). In the Southern city the Negro victim rate (49.0) and the offender rate (48.0) were approximately twice as high as the rates for Philadelphia Negroes (22.5; 25.6). In Birmingham, white victim and offender rates (5.8) were three times greater than those for Philadelphia whites (1.8; 1.9).[26] Hence, in order to determine propensity to commit criminal homicide, the rate per population unit is necessary.

Rape is one other type of offense in which the relationship between victims and offenders is an important aspect, but unfortunately little research has ever been done on it. Like homicide and other assaults, rape is overwhelmingly intraracial and intragroup. Generally, the nonwhite arrest rate is three to four times higher than the white arrest rate.[27] Donald R. Taft noticed this for 1927, as have many other writers up to Thorsten Sellin in 1962.[28-34] James E. McKeown, who related rates of rape with the proportion of Negroes in a community, contended that there was so much variation from year to year and from city to city that no conclusion could be justified regarding the association.[35]

It was at first suggested that rape rates for blacks were high only in the South. Edward B. Reuter showed that, for the first decade of the present century, Negroes accounted for 66 per cent of rapes in that region, but only 13 per cent in the North, a proportion about the same as the black population in the North. But more recently, other references—for Philadelphia, Washington, California, Ohio and Michigan—show more non-whites committing rape than they represent in these respective populations.[36-41]

Some reports suggest that Negroes commit rape less frequently than whites.[42-51] Most of the latter studies, however, have used prison statistics or selected groups seen in clinics to which courts have made referrals. Perhaps Taft's conclusion comes closest to what studies indicate—that although the Negro is punished for rape far more than the white, the reason is that blacks, more often than whites, are charged with rape regardless whether the victim is Negro or white.

In Menachem Amir's study of rape in Philadelphia for a two-year period, 1958 and 1960, the race of victim and of offender in each situation was noted, an aspect of research design rarely considered.[52] Of 616 cases of known relationships, 497, or 77 per cent, were black-black; 105, or 16 per cent, were white-white. Among the 44 cases in which the offender was of one race and the victim of another, 23, or 3.6 per cent, contained a white male offender and a Negro victim, and 21, or 3.3 per cent, had a Negro offender and a white victim. Once again, the amount of race crossing is small, and the danger to white women is as minimal as to Negro women—probably much less if we stretch beyond officially recorded statistics and refer to the history of race relations from the days of slavery to recent times.

White males have long had a nearly institutionalized access to Negro women without much fear of reprisal or retribution. In the social tradition of the South, the reverse has always been considered an anathema. In North and South alike (as well as East and West), there is probably greater white male accessibility to Negro girls through subterranean associations such as houses of prostitution, street walkers and call girls. Even with, or perhaps because of, these options of opportunity, there are numerically as many rapes of Negro women by white men as occur in the reverse relationship. One would expect in a society where the law, the police, and the courts are dominated by whites, that if immunity exists, if justice is not always equal, white rapists will be less frequently arrested and convicted. Aside from this reasonable assumption, the total amount of interracial rape recorded is small.

The Chicago victim study mentioned earlier, in addition to identifying the victims of crime, explored victim-offender relationships for crimes of rape, robbery and assault.[53] It was noted that a white woman's risk of being attacked by a black is less than half that of being victimized by a white. Moreover, a white woman is more likely to be victimized by another white woman than by a black woman, and a black woman is more likely to be victimized by a black woman than by a white man or woman. Similarly, white and black men are both more likely to be victims of their own race than of another race.

These findings are consistent with André Normandeau's very detailed study of 1,722 cases of robbery that occurred in Philadelphia between 1960 and 1966. He reported that 76 per cent of the robberies were intraracial: in 63 per cent Negroes robbed Negroes, and in 13 per cent whites robbed whites.[54] For these serious crimes of violence (rape, robbery, aggravated assault) as well as homicides, the victim and offender were usually of the same race.

Gang violence is another type of intraracial crime. Not only are there structured juvenile gangs, made up primarily of minority-group youth, but their victims, too, are minority-group members.[55] One study comparing the patterns of delinquency of organized gangs and spon-

taneously formed groups in Philadelphia found that 96 per cent of all delinquent gangs (104) were black.[56] Only four of the gangs were white. Equally revealing, the overwhelming majority of victims were also black. Virtually 100 per cent of the gang assaults involved victims and offenders of the same race. Negro boys were almost 100 times more likely to be assaulted by gangs than white boys, and black girls ran a three-and-one-half times greater risk than white boys. Not a single white girl was attacked by a gang.

In summary, the major facts about victims and offenders in crimes of violence are as follows:[57]

1) Whites are much less likely than blacks to be victims of major violent crimes.
2) An individual, black or white, has most to fear from persons of his own race.
3) Both men and women are most likely to be victimized by men of their own race.
4) White women are least likely to be victims of major violent crimes, but Negro women run a risk substantially greater than do white men.
5) Among the few crimes that cross racial lines, Negro men are the most likely offenders.
6) In cases of robbery, whites are most likely to be victimized by Negroes.
7) In interracial crimes of assault and battery, more Negroes are victimized by whites. That is, whites attack and assault blacks more often than blacks attack and assault whites.
8) Negro women are the most likely victims in forcible rape and assault with intent to rape.
9) Negro men are the most likely victims in cases of robbery and major assaults with a dangerous weapon resulting in injury.
10) Negroes figure most frequently in major crimes against the person, both as victims and as offenders.

FEARS AND REALITIES

How do these facts compare with people's fears about crime? During 1966, 511 randomly selected adults in three police precincts in the District of Columbia were interviewed on this subject.[58] An index of anxiety was constructed, reflecting both concern for personal safety in an individual's immediate surroundings as well as a more generalized concern about crime. The scale items included safety as a criterion for choosing a place to live, perception of personal safety in a neighborhood, desire to more to a less dangerous location, belief that neighbors create disturbances and belief that crime was increasing.

The responses indicated that, in general, blacks were more worried about crime than whites. Negro women expressed the greatest concern (56 per cent scored high in the anxiety category compared to 47 per cent for white women), and Negro men had the next highest anxiety score (53 per cent compared to 29 per cent for white men). Moreover, the fear of crime was highest among poor Negroes, in whose neighborhoods the rates of crime are indeed highest.

The victim survey also studied what people actually do in order to protect themselves from crime.[59] A person's perception of crime tends to affect his personal behavior. Fear and anxiety about crime prevent some people from walking in the streets at night, particularly if they were from going out alone in the evening. People who fear for their personal safety may spend more of their income for taxi fare instead of traveling by bus or subway. They may use additional locks in their houses or apartments, and keep the lights on to scare away potential intruders. Some people keep firearms for protection—a measure that, in fact, appears to increase the likelihood of being injured. Most people, the findings show, take precautions against personal attacks rather than against property theft. As might be expected, respondents were much more afraid of being assaulted in the streets at night, particularly if they were alone, than of being victimized by theft, fraudulent business practices or other white-collar or organized crime.

Because Negroes are the victims of murder, rape, robbery and assault much more often than whites, we might expect them to be more concerned with self-protection. The survey found this true for black women, but not for black men. While 67 per cent of Negro women had high self-protection scores, only 33 per cent of the Negro men did so (compared to 65 per cent for white women and 50 per cent for white men). In general, according to the survey, Negro women are more influenced by their perceptions and fears of crime than any other group.

NOTES

1. *Crime in the United States: Uniform Crime Reports,* 1967, Washington, D.C.: U.S. Department of Justice, 1968.
2. Philip H. Ennis, *Field Surveys II: Criminal Victimization in the United States, op. cit.*
3. Albert J. Reiss, Jr., *Field Survey III: Studies in Crime and Law Enforcement in Major Metropolitan Areas. Volume I.* The University of Michigan; especially pp. 29-65.
4. Ibid.
5. Marvin E. Wolfgang, *Patterns in Criminal Homicide,* Philadelphia: University of Pennsylvania Press, 1958; expecially Ch. 12, pp. 222-237.
6. Edwin H. Sutherland, *Principles of Criminology,* 4th ed., Philadelphia: J. B. Lippincott Co., 1947, p. 25.
7. Austin L. Porterfield, R. H. Talbert, H. R. Mundhenke, *Crime, Suicide and Social Well-Being in Your State and City,* Fort Worth: Leo Potishman Foundation, 1948, p. 102.
8. Harrington C. Brearley, *Homicide in the United States,* Chapel Hill: The University of North Carolina Press, 1932, p. 100.
9. Frederick L. Hoffman, *The Homicide Problem,* Newark: The Prudential Press, 1925.
10. Computed from figures given by A. A. Bruce and P. S. Fitzgerald, cited by Hans von Hentig, *The Criminal and His Victim,* New Haven: Yale University Press, 1948, p. 394.
11. Ibid., p. 101.
12. *The Illinois Crime Survey,* Chicago: Illinois Association for Criminal Justice and the Chicago Crime Commission, 1929, p. 625.
13. Harold Garfinkel, "Research Note on Inter- and Intra-Racial Homicides," *Social Forces* (1949), 27:369-381.
14. Arthur C. Meyers, Jr., "Murder and Non-Negligent Manslaughter: A Statistical Study," Unpublished manuscript, St. Louis University, 26 pp.
15. David J. Pittman and William Handy, "Patterns in Criminal Aggravated Assault." December 1964, Vol. 55, no. 4, pp. 462-470.
16. Howard Harlan, "Five Hundred Homicides," *Journal of Criminal Law and Criminology* (1950), 40:736-752.
17. Harwin L. Voss and John R. Hepburn, "Patterns in Criminal Homicide in Chicago," *The Journal of Criminal Law,*

Criminology and Police Science, December 1968, 59: 499-508.

18. Larry Howard Weiss, "Homicide: Queens County 1967," Unpublished paper.

19. Wolfgang, *op. cit.*

20. For a bibliography of these studies with an analytical review, see Wolfgang, *op. cit;* for additional European and psychological literature on homicide, see Franco Ferracuti, "La personalità dell'omicida," *Quaderni di Criminologia Clinica* (1961), 3:419-456.

21. Sutherland, *op. cit.,* pp. 134-135.

22. Harlan, *op. cit.* Rates were computed from Table 1, p. 737.

23. George Bryan Vold, "Extent and Trend of Capital Crimes in the United States," *The Annals of the American Academy of Political and Social Science* (November 1952: *Murder and the Penalty of Death*), 284:1-7.

24. Ibid., p. 5.

25. Harlan, *op. cit.,* p. 737.

26. Ibid. Rates for Birmingham computed from Harlan's work.

27. For much of the following review of rape studies, the author is indebted to Menachem Amir, who has written a dissertation on the topic, "Patterns of Rape and the Female Victim," Ph.D. thesis, University of Pennsylvania, 1966.

28. Donald R. Taft, *Criminology,* 3rd ed., New York: The Macmillan Co., 1956, Ch. 7.

29. Hans von Hentig, "The Criminality of the Negro," *Journal of Criminal Law and Criminology* (1940), 30:622-680.

30. Guy B. Johnson, "The Negro and Crime," *The Annals of the American Academy of Political and Social Science* (1941), 217:93-104.

31. Willem A. Bonger, *Race and Crime,* New York: Columbia University Press, 1943.

32. Vold, *loc. cit.*

33. Korn and McCorkle, *op. cit.,* Ch. 4.

34. Thorsten Sellin, "Crime and Delinquency in the United States, an Overall View," *The Annals of the American Academy of Political and Social Science* (1962), 339: 11-24.

35. James E. McKeown, "Poverty, Race and Crime," *Journal of Criminal Law and Criminology* (1948), 39:480-483.

36. Edward B. Reuter, *The American Race Problem,* New York: The Thomas Y. Crowell Co., 1927.

37. George G. Brown, *Law Administration and Negro-White Relationships in Philadelphia,* Philadelphia Bureau of Municipal Research, 1947.

38. John B. Williams, "Where Is the Reign of Terror?" Washington, D.C.: U.S. Congress, House of Representatives, 84th Congress, 2nd Session, March 27, 1950.

39. *California Sexual Deviation Research: A Report,* 1952, pp. 12-17.

40. Robert M. Frumkin, "Race of Men Serving Life Sentences in the Ohio Penitentiary," *Journal of Negro Education* (1955), 24:506-508.

41. Vernon Fox and Joann Volakakis, "The Negro Offender in a Northern Industrial Area," *Journal of Criminal Law and Criminology* (1956), 46:641-648.

42. Frank W. Hoffer, *The Jails of Virginia,* New York: Appleton-Century Co., Inc., 1933.

43. Ira DeA. Reid, "A Study of 200 Negro Prisoners in the Western Penitentiary of Pennsylvania," *Opportunity* (1925), 3:168-174.

44. *The Negro in New Jersey,* a report of the Survey of the Interracial Committee of the New Jersey Conference of Social Work, Newark, December 1932.

45. Lewis J. Doshay, *The Boy Sex Offender and His Later Career,* New York: Grune & Stratton, Inc., 1943, p. 82.

46. *Report of the Mayor's Committee for the Study of Sex Offenders,* New York, 1940, p. 81.

47. Herman B. Canady, "The Negro in Crime" in V. C. Branham and S. B. Kutask, *Encyclopedia of Criminology,* New York: Philosophical Library, Inc., 1949, pp. 267-277.

48. John L. Gillin, *The Wisconsin Prisoner,* Madison: University of Wisconsin Press, 1946, Table 28, p. 227.

49. David Abrahamsen, *The Psychology of Crime,* New York: Columbia University Press, 1960, p. 157.

50. Walter Bromberg, *Crime and the Mind,* Philadelphia: J. B. Lippincott Co., 1948, p. 85.

51. Manfred S. Guttmacher, *Sex Offenses,* New York: W. W. Norton & Co., 1951, pp. 59-60.

52. Amir, *loc. cit.*

53. Reiss, *op. cit.*

54. André Normandeau, *Trends and Patterns in Crimes of Robbery,* Unpublished dissertation, University of Pennsylvania, 1968.

55. Bernard Cohen, *Internecine Violence: A Sociological Investigation of 199 Gangs and Groups,* Ph.D. dissertation, University of Pennsylvania, 1968; "The Delinquency of Gangs and Spontaneous Groups" and "Internecine Conflict: The Offender," in Thorsten Sellin and Marvin E. Wolfgang, *Delinquency: Selected Studies,* New York: Wiley & Sons, 1969, pp. 61-137; and J. F. Short and F. L. Strodtbeck, *Group Process and Gang Delinquency,* Chicago: University of Chicago Press, 1965.

56. Cohen, *op. cit.*

57. Reiss, *op. cit.,* pp. 48-65.

58. Albert D. Biderman, Louise A. Johnson, Jennie McIntyre, and Adraianne W. Weir, *Field Surveys I. Report on a Pilot Study in the District of Columbia on Victimization and Attitudes Toward Law Enforcement,* Washington, D.C.: Bureau of Social Science Research, 1967, p. 121.

59. Ibid., pp. 129-132.

D □ *A national perspective of elderly crime victimization*

NINETY-FIFTH U.S. CONGRESS, SELECT COMMITTEE ON AGING

In 1968 the Law Enforcement Assistance Administration (LEAA) was added to the Department of Justice. It was created to assist and supplement local law enforcement agencies. One of its functions is to conduct studies and gather data on the incidence of crime. LEAA utilizes a survey[1] method for data collection, unlike the FBI's method of relying on incidents reported to the police. Its statistics on the extent of crime vary considerably from the FBI Uniform Crime Reports. One of its findings reveals that the number of unreported crimes is twice the amount reported to the police.

The National Crime Panel of LEAA has undertaken five surveys on criminal victimization in the United States.[2] These reports constitute the most extensive attempt to document the risk of being victimized that different groups in our society encounter. The crimes which are measured are those considered most serious by the general public and those which lend themselves to measurement by the survey method.[3] For individuals, these are: rape, robbery, assault, and personal larceny; for households: burglary, larceny, and motor vehicle theft.

The victimization rates derived from the national study reveal that the elderly are victims of violent crimes at a rate of 8 per 1,000 population, while the rate for the general population is 32 per 1,000 population. For crimes of theft, the elderly are victimized at a rate of 22 per 1,000 as compared to 91 per 1,000 for the general population. In household crimes, the elderly experience victimization rates of 107 per 1,000 households while the general population has a rate of 217 per 1,000 households, Therefore, according to the survey data, national victimization rates are lower for the elderly than for the general population.

In the three surveys, "Criminal Victimization Surveys in the Nation's Five Largest Cities," "Crime in Eight American Cities," and "Criminal Victimization Surveys in 13 American Cities"[4] (hereafter to be referred to as the "city" studies), LEAA included an analysis of victimization by age. These surveys also indicate that the elderly are not disproportionately victimized. The subcommittee believes that the general figures mask certain crime categories in which the elderly experience high victimization rates. According to "Criminal Victimization Surveys in the Nation's Five Largest Cities," the elderly have the highest rate of larceny with contact in four out of the five cities. In "Crime in Eight

Excerpted from *In Search of Security: A National Perspective on Elderly Crime Victimization*, Report by the Subcommittee on Housing and Consumer Interests of the Select Committee on Aging, 95th Congress, First Session (Washington: U.S. Government Printing Office, 1977). Footnotes and tables have been renumbered from the original for internal consistency.

[1] The survey consists of a representative probability sampling of households and commercial establishments. It has two main elements—a continuous national survey and surveys taken periodically in selected central cities. The surveys are designed and conducted for the LEAA by the U.S. Bureau of the Census.

[2] Victimization surveys: "Criminal Victimization in the United States: 1973 Advance Report;" "Crimes and Victims: A Report on the Dayton–San Jose Pilot Survey of Victimization;" "Criminal Victimization Surveys in the Nation's Five Largest Cities: National Crime Panel Surveys in Chicago, Detroit, Los Angeles, New York, and Philadelphia;" "Crime in Eight American Cities: National Crime Panel Surveys in Atlanta, Baltimore, Cleveland, Dallas, Denver, Newark, Portland, and St. Louis—Advance Report;" and "Criminal Victimization Surveys in 13 American Cities: National Crime Panel Surveys in Boston, Buffalo, Cincinnati, Houston, Miami, Milwaukee, Minneapolis, New Orleans, Oakland, Pittsburgh, San Diego, San Francisco, and Washington, D.C."

[3] The category of murder cannot be included because the victims cannot be surveyed.

[4] See "Elderly Crime Victimization (Federal Law Enforcement Agencies—LEAA and FBI)" p. 4.

Table 1. Personal and household crimes: victimization rates for the general and elderly populations, United States, 1973

Type of crime	Rate for the general population (age 12 and over)	Rate for the elderly population (age 65 and over)
Personal crimes*		
Crimes of violence†	32	8
Robbery	7	5
Robbery with injury	2	2
Robbery without injury	4	3
Assault	25	3
Aggravated assault	10	1
Simple assault	15	2
Crimes of theft	91	22
Personal larceny with contact‡	3	3
Personal larceny without contact	88	19
Household crimes§		
Burglary	91	55
Household larceny	107	47
Motor vehicle theft	19	5

*Each rate is based on 1,000 persons within that particular age group.
†Includes data on rape, not shown separately.
‡Includes purse snatching and pocket picking.[4]
§Each rate is based on 1,000 households headed by persons within that particular age group.
Note: Detail may not add to total shown because of rounding.

American Cities," it is revealed that while the victimization rate for the general population for personal larceny with contact is 317 per 100,000, the rate for those 50–64 is 342 per 100,000 and 362 per 100,000 for those 65 and older. In three of the eight cities, robbery with injury was highest for those 50 and above—except for persons under 20 years of age.[5]

The victimization rates for burglary are substantially higher than those for personal larceny with contact: 5,526 per 100,000 households for those 65 years old and above and 7,188 per 100,000 households for those 50–64 years of age. Although these figures are lower than the 9,267 per 100,000 households for the total population, this shows a very substantial number of elderly persons being burglarized.

Although the elderly appear to be less victimized in most of the crime categories of the LEAA

survey than persons in younger age groups, this is just one way of viewing the data. Another way to utilize the data is to examine the raw figures. In the subcommittee hearing held on April 12, 1976, in Washington, D.C., Henry F. McQuade, Deputy Administrator for Policy Development of the Law Enforcement Assistance Administration, provided the following figures:[6]

1. In crimes of violence, the elderly experience 8 victimizations per 1,000 population;
2. In crimes of theft, 22 victimizations per 1,000 population; and
3. In household crimes, 107 victimizations per 1,000 population.

If the elderly population at the time was approximately 20 million, in a 1-year period, the elderly experienced 160,000 violent crimes,

[5]U.S. Department of Justice, Law Enforcement Assistance Administration, "Criminal Victimization in Eight American Cities," April 1975, p. 431.

[6]See "Elderly Crime Victimization (Federal Law Enforcement Agencies—LEAA and FBI)," p. 3.

440,000 crimes of theft, and 2,140,000 household crimes. Combining these figures, one finds that the elderly experienced 2,740,000 per 20 million population. This means that an elderly person stands a little better than one chance in ten of being the victim of a crime in a 1-year period.

Another valuable use of these data is a comparison of the victimization rates of the elderly for consecutive years to determine any changes over time. The report, "Criminal Victimization in the United States: A Comparison of 1973 and 1974," states that Americans 65 years of age and older experienced the greatest overall increase in crimes of violence (except for males 16–19). There was a 46 percent increase in assault during that 1-year period. Although robbery for males without injury decreased 28.4 percent, robbery with injury for males increased 25.4 percent, personal larceny with contact increased 14.4 percent and personal larceny without contact increased 11.2 percent for females. In the aggregate figure for crimes of violence for both sexes, there is a 6.5 percent increase between 1973 and 1974 (males 10.9, females 1.8). The aggregate figure for crimes of theft shows a decrease of 1.9 percent. This figure is deceiving, however, because a breakdown by sex shows that although males have experienced a decrease of 14.3 percent, theft against females increased by 11.7 percent. In fact, the increase in theft for females 65 and older is higher than for any age group in the survey.

The most significant decreases have been robbery for females 65 and over (30.8 percent) and crimes of theft for males 65 and over (14.3 percent).

SUBCOMMITTEE ANALYSIS OF LEAA SURVEYS

The subcommittee believes that there are some methodological problems in the LEAA survey data which affect their application to the elderly. These include:

1. Reporting method. The use of an aggregate figure can mask important rates from subsamples and variables which are lost when the data is averaged to form that aggregate. An example of this was found in the LEAA 1973–1974 comparison findings. The aggregate figure cited for crimes of theft showed a decrease of 1.9 percent. When this figure was refined by sex variables, one can see that although males experienced a 14.3 percent decrease, females experienced an 11.7 percent increase in theft. As has been previously mentioned, the increase in theft for females 65 and over is higher than for any other age group in the survey.

2. Crime categories. The elderly by virtue of age, health, and economics are less susceptible to some of LEAA crime categories than the general population, e.g., rape and auto theft. On the other hand, the elderly are considered to be more vulnerable to crimes that were not included,[7] e.g., fraud, bunco,[8] medical quackery, and harassment by teenagers.

3. Age intervals. Every age interval in the survey is a closed interval (e.g., 12–15, 35–49) except that of the elderly. It includes all those 65 and over. This category is too large and undifferentiated. As gerontologists explain, this category includes the young-old, middle-old, and old-old (as distinguished by their health, habits, and lifestyles). Many people in this expanded group are not "at risk" in street crimes since they are too old and frail to leave their residences. Most studies show that crime decreases at the highest end of the aging spectrum. Carl L. Cunningham elaborates on this aspect:

The distribution of victimization over elderly age groups (Table 2) reveals that the youngest (60–64) group suffers the highest overall rates of victimization compared to other age groups. For the three following age groups (65–69, 70–74, 75–79), the combined rate of victimization remains at a relatively stable level and then declines substantially for the oldest group (80 and older). This general trend is somewhat a function of the activity levels of these age groups. The youngest age group (60–64) is more

---

[7]From article by Jack Goldsmith and Noel E. Tomas, "Crimes Against the Elderly: A Continuing National Crisis," Aging, June/July, 1974, p. 4.

[8]Bunco—1. slang term for confidence games; 2. confidence games include home improvement frauds, fraudulent sales schemes and fraudulent advertisement.—Washington, D.C., Police Department.

Table 2. Type of crime by age of victim, Sept. 1, 1972 through Apr. 15, 1975*[10]

	60-64			65-69		
Type of crime	Number	Percent	Rate per 1,000	Number	Percent	Rate per 1,000
Burglary	592	60.5	25.86	421	62.5	21.48
Robbery	228	23.3	9.96	153	22.6	7.80
Armed	(117)	(12.0)	(5.11)	(71)	(10.5)	(3.62)
Strong-arm	(111)	(11.3)	(4.85)	(82)	(12.1)	(4.18)
Nonpurse snatch	(54)	(5.5)	(2.36)	(40)	(5.9)	(2.04)
Purse snatch	(57)	(5.8)	(2.49)	(42)	(6.2)	(2.14)
Larceny, purse snatch	72	7.4	3.15	54	8.0	2.76
Assault	67	6.8	2.93	30	4.5	1.53
Fraud	16	1.6	.70	14	2.1	.71
Homicide	1	.1	.04	1	.1	.05
Rape	3	.3	.13	1	.1	.05
ALL CRIMES	979	100.0	42.77	674	99.9	34.38

*Crime categories containing fewer than 30 observations should be interpreted cautiously.
[10]Ibid., p. 51.
Note: Percentages may not sum to 100 percent due to rounding.

likely to be employed and more mobile. This mobility presents opportunities for victimization that are not as prevalent in the older age groups. For example, because the younger victim is more likely to be employed, he or she will be away from home, which increases the probability of being burglarized. Furthermore, being away from the house the entire work day implies that the employed person will be in situations —on the street, in parking lots—that would increase his or her probability of being robbed or assaulted.[9]

4. Qualitative vs. quantitative measures. Every professional that testified before this subcommittee bore witness to the fact that although there is controversy regarding the quantitative measures of elderly victimization, it is clear that the elderly suffer disproportionately in qualitative measures. Clarence M. Kelley told this subcommittee on April 13, 1976, "Psychologically, financially, and physically, no group of citizens suffers more painful losses than our Nation's elderly do at the hands of America's criminal predators."[11]

Mr. McQuade stated on April 12, 1976:

While there may be some uncertainty about crime victimization among senior citizens, there is, I believe, little question about their vulnerability—physical, psychological, and financial.

Take, for example, the instance of the theft of a television set. The effect upon a younger person does not carry the same impact as it does upon a person who is 65 years and older and of limited means.

Take the instance of physical violence. It has a particularly debilitating effect on the older person.

The theft of a social security check has a tremendous impact upon a person of lower income.[12]

Mr. George Sunderland, Coordinator of the Crime Prevention Program of the National Retired Teachers Association/American Association of Retired Persons (NRTA/AARP), explained:

Although the incidence of crime has risen throughout society in general, we are finding that crimes against older persons are becoming more prevalent and more frequent. This is particularly important to note because crime impacts most heavily on older persons. Financially and physically, they are least able to cope with the loss or injury resulting from a crim-

[9]Report by Carl L. Cunningham, Midwest Research Institute, Kansas City, *Patterns of Crimes Against Older Americans*, Dec. 12, 1975, pp. 49 and 51.
[11]See "Elderly Crime Victimization (Federal Law Enforcement Agencies—LEAA and FBI)," p. 24.

[12]Ibid., p. 5.

70-74			75-79			80 or older			
Number	Percent	Rate per 1,000	Number	Percent	Rate per 1,000	Number	Percent	Rate per 1,000	Median age
314	57.1	19.64	226	55.3	19.41	191	55.7	15.51	67.8
132	24.0	8.26	111	27.1	9.53	85	24.8	6.90	68.6
(58)	(10.5)	(3.63)	(42)	(10.3)	(3.61)	(30)	(8.7)	(2.44)	(64.5)
(74)	(13.5)	(4.63)	(69)	(16.8)	(5.92)	(55)	(16.1)	(4.47)	(69.7)
(34)	(6.2)	(2.13)	(28)	(6.8)	(2.40)	(27)	(7.9)	(2.19)	(69.2)
(40)	(7.3)	(2.50)	(41)	(10.0)	(3.52)	(28)	(8.2)	(2.27)	(70.1)
68	12.4	4.25	47	11.5	4.04	31	9.0	2.52	70.2
20	3.6	1.25	15	3.7	1.29	13	3.8	1.06	65.4
12	2.2	.75	8	2.0	.69	17	5.0	1.38	71.0
2	.4	.13	0	0	.0	4	1.2	.33	(**)
2	.4	.13	2	.5	.17	2	.6	.16	(**)
550	100.1	34.41	409	100.1	35.13	343	100.1	27.86	68.2

inal act. No one would argue that the time has come to give more serious consideration to crimes against the elderly.

I travel across the country, as do all members of my staff.

Last year, I took 56 trips outside of Washington. Every time something is brought to my attention either I go, or a member of my staff goes, to observe it. I do see a change in crimes against the elderly. That is in addition to the economic gain. I see a trend toward unprovoked violence. This concerns me greatly.

For the older victim who quite often has worked all his life and has fallen into the crunch between inflation and reduced fixed income, being criminally victimized is the "last betrayal."[13]

CONDITIONS INCREASING THE ELDERLY'S VULNERABILITY

The data from these reports, however, do not fully discuss some conditions inherent in the aging process that increase the elderly's vulnerability to criminal victimization. The following are factors which the subcommittee feels are

[13]See pp. 13 and 17 of hearing, "Elderly Crime Victimization (Crime Prevention Programs)," held before the Subcommittee on Housing and Consumer Interests of the House Select Committee on Aging, Mar. 29, 1976.

vitally important in understanding the relationship of crime to the elderly person.

Economic factors

Almost half of the population 65 and over are retired, and live on a fixed income at or below the poverty level. In 1973, the poverty threshold for a couple was set at $2505 and at $1974 for an individual. In all older families, 12 percent were below the poverty level; for the older person living alone or with nonrelatives, 37 percent were below the poverty level. The Bureau of Labor Statistics indicated that it costs a retired couple a minimum of $5414 a year to maintain an "intermediate" standard of living in an American city. Half the aged couples could not afford this "modest but adequate" standard of living.

Elderly crime victims are poor both relatively and absolutely. The theft of $20.00 from an elderly person on a fixed income can represent a much greater relative loss than the same amount stolen from an employed person. Many older people have no bank accounts from which they can withdraw funds in an emergency, e.g., if robbed. They must often wait until their social security, pension, or supplemental security income checks arrive in the following month.

This protracted loss also occurs when an older person's property is stolen or damaged. The elderly generally do not have the financial capability to replace or repair the property. The dollar loss or theft of a television set may not appear significant in terms of the FBI Crime Index—but the consequences of the loss for the elderly person may be dramatic. The losses experienced by the elderly victim can have implications that are far more dramatic than a purely economic evaluation would reveal.

Physical factors

There are some normal conditions in the aging process which cause the older person to be more vulnerable to criminal abuse. Diminished physical strength and stamina are experienced by all older people. With advanced age there is also a greater possibility of incurring physical ailments such as visual or hearing losses, arthritis and circulatory illnesses. Another condition of advanced age is osteoporosis which causes bones to be more brittle, more easily broken, and less quick to heal.

Criminals, particularly teenagers, are aware of the diminished strength and physical weaknesses in the aging population and often seek this more vulnerable group as targets. If the older person is physically harmed as the result of crime, it is difficult to assess the full extent of the injury.

A leg or hip that is broken in a fall during a mugging or purse snatching can mean immobility and dependency for a prolonged period. It can result in being permanently confined to a wheelchair or even an institution.[14]

Environmental factors

One of the key factors in the elderly's vulnerability to crime stems from their location in urban areas, and particularly, their residence in neighborhoods with high crime rates. More than 60 percent of the elderly live in metropol-

itan areas, and most of these reside in the central city. Many have been living in an area for decades and either for cultural, emotional, or economic reasons have not moved. Many older people live in the central city because they cannot afford housing in the surrounding areas or suburbs. They are often people who are dependent on public transportation. For whatever reason, the urban elderly often find themselves in close proximity to the people most likely to victimize them—the unemployed and teenage dropouts. The dates that the elderly receive social security, SSI and pension checks are well known in these areas. Criminals know the most likely days that the elderly will have larger sums of cash on their person and in their homes. Older people are also more likely to be victimized repeatedly—frequently the same crime by the same offender.[15] Because older persons are often unable to move from the area, they do not report the assailant for fear of reprisals.

Social factors

There are some social conditions, more prevalent in the aging population, which increase their chances of victimization. Statistically, elderly people are more likely to live alone. The criminal is more apt to select a home for burglary that is inhabited by only one elderly person. Older persons are frequently alone on the streets and on public transportation. This again makes them easier targets.

There is indication that older people are particularly susceptible to fraud, bunco, and confidence games. This may be related to the social isolation experienced by many older Americans.

Psychological factors—fear of crime

Fear of crime among the elderly is as debilitating as victimization. Charles R. Work, Deputy Administrator of LEAA, told the Senate Special Committee on Aging, "Fear of crime keeps many of the elderly in our cities virtually prisoners in their homes and apartments." The quality of life for thousands of senior citizens is diminished as they curtail their movement

---

[14]From article by Jack Goldsmith, "Community Crime Prevention and the Elderly: A Segmental Approach," *Crime Prevention Review*, California State Attorney General's Office, July 1975, p. 19.

[15]Ibid., pp. 1 and 2.

and activities. The issue of fear is so complex that an entire chapter is devoted to it.

VARIABLES THAT AFFECT FEAR

One aspect of the problem that needed to be determined was how fear is distributed in the elderly population. Are there groups that experience more fear than others? Can the conditions that cause this fear be determined? If it is possible to refine this problem into its component parts, policies and programs can be directed to the areas where the greatest need exists.

A number of recent research projects have attempted to answer these questions. Although each study may weigh or prioritize the variables differently, most cite the following as important components in their relationship to fear in the elderly population: sex, economics, race, and community size.

Sex

All studies reviewed by the subcommittee revealed that women have a higher rate of fear than men. This pattern holds true for the elderly, although the gap between the sexes is reduced. Data from the 1973 and 1974 General Social Surveys, conducted by the National Opinion Research Center (NORC) at the University of Chicago, indicated that:

19 percent of non-aged males reported fear of crime.

60 percent of non-aged females reported fear of crime.

(The difference between non-aged males and females is 41 percent.)

34 percent of aged males reported fear of crime.

69 percent of aged females reported fear of crime.

(The difference between aged males and females is 35 percent.)[16]

Economics

People at lower income levels express more fear of crime than people in higher economic strata. The Louis Harris poll reports that of those people with incomes under $3,000 per year, 31 percent felt that fear of crime was a major social problem as compared to 17 percent of those with incomes of $15,000 per year or more. This relationship between economics and fear may be justified in light of the fact that poorer people generally live in the inner cities and experience higher victimization rates than their wealthier, suburban cohorts.

An article written by Frank Clemente and Michael B. Kleinman also shows a relationship between fear of crime and income. Of the elderly population with incomes of $7,000 per year or less, 51 percent indicated a fear of crime. On the other hand, 43 percent of older Americans with incomes above $7,000 per year expressed significant fear.[17]

Race

Virtually all studies indicated a higher fear of crime in the elderly black population than in the elderly white population. The 1974 Louis Harris survey showed that of those people over 65, 21 percent of the white population as compared to 41 percent of the black population reported crime as a "serious problem for them personally." A further refinement of these statistics made a correlation between race and income. Of those 65 years and over with incomes under $3,000 per year, 28 percent of the whites and 44 percent of the blacks listed fear of crime as a very serious social problem. These rates declined to 18 percent for the white population and 33 percent for the black population when incomes were over $3,000.

The Clemente and Kleiman study indicated that while approximately 47 percent of the elderly white population was afraid to walk alone in their neighborhoods at night, this figure increased to 69 percent in the elderly black population.

Community

Community size is positively related to a person's fear of crime.[18] The greater the size of

---

[16]From paper by Frank Clemente and Michael B. Kleiman, "Fear of Crime Among the Aged," The Gerontologist, June 1976, p. 209.

[17]Ibid.
[18]From article by Sarah L. Boggs, "Formal and Informal Crime Control: An Exploratory Study of Urban, Suburban, and Rural Orientations," in The Sociological Quarterly, Summer 1971, pp. 320-326.

the community, the higher the level of fear, according to the Harris polls of 1964, 1966, 1967, 1969, and 1970, and Gallup polls of 1967, 1968, and 1972. This fact holds true for all age levels in the population, but is most acute among the elderly.

The Clemente and Kleiman study shows that fear in the elderly "decreases in a clear step pattern as one moves from large cities to rural areas."[19] The study produced the following data showing the percent of the elderly who expressed fear in cities of various sizes:

ELDERLY EXPRESSING FEAR

Percent	City size
76	Larger cities (250,000+).
68	Medium cities (50,000–250,000).
48	Suburbs of large cities.
43	Small towns (2,500–50,000).
24	Rural locations (under 2,500).

These percentages become even more glaring when compared with the nonelderly respondents (under 65) who expressed fear of crime:

NONELDERLY EXPRESSING FEAR

Percent	City size
57	Larger cities.
47	Medium cities.
39	Suburbs of large cities.
40	Small towns.
25	Rural location.

These data clearly indicate that fear of crime is highest in the elderly urban resident. Even when holding the income variable constant, the Clemente and Kleiman study shows urban resi-

[19]See "Fear of Crime Among the Aged," p. 209.

dents are more afraid than those living in rural areas.

Richard A. Sundeen and James Mathieu compared the fear of crime of the elderly in a central city environment, an urban middle class municipality, and a suburban retirement community. Their findings also supported the view that central city residents have a significantly higher fear of criminal victimization in their immediate neighborhood than the other two groups.

An interesting fact brought out in their study was that the residents of the guarded security-walled retirement community expressed similarly high fears of victimization in areas that were beyond their compound.[20]

The necessity of analyzing fear and its attendant variables became clear when the subcommittee looked at a study of "Age and Fearfulness," conducted by Barry D. Lebowitz.

When this study measured age and fear generically—without consideration of variables (e.g., sex, race, and city size)—the results were:

PERCENT OF FEAR BY AGE

Age	Percent
Under 40	38.0
40—59	39.5
Over 60	45.0

These results are not substantial nor statistically significant. When these same data were analyzed holding a third variable (residence) constant and "inspecting the conditional dis-

[20]From article by Richard A. Sundeen and James T. Mathieu, "The Fear of Crime and Its Consequences Among Elderly in Three Urban Communities," The Gerontologist, 1976, p. 215.

Table 3. Age and fearfulness (Percentage fearful by age and place of residence)[21]

Age	Place of residence				
	Rural	Small city	Suburb	Medium city	Large city
Under 40	24% (135)	38% (168)	31% (97)	44% (88)	53% (184)
40 to 59	23% (108)	37% (110)	42% (94)	48% (79)	60% (106)
Over 60	19% (101)	39% (66)	50% (34)	63% (35)	71% (78)

Numbers in parentheses represent totals.

[21]From article by Barry D. Lebowitz, "Age and Fearfulness: Personal and Situational Factors," Journal of Gerontology, November 1975, p. 699.

tributions on a multidimensional table," the results are quite different (see Table 3).

The difference between fear of crime of the elderly in rural areas (19 percent) and in large cities (71 percent) is apparent from the table. These data were obscured in the generic study because fearfulness is low for the rural residents and high for urban residents; when these figures are combined, they averaged out to a "zero" effect. In other words, the age/fear relationship was suppressed or obscured by the lack of control for place of residence.

These same data were analyzed holding other variables constant—sex, presence of others in household, and income. The results are not as

Table 4. Percentage fearful by age, sex, and others in household[22]

Age	Sex	
	Male	Female
Under 40	17% (316)	59% (356)
40 to 59	21% (218)	58% (279)
Over 60	25% (161)	65% (153)

Age	Others in household	
	None	One or more others
Under 40	46% (41)	39% (630)
40 to 59	42% (31)	40% (466)
Over 60	56% (77)	41% (237)

Numbers in parentheses represent totals.
[22]Ibid., pp. 697 and 698.

Table 5. Percentage fearful by age and income[23]

Age	Income*		
	Low	Moderate	High
Under 40	37% (111)	41% (182)	38% (347)
40 to 59	48% (58)	36% (107)	41% (295)
Over 60	48% (134)	44% (73)	35% (71)

*Low: Under $5,000 annual family income in 1972; Moderate: $5,000 to $10,000 annual family income in 1972; High: Over $10,000 annual family income in 1972.
Numbers in parentheses represent totals.
[23]Ibid., p. 698.

substantial as community size, but are noteworthy. Sex is clearly an important predictor of fear.

Thus the research data indicate that there is a strong fear of crime among the elderly. It is, therefore, important to examine the effect of that fear upon the quality of life of the elderly. Are older Americans in any way altering their behavior or reflecting emotional stress due to the fear of victimization? The following studies address this issue.

RESULTS OF FEAR OF CRIME AND/OR VICTIMIZATION

A current study is being undertaken by Dr. Marlene A. Young Rifai in Multnomah County, Oregon. A central aspect of the research is behavioral changes in the elderly caused by fear of crime. Dr. Rifai stated that, "The general perception of crime by older persons seemed to reflect a great deal of concern."[24] Some of her findings are:

1. Eighty-four percent would not walk [outside] after dark, with 62 percent attributing this directly to the fear of crime.
2. Almost 25 percent of all those interviewed avoided certain areas in their own neighborhoods due to fear.
3. Sixty-six and two-thirds percent felt their homes would be burglarized.
4. Fifty-four percent avoided certain areas of the city because they felt them to be unsafe, and their perception of the city as a whole was fraught with anxiety.

Dr. M. Powell Lawton, et al, studied the elderly and the psychological aspects of crime. They explained that the normal aging process is punctuated by a series of losses. The elderly are generally faced with a reduction in income and with the consequent limited ability to purchase goods and services. While 12–15 percent are partially or totally disabled, 85 percent have one or more chronic illnesses. A significant number of the elderly live in inadequate housing; many have constraints in their access to transportation or difficulty with mobility. Many suffer from poor nutrition. There is a constant

[24]See "Older Americans Crime Prevention Research," p. 7.

reduction in the social network—often loss of spouse, loss of meaningful peer relationships, and loss of role. Any one or combination of these losses is associated with a devaluation of one's self image and a heightened susceptibility to stress.[25]

The report explained how these conditions are related to the threat of a crime. A threat is perceived whether in terms of doubt in one's ability to deal with a problem or the magnitude of the problem. Maintaining a state of appraised threat is always experienced as a "cost" to the person in terms of strain and anxiety, and in extreme situations, this can even result in psychological and physical symptoms.

Living in a high crime-ridden neighborhood poses a chronic threat, requiring constant vigilance to maintain safe, appropriate behavior. This adds enormous stress to an already vulnerable group of people. Any time a threat is perceived, behavior is modified to cope with the threat. The coping mechanism, however, can be adaptive or maladaptive. Many people respond to fear of crime by minimizing their exposure. Many curtail participation in activities and limit their trips away from home to bare necessities. Although in one sense this reduces the elderly's opportunity for victimization, there are attendant social and psychological losses. By limiting their opportunities for social relationships and essential trips (i.e., doctors, shopping, etc.), many important areas of life satisfaction are blocked, and self-esteem is diminished.

The Harris poll attested to this condition of restricted activity when it disclosed that approximately 25 percent of older people significantly limited their own mobility.

Carl L. Cunningham, in the Kansas City study, analyzed fear of crime through interviews with victims. Some of his major observations were:

1. The most common response of elderly burglary victims was a reluctance to leave home with a heightened fear of remaining alone in it. Some suffered acute anxiety.
2. Elderly victims of burglary, almost without exception, displayed a long-lasting fear that obviously emanated from a sense of anonymous invasion and latent threat.
3. Criminal invasion of the home, regardless of outcome or loss, usually assumed larger dimensions in the victim's mind than a crime or accident that occurred elsewhere.
4. The majority of burglary victims reported anxiety and a high incidence of voluntary restriction of activity motivated by a generalized fear of crime.
5. Nearly 40 percent of the total burglary and robbery victims did not go places nor engage in certain activities due to a fear of crime.
6. Slightly over 12 percent moved from their homes or sold businesses, citing the burglary and general threat of crime in the neighborhood as the reasons.
7. The most common response to robbery was a general fear and nervousness.
8. About 10 percent of robbery victims changed their work schedules and some abandoned employment as a result of the robbery.
9. The most drastic event was that several reported abandonment of their homes following a robbery or burglary.[26]

MORALE AND ENVIRONMENT

It is only recently that studies have been conducted on the relationship between morale and environment in the elderly population. In 1970 a national study of approximately 4,000 people 65 years of age and older demonstrated the importance of environmental factors to morale. The findings suggest that environmental characteristics are more central to maintaining morale than social relationships.[27] A 1973 study showed "security in one's residence"

---

[25]From article by M. Powell Lawton, Lucille Nahemow, Silvia Yaffe, and Steven Feldman, "Psychological Aspects of Crime and Fear of Crime," in *Crime and the Elderly: Challenge and Response* edited by Jack Goldsmith and Sharon S. Goldsmith, D. C. Heath, Lexington Books, Lexington, Mass., 1976, pp. 21 and 22.

[26]See "Patterns of Crimes Against Older Americans," pp. 38-55.

[27]From article by Kermit K. Schooler, "Effect of Environment on Morale," The Gerontologist, Autumn 1970, p. 196.

to be one of the three most significant correlates to quality of life.[28] A study of inner city elderly in Philadelphia revealed deprivations in both income and health. Physical security, however, was evaluated by these residents as their most important need. Lawton and Kleban claim that ". . . their spontaneous comments reveal how urgently they fear threats to their physical safety and how deeply this insecurity underlies their difficulty in gaining satisfaction in other areas."[29]

[28]From article by J. E. O'Brien, "Component of Quality of Life Among Severely Impaired Urban Elderly," The Gerontologist, 1973.
[29]From article by M. Powell Lawton and Morton H. Kleban, "The Aged Resident of the Inner City," The Gerontologist, Winter 1971, p. 283.

The subcommittee is convinced that fear of crime is a pervasive and onerous problem for older Americans. Women, blacks, and inner-city residents are the groups most profoundly and adversely affected by this fear.

It is also clear that the quality of life for senior citizens is diminished by fear. Many older people limit their participation in social and recreational activities because they are afraid to be on the streets. Some limit their outside activities to only essential trips for food or medical attention. The subsequent losses in life satisfaction and self-esteem are pernicious.

E □ *Violent schools—safe schools*

Overview

NATIONAL INSTITUTE OF EDUCATION

Student misbehavior, lack of interest or attention, disrespect for teachers or rules, and other difficulties of classroom management have long been problems in American education. In the last decade, however, public concern over evidence of more serious problems—those of crime and violence in schools—has heightened. In the early 1970's, the Senate Subcommittee to Investigate Juvenile Delinquency, chaired by Senator Bayh, noted mounting evidence of school violence and vandalism. Increasingly, newspapers and other media have presented stories of violent encounters in schools—robberies, gang fights, even murders—and of massive property destruction. Parents, teachers, and

Excerpted from U.S. Department of Health, Education, and Welfare, National Institute of Education, *Violent Schools —Safe Schools: The Safe School Study Report to Congress*, vol. 1 (Washington: U.S. Government Printing Office, January, 1978), pp. 1-9.

school administrators have voiced serious concern about the problem, both to Congress and through the media. Yet systematic data have not been available to assess the magnitude of the problem or to describe the nature, extent, and cost of school crime for the nation as a whole. To provide such information, the "Safe School Study Act" was introduced in the House of Representatives by Congressmen Bingham of New York and Bell of California. Following similar initiatives in the Senate by Senator Cranston, the Ninety-third Congress, as part of the Education Amendments of 1974 (Public Law 93-380), mandated that the Secretary of the Department of Health, Education, and Welfare (HEW) conduct a study to determine the incidence and seriousness of school crime; the number and location of schools affected; the costs; the means of prevention in use, and the effectiveness of those means.

In response to this legislation, the National Institute of Education (NIE) designed a three-part study. In Phase I, a mail survey, principals in a representative national sample of more than 4,000 public elementary and secondary schools were asked to report in detail on the incidence of illegal or disruptive activities for selected 1-month periods between February 1976 and January 1977, and to provide other information about their schools. The nine 1-month reporting periods (summer months not included) were assigned to participating schools on a random basis.

In Phase II, a nationally representative sample of 642 public junior and senior high schools was surveyed. The Phase II data collection was conducted on site by field representatives rather than by mail. Once again, principals were asked to keep a record of incidents during the reporting month and to supply additional information about their schools. Students and teachers were also surveyed and asked to report any experiences they had had as victims of violence or theft in the reporting month. They also provided information about themselves, their schools, and their communities, which was later used in statistical analyses to sort out some of the factors that seemed to affect school crime rates. The Phase I and Phase II samples were selected to be representative of schools in large cities, smaller cities, suburban areas, and rural areas.

In Phase III, 10 schools were selected for more intensive, qualitative study. Most of the Phase III schools had had serious problems with crime and violence in the past and had changed rather dramatically for the better in a short period of time. A few continued to have serious problems. Each Phase III report is a small case study that focuses concretely on the ways in which schools coped or failed to cope with incidents of crime and disruption, and with what consequences.

This report is based primarily on the NIE study, but it also includes information from a companion survey conducted by the National Center for Education Statistics (NCES) in 1975, and from other studies as well. The organization of topics in this summary corresponds

roughly to the organization of chapters in the report and addresses the following broad questions:

- How serious is the problem of crime and disruption in schools?
- How many schools, students, and teachers are affected, in what ways, and to what extent?
- When and where are the risks of crime and violence highest?
- Who are the victims and offenders?
- What are the attitudes and experiences of the victims?
- What factors are associated with violence and vandalism in schools?
- What measures are schools using to reduce or prevent crime?*
- What measures do principals, teachers, and students recommend?*
- What are the implications of this research for policy?*

HOW SERIOUS IS THE PROBLEM OF CRIME AND VIOLENCE IN SCHOOLS?

This question can be approached in several different ways. One is to compare the extent of the problem in different time periods. Another is to compare the risks of violence in school with the risks in other places. A third method is to ask knowledgeable people in schools whether they think their schools have a crime problem, and if so, to what extent. Yet a fourth is to use some arbitrary but reasonable criterion of seriousness. All four methods were used in the study.

Time trends

Are crime and violence in schools more prevalent today than in the past? The evidence from a number of studies and official sources indicates that while acts of violence and property destruction in schools increased from the early sixties to the seventies, both increases leveled off after the early 1970's. Safe School Study data are consistent with these findings. Prin-

---

*Editors' note: The discussion of these issues has been omitted from this excerpt.

cipals' assessments of the seriousness of violence and vandalism in their schools for the years 1971-1976 showed no overall change and some improvement in urban areas. For the offenses usually summed up in the terms "violence" and "vandalism," then, the data from these studies do not indicate that the situation is growing worse, and there are some hints that it may be getting better.

In attempting to explain the increased amount of school violence and vandalism in the late sixties and early seventies, respondents in the case studies often observed that these were times of protest and discontent, particularly among young people. The protest against the war in Vietnam, together with racial conflict and a growing youth movement, were said to have been associated with a general rebellion against school authority which sometimes entailed conflict and property destruction in schools.

Underlying much of the discontent among young people in this period may have been an important demographic change. As "baby boom" children became adolescents in the 1960's, the amount of disruption in schools increased. As the crest of the wave passed in the 1970's, the amount of disruption leveled off and may be showing modest signs of decline. The size of this age group relative to the rest of the population and to schools may have been a factor in the growth of disruption in schools. The growth of the youth cohort relative to the general population seems to have been accompanied by an increasing sense of group consciousness—youth versus adults—and by an increasing sense of the power or potential of youth, which schools, as adult-controlled institutions, were sometimes seen as inhibiting.

We do not know to what extent the growth and decline of the adolescent age cohort has in fact affected the amount of disruption in schools. But to the extent that it has, we would expect the leveling off which began in the early 1970's to turn into a definite decline. Whether or not a definite decline occurs is a question for the future, however. The problem today is as serious as it has ever been.

The second way to assess seriousness is to compare risks at school with those elsewhere. An analysis of data from 26 cities in the Law Enforcement Assistance Administration's National Crime Survey provides substantial evidence that the risk of violence to teenage youngsters is greater in school than elsewhere, when the amount of time spent at school is taken into account. (Data from another nationwide study support this finding.) Although teenage youth (ages 12 to 19) may spend, at most, 25% of their waking hours in school, data show that 40% of the robberies and 36% of the assaults upon teenagers occur in schools. Most of this discrepancy is accounted for by young adolescents, aged 12 to 15. A remarkable 68% of the robberies and 50% of the assaults on youngsters of this age occur at school. No doubt there are certain places where the risks are higher; other evidence from the Safe School Study indicates that schools in high crime areas are safer than their surroundings. But in general, young urban adolescents face higher risks at school than elsewhere.

This situation is probably not new and should not be surprising, considering that young teenagers are more likely than people in other age brackets to commit violent acts and that attendance at school greatly increases the amount of contact among them.

In the third approach to gauging the seriousness of school crime, we relied on the assessments of elementary and secondary school principals. Some 8% of them, representing about 6,700 schools, reported having a serious problem. The proportion reporting a serious problem ranged from 6% in rural areas to 15% in large cities; secondary schools were more likely to have problems than elementary schools. While the largest *proportion* of seriously affected schools is in the cities, the largest *number* is in suburban and rural areas (where four out of five schools altogether are located); seriously affected suburban and rural schools outnumber seriously affected urban schools two to one. About the same results were obtained using the fourth approach, in which schools reporting five or more incidents in a month were classified as having a serious problem.

In sum, the problem is as serious as it has ever been, the risks of violence for young adolescents in cities are greater at school than elsewhere, and around 6,700 schools are seriously affected by crime. While the problem is most pronounced in urban areas, it cannot be seen as strictly urban. Now let us look more closely at measures of crime and disruption in schools.

HOW MANY PEOPLE AND SCHOOLS ARE AFFECTED?

Our survey data enable us to assess the risks of offenses against persons and against schools, and also to say something about the prevalence of "victimless offenses," particularly drug and alcohol use. For the personal offenses we have calculated estimates of the risks of personal theft, attacks, and robbery from students' and teachers' reports of their own experiences. The figures presented here are estimates from a sample. Such estimates inevitably contain some degree of error, and estimates of crime are especially difficult to make with confidence. In the case of data from teachers and students, a careful examination of the methods used and the results obtained suggests that the estimates are probably somewhat high. Nevertheless, they give us some idea of the dimensions of the problem.

The reports of students

Theft is clearly the most widespread of the offenses measured. Eleven percent of students have something worth more than $1 stolen from them in a month. This represents about 2.4 million of the nation's 21 million secondary students. Most of the reported thefts involved items such as small amounts of money, sweaters, books, notebooks, and other property commonly found in lockers. Only one-fifth of the thefts involved losses of more than $10. No significant differences were apparent between school levels, and differences among locations were not pronounced. Petty theft appears to be commonplace throughout secondary schools.

An estimated 1,3% of secondary school students report that they are attacked at school in a typical 1-month period, representing some 282,000 students. More than two-fifths of the attacks (42%) involved some injury, although most of the injuries were minor. Only 4% of the attacks involved injuries serious enough to require medical attention. The proportion of junior high school students reporting attacks was about twice as great as that of senior high students (2.1% vs. 1%). While the risk of minor attacks is about the same, regardless of location, the risk of serious attack is greater in urban areas than elsewhere.

An estimated one-half of 1% of all secondary students have something taken from them by force, weapons, or threats in a typical month, representing some 112,000 students. (This description includes robberies and petty extortion, or shakedowns.) Eighty-nine percent of the robberies involved no injury to the victim; 11% involved some injury, but only 2% were serious enough to require a doctor's attention. The risks are again greater in junior than in senior highs, and greater in urban areas than elsewhere. While attacks, robberies, and shakedowns affect a large number of students each month, most are minor offenses. Still, their consequences in terms of personal fear and disruption of the educational process can be considerable.

The reports of teachers

The proportions of public secondary school teachers victimized by theft, attack and robbery are roughly similar to those of students. In a typical month, an estimated 12% of the nation's 1.1 million secondary teachers (around 130,000) have something stolen from them worth more than a dollar. As with students, about one-fifth of these thefts involve the loss of things worth $10 or more. The risks to teachers in junior and senior highs are the same, but unlike students, teachers have higher risks of theft in larger communities.

An estimated one-half of 1% of the teachers are physically attacked at school in a month's time. Although this proportion is small, it represents some 5,200 teachers. Most of the attacks reported by teachers did not result in serious injury; about one-fifth (19%) required treatment by doctors. However, this is a much higher percentage than for students (4%), indicating that attacks on teachers are almost five times as likely as those on students to result in serious injury. Thr proportion of teachers attacked declines as we move from large cities to rural areas, and junior high schools show higher percentages than senior highs.

A little more than one-half of 1% of all secondary school teachers are estimated to have had something taken by force, weapons, or threats at school in a month. This represents about 6,000 teachers. Once again, large cities show the highest percentages and rural areas the lowest. The differences between school levels are significant only in large cities, where junior high school teachers are more vulnerable than those in senior high schools. The estimate of the proportion of teachers raped in a month is very low (4/100ths of 1%) and is not very reliable, except in terms of orders of magnitude.

Offenses against the school

Estimates of offenses against schools, rather than persons, come from the principals' reports and are no doubt conservative, because some time and effort were necessary to fill out each incident sheet. Most widespread are the property offenses—trespassing, breaking and entering, theft of school property, and deliberate property destruction, sometimes called vandalism. Of these, property destruction is the most prevalent. Some 24,000 of the nation's 84,000 public elementary and secondary schools report some vandalism in a month. The risks are greater than one out of four, and the average cost of an act of vandalism is $81. In addition, around 8,000 schools (1 out of 10) are broken into in a month, the average cost of a school burglary being $183. The rate of burglary for schools is about five times as high as that for commercial establishments such as stores, which have the highest burglary rates reported in the National Crime Survey.

In contrast to property crimes, disruptive/damaging offenses—fires, false alarms, bomb threats, and disruptive behavior—primarily affect the school routine. While fires are usually regarded as property offenses, our data show that the costs typically associated with these acts are negligible. Most of them are probably wastebasket or trash fires. (This is not to minimize the amount of property loss due to serious arson. Other data indicate that arson is a major contributor to the cost of school crime. But the number of such cases is too small to estimate from this survey.) While school property offenses, such as vandalism and burglary, affect between 1 in 4 and 1 in 10 schools (respectively) in a typical month, any one of the disruptive/damaging offenses affects fewer than 1 in 40 schools.

Estimates of the annual cost of school crime run from $50 million to $600 million, with most clustering in the $100-$200 million range. Our best estimate, based on NCES data, is around $200 million in yearly replacement and repair costs due to crime.

There is a consistent tendency for the risks of antischool offenses to be higher in the Northeast and West than in the North Central and Southern regions. While there is some tendency for urban schools to have more property offenses, the risks of these and disruptive/damaging acts do not differ much throughout metropolitan areas (cities and suburbs) and are about the same in junior and senior high schools. The per-capita cost of school crime is higher in the suburbs than in the cities. Moreover, according to secondary school students, beer, wine, and marijuana are also widely available throughout metropolitan areas, especially in senior high schools.

As a rule, then, the risks of personal violence are greater in junior highs and large communities; the risks of antischool offenses are about the same for both junior and senior highs throughout metropolitan areas; the availability of alcohol and marijuana is greatest in senior highs but does not differ from cities to suburbs. Elementary and rural schools tend to have the fewest problems with these various offenses, though there are some minor exceptions. Clearly, though, the problems of school crime and disruption are not specifically urban phenomena.

Reporting of offenses to police

Only a small portion of violent offenses are reported to the police by the school. One-sixth of the attacks and robberies recorded by principals for the survey were reported. Even where serious violence is involved, as with attacks requiring medical treatment, only a minority—about one-third—of the offenses are reported to police. On the other hand, the majority of certain offenses against the school—especially burglaries—are reported to police. School principals are not unique in the tendency to avoid involving the police. Other studies have shown that people in general are reluctant to call in police unless the offense is serious.

Nevertheless, the nonreporting of violent offenses in schools is a finding that deserves consideration by school districts. The schools and police have traditionally had an arm's-length relationship, and much can be said for schools' handling of their problems internally, if they are not too serious. But districts in which violence is a serious problem may find it useful to assess and enforce reporting requirements and, in planning efforts, to rethink the respective roles of the police and the schools, especially with regard to the question of when the police should become involved and when not.

Other signs of trouble in schools

In addition to the actual costs in human and dollar terms which crime and disruption create wherever they occur, they have added significance when they take place in the schools. Teachers who must attempt to carry out their responsibilities under fear for their personal safety find such conditions detrimental to effective teaching, to say the least, and students who spend their days at school afraid are not likely to learn much. We found that:

- 22% of all secondary students reported avoiding some restrooms at school because of fear.
- 16% reported avoiding three or more places at school for the same reason.
- 20% of the students said they are afraid of being hurt or bothered at school at least sometimes.
- 3% reported that they are afraid most of the time, representing around 600,000 secondary students.
- 4%, or around 800,000 stayed home from

school in the previous month because they were afraid.

- 12% of the secondary school teachers, representing some 120,000, said they were threatened with injury by students at school.
- 12% of the teachers said they hesitated to confront misbehaving students because of fear.
- Almost half (48%) of the teachers reported that some students had insulted them or made obscene gestures at them in the last month.

With few exceptions, these attitudes and experiences are most prevalent in junior high schools in urban areas and least so in senior high schools in rural areas. At both the individual and the school level there is an association between these indications of trouble and actual violence.

The statistics on incidence, frequency, and seriousness of the problem are sufficiently compelling to make clear the dimensions of the problem and the need for concerted action to remedy it.

TIME AND PLACE OF INCIDENTS

The analysis of school crime data by time and place illustrates how "risk profiles," which may be of considerable use to school systems and schools in planning the allocation of preventive measures, can be developed. The analysis of national-level data should not be used for local planning purposes, however. It can only clarify broad patterns and illustrate approaches that school districts may want to employ in assessing and planning ways to reduce school crime.

The risks of personal violence, personal theft, and disruptive/damaging acts against the school are highest during regular school hours and tend to occur more frequently during midweek. Four-fifths of all personal violence at school takes place during the schoolday.

The risks of breaking and entering, on the other hand, are highest on weekends and secondarily during other nonschool hours. The importance of the absence of witnesses to such acts is highlighted by the fact that two-thirds of all school property offenses other than break-ins (theft of school property, vandalism, and trespassing) also occur on weekends and during other nonschool hours. Thus, the occurrence of school property offenses and personal violence tends to be complementary throughout the week, the former taking place more often on weekends and abating during the week, the latter starting low on Mondays, rising to a peak at midweek, and declining toward the end of the week.

Personal violence and school property offenses also tend to be complementary across months of the school year, one being high when the other is low. During the spring semester, school property offenses stay at or below the average for the year, with one exception. However, in the fall semester these offenses rise from a low in September to a high in December. Perhaps because of Christmas vacation, the risks of property offenses in December are much higher than in any other school month.

In a pattern the opposite of that for school property offenses, the relative monthly frequency of violent incidents begins high in February and drops systematically thereafter, reaching its low point in December. There is some evidence, then, that the incidence of both types of offenses is cyclical. Just as school property offenses occur in a mirror image of offenses against persons over the days of the week, they also do over months of the year.

For students, the classrooms are the safest places in school, considering the amount of time spent there. The risks are highest during the between-class crush in the hallways and stairs. Other places that pose substantial risks are the restrooms, cafeterias, locker rooms, and gyms. In the Phase III Case Studies, we found that the locus of much violence and disruption —the stairways, hallways, and cafeterias—were areas of crowding. One frequently heard comment from school personnel was that control of students, once they were in the classroom, was easier, and a relief from the chaos and disorder of the halls and stairs during change of classes.

WHO ARE THE VICTIMS AND OFFENDERS IN SCHOOL CRIME AND DISRUPTION?

A knowledge of who the victims and offenders are can be useful for policy purposes. For example, if most of the offenders are nonstudent outsiders, then measures to keep them out of school should be stressed. If most of the offenses involve older students preying on younger ones, then perhaps a separation of older and younger students is needed. If interracial violence is prevalent, then measures to reduce racial conflict would be appropriate.

Student status of offenders

The data provide clear answers to these and related questions. First, with the exception of trespassing and breaking and entering, the great majority of all reported offenses in schools were committed by current students at the school. All respondents agree on this. In most attacks and robberies at school, the offender is recognized by the victim; in most attacks the victim knows the offender by name (75%), but in most robberies he does not (43%). Since current students are responsible for most offenses, the schools' primary emphasis should be on internal problems.

Age and grade level of victims and offenders

The data are equally clear on the relative ages of victims and offenders. In three-fourths of all attacks and robberies of students, the victims and offenders were roughly the same age. In the other cases there was a slight tendency for older students to pick on younger ones, but not nearly enough to regard the separation of older and younger students as a viable means of reducing school violence.

With minor exceptions, the risks of being a victim of either attack or robbery in secondary school decline steadily as grade level increases. It is 7th graders who are most likely to be attacked or robbed and 12th graders who are least so. Since grade level is closely associated with age, the risks of violence also decline as the student's age increases. The lower the age and the lower the grade level, the greater the

risk of being the victim of either attack or robbery. One striking exception, however, is the
evidence that students 19 years old and above
have a much higher probability of being victimized than students a year or two younger.
The probable explanation is that those older
students have failed a year or more at school,
may have greater difficulty getting along with
their younger classmates, and may be targets
(and perhaps initiators) of aggressive behavior
because of their marginal status.

Why are the risks of violence at school greater
for the younger secondary students in the lower
grades? There are a number of possible explanations. The higher risks may be due to: (1)
biological and related emotional changes which
some believe make early adolescence a volatile
age; (2) socialization—as children grow older,
society increasingly teaches them acceptable
forms of behavior; it also becomes less tolerant
of violent behavior; (3) adaptation to secondary
school—the younger students have to learn
the ropes in a new environment; (4) the separation of younger, more volatile students (in junior
high schools) from the moderating influence of
older students; and (5) the dropping out of problem students as they grow older than the mandatory schooling age.

Disentangling (1) biological and (2) socialization effects is beyond the scope of this study.
The data do show that (3) the longer a student
attends a given school, the lower the risks of
violence, which suggests that learning the ropes
may be a factor. More interesting, we find that
(4) the isolation of young adolescents in junior
high or middle schools may be a factor: 7th
and 9th graders in comprehensive high schools
(grades 7-12) have lower risks than those in
junior high and middle schools, even taking
location into account. The dropout argument (5)
is not supported by the data: after other factors are taken into account, the proportion of
dropouts reported by schools is not related to
the levels of violence they experience; neither
is the number of students identified by teachers
as behavior problems. This suggests that removing problem youngsters from regular
schools is not necessary to reduce violence.

Racial/ethnic characteristics and school violence

Three assumptions are generally made about
the relation between racial/ethnic status and
violence in schools: (1) that the risks of violence are greater in minority (nonwhite) than
in white schools; (2) that court-ordered desegregation contributes to school violence; and
(3) that most violence in schools is interracial.
What support do these assumptions receive
from the data?

First, except for attacks in general, the risks
of violence are greater in schools that are less
than 40% (non-Hispanic) white. The risks are
higher for all robberies of students and teachers,
attacks on teachers, and serious robberies and
attacks on students.

Does this mean that a school's racial composition itself contributes to (or reduces) violence?
Statistical analysis shows that when other factors are taken into account, the proportion of
minority students in a school cannot be seen
as a cause of the general level of student violence (attacks and robberies combined). The
important factor seems to be the amount of
crime in the attendance area of the school. A
minority school in a low-crime area has a little
less violence than a white school (more than
70% white) in a low-crime area. Whether the
same results hold for serious violence against
students and for violence against teachers is
a question for further research.

Second, court-ordered desegregation is associated with slightly higher levels of violence in
schools, but there is no relation between the
numbers of students bused for desegregation
purposes and school violence, and there is suggestive evidence linking violence to the *recency*
of initial desegregation efforts. Taken together,
the data suggest that while the beginning of
the desegregation process is associated with
some increase in violence, things quiet down
as time goes on and the process continues.

Third, the majority of violent incidents
against students are not interracial, but a substantial proportion (42% of the attacks and 46%
of the robberies) are interracial. However, this
is not more than would be expected to occur

by chance alone. It seems that the smaller the racial or ethnic minority in the school, the greater the chances that an attack on a member of that minority will be by someone of another racial or ethnic group. For example, more than two-thirds of the attacks on white students were committed by whites, while more than two-thirds of the attacks on Hispanic students were committed by members of other racial/ethnic groups.

Contrary to some research findings, our data indicate that the chances of violence are not greatest in substantially integrated schools (40%-69% white), but at least as great in schools in which either whites or racial/ethnic minority students are numerically predominant; there is some suggestion that risks may be highest for minority students in white schools and white students in minority schools. Numerical predominance by one group in a school appears to increase the risks for others.

Experiences and attitudes of student victims

When students victimized by attack or robbery are compared with other students, they are more likely to report having low grades and having failed at school. They are also more likely to be in trouble at school. Half again as many victims as other students report having been suspended, and twice as many were expelled from other schools. These findings and others suggest that the victims of attack and robbery are also more likely than most students to be offenders. They tend to be youngsters who are in trouble, and part of the trouble may well be that they get into fights and other situations in which their chances of being victimized increase.

Compared to other students, victims of attack or robbery in schools are more likely to live in high crime neighborhoods and are much more apt to say that they are afraid on the way to school and at school. They are also more likely to avoid places at school because of fear, to stay home out of fear of being hurt, and to be absent for whatever reason.

Within the school, they tend to have fewer close friends and are more likely to turn to counselors and teachers for advice on personal problems than do other students. Those victimized by attack or robbery tend to say that they do not like their school, the students, the principal, or the classes. They also tend to see the rules of the school as unfair, inconsistent, and arbitrary, and to report corporal punishment and demeaning treatment of students. More than twice as high a proportion of victims as others say their schools are "not nearly as good" as other schools in the area.

These assessments should not be regarded simply as reflections of more negative attitudes on the part of student victims. They may also be realistic appraisals of schools which are badly run and in which a good deal of violence and illegal behavior occurs.

Characteristics of victimized teachers

Many of the demographic variables associated with student victims do not apply to teachers. Male students are twice as likely to be attacked as females, but for male and female teachers the risks are the same. Young (secondary) students are much more likely to be attacked than older students, but age is not consistently related to a teacher's risk of attack. In general, a teacher's attitudes and actions may have more to do with his or her risks than any demographic characteristics.

Class size does seem to be related to teacher victimization, for the higher the average number of students in the classes they teach, the higher the risk of being attacked and robbed. Teachers with high proportions of (1) low-ability students, (2) underachievers, (3) behavior problems, and (4) minority youngsters are also more likely to be victims than others.

The picture of the school and its surroundings drawn by the victimized teachers is similar to that of their student counterparts. More than other teachers, they report that crime is a problem in the neighborhood around the school. Like the students, their assessment of their schools tends to be much more negative than that of other teachers. Their view of students is also negative. Like the victimized students, they are probably describing accurately school and neighborhood environments in which violence is fairly common, and in which efforts to reduce violence are generally ineffective.

FACTORS ASSOCIATED WITH SCHOOL VIOLENCE AND VANDALISM

Statistical analysis has shown that 22 factors are consistently associated with school violence and property loss, even after each factor is weighed against others. The 10 factors associated with violence are:

1. The crime rate and the presence or absence of fighting gangs in the school's attendance area. It seems that the more crime and violence students are exposed to outside of school, the greater the violence in the school.
2. The proportion of students who are male. Since males commit more violent offenses than females, schools with higher proportions of males have more violence.
3. The grade level in secondary school and the age of the students. The lower the grade level and the younger the students, the more violence in the school. Possible reasons for this have already been discussed.
4. The size of the school. The larger the school, the greater the risk of violence, though the association is not strong.
5. The principal's firmness in enforcing rules and the amount of control in the classroom. The more firmly a school is run, the lower the incidence of violence.
6. Fairness in the enforcement of rules. The absence of fairness, as perceived by students, seems to provoke violence.
7. The size of classes and the number of different students taught by a teacher in a week. Apparently the implication is not only that teachers have better control over smaller classes, but that more continuous contact with the same students helps reduce violence.
8. The relevance of academic courses. Schools where students say the teachers

are not "teaching me what I want to learn" have more violence. Students "turned off" by school seem to cause trouble.
9. The importance of grades to students. Schools where students say that teachers grades have less violence.
10. The students' feelings of control over their lives. Schools in which students feel they have little control over what happens to them have more violence.

In addition, there are 12 factors consistently associated with property losses due to crime in schools:

1. The crime rate in the attendance area.
2. Residential concentration around the school. The school's proximity to students' homes may make it a convenient target for vandalism.
3. The presence of nonstudent youth around school, cited by principals as a problem. Evidently, they increase the school's risk of property loss.
4. Family intactness and family discipline. Schools having higher proportions of students from families in which both parents are present, and in which discipline is firm, suffer less property loss due to vandalism and other offenses.
5. School size. In larger schools, where there is more to steal or destroy, property losses will be higher.
6. Rule enforcement, classroom control, and nonclassroom supervision. These again indicate that the more firmly a school is run, the fewer offenses it has.
7. Coordination between faculty and administration. This is another measure of how well the school is run.
8. Hostile and authoritarian attitudes on the part of teachers toward students. As a response to such attitudes, students apparently take it out on the school.
9. Students' valuing their teachers' opinions of them. Schools in which students identify with their teachers have less vandalism.
10. The manipulation of grades as a disciplinary measure. This practice may be

seen by students as arbitrary and unfair, with the result that the school again is the victim.

11. The importance of grades to students. Schools where students strive to get good grades have *more* vandalism.

12. The importance of leadership status to students. Schools where there is intense competition for leadership have greater property losses.

In considering these 22 factors, certain themes emerge. The first is that while community and other background factors have a substantial influence on the amount of violence and property loss, schools are by no means the helpless victims of their circumstances. Many school factors seem to influence the amount of crime that schools experience. A sense of helplessness about the situation may even contribute to the problem by undercutting the positive steps that could be taken.

Second, systematic discipline and strong coordination between faculty and administration, both important factors in school governance, can have a substantial effect in reducing a school's problems.

Third, fairness in the administration of discipline and respect for students is a key element in effective governance. The absence of this characteristic in a school can lead to frustration and aggressive behavior by students.

Fourth, while size and impersonality are associated with school vandalism and violence, impersonality seems to be the more important of the two. Evidently, the closer and more continuous the personal bonds between teachers and students, the lower the risks of violence. In the Phase III Case Studies, respondents frequently mentioned the importance of personal contact. Not only does it increase a teacher's influence with students, but if students are known and can be identified, they are less likely to commit violent offenses. Further, close personal ties between teachers and students may increase the students' commitment to and involvement with the school.

Fifth, the perceived relevance of academic courses is a factor in the amount of violence a school experiences. Sixth, the discovery that striving for good grades at school seems to reduce violence while increasing vandalism does not mean that violent schools are faced with the difficult choice of trading violence for vandalism. There seem to be two syndromes—one for violence and another for vandalism—involving different kinds of students. In particularly violent schools, students are likely to be apathetic about grades, to have given up on school, and to feel that they have little control over their lives. Emphasizing academic achievement in such schools, as seen in the Phase III case studies, is part of the process of building school pride and student commitment, both of which are ingredients in turning violent schools into orderly ones. Many "turned off" students can be turned on again.

The vandalism syndrome, on the other hand, seems more likely to involve students who care about school, but who are losing out in the competition for grades and leadership positions, or who perceive grades as being unfairly manipulated for disciplinary purposes. Denied what they consider fair and adequate rewards by the school, they take aggressive action against it.

If a school is large and impersonal, discipline lax and inconsistent, the rules ambiguous and arbitrarily or unfairly enforced, the courses irrelevant and the reward system unfair, the school lacks a rational structure of order and the basic elements necessary to maintain social bonds, both among students and between students and school. In the absence of these, acts of violence and vandalism, whether for immediate gratification or rebellion, are likely to be common.

Selected readings for Chapter 5

Bartollas, Clemens, Stuart J. Miller, and Simon Dinitz. *Juvenile Victimization: The Institutional Paradox* (New York: Halsted Press, 1976).

> Participant observation and in-depth interviewing was used to study victimization of youth in a juvenile correctional institution. A variety of sources of victimization are analyzed—youth victimized by other youth, by staff, and by the organizational and processing procedures.

Brownmiller, Susan. *Against Our Will: Men, Women, and Rape* (New York: Simon & Schuster, Inc., 1975).

> An analysis of rape, including historical material, from a feminist perspective. Rape is primarily a crime of violence and aggression toward women rather than sexual in nature; women are vulnerable because of historical and cultural sex role definitions of women as objects to be controlled and used by men.

Cook, Fay L., and Thomas D. Cook. "Evaluating the Rhetoric of Crisis: A Case Study of the Victimization of the Elderly," *Social Service Review* **50:**632-646, 1976.

> The rhetoric suggests that crimes against the elderly have reached crisis proportions. The elderly are less likely to be victimized by personal crimes than younger age groups. The crisis may occur when the elderly actually experience victimization; they appear to suffer more than younger persons. Also, fear of crime is higher among elderly than among younger people.

Drapkin, Israel. "The Prison Inmate as Victim," *Victimology* **1:**98-106, 1976.

> Prison inmates are deprived of many rights beyond those specific deprivations intended as punishment. Their treatment—especially violations by other inmates, unnecessary suffering and death from acute disease, and chronic depression leading to suicides and homicides—leads to the conclusion that inmates should be viewed as victims.

Goldsmith, Jack, and Sharon S. Goldsmith, eds. *Crime and the Elderly: Challenge and Response* (Lexington, Mass.: D. C. Heath & Co., 1976).

> A collection of 16 papers prepared for the National Conference of Crime Against the Elderly, held in 1975. Several dimensions of the problem are addressed, including patterns of victimization, plight of the older victim, and response to the problem. Crime and fear of crime often tragically affect the quality of life for older Americans.

Gubrium, Jaber F. "Victimization in Old Age," *Crime and Delinquency* **20:**245-250, 1974.

> Analysis of data suggests that the aged are not victimized more frequently than other age groups. The impact of housing protectiveness and age concentration, concern about crime, and fear may reduce exposure of the aged to victimization situations.

Huston, Ted L., Gilbert Geis, Richard Wright, and Thomas Garrett. "Good Samaritans as Crime Victims," *Victimology* **1:**284-294, 1976.

> An exploratory study of persons who come to the aid of others being criminally victimized. The good samaritan interventions seem motivated by attitudes toward crime, criminals, and the police rather than direct concern for the victim. Questions are raised about the value of encouraging good samaritan behavior in regard to crime.

Rifai, Marlene A. Young, ed. *Justice and the Older American* (Lexington, Mass.: D. C. Heath & Co., 1977).

> A collection of 19 articles analyzing the victimization of older Americans, society's response to the victimization of the elderly, and the politics of providing justice to the older Americans.

Russell, Diana E. H. *The Politics of Rape* (New York: Stein & Day, Publishers, 1975).

A collection of women's accounts of their rape experiences. Ninety women were interviewed, and each of the accounts expresses the feelings of rape victims.

Sagarin, Edward, and Donal E. McNamara. "The Homosexual As Crime Victim," *International Journal of Criminology and Penology* **3**:13-25, 1975.

This article examines the special vulnerability of the homosexual as a crime victim. The authors note the particular difficulties associated with trying to obtain accurate information on the incidence of homosexual victimizations, discuss the relationship between such victimizations and victim precipitation, and offer some thoughts on the outlook for this type of victimization in the fast-changing sexual scene in America.

Schultz, Leroy G., ed. *Rape Victimology* (Springfield, Ill.: Charles C Thomas, Publisher, 1975).

A collection of readings, including victims' perceptions of rape, social aspects of rape victimization, legal aspects of rape, child sex victims, and suggested public policy changes.

Chapter 6

VICTIM CULPABILITY

A □ *The culpability of the victim*
LeROY LAMBORN

B □ *Victim precipitation and violent crime*
LYNN A. CURTIS

C □ *Victimology revisited: a critique and suggestions for future direction*
CLYDE W. FRANKLIN II and ALICE P. FRANKLIN

D □ *The resisting victim: extending the concept of victim responsibility*
DANIEL S. CLASTER and DEBORAH S. DAVID

A □ *The culpability of the victim*

LeROY LAMBORN

It is unusual for the victim of crime to be considered as other than an appropriate subject for sympathy and assistance. That attitude is the natural concomitant of society's positive condemnation of the conduct of the criminal with the most powerful sanctions at its command. The injury to society and to the individual victim is thought to be so serious that mere social disapproval or the opportunity for civil recovery is deemed to be an inadequate deterrent to such conduct. If the criminal has

breached society's standards to the extent that his conduct constitutes a crime, it is reasonable to assume that the victim of the criminal's conduct is deserving of assistance and of sympathy. Such an assumption would meet with virtually unanimous approval were it also assumed that all victims are blameless for their plights. In some cases, however, the victim is entirely responsible for the injury inflicted upon him by the criminal, and in many instances the victim and the criminal share the blame. Nevertheless, even a high degree of victim responsibility for the crime does not eradicate the criminality of the conduct; for even the victim's

Excerpted by permission of the publisher from *The Rutgers Law Review* 22:760-765, 1968.

consent to and desire for the commission of the crime against him do not change the attitude of society toward that conduct. What is desirable or undesirable in the area of criminal law rests upon a societal judgment, not the subjective evaluation of the individual. It is the relationship between two individuals—an actor whose conduct is forbidden by the state and the person who is the object of the conduct—that makes the one a criminal, the other his victim. For that reason, the victim of the victimless crime is in this article deemed a victim, although it is occasionally difficult to distinguish the criminal from the victim, and although it is recognized that the victim may well be a very willing victim. However, such a victim's willingness to participate in the crime should be considered in mitigation of the punishment of the criminal and in limitation of the compensation to the victim for any injury received.

Many crimes can be blamed solely upon the criminal, the victim having no prior contact with the criminal or reason to suspect that he was in danger. After the discussion of the relationship of the victim to the criminal, however, the question arises of how much blame is to be imputed to the victim for the fact that he lives in a high crime-rate area, or is a nonwhite, or is married to an easily excitable woman. Such factors can most conveniently be considered through a classification of six levels of victim responsibility. The importance of apportioning the responsibility for the commission of crime lies in its effect upon the treatment to be given the criminal and that to be given the victim. In the light of the frailty of human nature, it would seem desirable to decrease the severity of the punishment of the criminal as the relative responsibility of the victim increases. Similarly, it would seem desirable to decrease the extent of compensation to be provided the victim as his relative responsibility increases, in order to deter potential victims from following his example. To a certain variable extent, it can be said that each member of society is responsible for crime, inasmuch as he allows society to continue to permit, if not encourage, criminal conduct. Because the programs that might be undertaken to prevent crime are expensive and unproven, they have not received the full support of the community. A victim orientation, which would vividly illustrate the cost of crime to the individual victim and to society as a whole, might well engender broader support for crime prevention programs. That type of responsibility for crime will not be pursued here because it is common to victim and nonvictim alike.

The first level of victim responsibility for crime is that of invitation, the victim's knowing and unnecessary entry into a dangerous situation. The nature of the danger involved can range from death to a bloody nose; from the loss of the nominally valuable to the loss of the invaluable. The probability of the criminal danger coming into fruition can also vary from the almost impossible to the nearly certain. The variety of dangerous situations can be considered in a few categories. Physical entry into geographic and social situations conducive to a high crime rate is one way of entering a dangerous situation. The person who enters on foot certain public parks at late hours has a greater chance of being robbed and beaten than the person who walks around the park or the person who drives through. The white man who enters certain nonwhite neighborhoods or establishments at late hours has a greater chance of being attacked than the nonwhite stranger. Each of those potential victims may be engaged in entirely legal and moral activities that may well be desirable, or on the other hand, they may be acting whimsically, in a spirit of adventure, in a state of apathy, or under a delusion of invulnerability. The conscious creation of risk may well be a reaction to the tedium of life. However, some victim responsibility may be unknowing, as in the unconscious tempting of the offender by the potential rape victim. The use of alcohol added to entry into a dangerous geographic or social situation, or even in otherwise neutral circumstances, is conducive to the occurrence of crime. Not only does alcohol render the imbibers less inhibited, it can also be used to dull the senses of the victim and to increase the courage of the criminal. The search for sexual adventure is also conducive to crime. Much nonmarital sexual activity is illegal, is therefore apt to be carried out in neighborhoods of marginal safety, and may be the basis for blackmail; the passions are apt to be aroused beyond control, increasing the likelihood of violent confrontations. The use of narcotics is even more likely to arouse crime. Most nonmedical usage is illegal, controlled by criminals, produces a psychological and physiological need for narcotics that is not deterable by ordinary means, and renders the user more susceptible to harm by others. Thus the potential victim who enters areas where drugs are used, or who uses them himself, is likely to become an actual victim of crime. Other illegal, or even merely immoral, activity on the part of the potential victim can also have a high probability of causing him criminal injury. For example, it has been said by men convicted of fraud that they could never cheat a person who was not himself seeking illicit gain. Just as crimes of passion are caused by the opportunity for friction realized, the probability of other types of crimes may be increased by close contact with those who have committed such crimes in the past.

Victim responsibility at the invitation level is not sufficient to relieve the criminal of his responsibility. Such an invitation merely renders the victim more accessible to the criminal; it does not imply a desire by the victim that the crime be committed. Nor should victim responsibility at this level decrease the compensation that would otherwise be due the victim for criminal injuries to the person. A reduction of compensation, when warranted, is not based upon a decrease in need; it is justified by the belief that the potential victim's knowledge that he will not receive full compensation for criminally inflicted injuries for which he is substantially responsible will deter him from conduct that is conducive to crime. The victim's interest in his own physical welfare should prevent him from taking too many chances; few men will enter a brawl for the reason that they know that a broken arm will ensure them of a paid holiday. In this case of injury to property, however, knowledge of compensation for its loss might well encourage carelessness and fraud. It would therefore appear appropriate for com-

pensation for injury to property, if such a loss is to be included in a compensation program, to be decreased in amount according to the extent of victim responsibility for the crime. It then becomes necessary to consider the standard of care to be used. If the ordinary man would have known that the situation was dangerous, and in light of the nature of the danger, the probability of harm occurring and the importance of the proposed conduct, would have entered into the dangerous situation, then the victim's compensation should not be decreased. The standard is that of the ordinary man rather than the particular individual involved because the stricter standard should serve as a more effective deterrent.

The second level of victim responsibility for crime is that of facilitation, the victim's failure to take reasonable precautions to prevent the crime. Once a person enters a dangerous situation, known by him to be dangerous, he is to some extent responsible for the occurrence of the crime if he does not take steps to prevent it. The person who is forced by economics to live in a high crime-rate area is able to safeguard himself by traveling with friends, by restricting late-hour walks, or perhaps by arming himself. The owner of property can discourage theft by installing dead locks rather than snap locks on his doors, by keeping his valuables in a safe, and by making use of the locks when they have been installed. The employer hiring a person for a position of trust can prevent embezzlement by intensive investigation of the potential employee's past. As was the case with invitation, the victim's facilitation of the crime does not exculpate the criminal. Similarly, although compensation for injury to the person should not be reduced, compensation for injury to property should be decreased.

The third level of victim responsibility for crime is that of provocation. Provocation is the victim's active inducement of a criminal response, that is, conduct in the nature of a dare. Provocation can be physical or verbal. The sarcastic remark, the insulting gesture, the leer, and the threat can be just as provocative as the more widely recognized shove, drawn knife, or punch. Although words alone are not generally accepted as provocation adequate to reduce murder to manslaughter, or to place the criminal's response in the category of self-defense, in many segments of the community certain phrases are known to, and even expected to, arouse antagonism to the extent of the use of force. The nature of those "fighting words" may vary from locale to locale; their existence may not even be recognized by the authorized decisionmakers. The victim's knowledge that his conduct is likely to arouse the criminal and his subsequent carrying out of that conduct place some responsibility on him for the criminal's response to it. Again, it may well be that the victim's conduct is lawful, moral, and proper; that does not relieve him of responsibility. If the ordinary man would have been provoked by the victim's conduct, the criminal should be relieved of some liability because he did that which any man would have done. Perhaps if the particular criminal was actually provoked he should be relieved of liability even if the ordinary man would not have been provoked. Compensation for injury to the person should be decreased if the particular victim realized that his conduct was provocative. Compensation for injury to property should be decreased if the ordinary man would have realized that the conduct was provocative. The difference in treatment of the two types of injuries is the result of sympathy outweighing cost in the first instance and not in the second.

The fourth level of victim responsibility is that of perpetration, the victim's initiation of a crime against another. The difference between provocation and perpetration is that of the culpability of the victim's intent. Provocation implies that the victim does not seek to injure, or to be injured, but knows that his conduct is likely to excite the criminal. Perpetration, on the other hand, involves the victim's intention of injuring the criminal and his use of force or guile to that end. That the criminal's response to the victim's use of force is overwhelming results in his being deemed the criminal, rather than the victim. Although the victim's attack justifies a forceful response, the response will be deemed criminal, and not in self-defense or the result of provocation adequate to reduce

murder to manslaughter, unless the ordinary man would have been provoked to respond in that manner and the force of the response was not unreasonable. Because of the uncertainty regarding the extent of force that is necessary to repel, but not to escalate, an attack, it would seem that it is often a matter of chance which of the persons involved is the eventual victim and which the eventual criminal. The victim of fraud, cheated while attempting to cheat the criminal, is another example of the perpetrating victim. Certainly the victim's responsibility at this level is extensive enough to justify mitigation of the criminal's punishment and decrease of the victim's compensation.

The fifth level of victim responsibility is that of cooperation, the victim's consent to the crime. That type of responsibility is especially prevalent in the area of the so-called "victimless" crimes, those involving homosexuality, narcotics, and gambling, but also occurs in cases in which masochistic individuals feel the need to be punished, whether by an authorized or unauthorized decisionmaker.

The sixth level of victim responsibility is that of instigation, the victim's active encouragement of the crime. The crimes specified in the fifth level and abortion* can also be included at this level if it is the victim who initiates the proscribed conduct. It would also seem appropriate to include suicide and attempted suicide in this category, inasmuch as no other person is directly responsible for the criminal conduct. In the case of both cooperation and instigation we encounter the problem of crime. Certainly society feels that an individual is injured in those crimes in which individuals can be victims; for direct or indirect injury to an individual is a prerequisite to injury to society as a whole. At this level of victim responsibility, however, it may be difficult to sympathize with the victim or to feel a need to compensate him. However, the reasons for his consenting to what he does not consider

---

*Editors' note: Decisions of the U.S. Supreme Court have changed the legal status of abortion since this article was originally published.

immoral may be compelling, and it should be realized that sympathy is a very subjective emotion that will be aroused at different points in different persons. When the responsibility of the victim is equal to or greater than that of the criminal, it would seem proper that consideration should be given to making the conduct noncriminal, or at least to drastically reducing the punishment of the criminal. Similarly, the victim's desire for the criminal conduct has the result of lessening sympathy for him and compensation to him. The victim's cooperation or instigation is highly likely to mean that no actual injury to him is possible. In that case, of course, no compensation is needed, and a reduction need not be contemplated. When an injury results from an undesired but allied crime, the cooperating or instigating victim can be treated as a victim of that crime with a lower level of responsibility. However, in the situation in which the victim cooperates in or instigates a crime involving actual injury to the person he is more than likely suffering from mental disability and probably should receive compensation and treatment on that basis.

B □ *Victim precipitation and violent crime*

LYNN A. CURTIS

SUMMARY OF THE NATIONAL SURVEY

. . . It is not difficult to imagine a contribution by the victim to each of the major violent crimes. During an altercation, one party hands the other a gun and, knowing full well the other's hostile mood, accuses him of not having the "guts to shoot." A young woman agrees to intercourse and engages in heavy petting but resists her date at the last moment. A man flashes a great deal of money at a bar and then staggers home alone on a dark street late at night.

The extent to which culpability is legally recognized when situations such as these lead to acts reported to the police varies considerably according to the type of crime. American homicide laws recognize provocation by allowing for mitigation of the offense from murder to excusable homicide. Comparable outcomes are allowed in felonious assaults not resulting in

Reprinted by permission of the publisher, from Lynn A. Curtis, *Criminal Violence: National Patterns and Behavior* (Lexington, Mass.: Lexington Books, D. C. Heath and Company, Copyright 1974, D. C. Heath and Company).

death, but there is no acknowledgment of culpability in robbery. Statutory recognition of the victim's role in rape has mainly been entered through corroboration rules. At one extreme, New York State law long provided that every material element of a rape—penetration, force, and the identity of the rapist—had to be corroborated by evidence besides the victim's testimony. Largely as a response to pressures from feminists and other groups, the corroboration requirement was removed from the books in March 1974 for all sex offenses where lack of consent results from "forcible compulsion" or "physical helplessness."[1] There are now only a few remaining jurisdictions with corroboration rules.

From a behavioral science point of view, the concept of victim precipitation was probably first suggested by Von Hentig in the 1940s. He observed that "the victim shapes and moulds the criminal" and that "the victim may assume the role of the determinant."[2] The actual term "victim precipitation" was later coined by Wolfgang.[3] Over recent years, there has been increased interest in the role of the victim in the

Table 1. Victim precipitation by type of crime, 17 American cities, 1967, clearances (percent)

Presence of victim-precipitation	Major violent crime type				
	Criminal homicide	Aggravated assault	Forcible rape	Armed robbery	Unarmed robbery
Victim pre-cipitation	22.0	14.4	4.4	10.7	6.1
No victim pre-cipitation	33.8	34.6	82.9	81.4	83.8
Unknown	44.2	51.0	12.6	7.9	10.1
TOTAL	100.0	100.0	100.0	100.0	100.0
	(668)	(1493)	(617)	(509)	(502)

Base: Interactions

etiology of crime, culminating in the First International Symposium on Victimology held in Jerusalem in 1973. Seeking to examine the empirical validity of victim precipitation, the national survey tailored a definition of the term to each of the violent crimes and used as guides the definitions in earlier studies wherever possible. The coders reading the police reports then judged for presence or absence of provocation.[4] On the basis of the definitions used, precipitation appeared not uncommon for homicide and assault, less frequent but still empirically noteworthy for robbery and perhaps least relevant for rape. Table 1 has the data on clearances.

CRIMINAL HOMICIDE
The United States

From a psychoanalytic perspective, there is much to theorize about the death wish and a victim's precipitative inclinations, but mapping the unconscious was hardly amenable to operationalization in the survey. The definition had to be more overt, and so, following Wolfgang, provocation was considered to occur whenever the victim was first to use physical force against the subsequent slayer.

As originally conceived by Wolfgang, this straightforward definition, relatively easy to operationalize, seeks a level of behavioral technicality and political neutrality. It does not automatically assume that certain situational contexts (such as gang fights for homicide-assault or hitchhiking for rape) are precipitative per se. There is further inquiry into what precisely happens when the participants meet. Each offender-victim interaction is examined to see whether the victim engages in a specific kind of behavior at a specific time. In addition, the decision on whether or not an event is precipitated is made by a coder reading a police report and implementing a predetermined definition. It is not based on the offender's judgement of self-perceived precipitation, nor the victim's judgment. Degrees of precipitation are not operationalized.

Here are some illustrations of precipitation as defined in this way by Wolfgang and replicated in the national survey:

• A husband accused his wife of giving money to another man, and while she was making breakfast, he attacked her with a milk bottle, then a brick, and finally a piece of concrete block. Having had a butcher knife in hand, she stabbed him during the fight.

• During a lover's quarrel, a man hit his mistress and threw a can of kerosene at her. She retaliated by throwing the liquid on him, and then tossed a lighted match in his direction. He died from the burns.

• A drunken husband, beating his wife in their kitchen, gave her a butcher knife and dared her to use it on him. She claimed that if he should strike her once more, she would use the knife, whereupon he slapped her in the face and she fatally stabbed him.

• During an argument in which a man called a woman many vile names, she tried to telephone the police. But he grabbed the phone from her hands, knocked her down, kicked her, and hit her with a tire gauge. She ran to the kitchen, grabbed a butcher knife, and stabbed him in the stomach.[5]

Unfortunately, there was not enough information for coders to make a judgement on many reports in the national survey, but 22 percent of all the clearances and 14 percent of the non-clearances were determined to be precipitated.[6] Wolfgang found 26 percent of the Philadelphia slayings he studied to be provoked[7] and, using the same definition, Voss and Hepburn put the figure at 38 percent in Chicago.[8] Complementary results were provided when the national survey data were grouped by region; higher frequencies of precipitation fell in the North Central cities than in the Northeast.[9] It would be interesting to explore the extent to which these differences reflect truly divergent behaviors rather than idiosyncracies in police reporting.

Among the race specific patterns, precipitation was lowest (6 percent) when the offender was black and the victim white, a finding consistent with an initial motive of robbery and the absence of previous relationships—typical indicators of interracial killings. Of the all-black killings, 28 percent were judged precipitated, as against 20 percent of the all-white killings, but there were high percentages of unknowns.[10]

Males of both races were considerably more likely than females to precipitate cleared homicides in the survey. Age, relationship, and location were not important considerations.[11] Wolfgang's results were about the same,[12] but variations in Chicago included frequencies of precipitation for non-white victims that were higher than in the national survey.[13]

Foreign comparisons

Several bits of information begin to validate the cross-cultural significance of precipitation in homicide.

Examining homicides in Scotland and sensitive to both intent and motive, Avison distinguishes three categories that in reality blend into one another along a continuum: crimes with no victim involvement or minimal involvement, crimes with some degree of "participation" and crimes where there is clear victim responsibility.[14]

The first group is largely characterized by deliberate offender premeditation—as in "problem solving homicides." The second group is perhaps best illustrated by quarrels that escalate from verbal to physical violence and end in a fatal assault. Alcohol consumption is a common correlate. There is usually an absence of intent, and the offender is commonly remorseful afterwards. The third category covers incidents where the subsequent victim seeks to detain a criminal or intervenes in a fight, the victim colludes in a criminal act and disregards the possibility of being killed (e.g., a woman in an illegal abortion), the victim seeks revenge after a quarrel or over a long series of episodes, or the victim is a member of a gang attacked by another group. Intent usually is present.

Notice that the first category, of little victim involvement, and the third, of considerable involvement, both usually witness intent by the offender, whereas the role of both offender and victim are typically more ambiguous in the second grouping. In addition, there is a tendency for Avison's instances of clear precipitation to more away from Wolfgang's offender-victim specifics and toward a definition in terms of certain situational contexts per se.

Avison found that two-thirds of the homicides studied fell into categories two or three. He does not further distinguish this proportion—presumably because the emphasis on a continuum of participation often made it difficult to neatly classify an event as either group two or three. His conclusion is that "the phenomenon of participation is far more widespread than has been indicated [in prior research]."[15]

In another study, Holyst refers to a "predestined guilty victim group" within a total of 470 Polish homicides, although the exact proportion is not given. These victims engaged in illegal or quasi-illegal activities (for example, prostitution), experienced personal problems (alcoholism), acted anti-socially (through, for example, "brutal behavior"), worked in target-prone legal jobs (taxi drivers, police officers, cashiers) and were "incidentally" or "permanently" careless, according to whether or not exposure to danger occurred regularly.[16]

The question of provocation is explored within this unspecified "predestined guilty" subsample. No formal definition of "victim precipitation" is given, but a much broader conception than used here becomes apparent. In illustrating his range of precipitation, Holyst specifies active and passive forms, conscious and unconscious provocation, and from the point of view of "moral and social criteria," "pejorative, positive and indifferent provocation." So conceived, "provocation" was applicable to 49 percent of the Polish cases with "predestined guilty" victims.[17]

Using a definition more in keeping with Wolfgang's and ours, Pecar found that the victim verbally or physically provoked homicide in 51 percent of the 271 cases studied in Slovenia between 1954 and 1967.[18]

Palmer uses a broader definition, but one that still focuses on specific offender-victim transactions. He found that the victim made "the first aggressive move physically or orally or by gesture" in over half of the homicides in 15 of the 29 non-literate societies examined.[19]

A final source of information is derivable from the case-by-case summaries included in the survey of African homicides by Bohannon and in Elwin's classic account of killings among the Maria tribe in India. We have judged these cases for presence of victim precipitation as defined in the national survey. The results are in Table 2. The only primitive societies that seemed to approach the American figures for precipitation were the Gisu and Luyia tribes in Africa (where 20 to 16 percent of the cases, respectively, were judged to be precipitated). No differences in traditions or institutions encouraging physical provocation could be discerned from the available information to make these cultures unique when set against the other primitive societies. More detailed work is necessary—it would be a valuable undertaking—before any conclusions can be reached on the quality and extent of assaultive provocation in American ghettos, say, compared to experiences in Africa.

Table 2. Victim precipitation in criminal homicide estimated for United States and primitive tribes (percent)

Country:	United States	Africa[a]						India[b]
Geographic scope:	Urban (17 city survey, clearances)	Rural						Rural (Maria tribe)
		Gisu	Luo	Luyia	Nyoro	Soga	Tiv	
Year:	1967	1948-1954	Years not available	1949-1954	1935-1955	1952-1954	1931-1949	1921-1941
Presence of victim precipitation								
Victim precipitation	22.0	20.2	4.5	15.8	0	7.0	9.9	11.0
No victim precipitation	33.8	53.5	59.1	64.9	97.1	72.0	78.9	76.0
Unknown	44.2	26.3	36.4	19.3	2.9	21.0	11.2	13.0
TOTAL	100.0	100.0	100.0	100.0	100.0	100.0	100.0	100.0
	(668)	(99)	(44)	(114)	(34)	(100)	(122)	(100)

[a]Compilation from case summaries in Bohannon's (1960) Appendix.
[b]Compilation from case summaries in Elwin's (1943) Appendix.

AGGRAVATED ASSAULT
The United States

Victim precipitated aggravated assault was defined in the national survey as occurring when the victim was first to use either physical force or insinuating language and gestures against the subsequent attacker. Large numbers of unknowns remained a problem, but 14 percent of the clearances and 21 percent of the non-clearances[20] were judged to be precipitated.

There have been no other estimates of provocation in assault to triangulate with these results, but the congruence with homicide is attested by clinical observations on the similar personality types of many assault and homicide victims, particularly when the offender is a friend or intimate. For example, Schultz has observed that many victims in both homicide and assault have aggressive-tyrannical personality types. They often complement submissive-passive offender types, who seek to avoid conflict whenever possible and will play the masochistic role if it gains them affection. But the eventual victim sadistically exploits these traits in the eventual offender by threatening to withhold love and affection. Finally, the victim oversteps the offender's "previously overcontrolled hostility threshold."[21]

As in homicide, precipitation in national survey assault clearances was not drawn to any particular victim age range, blacks invited attacks more than whites and men more than women.[22]

Foreign comparisons

No international material has been found for provocation in assault.

FORCIBLE RAPE
The United States

Precipitation is a particularly volatile question for rape. Illustrating attitudes that are commonly revealed, one man recently ventured on a Los Angeles television program that "in the majority of women who are raped, I think that probably 75 percent of them are actually enjoying it or are asking for it."[23]

Victim-precipitated rape was defined in the national survey as a situation ending in forced intercourse where a female first agreed to sexual relations, or clearly invited them verbally and through gestures, but then retracted before the act. Amir used this conception in his Philadelphia study. It can be argued that there is clear bias toward the offender, that too much is necessarily labeled precipitative. Does not a woman have the right to be receptive, but up to a point? Nonetheless, the definition is still closer to seeking offender-victim specifics than to blanketing certain situational contexts as precipitative per se.

Whereas Amir judged 19 percent of the rapes studied in Philadelphia to be precipitated,[24] only 4 percent of the survey clearances at the national level and 6 percent of the non-clearances were so designated by the coders.[25] The survey sample of clearances from Philadelphia (N = 44) was lower still: 2 percent of the interactions were judged to be precipitated, 96 percent not, and 2 percent could not be determined.

It is plausible to argue that Amir's results are more reliable than the survey frequencies. He was able to review backup material in the Philadelphia police records, whereas all the information was often not sent for cases with extensive write-ups in the national survey. Amir's definition is sufficiently vague to raise questions of accurate replication. A number of different coders worked on the rapes in the survey, and Amir, working alone, might have built up a deeper understanding and more sensitive decision-making ability. Clinical material on sexual precipitation—for example, the work of Weiss, Halleck and Schultz[26]—can be found.

Amir also asked whether rape victims had a "bad reputation"—whether they were known as promiscuous, admitted having sexual relations before with the offender, admitted having sexual relations before with anyone (for young women under age 18), or admitted being raped before but didn't prosecute. On this basis, 19 percent of the black women and 23 percent of the white victims had "bad reputations."[27] Although the D.C. Crime Commission did not measure for provocation, it did inquire into "poor reputations." Determination of "poor reputation" was based on whether the victim engaged in a criminal occupation; had a prior record for sex offenses, habitual drunkenness, disorderly conduct and drug offenses; or had a history of prior specious complaints of sexual assault. Also used were substantiated statements by the offender(s) that the victim was known to be a "loose or easy object of sexual assault."[28] By these criteria, 24 percent of the black victims and 25 percent of the whites had "poor reputation."[29] If one interprets bad or poor reputation as associated with the likelihood of precipitation, then added support is given Amir's position.[30]

A decline in Philadelphia and perhaps national victim precipitated rapes from Amir's 1958 to 1960 period to 1967 might be theorized to explain some of the discrepancy with the survey findings, but the institutional filters that help confound the results should always be remembered. . . . The gap between true and reported levels of rape is as great as or greater than the gap for the other serious violent crimes (or any of the FBI Index crimes), so our confidence—as well as Amir's—about any reported rape configuration is commensurably weakened. Police are usually more skeptical about the victim in rape than homicide, assault, or robbery, because, among other reasons, rape is such a personal crime, often lacking witnesses and therefore squarely pitting the victim's word against the defendant's.

One possible consequence—there is little proof—might be that the low level of precipitation registered in some cities in the national survey reflected police rejection of questionable complaints because they assumed the cases would not survive the criminal justice process. Yet, one can argue in the other direction that police bias against the victims in some cities resulted in their filing more reports interpretable as precipitative by our coders than were warranted. Some police departments are skilled and tactful in their interrogation of the victim and construction of offense reports, yet accounts of insensitive treatment are common, and many feminists are outraged at what they see as the unfairness of the criminal justice system. They argue that there can be no clearer example of women's place in society. When a person is robbed or murdered, the offender is put on trial. "But when a woman is raped, it is the woman and not the rapist who is put on trial."[31] Although opinion abounds, there is in fact little objective evidence that victims in rape lie more than, say, victims in robbery. The procedural need is for a better balance, eliminating the second class citizenship pressed on many rape victims while still protecting offenders from grave injustice. The New York Police Department's largely female staffed and directed Sex Crimes Analysis Unit is an example of welcome reform in this direction.[32]

The national survey departure from Amir need not be written off, then, as long as it is recognized that issues of factual accuracy are interwoven with biases from institutions filtering the data. In addition, compared to homicide and assault, the frequency of unknowns in estimating national survey rape precipitation was relatively low; the coders seemed to be expressing some degree of confidence. They were all males, which discounts the possibility of female coders intentionally not recording precipitation. Because precipitation was low both in non-clearances (where only accounts by victims are recorded) and clearances (where offenders accounts may be attached), it cannot be claimed that the findings reflect a victim reporting bias. Perhaps Amir projected biases; with a number of recorders, the survey gained a better chance of having subjective currents neutralized or diluted. Feminists can easily shoot down the material on bad and poor reputations on the basis of sexism[33] and point out thet white males have done most of the clinical studies—which, in addition, have meager generalizability because of few subjects.

The jury is far from in, and may never be, on whether the occurrence of provocation in rape follows the minority but still highly significant pattern apparent in homicide and assault, gravitates towards insignificance or holds a middle course. Yet, at present, there is sufficient reason to de-emphasize the typical rape victim's contribution. This tentative conclusion will be useful in the conceptual discussion of rape in *Violence, Race and Culture*.

The 15 to 17 age range had a higher proportion of precipitating victims than other ages in the national survey, but no clearcut interracial or intraracial patterns could be specified with confidence. Amir's results on age were generally consistent, but 29 percent of his white victims precipitated rape, against 17 percent for black females. His all-white versus all-black precipitation figures were 41 and 14 percents, respectively.[34]

The survey frequency of precipitation was higher between close friends, paramours, and the like than when the rapist was a relative or when the relationship was non-primary. Amir concurred. It is, of course, consistent with accepted sexual behavior among blacks and whites as well for a female to assume a more receptive posture to the advances of a boy friend than an uncle or stranger. Provocation was slightly more common nationally in home locations than when the rape happened elsewhere. Amir, however, found Philadelphia precipitation higher in outside places excluding cars than in residences or in cars. When the victim was injured in the survey, she was about as likely to have provoked attack as when she was not, but Amir found more precipitation in cases where the offender used physical force than when he did not.[35]

In a later study, Amir, with Nelson, found that 20 percent of the rapes sampled in Berkeley from 1968 to 1970 involved hitchhiking. The Philadelphia definition of precipitation is not applied in this research. Rather, the authors conclude that hitchhike rape "is interesting because it is a 'victim precipitated' offense, in which the victim's behavior contributes to her victimization."[36] As with evidence that some law enforcement officials consider prior association by white women with black men as tantamount to a request for rape,[37] here is a good illustration of precipitation defined in terms of a situational context per se.

Foreign comparisons

Empirical findings are not readily available, but several different conceptual approaches to provocation come to light.

Consider again LeVine's work on the Gussi

tribe of Kenya. The reported rape in Gugiland is very high (for example, 47 per 100,000 in 1955, compared to 15 per 100,000 in the United States for the same year). Much, perhaps most, of the reason may prove to be embedded in reporting discrepancies. But courting traditions, acceptable feminine role-playing, familial obligations, and religious interdicts coalesce to produce incidents that might reasonably be called victim precipitated rape:

Gusii girls who have no desire for sexual relationships deliberately encourage young men in the preliminaries of courtship because they enjoy the gifts and attention they receive. Some of them act provocative, thinking they will be able to obtain the desired articles and then escape the sexual advances of the young man. . . . An agressive conclusion is particularly likely if the girl is actually married. In the early stages of marriage brides spend a good deal of time in their home communities visiting their parents. Such a girl may . . . pretend to be unmarried in order to be bribed and flattered. No matter how emotionally and financially involved in her a young man becomes, the bride is too afraid of supernatural sanctions to yield to him sexually. After she fails to appear at several appointments . . . he may rape her in desperation the next time they meet, and she will report the deed.[38]

Had LeVine been interested in operationalizing a definition of precipitation, it seemingly would have concentrated on offender-victim specifics. What he does contribute is some sense of the developmental history of the relationship that touches more on offender motive than intent. If such information had been available on the national survey police reports, instead of data covering a very discrete segment of time, more accurate judgements on precipitation might have emerged. Thus, behavior during a single recorded incident that could be interpreted as woman's right takes on different implications if repeated again and again.

By contrast, the following illustrations have affinities to Nelson and Amir's assumption that certain contexts are precipitative per se.

In Nigeria, Nkpa describes an incident among the Igbo people in which a girl came to market wearing a mini skirt. When she bent down, her thighs and underwear were exposed.

Seeing this, a young man "lost control of himself" and raped her. Nkpa says the girl "prepared the ground" for the assault because of her dress, which contrasts to the traditional Igbo garment, flowing down almost to the ankle.[39]

Among orthodox Moslems in many less Westernized Mideast and Central Asian Countries, like Afghanistan and Pakistan, a woman must wear the traditional veil, or burqa, when she leaves home. This is part of "purdah," the nunlike existence in which women are shut off from contact with all but their closest relatives. Orthodox Moslem men see purdah as protecting women and preserving their sanctity. When several young Pakistanis were recently asked by a reporter what would happen if the veil were taken away, one member replied that "men would become crazy. They couldn't control themselves. There would be nothing but crime and anarchy—the same as in [the United States]."[40]

In Bangladesh, Roy interviewed a sample of women raped by Pakistani soldiers during the 1971 war for liberation. He reports that the victims did not know their offenders, had no prior contacts with them, and were fearful of any kind of direct or indirect involvement with the Pak army. Roy concludes that victims therefore were "not responsible for their victimization either consciously or by default. No rape event can thus be said to have been precipitated by victims."[41]

The status quo is threatened by change in the first two examples. In the eyes of men, who establish the standards of behavior, the change is associated with a Westernizing influence in the dress of women. Rather than recognizing the possibility of or adjusting to the change, the response is to label it remissive. There is also a renunciation of social responsibility for what is predicted to happen if the behavior continues—based on an assumption that men have an innate sexual appetite that is difficult to control. The potential importance of a particular cultural setting in the definition of precipitation is clearly brought out. . . .

Whereas the first two examples show how victim precipitation can be used to defend the existing social order, the last illustration, where an entire context is defined as *non*-precipitative per se, demonstrates how the provocation concept can be reversed and used as a tool with which to attack the offender. The central assertion in Roy's paper, which his discussion of precipitation helps make, is that rape by soldiers was ordered by the top Pakistani commanders as part of an overall military strategy to terrorize a rebellious people.

ROBBERY
The United States

Victim precipitation in armed and unarmed robbery was defined in terms of "temptation-opportunities" where the victim clearly had not acted with reasonable self-protective behavior in handling money, jewelry, or other valuables. The orientation was to personal victims, but applicability to institutions was not ruled out. This conception was taken from Normandeau. As with Amir's original definition of precipitation in rape, the emphasis here is more on accepting Wolfgang's use of case-by-case offender-victim specifics rather than on assuming that all events of a certain context are precipitated per se. But, also as for rape, the definition for robbery has more conceptual and operational ambiguities than for homicide. There is not that cutting point neatness of the subsequent victim striking the first blow.

Careless, precipitating behavior was determined to be present in 11 percent of the national survey armed clearances, 5 percent of the non-clearances, 6 percent of the unarmed clearances, and 10 percent of the unarmed non-clearances.[42] Unknowns were low. Normandeau found a roughly compatible 11 percent of his Philadelphia robberies to fit the description.[43]

In his recent Boston study, Conklin confirms that robbers look for such invitations. Less skilled, non-career robbers, who casually stole on the street as the opportunity arose, were concerned with obvious signs of vulnerability in personal victims, such as being old and out alone at night. Their level of awareness in effect converged quite closely to the transactions recorded as precipitative in the survey. But Conklin also found that career professionals, who were usually older and had a relatively greater interest in robbing institutions, conceived of vulnerability in broader terms, as circumstances that might yield potential payoffs after careful planning. Thus, a vulnerable bank might have a rear exit, a poor alarm system and a highway nearby.[44]

DeBaun, writing while serving a sentence for armed robbery, has described how such professionals find their "marks." Some targets are sought out by the professional himself—e.g., armored cars making deliveries or women appearing in public "festooned like Christmas trees." Other "marks" are tipped off by ostensibly honest people, and more than a few are prearranged: the truck driver wishing to share the value of the cigarettes or whiskey he is carrying; the jeweler wanting to beat his insurance company; the bank manager seeking to cover his embezzlements.[45]

The high degree of emotion and irrationality in homicide and assault would seem to make warnings against precipitating attack rather futile. In spite of the seemingly lower prevalence of provocation in robbery, a public response, in terms of greater personal care and public and private target hardening, is more feasible. Thus, Camp concludes that banks could do much to make thefts more difficult[46] and Normandeau lectures on the responsibilities of individuals. . . .[47]

Male victims precipitated armed robbery more than female victims, and the percentage was higher for blacks than whites in the national survey. Temptation opportunities appeared to surface more in all-black than all-white or black-on-white situations. Victims 18 to 20 and 26 to 30 were more likely to invite armed robbery than other ages, and offenders were almost invariably strangers. Interestingly, victim precipitation took place almost entirely in all-white clearances for unarmed robbery.[48]

There was a higher percentage of armed robbery temptation opportunities in the Northeast (19 percent) than in the north central (5 percent) and western (6 percent) cities and a greater proportion of victim precipitated unarmed robberies in the West (10 percent) and Northeast (8 percent) than in the north central

region (1 percent). The sample size was too small to say anything about the South. The relatively high overall noneastern figure invites futher work to test the hypothesis that the location, physical structure, and practices of businesses handling money as well as the habits of private individuals with money make them more robbery prone in Bos-Wash than in other parts of the country.[49]

Foreign comparisons

In the absence of international findings of an empirical nature for robbery, two examples serve to demonstrate how the concept of precipitation has been employed qualitatively in the analysis of foreign data and how the search for robbery victims carries across national and cultural boundaries.

McClintock and Gibson conclude that many London robberies could have been avoided if victims had taken very elementary precautions. In spite of police warnings to merchants and others against making the same journey with money at the same time each week, a sizeable number of robberies were carefully planned precisely because offenders were able to observe the regular movements of subsequent victims. Other victims walked across parks, commons, or poorly lit side streets late at night instead of taking longer routes along main thoroughfares.[50]

In Nigeria, Nkpa described how "easy marks" for robbery are sought out among the Igbo. The emphasis on material success is so great in Igbo society, says Nkpa, that many people will go to any length to achieve it. One manifestation is acceptance—indeed, often approval—of theft, as long as it is conducted in towns other than where one is born.[51] Here, then, the impact of interceding cultural interdicts seems to result in a very broad perception of precipitation in robbery by potential offenders outside village boundaries that sharply diminishes with declining distance to the village—until there is minimal or no response to even the easiest of marks.

DISCUSSION

Based on the data and definitions in the national survey, the ranking of homicide-assault, robbery, and rape in terms of greatest to lesser precipitation by the victim is attenuated by the definitional, conceptual and operational questions that have been raised.

One step in conceptually refining precipitation as a notion applicable to all crimes with victims would be to standardize a scale of victim availability as a replacement for Wolfgang's either-or version replicated here. Even though both incidents can be considered precipitative, there is surely a difference in degree between a person walking alone through Central Park late at night and someone who hands his assailant a gun and dares him to shoot. Von Hentig's original thought on provocation in fact acknowledged a victim range from "complete indifference to conscious impulsion."[52]

A modest innovation would follow Avison into three categories of precipitation, from deliberate provocation to some degree of involvement to little or no involvement. (Figure 1.) But most past work–Avison excluded–may be deficient in not systematically recognizing that victim precipitation simultaneously must be defined by offender intent. Figure 1 does this. There are five categories: 1—"pure victim precipitation" (clear victim provocation and little or no offender intent); 2—events short of this extreme, where victim involvement is still more pronounced than offender intent; 3—events where the involvement-intent levels are roughly equivalent; 4—events, short of the extreme, where offender intent is more pronounced than victim involvement; and 5—"total offender responsibility" (deliberate offender premeditation and little or no victim involvement). Whereas those following the Wolfgang approach might concentrate on all events in the column headed "clear provocation" (and also possibly events in the column headed "some involvement"), this scheme asserts that only in category 1 can one think confidently in terms of distinct victim responsibility alone. The relative focus remains on the victim in category 2, though the offender intent-victim responsibility disparity is not as clearcut. In part, category 3 argues that even if there is clear provocation or at least some involvement by the victim, it may be misleading from conceptual and policy viewpoints to collapse into category 1 events where there is a standoff in terms of responsibility.

Conceptually, a distinction might be made between a homicide where the victim hands the offender a gun and dares him to shoot (category 1) and a gang shootout where the victim wings the offender first but then is killed (category 3A). For rape, the distinction might be between an event where the victim, after drinking a great deal, succumbs or agrees to inter-

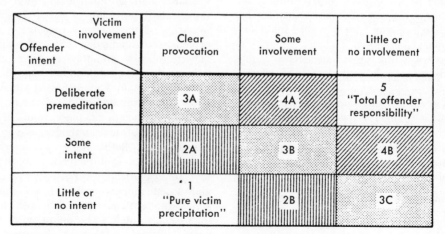

Offender intent \ Victim involvement	Clear provocation	Some involvement	Little or no involvement
Deliberate premeditation	3A	4A	5 "Total offender responsibility"
Some intent	2A	3B	4B
Little or no intent	1 "Pure victim precipitation"	2B	3C

Key: see text

Figure 1. Offender intent and victim involvement.

course with her boss but then claims rape when discovered by her husband (category 1) and a party where the victim, when dancing, physically encourages a stranger on the make, who then takes her into a bedroom and forces sex against her will (category 3A). For robbery, compare a scene where a dude happens on a drunken older man and, on the spot, decides to take advantage of him (category 1) and the planned postal office heist of a professional robber that is facilitated by most of the staff being asleep (a category 3A event that has been reported in Italy). Similar distinctions are possible between cells 3B or 3C, on the one hand, and cell 1 on the other. A mirror image analysis in terms of offender responsibility can be done with categories 3, 4, and 5.

The potential implications for victim compensation illustrate the policy relevance that might be developed from this scheme. If policy were to look at the victim alone, then an event falling into cell 4A, with some victim involvement, would not promise much compensation for the victim. But if the relatively higher level of offender intent were jointly taken into account, the victim could expect more favorable consideration.

A modification of Figure 1 might also consider how voluntarily the victim entered into the episode concluding in rape. Thus, it can be argued that a woman who voluntarily accepts a hitch has more responsibility for her attack than a woman who is pushed into a car. The crucial query then becomes whether or not degree of voluntariness is necessarily always positively associated with degree of precipitation.

Another critical question is the perspective from which victim precipitation should be defined. The studies . . . are based on the researcher's definition, applied to a reading of police reports. But Silverman offers a definition in terms of the offender's perception:

Victim precipitation occurs when the offender's action in committing or beginning to commit a crime is initiated after and directly related to an action (be it physical or verbal, conscious or unconscious) on the part of the victim. The offender perceives the victim's behavior as a facilitating action (including

temptation, invitation) to the commission of the crime. The action of the victim might be said to have triggered the offender's behavior.

An advantage to Silverman's definition is that it acknowledges the demonstrably important role of culture but still avoids automatic conclusions that certain contexts are precipitative per se. The normative standards held by the offender presumably help mold his perception of what is precipitating behavior. Thus, for example, leaving a car door unlocked in a small town may not be perceived as a temptation opportunity, but this may indeed be the case in a large city.[54] Or, applying Igbo values, the unlocked car is not a temptation opportunity in one's own small town, but it is in the small town just across the river.

Yet does Silverman place too much importance on the offender? His definition threatens to yield figures for victim precipitation that are so high as to severely reduce any discriminating capacity the concept may have. A short skirt—even (or especially) in Los Angeles—might do for rape. If, after reading the paper, a professional thief decides to rob the latest lottery winner, is this not the genesis of a victim-precipitated episode? At the extreme, the offender may interpret the mere existence of an individual as victim precipitation—for example, a child not wanted by an unmarried woman.[55] With as much justification, an argument might be made to define precipitation in terms of the *victim's* perception (except, of course, in homicide). Thus, Conklin interviewed robbery offenders on their perceived vulnerability,[56] and it would be easy to proceed a bit further into a more formal victimization survey on self-interpreted involvement.

Victim-defined precipitation would likely produce figures as low as offender-defined figures may be high. Both versions incorporate cultural influences—yet the relativity of the definition to a participant's normative references and social milieu means that comparisons across different cultures will be difficult if not impossible to make. The definition of precipitation will change. Here is where a constant, researcher-defined concept . . . has greatest advantage.

The implication is that there is no "correct" definition of precipitation. Each version has advantages and disadvantages. Accordingly, why not triangulate offender-, victim-, and researcher-based definitions and incorporate into each some kind of more refined scale of degrees of victim involvement like the one suggested? A comparative analysis could then identify the upper- and lower-bound percentage figures of precipitation in a specified sample, depending on the different definitions. Although it may not necessarily be the ideal toward which researcher should aim, a more unified consensus definition of precipitation could emerge from such analysis. One might even conceive of a Delphi exercise among offenders, victims, and researchers.

The discussion has mainly been conceptual. But it will not be easy to measure and compare even sizeable gradations of offender intent and victim involvement. Investigations that apply several definitions will have to face difficult problems of operationalization and replication. At least for researcher-defined precipitation, it may be that only blatant physical actions, like striking the first blow, are employable and that "suggestive gestures," "temptation opportunities," and the like are too subtle to be captured and replicated.

However, in spite of the crude measurement tools presently available to social science, much progress can be made simply if better data are obtained. Future research on victim precipitation should avoid police reports and other institutional filters. Instead, the need is for detailed clinical interviewing and projective testing of incoming victims and offenders on a scale large enough to retain a significant and stratified sample. Whenever possible, the developmental history of any prior relationship between offender and victim should be reconstructed from accounts by the participants as well as significant others. Teams of researchers with different personal attributes should be used for interviewing. Will, for example, conclusions by investigators of the same race and sex of the offender or victim be greatly different from what is now mainly viewed through the eyes of white male scholars? In addition, comparisons of persons who, faced with an offender, have escaped victimization to those who have succumbed may yield valuable insights—for instance, on the merits of aggressiveness by women against rapists. (Touching on this question, Reiss found that the "completion rate" for Chicago rapes in public places was higher for black than white women. Whether white women were in fact more skilled at thwarting attacks could not be determined.[57])

This course of proposed research embraces the writer's preference for a relatively more neutral, Wolfgang-type approach to precipitation based on offender-victim specifics, rather than one blocked out of certain contexts defined as precipitative per se. We believe that the latter path assumes too much, that precipitation should be based on the details of what actually happened and on the participants' perceptions, not on blanket assumptions of increased risk and responsibility for all situations of a given kind. Such assumptions are likely to be unequally applied to different crimes. Thus, is there something about the kind and intensity of sexual as against economic values in the United States that dissuades those who perceive of short skirts and hitchhiking as sexually precipitative per se from adding that the same might apply in robbery to women whose purses are observable on the street? In addition, the same extreme positions that could result from a definition based on offender perception alone are possible from the blanket definitions. To give the most volatile current political example: for some, the mere existence of Israel may be ground for attack.

Nonetheless, situational context definitions can be expected as long as man remains subjective and political. And such definitions should be encouraged, as interpretations of classes of behavior rather than criteria or standards in any absolute sense. An unlimited variety of new definitions begins to unfold as the sphere of conceptual relevance expands beyond the offender-victim interaction and encompasses the moral demand systems of any society or subgroup within it. By blaming a woman for her own rape, by parallel application to other crimes, the notion of precipitation can be used to resist change and defend the institutionalized order. But victim precipitation has considerable potential for use by the political left as well. The view that the student of victims shares with the labeling theorist invites turning conventional wisdom inside out and criticizing the established dominant cultural value system. As discussed in *Violence, Race and Culture*, what does precipitation mean if we see American blacks less as violent crime offenders and more as casualties of institutional racism, adapting to economic and racial constraints with contracultural responses that use physical violence to pass the victim identity onto others? To the extent that violent crimes encourage governmental repression, reactive police measures, massive expenditures on hardware, and reaffirmed institutional racism rather than social change, these crimes themselves can be interpreted as precipitative.

NOTES AND REFERENCES

1. Forcible compulsion is defined as "physical force that overcomes earnest resistance or a threat, express or implied, that places a person in fear of immediate death or serious physical injury to himself or another person or in fear that he or another person will immediately be kidnapped." Physical helplessness means ". . . that a person is unconscious or for any other reason is physically unable to communicate unwillingness to an act." Corroboration is still required when the victim is less than 17 years or when she is mentally defective or incapacitated. Proof of penetration (usually supplied by a sperm test) is still required. (*Legal Division Bulletin,* 1974.) See also Lear (1972).
2. Von Hentig (1949, p. 384). See also Von Hentig (1940). The historical development of victim precipitation is summarized in Silverman (1973).
3. Wolfgang (1958).
4. Coders were instructed to record "unknown" unless they were reasonably certain from the information provided that an interaction definitely did or did not involve victim precipitation.
5. From Wolfgang (1958, p. 253).
6. For the tables on non-clearances, see Curtis (1972).
7. Wolfgang (1958, p. 252).
8. Voss and Hepburn (1968, p. 506).
9. See Curtis (1972) for the supporting tables.
10. See Curtis (1972) for the supporting tables.
11. See Curtis (1972).
12. Wolfgang (1958, pp. 256-7).
13. Voss and Hepburn (1968, pp. 506-7).
14. Avison (1973).
15. Avison (1973, p. 8).
16. Holyst (1967, p. 79).
17. Hoylst (1967, p. 80).
18. Pecar (1971).
19. Palmer (1973).
20. See Curtis (1972) for the supporting tables on non-clearances.
21. Schultz (1969, pp. 139-40).
22. See Curtis (1972) for the supporting tables.
23. Csida and Csida (1974, p. 18).
24. Amir (1967, p. 533).
25. For the supporting tables on non-clearances, see Curtis (1972).
26. Weiss et al. (1955), Halleck (1965), Schultz (1968).
27. Amir (1965, p. 250).
28. D.C. Crime Commission (1966, p. 941).
29. D.C. Crime Commission (1966, p. 50).
30. Peters (1973) also discloses from the first interviews in an ongoing study of rape in Philadelphia that adolescent victims (aged 13 to 17) were judged by the social workers "to lack discretion or have some complicity in over 40 percent of the cases." However, the N was low (47) and the figure was 10 percent for adults (N = 84).
31. Anderson (1971). As indicated here, criticism is not limited to police but to the entire criminal justice system. In fact, Holmstrom and Burgess (1973)—both women—found in their Boston study that, contrary to stereotype, two-thirds of the rape victims interviewed believed the police to have treated them well. The authors conclude that, at least in Boston, more painful to the victim and more in need of reform than treatment by police is the experience in court, particularly cross-examination by the defense lawyers.
32. *Time Magazine* (1973).
33. The National Organization for Women argues that a woman's activities with men other than the accused are irrelevant. Consonant with this position, Iowa and California have recently passed laws barring defense lawyers from asking questions in court about a woman's past sexual conduct; in Florida, such queries must first be screened in the judge's chambers. (*Time Magazine,* 1974.)
34. Amir (1965, p. 546). See Curtis (1972) for the national survey tables supporting this paragraph.
35. See Curtis (1972) for the tables supporting the survey results and reported in this paragraph. The references to Amir are (1965, ppp. 550-1).
36. Nelson and Amir (1973, p. 26).
37. See, for example, Peterson (1973).
38. LeVine (1959, p. 988).
39. Nkpa (1973).
40. Bordewich (1973).
41. Roy (1973, p. 6).
42. For the supporting tables on non-clearances, see Curtis (1973).
43. Normandeau (1968, pp. 291-2).
44. Conklin (1972, pp. 89-90).
45. DeBaun (1950, p. 70).
46. Camp (1967).
47. Normandeau (1968, p. 290).
48. See Curtis (1972) for the supporting tables.

49. See Curtis (1972) for the supporting regional breakdown tables.
50. McClintock and Gibson (1961, p. 23).
51. Nkpa (1973).
52. Von Hentig (1948).
53. Silverman (1973, p. 17).
54. Silverman (1973).
55. Avison (1973).
56. Conklin (1972).
57. Reiss (1967, p. 106).

C □ *Victimology revisited*

A critique and suggestions for future direction

CLYDE W. FRANKLIN II and ALICE P. FRANKLIN

Victimology as an area within criminology or as a separate perspective had its beginnings in the published works of Hans von Hentig (1941, 1948), and B. Mendelsohn (1947).[1] Exploring the role of the victim in crime, von Hentig contended that some victims may bring about their own victimization through manifest expressions of wishes, attitudes, and personalities which appear to initiate criminal activity (Reckless, 1973). Following the initial works by von Hentig and Mendelsohn, significant theoretical and research contributions to victimology were made by Mendelsohn (1956, 1963), Ellenberger (1954), and Wolfgang (1957) among others.

While nearly three decades have passed since von Hentig's initial exploration into the phenomenon, students of victimology generally have remained faithful to the basic assumptions underlying his initial works. In fact, many of the later theoretical contributions to victimology have been restatements and/or reportings of the positions taken by the pioneer thinkers (Nagel, 1963; Quinney, 1972; Glaser, 1970; and Silverman, 1974). Few attempts have been made to evaluate the logical adequacy of victimology or any of its various dimensions. What has been done has centered around either the "boundaries of victimology" or the "victim typologies" rather than the assumptions underlying the perspective.

This paper is devoted to an identification, explication, and evaluation of selected assumptions underlying the victim-precipitation dimension of victimology. Specifically, these assumptions are: (1) some criminal deeds can be explained by the precipitative behavior of the victims; (2) the criminal is in a passive state and set into action by the victim's behavior; (3) the victim's behavior is both a necessary and sufficient condition for the criminal act; and (4) the intent of the victim can be assumed from his/her resultant victimization.[2]

ASSUMPTION I: CRIMINAL DEEDS CAN BE EXPLAINED BY THE PRECIPITATIVE BEHAVIOR OF THE VICTIM

According to victimology literature, behaviors such as apathy, lethargy, submission, cooperation, and provocation constitute precipitative behaviors which are responsible for a large proportion of criminal deeds. Such behaviors, which range from complete indifference to conscious impulsion, are thought to be crime precipitators which if displayed by potential

"Victimology Revisited: A Critique and Suggestions for Future Direction" by Clyde W. Franklin II and Alice P. Franklin is reprinted from *Criminology*, Vol. 14, No. 1 (May 1976), pp. 177-214 by permission of the Publisher, Sage Publications, Inc.

victims actually cause their own victimization. Illustratively, based on the victimology perspective, a woman who walks alone toward her car on an unlighted street at night causes her own rape as surely as the man who precipitates his car theft by accidentally leaving his car keys in the car ignition or the man who slaps his wife and brings about his own demise.[3]

To be sure, differences may exist between the illustrative behaviors with respect to intent. However these differences, until recently, had not been explored nor emphasized in explications of victimology.[4] This is substantiated by the fact that all such behaviors at one time or another have been labeled as instances of victim precipitation (Wolfgang, 1957; Mendelsohn, 1963; Schafer, 1968; Reckless, 1973). Just as important as the labeling of behavior and the attributes of intent (these topics are explored later in this paper) are the explanations generally offered by victimologists for the occurrences of criminal acts. Using the above illustrations, occurrences of these crimes, from a victimology viewpoint, could be explained by the fact that in each case, the victim (woman walking alone at night, man leaving his car keys in the car ignition, and man slapping his wife) displayed specific behaviors which caused the criminal deed (rape, car theft, and homicide). Furthermore, an explanation of why the victims' behaviors caused the criminal deeds lies in the precipitative nature of the victim's behavior. *In sum, the victims' precipitative behaviors led to the criminal deeds because the victims' behaviors were precipitative.*

Unfortunately, this kind of circular reasoning cannot be avoided if the victimology framework is used to explain the causes of criminal acts. A major reason for this unfortunate occurrence lies in the lack of independence between the presumed causative factor (victim-precipitative behavior) and the resultant condition (victimization). Weiss and Borges (1973: 72) alluded to the interrelatedness of the definitions of the concepts although they did not explore the problems created by the lack of concept independence. They define victimization as "societal processes that occur before, during and after the event simultaneously rendering the victim defenseless and even partly responsible for it."

The interrelatedness of the independent and dependent variables "victim precipitation" and "victimization" becomes more apparent when an attempt is made to identify victim precipitation in the absence of victimization. For example, a woman walking alone at night on an unlighted street under present conceptions of victimology can hardly be thought of as engaging in crime-precipitative behavior if no criminal act takes place.[5] Similarly, the woman who walks alone at night on an unlighted street who is an expert in the art of karate and can defeat the vast majority of attackers is not engaging in victim-precipitative behavior—that is, unless she meets an attacker who is superior in the art of karate and succeeds in assaulting her. To drive the point home even more, based on current thinking in victimology even though a man beats his wife regularly, his behavior can hardly be defined as victim-precipitative until she murders him following a beating incident.

Whether victimology can provide a framework wherein logically adequate theoretical expositions can be developed seems to hinge, in part, on the construction of a clear distinction between victimization and victim precipitation. One step in the direction of concept distinction would seem to be an empirical attempt to identify and define behaviors which may be labeled precipitative even if their emissions do not result in social, physical, or symbolic harm or injury to the person displaying the behaviors.[6] Certainly, this is a very difficult task to accomplish, since such behaviors must lead to victimization and yet remain conceptually distinct from the process. Operationally this means that it should be possible for victim precipitation to occur and some intervening variables to follow which resulted in either nonvictim-precipitated victimization or nonvictimization. While this suggestion may not be very appealing to victimologists, the alternative to developing the perspective in this direction is much less appealing, since it entails dispensing with the use of victim-precipitation explanations because of the obvious logical fallacy.

[Handwritten marginalia at top: "★ victim-precipitation — "victim generates criminal behavior in the doer." ↓ converting a potential doer into an actual doer."]

ASSUMPTION II: THE CRIMINAL IS IN A PASSIVE STATE AND SET INTO ACTION BY THE VICTIM'S BEHAVIOR

[Handwritten marginalia: "S-R sequence"]

Reckless (1973), drawing upon the works of von Hentig, Ellenberger, and Mendelsohn, defines the victim-precipitation perspective as the model of criminology which assumes that "the victim generates criminal behavior in the doer"—converting a potential doer into an actual doer. It does not take much imagination to reach the conclusion that one underlying assumption in victimology is that human behavior is characterized by a stimulus-response sequence.[7] While Reckless' comments indicate clearly that this sequence is a characteristic of victimology, other contributions have been more subdued with respect to emphasizing this assumption. For example, Wolfgang (1957) varied his operational definition of victim precipitation in his study of "victim-precipitated" homicides. In Wolfgang's study, the victim's "direct, positive precipitation in his/her crime" was operationalized to mean that the victim must have been the first one to use physical force in the homicide drama. This connotation of "victim-precipitated" homicide is apparent in an illustration of the cases used, which included homicide in self-defense, accidental homicide and, perhaps, homicide during the heat of passion.

A cursory glance at the sample of homicide cases presented by Wolfgang reveals that at least four of the nine could not have been defined as victim-precipitated unless a stimulus-response model of human behavior was assumed. While five of the cases show clearly that the victim used physical force to the extent of threatening the life of the offender, cases 4, 5, 6, and 8 do not show this. While the concept "victim precipitation" does not require "excessive" behavior by the victim, it does seem to require a motive of "intent." We will explore this point later. Returning to Wolfgang's cases, at least one of the cases shows clear evidence that the victim was *not* engaging in extraordinary behavior (to the contrary, the victim is reported to have beaten his wife on numerous occasions prior to the homicide). Therefore, it seems inadequate to explain the offender's act as a response to the victim's precipitative act. To the contrary, the offender may have mapped out a course of action to follow given a certain kind of interaction between herself and the victim prior to the homicide drama. A crucial explanatory variable in this homicide case would seem to be the offender's *interpretation* of the social interaction situation. We submit that many so-called victim-precipitated homicides may, in actuality, have been planned and/or mapped out at some points prior to the acts.[8] If this is the case, then such homicides occur not because of victim precipitation but because the offender *decides*, between alternative courses of action, to engage in victimization. Information regarding the interpretation and/or choice between alternative variables can be gleaned from an assessment of prior interaction patterns between the victim and the offender. However, instead of interpreting a priori certain interaction patterns, the investigator may want to attempt to determine whether such interaction patterns are "ordinary" for the persons involved.

The suggestion offered above to researchers using the victimology perspective is important in the sense that stimulus-response assumptions may be inadequate for human behavior because they suggest that the offender is inert, and waiting for a stimulus to set him/her into action. Such an assumption is diametrically opposed to basic tenets in most of the social and behavioral sciences which indicate that humans are active beings who interpret, make judgments, suspend judgments, act upon, and so on. Stimulus-response ideas deny the dynamic nature of human beings which is crucial to an understanding of the individual's behavior in social and nonsocial situations. In addition, stimulus-response interpretations of human behavior imply that specific stimuli can be linked with specific responses. While this appears to be true for certain reflexive behaviors, there is little evidence to support such explanations for social behavior.[9] In other words, a woman walking alone at night may be either robbed, raped, murdered, or she may fall victim to all three crimes. As an examination of crime statistics will show, these offender responses as well as others are possible. Therefore to explain the occurrence of any one response as a function of walking alone at night (precipitative behavior or stimulus) is not only inadequate but empirically unfounded.

ASSUMPTION III: BEHAVIORS DISPLAYED BY A VICTIM ARE NECESSARY AND SUFFICIENT FOR CRIMINAL ACTS

According to the victim-precipitation model in victimology, a man who leaves his car unattended with the keys in the ignition engages in behavior which is necessary and sufficient for certain kinds of car theft. Presumably such behavior provides not only a necessary condition for certain kinds of car theft, but also, regardless of anything else, is the cause of the crime. Interestingly, some researchers of victim-precipitated homicides have recognized the potential problems which may be encountered if a wide variety of symbolic behaviors are labeled precipitative with the underlying assumption of "sufficiency." As a result, in some instances, these researchers have limited "sufficient" cause to the initiation of physical force against the offender. When such an approach has been taken, however, still there has been a neglect of the interpretative variables surrounding the situation which may be crucial to an understanding of the resultant act. In other words, limiting the scope of behaviors which are defined as precipitative does not enable one to assume that such behaviors are sufficient for the criminal act. This assumption is arbitrary and must be recognized as such by victimologists. Succinctly, there is a difference between justification for a criminal act and sufficient cause for the occurrence of the act. The former constitutes a judgment in the legal sense, while the latter is a theoretical assertion which should be tested empirically.

Perhaps the main problem faced by those who must determine what specific behaviors by the victim caused the occurrence of a criminal act is the mass of evidence which may point to a contrary conclusion. Such evidence may be derived from an assessment of the behaviors of numerous persons which are similar in appearances but which result in vastly different outcomes. This evidence alone indicates that any assertion suggesting that a victim's behavior alone leads to a particular criminal deed may be premature. In all fairness to von Hentig, he recognized that there were many causative factors in the victim precipitation-victimization sequence; however, contributions to the development of the perspective seem to have ignored these factors. The reason why this has occurred is due to a failure on the parts of researchers and theorists to take both the victim and the criminal into account—their initial responses (both covert and overt), their interpretations of each others' responses, their interpretations of the situation, and their *joint* resulting action. The implication of this criticism is that more elaborate conceptualization is necessary in victimology which emphasizes not only behavior but also symbolic, perceptual, and interpretative variables. Unless this is done, we will be unable to explain why some acts which seem to be sufficient for criminal deeds on some occasions are insufficient on other occasions.

ASSUMPTION IV: THE INTENT OF THE VICTIM CAN BE ASSUMED FROM HIS/HER RESULTANT VICTIMIZATION

A final assumption underlying the dimension of victimology devoted to victim-precipitation discussed in this paper concerns the attribution of intent to the victim. Nowhere is this assumption more apparent than in the following statement: "It is suspected that a large percentage of murder victims initiated the action which led to assault and death, almost as if they wanted to commit suicide and could not" (Reckless, 1973). The attribution of criminal intent is implied also in the observation by Porterfield and Talbert (1954) that in some cases there is almost perfect cooperation by the victim with the killer in the process of getting killed. In fact, the tendency to attribute intent to the rape victim has become so commonplace that Weiss and Borges (1973) felt compelled to devote a paper to the subject entitled "Victimology and Rape: The Case of the Legitimate Victim" in which they questioned the tendency to attribute intent to rape victims.

Upon closer analysis of the victim-precipitation concept, it is not surprising that attribution of intent to the victim is an underlying assumption. Because the potential criminal is "converted" into a criminal by the behavior of the victim, some interpretation of the total act must be made. In an effort to escape the circularity of reasoning mentioned earlier, some students of victimology have attributed a desire or wish for the act to the victim as evidenced by the victim's victimization. Thus, the tautological explanation is extended in that *the victim's precipitative behavior led to the crime because the victim's behavior was precipitative; and, the victim's behavior was precipitative because the victim intended for the crime to occur.* Needless to say, in many instances the only evidence available that the victim "intended" for the crime to occur is the resultant victimization.

It is quite probable that some so-called "victims" actually are desirous of the criminal acts directed toward them. An identification of such "victims," however, must be made independent of the resultant victimization. If this cannot be done, then any relationship drawn between the crime and the intent of the victim may be a function of the imagination of the interpreter rather than the reality of the situation. Again, it is suggested that adequate explanations of the criminal act can emerge only from an intensive exploration of the roles of the victim *and* the criminal.

CONCLUSIONS

Within recent years there has been increased interest in victimology. This interest has centered around phenomena such as victim proneness, victim compensation, victim risk, and victim precipitation among others. We have been concerned with only one aspect of victimology—victim precipitation. Victim precipitation was chosen as the central focus of this discussion because of the increasing number of theoretical and research efforts using victim-precipitation assumptions.

The point of departure in this paper was an identification of the assumptions underlying the victim-precipitation explanatory frameworks which included the following: (1) criminal deeds can be explained by the precipitative behavior of the victim; (2) the criminal is in a passive state and set into action by the victim's behavior; (3) behaviors displayed by a victim are necessary and sufficient for criminal acts; and (4) the intent of the victim can be assumed from his/her resultant victimization.

The results of our evaluation suggested the necessity for theory revision and reconceptualization of victim-precipitation explanatory formulations in victimology. This was due to several fallacies which appear to plague the underlying assumptions of victim-precipitation explanations including circular reasoning, stimulus-response interpretations of human interaction, incongruence between theoretical explanations of victim behaviors and the empirical reality of these behaviors, and inadequate assessment of victim-precipitative behaviors. While an alternative theoretical perspective is not offered, we do suggest directions that can be taken to reconceptualize and revise victim-precipitation explanatory frameworks. Finally, revision and reconceptualization along the lines suggested should contribute immensely to the development of victimology as a perspective in criminology or as a separate discipline.

NOTES

1. There has been some debate over who founded victimology and whether victimology should be considered as a subfield of criminology or as a distinct discipline. The latest major work in victimology (Drapkin and Viano, 1974) does not resolve either issue.

2. The assumptions stated in this paper are drawn from discussions of victimology by Reckless, von Hentig, Mendelsohn, and Ellenberger. Also used as a source for the assumptions presented was *Victimology*, edited by Drapkin and Viano.

3. The examples of crimes provided here have been used by scholars writing in the general area of victimology to illustrate victim precipitation.

4. A recent article by Weiss and Borges (1973) is an exception in that they attacked victim-precipitation explanations of rape indicating among other things that there may very well be an underlying sex bias in the explanatory framework.

5. While some may be tempted to quarrel with this statement, support for this interpretation can be found in von

Hentig's apparent endorsement of the statement that some young girls do not resist sexual advances because of such factors as curiosity, fear, intellectual challenge and thus do not *try* to escape from being victims. It is only axiomatic, then, that if she does escape, her behavior is defined as nonprecipitation.

6. While it would be possible to subsume victim-precipitation under the general category of risk-taking behavior, we have chosen to criticize victim precipitation as a subcategory of the victimology perspective rather than as a subcategory of the aforementioned.

7. For purposes of clarity, a distinction should be made between stimulus-response and response-stimulus-response-models. A stimulus-response model implies that the stimulus is antecedent to the response. In the response-stimulus-response model, the response is antecedent to the stimulus, and in actuality the stimulus becomes an intervening variable. Much of the research on humans in behavioral psychology since the 1930s has used the response-stimulus-response perspective rather than the stimulus-response model. Therefore, more recent discussions of behaviorism are not cited in this paper.

8. Ordinarily, one would not think that offender "interpretation of the situation" negates the possibility of victim-precipitated crimes. However, because victim precipitation, as conceived presently by most of those writing in the area, is stimulus-response based, offender "interpretation of the situation" does exclude the possibility of victim-precipitated crimes.

Such a view is consistent with the general assumptions underlying the Symbolic Interaction perspective in Social Psychology which are (1) that persons react to objects on the basis of the meaning that objects have for them, (2) meaning arises from social interaction, and (3) meaning is modified by individual interpretation (Blumer, 1969).

9. R.E.L. Faris presents an excellent discussion in *Social Psychology* which epitomizes the position of many with regard to stimulus-response psychology.

REFERENCES

Blumer, H. (1969) Symbolic Interactionism: Perspectives and Method. New York: Prentice-Hall.

Drapkin, I. and E. Viano (1974) Victimology: A New Focus. Vol. 1. Lexington, Mass.: D. C. Heath.

Ellenberger, H. (1954) "Psychological relationships between the criminal and his victim." Rèvue Internationale de Police Technique 2:103-121.

Faris, R.E.L. (1952) Social Psychology. New York: Ronald.

Glaser, D. (1970) "Victim survey research: theoretical implications," pp. 136-146 in A. L. Guenther (ed.) Criminal Behavior and Social Systems: Contributions of American Sociology. Chicago: Rand McNally.

Hentig, H. von (1948) The Criminal and His Victim: Studies in the Sociobiology of Crime. New Haven, Conn: Yale Univ. Press.

———(1941) "Remarks on the interaction of perpetrator and victim." J. of Criminal Law, Criminology and Police Sci. 31 (March/April): 303-309.

Mendelsohn, B. (1963) "The origin of the doctrine of victimology." Excerpta Criminologica 3, 3 (May/June):239-244.

———(1956) "The victimology." Etudes Internationales de Psycho-Sociologie Criminelle (July-September):25-26.

———(1947) "New bio-psycho-social horizons: victimology." Communication read to the Roumanian Society of Psychiatry in Bucharest. (unpublished)

Nagel, W. H. (1963) "The notion of victimology in criminology." Excerpta Criminologica 3, 3 (May/June):245-247.

Porterfield, A. L. and R. H. Talbert (1954) Mid-Century Crime in Our Culture: Personality and Crime in the Cultural Patterns of American States. Fort Worth, Texas: Leo Potishman Foundation.

Quinney, R. (1972) "Who is the victim?" Criminology 10, 3:314-323.

Reckless, W. (1973) The Crime Problem. New York: Appleton-Century-Crofts.

Schafer, S. (1968) The Victim and His Criminal. New York: Random House.

Silverman, R. (1974) "Victim typologies: overview, critique and reformulations," pp. 55-65 in Israel Drapkin and Emilio Viano (eds.) Victimology: A New Focus. Vol. 1. Lexington, Mass.: D. C. Heath.

Weiss, K. and S. S. Borges (1973) "Victimology and rape: the case of the legitimate victim." Issues in Criminology 8, 2 (Fall).

Wolfgang, M. (1957) "Victim-precipitated homicide." J. of Criminal Law, Criminology and Police Sci. 48, 1:1-11.

D ◪ *The resisting victim*

Extending the concept of victim responsibility

DANIEL S. CLASTER and DEBORAH S. DAVID

Victimology's major contribution to date is not that it has supplied answers to questions that baffled traditional criminologist, but rather that it has raised questions which criminologists previously ignored. For example, Mendelsohn (1956) and Von Hentig (1948) did not simply supply categories to explain the role of the victim in crime; their contributions are equally important for their criticism of traditional criminology for attributing responsibility to the offender alone. They both described ways in which victims may be responsible for their victimization and called attention to the significance of such factors for a fuller understanding of crime.

Just as victimology extended the idea of responsibility for crime to include the victim as well as the offender, the present paper seeks to extend the idea of victim responsibility to include responsibility for thwarting the act as well as for encouraging it. Thus we shall be dealing with victim *resistance*. Resistance is considered here as *action by a potential victim during a confrontation, which is designed to interfere in any way with completion of the criminal act or escape.*[1] Thus it may comprise active conduct, like physical retaliation or calling for help, but it can also include a refusal to meet the demands of an offender, similar to the passive or nonviolent resistance made famous by Mahatma Gandhi and his followers.

In what follows, we shall indicate some of the ways in which the study of resistance may contribute to victimology. Resistance will be discussed in relation to social power insofar as power affects the impact of resistance upon the outcome of criminal confrontations. Some data from a pilot study of elderly robbery victims in a large metropolitan area will be presented, to illustrate the application of this formulation in empirical research.

RESISTANCE AND VICTIMOLOGY

At the outset, in discussing the place of resistance in victimological theory, we should distinguish between successful and unsuccessful resistance. Sometimes unsuccessful resistance may have no effect at all—that is, the offender may end up doing just what he or she would have done had no resistance been offered. And in studying some cases of unsuccessful resistance, we meet the kind of situation described by Von Hentig (1948:438) who noted that a "fighting victim" may sustain more serious injury than one who has done nothing, and thus may in some sense be responsible for his or her victimization.[2] But what of the successful resister, who actually does succeed in thwarting the offender? Why should victimology study someone who is not really a victim?

One response to this question may be given by analogy. The study of natural immunity from disease is one very useful strategy for understanding the disease itself. By comparing factors present and absent in immune and susceptible organisms, one arrives at an explanation. Closer to our field of present interest are studies of the "good boy" in a high delinquency neighborhood—studies whose value

---

Reprinted by permission from Victimology: An International Journal, vol. 2, no. 1, pp. 109-117, © Visage Press Inc. All rights reserved.

[1]This definition limits the term to behavior initiated during the confrontation, after the victim has been selected by an offender. Resistance may thus be distinguished from prevention, which usually refers to behavior by one who has not been selected as a victim, to avoid being so selected. Since the scope of the present paper is limited to confrontation situations, it will not treat prevention.

[2]See Schafer (1968) for an extended discussion of the meanings of responsibility in victimology.

lies in more clearly pinpointing the distinctive characteristics of delinquents (Reckless et al., 1957). Similarly, it may be anticipated that study of behavior which repels a criminal act would lead to clearer delineation of that which promotes it.

Moreover, to dichotomize resistance as succesful or unsuccessful may be a useful shorthand procedure, but it may also obscure important gradations. In this connection it seems useful to offer a definition of victimization, as the *degree* of harm resulting from a criminal act. Thus we treat it, not as an all-or-none attribute, but as a variable—specifically, one that reflects the amount of injury done. Such a definition is consistent with the Sellin-Wolfgang typology (1964), which reflects the degree of such harm. In light of this definition we suggest, as a second reason for studying the "successful" resister within a victimological framework, that he or she may be successful only in having avoided one kind of injury, but that we should allow for the possibility of more subtle, and possibly greater damage than simply the loss of a wallet or ring—damage in terms of increased anxiety, leading to reluctance to go outside one's home or neighborhood, in turn depriving the individual of social satisfactions, and so on.[3] Thus an overtly successful resister may still be a victim.

More generally, then, our rationale for studying resistance is that it may affect victimization in one way or another (Conklin, 1972). With Schafer (1968) we consider that the issue of responsibility lies at the core of the study of victimology. As usually interpreted, victim responsibility applies to the guilty victim. The guilty victim has been regarded as one who has done something, and that something has led to the victimization. In that sense he or she is responsible, in contrast to the innocent victim, who has done nothing and nevertheless suffers at the hands of a criminal (Mendelsohn, 1956). What such a formulation does not consider, as suggested by examples above, is the possibility that action, as well as promoting victimization, may thwart the criminal act, in which case we would be dealing with a potential victim who is responsible for minimizing his or her victimization, in contrast to the provocateur, who contributes to his or her own suffering. Put differently, we may identify potential victims in three ways rather than two: (1) those who contribute to their own suffering, (2) those who do nothing to affect it, and (3) those who minimize it. If victim responsibility represents a significant focus in victimology, as is generally accepted, then it seems only reasonable to study the effects of all three alternatives.

Victim responsibility

To spell out a research strategy, a goal that is implied above, we need to clarify our sense of the word responsibility as it relates to the concept of resistance. Without pursuing all the ramifications dealt with by Schafer, we may note two senses in which the term responsibility is used. One sense is illustrated in the sentence "The storm was responsible for a million dollars worth of damage." A second sense is expressed when we speak of a person who "takes on the responsibility" to accomplish some goal. In the first sense, responsibility is retrospective: after the damage occurred, we attribute it to the storm. The example makes clear that the term need not imply motivation, since of course a storm is not "motivated" in the ordinary sense of that term. In the second phrase, on the other hand, the outcome is unknown, but we use the term "responsibility" in the sense of *intention*—to indicate that someone acts with a view toward accomplishing a goal.

For purposes of research in victimology, we advocate confining use of the term responsibility to the second sense connoting intention. Congruent with this, resistance has been defined above as action which "is designed to interfere . . ." It is therefore a subjective definition. Admittedly this presents a problem insofar as it may represent different actions in different cases. But we choose it in preference to a definition that is tied to the results of the action,

---

[3]At the same time we cannot ignore the possibility that successful resistance can bring positive rewards, like social recognition, or a feeling of competence that diminishes previous fears.

since it is precisely the results with which we wish ultimately to correlate acts of resistance.

Power

A crucial factor impinging upon the potential victim, affecting his or her behavior vis-a-vis a criminal adversary, is that of social power, as Schafer has pointed out (1968:8). In formulating a research design, it is thus relevant to take account of the power relationship between victim and offender. The actual power relationship may be reflected, for example, by comparing physical size, occupation, sex, age, or number of participants for both parties. Relevant as well is the *perceived* power relationship. While the objective facts ordinarily have a strong influence on subjective perception of power, it is interesting to consider cases where there is a discrepancy. Of particular interest in the study of resistance are victims who appear to be at a disadvantage in relation to an offender who confronts them, but who nevertheless make an effort to fight back, to stall, or to call for help even when they are threatened with physical harm.

In order to hold constant the objective power situation, so that we might pursue variations in perceived power, we chose elderly persons as research subjects. Since they are not well equipped to run or fight back in a robbery situation, they are likely to be chosen as targets when they venture out of their houses, and when chosen, are at a greater disadvantage than younger people (Cunningham, 1973). And yet many elderly people appear not to take account of discrepancy. For example, in an early interview we encountered a retired schoolteacher who had been accosted by two young adolescents demanding her purse, while she was leaving a supermarket. She responded angrily, "I'll give you your head," and raised her cane as if to strike them. As they retreated she yelled, "Don't go away, the cops are coming."

Because of the variability in response to victimization among the elderly, we began to consider the range of factors that would lead some of these people to offer resistance, and others to comply. Our orientation in selecting factors related to resistance was guided by work on disengagement among the elderly (Cumming, 1963; Hochschild, 1975). We anticipated that disengaged senior citizens—those who are less integrated into friendship networks, family, formal organizations and other social groups—would be less likely to offer resistance in a criminal confrontation because they feel that their own actions will have no impact on the outcome.

Methods

For briefing us on the nature of robberies in which senior citizens are victims, and for assistance in contacting respondents, we benefited from the cooperation of the Senior Citizens' Robbery Unit (SCRU) of the New York City Police Department, located in the 48 Precinct, Bronx, New York.[4] This is a group of ten police officers concerned with investigating robberies against persons over age 60 that take place inside buildings (as opposed to street crimes). The cases are referred to the SCRU from all precincts in the Bronx. Occasionally, a case comes to the attention of the police only after the victim has gone to a social agency to remedy a loss sustained in a crime, such as getting a new Medicare card. In these situations, the agency will notify the police. The officers investigate by interviewing the victims and showing them photographs of suspects or known offenders. They go beyond usual police routine in transporting the victims back and forth to both police headquarters and the courts, for investigation and/or testimony. In addition, these police officers perform a variety of social services, for example, making repeated call-backs if the victim is too upset to discuss the incident at the time the officers call on her or him, or helping a victim find a new apartment to move to. The officers from SCRU also work closely with the various senior citizens groups in the Bronx and conduct demonstration-lectures for the elderly

[4]We wish to express our appreciation to the personnel of the Bronx Senior Citizens' Robbery Unit, and various social agencies who shared their insights with us and facilitated our interviews. We owe a special debt to Detective Thomas Sullivan for his many contributions to this project. We are grateful to the respondents in this study for their willingness to be interviewed.

on ways to protect themselves against crime.

Through the cooperation of the SCRU, we embarked on a pilot study of robbery victims listed in their files. As background, we held discussions with the police officers and personnel in social agencies who deal with these victims, and exploratory group interviews with victims at several senior citizens' centers. The preliminary data we present here are based on 20 structured interviews with persons who were victimized during June, 1976. This last group was selected from a list given to us by the SCRU of all such elderly known to them. The only proviso was that any open cases not be interviewed. We attempted to set up appointments for face-to-face interviews with the victims, but in several instances they were unwilling to have us interview them, failed to keep appointments, or in one case, the daughter of the victim called the police to request that her mother not be interviewed for reasons of health. Therefore, we found it expedient to interview victims when we first reached them by telephone, if they were willing. As a result, 17 are telephone interviews and three are face-to-face.

In constructing an interview guide for use in the pilot study, we included a number of questions about membership and attendance at formal organizations, including church, senior citizens' centers, etc. We also asked about the frequency of contacts with relatives and friends, both in person and by telephone.

Another series of questions dealt with the respondents' experience with crime. As indicated below, we selected respondents who were recorded by the police as recent robbery victims. A number of questions were included to get at the details of the confrontation—its location, who said what and did what, and the outcome, in terms of financial loss and physical injury. We also inquired into the phenomenon of "vulnerability conversion" (Lejeune and Alex, 1973): how frightened the victims were thereafter, whether or not they were less willing to venture outside their apartments, to what extent they took greater security precautions, etc. Generally the interview guide provided a means to classify respondents with respect to disengagement, social power, resistance or compliance, and effects. Our plan for analysis centered on factors affecting resistance, and the consequences of resistance.

Findings

We found that in seven of the cases, the circumstances were such that resistance was precluded. In these cases the confrontations were very transitory with a strong element of surprise, in which a pocketbook was snatched or the victim was grabbed from behind and rendered immobile while being relieved of purse, wallet, or other valuables. The presence of resistance was ambiguous for three respondents. In two cases there was complete compliance with explicit demands of the robbers. Of the five instances where victims resisted, two did so by calling for help during the confrontations, and a third victim withheld information as to the location of money. The fourth resister, being choked from behind, so that he could not call out, kicked and pulled his assailant's hair, until the assailant loosened his grip, and then he called for help. The fifth resisting victim had been followed home from a bank after withdrawing $400. The criminal accompanied the victim into the apartment house elevator. As the victim stepped out at his floor:

He [the robber] made a grab for my side pocket where I had the envelope. He said, "Give me what you got in that pocket." I think I said, "No you don't," and grabbed his arm. I called to my wife to bring a bat. We struggled.

From this small group of respondents, there emerged no clear relationship between resistance and disengagement. All but two of the respondents had almost daily contact with either acquaintances, friends, or relatives. The patterns of resistance for these two victims were no different from those of the victims with more integrated social networks. A larger sample might, however, reveal some differences.

A major focus of our research had to do with the impact of the event on the lives of the victims. In the majority of cases, property loss was not great (less than $50). As for physical injury, there was one case where the victim sustained serious enough injury to require extended hospitalization. In regard to the impact on their day-to-day lives, most victims were not affected. This is not to say that they were not fearful of crime, but for many the effect of this occurrence was to heighten previously existing concern, rather than initiate fear. Typically our respondents report that they were more careful about entering elevators with strangers after their victimization than before. However, when we asked them whether they had begun to avoid going out at certain hours after the incident, most indicated that their practice was to avoid going out after dark before they had personally been robbery victims, and continued that practice after the incident.

Implications

The practical question which arises for the person on the street is, "How should I act if I am a victim?" At an early stage in formulating our study we were impressed by some dramatic press reports of resistance by elderly victims that were successful in thwarting attempted robberies. We were told of a case handled by the Senior Citizens' Robbery Unit in which two young offenders inflicted serious physical injuries for no apparent reason upon a series of nonresisting victims after they had robbed them, but then encountered one forceful woman victim who, although she yielded her property, said to them, "I'm giving you the money now, but I'll see you in jail later." Significantly, she alone, among the victims of these offenders who were known to the police, was not assaulted in the course of the robbery.

On the other hand, there are clearly forms of resistance that do provoke the offender. One of our interviewees had already told the robber where she kept fifty dollars to pay her utilities bill. He then demanded more money and threatened, for the second time, to kill her. She said, "Don't you have a mother?" At that, he began to choke her with a towel that he had put over her head earlier, simply so that she would be unable to identify him. Fortunately she was not injured, but the choking did serve to stop her from talking—conceivably, because "mother" was an emotionally loaded symbol for the robber. The detectives assigned to the SCRU indicated that

they were struck by the demeanor of the robbers they encountered, contrasting sharply with offenders against younger victims. These robbers, most of them adolescents, showed none of the cockiness or wise-guy attitudes that the police ordinarily encounter, possibly because victimizing the elderly evokes a feeling of guilt within the offender. It seems apparent that the social power variable needs to be carefully taken into account in this connection, and we plan to measure it more explicitly in our continuing research.

But beyond the practical implications of resistance in the context to which our pilot study is limited, the effect of resistance by victims in a variety of situations deserves to be studied. It may be profitably investigated in any of the traditional crimes against the person, and there has been some attention to it in crimes other than robbery, for example, in the case of rape (Chappell and James, 1976). And it is of course also relevant for political crime. The issue of resistance—its presence or lack—remains a burning issue among students of the Jewish reaction to the Nazi holocaust (Hilberg, 1961; Suhl, 1967). It is hoped that a general theory of resistance, applicable to situations ranging from traditional crimes against the person to genocide, will be developed within victimology.

REFERENCES

Chappell, Duncan and Jennifer James
　1973 "Victim Selection and Apprehension from the Rapist's Perspective," paper presented at Second International Symposium on Victimology, Boston.
Conklin, John
　1972 *Robbery and the Criminal Justice System.* Philadelphia: Lippincott.
Cumming, Elaine
　1963 "Further Thoughts on the Theory of Disengagement." *International Social Science Journal* 15: 377-93.
Cunningham, Carl L.
　1973 "Crime and the Aging Victim." *Midwest Research Institute Quarterly,* Spring: 4-9.
Hentig, Hans von
　1948 *The Criminal and His Victim.* New Haven: Yale University Press.
Hillberg, Raul
　1961 *The Destruction of the European Jews.* Chicago: Quadrangle.

Hochschild, Arlie
   1975 "Disengagement Theory: A Critique and Proposal," *American Sociological Review* 40 (Oct.):553-69.
Lejeune, Robert and Nicholas Alex
   1973 "On Being Mugged: The Event and Its Aftermath," *Urban Life and Culture* 2 (Oct.):259-87.
Mendelsohn, B.
   1956 "The Victimology," *Etudes Internationales de Psycho-Sociologie Criminelle* 1 (July-Sept):25-36.
Reckless, Walter C., Simon Dinitz, and Ellen Murray
   1957 "The 'Good Boy' in a High Delinquency Area," *Journal of Criminal Law, Criminology, and Police Science* 48 (May-June):18-25.

Schafer, Stephen
   1968 *The Victim and His Criminal*. New York: Random House.
Sellin, Thorsten and Margin E. Wolfgang
   1964 *The Measurement of Delinquency*. New York: Wiley.
Singer, Simon
   1976 "The Seriousness of Crime and the Elderly Victim," Paper presented at Second International Symposium on Victimology, Boston.
Suhl, Yuri
   1967 *They Fought Back*. New York: Crown.

Selected readings for Chapter 6

Amir, Menachem. *Patterns in Forcible Rape* (Chicago: University of Chicago Press, 1971).
> A study of social characteristics and social relationships of 1,292 offenders and 646 victims of rape reported in Philadelphia between 1958 and 1960.

Baldwin, John. "The Role of the Victim in Certain Property Offences," *The Criminal Law Review* (England), 1974, pp. 353-358.
> Data collected from 1966 police crime records for Sheffield, England, for the offences of housebreaking, taking motor vehicles without the owner's consent, and stealing from unattended cars. Many victims were found to be careless and failed to take minimal precautions to avoid loss of property, but the data did not show that the carelessness directly contributed to the actual offenses. Whether persons who are victimized by property offenses are more careless than the general population is not known.

Gobert, James J. "Victim Precipitation," *Columbia Law Review* **77:**512-553, 1977.
> The law fails to recognize the concept of victim or third-party precipitation; this recognition needs to occur and should be followed by a definition of the role of precipitation in criminal law. Precipitation offenders should be subjected to criminal sanctions, but the sentence might be reduced based on the precipitation. Precipitators themselves might also be subject to legal sanctions.

Johnson, Joan H., et al. *The Recidivist Victim: A Descriptive Study,* Criminal Justice Monograph, vol. 4, no. 1, Institute of Contemporary Corrections and the Behavioral Sciences, Sam Houston University, Huntsville, Texas, 1973.
> A descriptive study of crime victims seeking services at the emergency ward of a hospital for treatment from gunshot wounds; about 20% of the victims had previously been treated at the same hospital for gunshot wounds resulting from earlier crime victimizations.

Silverman, Robert A. "Victim Precipitation: An Examination of the Concept," in Drapkin, Israel, and Emilio Viano, eds. *Victimology: A New Focus,* vol. 1, *Theoretical Issues in Victimology* (Lexington, Mass.: D. C. Heath, 1974), pp. 99-109.
> Examines the variety of definitions and conceptual ambiguities in the use of the term *victim precipitation* and suggests a common conceptual definition.

Silverman, Robert A. "Victim-Offender Relationships in Face-to-Face Delinquent Acts," *Social Problems* **22:**383-393, 1975.
> Police and court records were reviewed for juvenile offenders from a large eastern city for 1969; a 5% systematic random sample yielded a total of 572 cases, of which 168 involved victimizations in which the victim had visual contact with the offender. These records were further analyzed to study the interpersonal relationships of the 168 juvenile offenders and their victims.

Wolfgang, Marvin E. *Patterns in Criminal Homicide,* (New York: John Wiley & Sons, Inc., 1958).
> A study of 588 homicides occurring in Philadelphia from 1948 to 1952; 588 homicides involved 621 offenders; 150 of the homicides were judged to involve victim precipitation.

Chapter 7

VICTIMS OF FAMILY VIOLENCE

A ☐ *Battered women: scope of the problem*
DEL MARTIN

B ☐ *The battered husband syndrome*
SUZANNE K. STEINMETZ

C ☐ *Significant findings in child abuse research*
MARC F. MADEN and DAVID F. WRENCH

A ☐ *Battered women*

Scope of the problem

DEL MARTIN

A problem—in this case, wife-battering—becomes significant and of public importance when it can be proved that it affects millions of people. Consequently, many of us have been forced to play the numbers game in order to make the public aware that wife abuse is indeed a very serious social problem. Accurately determining the incidence of wife beating, of course, is nigh unto impossible—not only because obvious sources of statistics (police, courts, doctors, social workers, and mental health professionals) don't keep such records, but also because of differences in defining the problem.

Reprinted from United States Civil Rights Commission, *Battered Women: Issues of Public Policy* (Washington D.C.: A Consultation Sponsored by the United States Commission on Civil Rights, January 30-31, 1978), pp. 3-18.

The police term "domestic disturbance" is not synonymous with "wife beating." A domestic disturbance may or may not involve actual physical violence. But even agreeing on a definition of "violence" poses a problem. Police seem to think that few domestic disturbances are really violent. They tend to define violence in terms of its effect. In the absence of blood and visible injury, they are apt to discount the wife's report of her husband's brutality.

The law, however, defines violence by the degree of its severity, and social scientists tend to measure violence by the degree of its acceptance. The fact that one-fifth of American adults in a Harris poll approved of slapping one's spouse on "appropriate" occasions is seen by the latter as "legitimizing" a certain amount of violence.[1]

For our purposes, marital violence will be described as "an act carried out with the intention of, or perceived intention of, physically injuring one's spouse." The act can include slapping, hitting, punching, kicking, throwing things, beating, using a weapon, choking, pushing, shoving, biting, grabbing, etc. And the cast of characters includes men and women who live together in an intimate relationship, whether or not they are legally married.

I deliberately called my book *Battered Wives* to focus on marriage as the institutional source and setting in which the violence is initiated and carried out.[2] Although many try to avoid its implications, to me, domestic violence cannot be fully understood without examining the institution of marriage itself as the context in which the violence takes place. The power relationship between husband and wife is culturally determined, and its imperatives necessarily affect other man-woman relationships despite attempts to avoid or escape its legalization by the marriage ceremony.

Another problem in gathering statistics on wife beating, besides the fact that it is one of the most unreported crimes, is that language in police reports and research studies often describes assailants and victims in non-specific terms. Gender is omitted.

Although many have rebelled against feminist attempts to de-sex the language, suddenly, for some reason, it becomes the vogue when discussing domestic violence. The Kansas City, Missouri, police study of 1971-72 refers to assailants and victims without specifying either their sex or marital role.[3] And social scientists speak of "family" violence and "intrafamily" murder. It should be made clear that what we are discussing is the battering of women by the men they love and live with.

A national survey of 2,143 couples, randomly selected and demographically representative, was conducted in 1976 by Murray Straus, Suzanne Steinmetz, and Richard Gelles to measure the magnitude of marital violence. From the results Straus estimates that, of the approximately 47 million couples living together in the United States in 1975, over 1.7 million had faced a husband or wife yielding a knife or gun, well over 2 million had been beaten up by their spouse, and another 2.5 million had engaged in high-risk injury violence.[4]

The findings showed a high rate of violence for wives, but the data did not indicate what proportion of violent acts committed by wives were in self-defense. Husbands showed a higher rate for the most dangerous and injurious forms of violence (beating or using a knife or gun) and for the repetitiveness of their brutal acts.[5]

Wives reportedly resort to violence mostly as a protective reaction—in self-defense or out of fear. Fighting back, they say, often results in even more severe beatings. Lenore Walker, who has isolated a "three-phase cycle" theory of marital violence, says that many wives, when they recognize the inevitability of an acute incident, may deliberately provoke it in order to get it over with and move on to the "calm, loving respite" stage that follows.[6]

The practice of wife beating crosses all boundaries of economic class, race, national origin, or educational background. It happens in the ghetto, in working-class neighborhoods, in middle-class homes, and in the wealthiest counties of our Nation.[7]

The often held assumption that violence occurs more frequently among lower class families could be due to variations in reporting. Having fewer resources and less privacy, these families are more apt to call police or seek the services of other public agencies. Middle or upper class wives and husbands have greater access to private support services and thus are less apt to come to the attention of authorities.[8]

Women who are treated for physical injuries or for severe depression are often victims who go undetected, since they do not volunteer the information out of fear or shame, and few doctors ask. One psychiatrist, who claimed that he had never encountered a case of marital violence in his practice, was challenged to ask his next 10 female clients. Eight out of the 10 proved to be victims.

Elaine Hilberman and Kit Munson, in their study of 60 women drawn from a rural health clinic, found that the history of physical abuse was known by the initial clinician in only 4 of the 60 cases, although most of the women and their children had received ongoing medical care at the clinic.[9]

The danger in our inability to identify victims is that violence unchecked often leads to murder. The husband in domestic homicides is almost as often the victim as the wife.[10] Since a woman doesn't have the physical strength of a man, she may—out of desperation to put a stop to the beating—pick up the nearest object and let her assailant/husband have it. The object may turn out to be a lethal weapon. In the last year the news media has reported a sizeable number of trials in which the wife murdered her husband after years of being subjected to constant beatings.

The sheer numbers of violent male-female relationships indicate that we would be foolhardy to regard domestic violence solely in terms of the personal interaction between the two parties involved. To understand why it is happening, we must also examine the social imperatives that influence their behavior. This includes a review of the history of marriage, prevailing attitudes towards women, sex role stereotyping, the expectations versus the realities of marriage, and the response of helping agencies in times of crisis. All of these factors have a powerful influence on what we usually think of as a "private" and very "personal" relationship.

Wife beating is not a new phenomenon. It has been going on for thousands of years. Frederick Engels placed its beginning with the emergence of the first monogamous pairing relationship and the patriarchal social and economic system.[11] Prior to the pairing marriage, women, as the only discernible parents, were held in high esteem among the clans. The new arrangement came about because women sought protection from what Susan Brownmiller called "open season on rape,"[12] and because men wanted to authenticate and guarantee their identity and rights as fathers. But the cost to women for their husbands' "protection" came high. The new "father right" brought about the complete subjugation of one sex by the other.

Although polygamy and infidelity remained men's privileges, the strictest fidelity was demanded of women, who became their husband's property. Women were confined to certain parts of the home, isolated, guarded, and restricted from public activity. A woman was duty bound to marry, satisfy her husband's lust, bear his children, and tend to his household. If a woman showed any signs of having a will of her own, the husband was expected by both church and state to chastise her for her transgressions.

Women were burned at the stake under many pretexts, including scolding and nagging, refusing to have intercourse, miscarrying (even though the miscarriage was caused by a kick or a blow from the husband), and for sodomy (even though the husband who committed it was forgiven).[13] Too numerous to mention here are the worldwide accounts of the inhumane and callous treatment of women in the name of the law, religion, and social custom—treatment that clearly indicates how deeply entrenched sexual inequality, at the least, and woman hating, at the extreme, is in human history.

In our own country a husband was permitted to beat his wife so long as he didn't use a switch any bigger around than his thumb.[14] In 1874 the Supreme Court of North Carolina nullified the husband's right to chastise his wife "under any circumstances." But the court's ruling became ambiguous when it added, "If no permanent injury has been inflicted, nor malice, cruelty, nor dangerous violence shown by the husband, it is better to draw the curtain, shut out the public gaze, and leave the parties to forgive and forget."[15]

The latter qualifying statement has become the basis of the American legal system. Laws against assault and battery are rarely invoked against husbands because the criminal justice system (which is male dominated) and victims of domestic violence (who are primarily female) differ in their interpretations of "serious injury," "malice," "cruelty," and "danger."

The police, mental health practitioners, emergency room attendants, prosecutors, and judges deal with isolated cases and the interrelationship of a particular couple. In this light, it is not surprising that they tend to view wife abuse as a personal dispute in which one or both individuals are to blame. This attitude, coupled with the concept of family as the basic unit of society which must be preserved at all costs, fosters the belief that mediation or professional counseling will restore peace and harmony and thus enforcement of laws against assault and battery will serve no useful purpose.

Police often say that they are called out of "vindictiveness"—that the caller tries to use the police as a counter-punch and get an authority figure to take her side in an argument. Police officers feel they have neither the time, competence, nor social mandate to deal with domestic disputes. Consequently such calls receive a low priority.

In a sample of 283 calls over a 2-month period in Vancouver, B.C., Donald Dutton and Bruce Levens found that a car was dispatched 53.8 percent of the time for man-woman fights. In only 10 percent of the cases did these calls receive priority one attention. If the caller mentioned violence the probability of a car being dispatched went up to 67 percent; this was true also if alcohol was mentioned. If violence and children were involved, a car was dispatched 73 percent of the time. The mention of these variables improved the chances of immediate police response—a decision which was not based on the availability of police personnel or vehicles, the researchers said, because the dispatch rate did not fluctuate with the time of day or the shift.[16]

The arrest rate in this study was about 7 percent.[17] The reluctance of police to make arrests is a common complaint of wife/victims. When a woman calls the police, it is an act of desperation. She expects immediate response and protection. At most the officer, if and when he does show up, may get the husband to leave the home for a cooling off period. Police, of course, can only make felony arrests for "probable cause" and must witness the offense in order to make an arrest for assault and battery misdemeanors.

The onus then is on the victim to make a citizen's arrest, but she may be in a state of trauma (having just been beaten) and incapable of making that decision or fearful of reprisal if she is the one to initiate criminal proceedings. Should she be insistent on her right to have her assailant arrested, the wife/victim is likely to be discouraged from doing so by the police.

At the training academy in Michigan officers are told to avoid arrests and appeal to the woman's vanity. They are told to explain the whole procedure of obtaining a warrant, that she is going to have to sign it and appear in court and should consider the loss of time and court costs. Police are also told to explain that victims usually change their minds before going to court, and perhaps she really ought to postpone any decision about making an arrest.[18]

The training bulletin of the Oakland, California, Police Department warns of the danger to the officer if he arrests the husband, who is apt to turn on him to save face in front of his family. The bulletin also states that when no "serious" crime has been committed but one of the parties demands arrest, the officer should explain the ramifications (like loss of wages and bail procedures) and encourage the parties to reason together.[19]

This policy has made the Oakland Police Department the defendant in a suit brought in Federal court by four battered women on the grounds that the nonarrest policy is a denial of their right to equal protection under the law and a breach of the duty of police to make arrests. A similar suit is pending before the Manhattan Supreme Court not only against the New York City Police Department, but also the clerk and probation employees of the family court. This suit was brought by 12 battered women, and 59 more have filed affidavits—a clear indication that many victims would follow through on their complaints if the criminal justice system were more responsive and less obstructive in its procedures.

In recent years family crisis intervention training for police has been highly touted as the means and mode of handling domestic violence cases. The concept, or at least the words, sound impressive, but the effectiveness solutionwise is questionable. While a reduction in repeat calls is attributed to this training, it may be that victims do not call back because they feel it would be useless to do so. Much of the training is to teach the officers how to protect themselves, and rightfully so.

The FBI statistics for 1974 show that one out of five officers killed in the line of duty died trying to break up a family fight.[20] Yet, ironically, police still dismiss domestic disturbances as mere "family spats." If they are dangerous to trained police officers, they must certainly be dangerous to a defenseless woman and her children.

Equally disconcerting is this reference in the training guide published by the Law Enforcement Assistance Administration of the U.S. Department of Justice: "Although the prevailing American culture tolerates a minimum of physical force as a reaction to anger, such physical force is the common response among certain ethnic groups. Therefore, whether or not the use of such force can be considered serious depends in part on the cultural background of the people using it."[21]

The guide goes on to say, "In some cultures the dominance of the father is especially noticeable. In Puerto Rican families, for example, the need to assert masculinity ('machismo') is very important to males and taught to them early."[22] Such an approach possibly reflects some racist assumptions. But, if indeed, some communities are more tolerant of family violence, that situation is part of the problem and should not obviate enforcement of the law.

The values and perceptions that become the excuse for doing nothing are those of male culture, which is, by and large, shared by male police officers. It does not necessarily reflect the perceptions of nor the acceptance by women who are victims of that culture.

Most police training guides refer to family disputes and rarely make direct references to wife beating. I did manage to find this single example under the heading "Illustrations of Dispute Situations Involving the Use of Authority, Negotiation and Counseling Approaches." "A married couple had an argument resulting in the wife's nose being broken by her husband. The officer asked the wife for her story, if she wanted her husband arrested, if she still loved her husband, and where he could find the husband. After locating the husband, the officer informed him that his wife was in pain, and asked him if he loved his wife, and what had happened. He then brought the two together and asked them to talk and apologize to each other.

He reminded them that their child would never forget incidents like the present one, and suggested that if one spouse began to argue, the other should remember her or his responsibilities and leave. He said that if they both acted like children there would be no one to govern their child. Reminding them that they were lucky this time—the husband had no charges brought against him; the wife had only a broken nose—the officer left."[23]

The benevolent nonarrest policy might be satisfactory in some instances if the husband/assailant responded to leniency and kindness by resolving never to resort to violence again. Unfortunately, the man is more apt to see this leniency as reinforcement for his abusive behavior. He quickly learns that lesser injuries, like a broken nose, are tolerated by the system and the probability of his being taken into custody is remote. In the Oakland case against the police, one complainant stated that her husband repeatedly handed her the phone and dared her to call police, knowing full well he was safe from arrest and prosecution.

Male prosecutors and judges react in much the same way as the police. District attorneys count stitches and witnesses before deciding if they have a "winning case." And judges, when the husband is found guilty, are likely to let him off with a warning, probation, or a small fine on his worthless promise that he won't do it again.

Although studies show that domestic violence, when it becomes an established pattern, often leads to homicide, police and others in the helping professions persist in viewing the violence as resulting from an argument or communications breakdown. The danger of escalation of the violence is all too often overlooked. Well, not entirely. There are social scientists who are speculating on what makes the difference between the man who merely wounds his wife and the man who kills her.[24] One researcher sees the murderer as a man less experienced in violence who can go too far when he loses control. Another says that alcohol could affect his judgment of the degree of battering a woman could take without dying.

Social service agencies are no more effective than the criminal justice system in offering battered wives help and protection. They are not open at night or on weekends when the violence usually occurs. Emergency housing for women with children, until recently, was virtually non-existent.

A 1973 survey in Los Angeles showed that there were 4,000 beds available for men, but only 30 for women with children, and none for mothers with sons over 4 years of age.[25] This is an indication of how outdated our social service system is. The assumption is that men may be transient and in need of shelter, but that women always have a home—with their husbands or their parents.

A woman who flees from a violent home in the middle of the night is usually without funds and has only the clothes on her back. If she seeks welfare, she may be turned down because her husband's salary disqualifies her. Unless she has filed for divorce or has established separate maintenance, technically she is neither home-less nor destitute. In St. Louis, Missouri, I am told, it takes from 4 to 6 weeks for the first wel-fare check to come, during which time the woman must have established a permanent resi-dence, been cleared by a social worker who makes a home visit, and provided the depart-ment of social services with proof of birth and social security numbers for herself and her chil-dren. To rent a place the woman needs money, and rent vouchers are difficult to obtain. If she is lucky enough to get one, however, she finds that most landlords won't accept rent vouchers. They want cash on the line. Without a place to go or means of support until she can become independent, the wife/victim is often forced to return to her violent husband.

A study of 100 battered wives in England re-vealed that 89 had fled their homes, 36 having fled four or more times, and some having left 10 or even 20 times.[26] They had returned home be-cause (1) they were found by their husbands who either threatened them with further abuse or promised to reform, or (2) none of the agen-cies they turned to for help could offer them pro-tection or a roof over their heads. Also, many of the women married right out of high school and had no job experience or marketable skills.

If a woman does manage to get away and ob-tains a divorce, she still has no guarantee of safety. Some ex-husbands continue to stalk and hunt down "their" women for years after a di-vorce, forcing their victims to move and change jobs continually. Despite the danger, judges continue to grant violent fathers visitation rights, and thus the opportunity to further in-timidate their ex-wives.

When a woman concludes that her husband isn't going to change and that she has no alter-native but to leave him, she is forced to face the cold, hard facts of the poverty of her existence. How is she going to support herself and her chil-dren? Even if she had worked before marrying, her lack of recent references counts against her. In all likelihood she will have to take a menial job at low pay to reestablish herself as a mem-ber of the work force. Discrimination against women in employment often precludes her from advancement in position and salary.

It is often said that a wife is one man away from welfare. Despite myths to the contrary, studies show that alimony is rarely awarded and most fathers do not even make child support payments as ordered by the court. In the first year after divorce, 62 percent fail to comply fully and 42 percent do not even make a single pay-ment. By the 10th year, 79 percent are in total noncompliance.[27] Without child support or child care, the divorced working mother may find that her "take home pay" is less than the minimal subsistence offered by welfare.

Instead of asking the all too frequent ques-tion, "Why does a woman stay in a violent mar-riage?" we should be asking, "What is it about marriage and society that keeps a woman cap-tive in a violent marriage?" I have already al-luded to historical attitudes toward wives as property of their husbands, to acceptance of lesser violence, like slapping, as "legitimate," and to public agency policy which offers vic-tims no alternative. But the basic problem, as I see it, is the institution of marriage itself and the way in which women and men are social-ized to act out dominant-submissive roles that in and of themselves invite abuse. Husband/as-sailants and wife/victims are merely the actors in the script that society has written for them.

Battered women are often perceived as somehow provoking their husbands to violence in order to fulfill a basic female masochistic need. Such theories evolve from the patriarchal structure of our society in which the dominant group (men) define acceptable roles for subordinates (women).

The superior role of men is maintained by definition of "masculinity" as strong, active, rational, aggressive, and authoritarian and "femininity" as submissive, passive, dependent, weak, and masochistic. These roles are incorporated into the culture by its philosophy, science, social and psychological theory, morality, and law. The inequality of the roles is obscured by calling them "natural" or "normal" and by training women to dependency upon men in order to maintain the nuclear family as the basic unit of society.

Women have been socialized to believe that their greatest achievement in life is marriage and motherhood and that failure of the marriage is the wife's personal failure. If the woman adopts the characteristics and role assigned to her, adapts to her husband's personality and submerges her own, she is called "normal" and "feminine." This was emphasized in the Broverman study in which professional therapists were asked to describe typical male and female behavior and to indicate what is normal adult behavior (sex unspecified). Not surprisingly, they described male and female behavior in stereotypical terms and equated the normal adult with accepted male characteristics.[28]

Ruth Pancoast and Lynda Weston point out that men experience no dichotomy between adulthood and manhood because society says the two are identical. But the woman who tries to be a healthy adult does so at the expense of being "feminine," and a woman who adjusts to her "normal" role does so at the expense of being a healthy adult. Society has then constructed a "no-win" situation for women.[29]

Furthermore, the feudal system of marriage described earlier is still existent today. Aaron Rutledge says, "Despite the age of jets and satellites, some people try to get by on a horse-and-buggy marriage. . . . Individuals who would not tolerate a feudal society still insist upon an owner-tenant type of family structure."[30]

The master-serf type of family is characterized by the husband/father as head of household who, as the breadwinner, gives his wife and children what they need, as he defines their needs. This "stay-in-your-place" family depends upon each member following preconceived roles and respecting the authority of the husband/father, who metes out punishment when the wife or children get out of line.

In early English common law husband and wife were considered one person: "The very being or legal existence of the woman is suspended during the marriage, or at least is incorporated and consolidated into that of the husband, under whose wing, protection, and cover she peforms everything."[31]

A 1944 Florida Supreme Court decision verified that a woman's legal status in the 20th century is no different: "A woman's responsibilities and faculties remain intact from age of maturity until she finds her mate; whereupon incompetency seizes her and she needs protection in an extreme degree. Upon the advent of widowhood she is reinstated with all her capabilities which had been dormant during her marriage, only to lose them again upon remarriage."[32]

In many states the husband has exclusive authority over "community" property, including all the wife's earnings, and can dissipate the family assets without the wife's prior knowledge or consent. The wife is at the mercy of her husband, whom the state presumes to be a benevolent despot. If he decides to give her no money and refuses to buy her clothing, she has no legal recourse.

In 1953 a Nebraska court ruled: "The living standard of a family are a matter of concern to the household. As long as the home is maintained and the parties are living as husband and wife it may be said that the husband is legally supporting his wife, and the purpose of the marriage relation is being carried out."[33]

The 1962 ruling of a Connecticut court was even more explicit about the wife's obligation to her husband "to be his help mate, to love and care for him in sickness, and to labor faithfully to advance his interests." She must also perform "her household and domestic duties . . . without compensation therefor. A husband is entitled to benefit of his wife's industry and economy."[34]

In marriage the woman loses her personhood and is identified in terms of her husband. With few exceptions, she takes her husband's name and his domicile. She must literally "love, honor and obey" or suffer the consequences. Her labor is a duty to be performed without value or compensation. Since the wages her husband earns belong to him, she is totally dependent upon his whim or generosity—a situation that leaves the wife vulnerable to abuse.

Needless to say, the expectations women have about marriage differ significantly from the reality of the marriage contract, which Lenore Weitzman points out is unlike most contracts. Its provisions are unwritten, its penalties unspecified, and its terms are unknown to the contracting parties, who are not allowed any options to its terms.[35]

A study conducted by Hernán San Martín in Chile on the reasons women and men marry showed that the women's chief motive stemmed from the desire to get out from under parental control and be free. They also married because of the consequences of not marrying. The reasons men gave for marrying were more in keeping with patriarchal imperatives: that marriage should incorporate fatherhood and provide the man with a "companion" to do the housework, take care of his sexual needs, and look after the children.[36]

Adherence to and reinforcement of stereotypical sex roles by legal and social sanctions obscure the patriarchal nature of society, which depends upon the subjugation and control of women and uses marriage as a routine means of enforcement.

Most research into marital violence concentrates on external influences on the husband's behavior. He was under stress, he lost his job, he drank too much, his mother had an extramarital affair. Whatever the rationalization, it serves to excuse the husband's behavior and remove him from responsibility for his own acts.

The reality of the wife's condition is not seen in its totality, but only in terms of what she may have said or done to provoke her husband's anger. Clinical approaches that attempt to change the husband's behavior by changing the wife's behavior only further victimize her. Such approaches reinforce the husband-over-wife feudal relationship, which we must come to realize as economically based if we are to find any long-lasting solutions to marital violence. Manifestations of psychological warfare and violence are reactions to the economic system that socializes men to be powerful and women to be dependent.

Donald Morlan says that separating out "battering men" from so-called "normal men" is to disregard the fact that virtually all men are angry at women and that a batterer is acting out an extreme of what most men feel, at least part of the time.

He attributes this anger to the restriction of men's emotional life and intimacy only with women, to the socialization of boys to repress emotion and exercise power, and to men's sense of failure when they find themselves weak rather than strong, or disoriented rather than clear and decisive. "Given the few number of men who really get to exercise power and the fact that we are all socialized to be powerful," Morlan says, "there are a lot of us walking around who are like pentup volcanoes." He concludes, "Our present economic system requires its quota of failures to keep us all obediently in our particular assembly lines working hard and grumbling little. . . . Men will be angry and find their anger channeled against women as long as all of us shackle our physical and emotional lives to an economic system which values impersonal profits more than whole persons."[37]

What can be done to alter this collision course between men and women? Family crisis intervention training, strengthening of and enforcement of protective orders, victim-witness advocacy programs, emergency hotlines, shelters for battered women and their children, and couples therapy are all services that have recently been developed to deal with the immediate crisis.

The shelter network, established by grassroots women's groups with its "underground railway" by which battered women can be transported from one state to another, affords the only real protection to the victim. The other measures may stop a particular incident and postpone or reduce further violence, but do not prevent its recurrence. As such, they are stop-gap Band-Aid measures.

An innovative judge in Hammond, Indiana, has named the wife/victim her husband's probation officer. The rationale is that the man won't hesitate to beat up his wife, but he might think twice about beating up an officer of the court.[38]

In Milwaukee, Wisconsin, a "first offender" is required to participate in a treatment program or face prosecution. The district attorney warns him that although the incident will be held confidential, the charge will also be "held open." A recurrence of the violence results in two counts of battery, arrest, and advice to the court that the man had already been given informal probation. Additionally, when a case is set for trial and the woman is under continuing threat of violence, the sheriff's department provides 24-hour protection.[39] This program seems to be one of the most effective deterrents for first offenders and does take into account necessary safety precautions.

In Ohio a bill was recently introduced so that a second offense against a spouse will be a felony so that police can make arrests for "probable cause," relieving the victim from responsibility for initiating criminal charges against her husband.

On November 30, 1977, the Texas Supreme Court abolished a 91-year old legal doctrine and ruled that a wife can sue her husband and collect damages for injuries he deliberately inflicted on her. The ruling was made retroactive to March 1971, the date of the incident and case that prompted the ruling. If a woman is awarded damages, the husband would have to pay her from his share of the community property or from his assets not considered community property.

Some see therapy rather than law as a solution. But what kind of therapy? Certainly not the traditional kind that is steeped in sex role stereotyping and sees rehabilitation of the family as the only goal. Wife beating is a traditional practice that has been exacerbated by traditional attitudes and institutions.

Solutions to the problem, therefore, call for nontraditional measures and radical change in approach, the impetus for which has come from women who are victims of tradition. Women have been developing their own support systems for victims based upon the concept of women helping women. They see their roles as advocates rather than as counselors.

Beside hotlines, response to the immediate crisis, emergency shelters, legal aid and other referrals, these women provide consciousness raising, assertiveness training, self-defense and feminist therapy—if, indeed, therapy is called for. The battered woman gains confidence and strength through peer counseling, sharing with other women who have suffered the same experience. The support group works to explore what part is her responsibility and what is imposed on her by society. The wife/victim becomes aware of options open to her, knowing that whatever she chooses she will have support from the other women.

Feminists insist that if anyone is mentally ill, it is not the victim but her assailant. What the women need is advocacy: first of all, someone to listen nonjudgmentally; second, assurance and support; third, someone to help them through the bureaucratic maze of the legal and social services. Psychotherapy, feminists believe, is based on patriarchal assumptions which are the cause of the wife/victim's plight and therefore is inappropriate in solving her problem.

Marya Grambs, co-founder of La Casa de las Madres, the shelter for battered women in San Francisco, says that intervention by a male therapist, whose authority in the therapeutic process duplicates the power relationship of husband and wife, thereby continues the cycle of the woman's dependency on men. What is needed, she says, is to help the victim make connections with other women and reduce her isolation. Some of the best therapy, Grambs claims, takes place in the shelter while doing dishes or during midnight raps. The function of La Casa is to help the women take power over their lives.

What we need are counterpart programs conducted by men who are liberated enough to have no need to prove their manhood, to work with battering husbands in much the same way as women are helping wife/victims. If men would stop making jokes about wife beating, if they would let batterers know in no uncertain terms that violence is not acceptable male behavior, if men would offer husband/offenders peer support and programs to help them change destructive patterns into constructive outlets for their hostility—we would move a lot faster towards ending marital violence.

Barry Shapiro of the Berkeley Men's Group, tells me that his and other men's groups affiliated with the National Conference on Men and Masculinity, which met in St. Louis during November 1977, are considering the formation of such programs. It is hoped that these men's groups will help to break down the impossible image of masculinity, which, Morlan says, dooms men to feelings of frustration and rage and puts women in the role of their projection targets. Men need to learn that it is all right to be vulnerable if they are ever going to be comfortable with their own unique mixtures of strength and weakness.

But coping with man-woman anger and hostility as it erupts is not enough. At the same time we need to deal with problems inherent in the institution of marriage itself and the economic and social structure of the society that creates, harbors, and festers the hostility. Monogamous marriage—or serial monogamy, at any rate—is still the accepted and expected relationship. While the divorce rate today is very high, the remarriage rate is also high.

Historically, marriage has four main functions: (1) reproduction and the guarantee of the father right; (2) economic provision for family members by the husband/father, who is designated head of household; (3) care of children and household maintenance by the wife/mother in return for bed and board; and (4) psychological security and social acceptance within society so long as the marriage remains intact. Survival needs, the need for a recognized position and status in society, and stigmatization of unmarried women have been compelling reasons for keeping battered wives silenced and locked in violent marriages.

The real problem with existing marriage and divorce law, according to Weitzman, is that it favors "structure, stability and security to the exclusion of flexibility, change and individual freedom."[40] Roles which the courts presently demand of husbands and wives are rigid, archaic, and arbitrary. They stem from material considerations and disregard personal ones.

The acting out of these roles (authoritarian husband and servile wife) and the imbalance of power they represent are largely responsible for marital conflict. Balance of power has long been a principle of international relations to prevent strong industrialized nations from taking over or victimizing weaker underdeveloped countries and to stave off war. By analogy, creating a balance of power—both economic and social—between marital partners could be the means of preventing one sex from taking advantage of the other and preventing the violence this imbalance provokes.

Seen in this light, marriage would be a partnership—an egalitarian relationship—in which both husband and wife have equal ownership and share management and control of the income, assets, and liabilities. To effect such a partnership, marriage laws would have to be redefined to allow the individuals involved to determine and agree upon their own roles and living arrangements according to their own particular needs and lifestyle. These agreements should not be the business of the state; the state's only interest should be to adjudicate disagreements.

"A man and woman could decide, in advance, on the duration and terms of their relationship, as well as conditions for its dissolution," Weitzman points out. "They could specify their respective rights and obligations for the financial aspects of marriage (support, living expenses, property, debts, etc.) as well as those for their more personal relations (such as responsibility for birth control, the division of household tasks, child care responsibilities). Further, they could make some decisions before entering the relationship while reserving others for later (such as domicile changes). They could also specify the process of making a later decision such as an agreement to use an arbitrator in the event of disputes."[41]

Whether these be contracts within or in lieu

of marriage, the couple could decide if they wanted to take turns working full time, or they could both work part time, allowing them to share necessary household chores and caring for the children. As Morlan says, "We need to stop being just Mothered and start being Parented from the moment of birth. All of us need a bisexual emotional foundation."[42]

One standard provision, without any option, which I would like to see written into every marriage contract is the restraining order. It should be built into the contract so that it is clearly understood by both parties at the outset that violence will not be tolerated and the restraining order will take effect immediately upon violation.

Allowing couples to draw up their own marriage contracts and to exercise options, of course, requires many changes; ratification of the Equal Rights Amendment; passage of the Full Employment Act, based on the principle that employment should be available to all adult Americans able and willing to work at fair rates of compensation; enforcement of "equal pay for equal work" laws and antidiscrimination employment policies; legislation to create part-time work, flexible work schedules, and shared jobs in civil service; education of the private sector to understand the advantages and value of such work flexibility; and provisions for on-the-job or community child care centers so that single-parent heads of household can earn a living wage and extricate themselves from the welfare system.

The more traditional marriage—having one partner remain in the home and take care of the household while the other works—should not be precluded as an option. But provisions should be made to protect the homemaker economically in the event of dissolution by social security coverage, divorce insurance, or such programs as the Displaced Homemakers Act, which provides for job counseling, training, and placement for the woman reentering the work force. Child support orders should have cost-of-living escalation clauses and should be backed up by Federal legislation enabling Social Security and Internal Revenue Service to locate missing spouses who renege on their payments.

These may sound like radical changes, but they really aren't. Some of them are already in process or are under consideration. Although individual marriage contracts have yet to be legalized, a few couples are already drawing up their own contracts, some provisions of which have been honored by the courts, while others have not been.

Legislation to alter inequities in our economy have already been introduced, and some attention is being paid to revisions of family law. What we are faced with is cultural lag and the resistance of bureaucratic institutions to social change.

Clearly the problem of domestic violence cannot be solved without addressing the foregoing economic issues or without revolutionary changes in attitudes towards the roles of women and men in our society. Without such changes we cannot ensure women "equal protection under the law," and without such protection they will remain vulnerable to their husbands' abuse.

NOTES

1. Stark, Rodney, and James McEvoy III. "Middle-Class Violence," *Psychology Today* (November 1970) pp. 30-31.
2. Martin, Del. *Battered Wives* (San Francisco: Glide Publications, 1976); paperback edition (New York: Pocket Books, 1977).
3. Northeast Patrol Division Task Force, Kansas City Police Department. "Conflict Management: Analysis/Resolution" (Original draft).
4. Straus, Murray. "Normative and Behavioral Aspects of Violence Between Spouses: Preliminary Data on a Nationally Representative USA Sample." (Paper [VA-2] Department of Sociology, University of New Hampshire, March 15, 1977), p. 7.
5. Ibid., p. 11.
6. Walker, Lenore. "The Battered Women Syndrome Revisited: Psycho-social Theories" (Paper presented at the American Psychological Association meeting, San Francisco, August 29, 1977), p. 5.
7. Martin, pp. 11-15, 54-55.
8. Whitehurst, Robert N. "Violence in Husband-Wife Interaction," in Steinmetz, Suzanne K., and Murray A. Straus, eds. *Violence in the Family* (New York: Dodd, Mead, & Co. 1975) pp. 78-79.
9. Hilberman, Elaine, and Kit Munsor. "Sixty Battered Women: A Preliminary Report." (Paper presented at American Psychiatric Association meeting, Toronto, May 5, 1977), p. 1.
10. Federal Bureau of Investigation. *Uniform Crime Reports,* 1973.

11. Engels, Frederick. *The Origin of Family, Private Property and the State* (Moscow: Progress Publishers, 1948), p. 42.
12. Brownmiller, Susan. *Against Our Will* (New York: Simon & Schuster, Inc., 1975) p. 16.
13. Davis, Elizabeth Gould. *The First Sex* (New York: G. P. Putnam's Sons, 1971) p. 255.
14. Calvert, Robert. "Criminal and Civil Liability in Husband-Wife Assaults," in Steinmetz and Straus, p. 89.
15. Ibid.
16. Dutton, Donald. "Domestic Dispute Intervention by Police" (Report on United Way Symposium on Family Violence, Vancouver, B.C., March 1977), p. III-23.
17. Ibid., p. III-24.
18. Eisenberg, Sue, and Patricia Micklow. "The Assaulted Wife: 'Catch 22' Revisited" (Unpublished paper, University of Michigan, 1974) p. 112.
19. City of Oakland Police Services. "Techniques of Dispute Intervention" (Training Bulletin III-J, June 19, 1975), pp. 2-3.
20. Murphy, Robert B., Ed McKay, Jeffrey A. Schwartz and Donald A. Liebman. "Training Patrolmen As Crisis Intervention Instructors" (Unpublished), p. 1.
21. Bard, Morton. *The Function of the Police in Crisis Intervention and Conflict Management* (Washington, D.C.: U.S. Department of Justice, Law Enforcement Assistance Administration, 1975), p. 6.9.
22. Ibid., p. 6.10.
23. Bard, Morton, and Joseph Zacker. *The Police and Interpersonal Conflict* (Washington, D.C.: Police Foundation, 1976), p. 58.
24. Gayford, J. J. "Battered Wives," *Medical Science Law,* vol. 15, no. 4, 1975, pp. 243-244.
25. Fisher, Trude, with Marion P. Winston. "The Grim Plight of Destitute Mothers Who Need Free Rooms on a Stormy Night," *Los Angeles Times,* March 12, 1973.
26. Gayford, J. J. "Wife Battering: A Preliminary Survey of 100 Cases," *British Medical Journal,* January 25, 1975, pp. 194-197.
27. Weitzman, Lenore J. "Legal Regulations of Marriage: Tradition and Change," *California Law Review,* vol. 62, no. 4, July-September 1974, p. 1195.
28. Broverman, I. K., D. M. Broverman, R. Clarkson, P. Rosenkrantz, and S. Vogel. "Sex Role Stereotypes and Clinical Judgments of Mental Health," *Journal of Consulting Psychiatry,* 1964.
29. Pancoast, Ruth Dreiblatt, and Lynda Martin Weston. "Feminist Psychotherapy: A Method for Fighting Social Control of Women," (Position statement of Feminist Counseling Collective, Washington, D.C., February 1974), p. 7.
30. Rutledge, Aaron L. "The Feudal System of Marriage," *San Francisco Chronicle,* May 26, 1977.
31. Blackstone, W. *Commentaries,* 1765, p. 442.
32. De Crow, Karen. *Sexist Justice* (New York: Random House, Inc., 1974) p. 169.
33. Ibid., pp. 164-65.
34. Weitzman, p. 1187.
35. Ibid., p. 1170.
36. San Martín, Hernán. "Machismo: Latin America's Myth-Cult of Male Supremacy," *Unesco Courier,* March 1975, p. 31.
37. Morlan, Donald W. "Why Are Men Angry at Women" (The Battered Women Conference Report, American Friends Service Committee, New York, 1977), pp. 16-17.
38. Van Gelder, Lawrence. "Giving Battered Wives a Little Legal Clout," *New York Times,* November 13, 1976.
39. "Needs of Battered Women Receive Special Attention from Milwaukee DA's Office," *Response,* vol. 1, no. 3, February 1977, pp. 1-2.
40. Weitzman, p. 1277.
41. Ibid., p. 1249.
42. Morlan, p. 17.

B □ *The battered husband syndrome*

SUZANNE K. STEINMETZ

HISTORICAL ACCOUNTS AND COMIC STRIPS

While the horrors of wife-beating are paraded before the public, and crisis line and shelters are being established, the other side of the coin—

Reprinted by permission from *Victimology: An International Journal,* vol. 2, nos. 3-4, pp. 499-508. © Visage Press Inc. All rights reserved.

husband-beating—is still hidden under a cloak of secrecy. But is husband battering *really* an unknown phenomenon, or is it simply another example of selective inattention? Some insights into a possible answer for this question can be gained by an examination of humor which exaggerates and brings into public view many aspects of life too personal to be discussed in a non-joking context. For example, the popularity of domestic-relation humor such as mother-in-law jokes; the wife's lack of cooking skills; the husband's incompetence as a fix-it man; and sexual incompatibilities—the staple of many stand-up comics' routines—suggests that these problematic areas of marriage are commonly shared yet tabooed problems.

The charivari, a post renaissance custom, was a noisy demonstration intended to shame and humiliate wayward individuals in public. The target was any behavior considered to be a threat to the patriarchal community social order. Thus in France, a husband who allowed his wife to beat him was made to wear an outlandish outfit, ride backwards around the village on a donkey while holding onto the tail. Beaten husbands among the Britons were strapped to carts and "paraded ignominiously through the booing populace." The husband beater was also punished by riding backwards on a donkey and being forced to drink wine and wipe her mouth with the animal's tail. The fate of these men in 18th century Paris was to kiss a large set of ribboned horns (Shorter, 1975).

The subject matter of comic strips, specifically those revolving around a domestic theme, is also revealing. A common theme is a caricature of husbands and wives in which the husband deviates from the ideal image of strong, self-assertive, and intelligent, and assumes the character traits which have been culturally ascribed to be feminine. The wife in these comics is justified in playing the dominant role and in chastising her erring husband, since he has not fulfilled his culturally prescribed roles. A contemporary example of this phenomenon is provided by Gelles (1974: 78-79) interview of a wife who explained how she retaliated against a drunken husband who slapped her for no apparent reason:

I know I was stronger than him, when he was drunk that is, so I gave him a good shove and kick—whatever I could kick—I didn't aim. And then he'd end up on the floor and I'd beat the daylights out of him.

Saenger's (1963) study of 20 consecutive editions of all comic strips appearing in the nine leading New York City newspapers during October 1950 provides additional insights. He found that 48 percent of the females and only 10 percent of the males in comic strips revolving around domestic relations exhibited mastery of all situations, while 19 percent of the males but only 4 percent of the females were pictured as helpless. He also noted that while husbands were the victims of hostility and attack in 63 percent of all conflict situations, wives were victims in only 39 percent. Furthermore while 10 percent of the males and 7 percent of the females initiated physical aggression acts, only one percent of the females, but 14 percent of the males were recipients of domestic physical aggression. Further analysis revealed that in 73 percent of the domestic strips the wives were more aggressive; in ten percent husband and wife were equal; and in only 17 percent of the strips were the husbands portrayed as being more aggressive than their wives.

Barcus (1963) in a survey of every comic strip appearing in March for the years 1943, 1953, 1958 in the bound files of *Puck: The Comic Weekly* and three Boston newspapers, a sample representing most of the major nationally syndicated Sundies, found that domestic relations was a theme in 41 percent of the comics examined. These domestic relations are presented as caricatures reflecting a stereotype of husbands as fatter, balder, less virile, and of wives as taller and bigger than their husbands (Barcus, 1963). This is most poignantly exhibited in the domestic comic strip "Bringing Up Father." This domestic comic, which originated in 1913, revolves around a newly-rich Irish immigrant (Jiggs) who prefers his former life-style of corn beef and cabbage and billiards, and who endures the physically violent attacks by his wife (Maggie) who is unsuccessfully attempting to emulate upper-class life styles.

The impact of comics is impressive. In one study covering a 12 year period, over 56 percent of both male and female readers ranked the category, comic strips, as "most frequently" read (Swanson, as cited in Robinson and White, 1963). The second ranking category, war, was listed by 35 percent of the respondents. Since a large portion of this survey occurred during World War II, it is surprising that the category "war" was a poor second to the comics.

Therefore, the portrayal of family life in comics not only reflects life styles but also is in a position to influence or reinforce family related behavior.

It is true that comics tend to be based on a distortion of reality. However, the consistent appearance of battered husbands in early court and community records both in Europe and the United States; the persistence of battered husbands as a dominant theme in comics; and the stability of the findings that husbands equal wives as victims of marital homicide—the most severe form of violence—reinforce our belief that husband battering is not a new phenomenon.

EMPIRICAL DATA ON BATTERED HUSBANDS

An examination of empirical data on wives' use of physical violence on their husbands suggests that husband-beating constitutes a sizeable proportion of marital violence.

We know, for example, that over three percent of 600 husbands in mandatory conciliation interviews listed physical abuse by their wife as a reason for the divorce action (Levinger, 1966). While this is far lower than the near-

ly 37 percent of wives who mentioned physical abuse, several factors should be noted. First, Levinger's study showed that women had nearly twice the number of total complaints as men. Therefore, unless one assumes that it is always the husband's fault when a marriage fails, it appears that women might be more comfortable voicing their complaints. A second, related factor is that the traditional role of husbands in a divorce action is to take blame for the failure. Thus, even if the husband desires the divorce, etiquette demands that he allow his wife to initiate the action. During a conciliatory interview it is reasonable then to expect the husband to be less ready to expose his wife's faults. Some support is provided for this position by examining the types of complaints commonly made by husbands, i.e., sexual incompatibility, and in-laws, both traditionally accepted male-oriented complaints. Finally the male in our society is under pressure to maintain a dominant position over a female (Balswick and Peek, 1971; Steinmetz, 1974). Thus given the psychological stress of recognizing the wife's physical dominance, it is unlikely that many men would be willing to admit their physical weakness to a third party.

Table 1. Comparison of physical violence used by husbands and wives in percent

	N	Throwing things		Pushing shoving		Hitting slapping		Kicking		Hit with something		Threatened knife or gun		Used knife or gun		Use of any violence	
		H	W	H	W	H	W	H	W	H	W	H	W	H	W	H	W
Gelles* (1974)	80	22	11	18	1	32	20	25	9	3	5	5	0	—	—	47	33
Steinmetz* (1977a)	54	39	37	31	32	20	20	—	—	10	10	—	—	2	0	47	43
Steinmetz* (1977b) Canada	52	21	21	17	13	13	13	—	—	10	12	—	—	—	—	23	21
Steinmetz* (1977c)	94	31	25	22	18	17	12	—	—	12	14	—	—	—	—	32	28
Straus, Gelles and Steinmetz**	2,143	3	5	11	8	5	5	2	3	2	3	.4	.6	.3	.2	12	12

*Incidents occurring throughout the duration of the marriage.
**Incidents occurring during 1975.

Based on police records and a random sample of families, it was estimated that 7 percent of the wives and .6 percent of the husbands would be victims of severe physical abuse by their spouse (Steinmetz, 1977c). Further evidence for the existence of battered husbands is provided by a comparison of physical violence used by husbands and wives to resolve marital conflicts in five studies (see Table 1).

Using two United States populations—a broadbased non-representative group and a random sample in New Castle DE—and a Canadian sample of college students, Steinmetz (1977c and b) found only small differences in the percentage of husbands and wives who resorted to throwing things, pushing or shoving, hitting with the hand, or hitting with an object. In fact the total violence scores, for these three studies, were very similar.

The data from the nationally representative sample (Straus et al., 1977), based on reports of violence that occurred during 1975, found wives to be slightly higher in almost all categories except pushing and shoving. The total violence scores, however were identical.

Only one study (Gelles, 1974) found husbands exceeding wives in the use of all types of violence except "hitting with something," a mode which de-emphasized physical strength. In this study, 47 percent of husbands had used physical violence on their wives, while only 33 percent of the wives had used violence on their husbands. However, half of the respondents were selected from the police blotter because of reported domestic violence or by the social service agency which selected families because it was suspected that violence might be occurring. This may explain why more wives than husbands were victims of physical violence in Gelles' study, since it is wives who report domestic violence to the police and seek help from social services and agencies.

While these data represent the percentage of husbands and wives who have used physical violence against a spouse, it does not tell us the frequency with which these acts occur. Surprisingly, the data suggest that not only the percentage of wives having used physical violence often exceeds that of the husbands, but that wives also exceed husbands in the frequency with which these acts occur. The average violence score of wives as compared with husbands were all higher in the Steinmetz studies: 4.04 vs 3.52 (Steinmetz, 1977a); 7.82 vs 6.00 (Steinmetz, 1977b); and 7.00 vs. 6.60 (Steinmetz, 1977c). The Straus' study found that wives committed an average of 10.3 acts of violence against their husbands during 1975, while husbands averaged only 8.8 acts against their wives. Only Gelles (1974) found husbands to exceed their wives in use of physically violent modes. He found that 11 percent of the husbands and 5 percent of the wives engaged in marital violence between two and six times a year, and 14 percent of the husbands and 6 percent of the wives used violence between once a month and daily. Wives exceed husbands in one category, however: eleven percent of the husbands, but 14 percent of the wives noted that they "seldom" (defined as between two and five times during the marriage) used physical violence against their spouse.

IGNORING THE BATTERED HUSBAND PHENOMENON

Given the data provided above, why has this area been ignored? First, the stigma attached to this topic, which is embarrassing for beaten wives, is doubly so for beaten husbands. The patriarchal concept of the husband's right to chastise his wife with a whip or rattan no bigger than his thumb is embedded in ancient law and was upheld by a Mississippi court in 1824, "in case of great emergency" and with "salutary restraints" (Bradley v. State, Walker, 158, Miss., 1824). This idea has provided some legal and social understanding for the woman who has suffered because her husband has gone beyond permissible bounds. Since there is no recognition of the woman's right to chastise her husband, there is little likelihood that society will recognize that the wife may go beyond that which is permissible. As one respondent, who had been terrorized by a knife-wielding spouse and had gone to work with deep fingernail gashes on his face related, "I never took the fights outside, I didn't want anyone to know. I told the guys at work the kids did it with a toy."

This fear of stigma also affects the official statistics collected on husband-wife violence. Curtis (1974) reported that while violence by men against women was responsible for about 27 percent of the assaults and 17.5 percent of the homicides, violence by women against men accounted for 9 percent of the assaults and 16.4 percent of the homicides in his study. Thus, while women commit only about one-third as many assaults against men as men commit against women, the number of cross-sex homicides committed by the two groups are nearly identical. Wilt and Bannon (1976: 20) warn that caution should be applied when interpreting the Curtis' findings. They note that "non-fatal violence committed by women against men is less likely to be reported to the police than is violence by men against women; thus, women assaulters who come to the attention of the police are likely to be those who have produced a fatal result."

Also helping to camouflage the existence of husband-beating is the terminology used to describe it. This can be illustrated by referring to Gelles' monograph *The Violent Home* (1974). An examination of the entries in the subject index shows that, while there is one page each devoted to "wife-to-husband" and "husband-to-wife" violence, seven pages under the heading "wife-beating," two under "battered wife," no corresponding listing can be found for "husband-beating." However, Gelles' data provides ample evidence that many wives do, in fact, beat their husbands. In addition to the data from Gelles' study summarized in Table 1, many quotes from his respondents support this. For example, one respondent noted, "He would just yell and yell—not really yell, just talk loudly, and I couldn't say anything because he kept talking, so I'd swing." (Gelles, 1974: 80)

Even though Gelles reports that one respondent, a retired cook, was often verbally and physically attacked by his jealous wife, and quotes another as saying, "My wife is very violent. It's a miracle that I didn't go out because she really put a hell of a dent in my head," these are not labeled as husband-beatings. Thus, although Gelles readily acknowledges that men are physically victimized by their wives, he does not provide a discussion of this phenomenon as a distinct parallel to wife-beating.

Why is so much attention given to wife-beating and so little to husband-beating? The answer partially is the relative lack of empirical data on the topic, the selective inattention both by the media and researchers, the greater severity of physical damage to women making their victimization more visible, and the reluctance of men to acknowledge abuse at the hand of women.

Why is there this difference in degree of physical damage—a difference which has tended to overshadow less violent attacks on women and most attacks on men? Popular culture has provided three different explanations. First, because of socialization, women are taught better impulse control and they stop aggressive behavior before any danger occurs. A second rationale suggests that women are more verbal than men, and therefore men resort more readily to physical means to support their dominant position. A third explanation focuses on the superior physical strength of men and their greater capability of causing more physical damage to their spouses than wives are capable of doing to their husbands.

In reality, the contention that woman are socialized for greater impulse controls appears to have little support, at least as far as marital fights are concerned. The data provided in Table 1, plus insights gained from the in-depth interviews, suggest that women are as likely to select physical violence to resolve marital conflicts as are men. Furthermore, child abusers are more likely to be women, and women throughout history have been the prime perpetrators of infanticide (Straus, Gelles and Steinmetz, 1973). While it is recognized that women spend more time with children and are usually the parent in a single parent home (which makes them prone to stress and strains resulting in child abuse); and that fathers in similar situations might abuse their children more severely, these findings indicate that women have the potential to commit acts of violence and that under certain circumstances they do carry out these acts.

Wolfgang (1958), in an investigation of homicides occurring between 1948 and 1952, found that spouses accounted for 18 percent of the incidents and that there were virtually no differences between the percent of husbands or wives who were offenders. According to FBI statistics, 15 percent of the homicides in 1975 were between husband and wife. In 7.8 percent of the cases the husbands were victims, while in 8.0 percent of the cases the victims were wives (Vital Statistics Reports, 1976).

The second point is also questionable. Although the myth of the verbally abusing, nagging woman is perpetuated in the media—mainly in comic form—the data do not support this myth. There appeared to be small random differences in the use of verbal violence in the families studied. Furthermove, Levinger (1966) in his study of divorce applicants found that wives were three times more likely to complain of verbal abuse than their husbands.

It appears that the last reason is more plausible. The data reported suggest that at least the intention of both men and women towards using physical violence in marital conflicts is equal. Identical percentages of men and women reported hitting or hitting with an object. Furthermore, data on homicide between spouses suggest that an almost equal number of wives kill their husbands as husbands kill wives (Wolfgang, 1958). Thus it appears that men and women might have equal potential towards violent marital interaction; initiate similar acts of violence; and, when differences of physical strength are equalized by weapons, commit similar amounts of spousal homicide. The major difference appears to be the male's ability to do more physical damage during nonhomicidal marital physical fights. When the wife slaps her husband, her lack of physical strength plus his ability to restrain her reduce the physical damage to a minimum. When the husband slaps his wife however, his strength plus her inability to restrain him result in considerably more damage.

An apt illustration is provided by a newspaper article describing the beating a physically weaker husband had received from his wife. This article noted that a wealthy, elderly New York banker had won a separation from his second wife who was 31 years his junior. During the 14-year marriage the husband had been bullied, according to the judge, by: "Hysteria, screaming tantrums, and . . . various physical violence practiced on a man . . . ill-equipped for fist-fights with a shrieking woman." The judge noted that the husband wore constant scars and bruises. Once his wife shredded his ear with her teeth; another time she blackened both his eyes; and on another occasion, injured one of his eyes so badly that doctors feared it might be lost (Wilmington Evening Journal, April 21, 1976: 2).

WHY DO HUSBANDS STAY?

Gelles (1975: 659), asks the question, "Why would a woman who has been physically abused by her husband remain with him?" His analysis suggests that there are three major factors influencing wives' decision to leave abusing husbands. The less severe and the less frequent the violence, the more the wife experienced violence as a child; and the fewer the resources and power the wife has, the more likely she is to stay with her husband. These three factors were also found to influence the husbands' decision to stay.

Lower levels of violence were not likely to be considered a major concern. Only when the violence appeared to be affecting the children, rather than affecting the husband's physical safety, did the husband consider leaving. The background of violent wives is often characterized by violence and trauma. One violent wife, as a child, witnessed her own father force her mother, who was in the last stages of pregnancy, to walk home in the snow carrying bags of groceries. The father drove behind his wife in a car, bumping her with the car to keep her moving and beating her when she stopped or stumbled. Another wife felt responsible for her father's suicide which occurred when she was ten. Still another wife as a teenager slept with weapons under her pillows and lived in constant fear of brutal beatings from her alcoholic father.

The perceived availability of resources also affects the man's decision to leave. According to most studies (as well as popular knowledge), women remain because they feel that the children will be worse off if they leave. Not only does the wife often lack the economic resources to provide adequately for the children, but she feels that separation will have a more harmful effect on the children than would remaining with her abusive spouse. It is always assumed that the husband's greater economic resources could allow him to more easily leave a disruptive marital situation. Not only do men tend to have jobs which provide them with an adequate income, but they have greater access to credit and are not tied to the home because of the children. This perspective rests on erroneous sexist assumptions. Although males, as a group, have considerably more economic security, if the husband leaves the family, he is still responsible for a certain amount of economic support of the family in addition to the cost of a separate residence for himself. Thus the loss in standard of living is certainly a consideration for any husband who is contemplating a separation. Furthermore, it is assumed that because wives are "tied to their homes," they would be the ones who would most likely regret it if they moved. Until recently, custody was almost always awarded to mothers, thus mother remained in the family home while father sought a new residence. Interviews with abused men suggest that leaving the family home means leaving many hours of home improvements, family rooms, dens, workshops, in other words the comfortable and familiar, that which is not likely to be reconstructed in a small apartment.

Probably the most erroneous assumption, however, is that husbands' decisions to leave would not be influenced by concerns over the children. Often the husband becomes the victim when he steps in to protect the children and becomes the target of abuse. These men are afraid to leave for fear that further violence would be directed towards the children. Recognizing that men are not likely to receive custody of the children, even in an era of increased recognition of their ability to care for them, they feel that by staying they are providing some protection for them. These men also express the idea that keeping the family together at all costs is best for the children. Another man, who lived in terror for two years and did not know when his wife would attack him with knives and other objects,

an almost daily occurrence, remained because as an orphan, he knew what it was like to be without a father. Also he considered his wife to be attractive, personable, a good housekeeper and mother and, except for her violent attacks, a good wife. The wife, however, was insecure, dissatisfied with herself, had low self-esteem, and was uncomfortable with her low position as a secretary, and with a paycheck which was smaller than her husband's. She wanted a career and to be the economically dominant partner.

Why, then, do these husbands not protect themselves? Several reasons evolve. The first, based on chivalry, considers any man who would stoop to hit a woman to be a bully. The second, usually based on experience, is a recognition of the severe damage which a man could do to a woman. In fact, several men expressed the fear that if they ever lost control, they could easily kill their wives. One husband noted that he hit wife only once, "in retaliation with hands and fists, and smacked her in the mouth. She went flying across the room into the chest." Because he realized how badly he could hurt his wife, he continued to take the physical abuse. He noted, with hindsight, that probably she continued her abuse because she knew she could get away with it.

A final reason expressed by these beaten men is perhaps a self-serving one. The combination of crying out in pain during the beating and having the wife see the injuries, which often take several weeks to heal, raises the wife's levels of guilt which the husbands consider to be a form of punishment.

CONCLUSION

Although the data discussed do not represent, for the most part, a systematic investigation of representative samples of battered husbands, it is important to understand husband-beating because of the implications for social policies to help resolve the more global problem of family violence.

This paper is not intended to de-emphasize the importance of providing services to beaten wives, but to increase our awareness of the pervasiveness of all forms of family violence.

When the focus remains on the battered wife, the remedies often suggested revolve around support groups, crisis lines, and shelters for the woman and her children. This stance overlooks a basic condition of violence between spouses— a society which glorifies violence if done for the "right reasons:" the good of society, or that of one's own family. It is critical to shift at least some of the blame from individual family members to basic socio-cultural conditions so that more resources will become available to help families and a greater emphasis will be placed on changing the attitudes and values of society.

REFERENCES

Balswick, J. O. and Peek, C.
1971   "The Inexpressive Male: A Tragedy of American Society," Family Coordinator, 20(4):363-368.
Barcus, Frances E.
1963   "The World of Sunday Comics." Pp. 190-218 in D. M. White and R. H. Abel, The Funnies, An American Idiom. Glencoe: The Free Press.
Curtis, Lynn A.
1974   Criminal Violence: National Patterns and Behavior. Lexington, Mass.: Lexington Books.
Gelles, Richard J.
1974   The Violent Home. Beverly Hills, California: Sage.
Levinger, George
1966   "Sources of Marital Dissatisfaction Among Applicants for Divorce," American Journal of Orthopsychiatry 35(5):556-598.
Robinson, Edward J. and David Manning White
1963   "Who Reads the Funnies—and Why" Pp. 179-232 in P. M. White and R. H. Abel, The Funnies, An American Idiom. Glencoe: The Free Press.

Saenger, Gerhart
1963   "Male and Female Relations in the American Comic Strips" Pp. 219-231 in D. M. White and R. H. Abel, The Funnies, An American Idiom. Glencoe: The Free Press.
Shorter, Edward
1975   The Making of the Modern Family. New York: Basic Books.
Steinmetz, Suzanne K.
1974   "Male Liberation—Destroying the Stereotypes." Pp. 55-67 in Powers, E. and Lee, M. (eds.) The Process of Relationships. Minneapolis: West.
1977a The Cycle of Violence: Assertive, Aggressive and Abusive Family Interaction. New York: Praeger.
1977b Secondary analysis of data from a United States-Canadian Comparison of Intrafamily Conflict. Canadian Conference on Family Violence, Simon Fraser University, April.
1977c Secondary Analysis of data from the study "The Use of Force for Resolving Family Conflict: the Training Ground for Abuse." Family Coordinator. 26 (January): 19-26
Straus, M. A., Gelles, R. J. and Steinmetz, S. K.
1973   "Theories, Methods and Controversies in the Study of Violence between Family Members." Paper presented at the annual meeting of American Sociological Association, New York (mimeo).
1977   Preliminary Data. Study of Physical Violence in American Families. Report by M. A. Straus to the International Society for the Study of Family Law, Montreal.
Vital Statistics Reports
1976   Annual Summary for the United States. Vol. 24, No. 13 Washington DC: National Center for Health Statistics.
Wilt, G. M. and Bannon, J. D.
1976   Violence and the Police: Homicides, Assaults, and Disturbances. Washington DC: The Police Foundation.
Wolfgang, Marvin E.
1958   Patterns in Criminal Homicide. New York: Wiley.

C □ *Significant findings in child abuse research*

MARC F. MADEN and DAVID F. WRENCH

DEFINITION

A fundamental problem among contemporary researchers is disagreement about what constitutes child abuse (Gelles, 1975). Originally, the meaning of child abuse was restricted to a medical diagnosis designated by Kempe et al. (1962) as the "battered child syndrome." However, many researchers (e.g. Simons et al., 1966; Zalba, 1966; Currie, 1970; Gil, 1970) found that the battered child syndrome inaccurately categorized all forms of child abuse under a restrictive definition. Since unexplained physical injury constitutes the *sine qua non* of child abuse and almost all studies agree that nonaccidental physical injury requiring medical attention constitutes child abuse, this review[1] follows such definition. More specifically, sexual molestation, infanticide, and neglect have been excluded from the definition because they appear to be discrete phenomena. (See Burt Associates, 1975; Sussman and Cohen, 1975 for a complete discussion of the problem of defining child abuse.)

Both Gil (1970) and Steele (1970) distinguish sexual abuse on etiologic and dynamic grounds. Studies find that frequently sexual abuse is a single episode (De Francis, 1971), that it often involves a stranger (Fisher and Howell, 1970; McCaughy, 1971), and that it is more often ac-

Reprinted by permission from *Victimology: An International Journal*, vol. 2, no. 2, pp. 196-224. © Visage Press Inc. All rights reserved.

[1]The original research reported in this article was supported by a grant from the Western Interstate Commission on Higher Education (WICHE) to the Rosenfeld Center for the Study and Treatment of Child Abuse at the Oregon Health Sciences Center. Subsequent support was provided by the Dan Davis Fellowship and the Maurie Clark Fellowship, School of Urban Affairs, Portland State University. We want to express our appreciation to Dr. Harold Boverman, Dr. Stan Cohen, Dr. Robert Jones, Dr. Barry Anderson, Dr. Nohad Toulan and the Office of Graduate Studies for their generous help in bringing this project to fruition.

companied by physical coercion when it involves strangers (McCaughy, 1971). These features contrast with those typical of child abuse. DeFrancis' (1971) finding that only 11 percent of sexual abuse was accompanied by physical child abuse also supports a conclusion that sexual abuse is etiologically different.

While Bakan (1971), Adelson (1972), and Solomon (1973) place infanticide on the child abuse spectrum, most . authors join Kempe (1973) in affirming that child abusers do not willfully mean to murder children. Both Resnick (1969, 1970) and Meyers (1970) show that the most common modes for infanticide are suffocation, strangulation, and head trauma, indicating that death was caused by a single, direct attack. In contrast, as will be discussed later, most injuries stemming from child abuse are bruises, welts, and long bone fractures. The context of the attack, the mode of assault, and the type of injury inflicted appear to support the hypothesis that infanticide is etiologically distinct from child abuse (Currie, 1970).

Several authorities (Fontana, 1964, 1973; Gil, 1970; Kempe and Schmidt, 1974) conclude with Silver et al. (1969) that neglect and physical abuse are parts of the same child abuse spectrum and not mutually exclusive. While Currie (1970) recognized considerable overlap between abuse and neglect, he and others (Chesser, 1952; Young, 1964; Makover in Gil, 1970; Polansky, 1975) believe that they are symptomatically, if not etiologically, distinguishable. Giovannoni (1971: 650) observes that "neglect appears to be more closely associated with those stresses emanating directly from poverty" while abuse appears to "be associated with interpersonal and intrapsychic kinds of stresses." Steele and Pollock (1968: 99) propose that the neglecting parent reacts to a perceived failure of the child by withdrawing from and "abandoning efforts to even mechanically care for the child." In contrast, they believe that the abusing parent overresponds to disappointment with a child and "moves in to punish it for its failure and to make it 'shape up' and perform better." Comparative data from several studies (Young, 1964; Togut et al., 1969; Kent, 1973) lend support to these observations. While O'Neill (1973) and Smith (1975) confirm impressions by Fontana (1964) and others that neglect and malnutrition constitute a part of the child abuse syndrome, other authorities (Zalba, 1966 citing Chesser, 1952; Giovannoni, 1971; Kadushin, 1974) consider the pattern to be discrete. Consequently this review excludes neglect from the child abuse definition. Additionally, maternal deprivation, failure to thrive, and all forms of emotional injury are excluded on the basis that their relationship to child abuse has not been clearly established (Sussman, 1974). In sum, child abuse will be defined as a deliberate attack against a child resulting in physical injury perpetrated by any person exercising his responsibility as a caretaker.

RESEARCH FINDINGS
Incidence

According to Smith (1975) child abuse is prevalent in Western Europe, Scandinavia, Australia and New Zealand as well as the United States, and has been reported in India and Uganda. No comparable data on incidence are available, although Viano's (1975) compilation of European fatality rates indicates that child abuse is at least as serious in those countries as in the United States, Canada and New Zealand (Maden, 1975; MacKeith, 1975). In their recent study on the incidence of child abuse in the United States, Cohen and Sussman (1975) simply conclude that accurate data do not exist. Most incidence estimates rely on reports that suffer from variations in the definition, interpretation, and administration of fifty state statutes. One recent estimate extrapolated the number of confirmed reports of child abuse from the ten largest states and yielded a national projection of 41,105 cases (Cohen and Sussman, 1975). Gil (1969: 851), however, recognized that "legally reported incidents may constitute only a part of the total universe of child abuse inci-

dents." Consequently, Gil (1970) estimated incidence by creating and then surveying a random sample to determine personal knowledge about physical child abuse. Extrapolating to the adult of the United States, Gil estimated that between 2.53 and 4.07 million individuals had personal knowledge of a child-abusing family during the preceding year. Light (1973) attempted to control for the possibility that the same case was known by more than one of Gil's survey subjects; he offered a revised estimate of 500,000 incidents based on 1970 census data. Most recently, Gelles (1977) interviewed a national probability sample of 1,146 families with children between the ages of three and seventeen. On the basis of extrapolated frequencies, the study estimated that between 1.2 and 1.7 million children were kicked, hit or punched and between 460,000 and 750,000 children were beaten up in 1975 alone. The study estimated generally that between 1.4 and 1.9 million children "were vulnerable to physical injury from violence in 1975" (1977: 18). Whatever the actual incidence of child abuse, the rate appears to be increasing (Gil, 1970; Fontana, 1973b; Cohen and Sussman, 1975). Smith (1975) speculates that the increase in child abuse is associated with the documented increase in illegitimacy and teenage parenthood. Given the recent increasing interest in the child abuse problem resulting in comprehensive reporting statutes and a higher index of suspicion, it is more likely that incremental incidence rates reflect the fact that a larger proportion of the child abuse population is identified (Gil, 1970; Johnson, 1974; Cohen and Sussman, 1975).

Authorities disagree about the incidence and distribution of child abuse within the family (Silver, 1969; Smith, 1975). A number of authors observed that only one child in the family was subjected to abuse (Merrill, 1962; Boardman, 1962; Zalba, 1966; Steele and Pollock, 1968; Brown and Daniels, 1968). Other studies reported that siblings were also mistreated (Silver, 1969; Skinner and Castle, 1969; Gil, 1970; Lauer et al., 1974; Friedman and Morse, 1974; Smith and Hanson, 1974; Baldwin and Oliver, 1975; Sturgess and Heal, 1976; Lynch, 1976).

Two studies with relatively complete data on sibling abuse indicate that when first-born children are abused, subsequent children carry significant risk as well (Skinner and Castle, 1969; Baldwin, Oliver, 1975). Incomplete data may also account for conflicting findings about the ordinal position of the abuse victim. Several studies found that older, especially first-born, children were more frequently abused (Gregg and Elmer, 1969; Thomson et al., 1971; Burland et al., 1973) while other studies indicated that the youngest child was more susceptible (Johnson and Morse, 1968; Bennie and Sclare, 1969; Corey et al., 1975; Holman and Kanwar, 1975, Lynch, 1976). Both Gil (1970) and Smith (1975) found that the polar positions in the sibship were at risk. None of these studies apparently controlled for family size. Smith (1975: 206) found that "when birth order is properly related to family size, the suggestion that a child's particular ordinal position carries more risk of battering does not hold." Three other studies, Skinner and Castle (1969), Sturgess and Heal (1976) and Baldwin and Oliver (1975) support the Smith (1975) finding.

Age, sex, race

Age. Most clinical studies indicate that abuse victims are infants and younger children (for example, Kempe et al., 1962; Currie, 1970; Skinner and Castle, 1969; Baldwin and Oliver, 1975), whereas surveys produce a more even age distribution (for example, Gil, 1970; Fergusson et al., 1972; Johnson, 1974). Several factors contribute to these differences. Clinical studies often arbitrarily restrict the age of the sample (Johnson and Morse, 1968; Skinner and Castle, 1969; Lauer et al., 1975; Baldwin and Oliver, 1975; Smith, 1975) or rely on case records from pediatric services that exclude older children, whereas surveys include reports from sources that have contact with older children and adolescents (Sussman, 1974). Also, abuse in young children is more likely to be detected and less likely to be confused with accidental injury (Lauer et al., 1974). Despite these biases, the evidence supports the conclusion that abuse victims more often fall into the younger age categories. Three surveys (Gil, 1970; Fergusson et al., 1972; Johnson, 1974) reported that the majority of abused children were younger than six. In addition, surveys that include older children and adolescents run the risk of incorporating sexual molestation reports. All three cited surveys report higher percentages of abused females in age categories over ten. In view of expanded mandatory reporting statutes and a higher level of suspicion among, for example, school officials, future data may indicate more physical mistreatment of older children. Infants and young children, however, will probably continue to constitute the majority of abuse victims, particularly if the early identification and subsequent foster placement of abused children depresses the percentage of older victims (Fergusson et al., 1972).

Sex. Nearly all surveys agree that very slightly more males than females are abused (Gil, 1970; O'Neill, 1973; Lauer et al., 1974; Johnson, 1974). However, three major surveys (Gil, 1970; Fergusson et al., 1972; Johnson, 1974) indicate that the sex and age of the victim are related, with females outnumbering males in adolescent age groups. Gil (1970) hypothesized that this pattern reflects culturally differentiated childrearing practices for males and females. He suggested that females were more quickly socialized into culturally assigned passive roles, and were thus subject to less physical punishment but that they became subject to it when they became involved in heterosexual relationships during adolescence. Both Elmer (1967) and Straus (1971) provide evidence to refute this hypothesis. The former reported that girls were more frequently punished at an earlier age, and tentatively, disciplined with greater severity. The latter found that among a sample of college students recalling high school experiences, boys had been punished twice as frequently or severely as girls.

Four studies (Thomson et al., 1971; Scott, 1973; Lauer et al., 1974; and Johnson, 1974) indicate that female abuse victims sustain a significantly higher risk of fatality. While males constitute the majority of reported abuse cases, females are more likely to be confirmed abuse victims (Johnson, 1974). These results suggest that abuse of females may need to be more severe before it is reported.

Race. Four major surveys (Gil, 1970; Thomson et al., 1971; Fergusson et al., 1972; Johnson, 1974) and numerous clinical studies have found a disproportionate number of nonwhites among the abuse sample. The majority of these studies draw upon nonrandom samples with disproportionate nonwhite populations (for example, Young, 1964; Elmer, 1967). The surveys also incorporate biases in the original recording of the cases. For example, Thomson et al. (1971) surveyed child abuse in Erie County, New York, and reported that 37 percent of the abused children were nonwhite. However, 74.1 percent of the total cases were reported in Buffalo, a city which contains only 39.6 percent of the total child population of Erie County. Since 93.2 percent of the nonwhite children live within the city of Buffalo, this produces a considerable over-representation of nonwhites. Where

clinical studies have compared the abuse sample with the population actually served by the facility, they have generally found no significant over-representation of nonwhites in the abuse population (Elmer, 1967; Heins, 1969; Silver et al., 1971; Lauer et al., 1974; Martin et al., 1974).

Perinatal history

Numerous studies establish a relationship between abuse and a higher incidence of prematurity and/or complications stemming from birth (Table 1). Several studies (e.g., Simons et al., 1966; Elmer, 1967; Fitch et al., 1977) lack appropriate control groups and one (Corey et al., 1975) fails to find a relationship. However, a number with adequate controls (Smith and Hanson, 1974; NSPCC, undated; Lenoski, 1974; Lynch, 1976) do sustain the relationship. Lenoski, with very large index and control groups, found not only that the abused children

Table 1. Perinatal history of abused children

	Sample population (%)		Control population (%)
Low birth weight			
Elmer and Gregg (1967)	31.8	$N = 22$	
Simons et al. (1966)	20.0	$N = 313$	10.0 New York City
Terr (1970)	20.0	$N = 10$	
McRae (1973)	12.0	$N = 132$	
*Lenoski (1974)	22.0	$N = 674$	10.0 $N = 500$ pediatric admissions
Elmer et al. (1971)	37.0	$N = 24$	
Skinner and Castle (1969)	13.0	$N = 78$	6.5 Great Britain
*Klein and Stern (1971)	23.5	$N = 51$	10.0 Montreal indigent population
Martin et al. (1974)	19.0	$N = 58$	9.2 Colorado
Baldwin and Oliver (1975)	21.0	$N = 60$	6.7 Perinatal Mortality Survey (1963)
Smith and Hanson (1974)	24.0	$N = 134$	5.6 Great Britain
*Lynch (1976)	60.0	$N = 25$	20.0 Siblings
*NSPCC (undated)	28.4	$N = 81$	7.2 Great Britain social class IV & V
*Fitch et al. (1977)	21.7	$N = 92$	6.5 matched by age and race, not SES
Congenital defects			
Baldwin and Oliver (1975)	10.0	$N = 60$	3.0 national surveys
Birrell and Birrell (1968)	26.0	$N = 42$	
Smith and Hanson (1974)	7.5	$N = 134$	1.8 national population
Birth complications			
Terr (1970)	60.0	$N = 10$	
*Lenoski (1974)	9.0	$N = 674$	4.2 $N = 500$ pediatric admissions
*Lynch (1976)	50.0	$N = 25$	5.7 Siblings

*Statistically significant.

were twice as likely to be premature but also that 24 percent of them were delivered by Caesarean section compared with 3.2 percent of the controls. In the most comprehensive perinatal study of abused children and their own non-abused siblings, Lynch (1976) found that the subject group suffered significantly more abnormal pregnancies and deliveries, neonatal separations, and postnatal illnesses than the control sample.

While premature children run a higher than average risk of abuse, this does not seem to be because physical immaturity makes them more susceptible to injury (Elmer, 1967; Klein and Stern, 1971). Several authors, however, regard the "failure to thrive" syndrome as a precursor to abuse (Koel, 1969; Van Stolk, 1972; Smith and Hanson, 1974; Smith, 1975). Possible causal connections between abnormal birth history and child abuse are discussed by Parke and Collmer (1975). Steele and Pollock (1968) speculate that low birth weights, congenital defects or birth complications may trigger parental disappointment over the newborn. Another possibility is that parental contact immediately after birth may have important consequences for the later parent-child relationship. Klaus and Kennell (1976) report that the amount of separation between mothers and neonates even after normal pregnancy and delivery has negative effects on the mother-infant relationship. Mothers given extended contact with their infants during the first three days after delivery were found to spend more time fondling them and making eye contact with them a year later when compared to a control group. Leiderman (1974) and Gray et al. (1976) report improved mothering and decreased probability of abuse as a result of similar interventions with high risk populations.

Injuries

Substantial data have been aggregated on trauma sustained by abused children (Maden, 1975). The principal modalities of attack are beating with hands, assault with a blunt instrument, and burning. Superficial injuries including bruises, welts, and lacerations are the most frequent injuries, as indicated in Table 2.

When compared with surveys, clinical studies find a higher percentage of serious and fatal injuries including cranial trauma, bone fractures, and internal injuries. Several factors account for most of the difference. Gil (1970), Martin et al. (1974), and Johnson (1974) all confirm that infants and young children sustain more serious injuries. As previously noted, clinical studies often exclude older children and adolescents and also draw their samples from pediatric services which attend to serious trauma. Compared with Lenoski's (1974) clinical data on accidental childhood injuries, however, it is clear that abused children suffer a disproportionate number of serious injuries largely attributable to a history of escalating abuse. Authorities agree that a high proportion of abused children have had a history of mistreatment, (see Table 3), and that, without effective intervention, they can expect future abuse not infrequently escalating to permanent damage or fatality (Perrin, 1970; Raffalli, 1970; Martin, 1972; Fontana, 1973; MacKeith, 1975). Parke and Collmer (1975) present a comprehensive

Table 2. Severity of child abuse injuries

Four selected clinical studies and surveys	Sample	Fatal	Serious	Not serious	No injury/ unknown
Studies					
Skinner and Castle (1969)	N = 78	1.5	73.0	25.5	
Smith and Hanson (1974)	N = 134	8.0	61.0	23.0	8.0
Surveys					
Gil (1970)	N = 1380	3.4	41.1	53.3	2.2
Fergusson et al. (1972)	N = 255	2.7	13.8	71.4	12.2

Table 3. Previously abused children

Study	N	Previous abuse (%)
Simons et al. (1968)	313	33.0
Morse et al. (1970)	23	35.0
Morse and Johnson (1968)	101	40.0
Lauer et al. (1974)	130	43.8
Ebbin et al. (1969)	50	50.0
Thomson et al. (1971)	376	61.3
O'Neill (1973)	110	80.0
Terr (1970)	10	80.0
Smith and Hanson (1974)	139	54.0
Baldwin and Oliver (1975)	38	70.0

review and evaluation of current programs to control and prevent child abuse. However, Young (1964), Skinner and Castle (1969), Silver et al. (1971), Oliver and Cox (1973), Smith (1975) and Sussman (1975) all reported considerable failure to prevent subsequent abuse despite various forms of intervention.

Victim: functioning

Physical functioning. Studies indicate significant proportions of abused children suffer neurologic impairment from the abuse (Fergusson et al., 1972; Martin, 1972; Caffey, 1972, 1974; Martin et al., 1974; Baldwin and Oliver, 1975; Cooper, 1975). Other frequent consequences include ocular damage (Heins, 1969; Mushin, 1971; Caffey, 1974; Smith and Hanson, 1974), and growth failure (Elmer, 1967; Ebbin et al., 1969; Morse, 1970; Terr, 1970; Martin, 1972; Kent, 1973; O'Neill, 1973; Smith and Hanson, 1974; Martin et al., 1974). More qualitative measures of physical dysfunction include: atypical behavior (Gil, 1970; Fergusson et al., 1972; Smith and Hanson, 1974; Baldwin and Oliver, 1975); chronic illness (Lebsack cited in Zadnick, 1973); physical unattractiveness (Fergusson et al., 1972; Baldwin and Oliver, 1975); and subsequent injuries. While the majority of physical dysfunctions of abused children are the result of abuse, there also remains the possibility that some of them antedate and contribute to the abuse. The extent to which physical dysfunctions of abused children derive from prematurity, congenital defects, and

other neonatal diseases has not been determined.

Cognitive functioning. Despite control problems, researchers concur that a significant proportion of child abuse victims have impaired cognitive functioning as a consequence of the abuse (Elmer and Gregg, 1967; Smith and Hanson, 1974; Sandgrund et al., 1974; Cooper, 1975; Baldwin and Oliver, 1975). It is unclear, however, that the impaired functioning is primarily the result of head trauma. Two studies (Martin et al., 1974; Smith and Hanson, 1974) found that while neurologic dysfunction is highly related to intellectual performance, the relationship between head trauma and neurologic impairment is equivocal. Further, both studies report that children with sustained growth failure score markedly lower on intelligence tests than other abused children.

The Elmer et al. (1975) controlled, eight-year follow-up study found considerable intellectual dysfunction both among the abuse sample and among the accident and nonabuse control groups. The authors concluded that "the effects of abuse on child development were insignificant in comparison to the effects of membership in the lower classes." (Elmer et al., 1975) However, Sangrund et al. (1974) matched abuse, neglect, and control groups according to socioeconomic status, ethnicity, and age and found that the proportion of abused and neglected children with subnormal scores was nearly ten times the number of control subjects. Kent's (1973) follow-up data on I.Q. scores of abused and neglected children showed that whereas the former group improved, the latter group maintained their low intelligence scores. Other follow-up data indicate that abused children suffer delayed cognitive development manifested by language delay (Elmer, 1967; Johnson, 1968; Martin et al., 1974; Smith and Hanson, 1974; Elmer et al., 1975) and poor performance in school (Gil, 1970; Kline and Christiansen, 1975). Although the etiology of impairment has not been clearly established, the data clearly indicate that child abuse causes significant impairment in cognitive functioning.

Psychosocial functioning. Studies without controls uniformly report significant social psychological dysfunctions including deviant behavior (Young, 1964; Elmer, 1967; Johnson and Morse, 1968; Green, 1968; Gil, 1970; Ounsted et al., 1975) and defective relationships (Delsordo, 1963; Steele and Pollock, 1968; McRae et al., 1973). Not only is it unclear whether the deviance results from or contributes to the abuse (Friedrich and Boriskin, 1976); it is often unclear whether it exists other than in the eye of the observer. It is interesting to note that abusing mothers perceive their children to be more difficult than normal (Galdston, 1965; Gregg and Elmer, 1969; Smith and Hanson, 1974; Ounsted et al., 1975), even though observations by Gregg and Elmer (1969) and Smith and Hanson (1974) indicate that they may be easier to care for than controls. Perhaps most significantly, retrospective studies of juvenile offenders and violent criminals indicate an important association with antecedent child abuse (Shephard, 1965; Kent, 1973; Fontana, 1973 cited by Sussman and Cohen, 1975; Howell, 1975; Steele, 1975). Any but tentative conclusions must await better controlled and longitudinal data.

Perpetrator: identity, age, sex

Identity. Authorities agree that the large majority of child abusers are natural parents or their substitutes (Maden, 1975). Several authors (Paulson and Blake, 1969; Gil, 1970; Fergusson et al., 1972) suggest that many abusers are stepparents, adoptive parents, foster parents or companions. Johnson (1974) notes that abuse reports are more often confirmed when the victim was with a stepparent.

Sex. Perhaps because of greater contact, studies generally find that more mothers than fathers assault their children (Gelles, 1973), particularly younger children (Schloesser, 1964; Silver et al., 1971; Theisen, 1975). If the father is unemployed, Steele and Pollock (1969) and Schmidt and Kempe (1974) suspect that the differential incidence is eradicated. Indirect support of this idea is given by Light's (1973) finding that unemployed fathers assault younger as well as older children. In any case, most authors agree that both parents share complicity in child abuse even if one parent actually commits the

reported abuse (Steele and Pollock, 1968; Brown and Daniels, 1968; Silver, 1968; McRae et al., 1973; Sturgess and Heal, 1976). However, Sturgess and Heal (1976) discovered that among a sample of previously abused children, mothers were most often responsible for the initial assault whereas both parents were equally likely to commit subsequent abuses.

Age. The finding that abusing parents are likely to be young (Lauer et al., 1974; Smith et al., 1974) may be an artifact of the age of the victim population particularly in clinical studies (Maden, 1975). Alternately, this finding may reflect Smith's (1975) hypothesis that child abuse is related to teenage marriages.

Parent functioning: intellectual, social, psychiatric

Intellectual. Numerous studies (Sheridan, 1956; Bennie and Sclare, 1969; Gil, 1970; Baldwin and Oliver, 1975) reported a high incidence of intellectual subnormality among abusing samples, but appropriate controls accompanied none of them. Other uncontrolled studies (Kempe et al., 1962; Cameron et al., 1966; Steele and Pollock, 1968; Holter and Friedman, 1968b; and Fergusson et al., 1972) found that abuse was not related to intelligence. Both Smith et al. (1973b) and Wright (1976) compared abusing with nonabusing parents and reported that the former group scored significantly lower on intelligence tests. Hyman (1976) confirmed the direction but not the significance of the Smith et al. finding, attributing the discrepancy to small sample size, the manipulation of subtest scores and the influence of socioeconomic status. In sum, the data are not now adequate to demonstrate a relationship between intelligence and abuse.

Social. A composite of the data indicates that child abusing mothers and fathers have a consistent but differentially patterned history of antisocial behavior. Many studies uncovered an extensive record of criminal activity particularly among male abusers (Young, 1964; Bennie and Sclare, 1969; Gil, 1970; Scott, 1973; Smith et al., 1973b; Baldwin and Oliver, 1975). Fergusson et al. (1972) found that a disproportionate number of male abusers had been convicted of crimes excluding mistreatment of children, compared with the nonabusing population, a finding supported by Baldwin and Oliver (1975). The data support the conclusion that previous criminal activity, at least for males, is significantly related to child abuse. Smith (1975) provides the most comprehensive data on the social relationships of abusing mothers compared with nonabusing peers. That study reported that a significant proportion of index mothers had only rare contact with parents, relatives, neighbors, and friends. Moreover, a significant number of abusing mothers compared with index fathers and control parents engaged in no social activities. Other studies find that abusers are unusually mobile (Schloesser, 1964; Johnson and Morse, 1968; Birrell and Birrell, 1968; Gil, 1970; Smith et al., 1974; Lauer et al., 1974); maintain unlisted telephones (Lenoski, 1974); refuse to allow their children to engage in normal educational and recreational activities (Young, 1964); and do not voluntarily avail themselves of support from community organizations (Morris and Gould, 1963; Young, 1964; Holter and Friedman, 1968b; Gil, 1970; Smith et al., 1974; Holman and Kanwar, 1975).

Several well-controlled studies indicate that abusing families have more than the average number of children, making it likely that this finding is not simply due to oversampling of large nonwhite families. Light (1973) provides an international survey—United States, Great Britain, and New Zealand—of the family size of abusing families accompanied by respective national census figures. In all three countries fewer abusing families had only one child, while in the United States (Gil, 1970) and New Zealand (Fergusson et al., 1972), significantly more abusing families had four or more children. Although both Gil and Fergusson include a disproportionate number of nonwhite families in their surveys, the latter partialed out the nonwhite families and still found a marked difference in family size between abusing and nonabusing families. In reanalyzing Gil's data, Light (1973) controlled for family income, ethnicity, and the father's education level and found, nevertheless, that abusing families have

more children. Findings by Lenoski (1974) that abusing mothers have a stronger desire for pregnancy, and by Smith (1975) that they have a negative attitude towards contraception, amplify the relationship between family size and child abuse.

Numerous studies indicate a significant number of separations, divorces, and single parent households among abusing families (Ebbin et al., 1969; Gil, 1970; McRae, 1973; Smith et al., 1974; Baldwin and Oliver, 1975). As Simons et al. (1966), Steele and Pollock (1968), and Corey et al. (1975) show, however, the marital situation of abusing families may not be significantly different from nonabusing families drawn from the same socioeconomic class. In any case, researchers report substantial domestic discord between child abusing parents or stepparents (Simons et al., 1966; Fergusson et al., 1972; Smith et al., 1974; Smith and Hanson, 1975). Measurement of the relationships between and among parents, abuse victims and siblings indicate high levels of violence (Lenoski, 1974; Martin et al., 1974; Brown and Oliver, 1975), punitiveness (Elmer, 1967; Martin et al., 1974; Smith and Hanson, 1975), and rejection or hostility (Young, 1964; Morse and Hohnson, 1968; Martin et al., 1974; Smith and Hanson, 1975).

Psychiatric. Although most studies find a high prevalence of psychiatric dysfunction among child abusers, the data frequently suffer from diagnostic and interpretive distortions (Friedman, 1972; Gelles, 1973; Walters, 1975). For example, numerous studies relate alcoholism and more recently, drug addiction to child abuse (Young, 1964; Birrell and Birrell, 1968; Johnson and Morse, 1968; Gil, 1970; Wertham, 1972; Fontana, 1973; Blumberg, 1974; Baldwin and Oliver, 1975). However, Simons et al. (1966) and Smith (1975) found that these problems were no more common among the abusing sample than among the general population from which they were drawn. Fergusson et al. (1972) found comparably high drinking rates among abusing and nonabusing parents but noted that nearly half the heavy drinking fathers were personally responsible for injuring the child. Gil (1970) reported that 12.9 percent of the child abuse perpetrators in his large sample were intoxicated. The data indicate that alcoholism is a precipitating factor in child abuse (Starr, 1976). The prevalence of psychosis among child abusers is not great (Wasserman, 1967; Fleming, 1967; Steele and Pollock, 1968; Spinetta and Rigler, 1972; Caffey, 1972b; Kempe, 1973; O'Neill, 1973; Ounsted et al., 1975; Smith, 1975). However, a larger proportion of child abusers had histories of mental illness reflected in medical diagnosis, psychosomatic illness, psychiatric treatment, or institutionalization (Gil, 1970; Smith, 1975; Ounsted et al., 1975; Holman and Kanwar, 1975; Baldwin and Oliver, 1975; Smith and Hanson, 1975). In two controlled studies, Fergusson et al. (1972) found that significantly more mothers suffered severe mental illness whereas Smith (1975) found that significantly more fathers were considered psychopathic while mothers were frequently diagnosed with less severe mental illnesses.

While authorities have not identified a coherent abusing personality structure (Katz, 1970; Steele, 1970a; Gelles, 1973; Paulsen et al., 1974), they observe common personality deficiencies of abusing parents: unmet dependency needs (Cohen, 1966; Steele and Pollock, 1968; Court, 1970; Kempe, 1973; Green et al., 1974); lack of identity (Elmer, 1967; Brown and Daniels, 1968; Steele and Pollock, 1968; Green et al., 1975); reversal of roles (Morris and Gould, 1963; Bryant, 1963; Galdston, 1965; Elmer, 1967; Brown and Daniels, 1968; Steele, 1970; Stolk, 1972; Blumberg, 1974; Green et al., 1974); impaired impulse control (Cohen, 1966; Johnson, 1968; Green et al., 1974; Smith and Hanson, 1975); and rigid or inadequate defenses (Cohen, 1966; Steele and Pollock, 1968; Melnick and Hurley, 1969; Elmer, 1967, 1970; Scott, 1973; Green et al., 1974; Ounsted, 1975). Inadequate personalities have been related to physical and emotional neglect and abuse during the childhood of the abuser (Johnson and Morse, 1968; Steele and Pollock, 1968; Currie, 1970; Spinetta and Rigler, 1972; Green et al., 1974; Baldwin and Oliver, 1975; Smith and Hanson, 1975). Steele and Pollock (1968) suggest that child abuse is best described as a pattern of behavior rather than a psychiatric entity. Several studies have attempted to corroborate psychiatric observations with quantitative data from psychological test instruments. Steele and Pollock (1968), using standard diagnostic tests, uncovered considerable oral dependency, underlying depression, and unresolved identity conflict. Melnick and Hurley's (1969) small but well-controlled study of personality features of abusing mothers supported earlier findings. Scores from the California Test of Personality (CTP), the Family Concept Inventory (FCI), and the Thematic Apperception Test (TAT) indicated that the subjects feel frustrated in their emotional needs and find it difficult to manage responsibilities of life, particularly child caring activities, as well as scoring higher on the TAT Pathogenic Index. Evans (1976) supports these general findings. Other generally supportive findings were reported by Paulson et al. (1974, 1975a, 1975b) and Wright (1976). However, Melnick and Hurley (1969) also found that abusing mothers scored lower than controls on Manifest Rejection, suggesting more rigid defense against hostile impulses. Similarly, Wright (1976) reported that battering parents scored significantly higher on the Rosenzweig group conformity rating and lower on Rorschach bizarre content. He speculates that battering parents actively disguise their psychopathology, a pattern he has named the "sick but slick" syndrome. In sum, the data sustain the conclusion that abusing parents exhibit considerable psychological dysfunction when compared with control groups.

Environment

Financial factors. Child abuse studies generally draw samples from the lower socioeconomic strata. In the two studies which matched abusing families with a sample of nonabusing pediatric admissions (Elmer, 1969; Smith, 1975), child abusing families were rated lower on the Hollingshead Two-Factor Index. Generally, the data sustain the well established association between and among income, occupation, education, and housing in the child abusing population. Researchers find that a large proportion of reported child abusing families have poverty incomes (Elmer, 1969; Gil, 1970) and are eligible for public assistance although some of them do not avail themselves of it (Simons et al., 1966; Johnson and Morse, 1968; Smith and Hanson, 1974). Many authors report that abusing families are characterized by unemployment, underemployment, or discontinuous employment (Young, 1964; Simons et al., 1966; Holter and Friedman, 1968; Johnson and Morse, 1968; Steele and Pollock, 1968; Gil, 1970; Baldwin and Oliver, 1975). Re-analyzing Gil's (1970) data, Light (1973) sustained the observation that fathers without employment are likely child abusers (Galdston, 1965; Gelles, 1973; Scott, 1973). Employed abusers fall predominantly in the manual or unskilled occupation categories (Schloesser, 1964; Johnson and Morse, 1968; Gil, 1970; Scott, 1973; Smith et al., 1974), although both Steele and Pollock (1968) and Paulsen and Blake (1969) found that the occupation pattern mirrored the general population from which the abusing sample was drawn.

The data indicate that child abusers most frequently occupy rental housing and characterize their accommodations as substandard (Holter and Friedman, 1968; Johnson and Morse, 1968; Gil, 1970; Light, 1973; Baldwin and Oliver, 1975). In contrast to Sattin and Miller (1971), Light (1973) found that even when occupation is controlled, abusing families are more likely to live in apartment houses and less likely to share living quarters than nonabusing families. Other studies indicate that living conditions among abusing families generally do not appreciably differ from those of the other households in the surrounding area (Smith et al., 1974; Holmer and Kanwar, 1975).

In sum, it is evident that a disproportionate number of the reported cases of child abuse come from the lower socioeconomic classes. Determining whether there is a significant relationship between poverty and child abuse or whether child abusing parents are simply more likely to be detected if they are poor requires more adequate research designs. In any event, employment problems emerge as the most significant socioeconomic factor associated with child abuse.

Sociocultural environment. Parke and Collmer (1975) comprehensively review the literature pertaining to the relationship between the level of violence and child abuse and conclude that violence is endemic to American society and is reflected in comparative homicide and assault and battery rates, levels of violence portrayed on television, and assessments of intrafamily aggression. Relating social and family levels of violence, they cite Bellak and Antell who found correspondingly high homicide and suicide rates and levels of parental and child aggression in several European cities; and Steinmetz who reported lower rates of criminal aggressive activity and lower levels of intrafamily aggression in Canada. Similarly, Straus (1971:61) presents data to support his conclusion that "the United States is a society that practices and approves of violence." Following his review of pertinent American studies, Brofenbrenner related membership in the lower socioeconomic classes to higher levels of violence specifically including the use of corporal punishment, a topic also discussed by Elmer (1967) and Giovannoni (1971).

More recently, Erlanger (1974a) re-analyzed the research data on social class and corporal punishment in childrearing and reviewed additional studies (1974b). He concluded that there is an insignificant correlation between social class and the use of physical punishment. Studies by Straus (1971) and Steinmetz (1974) found that corporal punishment was equally pervasive among lower and middle class families. More specifically, Erlanger (1974a: 157) cites Gil and Noble's findings that the "mistreatment of children finds no support among the mass of low-status parents," and that they "are just as concerned about child abuse as high-status persons" and "favor more strict measures to help abused children."

CONCLUSIONS

This survey has both provided solid evidence for many things which were previously believed about child abuse and also identified several areas where previously unanticipated findings point to the need for more research. The victims of child abuse are generally young children and are not significantly distinguished by sex or race. Bruises and lacerations are the most common injury, but head injuries and bone fractures are not uncommon, especially among infants and young children. The majority of abused children have a history of mistreatment and, without effective intervention, can expect a future of abuse escalating to serious, permanent, or fatal injury. While it is not clear to what extent the dysfunction preceded the abuse and to what extent it followed it, most victims exhibit considerable deviance in physical, cognitive, and psychosocial functioning.

Most perpetrators are young, biological parents of the abused children, and parents of larger than average sized families. Where the abused child is young, the perpetrator is more likely to be the mother than the father. The perpetrators frequently have a history of personal problems and, in the case of males, a record of antisocial behavior. Families are frequently drawn from the lower socioeconomic classes, and are characterized by excessive mobility, social isolation, and lack of community affiliation. In addition to these findings supporting what was generally known about child abuse, there are a number of findings supporting significant features of each of the two major theories in the area (Steele and Pollock, 1968; Gil, 1969, 1970, 1971, 1975a, 1975b). Gil's theoretical emphasis on situational stresses is supported by many findings. Unemployment emerges as one of the most unequivocal factors in child abuse. The observations that housing conditions may be significantly related to abuse even when socioeconomic status is held constant, that abusing families are cut off from many forms of social support and help, and that they frequently are young parents with large numbers of children are also consistent with an emphasis on situational factors.

Present findings are also consistent with Gil's emphasis on the cultural transmission of violence. The clearest evidence for this at present comes from the study of abusing families who are characterized by histories of violence in general and conviction of males for crimes of interpersonal violence in particular. That delinquency and subsequent criminal activity can be expected from many victims of child abuse suggests the transmission of a culture of violence from generation to generation. Similarly, a number of aspects of Steele and Pollock's theory find support in the findings. That the victims of abuse are generally young, that they are liable to repeated abuse, and that their attackers are frequently maladjusted, isolated, and subject to various situational pressures are all findings which support the original observations made by Steele and Pollock.

Finally, several of the results reported here point to the need for both more empirical research and more theoretical development, including findings on sex differences in reported abuse, on first and subsequent abuse, and on mother-child bonding. We have noted that among young children, girls are more controlled by parents than are boys. We have also seen that boys are more likely to be reported as cases of child abuse, but that a higher proportion of the female cases are likely to be confirmed or even fatal. These findings suggest that the same act which is seen as abuse when applied to a young male child may be interpreted as appropriate discipline of a girl. Since sexual discrimination is well established in many areas of American life, it should not surprise us if one of its forms is greater cultural tolerance of aggression against females than against males.

A second finding which seems to demand more research is the observation that mothers are most frequently the first abuser of a child, but that the subsequent acts of abuse are frequently committed by the father. This finding, together with the ones earlier referred to on differences between male and female abusers, points to the necessity of research on the different dynamics which may underlie abuse by males and by females. Neither of the two theories which we have considered lays primary stress on the social norms existing within the family in understanding child abuse. Yet what seems a probable explanation of this finding highlights their possible importance. We have seen that abusing mothers are likely to have unmet neurotic needs, to be socially isolated, and to have a great deal of contact with a young infant. Under these circumstances, attack on the child might take place. We have also seen some evidence that abusing fathers are more often characterized by an antisocial acting out of aggression. This aggression might initially have been kept in check within the family by the social norm that it should not be expressed against young children. The mother's attack on the child might then communicate to the father that this was a permissible way to express aggression. While this account is highly speculative, the mere existence of evidence for different dynamics in male and female abusers suggests the importance of studies of how these dynamics are acted out within the context of the family.

The third important finding is one which perhaps holds out great potential for the reduction of child abuse. We have seen that there is a significant relationship between abuse and such perinatal factors as prematurity or birth by Caesarean section. There are a number of possible causal relationships which could underlie this finding. There is increasing evidence, however, that at least one of them is interference with the process of emotional attachment of the mother to the infant immediately after birth. With only a few studies yet done in the area, there are already preliminary findings indicating both that child abuse may be reduced by facilitating bonding in high risk cases, and that mother-child relationships in the general population may be improved by changing hospital routines to provide greater mother-child contact immediately after birth. Since neither of the theories stresses mother-child bonding as a theoretical variable, the emerging findings in this area point to the need for theoretical revision, as well as for both further research and the application of that research.

REFERENCES

Adelson, L.
1972 "The Battering Child." Journal of the American Medical Association 222(2):159-161.

American Humane Association, Children's Division
1976 Highlights of 1974 National Data. Denver, Colorado.

Bakan, David
1971 Slaughter of the Innocents: A Study of the Battered Child Phenomenon. San Francisco: Jossey-Bass.

Baldwin, J. A. and J. E. Oliver
1975 "Epidemiology and Family Characteristics of Severely Abused Children." British Journal of Preventive Social Medicine 29(4):205-221.

Banagale, P. C. and M. S. McIntire
1973 Child Abuse and Neglect. A Study of Cases Reported to Douglas County Child Protective Service from 1967-1973. Creighton University, Omaha, Nebraska, Department of Pediatrics.

Baron, Michael A., Bejar, R. L. and P. J. Sheaff
1970 "Neurologic Manifestations of the Battered Child Syndrome." Pediatrics 45(6):1003-1007.

Bennett, A. N.
1974 "Children Under Stress." Journal of the Royal Naval Medical Service 60(1-2):83-87.

Bennie, E. and A. Sclare
1969 "The Battered Child Syndrome." American Journal of Psychiatry 125(7):975-979.

Birrell, R. G. and J. H. Birrell
1968 "The Maltreatment Syndrome in Children: A Hospital Survey." The Medical Journal of Australia 2:1023-1029.

Bethschneider, J. L., Young, J. P., Morris, P. and D. D. Hayes
1973 "A Study of Father-Daughter Incest in the Harris County Child Welfare Unit." Criminal Justice Monograph 4(4):1-131.

Bloch, Harry
1973 "Dilemma of 'Battered Child' and 'Battered Children'." New York State Journal of Medicine 73: 799-800.

Blumberg, Marvin
1974 "Psychopathology of the Abusing Parent." American Journal of Psychotherapy 28(1):21-29.

Blumberg, Myrna
1964 "When Parents Hit Out." Twentieth Century 173: 39-44.

Boardman, Helen E.
1962 "A Project to Rescue Children From Inflicted Injuries." Social Work 1:43-51.

Boisvert, M. J.
1972 "The Battered-Child Syndrome." Social Casework 53(8):475-480.

Borgman, Robert
1974 Research Practice in Child Protective Services: Realities and Frustrations. In: Protective Services to Abused and Neglected Children and Their Families, Official Proceedings, National Institute for the Training of Trainers. Denver, Colorado. Graduate School of Social Work, University of Denver, Colorado.

Brown, John A. and Robert Danels
1968 "Some Observations in Abusive Parents." Child Welfare 47(2):89-94.

Bryant, Harold
1963 "Physical Abuse of Children—An Agency Study." Child Welfare, pp. 125-130.

Burland, Alexis J., Andrews, R. G. and S. J. Headsten
1973 "Child Abuse: One Tree in the Forest," Child Welfare 52(9):585-592.

Burt Associates, Inc.
1975 Report and Plan on Recommended Approaches and Methods for Determination of National Incidence of Child Abuse and Neglect. Volume I. (Report prepared for the National Center on Child Abuse and Neglect). National Technical Information Service, Springfield, Virginia.

Caffey, John
  1946 "Multiple Fractures in the Long Bones of Infants Suffering from Chronic Subdural Hematoma." American Journal of Roentgenology 56(2):163-173.
Caffey, John
  1972a "On the Theory and Practice of Shaking Infants." American Journal of Diseases of Children 124(2): 161-169.
Caffey, John
  1974 "The Whiplash Shaken Infant Syndrome." Pediatrics 54(4):396-401.
Cameron, J. M.
  1966 "The Battered Child Syndrome." Medical Science Law 6:2-21.
Cameron, J. and J. Rael
  1975 Atlas of the Battered Child Syndrome. Edinburgh, Scotland: Churchill Livingstone.
Cavallin, H.
  1966 "Incestuous Fathers: A Clinical Report." American Journal of Psychiatry 122:1132.
Chesser, Eustace
  1952 Cruelty to Children. New York: The Philosophical Library.
Clemenger, F.
  1974 Part I: A Study of the Effectiveness of the Reporting of Child Abuse by the City of Houston Public Health Nurses. Part II: Survey of the Available Source for the Prevention and Treatment of Child Abusers in Harris County, Texas. Houston University, Texas. Graduate School of Social Work.
Cohen, M.
  1966 "Psychological Aspects of the Maltreatment Syndrome of Childhood." Journal of Pediatrics 69(2): 279.
Cohen, Stephen and Alan Sussman
  1975 "The Incidence of Child Abuse in the United States." Child Welfare 54(6):432-443.
Cooper, Christine
        "The Doctor's Dilemma—A Pediatrician's View." Pp. 21-29 in A. Franklin (ed.), Concerning Child Abuse. Edinburgh, Scotland: Churchill Livingstone.
Corey, Eleanor J., Miller, Carol and Frederic Widlack
  1975 "Factors Contributing to Child Abuse." Nursing Research 24(4):293-295.
Court, Joan
  1970 "Psycho-social Factors in Child-Battering." Journal of Medical Women's Federation 52:99-104.
Currie, J. R. B.
  1970 "A Psychiatric Assessment of the Battered Child Syndrome." South African Medical Journal, pp. 635-639.
DeFrancis, Vincent
  1971 "Protecting the Child Victim of Sex Crimes Committed by Adults." Federal Probation 35(3):15-20.
Delsordo, James D.
  1963 "Protective Casework for Abused Children," Children 10(6):214.
Ebbin, A. J., Gollub, M. H., Stern, A. M. and M. G. Wilson
  1969 "Battered Child Syndrome in Los Angeles General Hospital." American Journal of Diseases of the Child 118:660-667.

Elmer, Elizabeth, Evans, Sue Reinhart, John B. Lachin, John and Frank Wimberly
  1975 Follow-Up Study of Traumatized Children (Final Report). Pittsburgh Child Guidance Center.
Elmer, Elizabeth, Gregg, G., Wright, B., Reinhart, J. B., McHenry, T., Geisel, P. and C. Wutenberg
  1971 Studies of Child Abuse and Infant Accidents, Mental Health Program Reports. Washington, D.C.: U.S. Government Printing Office, 58-59.
Elmer, Elizabeth
  1967 Children in Jeopardy: A Study of Abused Minors and Their Families. Pittsburgh: University of Pittsburgh Press.
Elmer, E. and G. S. Gregg
  1967 "Developmental Characteristics of Abused Children," Pediatrics 40(4):596-602.
Erlanger, Howard S.
  1974a "Social Class Differences in Parents' Use of Physical Punishment." In S. K. Steinmetz, and M. Straus, eds., Violence in the Family. New York: Dodd, Mead. Pp. 150-158.
  1974b "Social Class and Corporal Punishment in Childbearing: A Reassessment." American Sociological Review 39:68-85.
  1974c "The Empirical Status of the Subculture of Violence Thesis." Social Problems 22(2):280-292.
Evans, Phillip
  1968 "Infanticide." Proceedings of the Royal Society of Medicine 61:1296-1298.
Fanaroff, Avroy A., Kennell, John and Marshall Klaus
  1972 "Follow-up of Low Birth Weight Infants—The Predicative Value of Maternal Visiting Patterns." Pediatrics 49:287-290.
Fergusson, David M., Fleming, John and David O'Neill
  1972 Child Abuse in New Zealand. Wellington, New Zealand; Research Division, Department of Social Work.
Fisher, G. and L. M. Howell
  1970 "Psychological Needs of Homosexual Pedophiliacs." Diseases of the Nervous System 31(1):623-625.
Fitch, Michael, Cadol, Roger, Goldson, Edward, Jackson, Elaine K., Swartz, Darlene and Theodore Wendell
  1977 Perspective Study in Child Abuse: The Child Study Program. Denver Department of Health and Hospitals.
Fleming, G. M.
  1967 "Cruelty to Children." British Medical Journal 2: 421-422.
Flynn, William R.
  1970 "Frontier Justice: A Contribution to the Theory of Child Battery." American Psychiatry 127(3):375-379.
Fontana, Vincent J.
  1964 "The Neglect and Abuse of Children." New York Journal of Medicine 64:215-224.
  1973 "The Diagnosis of the Maltreatment Syndrome in Children." Pediatrics Supplement 51(4):780-782.
  1973 Somewhere a Child is Crying. New York: Macmillan.
Friedman, Stanford B.
  1972 "The Need for Intensive Follow-up of Abused Chil-

dren." Pp. 79-92 in C. H. Kempe and R. Helfer (eds.), Helping the Battered Child and His Family. Philadelphia: Lippincott.

Friedman, S. B. and Carol Morse.
1974 "Child Abuse: A Five Year Follow-up of Early Case Finding in the Emergency Department." Pediatrics 54(4):404-443.

Friedrich, William N. and Boriskin, Jerry A.
1976 "The Role of the Child in Abuse: A Review of the Literature." American Journal of Orthopsychiatry 46(4):580.

Galdston, R.
1965 "Observations of Children Who Have Been Physically Abused by Their Parents." American Journal of Psychiatry 122 (4):440-443.

Garbarine, J.
1976 "Some Ecological Correlates of Child Abuse. The Impact of Socioeconomic Stress on Mothers." Child Development 47(1):178.

Gelles, Richard J.
1973 "Child Abuse as Psychopathology: A Sociological Critique and Reformulation." American Journal of Orthopsychiatry, 43(4):611-621.
1975 "The Social Construction of Child Abuse." American Journal of Orthopsychiatry 45(3):363-371.
1977 "Violence Towards Children in the United States." Paper presented at the meeting of the American Association for the Advancement of Science, Denver, Colorado.

Gil, David G.
1969 "Physical Abuse of Children: Findings and Implications of a Nationwide Survey." Pediatrics (Supplement) 44:857-864.
1970 Violence Against Children: Physical Child Abuse in the United States. Cambridge, Massachusetts: Harvard University Press.
1971 "Violence Against Children." Journal of Marriage and the Family 33(4):637-648.
1975a "Unraveling Child Abuse." American Journal of Orthopsychiatry 45(3):346-356.
1975b "A Holistic Perspective on Child Abuse and Its Prevention." American Journal of Orthopsychiatry.

Gil, David and John Noble
1969 "Public Knowledge, Attitudes, and Opinions about Physical Child Abuse in the United States." Child Welfare 48(7):395-426.

Giovannoni, Jeanne M.
1971 "Parental Mistreatment: Perpetrators and Victims. Journal of Marriage and the Family 33:649-657.

Gray, Jane, Cutler, Christy, Dean, Janet and C. Henry Kempe
1976 "Prediction and Prevention of Child Abuse." Pediatric Research 10(4):103.

Green, Arthur H.
1968 "Self Destructive Behavior in Physically Abused Schizophrenic Children." Archives of General Psychiatry 19:171-179.

Green, A. H., Gaines, R. W. and A. Sandgrund
1974 "Child Abuse: Pathological Syndrome of Family Interaction." American Journal of Psychiatry 131(8):882-886.

Gregg, Grace S. and Elizabeth Elmer
1969 "Infant Injuries or Abuse?" Pediatrics 44(3):434-439.

Harder, T.
1967 "The Psychopathology of Infanticide." Acta Psychiatrica Scandinavica 43:196-891.

Heins, Marilyn
1969 "Child Abuse—Analysis of a Current Epidemic." Michigan Medicine 68(17):887-891.

Helfer, Ray
1973 "The Etiology of Child Abuse." Pediatrics (Supplement) 51(4):777-779.

Helfer, Ray and C. Henry Kempe
1968 The Battered Child. Chicago: University of Chicago Press. (Second edition, 1974).

Holland, Cathleen G.
1973 "An Examination of Social Isolation and Availability to Treatment in the Phenomenon of Child Abuse. Smith College Studies in Social Work 44(1):74-75.

Holmar, R. R. and S. Kanswar
1975 "Early Life of the 'Battered Child'" (letter). Archives of Disease in Childhood 50(1):78-80.

Holter, H. C. and S. B. Friedman
1968a "Principles of Management in Child Abuse Cases." American Journal of Orthopsychiatry 38(1):127-136.
1968b "Child Abuse: Early Case Finding in the Emergency Department." Pediatrics 42(1):128-138.

Hyman, Clare A.
1973 "I.Q. of Parents of Battered Babies." British Medical Journal 4:749.

Johnson, Betty and Harold Morse
1968 The Battered Child: A Study of Children with Inflicted Injuries. Denver, Colorado: Denver Department of Welfare.

Johnson, C. L.
1974 Child Abuse in the Southeast: An Analysis of 1172 Reported Cases. Georgia University, Athens: Welfare Research.

Kadushin, Alfred
1974 Child Welfare Services, 2nd edition. New York: Macmillan.

Katz, Julian
1970 "The Battered Child Syndrome—Psychiatric Aspects." Australian Journal of Forensic Sciences 3(2):71-78.

Kempe, C. Henry, Sherman, F. N., Steele, B. F., Droegemueller, W. and H. K. Silver
1962 "The Battered Child Syndrome." Journal of the American Medical Association 181:107-112.

Kempe, C. Henry and Ray Helfer
1972 Helping the Battered Child and His Family. Philadelphia: Lippincott.

Kempe, C. Henry
1973 "A Practical Approach to the Protection of the Abused Child and Rehabilitation of the Abusing Parent." Pediatrics 51(11):804-809.

Kent, James T.
1973 Follow Up Study of Abused Children. Los Angeles, California: Los Angeles Children's Hospital, Division of Psychiatry.

Klaus, Marshall and John Kennell
  1976   Maternal-Infant Bonding. St. Louis: Mosby.
Klein, Michael and Leo Stern
  1971   "Low Birth Weight and the Battered Child Syn-
         drome." American Journal of Diseases of Children
         122:15-18.
Kline, D. F. and M. A. Hopper
  1975   Child Abuse: An Investigation of the Literature and
         a Concept Analysis with Recommendations for Edu-
         cational Research. Prepared for: Bureau of Educa-
         tion for the Handicapped (DHEW), Washington,
         D.C.
Koel, Bertram S.
  1969   "Failure to Thrive and Fatal Injury as a Contin-
         uum." American Journal of Diseases of Children
         118:565-567.
Ladowitz, Annette
  1975   Child Abuse, Why Physicians Don't Report It. Mas-
         ter Thesis, Department of Social Work, San Jose
         University of California.
Lauer, Brian
  1974   "Battered Child Syndrome: Review of 130 Patients
         with Controls," Pediatrics 54(1):67-70.
Leiderman, P. Herbert
  1974   "Mothers at Risk: A Potential Consequence of the
         Hospital Care of the Premature Infant." In E. J.
         Anthony and C. Koupernik (eds.), The Child in His
         Family: Child at Psychiatric Risk. New York:
         Wiley.
Lenoski, Edward F.
  1974   Translating Injury Data into Preventive and Health
         Care Services—Physical Child Abuse. Draft, Uni-
         versity of Southern California School of Medicine,
         Los Angeles.
Light, Richard J.
  1973   "Abused and Neglected Children in America: A
         Study of Alternative Policies." Harvard Educational
         Review 43(3):556-598.
Lukianowicz, N.
  1971   "Battered Children." Psychiatric Clinic 4:257-280.
Lynch, Margaret
  1976   "Risk Factors in the Child: A Study of Abused Chil-
         dren and Their Siblings." Pp. 43-56 in H. Martin
         (ed.), The Abused Child. Cambridge, Mass.: Ballin-
         ger.
McCaghy, C. H.
  1971   "Child Molesting." Sexual Behavior 1:16-24.
McCrae, K. N., Ferguson, C. A. and R. S. Lederman
  1973   "The Battered Child Syndrome." Canadian Medical
         Association Journal 108(7):859-866.
MacKeith, Donald
  1975   "Speculations on Some Possible Long-Term Ef-
         fects." Pp. 63-68 in A. Franklin (ed.), Concerning
         Child Abuse. Edinburgh, Scotland: Churchill
         Livingstone.
Maden, M. F.
  1975   Toward A Theory of Child Abuse: A Review of the
         Literature, Masters Abstracts; Ann Arbor, Mich.:
         University Microfilms.

Martin, Harold
  1972   "The Child and His Development." Pp. 93-114 in
         C. H. Kempe and R. Helfer (eds.), Helping the
         Battered Child and His Family. Philadelphia: Lip-
         pincott.
Martin, Harold, Beezley, Patricia, Conway, Ester F., Kempe,
C. Henry
  1974   "The Development of Abused Children." Advances
         in Pediatrics 21:25-73.
Martin, Harold P.
  1976   The Abused Child: A Multidisciplinary Approach to
         Developmental Issues and Treatment. Cambridge,
         Mass.: Ballinger.
Maurer, A.
  1974   "Corporal Punishment." The American Psychologist
         29(8):614-626.
Menick, Barry and John R. Hurley
  1969   "Distinctive Personality Attributes of Child-abusing
         Mothers." Journal of Consulting and Clinical Psy-
         chology 33(6):746-749.
Morris, Marian and R. Gould
  1963   "Role Reversal: A Necessary Concept in Dealing
         With the 'Battered Child Syndrome'." American
         Journal of Orthopsychiatry 33:298-299.
Merill, Edgar, T.
  1962   "Physical Abuse of Children—An Agency Study."
         In: Protecting the Battered Child. Denver: Ameri-
         can Humane Association, pp. 1-16.
Morse, Carol W., Sahler, O. J. Z. and S. B. Friedman
  1970   "A Three-Year Follow-Up Study of Abused and
         Neglected Children." American Journal of Diseases
         of Children 120:439-446.
Mushin, A. S.
  1971   "Ocular Damage in the Battered-baby Syndrome."
         British Medical Journal 3:402.
Myers, Steven A.
  1970   "Maternal Filicide." American Journal of Diseases
         of Children 120:534-536.
National Society for the Prevention of Cruelty to Children
         (NSPCC) Registers of Suspected Non-Accidental
         Injury. London: NSPCC.
Newberger, E. H., Reed, R. B., Daniel, J. H., Hyde, J. N. and
         M. Katelchuck
  1974   Draft Report of Phase I of the Family Develop-
         ment Study. Children's Hospital Medical Center,
         Boston, Massachusetts.
New York State Department of Social Services
  1973   Trends in Child Abuse Reporting in New York
         State, 1966-1972. Publication No. 1157.
Oliver, J. E.
  1975   "Microcephaly Following Baby Battering and Shak-
         ing." British Medical Journal 2:262.
Oliver, J. E. and Jane Cox
  1973   "A Family Kindred with Ill-Used Children. The Bur-
         den on the Community." British Journal of Psychi-
         atry 123:81-90.
O'Neill, James A., Meachem, W. F., Griffin, P. P. and J. L.
         Sawyers
  1973   "Patterns of Injury in the Battered Child Syn-
         drome." Journal of Trauma 13(4):332-339.

Ounsted, Christopher, Oppenheimer, R. and J. Lindsay
  1975 "The Psychopathology and Psychotherapy of the Families: Aspects of Bonding Failure." Pp. 30-40 in A. Franklin (ed.), Concerning Child Abuse. Edinburgh, Scotland: Churchill Livingstone.
Parke, Ross D. and Candace W. Collmer
  1975 Child Abuse: An Interdisciplinary Analysis. Chicago: University of Chicago Press.
Paulson, Morris J. and Philip R. Blake
  1967 "The Abused, Battered and Maltreated Child: A Review." Trauma 9:1-136.
Paulson, Morris J. and Phillip R. Blake
  1969 "The Physically Abused Child: A Focus on Prevention." Child Welfare 48(2)86-95.
Paulson, M. J., Affi, A. A., Thomason, M. L. and A. Chaleff
  1974 "The MMPI: A Descriptive Measure of Psychopathology in Abusive Parents." Journal of Clinical Child Psychology 30(3):387-390.
Paulson, M. J., Abdelmonem, A., Chaleff, A. A., Thomason, M. L. and V. Y Liu
  1975a "An MMPI Scale of Identifying 'At Risk' Abusive Parents." Journal of Clinical Child Psychology 4(1):22-24.
Paulson, M. J., Abdelmonem, A., Chaleff, A., Liu, V. and M. Thomason
  1975b "A Discriminant Function Procedure for Identifying Abusing Parents." Suicide 5(2):104-114.
Peckham, Catherine
  1974 "The Dimensions of Child Abuse." Pp. 19-27 in J. Carter, (ed.), The Maltreated Child. London: Priory Press.
Perrin, Helen J.
  1974 Child Abuse in Naval Regional Medical Centers: San Diego and Long Beach. California Academic Press.
Polansky, N. A., Hally, C. and N. F. Polansky
  1975 Profile of Neglect: A Survey of the State of Knowledge of Child Neglect. Community Services Administration (DHEW). Washington, D.C.
Pollock, Carl and Brandt Steele
  1972 "A Therapeutic Approach to the Parents." Pp. 3-21 in C. H. Kempe and R. Helfer (eds.), Helping the Battered Child and His Family. Philadelphia: Lippincott.
Radbill, S. X.
  1968 "A History of Child Abuse and Infanticide." Pp. 3-17 in R. Helfer and C. H. Kempe (eds.), The Battered Child. Chicago: University of Chicago Press.
Raffali, Henri C.
  1970 "The Battered Child: An Overview of a Medical, Legal and Social Problem." Crime and Delinquency 16(2):139-150.
Resnick, Phillip J.
  1969 "Child Murder by Parents: A Psychiatric Review of Filicide." American Journal of Psychiatry 126(3): 325-334.
Resnick, P. J.
  1970 "Murder of the Newborn: A Psychiatric Review of Neonaticide." American Journal of Psychiatry 25: 1414-1420.

Sandgrund, A., Gaines, R. W. and A. H. Green
  1974 "Child Abuse and Mental Retardation: A Problem of Cause and Effect." American Journal of Mental Deficiency 79(3):327-330.
Sattin, Dane B. and John K. Miller
  1971 "The Ecology of Child Abuse Within a Military Community." American Journal of Orthopsychiatry 41:675-681.
Schloesser, P. T.
  1964 "The Abused Child." Bulletin of the Menninger Clinic 28:261-268.
Schmitt, Barton and C. Henry Kempe
  undated "The Battered Child Syndrome." Unpublished.
Scott, P. D.
  1973 "Fatal Battered-baby Cases." Medical Science and Law 13(3):197-206.
Sheridan, Mary
  1956 "The Intelligence of 100 Neglectful Mothers." British Medical Journal.
Silver, Larry B.
  1968a "Child Abuse Syndrome: A Review." Medical Times 96(8):803-820.
Silver, L. B.
  1968b "The Psychological Aspects of the Battered Child and His Parents." Clinical Proceedings 24(11):355-364.
Silver, L. B., Dublin, C. C. and R. S. Lourie
  1969 "Child Abuse Syndrome: The 'Gray Areas' in Establishing a Diagnosis." Pediatrics 44(4):594-600.
Silver, Larry B., Dublin, C. C. and R. S. Lourie
  1971 "Agency Action and Interaction in Cases of Child Abuse." Social Casework 52(3):164-171.
Silverman, F. N.
  1953 "The Roentgen Manifestations of Unrecognized Skeletal Trauma in Infants." American Journal Roentgenology, Radium Therapy, and Nuclear Medicine 69:413-427.
Simons, Betty, Downs, E. F., Hurster, M. M. and M. Archer
  1969 "Child Abuse: Epidemiologic Study of Medically Reported Cases." New York State Journal of Medicine 66:2738-2788.
Skinner, Angela and Raymond Castle
  1969 Seventy-Eight Battered Children: A Retrospective Study. London: National Society for the Prevention of Cruelty to Children (NSPCC).
Smith, S. M.
  1975 The Battered Child Syndrome. London: Butterworths.
Smith, S. M. and R. Hanson
  1975 "Interpersonal Relationships and Childbearing Practices in 214 Parents of Battered Children." British Journal of Psychiatry 127:513-525.
Smith, S. M. and R. Hanson
  1974 "Battered Children: A Medical and Psychological Study." British Medical Journal 3:666-670.
Smith, S. M., Hanson, R. and S. Noble.
  1974 "Social Aspects of the Battered Baby Syndrome." British Journal of Psychiatry 125:568-582.

Smith, S. M., Honigsberger, L. and C. A. Smith
1973a "E.E.G. and Personality Factors in Baby Batterers." British Medical Journal 3:20-22.

Smith, S. M., Hanson, R. and S. Noble
1973b "Parents of Battered Babies: A Controlled Study." British Medical Journal 5(5889):388-391.

Solomon, T.
1973 "History and Demography of Child Abuse." Pediatrics 51(4):773-776.

Spinetta, J. and D. Rigler
1972 "The Child Abusing Parent: A Psychological Review." Psychological Bulletin 77(4):296-304.

Starr, R. H.
1976 "The Controlled Study of the Ecology of Child Abuse and Drug Abuse." Paper presented at the N. P. Masse Research Seminar on Child Abuse, Centre International de l'Enfance, Paris, France.

Starr, R. H.
1976 "What Child Abuse Researchers Don't Tell About Child Abuse Research." Journal of Pediatric Psychology. Pp. 50-53.

Steele, B. F.
1970a "Parental Abuse of Infants and Small Children." In E. J. Anthony and T. Benedel (eds.), Parenthood: Its Psychology and Psychopathology. Boston: Little, Brown.
1970b "Violence in Our Society." Pharos. pp. 42-48.
1975 Working with Abusive Parents From a Psychiatric Point of View. Children's Bureau, (DHEW) National Center on Child Abuse and Neglect, Washington, D.C.

Steele, Brandt and Carl Pollock
1968 "A Psychiatric Study of Parents Who Abuse Infants and Small Children." Pp. 103-148 in R. Helfer and C. H. Kempe, The Battered Child. Chicago: University of Chicago Press.

Steinmetz, Suzanne, K.
1974 "Occupational Environment in Relation to Physical Punishment and Dogmatism." Pp. 166-172 in S. Steinmetz and M. Straus (eds.), Violence in the Family. New York: Dodd, Mead.

Straus, Murray A.
1971 "Some Social Antecedents of Physical Punishment: A Linkage Theory Interpretation." Journal of Marriage and the Family. Pp. 658-663.
1974 "Cultural and Social Organizational Influences on Violence Between Family Members." Pp. 53-69 in R. Prince and D. Barried, Configurations: Biological and Cultural Factors in Sexuality and Family Life. Lexington MA: D. C. Heath.

Strugess, T. and K. Heal
1976 Non-accidental Injury to Children Under the Age of 17: A Study to Assess Current Probation Service Involvement With Cases of Non-accidental Injury. (Res. 663/2/25) Home Office Research Unit. House of Commons Select Committee on Violence in the Family. Session #350.

Sussman, A.
1974 "Reporting Child Abuse: A Review of the Literature." Family Law Quarterly 8(3):245-313.

Terr, Lenore C.
1970 "A Family Study of Child Abuse." American Journal of Psychiatry 127(5):125-131.

Theisen, William M.
1973 Implementing Child Abuse Law: An Inquiry into the Formulation and Execution of Social Policy. Dissertation Abstracts International, Ann Arbor, Michigan: University Microfilms No. 73-13716.

Thomson, E. M., Paget, N. W., Bates, D. W., Mesh, M. and T. I. Putnam
1971 Child Abuse: A Community Challenge. East Aurora, New York: Henry Skewart, p. 169.

Togut, Myra R., Allen, J. E. and L. Lelchuck
1969 "A Psychological Exploration of the Nonorganic Failure-To-Thrive Syndrome." Developmental Medicine and Child Neurology 11:601-607.

Van Stolk, Mary
1972 The Battered Child in Canada. Toronto: McClelland and Stewart, pp. 127.

Viano, Emilio C.
1975 "The Battered Child: A Review of Studies and Research in the Area of Child Abuse." Pp. 145-164 in I. Drapkin and E. Viano (eds.), Victimology: A New Focus, Vol. IV. Lexington, MA: D. C. Heath.

Walters, David R.
1975 Physical and Sexual Abuse of Children: Causes and Treatment. Bloomington: Indiana University Press.

Wasserman, S.
1967 "The Abused Parent of the Abused Child." Children 14:175-179.

Wertham, Frederic
1972 "Battered Children and Baffled Parents." Bulletin of the New York Academy of Medicine 48:888-898.

Woolley, P. V. and W. A. Evans
1955 "Significance of Skeletal Lesions in Infants Resembling Those of Traumatic Origin." Journal of the American Medical Association 158:538-543.

Wright, Logan
1971 "The 'Sick But Slick' Syndrome as a Personality Component for Parents of Battered Children." Journal of Clinical Psychology 32(1):41-45.

Young, Leotyne.
1964 Wednesday's Child: A Study of Child Neglect and Abuse. New York: McGraw-Hill.

Zadnick, Donna
1973 "Social and Medical Aspects of the Battered Child with Vision Impairment." New Outlook for the Blind 67(6):241-250.

Zalba, Serapio
1966 "The Abused Child: I. A Survey of The Problem." Social Work, 11(4):3-16.
1967 "The Abused Child: II. A Typology for Classification and Treatment." Social Work 12(1):70-79.

Selected readings for Chapter 7

Fontana, Vincent J. *Somewhere a Child is Crying: Maltreatment Causes and Prevention* (New York: The New American Library, Inc., 1976).
> A moving analysis of the impact and scope of child abuse. Documents the problem with excellent case illustrations and suggests intervention and prevention strategies. Provides little information regarding the causes of child abuse.

Gelles, Richard J. *The Violent Home* (Beverly Hills, Calif.: Sage Publications, Inc., 1974).
> A descriptive study of family violence, especially between spouses. Samples of 40 families known to have reported violence were drawn (20 from social agency files and 20 from police files). Forty neighbors (for whom there were no reported incidents of violence) were also sampled. Informal interviews were conducted with spouses in each of the 80 households to gather data regarding the extent and nature of family violence.

Gil, David. *Violence Against Children* (Cambridge, Mass.: Harvard University Press, 1970).
> Report of a national study of the causes, incidence, and attitudes regarding child abuse. Violence against children is thought to reflect prevailing attitudes regarding the use of force and may result from the need to socialize children in a competitively rather than a cooperatively oriented culture.

Martin, Del. *Battered Wives* (San Francisco: Glide Publications, 1976).
> A dispassionate description of the plight of battered wives, with material regarding the historical roots of the mistreatment of women, social and psychological etiology of wife battering, and the inadequacies of the present legal and social service systems to respond to this problem. A guide is provided for the development of safe shelters for battered women, the service that is most immediately needed.

Steinmetz, Suzanne K., and Murray A. Straus, eds. *Violence in the Family* (New York: Dodd, Mead & Co., 1974).
> A collection of articles providing theoretical material, research reports, and summaries of research. The material examines violence between spouses, violent parents, and the family as a training ground for social violence.

Tooley, Kay M. "The Young Child as a Victim of Sibling Attack," *Social Casework* **58**:25-28, 1977.
> Describes family structures in which older siblings may abuse younger children without parental intervention or reporting of the incidents.

U.S. Commission on Civil Rights. *Battered Women: Issues of Public Policy* (Washington, D.C.: U.S. Government Printing Office, 1979).
> Report of a consultation held in 1978; contains testimony and several papers regarding the extent of the problem, causes of the problem, and responses of social service and criminal justice agencies to spouse abuse.

U.S. Department of Health, Education, and Welfare, Office of Human Development Services, Administration for Children. *1978 Annual Review of Child Abuse and Neglect Research* (Washington, D.C.: U.S. Government Printing Office, 1978).
> Broad overview of the status of research on child abuse and neglect. The report is based on completed and ongoing research abstracted and contained in the computerized data base of the National Center on Child Abuse and Neglect, U.S. Children's Bureau.

U.S. Department of Health, Education, and Welfare, Office of Human Development Services, Administration for Children. *Child Sexual Abuse: Incest, Assault, and Sexual Exploitation* (Washington, D.C.: U.S. Government Printing Office, 1978).

> A brief overview of recent research findings about the nature, extent, dynamics, and effects of child sexual abuse; suggests some promising preventive and treatment techniques.

Viano, Emilio, ed. *Spouse Abuse* (Washington, D.C.: Visage Press, Inc., 1977).

> A collection of materials regarding the problem of wife battering internationally and cross-culturally. Violence against women is a violation of human rights that women should no longer tolerate. Violence against women is a worldwide problem but is most likely to be reported in industrialized nations.

Victimology, vol. 2, no. 2, 1977.

> A special issue of articles, research and project notes, and book reviews regarding child abuse and neglect.

Victimology, vol. 2, nos. 3-4, 1977-1978.

> A special issue devoted to articles, research notes, and book reviews regarding spouse abuse.

SECTION THREE

Implications for the justice system

The three chapters in this section deal with implications of a victim perspective for the administration of justice. Included here are discussions of the alternative types of roles that victims might play in the justice system, the types of programs and practices corresponding to these roles, and the likely implications for the justice system of moving toward a focus on victims. All the papers agree that the crime victim has been neglected by officials in the justice system and that the results have been far from benign. What they disagree on is how the victim can best be reintroduced as a central actor in the administration of justice. Different writers place different emphases on different kinds of victim roles, among these being the victim as litigant, as partner, and as decision maker.

The administration of criminal justice has emphasized the roles played by specialized third parties, such as prosecutors, defense attorneys, and judges. At the same time that third parties have assumed an increasingly important place in the criminal justice system, the victim's role has become more peripheral and the victim has been treated by the system as largely irrelevant. Chapter 2 dealt with the often shabby treatment received by victims, and the three papers in Chapter 8 offer some alternatives for making the crime victim a more central actor in the administration of criminal justice.

In the first article in Chapter 8, the Norwegian criminologist Nils Christie makes the analogy between conflicts and pieces of property and suggests that the root problem of the administration of justice is that conflicts have become the property of professionals rather than of the people. By taking over ownership of disputes between people, professionals have taken the community's opportunity to learn from individual disputes and develop structures for improving the situation. Central to Christie's argument is the importance of disputants' retaining control over their dispute-property by being intimately involved in the decision-making process. Clearly, any discussion about structuring opportunities for victims to become involved in settling criminal disputes is likely to lead toward a focus on victim loss and how this might be made up in the form of restitution—the offender paying back the victim for the loss sustained in the criminal incident. Christie acknowledges the importance of restitution in his victim-oriented system of justice; the second paper, by Randy Barnett, presents a detailed series of arguments in support of a restitution model of criminal justice.

Randy Barnett is a prosecuting attorney with wide experience in criminal matters. He suggests that the dominant paradigm of the criminal justice system is based on punishment and that this approach is neither morally legitimate nor practically effective and needs to be replaced by a system based on restitution. Restitution becomes both the means and the goal of the administration of criminal law and requires the direct involvement of the victim in the resolution of the conflict.

One way both Christie and Barnett suggest that victims might be directly involved in dispute settlements is in arbitration programs. Such programs operate as alternative forums to the formal court system for resolving disputes between people. Complex court procedures with a focus on finding blame are seen as inadequate for resolving many disputes.

The third article in Chapter 8 describes the operation of a program that acts as a simple alternative to the criminal justice process. John Palmer is a professor of law who was instrumental in the development and operation of the Night Prosecutor Program in Columbus, Ohio. This was one of the early citizen dispute-settlement programs in the country, and it has been replicated in dozens of jurisdictions. This type of program is based on the assumption noted by both Christie and Barnett that the people directly involved have ownership of the dispute and should be provided with structured opportunities to resolve it through an informal settlement process.

The four articles contained in Chapter 9 continue with the theme of victim involvement in the justice system, specifically in relation to the use of offender restitution. The first paper, by Ann Heinz and Wayne Kerstetter, describes the research approach and major findings of an experiment that involved including the victim, defendant, police officer, judge, and defense and prosecuting attorneys in the plea negotiation stage of the criminal process. To some extent this type of scheme amounts to moving the arbitration model of dispute settlement, as described in the previous chapter, into the formal arena of the criminal justice system. The major difference is that although victims are given an opportunity to be involved in the process of arriving at a settlement, they do not exercise veto power over the proposed settlement, as is the case in the arbitration type of program. The role of the victim is mainly one of commenting on the acceptability of the pretrial settlement, especially if this might involve a payment of restitution. Heinz and Kerstetter describe the benefits of involving the different parties in plea negotiations, particularly in terms of speeding the disposition of the case. At the same time, these authors point out problems involved in getting victims to participate in pretrial hearings and note that victims attended only 32% of all conferences that were scheduled. The major reason for their absence was that they had not been notified. In short, victim involvement at any state of the criminal process will depend on making contact with and notifying the victim about the scheduled hearing. Furthermore, if victim involvement is truly desired, procedures need to be established to make it convenient for victims to participate. The problems described in the papers by Mary and Richard Knudten and Gilbert Geis in Chapter 2 are particularly relevant here.

The second article in Chapter 9, by Burt Galaway, reviews current program applications and significant issues in the use of restitution. Galaway is a social worker who has had practical experience at implementing and evaluating restitution programs at different points in the juvenile and adult justice systems. Based on this experience, he suggests that such issues as the following require careful attention by those interested in applying or testing a restitution sanction: (1) what is meant by the concept of restitution, (2) what is the purpose to be accomplished by the use of this sanction, (3) how does restitution fit with other sanctions, and (4) what role should victims play in a restitution program? Running through Galaway's paper is the idea that the way the purpose of restitution is defined will have implications for most, if not all, issues associated with program planning and evaluation. This is likely to be especially the case in relation to questions about the role of victims in a restitution scheme. If the primary purpose of restitution is defined as benefitting offenders or the criminal justice system, as compared with providing compensation to crime victims, then different program emphasis is likely to be placed on such concerns as eligibility criteria for offender participation, the amount and type of victim losses to be compensated, the importance given to treatment interventions with offenders, the role of crime victims, and so on.

The final two papers in Chapter 9 move to a discussion of programming efforts at using a restitution sanction. In his paper, Romine Deming, a professor of criminal justice, lays out a theoretical rationale and program guidelines for incorporating restitution at different points in the justice system. The goal is one of managing conflict between victims and offenders through the use of restitution payments. In this scheme, corrections staff would be responsible for meeting with victims and offenders separately and, if possible, arranging for meetings between the respective parties. Out of such meetings would come a restitution agreement that specified the type of restitution to be made and the amount and schedule of payments. As Deming makes clear, this program approach would require criminal justice practitioners to take on different kinds of roles from those traditionally given to them. Rather than operating from the assumption that offenders are "sick" and in need of therapy, they would be viewed as persons who have made conscious decisions to engage in criminal acts and are responsible to the victim and the community for undoing the damage done. Program staff, whether probation and parole officers or institutional staff, would act as mediators between the parties and be responsible for the preparation of the restitution agreement, which would then be reviewed and approved by appropriate officials, whether judge or parole board.

The paper by Dorothy (Edmonds) McKnight describes the operation of a restitution program that illustrates many of the ingredients suggested by Deming. McKnight worked with the Victim-Offender Reconciliation Project in Kitchener, Ontario, Canada. This project emphasized direct meetings between victims and offenders for the purpose of arriving at agreements about the amount and repayment schedule of restitution. Among the many interesting features of this project described by McKnight were the apparent anxieties felt by offenders in meeting directly with their victims, the lack of hostile expressions made by victims to offenders, and the overall willingness of victims and offenders to directly involve themselves in structured meetings. Two problems are apparent, however; one having to do with the general use of a restitution sanction and the other with structuring victim-offender involvement as illustrated in this project. Because all restitution projects depend on some assessment of loss or damage sustained in the criminal incident, there is always a possibility that victims might inflate the amount of damage or loss, whereas offenders might underestimate it. The possibility of further victimization then becomes apparent. The amount of staff time required for planning and holding victim-offender meetings is a problem unique to projects emphasizing the direct involvement of the parties to the dispute. McKnight notes that substantial time is required for these meetings, which, in the case of an unwilling victim, will probably result in the staff's spending a lot of time identifying, locating, and contacting victims, some of whom will ultimately have no interest in participating.

The four articles in Chapter 10 deal with the accountability of the criminal justice system to the victim. Marvin Wolfgang describes the general lack of accountability of justice system officials to either officials in other agencies in the system or to the crime victim. He suggests that each component of the system—police, court, and corrections—should be held responsible for reporting to preceding components as well as to the victim, offender, and public at large. Wolfgang advocates that victims be given timely information about the status of the case and be treated with consideration and respect.

Frank Carrington, Executive Director of Americans for Effective Law Enforcement, discusses litigation as a specific way of holding criminal justice officials accountable to crime victims. As described by Carrington, victim rights litigation involves the use of civil suits by victims against either the perpetrator of the crime or against a third party, such as a criminal justice official, who was negligent in completing a duty owed to the victim. Included are cases involving the liability of the government for failing to protect citizens, the liability of landlords or innkeepers for criminal acts on their premises, and the liability of criminal justice officials for negligent handling of offenders. Carrington describes significant case law developments and key legal issues in this area and offers some implications for the administration of justice. An obvious result of such litigation would be to stimulate criminal justice officials to more carefully consider their responsibility to potential victims.

A somewhat different approach to system accountability to crime victims is offered in the final paper in Chapter 10, by Donald Hall. Hall gives attention here to the manner and extent to which the actions of criminal justice officials can be influenced by crime victims. He traces the course of criminal cases from investigation to arrest through to parole release and executive clemency decisions and notes that the common denominator in all cases is the exercise of discretionary authority by officials. Discretionary authority exists whenever officials are free to choose an alternative course of action and the decision that is made is not open to the review of others. Decisions of the police to arrest, prosecutor to charge, judge to adjudicate, parole boards and the executive to release or grant clemency, are all, by their very nature, open to being influenced by crime victims, among others. Thus, although on the one hand officials need to give consideration to crime victims and their unique situation, on the other hand there is a need for limiting and structuring official discretion so as to better assure fair and consistent justice. How these two concerns are balanced to achieve fairness and consistency in the administration of justice is likely to be an ongoing issue.

Chapter 8

TOWARD A VICTIM ORIENTATION

A □ *Conflicts as property*
NILS CHRISTIE

B □ *Restitution: a new paradigm of criminal justice*
RANDY E. BARNETT

C □ *The Night Prosecutor: Columbus finds extrajudicial solutions to interpersonal disputes*
JOHN W. PALMER

A □ *Conflicts as property*

NILS CHRISTIE

INTRODUCTION

Maybe we should not have any criminology. Maybe we should rather abolish institutes, not open them. Maybe the social consequences of criminology are more dubious than we like to think.

I think they are. And I think this relates to my topic—conflicts as property. My suspicion is that criminology to some extent has amplified a process where conflicts have been taken away from the parties directly involved and thereby have either disappeared or become other people's property. In both cases a deplorable out-

come. Conflicts ought to be used, not only left in erosion. And they ought to be used, and become useful, for those originally involved in the conflict. Conflicts *might* hurt individuals as well as social systems. That is what we learn in school. That is why we have officials. Without them, private vengeance and vendettas will blossom. We have learned this so solidly that we have lost track of the other side of the coin: our industrialised large-scale society is not one with too many internal conflicts. It is one with too little. Conflicts might kill, but too little of them might paralyse. I will use this occasion to give a sketch of this situation. It cannot be more than a sketch. This paper represents the beginning of the development of some ideas, not the polished end-product.

Reprinted by permission of the Institute for the Study and Treatment of Delinquency, Croydon, England, from the *British Journal of Criminology*, vol. 17, no. 1, pp. 1-15, January 1978.

ON HAPPENINGS AND NON-HAPPENINGS

Let us take our point of departure far away. Let us move to Tanzania. Let us approach our problem from the sunny hillside of the Arusha province. Here, inside a relatively large house in a very small village, a sort of happening took place. The house was overcrowded. Most grown-ups from the village and several from adjoining ones were there. It was a happy happening, fast talking, jokes, smiles, eager attention, not a sentence was to be lost. It was circus, it was drama. It was a court case.

The conflict this time was between a man and a woman. They had been engaged. He had invested a lot in the relationship through a long period, until she broke it off. Now he wanted it back. Gold and silver and money were easily decided on, but what about utilities already worn, and what about general expenses?

The outcome is of no interest in our context. But the framework for conflict solution is. Five elements ought to be particularly mentioned:

1. The parties, the former lovers, were in *the centre* of the room and in the centre of everyone's attention. They talked often and were eagerly listened to.

2. Close to them were relatives and friends who also took part. But they did not *take over*.

3. There was also participation from the general audience with short questions, information, or jokes.

4. The judges, three local party secretaries, were extremely inactive. They were obviously ignorant with regard to village matters. All the other people in the room were experts. They were experts on norms as well as actions. And they crystallised norms and clarified what had happened through participation in the procedure.

5. No reporters attended. They were all there.

My personal knowledge when it comes to British courts is limited indeed. I have some vague memories of juvenile courts where I counted some 15 or 20 persons present, mostly social workers using the room for preparatory work or small conferences. A child or a young person must have attended, but except for the judge, or maybe it was the clerk, nobody seemed to pay any particular attention. The child or young person was most probably utterly confused as to who was who and for what, a fact confirmed in a small study by Peter Scott (1959). In the United States of America, Martha Baum (1968) has made similar observations. Recently, Bottoms and McClean (1976) have added another important observation: "There is one truth which is seldom revealed in the literature of the law or in studies of the administration of criminal justice. It is a truth which was made evident to all those involved in this research project as they sat through the cases which made up our sample. The truth is that, for the most part, the business of the criminal courts is dull, commonplace, ordinary and after a while downright tedious".

But let me keep quiet about your system, and instead concentrate on my own. And let me assure you: what goes on is no happening. It is all a negation of the Tanzanian case. What is striking in nearly all the Scandinavian cases is the greyness, the dullness, and the lack of any important audience. Courts are not central elements in the daily life of our citizens, but peripheral in four major ways:—

1. They are situated in the administrative centres of the towns, outside the territories of ordinary people.

2. Within these centres they are often centralised within one or two large buildings of considerable complexity. Lawyers often complain that they need months to find their way within these buildings. It does not demand much fantasy to imagine the situation of parties or public when they are trapped within these structures. A comparative study of court architecture might become equally relevant for the sociology of law as Oscar Newman's (1972) study of defensible space is for criminology. But even without any study, I feel it safe to say that both physical situation and architectural design are strong indicators that courts in Scandinavia belong to the administrators of law.

3. This impression is strengthened when you enter the courtroom itself—if you are lucky enough to find your way to it. Here again, the periphery of the parties is the striking observa-

tion. The parties are represented, and it is these representatives and the judge or judges who express the little activity that is activated within these rooms. Honoré Daumier's famous drawings from the courts are as representative for Scandinavia as they are for France.

There are variations. In the small cities, or in the countryside, the courts are more easily reached than in the larger towns. And at the very lowest end of the court system—the so-called arbitration boards—the parties are sometimes less heavily represented through experts in law. But the symbol of the whole system is the Supreme Court where the directly involved parties do not even attend their own court cases.

4. I have not yet made any distinction between civil and criminal conflicts. But it was not by chance that the Tanzania case was a civil one. Full participation in your own conflict presupposes elements of civil law. The key element in a criminal proceeding is that the proceeding is converted from something between the concrete parties into a conflict between one of the parties and the state. So, in a modern criminal trial, two important things have happened. First, the parties are being *represented*. Secondly, the one party that is represented by the state, namely the victim, is so thoroughly represented that she or he for most of the proceedings is pushed completely out of the arena, reduced to the triggerer-off of the whole thing. She or he is a sort of double loser; first, *vis-à-vis* the offender, but secondly and often in a more crippling manner by being denied rights to full participation in what might have been one of the more important ritual encounters in life. The victim has lost the case to the state.

PROFESSIONAL THIEVES

As we all know, there are many honourable as well as dishonourable reasons behind this development. The honourable ones have to do with the state's need for conflict reduction and certainly also its wishes for the protection of the victim. It is rather obvious. So is also the less honourable temptation for the state, or Emperor, or whoever is in power, to use the criminal case for personal gain. Offenders might pay for their sins. Authorities have in time past

shown considerable willingness, in representing the victim, to act as receivers of the money or other property from the offender. Those days are gone; the crime control system is not run for profit. And yet they are not gone. There are, in all banality, many interests at stake here, most of them related to professionalisation.

Lawyers are particularly good at stealing conflicts. They are trained for it. They are trained to prevent and solve conflicts. They are socialised into a sub-culture with a surprisingly high agreement concerning interpretation of norms, and regarding what sort of information can be accepted as relevant in each case. Many among us have, as laymen, experienced the sad moments of truth when our lawyers tell us that our best arguments in our fight against our neighbour are without any legal relevance whatsoever and that we for God's sake ought to keep quiet about them in court. Instead they pick out arguments we might find irrelevant or even wrong to use. My favourite example took place just after the war. One of my country's absolutely top defenders told with pride how he had just rescued a poor client. The client had collaborated with the Germans. The prosecutor claimed that the client had been one of the key people in the organisation of the Nazi movement. He had been one of the master-minds behind it all. The defender, however, saved his client. He saved him by pointing out to the jury how weak, how lacking in ability, how obviously deficient his client was, socially as well as organisationally. His client could simply not have been one of the organisers among the collaborators; he was without talents. And he won his case. His client got a very minor sentence as a very minor figure. The defender ended his story by telling me—with some indignation—that neither the accused, nor his wife, had ever thanked him, they had not even talked to him afterwards.

Conflicts become the property of lawyers. But lawyers don't hide that it is conflicts they handle. And the organisational framework of the courts underlines this point. The opposing parties, the judge, the ban against privileged communication within the court system, the lack of encouragement for specialisation—specialists cannot be internally controlled—it all underlines that this is an organisation for the handling of conflicts. *Treatment personnel* are in another position. They are more interested in *converting the image of the case from one of conflict into one of non-conflict*. The basic model of healers is not one of opposing parties, but one where one party has to be helped in the direction of one generally accepted goal—the preservation or restoration of health. They are not trained into a system where it is important that parties can control each other. There is, in the ideal case, nothing to control, because there is only one goal. Specialisation is encouraged. It increases the amount of available knowledge, and the loss of internal control is of no relevance. A conflict perspective creates unpleasant doubts with regard to the healer's suitability for the job. A non-conflict perspective is a precondition for defining crime as a legitimate target for treatment.

One way of reducing attention to the conflict is reduced attention given to the victim. Another is concentrated attention given to those attributes in the criminal's background which the healer is particularly trained to handle. Biological defects are perfect. So also are personality defects when they are established far back in time—far away from the recent conflict. And so are also the whole row of explanatory variables that criminology might offer. We have, in criminology, to a large extent functioned as an auxiliary science for the professionals within the crime control system. We have focused on the offender, made her or him into an object for study, manipulation and control. We have added to all those forces that have reduced the victim to a nonentity and the offender to a thing. And this critique is perhaps not only relevant for the old criminology, but also for the new criminology. While the old one explained crime from personal defects or social handicaps, the new criminology explains crime as the result of broad economic conflicts. The old criminology loses the conflicts, the new one converts them from interpersonal conflicts to class conflicts. And they are. They are class conflicts—also. But, by stressing this, the conflicts are again taken away from the directly involved parties.

So, as a preliminary statement: Criminal conflicts have either become *other people's property* —primarily the property of lawyers—or it has been in other people's interests to *define conflicts away*.

STRUCTURAL THIEVES

But there is more to it than professional manipulation of conflicts. Changes in the basic social structure have worked in the same way.

What I particularly have in mind are *two types of segmentation* easily observed in highly industrialised societies. First, there is the question of segmentation *in space*. We function each day, as migrants moving between sets of people which do not need to have any link—except through the mover. Often, therefore, we know our work-mates only as work-mates, neighbours only as neighbours, fellow cross-country skiers only as fellow cross-country skiers. We get to know them as *roles*, not as total persons. This situation is accentuated by the extreme degree of division of labour we accept to live with. Only experts can evaluate each other according to individual—personal—competence. Outside the speciality we have to fall back on a general evaluation of the supposed importance of the work. Except between specialists, we cannot evaluate how good anybody is in his work, only how good, in the sense of important, the role is. Through all this, we get limited possibilities for understanding other people's behaviour. Their behaviour will also get limited relevance for us. Role-players are more easily exchanged than persons.

The second type of segmentation has to do with what I would like to call our re-establishment of caste-society. I am not saying class-society, even though there are obvious tendencies also in that direction. In my framework, however, I find the elements of caste even more important. What I have in mind is the segregation based on biological attributes such as sex, colour, physical handicaps or the number of winters that have passed since birth. Age is particularly important. It is an attribute nearly perfectly synchronised to a modern complex industrialised society. It is a continuous variable where we can introduce as many intervals as we might need. We can split the population in two:

children and adults. But we also can split it in ten: babies, pre-school children, school-children, teenagers, older youth, adults, pre-pensioned, pensioned, old people, the senile. And most important: the cutting points can be moved up and down according to social needs. The concept "teenager" was particularly suitable 10 years ago. It would not have caught on if social realities had not been in accordance with the word. Today the concept is not often used in my country. The condition of youth is not over at 19. Young people have to wait even longer before they are allowed to enter the work force. The caste of those outside the work force has been extended far into the twenties. At the same time departure from the work force—if you ever were admitted, if you were not kept completely out because of race or sex-attributes—is brought forward into the early sixties in a person's life. In my tiny country of four million inhabitants, we have 800,000 persons segregated within the educational system. Increased scarcity of work has immediately led authorities to increase the capacity of educational incarceration. Another 600,000 are pensioners.

Segmentation according to space and according to caste attributes has several consequences. First and foremost it leads into a *depersonalisation* of social life. Individuals are to a smaller extent linked to each other in close social networks where they are confronted with *all* the significant roles of the significant others. This creates a situation with limited amounts of information with regard to each other. We do know less about other people, and get limited possibilities both for understanding and for prediction of their behaviour. If a conflict is created, we are less able to cope with this situation. Not only are professionals there, able and willing to take the conflict away, but we are also more willing to give it away.

Secondly, segmentation leads to destruction of certain conflicts even before they get going. The depersonalisation and mobility within industrial society melt away some essential conditions for living conflicts; those between parties that mean a lot to each other. What I have particularly in mind is crime against other people's honour, libel or defamation of character. All the Scandinavian countries have had a dramatic decrease in this form of crime. In my interpretation, this is not because honour has become more respected, but because there is less honour to respect. The various forms of segmentation mean that human beings are inter-related in ways where they simply mean less to each other. When they are hurt, they are only hurt partially. And if they are troubled, they can easily move away. And after all, who cares? Nobody knows me. In my evaluation, the decrease in the crimes of infamy and libel is one of the most interesting and sad symptoms of dangerous developments within modern industrialised societies. The decrease here is clearly related to social conditions that lead to increase in other forms of crime brought to the attention of the authorities. It is an important goal for crime prevention to re-create social conditions which lead to an increase in the number of crimes against other people's honour.

A third consequence of segmentation according to space and age is that certain conflicts are made completely invisible, and thereby don't get any decent solution whatsoever. I have here in mind conflicts at the two extremes of a continuum. On the one extreme we have the over-privatised ones, those taking place against individuals captured within one of the segments. Wife beating or child battering represent examples. The more isolated a segment is, the more the weakest among parties is alone, open for abuse. Inghe and Riemer (1943) made the classical study many years ago of a related phenomenon in their book on incest. Their major point was that the social isolation of certain categories of proletarised Swedish farm-workers was the necessary condition for this type of crime. Poverty means that the parties within the nuclear family became completely dependent on each other. Isolation meant that the weakest parties within the family had no external network where they could appeal for help. The physical strength of the husband got an undue importance. At the other extreme we have crimes done by large economic organisations against individuals too weak and ignorant to be able even to realise they have been victimised. In both cases the goal for crime prevention might be to re-create social conditions which make the conflicts visible and thereafter manageable.

CONFLICTS AS PROPERTY

Conflicts are taken away, given away, melt away, or are made invisible. Does it matter, does it really matter?

Most of us would probably agree that we ought to protect the invisible victims just mentioned. Many would also nod approvingly to ideas saying that states, or Governments, or other authorities ought to stop stealing fines, and instead let the poor victim receive this money. I at least would approve such an arrangement. But I will not go into that problem area here and now. Material compensation is not what I have in mind with the formulation "conflicts as property". It is the *conflict itself* that represents the most interesting property taken away, not the goods originally taken away from the victim, or given back to him. In our types of society, conflicts are more scarce than property. And they are immensely more valuable.

They are valuable in several ways. Let me start at the societal level, since here I have already presented the necessary fragments of analysis that might allow us to see what the problem is. Highly industrialised societies face major problems in organising their members in ways such that a decent quota take part in any activity at all. Segmentation according to age and sex can be seen as shrewd methods for segregation. Participation is such a scarcity that insiders create monopolies against outsiders, particularly with regard to work. In this perspective, it will easily be seen that conflicts represent a *potential for activity, for participation*. Modern criminal control systems represent one of the many cases of lost opportunities for involving citizens in tasks that are of immediate importance to them. Ours is a society of task-monopolists.

The victim is a particularly heavy loser in this situation. Not only has he suffered, lost materially or become hurt, physically or otherwise. And not only does the state take the compensation. But above all he has lost participation in

his own case. It is the Crown that comes into the spotlight, not the victim. It is the Crown that describes the losses, not the victim. It is the Crown that appears in the newspaper, very seldom the victim. It is the Crown that gets a chance to talk to the offender, and neither the Crown nor the offender are particularly interested in carrying on that conversation. The prosecutor is fed-up long since. The victim would not have been. He might have been scared to death, panic-stricken, or furious. But he would not have been uninvolved. It would have been one of the important days in his life. Something that belonged to him has been taken away from that victim.[1]

But the big loser is us—to the extent that society is us. This loss is first and foremost a loss in *opportunities for norm-clarification*. It is a loss of pedagogical possibilities. It is a loss of opportunities for a continuous discussion of what represents the law of the land. How wrong was the thief, how right was the victim? Lawyers are, as we saw, trained into agreement on what is relevant in a case. But that means a trained incapacity in letting the parties decide what *they* think is relevant. It means that it is difficult to stage what we might call a political debate in the court. When the victim is small and the offender big—in size or power—how blameworthy then is the crime? And what about the opposite case, the small thief and the big house-owner? If the offender is well educated, ought he then to suffer more, or maybe less, for his sins? Or if he is black, or if he is young, or if the other party is an insurance company, or if his wife has just left him, or if his factory will break down if he has to go to jail, or if his daughter will lose her fiancé, or if he was drunk, or if he was sad, or if he was mad? There is no end to it. And maybe there ought to be none. Maybe Barotse law as described by Max Gluckman (1967) is a better instrument for norm-clarification, allowing the conflicting parties to bring in the whole chain of old complaints and arguments each time. Maybe decisions on relevance and on the weight of what is found rele-

---

[1]For a preliminary report on victim dissatisfaction, see Vennard (1976).

vant ought to be taken away from legal scholars, the chief ideologists of crime control systems, and brought back for free decisions in the courtrooms.

A further general loss—both for the victim and for society in general—has to do with anxiety-level and misconceptions. It is again the possibilities for personalised encounters I have in mind. The victim is so totally out of the case that he has no chance, ever, to come to know the offender. We leave him outside, angry, maybe humiliated through a cross-examination in court, without any human contact with the offender. He has no alternative. He will need all the classical stereotypes around "the criminal" to get a grasp on the whole thing. He has a need for understanding, but is instead a nonperson in a Kafka play. Of course, he will go away more frightened than ever, more in need than ever of an explanation of criminals as nonhuman.

The offender represents a more complicated case. Not much introspection is needed to see that direct victim-participation might be experienced as painful indeed. Most of us would shy away from a confrontation of this character. That is the first reaction. But the second one is slightly more positive. Human beings have reasons for their actions. If the situation is staged so that reasons can be given (reasons as the parties see them, not only the selection lawyers have decided to classify as relevant), in such a case maybe the situation would not be all that humiliating. And, particularly, if the situation was staged in such a manner that the central question was not meting out guilt, but a thorough discussion of what could be done to undo the deed, then the situation might change. And this is exactly what ought to happen when the victim is re-introduced in the case. Serious attention will centre on the victim's losses. That leads to a natural attention as to how they can be softened. It leads into a discussion of restitution. The offender gets a possibility to change his position from being a listener to a discussion —often a highly unintelligible one—of how much pain he ought to receive, into a participant in a discussion of how he could make it good again. The offender has lost the oppor-

tunity to explain himself to a person whose evaluation of him might have mattered. He has thereby also lost one of the most important possibilities for being forgiven. Compared to the humiliations in an ordinary court—vividly described by Pat Carlen (1976) in a recent issue of the *British Journal of Criminology*—this is not obviously any bad deal for the criminal.

But let me add that I think we should do it quite independently of his wishes. It is not health-control we are discussing. It is crime control. If criminals are shocked by the initial thought of close confrontation with the victim, preferably a confrontation in the very local neighbourhood of one of the parties, what then? I know from recent conversations on these matters that most people sentenced are shocked. After all, they prefer distance from the victim, from neighbours, from listeners and maybe also from their own court case through the vocabulary and the behavioural science experts who might happen to be present. They are perfectly willing to give away their property right to the conflict. So the question is more: are *we* willing to let them give it away? Are we willing to give them this easy way out?[2]

Let me be quite explicit on one point: I am not suggesting these ideas out of any particular interest in the treatment or improvement of criminals. I am not basing my reasoning on a belief that a more personalised meeting between offender and victim would lead to reduced recidivism. Maybe it would. I think it would. As it is now, the offender has lost the opportunity for participation in a personal confrontation of a very serious nature. He has lost the opportunity to receive a type of blame that it would be very difficult to neutralise. However, I would have suggested these arrangements even if it was absolutely certain they had no effects on recidivism, maybe even if they had a negative effect. I would have done that because of the other, more general gains. And let me also add—it is not much to lose. As we all know today, at least

---

[2] I tend to take the same position with regard to a criminal's property right to his own conflict as John Locke on property rights to one's own life—one has no right to give it away (*cf.* C. B. MacPherson (1962)).

nearly all, we have not been able to invent any cure for crime. Except for execution, castration or incarceration for life, no measure has a proven minimum of efficiency compared to any other measure. We might as well react in crime according to what closely involved parties find is just and in accordance with general values in society.

With this last statement, as with most of the others I have made, I raise many more problems than I answer. Statements on criminal politics, particularly from those with the burden of responsibility, are usually filled with answers. It is questions we need. The gravity of our topic makes us much too pedantic and thereby useless as paradigm-changers.

A VICTIM-ORIENTED COURT

There is clearly a model of neighbourhood courts behind my reasoning. But it is one with some peculiar features, and it is only these I will discuss in what follows.

First and foremost; it is a *victim-oriented* organisation. Not in its initial stage, though. The first stage will be a traditional one where it is established whether it is true that the law has been broken, and whether it was this particular person who broke it.

Then comes the second stage, which in these courts would be of the utmost importance. That would be the stage where the victim's situation was considered, where every detail regarding what had happened—legally relevant or not— was brought to the court's attention. Particularly important here would be detailed consideration regarding what could be done for him, first and foremost by the offender, secondly by the local neighbourhood, thirdly by the state. Could the harm be compensated, the window repaired, the lock replaced, the wall painted, the loss of time because the car was stolen given back through garden work or washing of the car ten Sundays in a row? Or maybe, when this discussion started, the damage was not so important as it looked in documents written to impress insurance companies? Could physical suffering become slightly less painful by any action from the offender, during days, months or years? But, in addition, had the community

exhausted all resources that might have offered help? Was it absolutely certain that the local hospital could not do anything? What about a helping hand from the janitor twice a day if the offender took over the cleaning of the basement every Saturday? None of these ideas is unknown or untried, particularly not in England. But we need an organisation for the systematic application of them.

Only after this stage was passed, and it ought to take hours, maybe days, to pass it, only then would come the time for an eventual decision on punishment. Punishment, then, becomes that suffering which the judge found necessary to apply *in addition to* those unintended constructive sufferings the offender would go through in his restitutive actions *vis-à-vis* the victim. Maybe nothing could be done or nothing would be done. But neighbourhoods might find it intolerable that nothing happened. Local courts out of tune with local values are not local courts. That is just the trouble with them, seen from the liberal reformer's point of view.

A fourth stage has to be added. That is the stage for service to the offender. His general social and personal situation is by now well-known to the court. The discussion of his possibilities for restoring the victim's situation cannot be carried out without at the same time giving information about the offender's situation. This might have exposed needs for social, educational, medical or religious action—not to prevent further crime, but because needs ought to be met. Courts are public arenas, needs are made visible. But it is important that this stage comes *after* sentencing. Otherwise we get a re-emergence of the whole array of so-called "special measures"—compulsory treatments—very often only euphemisms for indeterminate imprisonment.

Through these four stages, these courts would represent a blend of elements from civil and criminal courts, but with a strong emphasis on the civil side.

A LAY-ORIENTED COURT

The second major peculiarity with the court model I have in mind is that it will be one with an extreme degree of lay-orientation. This is essential when conflicts are seen as property that ought to be shared. It is with conflicts as with so many good things: they are in no unlimited supply. Conflicts can be cared for, protected, nurtured. But there are limits. If some are given more access in the disposal of conflicts, others are getting less. It is as simple as that.

Specialisation in conflict solution is the major enemy; specialisation that in due—or undue—time leads to professionalisation. That is when the specialists get sufficient power to claim that they have acquired special gifts, mostly through education, gifts so powerful that it is obvious that they can only be handled by the certified craftsman.

With a clarification of the enemy, we are also able to specify the goal; let us reduce specialisation and particularly our dependence on the professionals within the crime control system to the utmost.

The ideal is clear; it ought to be a court of equals representing themselves. When they are able to find a solution between themselves, no judges are needed. When they are not, the judges ought also to be their equals.

Maybe the judge would be the easiest to replace, if we made a serious attempt to bring our present courts nearer to this model of lay orientation. We have lay judges already, in principle. But that is a far cry from realities. What we have, both in England and in my own country, is a sort of specialised non-specialist. First, they are used *again and again*. Secondly, some are even *trained,* given special courses or sent on excursions to foreign countries to learn about how to behave as a lay judge. Thirdly, most of them do also represent an extremely *biased sample* of the population with regard to sex, age, education, income, class[3] and personal experience as criminals. With real lay judges, I conceive of a system where nobody was given the right to take part in conflict solution more than a few times, and then had to wait until all other community members had had the same experience.

Should lawyers be admitted to court? We had an old law in Norway that forbids them to enter

the rural districts. Maybe they should be admitted in stage one where it is decided if the man is guilty. I am not sure. Experts are as cancer to any lay body. It is exactly as Ivan Illich describes for the educational system in general. Each time you increase the length of compulsory education in a society, each time you also decrease the same population's trust in what they have learned and understood quite by themselves.

Behaviour experts represent the same dilemma. Is there a place for them in this model? Ought there to be any place? In stage 1, decisions on facts, certainly not. In stage 3, decisions on eventual punishment, certainly not. It is too obvious to waste words on. We have the painful row of mistakes from Lombroso, through the movement for social defence and up to recent attempts to dispose of supposedly dangerous people through predictions of who they are and when they are not dangerous any more. Let these ideas die, without further comments.

The real problem has to do with the service function of behaviour experts. Social scientists can be perceived as functional answers to a segmented society. Most of us have lost the physical possibility to experience the totality, both on the social system level and on the personality level. Psychologists can be seen as historians for the individual; sociologists have much of the same function for the social system. Social workers are oil in the machinery, a sort of security counsel. Can we function without them, would the victim and the offender be worse off?

Maybe. But it would be immensely difficult to get such a court to function if they were all there. Our theme is social conflict. Who is not at least made slightly uneasy in the handling of her or his own social conflicts if we get to know that there is an expert on this very matter at the same table? I have no clear answer, only strong feelings behind a vague conclusion: let us have as few behaviour experts as we dare to. And if we have any, let us for God's sake not have any that specialise in crime and conflict resolution. Let us have generalised experts with a solid base outside the crime control system. And a

---

[3]For the most recent documentation, see Baldwin (1976).

last point with relevance for both behaviour experts and lawyers: if we find them unavoidable in certain cases or at certain stages, let us try to get across to them the problems they create for broad social participation. Let us try to get them to perceive themselves as resource-persons, answering when asked, but not domineering, not in the centre. They might help to stage conflicts, not take them over.

ROLLING STONES

There are hundreds of blocks against getting such a system to operate within our western culture. Let me only mention three major ones. They are:

1. There is a lack of neighbourhoods.
2. There are too few victims.
3. There are too many professionals around.

With lack of neighbourhoods I have in mind the very same phenomenon I described as a consequence of industrialised living; segmentation according to space and age. Much of our trouble stems from killed neighbourhoods or killed local communities. How can we then thrust towards neighbourhoods a task that presupposes they are highly alive? I have no really good arguments, only two weak ones. First, it is not quite that bad. The death is not complete. Secondly, one of the major ideas behind the formulation 'Conflicts as Property' is that it is neighbourhood-property. It is not private. It belongs to the system. It is intended as a vitaliser for neighbourhoods. The more fainting the neighbourhood is, the more we need neighbourhood courts as one of the many functions any social system needs for not dying through lack of challenge.

Equally bad is the lack of victims. Here I have particularly in mind the lack of personal victims. The problem behind this is again the large units in industrialised society. Woolworth or British Rail are not good victims. But again I will say: there is not a complete lack of personal victims, and their needs ought to get priority. But we should not forget the large organisations. They, or their boards, would certainly prefer not to have to appear as victims in 5000 neighbourhood courts all over the country. But maybe they ought to be compelled to appear. If the complaint is serious enough to bring the offender into the ranks of the criminal, then the victim ought to appear. A related problem has to do with insurance companies—the industrialised alternative to friendship or kinship. Again we have a case where the crutches deteriorate the condition. Insurance takes the consequences of crime away. We will therefore have to take insurance away. Or rather: we will have to keep the possibilities for compensation through the insurance companies back until in the procedure I have described it has been proved beyond all possible doubt that there are no other alternatives left—particularly that the offender has no possibilities whatsoever. Such a solution will create more paper-work, less predictability, more aggression from customers. And the solution will not necessarily be seen as good from the perspective of the policyholder. But it will help to protect conflicts as social fuel.

None of these troubles can, however, compete with the third and last I will comment on: the abundance of professionals. We know it all from our own personal biographies or personal observations. And in addition we get it confirmed from all sorts of social science research: the educational system of any society is not necessarily synchronised with any needs for the product of this system. Once upon a time we thought there was a direct causal relation from the number of highly educated persons in a country to the Gross National Product. Today we suspect the relationship to go the other way, if we are at all willing to use GNP as a meaningful indicator. We also know that most educational systems are extremely class-biased. We know that most academic people have had profitable investments in our education, that we fight for the same for our children, and that we also often have vested interests in making our part of the educational system even bigger. More schools for more lawyers, social workers, sociologists, criminologists. While I am *talking* deprofessionalisation, we are increasing the capacity to be able to fill up the whole world with them.

There is no solid base for optimism. On the other hand insights about the situation, and goal formulation, are a pre-condition for action. Of course, the crime control system is not the domineering one in our type of society. But it has some importance. And occurrences here are unusually well suited as pedagogical illustrations of general trends in society. There is also some room for manoeuvre. And when we hit the limits, or are hit by them, this collision represents in itself a renewed argument for more broadly conceived changes.

Another source for hope: ideas formulated here are not quite so isolated or in dissonance with the mainstream of thinking when we leave our crime control area and enter other institutions. I have already mentioned Ivan Illich with his attempts to get learning away from the teachers and back to active human beings. Compulsory learning, compulsory medication and compulsory consummation of conflict solutions have interesting similarities. When Ivan Illich and Paulo Freire are listened to, and my impression is that they increasingly are, the crime control system will also become more easily influenced.

Another, but related, major shift in paradigm is about to happen within the whole field of technology. Partly, it is the lessons from the third world that now are more easily seen, partly it is the experience from the ecology debate. The globe is obviously suffering from what we, through our technique, are doing to her. Social systems in the third world are equally obviously suffering. So the suspicion starts. Maybe the first world can't take all this technology either. Maybe some of the old social thinkers were not so dumb after all. Maybe social systems can be perceived as biological ones. And maybe there are certain types of large-scale technology that kill social systems, as they kill globes. Schumacher (1973) with his book *Small is Beautiful* and the related Institute for Intermediate Technology come in here. So do also the numerous attempts, particularly by several outstanding Institutes for Peace Research, to show the dangers in the concept of Gross National Product, and replace it with indicators that take care of dignity, equity and justice. The perspective developed in Johan Galtung's research group on World Indicators might prove extremely useful also within our own field of crime control.

There is also a political phenomenon opening vistas. At least in Scandinavia social democrats and related groupings have considerable power, but are without an explicated ideology regarding the goals for a reconstructed society. This vacuum is being felt by many, and creates a willingness to accept and even expect considerable institutional experimentation.

Then to my very last point: what about the universities in this picture? What about the new Centre in Sheffield? The answer has probably to be the old one: universities have to re-emphasize the old tasks of understanding and of criticising. But the task of training professionals ought to be looked into with renewed skepticism. Let us re-establish the credibility of encounters between critical human beings: low-paid, highly regarded, but with no extra power—outside the weight of their good ideas. That is as it ought to be.

REFERENCES

Baldwin, J. (1976) "The Social Composition of the Magistracy" *Brit. J. Criminol.*, **16**, 171-174.
Baum, M. and Wheeler, S. (1968). "Becoming an inmate," Ch. 7, pp. 153-187, in Wheeler, S. (ed.), *Controlling Delinquents*. New York: Wiley.
Bottoms, A. E. and McClean, J. D. (1976). *Defendants in the Criminal Process*. London: Routledge and Kegan Paul.
Carlen, P. (1976). "The Staging of Magistrates' Justice." *Brit. J. Criminol.*, **16**, 48-55.
Gluckman, M. (1967). *The Judicial Process among the Barotse of Northern Rhodesia* Manchester University Press.
Kinberg, O., Inghe, G., and Riemer, S. (1943). *Incest-Problemet i Sverige*. Sth.,
MacPherson, C. B. (1962). *The Political Theory of Possessive Individualism: Hobbes to Locke*. London: Oxford University Press.
Newman, O. (1972). *Defensible Space: People and Design in the Violent City*. London: Architectural Press.
Schumacher, E. F. (1973). *Small is Beautiful: A Study of Economics as if People Mattered*. London: Blond and Briggs.
Scott, P. D. (1959). "Juvenile Courts: the Juvenile's Point of View." *Brit. J. Delinq.*, **9**, 200-210.
Vennard, J. (1976). "Justice and Recompense for Victims of Crime." *New Society*, **36**, 378-380.

B □ *Restitution*

A new paradigm of criminal justice

RANDY E. BARNETT

This paper will analyze the breakdown of our system of criminal justice in terms of what Thomas Kuhn would describe as a crisis of an old paradigm—punishment. I propose that this crisis could be solved by the adoption of a new paradigm of criminal justice—restitution. The approach will be mainly theoretical, though at various points in the discussion the practical implications of the rival paradigms will also be considered. A fundamental contention will be that many, if not most of our system's ills stem from errors in the underlying paradigm. Any attempt to correct these symptomatic debilities without a reexamination of the theoretical underpinnings is doomed to frustration and failure. Kuhn's theories deal with the problems of science. What made his proposal so startling was its attempt to analogize scientific development to social and political development. Here, I will simply reverse the process by applying Kuhn's framework of scientific change to social, or in this case, legal development.[1]

In the criminal justice system we are witnessing the death throes of an old and cumbersome paradigm, one that has dominated Western thought for more than 900 years. While this paper presents what is hoped to be a viable, though radical alternative, much would be accomplished by simply prompting the reader to reexamine the assumptions underlying the present system. Only if we are willing to look at our old problems in a new light do we stand a chance of solving them. This is our only hope, and our greatest challenge.

Reprinted by permission of University of Chicago Press from *Ethics: An International Journal of Social, Political, and Legal Philosophy*, vol. 87, no. 4, pp. 279-301, July 1977; © 1977 by the University of Chicago. All rights reserved. Printed in the U.S.A.

This paper was made possible by a research fellowship from the Law and Liberty Project of the Institute for Humane Studies, Menlo Park, California. A somewhat expanded version of it appears in the book, *Assessing the Criminal: Restitution, Retribution, and the Legal Process*, eds. Randy E. Barnett and John Hagel III (Cambridge, Mass.: Ballinger Publishing Co., 1977). Also, I wish to extend my appreciation to John V. Cody, Davis E. Keeler, Murray N. Rothbard, and Lloyd L. Weinreb for their invaluable criticism and comments. I am greatly in their debt and hope to be able at some future time to make suitable restitution.

1. What immediately follows is a brief outline of Kuhn's theory. Those interested in the *defense* of that theory should refer to his book, *The Structure of Scientific Revolutions*, 2d ed., enl. (Chicago: University of Chicago Press, 1970). A paradigm is an achievement in a particular discipline which defines the legitimate problems and methods of research within that discipline. This achievement is sufficiently unprecedented to attract new adherents away from rival approaches while providing many unsolved questions for these new practioners to solve. As the paradigm develops and matures, it reveals occasional inabilities to solve new problems and explain new data. As attempts are made to make the facts fit the paradigm, the theoretical apparatus gradually becomes bulky and awkward, like Ptolemaic astronomy. Dissatisfaction with the paradigm begins to grow. Why not simply discard the paradigm and find another which better fits the facts? Unfortunately, this is an arduous process. All the great authorities and teachers were raised with the current paradigm and see the world through it. All the texts and institutions are committed to it. Radical alternatives hold promise but are so untested as to make wary all but the bold. The establishment is loath to abandon its broad and intricate theory in favor of a new and largely unknown hypothesis. Gradually, however, as the authorities die off and the problems with the old paradigm increase, the "young turks" get a better hearing in both the journals and the classroom. In a remarkably rapid fashion, the old paradigm is discarded for the new. Anyone who still clings to it is now considered to be antiquated or eccentric and is simply read out of the profession. All research centers on the application of the new paradigm. Kuhn characterizes this overthrow of one paradigm by another as a revolution.

THE CRISIS IN THE PARADIGM OF PUNISHMENT

"Political revolutions are inaugurated by a growing sense, often restricted to a segment of the political community, that existing institutions have ceased adequately to meet the problems posed by an environment they have in part created. . . . In both political and scientific development the sense of malfunction that can lead to crisis is prerequisite to revolution."[2] Kuhn's description of the preconditions for scientific and political revolutions could accurately describe the current state of the criminal law. However, simply to recognize the existence of a crisis is not enough. We must look for its causes. The Kuhnian methodology suggests that we critically examine the paradigm of punishment itself.

The problems which the paradigm of punishment is supposed to solve are many and varied. A whole literature on the philosophy of punishment has arisen in an effort to justify or reject the institution of punishment. For our purposes the following definition from the *Encyclopedia of Philosophy* should suffice: "Characteristically punishment is unpleasant. It is inflicted on an offender because of an offense he has committed; it is deliberately imposed, not just the natural consequence of a person's action (like a hangover), and the unpleasantness is *essential* to it, not an accompaniment to some other treatment (like the pain of the dentist's drill)."[3]

Two types of arguments are commonly made in defense of punishment. The first is that punishment is an appropriate means to some justifiable end such as, for example, deterrence of crime. The second type of argument is that punishment is justified as an end in itself. On this view, whatever ill effects it might engender, punishment for its own sake is good.

The first type of argument might be called the *political* justification of punishment, for the end which justifies its use is one which a polit-ical order is presumably dedicated to serve: the maintenance of peaceful interactions between individuals and groups in a society. There are at least three ways that deliberate infliction of harm on an offender is said to be politically justified.

1. One motive for punishment, especially capital punishment and imprisonment, is the "intention to deprive offenders of the power of doing future mischief."[4] Although it is true that an offender cannot continue to harm society while incarcerated, a strategy of punishment based on disablement has several drawbacks.

Imprisonment is enormously expensive. This means that a double burden is placed on the innocent who must suffer the crime, and, in addition, pay through taxation for the support of the offender and his family if they are forced onto welfare. Also, any benefit of imprisonment is temporary; eventually, most offenders will be released. If their outlook has not improved— and especially if it has worsened—the benefits of incarceration are obviously limited. Finally when disablement is permanent, as with capital punishment or psychosurgery, it is this very permanence, in light of the possibility of error, which is frightening. For these reasons, "where disablement enters as an element into penal theories, it occupies, as a rule, a subordinate place and is looked upon as an object subsidiary to some other end which is regarded as paramount. . . ."[5]

2. Rehabilitation of a criminal means a change in his mental *habitus* so that he will not offend again. It is unclear whether the so-called treatment model which views criminals as a doctor would view a patient is truly a "retributive" concept. Certainly it does not conform to the above definition characterizing punishment as deliberately and essentially unpleasant. It is an open question whether any end justifies the intentional, forceful manipulation of an individual's thought processes by anyone, much

2. Ibid., p. 92

3. Stanley I. Benn, "Punishment," in *The Encyclopedia of Philosophy*, ed. Paul Edwards (New York: Macmillan Publishing Co., 1967), 7:29 (emphasis added).

4. Heinrich Oppenheimer, *The Rationale of Punishment* (London: University of London Press, 1913), p. 255.

5. Ibid.

less the state. To say that an otherwise just system has incidentally rehabilitative effects which may be desirable is one thing, but it is quite another to argue that these effects themselves justify the system. The horrors to which such reasoning can lead are obvious from abundant examples in history and contemporary society.[6]

Rehabilitation as a reaction against the punishment paradigm will be considered below, but one aspect is particularly relevant to punishment as defined here. On this view, the visiting of unpleasantness itself will cause the offender to see the error of his ways; by having "justice" done him, the criminal will come to appreciate his error and will change his moral outlook. This end, best labeled "reformation," is speculative at best and counterfactual at worst. On the contrary, "it has been observed that, as a rule. . . ruthless punishments, far from mollifying men's ways, corrupt them and stir them to violence."[7]

3. The final justification to be treated here deterrence—actually has two aspects. The first is the deterrent effect that past demonstrations of punishment have on the future conduct of others; the second is the effect that threats of future punishment have on the conduct of others. The distinction assumes importance when some advocates argue that future threats lose their deterrent effect when there is a lack of past demonstrations. Past punishment, then, serves as an educational tool. It is a substitute for or reinforcement of threats of future punishment.

As with the goals mentioned above, the empirical question of whether punishment has this effect is a disputed one.[8] I shall not attempt to resolve this question here, but will assume *arguendo* that punishment even as presently administered has some deterrent effect. It is the moral question which is disturbing. Can an argument from deterrence alone "justify" in any sense the infliction of pain on a criminal? It is particularly disquieting that the actual levying of punishment is done not for the criminal himself, but for the educational impact it will have on the community. The criminal act becomes the occasion of, but not the reason for, the punishment. In this way, the actual crime becomes little more than an excuse for punishing.

Surely this distorts the proper functioning of the judicial process. For if deterrence is the end it is unimportant whether the individual actually committed the crime. Since the public's perception of guilt is the prerequisite of the deterrent effect, all that is required for deterrence is that the individual is "proved" to have committed the crime. The actual occurrence would have no relevance except insofar as a truly guilty person is easier to prove guilty. The judicial process becomes, not a truth-seeking device, but solely a means to legitimate the use of force. To treat criminals as means to the ends of others in this way raises serious moral problems. This is not to argue that men may never use others as means but rather to question the use of force against the individual because of the effect such use will have on others. It was this that concerned del Vecchio when he stated that "the human person always bears in himself something sacred, and it is therefore not permissable to treat him merely as a means towards an end outside of himself."[9]

Finally, deterrence as the ultimate justification of punishment cannot rationally limit its use. It "provides *no* guidance until we're told *how much* commission of it is to be deterred."[10] Since there are always some who commit crimes, one can always argue for more punishment. Robert Nozick points out that there must be criteria by which one decides how much deterrence may be inflicted.[11] One is forced there-

6. See Thomas Szasz, *Law, Liberty, and Psychiatry* (New York: Macmillan Co., 1963); id., "Psychiatric Diversion in the Criminal Justice System: A Critique," in *Assessing the Criminal: Restitution, Retribution, and the Legal Process,* eds., Randy E. Barnett and John Hagel III (Cambridge, Mass.: Ballinger Publishing Co., 1977), pp. 99-120.

7. Giorgio del Vecchio, "The Struggle against Crime," in *The Philosophy of Punishment,* ed. H. B. Acton (London: Macmillan Co., 1969), p. 199.

8. See, e.g., Samuel Yochelson and Stanton E. Samenow, *The Criminal Personality,* vol. 1, *A Profile for Change* (New York: Jason Aronson, Inc., 1976), pp. 411-16.

9. Del Vecchio, p. 199.

10. Robert Nozick, *Anarchy, State, and Utopia* (New York: Basic Books, 1974), p. 61.

11. Ibid., pp. 59-63.

fore to employ "higher" principles to evaluate the legitimacy of punishment.

It is not my thesis that deterrence, reformation, and disablement are undesirable goals. On the contrary, any criminal justice system should be critically examined to see if it is having these and other beneficial effects. The view advanced here is simply that these utilitarian benefits must be incidental to a just system; they cannot, alone or in combination, justify a criminal justice system. Something more is needed. There is another more antiquated strain of punishment theory which seeks to address this problem. The *moral* justifications of punishment view punishment as an end in itself. This approach has taken many forms.[12] On this view, whatever ill or beneficial results it might have, punishment of lawbreakers is good for its own sake. This proposition can be analyzed on several levels.

The most basic question is the truth of the claim itself. Some have argued that "the alleged absolute justice of repaying evil with evil (maintained by Kant and many other writers) is really an empty sophism. If we go back to the Christian moralists, we find that an evil is to be put right only by doing good."[13] This question is beyond the scope of this treatment. The subject has been extensively dealt with by those more knowledgeable than I.[14] The more relevant question is what such a view of punishment as a good can be said to imply for a system of criminal justice. Even assuming that it would be good if, in the nature of things, the wicked got their "come-uppance," what behavior does this moral fact justify? Does it justify the victim authoring the punishment of his offender? Does it justify the same action by the victim's family, his friends, his neighbors, the state? If so what punishment should be imposed and who should decide?

It might be argued that the natural punishment for the violation of natural rights is the deserved hatred and scorn of the community,

the resultant ostracism, and the existential hell of *being* an evil person. The question then is not whether we have the right to inflict some "harm" or unpleasantness on a morally contemptible person—surely, we do; the question is not whether such a punishment is "good"—arguably, it is. The issue is whether the "virtue of some punishment" justifies the *forceful* imposition of unpleasantness on a *rights violator* as distinguished from the morally imperfect. Any *moral* theory of punishment must recognize and deal with this distinction. Finally, it must be established that the state is the legitimate author of punishment, a proposition which further assumes the moral and legal legitimacy of the state. To raise these issues is not to resolve them, but it would seem that the burden of proof is on those seeking to justify the use of force against the individual. Suffice it to say that I am skeptical of finding any theory which justifies the deliberate, forceful imposition of punishment within or without a system of criminal justice.

The final consideration in dealing with punishment as an end in itself is the possibility that the current crisis in the criminal justice system is in fact a crisis of the paradigm of punishment. While this, if true, does not resolve the philosophical issues, it does cast doubt on the punishment paradigm's vitality as the motive force behind a system of criminal justice. Many advocates of punishment argue that its apparent practical failings exist because we are not punishing enough. All that is needed, they say, is a crackdown on criminals and those victims and witnesses who shun participation in the criminal justice system; the only problem with the paradigm of punishment is that we are not following it.[15] This response fails to consider *why* the system doggedly refuses to punish to the degree required to yield beneficial results and instead punishes in such a way as to yield harmful results. The answer may be that the paradigm of punishment is in eclipse, that the public lacks the requisite will to apply it in anything but the prevailing way.

---

12. For a concise summary, see Oppenheimer, p. 31.

13. Del Vecchio, p. 198.

14. See, e.g., Walter Kaufmann, *Without Guilt and Justice* (New York: Peter H. Wyden, Inc., 1973), esp. chap. 2.

15. See, e.g. "Crime: A Case for More Punishment," *Business Week* (September 15, 1975). pp. 92-97.

Punishment, particularly state punishment is the descendant of the tradition which imparts religious and moral authority to the sovereign and, through him, the community. Such an authority is increasingly less credible in a secular world such as ours. Today there is an increasing desire to allow each individual to govern his own life as he sees fit provided he does not violate the rights of others. This desire is exemplified by current attitudes toward drug use, abortion, and pornography. Few argue that these things are good. It is only said that where there is no victim the state or community has no business meddling in the peaceful behavior of its citizens, however morally suspect it may be.[16]

Furthermore, if the paradigm of punishment is in a "crisis period" it is as much because of its practical drawbacks as the uncertainty of its moral status. The infliction of suffering on a criminal tends to cause a general feeling of sympathy for him. There is no rational connection between a term of imprisonment and the harm caused the victim. Since the prison term is supposed to be unpleasant, at least a part of the public comes to see the criminal as a victim, and the lack of rationality also causes the offender to feel victimized. This reaction is magnified by the knowledge that most crimes go unpunished and that even if the offender is caught the judicial process is long, arduous, and far removed from the criminal act. While this is obvious to most, it is perhaps less obvious that the punishment paradigm is largely at fault. The slow, ponderous nature of our system of justice is largely due to a fear of an unjust infliction of punishment on the innocent (or even the guilty). The more awful the sanction, the more elaborate need be the safeguards. The more the system is perceived as arbitrary and unfair, the more incentive there is for defendants and their counsel to thwart the truth-finding process. Acquittal

becomes desirable at all costs. As the punitive aspect of a sanction is diminished, so too would be the perceived need for procedural protections.

A system of punishment, furthermore, offers no incentive for the victim to involve himself in the criminal justice process other than to satisfy his feelings of duty or revenge. The victim stands to gain little if at all by the conviction and punishment of the person who caused him loss. This is true even of those systems discussed below which despense state compensation based on the victim's need. The system of justice itself imposes uncompensated costs by requiring a further loss of time and money by the victim and witnesses and by increasing the perceived risk of retaliation.

Finally, punishment which seeks to change an offender's moral outlook, or at least to scare him, can do nothing to provide him with the skills needed to survive in the outside world. In prison, he learns the advanced state of the criminal arts and vows not to repeat the mistake that led to his capture. The convict emerges better trained and highly motivated to continue a criminal career.

The crisis of the paradigm of punishment has at its roots the collapse of its twin pillars of support: its moral legitimacy and its practical efficacy. As Kaufmann concludes, "the faith in retributive justice is all but dead."[17]

ATTEMPTS TO SALVAGE THE PARADIGM OF PUNISHMENT

"All crises begin with the blurring of a paradigm and the consequent loosening of the rules for normal research."[18] And yet until a new paradigm is presented, authorities will cling to the old one, either ignoring the problem or salvaging the paradigm with ad hoc explanations and solutions. Why are paradigms never rejected outright? Why must there always be a new paradigm before the old one is abandoned? Kuhn does not explicitly discuss this, but R. A. Childs hypothesizes "that, as such, paradigms may serve the function of increasing

16. This problem is examined, though not ultimately resolved, by Edwin M. Schur in his book *Crimes without Victims—Deviant Behavior and Public Policy, Abortion, Homosexuality, and Drug Addiction* (Englewood Cliffs, N.J.: Prentice-Hall, Inc., 1965).

17. Kaufmann, p. 46.
18. Kuhn, p. 82

man's sense of control over some aspect of reality, or some aspect of his own life. If this is so, then we would expect that a straightforward abandonment of a paradigm would threaten that sense of control."[19]

This psychological need for an explanation may in turn explain the many efforts to shore up the paradigm of punishment. The three attempts to be examined next have at their roots a perception of its fundamental errors, and at the same time they highlight three goals of any new paradigm of criminal justice.

1. Proportionate punishment. The king abandoned the composition system[20] for the system of punishment because punishment struck terror in the hearts of the people, and this served to inspire awe for the power of the king and state. But there was no rational connection between the seriousness of the crime and the gravity of the punishment and, therefore, no limit to the severity of punishment. Hideous tortures came to be employed: "But some of the men of the Enlightenment sought to counter the inhumanity of their Christian predecessors with appeals to reason. They thought that retributive justice had a mathematical quality and that murder called for capital punishment in much the same way in which two plus two equals four."[21]

The appeal to proportionality was one of the

early attempts to come to grips with deficiencies in the paradigm of punishment. It was doomed to failure, for there is no objective standard by which punishments can be proportioned to fit the crime. Punishment is incommensurate with crime. This solution is purely ad hoc and intuitive. We shall, however, find the *goal* of proportionate sentencing useful in the formation of a new paradigm.

2. Rehabilitation. It was noted earlier that the infliction of punishment tends to focus attention on the plight of the criminal. Possibly for this reason, the next humanitarian trend was to explore the proper treatment of criminals. Punishment failed to reform the criminal, and this led observers to inquire how the situation might be improved. Some felt that the sole end of the penal system was rehabilitation, so attention was turned to modifying the criminal's behavior (an obviously manipulative end). Emphasis was placed on education, job training, and discipline.

Unfortunately, the paradigm of punishment and the political realities of penal administration have all but won out. There is simply no incentive for prison authorities to educate and train. Their job is essentially political. They are judged by their ability to keep the prisoners within the walls and to keep incidents of violence within the prison to a minimum; as a result, discipline is the main concern. Furthermore, since he is sentenced to a fixed number of years (less time off for good behavior—so-called good time), there is no institutional incentive for the prisoner to improve himself apart from sheer boredom. Productive labor in prison is virtually nonexistent, with only obsolete equipment, if any, available. Except perhaps for license plates and other state needs, the prisoners produce nothing of value; the prisons make no profit and the workers are paid, if at all, far below market wages. They are unable to support themselves or their families. The state, meaning the innocent taxpayer, supports the prisoner, and frequently the families as well via welfare.

Rehabilitation has been a long-time goal of the penal system, but the political nature of government-run prisons and the dominance

---

19. R. A. Childs, "Liberty and the Paradigm of Statism," in *The Libertarian Alternative,* ed. Tibor Machan (Chicago: Nelson-Hall Co., 1974), p. 505.

20. Composition was the medieval version of a restitutionary system. For a fascinating outline of how such a system operated and how it came to be supplanted by state-authored punishment, see Stephen Schafer, *Compensation and Restitution to Victims of Crime,* 2d ed., enl. (Montclair, N.J.: Patterson Smith Publishing Corp., 1970); Richard E. Laster, "Criminal Restitution: A Survey of Its Past History and an Analysis of Its Present Usefulness," *University of Richmond Law Review* 5 (1970): 71-80; L. T. Hobhouse, *Morals in Evolution* (London: Chapman & Hall, 1951); Bruce Jacobs, "The Concept of Restitution: An Historical Overview," in *Restitution in Criminal Justice,* eds., Joe Hudson and Burt Galaway (Lexington, Mass.: D. C. Heath & Co., 1977), pp. 45-62; those interested in a cross-cultural historical analysis should see Laura Nader and Elaine Combs-Schilling, "Restitution in Cross-Cultural Perspective," in *Restitution in Criminal Justice,* pp. 27-44.

21. Kaufmann, p. 45.

of the paradigm of punishment has inevitably prevented its achievement. Prisons remain detention centers, all too temporarily preventing crime by physically confining the criminals.

3. Victim compensation. It is natural that the brutalities resulting from the paradigm of punishment would get first attention from humanitarians and that the persons subjected to those practices would be next. Until recently, the victim of crime was the forgotten party. Within the last few years a whole new field has opened up called victimology.[22] With it has come a variety of proposals, justifications, and statutes.[23]

Certain features are common to virtually every compensation proposal: (*a*) Compensation for crimes would be dispensed by the state from tax revenue. (*b*) Compensation is "a matter of grace" rather than an assumption by the state of legal responsibility for the criminal loss suffered by the victim. (*c*) Most proposals allow for aid only on a "need" or "hardship" basis. (*d*) Most are limited to some sort of crime of violence or the threat of force or violence. (*e*) None questions the paradigm of punishment.

The goal of these proposals and statutes is laudable. The victim *is* the forgotten man of crime. But the means proposed is the same tired formula: welfare to those in "need." In short, the innocent taxpayer repays the innocent victim (if the victim can prove he "needs" help) while the guilty offender is subjected to the sanction of punishment with all its failings. Like proportionate punishment and rehabilation, the goal of victim compensation is a recognition of very real problems in our criminal justice system, and at the same time it ignores the source of these problems: our conception

of crime as an offense against the state whose proper sanction is punishment. Until a viable, new paradigm is presented, *ad hoc* solutions like the ones discussed here are all that can be hoped for. And it is a vain hope indeed, for they attack the symptoms while neglecting the causes of the problem. What is needed is a new paradigm.

OUTLINE OF A NEW PARADIGM

The idea of restitution is actually quite simple. It views crime as an offense by one individual against the rights of another. The victim has suffered a loss. Justice consists of the culpable offender making good the loss he has caused. It calls for a complete refocusing of our image of crime. Kuhn would call it a "shift of worldview." Where we once saw an offense against society, we now see an offense against an individual victim. In a way, it is a common sense view of crime. *The armed robber did not rob society: he robbed the victim.* His debt, therefore, is not to society; it is to the victim. There are really two types of restitution proposals: a system of "punitive" restitution and a "pure" restitutional system.

1. Punitive restitution. "Since rehabilitation was admitted to the aims of penal law two centuries ago, the number of penological aims has remained virtually constant. Restitution is waiting to come in."[24] Given this view, restitution should merely be added to the paradigm of punishment. Stephen Schafer outlines the proposal: "[Punitive] restitution, like punishment, must always be the subject of judicial consideration. Without exception it must be carried out by personal performance by the wrong-doer, and should even then be equally burdensome and just for all, criminals, irrespective of their means, whether they be millionaires or labourers."[25]

There are many ways by which such a goal might be reached. The offender might be forced to compensate the victim by his own work,

---

22. For a brief definition of "victimology," see Emilo C. Viano, "Victimology: The Study of the Victim," *Victimology* 1 (1976):1-7. For an extensive collection of papers on various aspects of victimology, see Emilo C. Viano, ed., *Victims and Society* (Washington, D.C.: Visage Press, 1976).

23. For a discussion and list of symposiums, journal articles, and statutes concerning victim compensation, see Steven Schafer, pp. 139-57, and appendix; see also Joe Hudson and Burt Galaway, eds., *Considering the Victim: Readings in Restitution and Victim Compensation* (Springfield, Ill.: Charles C Thomas, 1975), esp. pp. 361-436.

24. Gerhard O. W. Mueller, "Compensation for Victims of Crime: Thought before Action," *Minnesota Law Review* 50 (1965):221.

25. Schafer, p. 127.

either in prison or out. If it came out of his pocket or from the sale of his property this would compensate the victim, but it would not be sufficiently unpleasant for the offender. Another proposal would be that the fines be proportionate to the earning power of the criminal. Thus, "A poor man would pay in days of work, a rich man by an equal number of days' income or salary."[26] Herbert Spencer made a proposal along similar lines in his excellent "Prison-Ethics," which is well worth examining.[27] Murray N. Rothbard and others have proposed a system of "double payments" in cases of criminal behavior.[28] While closer to pure restitution than other proposals, the "double damages" concept preserves a punitive aspect.

Punitive restitution is an attempt to gain the benefits of pure restitution, which will be considered shortly, while retaining the perceived advantages of the paradigm of punishment. Thus, the prisoner is still "sentenced" to some unpleasantness—prison labor or loss of X number of days' income. That the intention is to preserve the "hurt" is indicated by the hesitation to accept an out-of-pocket payment or sale of assets. This is considered too "easy" for the criminal and takes none of his time. The amount of payment is determined not by the *actual harm* but by the *ability of the offender to pay*. Of course, by retaining the paradigm of punishment this proposal involves many of the problems we raised earlier. In this sense it can be considered another attempt to salvage the old paradigm.

2. Pure restitution. "Recompense or restitution is scarcely a punishment as long as it is merely a matter of returning stolen goods or money. . . .The point is not that the offender deserves to suffer; it is rather that the offended party desires compensation."[29] This represents the complete overthrow of the paradigm of punishment. No longer would the deterrence, reformation, disablement, or rehabilitation of the criminal be the guiding principle of the judicial system. The attainment of these goals would be incidental to, and as a result of, reparations paid to the victim. No longer would the criminal deliberately be made to suffer for his mistake. Making good that mistake is all that would be required. What follows is a possible scenario of such a system.

When a crime occurred and a suspect was apprehended, a trial court would attempt to determine his guilt or innocence. If found guilty, the criminal would be sentenced to make restitution to the victim.[30] If a criminal is able to make restitution immediately, he may do so. This would discharge his liability. If he were unable to make restitution, but were found by the court to be trustworthy, he would be permitted to remain at his job (or find a new one) while paying restitution out of his future wages. This would entail a legal claim against future wages. Failure to pay could result in garnishment or a new type of confinement.

If it if found that the criminal is not trustworthy, or that he is unable ot gain employment, he would be confined to an employment project.[31] This would be an industrial enterprise, preferably run by a private concern, which would produce actual goods or services. The level of security at each employment project would vary according to the behavior of the offenders. Since the costs would be lower, inmates at a lower-security project would receive higher wages. There is no reason why many workers could not be permitted to live with

---

26. Ibid.
27. Herbert Spencer, "Prison-Ethics," in *Essays: Scientific, Political and Speculative* (New York: D. Appleton & Co., 1907), 3:152-91.
28. Murray N. Rothbard, *Libertarian Forum* 14, no. 1 (January 1972):7-8.
29. Kaufmann, p. 55

30. The nature of judicial procedure best designed to carry out this task must be determined. For a brief discussion of some relevant considerations, see Laster, pp. 80-98; Burt Galaway and Joe Hudson, "Issues in the Correctional Implementation of Restitution to Victims of Crime," in *Considering the Victim*, pp. 351-60. Also to be dealt with is the proper standard of compensation. At least initially, the problem of how much payment constitutes restitution would be no different than similar considerations in tort law. This will be considered at greater length below.
31. Such a plan (with some significant differences) has been suggested by Kathleen J. Smith in *A Cure for Crime: The Case for the Self-determinate Prison Sentence* (London: Gerald, Duckworth & Co., 1965), pp. 13-29; see also Morris and Linda Tannehill, *The Market for Liberty* (Lansing, Mich.: Privately printed, 1970), pp. 44-108.

their families inside or outside the facility, depending, again, on the trustworthiness of the offender. Room and board would be deducted from the wages first, then a certain amount for restitution. Anything over that amount the worker could keep or apply toward further restitution, thus hastening his release. If a worker refused to work, he would be unable to pay for his maintenance, and therefore would not in principle be entitled to it. If he did not make restitution he could not be released. The exact arrangement which would best provide for high productivity, minimal security, and maximum incentive to work and repay the victim cannot be determined in advance. Experience is bound to yield some plans superior to others. In fact, the experimentation has already begun.[32]

While this might be the basic system, all sorts of refinements are conceivable, and certainly many more will be invented as needs arise. A few examples might be illuminating. With such a system of repayment, victim *crime insurance* would be more economically feasible than at present and highly desirable. The cost of awards would be offset by the insurance company's right to restitution in place of the victim (right of subrogation). The insurance company would be better suited to supervise the offender and mark his progress than would the victim. To obtain an earlier recovery, it could be expected to innovate so as to enable the worker to repay more quickly (and, as a result, be released that much sooner). The insurance companies might even underwrite the employment projects themselves as well as related industries which would employ the skilled worker after his release. Any successful effort on their part to reduce crime and recidivism would result in fewer claims and lower premiums. The benefit of this insurance scheme for the victim is immediate compensation, conditional on the victim's continued cooperation with the authorities for the arrest and conviction of the suspect. In addition, the central-

ization of victim claims would, arguably, lead to efficiencies which would permit the pooling of small claims against a common offender.

Another highly useful refinement would be *direct arbitration* between victim and criminal. This would serve as a sort of healthy substitute for plea bargaining. By allowing the guilty criminal to negotiate a reduced payment in return for a guilty plea, the victim (or his insurance company) would be saved the risk of an adverse finding at trial and any possible additional expense that might result. This would also allow an indigent criminal to substitute personal services for monetary payment if all parties agreed.

Arbitration is argued for by John M. Greacen, deputy director of the National Institute for Law Enforcement and Criminal Justice. He sees the possible advantages of such reform as the ". . . development of more creative dispositions for most criminal cases; for criminal victims the increased use of restitution, the knowledge that their interests were considered in the criminal process; and an increased satisfaction with the outcome; increased awareness in the part of the offender that his crime was committed against another human being, and not against society in general; increased possibility that the criminal process will cause the offender to acknowledge responsibility for his acts."[33] Greacen notes several places where such a system has been tried with great success, most notably Tucson, Arizona, and Columbus, Ohio.[34]

Something analogous to the medieval Irish system of *sureties* might be employed as well.[35] Such a system would allow a concerned person,

32. For a recent summary report, see Burt Galaway, "Restitution as an Integrative Punishment," in *Assessing the Criminal: Restitution, Retribution and the Legal Process*, pp. 331-347.

33. John M. Greacen, "Arbitration: A Tool for Criminal Cases?" *Barrister* (Winter 1975), p. 53; see also Galaway and Hudson, pp. 352-55; "Conclusions and Recommendations, International Study Institute on Victimology, Bellagio, Italy, July 1-12, 1975," *Victimology* 1 (1976): 150-51; Ronald Goldfarb, *Jails: The Ultimate Ghetto* (Garden City, N.Y.: Anchor Press/Doubleday, 1976), p. 480.

34. Greacen, p. 53.

35. For a description of the Irish system, see Joseph R. Peden, "Property Rights in Medieval Ireland: Celtic Law versus Church and State" *Journal of Libertarian Studies* 1 (1977): 86; for a theoretical discussion of a similar proposal, ses Spencer, pp. 182-86.

group, or company to make restitution (provided the offender agrees to this). The worker might then be released in the custody of the surety. If the surety had made restitution, the offender would owe restitution to the surety who might enforce the whole claim or show mercy. Of course, the more violent and unreliable the offender, the more serious and costly the offense, the less likely it would be that anyone would take the risk. But for first offenders, good workers, or others that charitable interests found deserving (or perhaps unjustly convicted) this would provide an avenue of respite.

RESTITUTION AND RIGHTS

These three possible refinements clearly illustrate the flexibility of a restitutional system. It may be less apparent that this flexibility is *inherent* to the restitutional paradigm. Restitution recognizes rights in the victim, and this is a principal source of its strength. The nature and limit of the victim's right to restitution at the same time defines the nature and limit of the criminal liability. In this way, the aggressive action of the criminal creates a *debt* to the victim. The recognition of rights and obligations make possible many innovative arrangements. Subrogation, arbitration, and suretyship are three examples mentioned above. They are possible because this right to compensation[36] is considered the property of the victim and can therefore be delegated, assigned, inherited, or bestowed. One could determine in advance who would acquire the right to any restitution which he himself might be unable to collect.

The natural owner of an unenforced death claim would be an insurance company that had insured the deceased. The suggestion has been made that a person might thus increase his personal safety by insuring with a company well known for tracking down those who injure its policy holders. In fact, the partial purpose of some insurance schemes might be to provide the funds with which to track down the malefactor. The insurance company, having

paid the beneficiaries would "stand in their shoes." It would remain possible, of course, to simply assign or devise the right directly to the beneficiaries, but this would put the burden of enforcement on persons likely to be unsuited to the task.

If one accepts the Lockean trichotomy of property ownership,[37] that is, acquiring property via exchange, gifts, and *homesteading* (mixing one's labor with previously unowned land or objects), the possibility arises that upon a person's wrongful death, in the absence of any heirs or assignees, his right to compensation becomes unowned property. The right could then be claimed (homesteaded) by anyone willing to go to the trouble of catching and prosecuting the criminal. Firms might specialize in this sort of activity, or large insurance companies might make the effort as a kind of "loss leader" for public relations purposes.

This does, however, lead to a potentially serious problem with the restitutional paradigm: what exactly constitutes "restitution"? What is the *standard* by which compensation is to be made? Earlier we asserted that any such problem facing the restitutional paradigm faces civil damage suits as well. The method by which this problem is dealt with in civil cases could be applied to restitution cases. But while this is certainly true, it may be that this problem has not been adequately handled in civil damage suits either.

Restitution in cases of crimes against property is a manageable problem. Modern contract and tort doctrines of restitution are adequate. The difficulty lies in cases of personal injury or death. How can you put a price on life or limb, pain or suffering? Is not any attempt to do so of necessity arbitrary? It must be admitted that a fully satisfactory solution to this problem is lacking, but it should also be stressed that this dilemma, though serious, has little impact

---

36. Or, perhaps more accurately, the compensation itself.

37. For a brief explanation of this concept and several of its possible applications, see Murray N. Rothbard, "Justice and Property Rights," in *Property in a Humane Economy*, ed. Samuel L. Blumenfeld (La Salle, Ill.: Open Court Publishing Co., 1974), pp. 101-22.

on the bulk of our case in favor of a restitutional paradigm. It is possible that no paradigm of criminal justice can solve every problem, yet the restitutional approach remains far superior to the paradigm of punishment or any other conceivable rival.

This difficulty arises because certain property is unique and irreplaceable. As a result, it is impossible to approximate a "market" or "exchange" value expressed in monetary terms. Just as there is no rational relationship between a wrongfully taken life and ten years in prison, there is little relationship between that same life and $20,000. Still, the nature of this possibly insoluble puzzle reveals a restitutional approach theoretically superior to punishment. For it must be acknowledged that a real, tangible loss *has* occurred. The problem is only one of incommensurability. Restitution provides *some* tangible, albeit inadequate, compensation for personal injury. Punishment provides none at all.[38]

It might be objected that to establish some "pay scale" for personal injury is not only somewhat arbitrary but also a disguised reimplementation of punishment. Unable to accept the inevitable consequences of restitutional punishment, the argument continues, I have retreated to a pseudorestitutional award. Such a criticism is unfair. The true test in this instance is one of primacy of intentions. Is the purpose of a system to compensate victims for their losses (and perhaps, as a consequence, punish the criminals), or is its purpose to punish the criminals (and perhaps, as a consequence, compensate the victims for their losses)? The true ends of a criminal justice system will determine its nature. In short, arbitrariness *alone* does not imply a retributive motive. And while arbitrariness remains to some extent a problem for the restitutional paradigm, it is less of a problem for restitution than for punishment, since compensation has *some* rational relationship to damages and costs.

ADVANTAGES OF A RESTITUTIONAL SYSTEM

1. The first and most obvious advantage is the assistance provided to victims of crime. They may have suffered an emotional, physical, or financial loss. Restitution would not change the fact that a possibly traumatic crime has occurred (just as the award of damages does not undo tortious conduct). Restitution, however, would make the resulting loss easier to bear for both victims and their families. At the same time, restitution would avoid a major pitfall of victim compensation/welfare plans: Since it is the criminal who must pay, the possibility of collusion between victim and criminal to collect "damages" from the state would be all but eliminated.

2. The possibility of receiving compensation would encourage victims to report crimes and to appear at trial. This is particularly true if there were a crime insurance scheme which contractually committed the policyholder to testify as a condition for payment, thus rendering unnecessary oppressive and potentially tyrannical subpoenas and contempt citations. Even the actual reporting of the crime to the police is likely to be a prerequisite for compensation. Such a requirement in auto theft insurance policies has made car thefts the most fully reported crime in the United States. Furthermore, insurance companies which paid the claim would have a strong incentive to see that the criminal was apprehended and convicted. Their pressure and assistance would make the proper functioning of law enforcement officials all the more likely.

3. Psychologist Albert Eglash has long argued that restitution would aid in the rehabilitation of criminals. "Restitution is something an inmate does, not something done for or to him. . . . Being reparative, restitution can alleviate guilt and anxiety, which can otherwise precipitate further offenses."[39] Restitution, says Eglash, is an active effortful role on the part of the of-

---

38. That the "spiritual" satisfaction which punishment may or may not provide is to be recognized as a legitimate form of "compensation" is a claim retributionists must defend.

39. Albert Eglash, "Creative Restitution: Some Suggestions for Prison Rehabilitation Programs," *American Journal of Correction* 40 (November-December 1958): 20.

fender. It is socially constructive, thereby contributing to the offender's self-esteem. It is related to the offense and may thereby redirect the thoughts which motivated the offense. It is reparative, restorative, and may actually leave the situation better than it was before the crime, both for the criminal and victim.[40]

4. This is a genuinely "self-determinative" sentence.[41] The worker would know that the length of his confinement was in his own hands. The harder he worked, the faster he would make restitution. He would be the master of his fate and would have to face that responsibility. This would encourage useful, productive activity and instill a conception of reward for good behavior and hard work. Compare this with the current probationary system and "indeterminate sentencing" where the decision for release is made by the prison bureaucracy, based only (if fairly administered) on "good behavior"; that is, passive acquiescence to prison discipline. Also, the fact that the worker would be acquiring *marketable* skills rather than more skillful methods of crime should help to reduce the shocking rate of recidivism.

5. The savings to taxpayers would be enormous. No longer would the innocent taxpayer pay for the apprehension and internment of the guilty. The cost of arrest, trial, and internment would be borne by the criminal himself. In addition, since now-idle inmates would become productive workers (able, perhaps, to support their families), the entire economy would benefit from the increase in overall production.[42]

6. Crime would no longer pay. Criminals, particularly shrewd white collar criminals, would know that they could not dispose of the proceeds of their crime and, if caught, simply serve time. They would have to make full restitution plus enforcement and legal costs, thereby greatly increasing the incentive to prosecute. While this would not eliminate such crime it would make it rougher on certain types of criminals, like bank and corporation officials, who harm many by their acts with a virtual assurance of lenient legal sanctions.[43] It might also encourage such criminals to keep the money around for a while so that, if caught, they could repay more easily. This would make a full recovery more likely.

A restitutional system of justice would benefit the victim, the criminal, and the taxpayer. The humanitarian goals of proportionate punishment, rehabilitation, and victim compensation are dealt with on a *fundamental* level making their achievement more likely. In short, the paradigm of restitution would benefit all but the entrenched penal bureaucracy and enhance justice at the same time. What then is there to stop us from overthrowing the paradigm of punishment and its penal system and putting in its place this more efficient, more humane, and more just system? The proponents of punishment and others have few powerful counter-arguments. It is to these we now turn.

OBJECTIONS TO RESTITUTION

1. Practical criticisms of restitution. It might be objected that "crimes disturb and offend not only those who are directly their victim, but also the whole social order."[44] Because of this, society, that is, individuals other than the victim, deserves some satisfaction from the offender. Restitution, it is argued, will not satisfy the lust for revenge felt by the victim or the "community's sense of justice." This criticism appears to be overdrawn. Today most members of the community are mere spectators of the

40. Ibid.; see also Eglash's "Creative Restitution: A Broader Meaning for an Old Term," *Journal of Criminal Law and Criminology* 48 (1958): 619-22; Burt Galaway and Joe Hudson, "Restitution and Rehabilitation—Some Central Issues," *Crime and Delinquency* 18 (1972): 403-10.

41. Smith, pp. 13-29.

42. An economist who favors restitution on efficiency grounds is Gary S. Becker, although he does not break with the paradigm of punishment. Those interested in a mathematical "cost-benefit" analysis should see his "Crime and Punishment," *Journal of Political Economy* 76 (1968):169-217.

43. This point is also made by Minocher Jehangirji Sethna in his paper, "Treatment and Atonement for Crime," in *Victims and Society*, p. 538.

44. Del Vecchio, p. 198.

criminal justice system, and this is largely true even of the victim.[45] One major reform being urged presently is more victim involvement in the criminal justice process.[46] The restitution proposal would necessitate this involvement. And while the public generally takes the view that officials should be tougher on criminals, with "tougher" taken by nearly everyone to mean more severe in punishing, one must view this "social fact" in light of the lack of a known alternative. The real test of public sympathies would be to see which sanction people would choose: incarceration of the criminal for a given number of years or the criminal's being compelled to make restitution to the victim: While the public's choice is not clearly predictable, neither can it be assumed that it would reject restitution. There is some evidence to the contrary.[47]

This brings us to a second practical objection: that monetary sanctions are insufficient deterrents to crime. Again, this is something to be discovered, not something to be assumed. There are a number of reasons to believe that our *current* system of punishment does not adequately

deter, and for the reasons discussed earlier an increase in the level of punishment is unlikely. In fact, many have argued that the deterrent value of sanctions has less to do with *severity* than with *certainty*,[48] and the preceding considerations indicate that law enforcement would be more certain under a restitutional system. In the final analysis, however, it is irrelevant to argue that more crimes may be committed if proposal leaves the victim better off. It must be remembered: *Our goal is not the suppression of crime; it is doing justice to victims.*

A practical consideration which merits considerable future attention is the feasibility of the employment project proposal. A number of questions can be raised. At first blush, it seems naively optimistic to suppose that offenders will be able or willing to work at all, much less earn their keep and pay reparations as well. On the contrary, this argument continues, individuals turn to crime precisely because they lack the skills which the restitutional plan assumes they have. Even if these workers have the skills, but refuse to work, what could be done? Would not the use of force to compel compliance be

---

45. William F. McDonald, "Towards a Bicentennial Revolution in Criminal Justice: The Return of the Victim," *American Criminal Law Review* 13 (1976): 659; see also his paper "Notes on the Victim's Role in the Prosecutional and Dispositional Stages of the Criminal Justice Process" (paper presented at the Second International Symposium on Victimology, Boston, September 1976); Jack M. Kress, "The Role of the Victim at Sentencing" (paper presented at the Second International Symposium on Victimology, Boston, September 1976).

46. McDonald, pp. 669-73; Kress, pp. 11-15. Kress specifically analyzes restitution as a means for achieving victim involvement.

47. In two types of studies conducted for the Ventura County Board of Supervisors, Ventura, California, support for a restitutional program was indicated: "Both the citizen attitude survey and the Delphi goal-setting exercise revealed a strong concern for the *victim* as the 'forgotten man' of criminal justice. The Delphi panelists, in particular, emphasized the need for new kinds of criminal penalties in which the offender would be required to make restitution to his victim(s)" (*Development of a Model Criminal Justice System* [Santa Barbara, Calif.: Public Safety Systems, 1973], p. 85). The report recommends the implementing of a system of restitution. In the two cities mentioned earlier (Columbus and

Tucson), support, at least by the parties involved, appeared strong. In the thousands of cases arbitrated by trained law students in Columbus, only 4 percent proceeded further up in the criminal system. In Tucson after one year the program has been successful in all but nine of 204 cases (with the cost of handling each case at $304 compared with $1,566 required to process the average felony case). General approval of restitution in lieu of punishment was indirectly referred to in the *Columbia Law Review's* oft-cited study, "Restitution and the Criminal Law": "[E]ven where the complainant can be persuaded to continue the criminal case, after having received private satisfaction, his apathy is often so pronounced and his demeanor so listless that he becomes an extremely weak witness. . . . Also the knowledge of actual restitution seems to greatly assuage the jury. Even the knowledge of the existence of a civil suit can lead the jury to recomend leniency or acquittal" (39 [1939]: 1189; see also n. 31). Restitution, it seems, is accepted and preferred by the average person. Early studies indicate that, when properly administered, even offenders perceive a restitutionary sanction as fair (William Marsella and Burt Galaway, "Study of the Perceived Fairness of Restitution as a Sanction for Juvenile Offenders" [paper presented to the Second International Symposium on Victimology, Boston, September 1976]).

48. Yochelson and Samenow, pp. 453-57.

tantamount to slavery? This criticism results in part from my attempt to sketch an "ideal" restitution system; that is, I have attempted to outline the type toward which every criminal justice system governed by the restitution paradigm should strive. This is not to say that every aspect of the hypothetical system would, upon implementation, function smoothly. Rather, such a system could only operate ideally once the paradigm had been fully accepted and substantially articulated.

With this in mind, one can advance several responses. First, the problem as usually posed assumes the offender to be highly irrational and possibly mentally unbalanced. There is no denying that some segment of the criminal population fits the former description.[49] What this approach neglects, however, is the possibility that many criminals are making rational choices within an irrational and unjust political system. Specifically I refer to the myriad laws and regulations which make it difficult for the unskilled or person of transitory outlook[50] to find legal employment.[51] I refer also to the laws which deny legality to the types of services which are in particular demand in economically impoverished communities.[52] Is it "irrational" to choose to steal or rob when one is virtually foreclosed from the legal opportunity to do otherwise? Another possibility is that the criminal chooses crime not because of foreclosure, but because he enjoys and obtains satisfaction from a criminal way of life.[53] Though morally repugnant, this is hardly irrational.

Furthermore, it no longer can be denied that contact with the current criminal justice system is itself especially damaging among juveniles.[54] The offenders who are hopelessly committed to criminal behavior are not usually the newcomers to crime but those who have had repeated exposure to the penal system. In Kuhn's words, "Existing institutions have ceased to meet the problems posed by an environment *they have in part created.*"[55] While a restitutionary system might not change these hardcore offenders, it could, by the early implementation of sanctions perceived by the criminal to be just, break the vicious circle which in large part accounts for their existence.

Finally, if offenders could not or would not make restitution, then the logical and just result of their refusal would be confinement until they could or would. Such an outcome would be entirely in their hands. While this "solution" does not suggest who should justly pay for this confinement, the problem is not unique to a restitutionary system. In this and other areas of possible difficulty we must seek guidance from existing pilot programs as well as from the burgeoning research in this area and in victimology in general.

2. Distributionary criticisms of restitution. There remains one criticism of restitution which

---

49. For a discussion rejecting the usefulness of the latter description, see Szasz, pp. 91-146; for a recent study verifying Szasz's thesis, see Yochelson and Samenow, esp. pp. 227-35.
50. Edward C. Banfield put forth his controversial theory of time horizon in his book *The Unheavenly City* (Boston: Little, Brown & Co., 1970) and amplified it in *The Unheavenly City Revisited* (Boston: Little, Brown & Company, 1974) and, most recently, in "Present-orientedness and Crime," in *Assessing the Criminal*, pp. 133-42; see also Gerald P. O'Driscoll, Jr., "Professor Banfield on Time Horizon: What Has He Taught Us About Crime?" *ibid.*, pp. 143-62; and Mario Rizzo, "Time Preference, Situational Determinism, and Crime," *ibid.*, pp. 163-77. A contrary, but ultimately compatible view is presented by Yochelson and Samenow, pp. 369-72.
51. For example, minimum wage laws, and so-called closed-shop union protectionist legislation.
52. For example, laws prohibiting gambling, prostitution, sale of drugs, "jitney" cab services, etc.

53. "It is not the environment that turns a man into a criminal. Rather it is a series of choices that he makes at a very early age. . . . [T]he criminal is not a victim of circumstances" (Yochelson and Samenow, pp. 247, 249). This is in essence the main conclusion of their research. (For a concise summary of their provocative book, see Joseph Boorkin, "The Criminal Personality," *Federal Bar Journal* 35 [1976]: 237-41.) In *The Criminal Personality*, vol. 2, *The Process of Change* (New York: Jason Aronson, Inc., 1977) they relate and examine the methods they have employed to change the criminal thought pattern. Of course, such an approach can itself be subject to abuse.
54. See, e.g., Edwin M. Schur, *Radical Noninterventionism, Rethinking the Delinquency Problem* (Englewood Cliffs, N.J.: Prentice-Hall, Inc., 1973).
55. Kuhn, p. 92 (emphasis added).

is the most obvious and the most difficult with which to deal. Simply stated, it takes the following form: "Doesn't this mean that rich people will be able to commit crimes with impunity if they can afford it? Isn't this unfair?" The *practical* aspect of this objection is that whatever deterrent effect restitution payments may have, they will be less for those most able to pay. The *moral* aspect is that whatever retributive or penal effect restitution payments may have they will be less for those who are well off. Some concept of equality of justice underlies both considerations.

Critics of restitution fail to realize that the "cost" of crime will be quite high. In addition to compensation for pain and suffering, the criminal must pay for the cost of his apprehension, the cost of the trial, and the legal expenditures of *both* sides. This should make even an unscrupulous wealthy person think twice about committing a crime. The response to this is that we cannot have it both ways. If the fines would be high enough to bother the rich, then they would be so high that a project worker would have no chance of earning that much and would, therefore, have no incentive to work at all. If, on the other hand, you lower the price of crime by ignoring all its costs, you fail to deter the rich or fully compensate the victim.

This is where the option of arbitration and victim crime insurance becomes of practical importance. If the victim is uninsured, he is unlikely to recover for all costs of a very severe crime from a poor, unskilled criminal, since even in an employment project the criminal might be unable to earn enough. If he had no hope of earning his release, he would have little incentive to work very hard beyond paying for his own maintenance. The victim would end up with less than if he had "settled" the case for the lesser amount which a project worker could reasonably be expected to earn. If, however, the victim had full-coverage criminal insurance, he would recover his damages in full, and the insurance company would absorb any disparity between full compensation and maximal employment project worker's output. This cost would be reflected in premium prices, enabling

the insurance company which settled cases at an amount which increased the recovery from the criminal to offer the lowest rates. Eventually a "maximum" feasible fine for project workers would be determined based on these considerations. The "rich," on the other hand, would naturally have to pay in full. This arrangement would solve the practical problem, but it should not be thought of as an imperative of the restitutional paradigm.

The same procedure of varying the payments according to ability to pay would answer the moral considerations as well (that the rich are not hurt enough) and this is the prime motive behind *punitive* restitution proposals. However, we reject the moral consideration outright. The paradigm of restitution calls not for the (equal) hurting of criminals, but for restitution to victims. Any appeal to "inadequate suffering" is a reversion to the paradigm of punishment, and by varying the sanction for crimes of the same magnitude according to the economic status of the offender it reveals its own inequity. *Equality of justice means equal treatment of victims.* It should not matter to the victim if his attacker was rich or poor. His plight is the same regardless. Any reduction of criminal liability because of reduced earning power would be for practical, not moral, reasons.

Equality of justice derives from the fact that the rights of men should be equally enforced and respected. Restitution recognizes a victim's right to compensation for damages from the party responsible. Equality of justice, therefore, calls for equal enforcement of each victim's right to restitution. *Even if necessary or expedient, any lessening of payment to the victim because of the qualities of the criminal is a violation of that victim's rights and an inequality of justice.* Any such expedient settlement is only a recognition that an imperfect world may make possible only imperfect justice. As a practical matter, a restitutional standard gives victims an enormous incentive to pursue wealthy criminals since they can afford quick, full compensation. Contrast this with the present system where the preference given the wealthy is so prevalent that most victims simply assume that nothing will be done.

The paradigm of restitution, to reiterate, is neither a panacea for crime nor a blueprint for utopia. Panaceas and utopias are not for humankind. We must live in a less than perfect world with less than perfect people. Restitution opens the possibility of an improved and more just society. The old paradigm of punishment, even reformed, simply cannot offer this promise.

OTHER CONSIDERATIONS

Space does not permit a full examination of other less fundamental implications of such a system. I shall briefly consider five.

1. Civil versus criminal liability. If one accepts a restitutionary standard of justice, what sense does it make to distinguish between crime and tort, since both call for payment of damages? For most purposes I think the distinction collapses. Richard Epstein, in a series of brilliant articles, has articulated a theory of strict liability in tort.[56] His view is that since one party has caused another some harm and one of the parties must bear the loss, justice demands that it falls on the party who caused the harm. He argues that intention is only relevant as a "third-stage" argument; that notwithstanding some

fault on the part of the plaintiff (a second-stage argument), the defendant intended the harm and is therefore liable.[57] With a restitutional system I see no reason why Epstein's theory of tort liability could not incorporate criminal liability into a single "system of corrective justice that looks to conduct, broadly defined, of the parties to the case with a view toward the protection of individual liberty and private property."[58]

There would, at least initially, be some differences, however. The calculation of damages under the restitutionary paradigm which includes cost of apprehension, cost of trial, and legal costs of both parties would be higher than tort law allows. A further distinction would be the power of enforcers to confine unreliable offenders to employment projects.[59]

2. Criminal responsibility and competency. Once a criminal sanction is based not on the offender's badness but on the nature and consequences of his acts, Thomas Szasz's proposal that the insanity plea be abolished makes a great deal of sense,[60] as does his argument that "all persons charged with offenses—except those grossly disabled—[are fit to stand trial and] should be tried."[61] On this view, Epstein's

---

56. Richard A. Epstein, "A Theory of Strict Liability in Tort," *Journal of Legal Studies* 2 (1973): 151-204.
57. Richard A. Epstein, "Intentional Harms," *Journal of Legal Studies* 3 (1975): 402-8; see also his article "Defenses and Subsequent Pleas in a System of Strict Liability," ibid., 3 (1974): 174-85.
58. Epstein, "Intentional Harms," p. 441. Epstein himself would disagree. In a recent article, also notable for its well-reasoned rejection of victim compensation/welfare schemes, "Crime and Tort: Old Wine in Old Bottles," in *Assessing the Criminal,* pp. 231-57, he draws an emphatic distinction between tort and criminal law. He rests this distinction on two characteristics of the criminal law: (*a*) that its function is to punish (and therefore *mens rea* is required and more stringent procedural safeguards are appropriate), and (*b*) since the defendant is prosecuted by the state, fairness as between the parties is not relevant. From these assumptions, Epstein reasons quite correctly that the two systems are inherently different. It should be obvious that a restitutionary paradigm undermines both assumptions. Gilbert M. Cantor in his article, "An End to Crime and Punishment" (*Shingle* 39 [May 1976]: 99-114), takes precisely this view, arguing that "the time has come to abolish the game of crime and punishment and to substitute a paradigm of restitution and responsibility. I urge that we assign (reassign, actually) to the civil law our societal response to the acts or behaviors

we now label and treat as criminal. The goal is the *civilization* of our treatment of offenders. I use the word, 'civilization' here in its specific meaning: to bring offenders under the civil, rather than the criminal law; and in its larger meaning: to move in this area of endeavor from barbarism toward greater enlightenment and humanity;" (p. 107; emphasis in original).
59. It would seem that the only way to account for these differences would be an appeal to the *mens rea* or badness of the criminal as opposed to the unintentional tortfeasor. Yet such an approach, it might be argued, is not available to a restitutionary system which considers the moral outlook of an offender to be irrelevant to the determination of the proper criminal sanction. A possible response is that this overstates the restitutionist claim. That a criminal's mental state does not justify punishment does not imply that it is not relevant to *any* aspect of the criminal justice process. It may well be that it is relevant to the consideration of methods by which one is justified in extracting what, on other grounds, is shown to be a proper sanction, that is, restitution.
60. Szasz, pp. 228-30.
61. Ibid., pp. 228-29. "The emphasis here is on gross disability: it should be readily apparent or easily explicable to a group of lay persons, like a jury" (p. 229). But even the qualification of gross disablement might be unjustified (see Yochelson and Samenow, pp. 227-35).

concept of fairness *as between the parties* is relevant. A restitution proceeding like a "lawsuit is always a comparative affair. The defendant's victory ensures the plaintiff's [or victim's] defeat. . . . Why should we prefer the injurer to his victim in a case where one may win and the other lose? . . . As a matter of fairness between the parties, the defendant should be required to treat the harms which he has inflicted upon another as though they were inflicted upon himself."[62]

3. Victimless crimes. The effect of restitutional standards on the legality of such crimes as prostitution, gambling, high interest loans, pornography, and drug use is intriguing. There has been no violation of individual rights, and consequently no damages and, therefore, no liability. While some may see this as a drawback, I believe it is a striking advantage of the restitutional standard of justice. So-called victimless crimes would in principle cease to be crimes. As a consequence, criminal elements would be denied a lucrative monopoly, and the price of these services would be drastically reduced. Without this enormous income, organized crime would be far less able to afford the "cost" of its nefarious activities than it is today.

4. Legal positivism. What is true for victimless crimes is true for the philosophy of legal positivism. On the positivist view, whatever the state (following all the correct political procedures) says is law, is law; hence, whatever the state makes a crime is a crime. A restitutional standard would hold the state to enforcing individual rights through the recovery of individual damages.

5. Legal process. Because the sanction for crime would no longer be punitive, the criminal process could explore less formal procedures for dispute settlement. Also, the voice of the victim would be added to the deliberations. One possible reform might be a three-tiered verdict: guilty, not proven, and not guilty. If found "guilty," the offender would pay all the costs mentioned above. If the charges are "not proven," then neither party would pay the other. If found "not guilty," the defendant would be reimbursed by the enforcement agency for his costs and inconvenience. This new interpretation of "not guilty," would reward those defendants who, after putting on a defense, convinced the trier of fact that they were innocent.

These and many other fascinating implications of restitution deserve a more thorough examination. As any new paradigm becomes accepted, it experiences what Kuhn calls a period of "normal research," a period characterized by continuous expansion and perfection of the new paradigm as well as a testing of its limits. The experimentation with restitutionary justice will, however, differ from the trial and error of the recent past since we will be guided by the principle that the purpose of our legal system is not to harm the guilty but to help the innocent—a principle which will above all restore our belief that our overriding commitment is to do justice.

---

62. Epstein, p. 398. In his article "Crime and Tort: Old Wine in Old Bottles," he takes exactly this approach with the insanity defense in tort law.

C □ *The Night Prosecutor*

Columbus finds extrajudicial solutions to interpersonal disputes

JOHN W. PALMER

• Two employees of a Columbus, Ohio, factory began to argue over the previous Saturday's football game. One thing led to another, and blows began to fly. After the fight, the employee whose shift ended first went to the police station to file assault and battery charges against the other.

• A neighborhood dispute concerning minor children and their dogs caused a serious split in the neighborhood. One of the older residents threatened to shoot the next dog he saw on his property. Then an irate dog owner called the police and wanted to have his next door neighbor arrested.

• In downtown Columbus, a serious feud developed between two families: a total of seven felony and fourteen misdemeanor charges were filed against various family members who persisted in ambushing one another despite serious injuries sustained by both sides.

As these true examples illustrate, in interpersonal disputes, the person who files a criminal affidavit is frequently the party who won the race to the police station. Often, the complaining witness is equally guilty or the sole guilty party.

In these cases, a legal trial may obscure and distort the truth. The basic causes of the trouble are "irrelevant" or "immaterial" and inadmissible as evidence. Like the tip of an iceberg, the final criminal act may be identified, but the tensions and misunderstandings which caused it are never discovered, let alone dealt with. Consequently, criminal acts continue to be committed, with the formal criminal process serving only to aggravate the tension and hostility between the parties.

The city attorney's office of Columbus, Ohio, has developed a system, the Night Prosecutor's Program, for diverting many offenses resulting

Reprinted by permission from *Judicature,* the journal of the American Judicature Society, vol. 59, no. 1, pp. 23-27, June-July 1975.

from interpersonal disputes out of the court system. The Night Prosecutor's Program, so named because hearings are held in the evening, seeks to help antagonistic parties resolve their disputes in face to face confrontations as soon as possible after the commission of the overt act which caused the criminal complaint.

The goals of the program are (1) to speed the dispensation of justice to citizens who become involved in minor criminal conduct; (2) to reduce the criminal court backlog; (3) to ease community and interpersonal tensions; (4) to provide a forum for the working poor at times that do not interfere with their jobs; (5) to remove the stigma of an arrest record arising from minor personal disputes.

The program has been successful in all five areas. In 1974, its third year of operation, the program was designated an Exemplary Project by the National Institute of Law Enforcement and Criminal Justice of LEAA. Training sessions for communities interested in establishing similar programs were held in ten of the nation's LEAA districts.

OPERATION

The Office of the City Prosecutor in Columbus screens all criminal matters involving private citizens and decides which cases are appropriate for diversion into the Night Prosecutor's Program. In general, these are cases in which there is a continuing relationship, such as between families, neighbors, landlords and tenants, or employers and employees. The complainant does not necessarily consent to the diversion; however, should the Night Prosecutor fail to resolve the dispute, criminal remedies are still available.

When a case is sent to the Night Prosecutor, instead of an affidavit being prepared, signed, and filed with the clerk of courts, a complaint is taken and an administrative hearing scheduled for approximately one week later. This is a significant time saving for the complainant; it would probably take months for the case to reach trial. The complainant is told to appear at the hearing with his witnesses. Notice is sent to the person accused notifying him of the fact that a complaint has been made against him, the basic charges and the time of the hearing. This notice does not carry the legal force of a subpoena; however, if one party does not show up the other may file a criminal complaint.

All hearings are scheduled in half-hour blocks between the hours of six and ten p.m. Hearings are held in a private room in the office of the prosecutor. Present at the hearing are the hearing officer, the complainant, the respondent, attorneys (in rare cases) and witnesses, if there are any. The hearing officer conducts the hearing informally, inviting each party to tell his side of the story without interruption. The hearing officer may ask questions, and the parties or witnesses may talk with each other in an attempt to work out a solution to the underlying problem. The hearing officer acts as a mediator and conciliator. His job is to discover and expose the basic issues which have precipitated the original dispute.

Many people seem to come to the police station not to file charges, but because they have a serious social problem and do not know where else to go. Countless times the complainant says: "I don't want him arrested, I just want him to stop hitting me."

The most successful resolutions have proved to be those in which the parties themselves suggest and agree on a solution. Often, the most effective solution is suggested by a witness who, in many cases, is a friend of both parties. If, however, the parties are not able or willing to do this, the hearing officer will try to suggest a solution which is palatable to both sides.

An additional responsibility of the hearing officer is to inform the parties of the law and criminal sanctions. This may include criminal statutes or city ordinances which carry criminal penalties.

Occasionally the problem involves many parties or an entire neighborhood. In the case of the family feud mentioned at the beginning of this article, a dozen family members attended the hearing at which their dispute was resolved and the criminal charges dropped. In such cases, the hearing moves to a courtroom with the hearing officer at the judge's bench. These hearings may last up to an hour or more.

Hearings are free flowing without regard to rules of evidence, burdens of proof or other legalities. Emotional outbursts are common— it is the responsibility of the hearing officer to see that these do not get out of control. (On at least one occasion, an assault and battery occurred during the hearing.) It is this writer's firm conviction that without the opportunity for the controlled display of emotionalism, shouting, and other forms of confrontation, the basic truth often does not come to the surface.

Due to the volume of cases processed through the Night Prosecutor's Program, it was recognized that emphasis had to be on "quantity" rather than "quality." Hearings are scheduled for thirty minutes; but in many cases, additional time was needed. In order to fill this need, Catholic, Methodist, and Lutheran Seminaries in and around Columbus were asked to provide seminary students to work with difficult cases involving interfamily problems on a continuing basis. In 1974, 250 such cases were referred to family counseling sessions.

In addition to disputes involving interpersonal relationships, since July 1973, the Night Prosecutor's Program has provided facilities to handle bad check cases. Hearings on all bad check complaints from a particular company are scheduled for a single night, and a representative for that company must appear. The company representative and the hearing officer are assigned a room, and respondents are referred to them one by one to negotiate a settlement. More than 81 different retail establishments now process bad checks through the program.

In cooperation with an Apartment Owners Association, the Night Prosecutor's Program has arranged to process cases between landlords and tenants involving malicious destruction of property and theft (unlawful withholding of rent deposits). Sixteen such cases were processed in 1974.

STAFF

Early in the program, it became apparent that since few of the disputes involved questions of law, hearing officers required conciliatory ability more than extensive legal background. As a result, the project was revised to include law students as hearing officers with the Night Prosecutor acting as consulting supervisor.

The staff now includes a daytime coordinator, a secretary, two law student clerks and four law student hearing officers. The Family Counseling Division is staffed by seven seminary students.

Training sessions for staff are held periodically throughout the year. In 1974, a comprehensive training manual was prepared and distributed to all new participants.[1] Crisis intervention seminars are conducted by the Columbus Area Mental Health Center. Each member of the Night Prosecutor staff now has access to professional training in interpersonal dispute confrontations.

STATISTICS

In 1974, 6,180 interpersonal disputes were processed by the Night Prosecutor's Program and scheduled for hearing. Of these, only 3,274 or 52 per cent actually appeared so that hearings could be held. (In most "no shows" both parties fail to appear, and in this case no further action is taken. However, if only one party does not appear, the other may go ahead and file a criminal complaint.) Of all cases processed, only 328 criminal complaints were authorized and cases scheduled for court. The program also handled 4,227 bad check cases, of which only 237, or five per cent, resulted in the authorization of criminal complaints.

In gross figures, a total of 10,407 criminal complaints were processed by the Night Prosecutor's Program which resulted in only 565

authorized criminal complaints. A total of 9,842 cases were diverted from the criminal justice system.

The Franklin County Municipal Court has jurisdiction over all misdemeanors committed within the county as well as preliminary matters in felony cases. According to the clerk of the court, approximately 37,532 felony and misdemeanor cases, not including traffic offenses were put on the docket in 1974. But for the Night Prosecutor's Program, this number would have been approximately 21 per cent higher.

It has been estimated that the average cost of processing a case through the criminal justice system in the traditional manner is $200. The Night Prosecutor processed 10,407 cases a total cost of $60,000. The direct cost savings to Franklin County taxpayers was approximately $2,000,000. The indirect savings in fewer welfare payments, reduced family breakdowns and other social costs are incalculable.

It is expected that in 1975 these figures will be even higher. The last few months of 1974 showed an ever-increasing number of cases being referred to the Night Prosecutor's Program, averaging over 1,000 per month.

During 1974, a "call back" program was initiated. Approximately 30 days following a hearing, the parties are contacted by a hearing officer to determine whether or not the criminal activity is continuing. In more than 90 per cent of the cases called in 1974, a satisfactory solution had been achieved. In 10 per cent of the cases one of the parties said, "He's still at it!," but in only 1.2 per cent of all those called was there a further contact with the criminal justice system through a police run or by a new filing.

These encouraging statistics cause this writer to wonder whether perhaps recidivist criminal activity might not be to some degree a result of police or law enforcement supervision. Perhaps the low incidence of subsequent contact with the criminal justice system was because the parties were not placed under field supervision, as they would have been if they had been placed upon probation following conviction. Perhaps probation supervision is an unwarranted invasion of privacy, with probation violations occurring not because of so-called deviant behavior, but because the offender was

---

1. The Standard Operational Procedures Manual may be ordered from the Center of Law Enforcement and Correctional Justice, 9270 Hawthorn point, Westerville, Ohio, 43081. The price is $5.00. All forms used in Night Prosecutor's Program are included.

in close personal contact with an authority figure who had the power to make an arrest. Perhaps probation causes rather than reduces "criminal" behavior. These questions are left to future research.

Thus far, the Night Prosecutor's Program has concentrated on interpersonal disputes. However the concept of a prearrest diversionary program need not be limited to this one area. Jurisdiction has already been expanded to include bad check cases and could easily be adapted to the handling of shoplifting cases as well. Discussions are currently underway regarding the feasibility of using the Night Prosecutor's Program to handle welfare fraud cases.

Whatever future developments take place, the value of the Night Prosecutor's Program is firmly established. It is a proven benefactor not only to the system of criminal justice but to the citizens of Columbus as well.

Selected readings for Chapter 8

Brickman, Philip. "Crime and Punishment in Sports and Society," *Journal of Social Issues* **33:**140-164, 1977.
> Sports is an area in which penalties are equity based (designed to restore fairness), whereas the criminal law is seen as deterrent based, with penalties designed to prevent deviance. Advantages to victims, criminals, and society of using an equity-based system in criminal justice are outlined.

Conner, Ross F., and Ray Surette. *The Citizen Dispute Settlement Program* (Washington, D.C.: American Bar Association, 1977).
> An evaluation report on the Citizen Dispute Settlement Program of the Orange County (Florida) Bar Association. Presents information on the evaluation design, the findings, and the implications of these findings for the local criminal justice system.

Deming, Romine R. "Programs Advocating the Victim-Offender Relationship," *Victimology* **2:** 117-122, 1977.
> Summarizes research and program efforts in New England to involve offenders and victims in programs based on the ideas that the agencies were to prevent and resolve conflict and restore harmony between victims and offenders.

Kole, Janet. "Arbitration as an Alternative to the Criminal Warrant," *Judicature* **56:**295-297, 1973.
> Describes a program of the American Arbitration Association using arbitration between victims and offenders rather than criminal processing to resolve disputes.

McDonald, William F. "Towards a Bicentennial Revolution in Criminal Justice: The Return of the Victim," *American Criminal Law Review* **13:**649-673, 1976.
> This article traces the decline of the victim's importance in American justice and attempts to offer explanations for this decline. Presents information on the burdens that the contemporary criminal justice system forces victims to endure and examines some current reform movements to improve the lot of the victim.

McGillis, Daniel, and Joan Mullen. *Neighborhood Justice Centers: An Analysis of Potential Models* (Washington, D.C.: U.S. Government Printing Office, 1977).
> This report provides information on several dispute settlement programs that exist in the country. It presents an overview of the various dispute-processing mechanisms in use in the country and gives detailed case studies of six operating programs. Recommendations are offered for the design and implementation of neighborhood justice centers.

Chapter 9

VICTIM INVOLVEMENT

A ☐ Pretrial settlement conference

Evaluation of a reform in plea bargaining

ANNE M. HEINZ and WAYNE A. KERSTETTER

I. INTRODUCTION

In 1974 Norval Morris proposed that judges should play a more active role in plea negotiations and that the victims and defendants should also be invited to participate (1974:55-57). We are reporting a year-long test of that proposal carried out in Dade County, Florida (Kerstetter and Heinz, 1979). Using a field experiment design, we randomly chose 1074 cases: 378 were assigned to use a pretrial settlement conference; the remainder were the control group.

Plea bargaining—the primary mode of criminal charge disposition—has been under sustained attack for some time; the U.S. National Advisory Commission on Criminal Justice Standards and Goals recently urged that such negotiations should be abolished (1973:46-49). But despite criticism from many quarters, there is little indication that the practice is about to disappear.

The major criticism of plea bargaining is that it penalizes the defendant who wishes to assert his constitutional right to trial (U.S. National

Advisory Commission, 1973:48). As a consequence, innocent persons may plead guilty to avoid the more severe sanctions that follow conviction at trial. Thus a guilty person may receive a reduced sentence by pleading while an innocent person is severely punished for unsuccessfully asserting his innocence at trial.

The issue of judicial participation in plea bargaining has been part of this larger controversy. The American Bar Association Standards (1967: 71-77), Rule 11 of the Federal Rules of Criminal Procedure, and the U.S. National Advisory Commission on Criminal Justice Standards and Goals (1973:59-63) all state that trial judges should not be directly involved in plea negotiations though they may review a tentative settlement reached by the parties and indicate whether it is acceptable. This position is predicated on the belief that the role of the judge is so inherently coercive that his participation undermines the voluntariness of the defendant's acceptance of a plea agreement.

Morris challenges this view (1974:55-57). He points to the desirability of greater judicial knowledge of the facts and considerations behind the proposed plea. Traditional plea negotiations allow the judge little more than a veto power, which is itself constrained by caseload

Reprinted by permission of the Law and Society Association from *Law and Society Review*, vol. 13, no. 2, pp. 349-366, 1979.

The authors wish to thank the participants in the Dade County experiment, especially the judges and attorneys and their staffs, for their continued cooperation and interest in this project. Our research staff in Dade County, directed by Charlotte Boc, provided us with consistently high quality data in the face of substantial obstacles; without their perseverance the evaluation would never have been completed. The project was conducted at the Center for Studies in Criminal Justice of the University of Chicago Law School. Heinz was the senior methodologist and research associate; Kerstetter, the project director and Associate Director of the Center. We particularly wish to acknowledge the unfailing support and stimulus of the Center staff, and especially Frank E. Zimring, Ben S. Meeker, and Helen Flint.

The evaluation was prepared under Grant 76-NI-99-0088 from the National Institute of Law Enforcement and Criminal Justice, Law Enforcement Assistance Administration, United States Department of Justice. Points of view or opinions stated in this document are those of the authors and do not necessarily represent the official position or policies of the United States Department of Justice.

pressure. Alschuler, in his definitive survey of the arguments for and against judicial involvement, concludes:

Judicial control of the plea bargaining process would offer defendants a clear and tangible basis for reliance in entering their guilty pleas; it would, at least on occasion, permit effective regulation of the extent of the penalty that our criminal justice system imposes for the exercise of the right to trial; it would facilitate the introduction of new procedural safeguards; it would be likely to affect the tone and substance of the bargaining process in a variety of useful ways; and most importantly, it would restore judicial power to the judges. [1976:1154]

Rosett and Cressey (1976:170-72) argue that judicial participation will help to equalize the opportunity of all defendants to negotiate and will encourage the prosecutor and defense counsel to furnish the judge with information about the defendant's background, thereby leading to more individualized punishment.

Participation by the victim and the defendant in plea discussions has not received a great deal of attention. A *Yale Law Journal* Comment (1972:286) suggested including the defendant in a pretrial conference presided over by a judge. Rosett and Cressey (1976:173) also recommended that both defendant and victim participate in order to increase their understanding of the proposed settlement and encourage greater attention to the unique qualities of each case. Fredric DuBow and Theodore M. Becker (1976:147) assert that the victim's capacity to influence the outcome of the criminal case has declined over time, and that traditional plea bargaining has largely excluded victims. As a result, victims are dissatisfied with both the sentence imposed and their inability to participate meaningfully in the process.

If the victim is interested in retribution, he may be frustrated by the imposition of a low sentence without explanation of the reasons for leniency or the opportunity to participate meaningfully in the process of reaching a disposition. If the victim is not interested in retribution, there is little other satisfaction to be gained. Victims seldom get an apology, seldom are reconciled with the offender, and seldom receive restitution. [1976:150]

The proposal for a pretrial settlement conference envisions participation in all plea discussions by the judge, the victim, the defendant, and the police. It neither requires the judge to take an active role in the actual negotiations nor prohibits such a role. Victim and police officer are given an opportunity to be heard, not a veto power. The defendant retains all existing rights and acquires the option to participate, either as a passive observer or an active party.

In our search for experimental sites we discussed the proposal with attorneys and judges in over twenty jurisdictions. We were frequently met with dire predictions that the conference would absorb inordinate amounts of judicial time; that the presence of victims and defendants would lead to emotional or even violent confrontations; that the candid discussions between attorneys necessary to facilitate a settlement would be inhibited by the presence of lay participants; that victims and defendants would misunderstand the conference discussions and accuse judges of improper conduct; and that the dignity of the judge would be diminished by his involvement in the negotiations. In the context of such widespread misgivings, we

launched the conference procedure in Dade County (Miami), Florida.

II. METHODOLOGY
A. Research design

In order to determine if our proposal made any difference in the processing of criminal cases, we designed a field experiment[1] that compared post-arraignment cases where conferences were available with those where they were not (see Figure 1). Since we wanted to control the assignment of cases to the treatment condition, we required (i) random assignment of cases to judges and (ii) random assignment of cases from each judge's calendar to test or control conditions.[2]

We identified three (test) judges who agreed to use the conference in a random selection of those cases that survived arraignment and three others (comparison judges) who did not use the

---

[1]For a general discussion of field experiments, see Campbell and Stanley (1963); Weiss (1972). For their use in criminal justice research, see McCall (1975:13-20).

[2]For a more detailed discussion of the design, sample selection, instrumentation, and indices, see Kerstetter and Heinz (1979:136).

EVALUATION DESIGN

Judge	Prior to Intervention				Period of Intervention		
	T−n .....T−2	T−1		T	T+1	T+2 .....T+n	
A (Test)	R	O			R X O		
					R O		
B (Test)	R	O			R X O		
					R O		
C (Test)	R	O			R X O		
					R O		
D (Comparison)	R	O			R O		
E (Comparison)	R	O			R O		
F (Comparison)	R	O			R O		

O = Observation (Data Collection)
X = Treatment (Pretrial Settlement Conference)
T = Period of Intervention
R = Random Assignment

Figure 1

conference but allowed us to analyze their cases. Since the judges were not selected randomly, we do not argue that they represent the universe of judges in Dade County. Instead, we have considered the three test judges as three separate tests of the procedure. The cases of comparison judges serve to indicate possible changes in the court environment during the test period. Since the Dade County Circuit Court randomly assigns cases to individual judges for disposition, part of our requirements were satisfied prior to our intervention.

For the three test judges the research staff identified (i) 40 cases that closed prior to our intervention in January, 1977, (ii) approximately 130 cases that would be eligible for treatment (for which a conference date was set), and (iii) 75 control cases that were processed at the same time as the test cases but followed the court's usual procedures. For the control judges we divided cases into two categories: (i) approximately 40 cases that closed prior to our intervention and (ii) 75 cases disposed during the treatment period. Thus the design included three treatment conditions: pretreatment, test, and control for the test judges, and pretreatment and control for the comparison judges. We used the case rather than the defendant as our sampling unit because of the need to provide equal treatment to all members of multiple-defendant cases.

For the test and control categories we used prospective samples identifying cases from the arraignment calendars and following them until they closed. For the pretreatment category we used a retrospective sample, identifying closed cases by their proximity to the date of our intervention and tracking them back in time. Neither method imposed constraints on the length of time involved in processing the cases or on the types of offenses included. However, approximately eight percent of the prospective samples had not closed at the conclusion of the data collection period. All noncapital felonies that survived arraignment were eligible for selection.

B. Data sources

The research staff collected information from the court records concerning the nature of the offense, the timing of the process, and the method and type of disposition for each defendant in the sample.[3] A member of the staff also attended each conference and recorded the discussion. Structured twenty-minute interviews were conducted with victim, defendant, and police in test and control cases, after the cases were closed—in person for incarcerated defendants, otherwise by telephone. Among those respondents we could locate, we interviewed 54 percent of the defendants, 78 percent of the victims, and 63 percent of the police. Finally, senior staff conducted open-ended interviews with both test and comparison judges and attorneys.

III. THE SETTING
A. Criminal procedure

A 1972 amendment to the Florida Constitution streamlined the state court system. (American Judicature Society, 1973:174.) It established two tiers of trial courts, circuit and county. The Circuit Court has jurisdiction in all felony cases (crimes punishable by death or imprisonment in the state prison) and all misdemeanors where the defendant has also been charged with a felony. The Circuit Court in the 11th Judicial Circuit (Dade County) has a Criminal Division to which twelve judges are assigned.

The State Attorney is the prosecuting officer in all trial courts but municipalities may appoint officials to prosecute violations of their ordinances. The State Attorney's Office in Dade County employed 99 Assistant State Attorneys at the time of this study. Since 1974 the team of attorneys who present the case at the preliminary hearing also handle the case at trial, which has the advantage of encouraging them to review the cases carefully and screen out those that are inappropriate for felony prosecution.

The Public Defender is responsible for representing indigents. Assistant Public Defenders are assigned to specific courtrooms for extended periods of time. The Dade County Defender's Office had a staff of 57 attorneys at the time of this study.

---

[3] In multiple-defendant cases, one defendant was randomly selected to represent the case.

In the Dade County Circuit Court it takes about 30 days to process a felony case from arrest to arraignment. Approximately 15 days after arrest a nonadversarial preliminary hearing is held in County Court. The prosecutor presents the State's case and the defendant is bound over for trial if the judge finds probable cause. If the defendant indicates at the preliminary hearing that he wishes to plead guilty a public defender is appointed to represent him.

Discussions with attorneys and judges suggest that about 25 percent of felony cases are settled prior to arraignment. Defendants are normally arraigned on a felony information between 7 and 14 days after the preliminary hearing, depending on whether the defendant is in custody. If a public defender is necessary, the appointment is made no later than the time of arraignment. A local rule, normally invoked by oral motion at arraignment, provides for liberal discovery.

At arraignment the case is usually set for trial in 30 to 60 days. Many judges hold a "sounding" conference one week before the scheduled trial. The judges use the conference, which prosecutor and defense counsel attend, for a variety of purposes: most commonly to determine whether both parties are ready for trial, but also to explore the possibilities of a settlement, and even to urge the parties toward it. By providing a formal structure for judicial participation in plea discussions, this meeting is an antecedent to the pretrial settlement conference.

B. Experimental intervention

Discussions with Dade County officials led to the development of an agreement specifying the conference procedure in the context of the policies and practices of that jurisdiction. In order to minimize administrative problems we decided to use only those cases that survived arraignment. Project staff randomly selected the test cases from each test judge's arraignment calendar and notified the judge of the cases selected. At arraignment the judge informed prosecution and defense that the case had been selected and scheduled the settlement conference at a time that allowed for completion of pretrial motions and discovery. The defense attorney

was required to notify the prosecutor three court days in advance of the scheduled conference if he wished the conference to be held. Victims and police officers were invited by the prosecutor to attend the conference unless their eyewitness identification of the defendant was a crucial element in the case. The victims were neither subpoenaed nor compensated. The defendant could decide to attend with counsel, not to attend but to be represented by counsel, or fail to confirm the conference, thus canceling it.

At the conference the judge would indicate the purpose of the meeting and state that, for purposes of the discussion, the defendant's guilt of the charges would be assumed. The explicit statement of this assumption was necessary to make it clear that the defendant was not admitting guilt by participating in the discussion. The judge also advised the defendant that he was not required to make any statement supporting that assumption and could terminate the conference at any time. The judge advised the defense that no statement made at the conference could be used in a subsequent trial if settlement efforts failed. The conference discussed whatever issues the parties felt might contribute to a settlement. If a proposed settlement was reached between prosecutor and defense counsel, the judge had to decide whether it was appropriate, given the interests of all the parties and society. The defense counsel could consult with his client and report back later. If a settlement was reached and approved by the judge, the defendant entered a plea in open court. If no settlement was reached, the case was set for trial. A second conference could be held on the day of the trial, if necessary.

IV. FINDINGS
A. Dispositions

A conference date was scheduled for 378 cases and was held in 287 (76 percent);[4] of these, 26 percent were settled and another 46

---

[4]Cancellations were caused by scheduling problems, the timing of the session within the disposition process, and the likelihood of trial. There was some evidence that conferences involving more serious offenses were more likely to be canceled.

percent were tentatively settled.[5] In the remaining 28 percent the parties could not agree even in principle; slightly more than half of these were likely to go to trial, according to one or more participants; the remainder were continued for further discussions (although a second conference was scheduled only in one). In the 212 cases that did not reach a settlement, roughly 60 percent needed only to review the tentative settlement. For example, the defense counsel might say: "Three years probation makes sense to me but I will have to talk to my client. I'll be back and give you an answer." In one-third of these cases, timing problems were cited as the reason for failure to settle: additional motions to be filed, incomplete discovery, or other pending charges. Certainly the setting of a conference date reduces flexibility in scheduling. Nevertheless, judges and attorneys maintained that the conference did not interfere with pretrial preparation. In summary, the sessions were able to accomplish the task of working out a proposed settlement.

B. Attendance

A judge attended every conference. In 83 percent one or more lay parties was present. Most often, then, negotiations involved four or more participants rather than just the two attorneys. This reduced the cost of communicating information between judge and counsel and between professionals and nonprofessionals. Frequency of participation varied by role: defendants attended 67 percent of the conferences, police 28 percent, and victims 32 percent of those involving a crime against a victim. Attendance cannot be explained by the type of offense, personal characteristics, prior experiences with the courts, or general attitudes toward the criminal justice system.[6]

By far the most frequent reason given by those who did not attend was that they had not been notified; others said they were notified but told the conference would not take place. Although self-reports are difficult to interpret, the site director, attorneys, and the secretaries who handled the notification all confirmed that there were problems. Some were organizational: the task requires a level of persistence and imagination that may not be applied given the other duties of the secretarial staff. Often the information was inadequate: insufficient records, changes of address, lack of phone service, and absence from home during working hours made notification difficult.[7] Further, attendance was neither compulsory nor compensated. Some judges and attorney suggested that the low rates of attendance by victims and police indicated their lack of interest. Our findings show that notification problems must also be considered.

C. Conference

The following is a paraphrase of a pretrial settlement conference, drawn from observations made by one of the research staff.

Parties present: Judge, Assistant State Attorney, Assistant Public Defender, Defendant, and Victim

Judge: What is this case about?

A.S.A.: This is a larceny. The defendant stole television sets from a loading dock.

Judge: What about a prior record?

A.S.A.: Drugs and larceny.

Judge: Are you the victim?

Victim: Yes.

Judge: What did you lose?

Victim: Two TV's.

Judge: How old are you?

Defendant: Twenty-four.

Judge: Are you married?

Defendant: No.

Judge: Do you have a job?

Defendant: I'm a busboy.

Judge: What should happen in this case?

A.S.A.: I'd like to see two years.

Judge: What about you?

A.P.D.: He has a drug problem and has been in a treatment program. If he goes to prison it will hurt his recovery and he will lose his job. I'd recommend jail and probation.

---

[5]Tentative settlement is defined as a disposition to which the parties agreed but which one or more was unwilling to accept as binding at that time.

[6]Nevertheless, police who attended had a slightly more favorable attitude toward plea bargaining.

---

[7]Even after the research site director became somewhat more active overseeing the level of secretarial effort the attendance rates did not change substantially.

Judge: Do you have a drug problem?

Defendant: I used to; not any more.

Judge: I'll give one year and some probation with treatment and restitution. He has done this before and I have to protect society.

Judge: Do you have anything to say?

Victim: It's O.K. with me.

Judge: Can you come back this afternoon at the sounding?

A.P.D.: I'll have to consult with my client. Thanks for your time.

Time elapsed: 8 minutes

Case status: tentative agreement on some incarceration and probation.

Final disposition of the case: a guilty plea was entered the day of the conference. The sentence was 364 days in the county jail and 3 years probation with restitution; recommend drug treatment.

Virtually all conferences took place in the judge's chambers, with the judge wearing a business suit rather than judicial robes. The protocol and atmosphere were those of a business conference rather than a judicial proceeding. The conferences were generally short and to the point. One of our concerns was the amount of the time the conference might add to the disposition of cases but sessions averaged approximately ten minutes and only five percent took more than twenty minutes. Since the professional participants probably would otherwise engage in sequential bilateral discussions by phone or in person, the conference procedure did not substantially increase the time they devoted to case disposition.

The conference paraphrased above illustrates the type and quantity of information presented.[8] Virtually all conferences covered the facts of the case (96 percent), prior record (94 percent), and disposition recommendations (93 percent), however briefly. Roughly two-thirds dealt with the personal background of the victim or defendant. Office policy, statutory requirements, or the likely consequences of going to trial were rarely mentioned. Discussion was very superficial. The example presented above describes the crime by means of a mere statutory label and the object stolen. The assumption of guilt necessary to the conference may account for some of the lack of attention to factual detail; the danger of revealing one's case in the event of a trial was a further constraint. Disposition was also resolved expeditiously. Although the parties represented opposed interests, their recommendations generally were not widely divergent and were presented with little explanation. Contrary to the expectations of some observers the victims did not demand the maximum authorized punishment. Usually the victim was supportive of the disposition proposed by the attorneys and the judge.[9]

The judge appeared to play a pivotal role in the conference, typically controlling the discussion. In the example above, the judge initiated new subjects by asking questions: what were the facts, priors, defendant background, and recommendations? On average, the judge accounted for more than half of all subject changes. Further, it was the judge who most often made the recommendation that formed the basis for settlement. Within these parameters, there were differences among judges. One took an active role in developing consensus decisions. Another, after eliciting information, would announce the sentence without seeking the advice of any of the professional parties although he did consult with the lay participants. The third spent more time in establishing the factual basis for the decision.

The lay participants, by and large, provided information. The police took the most active part, particularly in giving facts of the case; the defendant said the least. Overall, 88 percent of the police but only 25 percent of the victims and 19 percent of the defendants made more than five comments during the course of the entire session. Although police and victim often gave recommendations, only a third of the defendants did so. As illustrated above, most recommendations were made at the request of the judge and amounted to an expression of approval of or acquiescence in the agreement achieved by the professional parties.

The professional participants reached differ-

---

[8]It is noteworthy that the participants were not introduced.

[9]Whether this resulted from prior consultation with the prosecutor we do not know.

ent conclusions about the utility of the information the lay parties provided. At the beginning of the project the three judges and many of the attorneys spoke optimistically about the value of this new resource. Toward the end of the project, two of the three judges concluded that the information was often either unnecessary or could be obtained elsewhere. The assumption that the defendant was guilty and the extensive experience of the professionals produced a very narrow definition of relevance that made the contribution of lay participants marginal.[10] The mere fact that lay parties participated in the conference without adding "relevant" information may have served to create the impression in the professionals that the lay parties rarely had anything to contribute.

In summary, most of the conferences ended with agreement on at least the outlines of a settlement. The process took an average of ten minutes. Most sessions had at least four participants: the judge, two attorneys, and one lay member. As a result, the structure of decision-making was generally different from the traditional mode of plea negotiation in criminal cases. The judge played the central role in the process by directing the information flow and determining sentence. Although the presence of lay participants changed the structure, their rate of attendance was lower than some professionals had hoped it might be, perhaps because of notification problems. Their role was limited to providing information requested by the professionals.

D. Effects of the conference on processing costs[11]

We expected that the conference procedure would reduce the time a case remained open. Joint negotiation by all of the parties in place of more traditional sequential series of discussions seemed likely to facilitate the settlement of cases. To test this we compared the number of

days from arraignment to disposition for the test and comparison judges for pretreatment, test, and control groups of cases. Tests were run for each courtroom among the three treatment conditions and between pairs of treatment conditions in order to pinpoint the location of differences as precisely as possible. Prior to the implementation of the conference procedure the average time from arraignment to disposition was 126 days, varying from 75 days to 208 days, among the three test judges. The conference procedure reduced the time to disposition in all three courtrooms by roughly three weeks. No similar reduction occurred in the cases handled by the comparison judges so the finding cannot be explained by some change in the court system.

In the total sample, approximately 10 percent of the cases went to trial and almost one-quarter were dismissed without adjudication. Although there is some evidence that the likelihood of trial or dismissal may have entered the decision to convene the conference, the overall distribution of trials, dismissals, and settlements was not changed by introduction of the conference.

Based on interviews with defendants, victims, and police we found that their participation in the conference did not affect the average number of contacts between lay and professional actors or the number of issues they discussed. However, those who attended the conference met more professionals and discussed more issues than those who did not.

An analysis of the costs of the conference involves several dimensions. We have already mentioned that the brevity of the session suggests a net savings. If notification of lay participants is to be improved and higher attendance achieved, more money will have to be spent for support staff. The accelerated disposition of cases and the brevity of the conference sessions appear to have several causes. First, the conference may have encouraged attorneys to review their cases carefully. The relative formality of the scheduling (it took place before a judge and then appeared on the court calendar) may make the attorneys less inclined to seek postponements. The presence of the lay participants

---

[10]When interviewed after the conclusion of the project, the judges could think of no information that was essential but *not* brought out at the conference.

[11]For a full presentation of our findings, see Kerstetter and Heinz (1979:chs. 7-9).

may have facilitated communication by reducing the need for subsequent consultation to review the proposed disposition. Nevertheless, the processing costs were not fundamentally altered: settlements did not increase nor were trials more attractive (for example, because the conference provided more information about the likely sentence following conviction at trial).

E. Effects of the conference on case dispositions

Defendants were found not guilty in 5 percent of the entire sample of closed cases. That figure was not significantly affected by the use of the conference. Almost half (46 percent) of those found guilty were incarcerated. The average sentence was 2.1 years.[12] We used a modification of the Diamond-Zeisel (1975:121) sentence severity scale (which incorporates fines, probation, and incarceration into a single score) to make comparisons among the treatment conditions and courtrooms. We found signficant differences among the courtrooms but little change that could be attributed to the use of the conference. Two judges modified their sentencing patterns (one imposed less severe sentences and the other ordered restitution more frequently) but the changes appear to be due primarily to changes over time since the control cases showed similar changes. The third judge did not change his basic sentencing pattern. The changes in sentencing may be due to spillover effects of the conference on the whole calendar.

Although the procedure did not contain an explicit sentencing philosophy, expanding the number of roles and reducing information costs might be expected to alter outcomes. Project findings did not support that expectation. Individual cases may have been affected by the conference but its introduction did not significantly change the pattern of adjudication or sentencing. Our review of the negotiation process suggested that it had not been significantly altered by the use of the conference. The absence of a significant change in either outcomes or sentences supports that conclusion.

F. Effects of the conference on lay attitudes

We expected a change in the attitudes and perceptions of defendants, victims, and police officers as a result of their participation in the conference: for instance, more knowledge about and more positive attitudes toward the specific disposition with which they were concerned. We tested these expectations by means of interview data with defendants, victims, and police, comparing those who did and did not attend for the effect of conference participation upon individuals and pretreatment and post-treatment cases for the systemic effects of the intervention.[13]

We were interested in whether the central actors in the criminal process knew the disposition of their cases. As expected, only two of the 297 defendants interviewed reported they did not know the outcome of their cases but half of the victims and one-third of the police reported ignorance. Since victim and police are not necessary to the closing of a case, some special effort by the courts would have been required to inform them unless they happened to be present at the disposition.

Introduction of the conference into the system did not significantly increase the level of knowledge of either victims or police.[14] Nevertheless, both the victims and the police who reported attending the conference were much more likely to feel they knew the disposition than those who did not.

The majority of each category of lay participants were generally positive in their evaluation of the attention given their cases by the

---

[12]After excluding suspended sentences and sentences that ran concurrently with those in earlier cases, the average was 1.7 years.

[13]The research design, with its random assignment of cases to test and control conditions, allows inferences about systemic efforts. Since attendance was not controlled in a similar manner, inferences about individual differences are more tenuous since those who attend may vary systematically from those who do not. However, they did not differ significantly in social and economic background and general attitudes toward the criminal justice system.

[14]Defendants were not included because virtually all knew the disposition.

judge and/or attorney. Defendants were the least satisfied and police the most, which is surprising given the common attitude among police that they are excluded from the subsequent processing of the arrests they make and that the judge is unsympathetic to their perspective.[15] The comparisons among respondents in the different treatment groups showed no significant treatment effects for defendants and police, but victims in the test category were somewhat more satisfied with the processing of their cases. Defendants and victims who attended a conference did not differ from those who did not, but police who attended were more satisfied.

All three categories of lay participants indicated general satisfaction with the disposition of their cases. Since they could be expected to have quite different perspectives, it is interesting to note the similarity in the overall ratings.[16] Among the defendants and victims there was no difference between test and control groups or between those who attended a conference and those who did not. Nevertheless, police who attended a session were more positive about the disposition and there was some evidence that police in the test group were more positive than those in the control.[17]

A major concern about judicial involvement in plea negotiations is that the role of the judge is inherently coercive. We explored this concern by comparing responses on whether defendants plead guilty because of fear of a more severe sentence if they go to trial. We found that 60 percent of the defendants interviewed felt that the possibility of a more severe sentence following a trial was an important or critical factor in their decision to plead.[18] Comparisons between test and control groups and between those who did and did not attend showed no differences in the salience of the issue that could be attributed to the use of the conference. Thus, concern about the inherent coerciveness of judicial participation is not supported by this study.

To argue that the conference procedure made an impact on attitudes and perceptions, consistent and significant differences need to be found. Out of fifteen sets of tests for treatment effects upon defendants, victims, and police, only one (or possibly two) showed significant differences. It therefore seems clear that the conference procedure did not substantially change the overall judicial environment. Out of the fifteen sets of tests for the effect of attendance, nine showed significant differences. These findings pose some difficult problems of interpretation. One must first come to grips with the reason for attendance. Perhaps those who attended were systematically different from those who did not—more satisfied with the courts, endowed with a greater sense of civic duty or from a higher socioeconomic stratum. On that basis one would interpret differences related to attendance as evidence of pre-existing differences. But our data show no significant difference in these characteristics between those who did and did not attend. Further, those in the test group who did not attend and those in the control group were similar in their degree of satisfaction and extent of knowledge but both differed from those who attended the conference. Because notification was not perfect and some conferences were canceled, we are inclined to view differences related to attendance as suggestive of effects on individuals, if not on the court system as a whole. The findings are consistent with the anticipated effects of making the negotiation procedures more open: participants generally had more information and

---

[15]We should note that the police and victims may come from what may be the more satisfied end of a continuum of victims and police, since they represent only cases that survived arraignment. The survival of these cases could be viewed by victims and police as a validation of their perceptions about the significance of the criminal event, with the result that they would be more disposed to view the court processing as a success.

[16]We are not suggesting that the three parties agreed in any given case but only that the overall pattern is similar. Further, these figures do not reflect the relationship between satisfaction and sentence. We are not saying that defendants who were imprisoned were as satisfied as those acquitted. We only measured the satisfaction of those who knew the disposition.

[17]Differences between test and control were statistically significant for one of the three judges.

---

[18]Whether there really is such a sentencing differential is a separate question, see Rhodes (1978).

were more satisfied with their treatment, but the gains were modest.

V. CONCLUSION

The pretrial settlement conference in Dade County, Florida, created a more open, formal arena for plea negotiations. The procedure increased the number of participants, including nonprofessionals, and thereby lowered information costs. Information needs were quite low. The sessions were brief, lasting an average of ten minutes. At the conclusion of the conference three-quarters of the cases had reached either a settlement or the outlines of a settlement.

The conference assumed the characteristics of an administrative proceeding whose goal was to fit the case into a category and then apply existing legal rules. Such a procedure appears appropriate for most criminal cases, where the issues in dispute are minimal. It also helped to identify the "difficult" cases (those that were most serious or where guilt was disputed) so that alternative procedures could be followed, such as further discovery and trial. This is facilitated by the presence of the disputing parties. For example, one defendant brought in a surprise witness which resulted in a continuance for further discovery.

The greatest impact of the conference procedure was to shorten the length of time it took to close cases. Furthermore, our data suggest that the conference certainly did not increase and may actually have decreased the total time invested by the court system. The conference did not cause significant changes in the proportion of litigated or settled cases or in the proportion of defendants found guilty, but there was some evidence that the imposition of restitution and incarceration was modified.

It seems unlikely that the conference procedure could change the environment in which the courts operate because lay attendance was so low. Nevertheless, the impact on individual police and victims who did attend was not insignificant.

The conference reduced the decision costs by achieving savings in time and by lowering the cost of obtaining information. These reductions benefit professionals (judge and attorneys) and lay parties as well, to the extent that processing costs concern all citizens. Further, because speedy dispositions are beneficial to innocent defendants, victims, and police, the conference procedure also enhances justice.

REFERENCES

Alschuler, Albert W. (1976) "The Trial Judge's Role in Plea Bargaining, Part I," 76 *Columbia Law Review* 1059.

American Bar Association: Project on Minimum Standards for Criminal Justice, Advisory Committee on the Criminal Trial (1967) *Standards Relating to Pleas of Guilty.* Chicago: American Bar Association.

American Judicature Society (1973) *Criminal Justice in Dade County: A Preliminary Survey,* vol. 3. Chicago: American Judicature Society.

Campbell, Donald T. and Julian C. Stanley (1963) *Experimental and Quasi-Experimental Designs for Research.* Chicago: Rand McNally.

Diamond, Shari and Hans Zeisel (1975) "Sentencing Councils: A Study of Sentence Disparity and Its Reuction," 43 *University of Chicago Law Review* 109.

DuBow, Fredric L. and Theodore M. Becker (1976) "Patterns of Victim Advocacy," in W. F. McDonald (ed.) *Criminal Justice and the Victim.* Beverly Hills: Sage Publications.

Kerstetter, Wayne A. and Anne M. Heinz (1979) *Pretrial Settlement Conference: An Evaluation.* Washington, D.C.: Government Printing Office.

McCall, George J. (1975) *Observing the Law: Applications of Field Methods to the Study of the Criminal Justice System.* Washington, D.C.: Government Printing Office.

Morris, Norval (1974) *The Future of Imprisonment.* Chicago: University of Chicago Press.

Rhodes, William (1978) *Plea Bargaining: Who Gains? Who Loses?* (PROMIS Research Project No. 14, Final Draft). Washington, D.C.: Institute for Law and Social Research.

Rosett, Arthur I. and Donald R. Cressey (1976) *Justice by Consent: Plea Bargains in the American Courthouse.* Philadelphia: Lippincott.

U.S. National Advisory Commission on Criminal Justice Standards and Goals (1973) *Courts.* Washington, D.C.: Government Printing Office.

Weiss, Carol H. (1972) *Evaluation Research: Methods for Assessing Program Effectiveness.* Englewood Cliffs, N.J.: Prentice-Hall.

Yale Law Journal (1972) "Comment: Restructuring the Plea Bargain," 82 *Yale Law Journal* 286.

B □ *The use of restitution*

BURT GALAWAY

The idea that the offender should make restitution as part of the penalty for wrongdoing was entrenched in primitive law systems.[1] Its historical de-emphasis, most scholars suggest, was a consequence of the development of strong centralized authority in England following the Norman invasion, the separation of criminal and civil law, and the state's superseding interest in the outcome of criminal proceedings.[2]

While weakened, the notion of restitution as a sanction for criminal wrongdoing was never entirely lost. Its use was advocated by Sir Thomas More, Jeremy Bentham, Herbert Spencer, Raffaele Garofalo, Enrico Ferri, and others.[3] More recent advocates include Giorgio del Vecchio, Stephen Schafer, Albert Eglash, Kathleen Smith, and Burt Galaway and Joe Hudson.[4] It has received limited attention in the past fifty years in the ideology of criminal justice and correction (at least as expressed in published

form), but its use as a probation condition has been authorized in statutes and has been reflected in the practice of courts ordering restitution as a condition of probation. Unfortunately the extent of this practice is not known, its rationale is not clearly articulated, and there appears to be little interest among correctional practitioners in considering its impact or examining its role in criminal justice.

Recent policy statements may indicate some shift in thinking. The National Advisory Commission's standard on "sentencing the nondangerous offender" states that the offender should not be imprisoned, if, among other favorable circumstances, he "has made or will make restitution . . . to the victim . . . for the damage or injury . . .,"[5] and it recommends that a fine not be imposed when it would interfere with the offender's ability to make restitution.[6] The second edition of the Model Sentencing Act explicitly

Reprinted, with permission of the National Council on Crime and Delinquency, from Burt Galaway, "The Use of Restitution," *Crime and Delinquency,* January 1977, pp. 57-67.

1. See, for example, Stephen Schafer, *The Victim and His Criminal* (New York: Random House, 1968), pp. 7-38; Richard E. Laster, "Criminal Restitution: A Survey of Its Past History and an Analysis of Its Present Usefulness," *University of Richmond Law Review,* Fall 1970, pp. 71-98, also in Joe Hudson and Burt Galaway, eds., *Considering the Victim: Readings in Restitution and Victim Compensation* (Springfield, Ill.: Charles C Thomas, 1975), pp. 19-28, 311-31; E. Adamson Hoebel, *The Law of Primitive Man* (Cambridge, Mass.: Harvard University Press, 1954).

2. See especially, Schafer, *op. cit. supra* note 1, and Laster, *supra* note 1.

3. Thomas More, *Utopia* [1516] (J. C. Collins ed., 1904), pp. 23-24; Jeremy Bentham, "Political Remedies for the Evil of Offenses" [1838], in Hudson and Galaway, *op. cit. supra* note 1, pp. 29-42; Herbert Spencer, "Prison Ethics" [1892], in Hudson and Galaway, *op. cit. supra* note 1, pp. 71-84; Raffaele Garofalo, "Enforced Reparation as a Substitute for Imprisonment" [1914], in Hudson and Galaway, *op. cit. supra* note 1, pp. 43-53; Enrico Ferri, *Criminal Sociology* (Boston: Little, Brown, 1917), pp. 498-520.

4. Giorgio del Vecchio, "The Problem of Penal Justice," in Hudson and Galaway, *op. cit. supra* note 1, pp. 85-101; Stephen Schafer, *Compensation and Restitution to Victims of Crime* (Montclair, N.J.: Patterson Smith, 1970); Albert Eglash, "Creative Restitution: A Broader Meaning for an Old Term," in Hudson and Galaway, *op. cit. supra* note 1, pp. 284-90; Albert Eglash, "Creative Restitution: Some Suggestions for Prison Rehabilitation Programs," *American Journal of Correction,* November-December 1958, pp. 20-22, 34; Paul Keve and Albert Eglash, "Payments on a 'Debt to Society,'" *NPPA News,* September 1957, pp. 1-2; Kathleen Smith, *A Cure for Crime: The Case for the Self-Determinate Prison Sentence* (London: Duckworth, 1965); Burt Galaway and Joe Hudson, "Restitution and Rehabilitation: Some Central Issues," *Crime and Delinquency,* October 1972, pp. 403-10; Burt Galaway and Joe Hudson, "Sin, Sickness, Restitution— Toward a Reconciliative Correctional Model," in Hudson and Galaway, *op. cit. supra* note 1, pp. 59-70.

5. National Advisory Commission on Criminal Justice Standards and Goals, *Corrections* (Washington, D.C.: U.S. Govt. Printing Office, 1973), Standard 5.2, p. 151.

6. *Id.,* Standard 5.5, p. 162.

recognizes restitution as a sanction to be used alone or in conjunction with other sanctions.[7] Restitution is recognized in standards enunciated by the American Bar Association[8] and was explicitly recommended as an alternative to imprisonment by the 1972 Annual Chief Justice Earl Warren Conference on Advocacy in the United States.[9] The Canadian Law Reform Commission is advocating use of restitution and negotiated settlements as methods for diverting offenders from the criminal justice system.[10]

In addition to these policy statements, a few projects have been developed in the 1970's which involve the explicit use of restitution.

The purpose of this paper is twofold: (1) to review contemporary examples of the use of restitution in pretrial diversionary programs, as a condition of probation, and as part of community-based, residential correctional programs which allegedly provide an alternative to the imprisonment of offenders; (2) to articulate a series of issues which emanate from the use of restitution. The issues relate to the lack of specificity of the concept of restitution, the purpose of restitution, the relation of restitution to other criminal justice sanctions, and the role of the victim in restitution programs.

Restitution is defined to mean a requirement, either imposed by agents of the criminal justice system or undertaken voluntarily by the wrongdoer but with the consent of the criminal justice system, by which the offender engages in acts designed to make reparation for the harm resulting from the criminal offense. This definition has three central components: action by the offender which may be either voluntary or co-

erced, knowledge and consent of agents of the criminal justice system, and the repairing of damages.

CONTEMPORARY APPLICATIONS

Restitution is applied in pretrial diversion programs, as a condition of probation, and as a part of the program of community correction centers established to provide an alternative to traditional imprisonment.

Pretrial diversion

While there is little published material, restitution has quite likely been used regularly and informally by police and prosecutors as a pretrial diversionary tactic. Permitting youth to return stolen merchandise or to pay for damage done as a result of vandalism exemplifies this use of restitution. Police and prosecutors may permit check offenders to make good in lieu of prosecution. Unfortunately, as is true of other early diversionary practices, this use of official discretion is informal, out of the public scrutiny, and usually not reported or recorded in any orderly way. An immediate need is information on the nature of restitution requirements imposed as a part of traditional, informal diversion practices.

Restitution components may also be built into new, structured pretrial diversion programs. Both Project de Novo in Minneapolis and Project Remand in St. Paul divert arrested juvenile, misdemeanor, and felony defendants into a work evaluation, training, and job placement program. In these projects restitution is a frequent condition of diversion, especially for property offenders.[11]

In Tucson, Ariz., the Pima County Attorney's Office administers an Adult Diversion Project for nonserious, first-time defendants who volunteer for the project and whose participation is approved by the victim, the arresting officers, and the prosecutor. If all approve, the victim and the offender meet in face-to-face confrontation to define the restitution obligations which are included along with other treatment obliga-

7. Council of Judges, National Council on Crime and Delinquency, "Model Sentencing Act" (2nd ed.), *Crime and Delinquency,* October 1972, § 9, p. 357, and commentary, pp. 358-59.

8. Herbert S. Miller, "The American Bar Association Looks at Probation," *Federal Probation,* December 1970, pp. 3-9.

9. Annual Chief Justice Earl Warren Conference on Advocacy in the United States, *A Program for Prison Reform* (Cambridge, Mass.: Roscoe Pound-American Trial Lawyers Foundation, 1972), p. 11.

10. Law Reform Commission of Canada, Working Paper No. 3: *The Principles of Sentencing and Dispositions,* pp. 7-10; Working Papers 5 & 6: *Restitution and Compensation; Fines,* pp. 5-15 (Ottawa: Information Canada, 1974).

11. Conversations with William Henschel, of Operation de Novo, and Kathryn Bleecker, of Project Remand.

tions that the defendant undertakes as a condition of diversion.[12]

The Community Youth Responsibility Program (CYRP) in East Palo Alto, Calif., provides services to juveniles as an alternative to juvenile court referral. Cases are reviewed by a Community Panel, consisting of neighborhood juveniles and adults, which may require the youth to make restitution to the victim or perform community services. While the orders do not carry legal authority, failure to comply creates the possibility of referral back to the court.[13]

Restitution is also one of the settlement procedures used by the Citizen Dispute Settlement Centers of the American Arbitration Association[14] and the Night Prosecutor Program in Columbus, Ohio.[15] Both of these programs were established to develop dispute-settlement procedures by means other than use of the criminal justice system and to provide noncriminal justice alternatives for handling private criminal complaints. Both involve efforts to bring the victim and the offender together and may utilize some form of restitution as a part of the settlement.

Probation condition

Statutes in several states permit courts to order payment of restitution as a probation condition, and, in other jurisdictions, courts are making use of this sanction as a part of their general power to establish reasonable probation conditions. There is some case law defining reasonableness of restitution and the beginning of judicial guidelines for courts in utilizing this

sanction.[16] Some courts have also been experimenting with use of community service requirements, especially for juvenile and misdemeanant offenders. Unfortunately there is no systematic reporting of these experiences or assessment of the extent of the practices. A research project is presently under way in Minnesota to determine the extent to which restitution has been used and to assess the views of judges, probation officers, offenders, and victims concerning the appropriateness of restitution requirements as a probation condition.[17]

In the Victims Assistance Program of the Pennington County (S. Dak.) Juvenile Court, restitution and work details are perceived as "therapeutic elements in court supervision" and are incorporated into court orders for juvenile probation.[18]

The West German code offers an interesting alternative for dealing with juvenile and young adult offenders. Judges may impose "corrective measures" on juvenile offenders for whom incarceration is thought unnecessary. Corrective measures may consist of a reprimand, imposition of particular requirements, or use of short-term (not to exceed one month), week-end, or intermittent detention. The particular requirements include making good the damage done, personally apologizing to the person injured, or making a financial contribution toward some useful public establishment. The young person can be required to contribute to a useful public establishment only to deprive him of the proceeds of his offense and only if the payment comes out of his own resources. In addition to corrective measures West German courts may make use of educational-welfare measures or youth imprisonment as sanctions for juvenile delinquency or young adult offenses. The

12. Herbert Edelhertz, *Restitutive Justice: A General Survey and Analysis* (Seattle, Wash.: Battelle Human Affairs Research Centers, 1975), pp. 57-59.

13. *Id.*, pp. 53-55.

14. Janet Kole, "Arbitration as an Alternative to the Criminal Warrant," *Judicature*, February 1973, pp. 295-97; Carl A. Eklund, "The Problem of Overcriminalizing Human Conflict: A Civil Alternative," paper presented to the American Society of Criminology Annual Meeting, Chicago, November 1974.

15. John W. Palmer, "Pre-Arrest Diversion," *Crime and Delinquency*, April 1975; U.S. Dept. of Justice, Law Enforcement Assistance Administration, *An Exemplary Project: Citizen Dispute Settlement* (Washington, D.C.: U.S. Govt. Printing Office, 1974).

16. See for example, William P. Jacobson, "Use of Restitution in the Criminal Process: People v. Miller," *UCLA Law Review*, 1969, pp. 456-75; Sol Rubin, *Law of Criminal Correction*, 2nd ed. (St. Paul, Minn.: West, 1973), pp. 229-32.

17. Minnesota Department of Corrections, "The Assessment of Restitution in the Minnesota Probation Services," Minnesota Governor's Commission on Crime Prevention and Control.

18. Edelhertz, *op. cit. supra* note 12, pp. 55-57.

money payment is the primary particular requirement imposed.[19]

Under provisions of the Criminal Justice Act of 1972, judges in Great Britain are permitted, in the instance of adult offenders (predominantly in the 18-to-25 age range), to order 40 to 240 hours of unpaid community service work in lieu of imprisonment. The community service order can be issued only with the consent of the offender, after a determination that suitable opportunities exist for the work and after consideration of the probation officer's report. The order must be carried out within one year and the work must be done in the offender's spare time.[20] Additionally, the Community Services Volunteers program in Great Britain has been providing opportunities for delinquent youth (both those residing in Borstals and those in after-care programs) to engage in voluntary community service activities which are beneficial to both the delinquent and the community.[21]

In 1973 Iowa legislation established a public policy of restitution as a condition of probation for all suspended or deferred sentences. Probation officers are expected to prepare and present restitution plans; payments are to be ordered to the extent of the offender's ability to make restitution.[22] Generally restitution payments are made to the clerk of the court, who forwards them to the victim to minimize the opportunity for direct victim-offender contact. The Restitution in Probation Experiment (RIPE), an LEAA-funded project in the Des Moines area, is building upon this policy by altering the practice of discouraging victim-offender contacts and bringing together the victim, the offender, and the probation officer to negotiate a restitution agreement, which is then presented to the court for consideration. The Iowa project introduces the variable of offender-victim communication into an existing restitution program.[23]

Residential community-correction center

Halfway houses, group homes, and other residential community correction facilities provide an additional setting for restitution. The Minnesota Restitution Center, established in 1972, is probably the prototype of this type of programing.[24] The Center receives adult male property offenders who have been admitted to the Minnesota State Prison and have served four months of their prison sentence. While in prison the offender, with the assistance of a staff member of the Restitution Center, meets with his victim face-to-face to develop a restitution agreement. After the agreement is prepared and the parole board concurs, the offender is released on parole to the Minnesota Restitution Center, where he lives, secures employment, and fulfills the terms of the restitution agreement. The offender resident may receive additional services, including mandatory group therapy, supervision in a community correction center, and assistance with securing employment. Most of the restitution agreements have involved a monetary exchange between the offender and the victim; in situations where the victim could not be located, was unwilling to participate, or had not suffered damage, restitution in the form of community service or a contribution to some community agency has been used. The trend has been away from community service and toward payment of money to a com-

---

19. Unfortunately data provided by the West German Ministry of Justice do not indicate what proportion of money payments went to the actual victims of crime and what proportion went to useful public establishments. Federal Republic of Germany, Ministry of Justice, "The Treatment of Young Offenders in the Federal Republic of Germany" (mimeo. in English; n.d.).

20. Howard Standish Bergman, "Community Service in England: An Alternative to Custodial Sentence," *Federal Probation*, March 1975, pp. 42-46.

21. Clementine, L. Kaufman, "Community Service Volunteers: A British Approach to Delinquency Prevention," *Federal Probation*, December 1973, pp. 35-41.

22. Iowa Senate File 26, 65th General Assembly (1973).

23. Polk County (Iowa) Board of Supervisors, "Restitution in Probation Experiment," grant application submitted to the Kansas City Regional Office of the Law Enforcement Assistance Administration, 1974.

24. Joe Hudson and Burt Galaway, "Undoing the Wrong," *Social Work*, May 1974, pp. 313-18; Burt Galaway and Joe Hudson, "Issues in the Correctional Implementation of Restitution to Victims of Crime," in Hudson and Galaway, *op. cit. supra* note 1, pp. 351-60.

munity organization as the preferred form of symbolic restitution.

Georgia has established four restitution shelters based partially on the Minnesota model. Generally men referred to these shelters come solely from courts and are on probation; in each case a court has ordered restitution as a probation condition. The offender has been ordered to live in the restitution shelter, secure and maintain work, and complete the court-ordered restitution. Georgia's program operates much like work-release shelters: the resident's salary checks are turned over to the shelter business manager, who deducts an appropriate amount for room and board, family support, a living-expenses allowance, and restitution. Victim-offender contacts are not a part of the program; the business manager mails the court-ordered restitution payment to the victim.[25]

ISSUES

Experiences to date with restitution in the criminal justice system suggest a series of issues that require clarification if it is to be more systematically utilized as a correctional tool. The issues can be grouped into four categories: de-

---

25. Georgia Department of Corrections and Offender Rehabilitation, "L.E.A.A. National Scope Project for Citizen Action," application for grant to the United States Department of Justice, Law Enforcement Assistance Administration, June 5, 1974. Personal interviews with Bill Read, Manager, and James H. Deal, Director, Rome Restitution Shelter, Georgia Department of Offender Rehabilitation, April 1975.

veloping a classification of restitution, specifying the purpose of restitution, clarifying the relationship of restitution to other criminal sanctions, and defining the role which victims might play in a restitution program.

Differing types

Even a cursory observation of existing programs reveals that the term *restitution* is applied to differing phenomena; sometimes adjectives are added, making references to *monetary* restitution, *symbolic* restitution, *community service* restitution, *moral* restitution, *creative* restitution, etc. An immediate need is the development of a conceptual framework that clearly specifies and defines different types of restitution.

A simple typology of restitution (see Figure 1) can be developed by using two variables: (1) the offender makes restitution in money or service and (2) the recipient of the restitution is the actual victim or some substitute victim. Four types of restitution can be identified by using these two variables:

Type I: Monetary-victim restitution refers to payment of money by the offender to the actual victim of the crime. This is probably the most common definition and actual use of restitution.

Type II: Monetary-community restitution involves the payment of money by the offender to some "substitute victim" (a useful public establishment). Examples are the Restitution Center and the West German

	Recipient of restitution	
	Victim	Community organization
Monetary	Type I Monetary-victim	Type II Monetary-community
Service	Type III Service-victim	Type IV Service-community

Form of restitution

Fig. 1. Typology of restitution.

corrective orders for juvenile and young adult offenders.

Type III: Service-victim restitution requires the offender to perform a useful service for the actual victim of the crime. Contemporary projects do not provide good examples of this type of restitution, although the Citizen Dispute Settlement Programs of the American Arbitration Association and the Night Prosecutor Program in Columbus, Ohio, are likely sources for this type of restitution. Both of these programs are designed to bring offenders and victims together to effect a noncriminal settlement of private criminal complaints. Although accounts of the settlements effected have not been published, the nature of the programs is consistent with Type III restitution.

Type IV: Service-community restitution involves the offender in performing some useful community service. Probation conditions requiring community service, the English program of substituting the community service for imprisonment, and the use of "symbolic" restitution in the first two years of operation of the Minnesota Restitution Center are all examples of Type IV restitution.

Any typology of restitution will become more complex as additional variables, such as victim-offender contacts or victim participation in developing the restitution contract, are considered. Whether the restitution is undertaken voluntarily or is coerced might be an important variable in a restitution typology. The Minnesota Restitution Center has developed agreements calling for the offender to make restitution for offenses (such as bad checks) of which, because of plea bargaining or for other reasons, he was not actually found guilty. The agreement containing such a provision clearly specifies that the restitution is a moral obligation only and that the offender's failure to adhere to it does not constitute a ground for parole revocation.

The restitution concept is broad and requires refinement. Different types of restitution must be clearly defined and distinguished from one another.

Purpose

Who or what is the intended beneficiary of a restitution program? Is it the victim? The offender? The community at large? The criminal justice system?

Promoting restitution to help crime victims is questionable. The vast majority of crimes go unsolved; in many, arrest of the offender does not result in conviction; and in other instances, even where conviction is secured, restitution may not be an appropriate sanction. Thus, a comparatively small number of crime victims will ever receive redress through a restitution program. If protecting the welfare of crime victims is the primary social aim, a public crime-victim compensation program is likely to be more effective than restitution.

Edelhertz notes that, historically, restitution was the mechanism whereby the offender and his kin group made amends to the victim and his kin group and thus avoided a more severe sanction that the victim's kin group could have legitimately imposed—in short, it benefited the offender rather than the victim,[26] as recently illustrated by a reported case in Minnesota.[27] An Ethiopian student who murdered his roommate, also Ethiopian, was found to be insane and was committed to a program for the criminally insane, after which the Immigration Service began deportation proceedings. The defendant requested a delay in his deportation until his family in Ethiopia could arrange a suitable settlement with the family of the victim (custom required that these negotiations could not begin until after a year of mourning had elapsed) so that he could return to Ethiopia without risk of being killed by the family of his victim.

A second purpose of restitution, consistent with its historic intent, is to provide a less severe and more humane sanction for the offender. This purpose is implicit in diversionary programs and is more or less explicit in the Minnesota and Georgia programs. The Minnesota Restitution Center is an alternative to imprisonment for property offenders, and the Georgia Restitution Shelters are part of a package of pro-

---

26. Edelhertz, *op. cit. supra* note 12, pp. 1-20.
27. Minneapolis *Tribune,* Nov. 15, 1974, p. 1.

grams that were funded to reduce the size of the state's prison population.

A third related but conceptually distinct purpose of restitution is aid in the rehabilitation of the offender, as advocated in the 1940s by the chief probation officer in New York City, in the 1950's by psychologist Albert Eglash, and more recently by Stephen Schafer (who sees restitution as an opportunity to integrate the punitive and rehabilitative purposes of the criminal law), O. Hobert Mower, and Galaway and Hudson.[28] The rationale for speculating that restitution might be more rehabilitative than other correctional measures includes the notion that restitution is related to the amount of damages done and thus would be perceived as more just by the offender, is specific and allows for a clear sense of accomplishment as the offender completes concrete requirements, requires the offender to be actively involved in the treatment program, and provides a socially appropriate and concrete way of expressing guilt and atonement. It maintains that the offender who makes restitution is likely to elicit a more positive response from persons around him than the offender who is sent to prison or is subjected to some other correctional sanction. Restitution is perceived as a sanction that enhances self-respect.

A fourth possible purpose for restitution is to benefit the criminal justice system by providing a fairly easily administered sanction permitting the reduction of demands on the system. The system can process offenders rather easily at the same time that it avoids a public appearance of doing nothing or being soft. While not articulated as a purpose, this rationale may be implicit in the use of restitution in informal diversion or as a probation condition.

A fifth purpose of restitution may be reduc-

tion of the need for vengeance in the administration of criminal law as offenders are perceived as responsible persons taking active steps to make amends for wrongdoing.

These five possible purposes—redress for the victim, less severe sanction for the offender, rehabilitation of the offender, reduction of demands on the criminal justice system, and reduction of the need for vengeance in a society—are not mutually exclusive. Individual restitution programs, however, can reasonably be expected to specify the purpose or purposes of their existence.

Relation to other sanctions

Is restitution a sufficient sanction for some types of crime? Does restitution detract from the effectiveness of other sanctions? Are there situations in which a restitution requirement may impose an injustice on the offender? These are some of the more troublesome questions in attempting to assess the relationship between restitution and other criminal justice sanctions.

With the possible exception of the community service programs in England, there is considerable reluctance to use restitution as the sole sanction for any identified group of offenders. (Some of the informal pretrial diversionary strategies, however, may be a *de facto* sole use of restitution as the sanction of wrongdoing.) The Minnesota Restitution Center imposes additional treatment requirements on residents (including mandatory group counseling) and, because of the comparatively small dollar damages done by residents, limits the monthly amount of repayment to hold residents in a treatment program for a specified period of time.[29] Restitution is generally perceived as one of a series of conditions which may be imposed on the wrongdoer. As experience is gained, perhaps restitution can be used as the only penalty for some specified kinds of offenses or offenders.

The prevailing view of the impact of restitution on other sanctions is that the restitution requirement may inhibit the offender's rehabilitation by weakening his ability to support himself and his family or to meet other financial

28. Irving E. Cohen, "The Integration of Restitution in the Probation Services," *Journal of Criminal Law, Criminology, and Police Science,* January-February 1944, pp. 315-21 (also in Hudson and Galaway, *op. cit. supra* note 1, pp. 322-39); Eglash, *supra* note 4; Schafer, *op. cit. supra* note 4; O. Hobert Mower, "Loss and Recovery of Community," in George M. Gazda, ed., *Innovations to Group Psychotherapy* (Springfield, Ill.: Charles C Thomas, 1968), pp. 130-48 (also in Hudson and Galaway, *op. cit. supra* note 1, pp. 265-83); Galaway and Hudson, *supra* note 4.

29. Hudson and Galaway, *supra* note 24.

obligations.[30] Some correctional staff maintain that focusing on restitution would interfere with their work on more important problems. Others have suggested that restitution is simply a bill-collecting procedure requiring little skill on their part and offering questionable help to the offender. When restitution is not the sole penalty, the challenge is to find ways of integrating its use with other correctional services and sanctions. In the 1940's, Irving Cohen suggested that restitution requirements provided a positive focus for the probation officer's work.[31] More recently, Kathleen Smith has proposed that financial restitution (both directly to the victim and also to the society in the form of a court-ordered discretionary fine) become the basis for determining the length of time that an offender would be incarcerated.[32] Essentially, the Smith proposal provides inmates with the opportunity to work at prevailing union rates. The prisoner would be charged a fee for room and board, would be required to contribute to support of his family, and would be discharged from prison upon completion of his restitution obligations.

Under certain circumstances restitution may be perceived as an unjust sanction—for example, when the damage is so extensive that even a lifetime of peak earnings would not be sufficient to make reparation.

The task is to begin specifying the kinds of offenders or the kinds of offenses for which restitution is an appropriate sanction. When is it appropriate as the sole sanction, when should it be used together with other sanctions, and when is it inappropriate?

Victim involvement

What role, if any, should the victims of crime play in a restitution program? If restitution is being used as a less severe sanction—e.g., as an alternative to imprisonment—what consideration should be given to the wishes of the victim

on this question? Some victims refuse to participate in the restitution process. Should this failure to participate be allowed to veto the use of restitution and, in effect, mandate a severe sanction? The Minnesota Restitution Center has resolved this issue, in the comparatively few times it has arisen, by permitting the substitution of community service or payment of restitution to a community organization for direct involvement of the victim. The Adult Diversion Project of Tucson, however, permits either the victim or the arresting officer to veto the defendant's entry into a pretrial diversionary program using restitution.

Existing programs range from attempts to involve the victim and the offender actively in direct communications to develop a restitution plan and to continue contacts as the plan is implemented (as in the Minnesota Restitution Center, the Iowa Restitution in Probation Experiment, and the Adult Diversion Project) to those in which court-ordered restitution is made through an intermediary to avoid victim-offender contacts (as in the Georgia Restitution Shelters). The Iowa program is an effort to introduce victim-offender involvement into a system in which restitution was already present but was being handled through court officials without victim and offender communication. The Minnesota program has had considerable success in securing the assistance of the victim in negotiating the restitution contract but less success in maintaining offender-victim communication once the contract is drawn up and the offender is actually implementing the agreement.[33]

The impact of victim-offender communication on both the victim and the offender is, at present, unknown. Can they engage in communication that would be beneficial to both? What does such communication do to the offender's perception of victims and the victim's perception of offenders? Would such communication reduce the need for scapegoating and cries for vengeance?

The question of victim involvement raises two further issues—differentiating types of victims and degrees of victim culpability. Victims range

30. See, for example, President's Commission on Law Enforcement and Administration of Justice, *Task Force Report: Corrections* (Washington, D.C.: U.S. Govt. Printing Office, 1967), p. 35; Rubin, *op. cit. supra* note 16, pp. 231-32.
31. Cohen, *op. cit. supra* note 28.
32. Smith, *op. cit. supra* note 4.

33. Galaway and Hudson, *op. cit. supra* note 24.

from individuals to large organizations. Should the type of victim be a consideration in determining the restitution obligation: How is "victim" to be operationalized in the case of large organizations? Does the type of victim influence the impact which restitution may be presumed to have on the offender? A growing body of evidence suggests that in some situations victims may be partially responsible for their own victimization.[34] What part, if any, should the issue of victim culpability play in imposing restitution requirements?

SUMMARY

Restitution has probably been fairly widely used, both as an informal diversionary strategy by police and prosecutors and as a probation condition by judges. During the last five years

it has been employed more systematically in pretrial diversion projects, in specialized probation projects, and as a part of programs of community correction centers serving as an alternative to imprisonment.

A number of issues have evolved from these uses of restitution, including need for a classification scheme to differentiate types of restitution and clarification of the purpose of restitution, the relationship between restitution and other criminal justice sanctions, and the role of the victim in the restitution process.

More adequate reporting of the nature of restitution and the extent of its use is badly needed. The publication of information on the extent of use of restitution in various jurisdictions and of description of restitution projects and how they can resolve the foregoing issues is essential to the orderly development of this concept and the appraisal of its place in the criminal justice system.

34. Lynn A. Curtis, *Criminal Violence: National Patterns and Behavior* (Lexington, Mass.: D. C. Heath, 1974).

C □ *Correctional restitution*

A strategy for correctional conflict management

ROMINE R. DEMING

As a divergent approach in contemporary corrections, a concept is proposed here which is founded on historical jurisprudence and contemporary research in behavioral science and criminal justice. Indeed, the concept of correctional restitution has a stronger basis realistically, historically, logically, and empirically than does much of contemporary corrections. Claims are not made for its success in reducing crime. However, it is a viable and valuable alternative concept that fits well into our contemporary processes of criminal jurisprudence.

Reprinted from *Federal Probation,* September 1976, pp. 27-32.

CORRECTIONAL RESTITUTION

As conceived by Schafer,[1] correctional restitution is the process of establishing, between the offender and the victim, a relationship which will raise the offender's sense of "functional responsibility" to society through a personal responsibility to the victim. The relationship is facilitated by the state through the court or parole board which sponsors, initiates, and monitors the relationship through its agents. Correctional restitution generates personal respon-

[1]The author is grateful to his colleague Stephen Schafer for the concept of correctional restitution and our valuable discussions.

sibility to the victim. It generates personal responsibility for the offense and reparation. Correctional restitution is something the offender must perform himself rather than having something done for, or to him. Correctional restitution requires the offender to maintain a relationship with the person whom he made a victim, until the victim's condition has been restored to the fullest extent possible. This concept holds a threefold promise in that it compensates the victim, relieves the state of some burden of responsibility, and permits the offender to pay his debt to society and to the victim.[2]

Perhaps most importantly, rather than permitting the criminal act to drive members of the community further apart, correctional restitution uses the criminal act to bring them functionally together. It reinforces the offender's sense of responsibility for the offense, and promotes a desire to be responsible for "righting the wrong." It may serve to educate both the individual offender and victim of their mutual responsibility to promote harmony in the social order. The parties work together to resolve the conflict for mutual benefit to the greatest extent possible. Lastly, correctional restitution is a means of promoting a sense of community in an impersonal mass society by personalizing the effects of the criminal act and the process of reparation.

THEORETICAL BASIS OF THE CONCEPT

Correctional restitution as conceived here seems to be rare. The Minnesota Restitution Center and a few new programs patterned after it, are noted exceptions.[3] However, restitution is often assessed incidental to probation.

The resistance to restitution programs is perhaps because they do not logically relate to deterministic theories of correctional treatment. For instance, if the offender is not responsible for the crime, he is not responsible for the consequences of the crime. The offender, as a party to the act, is minimized. If the offender is removed from consideration as an actor, then what rationale exists to consider the other actor, the victim? The crime is perceived as symptomatic of a social or psychological disease, not as it really is; a conflict relationship.

Another factor in the rarity of such programs, is the eclipsing of victim's rights by state's rights. Since the rise of the feudal barons and later the state, the business of crime control and punishing the offender has been assumed by the state. Property, or fines extracted as punishment were confiscated by the state as a logical process in punishment.

The offender-victim relationship is a conflict and there is a tendency to assume that those who conflict should be kept apart. There is a common aversion to conflict, even by those who should be scientifically and scholarly interested. As Lewis Coser points out, "Although the concept of social conflict is of central importance for an understanding of major areas of social relations, it has been almost wholly neglected by American sociologists in recent years."[4]

Although there is yet some degree of resistance to conflict, the turbulent late 1960's and early 1970's contributed to perceiving of social conflict as worthy of scientific analysis. A new interest in conflict sociology, and more specifically conflict criminology is emerging.[5]

Conflict criminology focuses on the relationship between the individual offender and the social order in general, and on the relationship between the offender and the victim specifically.[6] It does not focus on the offender per se. Conflict criminology progresses from the

---

[2]Stephen Schafer, *Restitution to Victims of Crime* (Chicago and London, 1960).

[3]Burt Galaway and Joe Hudson, "Issues in the Correctional Implementation of Restitution to Victims of Crime," in *Considering the Victim: Readings in Restitution and Victim Compensation,* eds. Joe Hudson and Burt Galaway (Springfield, Ill., 1975), pp. 351-360. Michael S. Serrill, "The Minnesota Restitution Center," *Corrections Magazine* 1:3, Jan.-Feb. 1975, pp. 13-20.

[4]Lewis Coser, *The Functions of Social Conflict* (New York, 1956).

[5]Romine R. Deming, "Evaluating Correctional Conflict Management," Prepublication. 1975.

[6]George Vold, *Theoretical Criminology* (New York, 1958) pp. 203-219. Raffaele Garofalo, *Criminology,* trans. Robert Wyness Millar (Boston, 1944). Enrico Ferri, *Criminal Sociology,* trans. Joseph I. Kelly and John Lisle (Boston, 1917).

assumption that there is nothing in the environment or in the individual that explicitly differentiates the criminal from the noncriminal.[7] The cause of crime is to be found in the existence of law. Crime is a relation of one person or persons, and another person or persons; or between a person or persons and the social order. Conflict criminology recognizes that although harmony is desirable within social systems, conflict is a normal and common social process. Rather than avoid the phenomenon of conflict, or deny its existence, conflict criminology recognizes its reality. It recognizes the natural and individual right of humans to conflict with the social order of the community. Lastly, it recognizes both the functional and dysfunctional potentials of conflict.

In conflict criminology, crime is viewed as conflict between an individual or individuals, and the social order. In addition, most crime is conflict between groups or individuals. The offender is viewed as a normal individual who is assumed to be capable of knowing the act is in conflict with the law. The offender is held responsible for the conflicting act. The social order has the right to establish rules (criminal law) and to hold members responsible for obeying the rules. The individual offender, however, has the inherent right not to obey the rules. On the other hand, the social order has the right to protect itself.

CORRECTIONAL CONFLICT MANAGEMENT

Crime is conflict defined by the state through the criminal code of the jurisdictional unit. Amelioration of these conflict situations is logically through conflict management processes. The concept of conflict management rather than conflict resolution is selected because it focuses on the process, rather than on the end result. In addition, the assumption that conflict is a natural social process suggests that realistically conflict will not be resolved. The necessary process of amelioration is the management of conflict so that the parties to the conflict

can function in the social system to benefit themselves and the system.[8]

Law is a formal means of interpreting and applying rules to specific conflict situations to define the actions of the parties and to make judgments of right and wrong regarding the parties. Although it is an excellent procedure to accomplish these ends, it suffers from the necessary limits of formality. More importantly, it determines right and wrong and who wins and who loses, but it does not address itself to facilitating harmony between the conflicting parties. In some situations, the advisory proceeding on right or wrong, win or lose, may heighten enmity between the parties whether offender and victim, or offender and the social order. However, it need not end here. The court has the authority and resources to sponsor, initiate, and monitor reparation between the offender and the victim and thereby facilitate the establishment of harmony in the community.

The goal of correctional conflict management is to intervene after the court determines right or wrong according to its interpretation of the rules of the social order; correctional conflict management then applies its resources to facilitate reparation between the parties to the conflict.

Correctional restitution is one of many strategies which holds promise for criminal conflict. These conflicts are categorized in a typology developed by the author and schematically presented here. The typology is illustrated in the recent study by an independent researcher who applied "The Offender-Victim Typology" to categorize all those who were serving sentences in Rhode Island during December 1975. The researcher applied the descriptive criteria to categorize the inmates on the basis of the offender-victim relationship occurring during the crime for which they were sentenced. In cases of multiple sentences, the offense for which the offender received the longest sentence was used.[9]

---

[7]Albert Cohen, Alfred Lindesmith, and Karl Schuessler (eds.) *The Sutherland Papers* (Bloomington, Ind., 1956).

[8]Stephen P. Robbins, *Managing Organizational Conflict* (Englewood Cliffs, N.J., 1974).

[9]Stanley Sheer, *A Study of the Criminal-Victim Relationship.* Unpublished thesis, 1976.

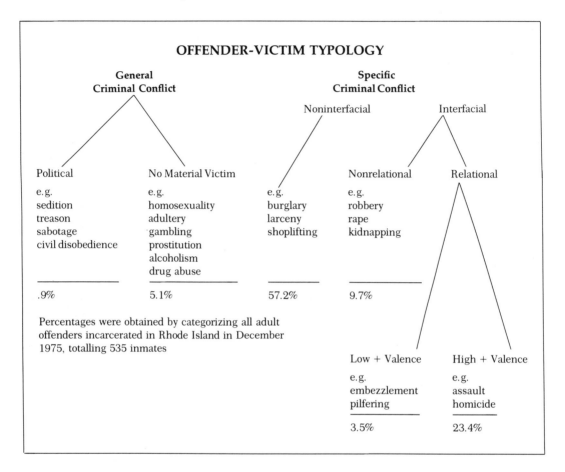

OFFENDER-VICTIM TYPOLOGY

General Criminal Conflict

Specific Criminal Conflict

Noninterfacial — Interfacial

Political | No Material Victim | | Nonrelational | Relational

e.g.
sedition
treason
sabotage
civil disobedience

e.g.
homosexuality
adultery
gambling
prostitution
alcoholism
drug abuse

e.g.
burglary
larceny
shoplifting

e.g.
robbery
rape
kidnapping

.9%   5.1%   57.2%   9.7%

Percentages were obtained by categorizing all adult offenders incarcerated in Rhode Island in December 1975, totalling 535 inmates

Low + Valence | High + Valence

e.g.
embezzlement
pilfering

e.g.
assault
homicide

3.5%   23.4%

To explain the typology, general criminal conflict is defined as conflict with the criminal law, or social order, not directly with any individual or group of individuals. This would include political crimes, such as sedition, treason, sabotage, and civil disobedience. Another category is the so-called victimless crimes in which there is no material victim and includes homosexuality, adultery, gambling, prostitution, alcoholism, and drug abuse. Specific criminal conflict is defined as crime in which there is a specific victim or group of victims. Noninterfacial criminal conflict is crime in which the offender and victim do not come into contact, but are anonymous to each other at the time of the act, as in crimes of burglary, larceny, and shoplifting. Interfacial criminal conflict is crime in which the offender and the victim interact during the criminal act. There are two kinds of interfacial crime. In nonrelational criminal conflict the offender and the victim have not been involved in a previously common social relationship. The act provides the basis for the interaction. This happens in such crimes as robbery, rape, and kidnapping. In relational criminal conflict, the parties to the act are acquainted. There are two types of relational criminal conflict. Low positive valence relational crimes are situations in which the parties to the conflict must interact, but are not strongly attracted to each other, as in the case of employer and employee. Typical acts are embezzlement and pilfering. High positive valence relational conflicts are situations in which the parties have been strongly attracted to each other as in the case of lovers, spouses, friends, or gang members. Typical acts are assault and homicide. The respective numbers and percentages are presented in the accompanying diagram. The largest categories are noninterfacial, and high positive valence relational.

The strategy of correctional restitution probably has the highest potential for success in crimes categorized as specific criminal conflict of a noninterfacial nature, the largest category. Consideration should not be excluded, however, for cases in the other categories.

STRATEGY OF CORRECTIONAL RESTITUTION

The correctional restitution strategy is especially well suited to be used in conjunction with the functions of diversion, presentence inquiry, pretemporary release, and preparole. However, opportunity and resources should be provided for those serving time and on probation and parole to be involved in reparation with their victims if they so desire. It also lends itself well as an adjunct to parole contracts as used by Wisconsin, California, and Minnesota. For illustration, it is presented here at the presentence stage.

Two documents are involved in the strategy of correctional restitution. A reparation plan is a written or oral statement of the offender's plan to accomplish the reparation of the victim. The restitution agreement is a formal agreement specifically stating the nature, amount, and schedule of restitution. It contains the signatures of the offender and the victim.

Effective application of the correctional restitution strategy is contingent upon the appropriate use of court authority. Rather than limiting the role of the court to levying punishment and mitigating punishment through probation, the inherent authority must be extended to facilitate an ameliorative relationship between the offended and offender. This is the principal court role in civil cases. However, in civil cases the action is initiated by the offended. The court is an advocate for justice. This does not necessarily restore harmony between the litigants. It merely settles the dispute. In addition, the civil court lacks officers to assist the

litigants to arrive at mutually satisfying agreements. In correctional conflict management, the court initiates the reparation as an advocate of the social order, and its enhancement through the facilitation of harmony, a subtle but major distinction which recognizes the necessity of the court's authority in correctional conflict management. This authority is likewise necessary of paroling authorities when correctional restitution is used in conjunction with parole.

The officer of the court, or agent, is indispensable to correctional conflict management. The appropriate philosophy of the agent is essential to effectively implement the correctional restitution strategy. The agent should have the orientation that crime is social conflict, and that social conflict is a normal social process. The agent must assume that the offender is responsible for the criminal act. In addition, the agent must assume the offender has a responsibility to the social order; but also accept the offender's inherent right to conflict. The agent must be an advocate for reparation between the offender and victim, and between the offender and the social order. The agent must be fully aware of the present relationship and society's desired relationship of offender and victim.

The agent in this position requires a set of skills different from those serving in deterministically oriented correctional programs, but no greater or less preparation than is generally required for incumbents in those programs. Incidentally, those who are renegades from those programs easily acquire the necessary skills for correctional restitution. The necessary skills include: creative problem solving in small groups, human relations skills, knowledge of group dynamics, social and individual analysis skills, and the ability to communicate the philosophical assumptions of the program. Lastly, the agent must generate trust and faith from and between the parties and thereby exercise the influence which is necessary for any successful conflict manager.

A prerequisite for the procedure is a noncoerced willingness of the offender to participate in a reparation plan. In some cases, the desire of the offender to reestablish his or her self-concept as a responsible member of the community may be sufficient. The possibility of receiving a favorable decision from the court or parole board will provide sufficient incentive for most offenders to enter into a relationship with the victim, to develop a reparation plan. However, care must be taken to give credit to the offender for his or her desire to be responsible for the action.

The first step after guilt is established is for the court to offer the offender the right to waive immediate sentence and meet with a corrections agent in conjunction with a presentence investigation, to attempt to work out a reparation plan and restitution agreement. The court explains the procedure simply and stresses that such a plan and agreement, if one is produced, will be considered by the court, but in no way encumbers the court from pronouncing the sentence; offer of waiver affects neither the quality, nor the length of sentence. Offer of waiver will, however, provide the offender with the opportunity, time and resources to develop a reparation plan in general and perhaps a specific restitution agreement.

The agent is either an officer of the court, or a staff member of a service agency to the court. The agent is directed by the court to serve as a resource person to the particular offender to assist him or her in drawing up a reparation plan and in gaining a restitution agreement.

The agent analyzes with the offender the nature of the act of criminal conflict, the attitudes prior to the act, the attitude toward the act, toward apprehension, toward the victim, and toward reparation and restitution. They examine the present relationship between the offender and victim and relationship before and at the time of the act.

The agent uses the authority of the court diplomatically to meet with the victim. The agent and victim together analyze the act, the attitudes, the relationship with the offender, and attitudes toward the relationship.

The agent uses the authority delegated by the court and the ability to generate trust and faith in the offender to influence, if possible, a parley. The parley is a meeting between the parties to the conflict.

The parley is a problem generated, goal oriented meeting or series of meetings. The prob-

lem is that the action of one person caused harm to another. The goal is the reparation of the relationship, or the returning of the victim and offender as nearly as possible to the previous status. Restitution is the primary resource. The specific goal of the parley is to generate a restitution agreement. The restitution agreement will vary in kind, amount, time span, and means of conveyance. Either party may consult with their attorney, however, it is important that only the principals to the conflict parley. The agent may not be able to establish a parley, for it is the right of the victim to refuse. However, the victim has an implicit responsibility to the social order to facilitate reparation. Coercion, however, is a violation of the victim's rights. Responsibility cannot be gained at the expense of individual rights.

If the parties are willing to parley, the agent convenes as many meetings as are necessary. The agent is a continuous advocate for reparation. The agent sets the tone of the meetings and influences the climate. He, or she, is responsible for the setting, both social and physical, in which the meeting occurs. The agent chairs the meeting and is responsible for keeping the discussion relevant, and serves as communication facilitator. Lastly, the agent directs energies toward a cooperative task oriented solution to the problem of restitution.

The agent is responsible for preparing the written Reparation Plan. The Plan will contain two alternatives, one to be used with a disposition of probation, and one for an institutional sentence. If a Restitution Agreement is obtained, a copy is signed by the parties and the agent as witness, and would be attached to the Plan. The Plan would then be presented to the offender for examination and signed when he or she is satisfied. The agent also signs the Plan as the preparer of the Plan. The agent then calendars the case for court appearance. Nothing in this procedure should be considered as excluding the victim from seeking remedies in civil court. Obviously the Restitution Agreement could be used by either party as evidence.

The court provides a disposition based on the criminal act, the circumstances and attitudes of offender and victim surrounding the act, the attitudes and commitments of the parties toward reparation. Thus, the unwillingness of the victim to parley or develop a Restitution Agreement is not necessarily damaging to the offender. The court will also examine the past criminal record and the need for incapacitating the offender, the specific or general deterrence effect of the particular disposition relative to the crime, and the anticipated sense of justice by the community. The court could sentence the offender to a community corrections center at which the offender could execute the Restitution Agreement while on work release.

If the offender is placed on probation, the Restitution Agreement is incorporated into the probation order. Provision is available for modifying the Restitution Agreement if all parties concur. If either party defaults, the agent has the responsibility to return the matter to court. When the Restitution Agreement is satisfied, the victim signs a Certificate of Satisfaction, and the agent calendars the case for discharge if an early discharge is merited and feasible. At least the agent and the person on probation must be present. The victim also has the right to appear in person, and may be invited by either the probationer or agent. The court then formally discharges the offender with an appropriate written court order, recognizing his or her reinstatement as a citizen.

The procedure is not designed with the objectives of preventing crime, or "rehabilitating the offender," as meritorious as these objectives are. The goal is to facilitate the offender taking responsibility for the offense, and in the reparation of the victim. Incidental to this may be, in fact, discontinuing criminal behavior. Evaluation of the procedure then is in relation to the realistic objective of reparation. Input data for assessment are:

(1) Number of Restitution Agreements drafted;

(2) Number of Restitutions completed;

(3) Number of Certificates of Satisfaction issued;

(4) Number of Early Discharges;

(5) Amount of Restitution made, stated in its appropriate form, i.e., hours, money, etc.;

(6) Objective attitude scale regarding the experience: (a) of the clients; (b) of victims;

(7) Client's attraction to the agent-client relationship;[10]

(8) Client's qualitative statement toward reparation and future behavior and relations.

CONCLUSION

Many, if not most, correctional personnel would agree that contemporary corrections is less than effective. This lack of effectiveness may be due to the positivistic and deterministic philosophy of contemporary corrections which negates the offender's responsibility for committing the act, and responsibility to the victim and community for the harm of the act. Correctional restitution is an alternative strategy of correctional conflict management which in turn is derived from conflict criminology theory. Conflict criminology views crime as social conflict and specifically recognizes crime as conflict between the offender and the community, and the offender and the victim. It recognizes the benefits of harmony to the social system. For this to occur, the relationship between the offender and the community and the victim must be brought back, as near as possible to the status prior to the criminal act. Correctional restitution is one strategy to accomplish this process.

Reparation will not occur naturally. In fact, contemporary jurisprudence and corrections may deter it by over emphasizing the advisory proceedings and punitive process. However, the courts and correctional agencies have the authority and resources necessary to facilitate reparation. The issue becomes one of desire and policy decision. Courts and correctional agencies can be the units to facilitate reparation. The orientation, the roles and specific procedures of the staff will probably have to be altered in many organizations. The alteration is not difficult to achieve.

Correctional restitution is not specifically aimed at the grand objective of reducing crime. Its objective is more immediate and specific, yet worthy—the reparation of the victim through facilitating a functional responsibility between the offender and his or her victim.

---

[10]Romine R. Deming, "Valence as a Measurement of the Effectiveness of the Probation Officer-Client Relationship," *The Journal of Criminal Justice*, Winter 1975. The Relationship Valence Scale is available through the author.

D □ *The Victim-Offender Reconciliation Project*

DOROTHY (EDMONDS) McKNIGHT

The Victim-Offender Reconciliation Project (VORP) was a joint venture of the Mennonite Central Committee of Ontario and the Province of Ontario Ministry of Correctional Services and was located in Kitchener, Ontario, Canada, a city of 130,000 in southwestern Ontario. The project was formulated by a local adult probation officer who was also a member of the Mennonite Central Committee; it was carried out under direction of a VORP Committee consisting of representatives of probation-parole services and the Mennonite Central Committee.

The VORP Committee defined project purposes as:

1. To provide an alternative method for dealing with crime in the community.
2. To bring the victim and offender together in an attempt to reach reconciliation and come to a mutual agreement regarding restitution.
3. To use a third party who could foster reconciliation between victim and offender.
4. To deal with crime as a conflict to be resolved.

The VORP approach to offenders and victims is based on the belief that "conflict is so central to life that it cannot be eliminated without eliminating life as we know it"[1] and that "peacemaking . . . does not require eliminating conflict . . . [but] requires effectively handling and resolving conflicts."[2] The VORP method of resolving conflict was negotiation, an ancient method that is used in labor disputes, marriage counseling, and internationally by the United Nations General Assembly. Victim and offender confrontation was used in VORP to arrive at a mutual agreement regarding restitution.

Experience with a few test cases generated encouragement and support from people within the judicial system and from the community. The VORP Committee then decided to apply for a government grant, which was approved, and a pilot project ran from fall 1975 until June 1976.

During the pilot project, VORP staff were involved with 61 offenders and 128 victims. Among the offenders were 45 adults and 16 juveniles, ranging in age from 13 to 42. Twenty-four of the offenders were referred by the court, 30 from the probation office, 2 from lawyers, and 5 from other sources. Since VORP involvement with an offender and victim usually came about as a result of a probation order, the VORP Committee recommended to the local judges this wording for the order:

The offender "will come to mutual agreement" with the victim regarding restitution, with the assistance of the probation officer or a person designated by the probation officer. If no agreement can be reached, the matter will be referred back to the court.

Of the 54 cases referred by the court and probation office, VORP was required to refer only two back to the court because the victim and the offender failed to reach an agreement. Types of offenses dealt with during the pilot project were predominantly breaking and entering, theft, and willful damage; a few cases involved mischief, fraud, assault, and possession of stolen goods. Victim-offender confrontations were not considered appropriate for all crimes, especially crimes of extreme violence.

A prerequisite for VORP involvement in a case was an identifiable victim or a representative of the victim. During the pilot project, the majority of victims were private individuals, although, if necessary, VORP dealt with large businesses, corporations, and insurance companies. These organizations varied in their responses. In rare incidences, a company would appear uninterested or unable to become involved. As a rule, VORP received a positive response, and one person from the organization would be appointed to handle all meetings and receive the restitution payments.

VORP dealt with six insurance companies.

In all cases the victim had been reimbursed before VORP involvement. Workers attempted to arrange a meeting between the offender and victim, to be followed by a meeting between the offender and a representative of the insurance company. Four insurance companies had their money refunded by the offender. In one of the cases, the insurance company considerably reduced the amount of the claim because the two offenders were young students. The fifth company declined any payment. In this case the company's representative had a fairly lengthy conversation with the two offenders involved. He spoke about the seriousness of the crime and the effect it could have on their futures. He then said, "If you promise to stay out of trouble in the future, I'm willing to accept that promise in good faith and forget about the money." He later told the VORP worker that handling the money would be more trouble than it was worth. The sixth company was not repaid because the two offenders had further charges laid against them.

A total of 48 offenders met with their victim or victims with the help of a VORP third party. Four victims refused to meet their offenders. Of these, two were victims of assault and two were victims of mischief, but there had also been prior conflict between victims and offenders. Two offenders refused to meet their victims because of prior conflict. The role of a third-party peacemaker was not one of enforcer. Although workers did advise both offender and victim of the merits of such a meeting, both parties were given equal opportunity to refuse.

At completion of the pilot phase of the project, 32 offenders had completed their restitution agreements and an additional 15 were making regular payments to their victims. The amount of cash paid to victims was $3262. Adult offenders paid $2921, and juvenile offenders paid $340. In addition, $658 was paid to insurance companies. Offenders worked a total of 130 hours for their victims and spent 180 hours on community work orders.

VICTIM-OFFENDER MEETINGS

Both victim and offender had an opportunity to meet separately with the third-party worker before a victim-offender meeting. Both were given a description of the intent and purpose of the victim-offender meeting. Goals and objectives were discussed and roles were defined. Each person was briefed regarding what to expect.

When the victims were given permission to ventilate their anger concerning the offender during this preparatory meeting, the amount of anger subsequently directed at the offender was frequently reduced. Empathetic listening was sometimes all that was needed. Some victims needed help in working through their emotions and other victims had resolved the issue on their own. Occasionally a victim would tell about his or a relative's having been in trouble with the law as a youth. In such cases the attitude was "anybody can make a mistake." Rarely was the victim totally vindictive.

Offenders were usually very apprehensive about meeting their victims. First meetings with a VORP workers frequently were held in a restaurant over a Coke or a cup of coffee. In the case of young offenders this was also a method of seeing them alone. For any age it was a neutral, informal, nonthreatening setting. If the third-party peacemaker could gain the trust of the offender, the victim-offender meeting became less frightening. Offenders were instructed on the importance of not cancelling the appointment and being on time for the victim-offender meeting.

Usually the victim decided on the location of the actual meeting between the victim and the offender. Frequently victims suggested that the meeting be held in the VORP Room because "it might be easier for him."

The VORP Room featured informality, both because of lack of funds and because it was non-threatening. The room defied the pretentious. The furniture was "early debris," painted, if paintable, in vivid orange, red, or purple, or a shiny black. The chesterfield had interesting valleys and knolls. The walls were painted off-white. No one was confronted by an office with a worker sitting behind a desk.

Some victims, however, insisted that the meeting be held in their homes. One victim described his reason, "If he wants to see me he can come here. I've been put out enough." In most victims' homes the offender was treated as graciously as any guest.

The issue of power parity had to be confronted. The victim and offender are in unequal power situations. The victim has a position of power, and the offender has little or no power. Richard Walton describes the situation:

Power parity in a confrontation situation is most conductive to success. Perceptions of power inequality undermine trust, inhibit dialogue, and decrease the likelihood of a constructive outcome from an attempted confrontation. Inequality tends to undermine trust on both ends of the imbalanced relationship, directly affecting both the person with the perceived power inferiority and the one with perceived superiority.[3]

One role of the third-party worker is to assist in finding a balance or equalization of this power and to assist the victim and the offender to reach an alliance or a point from which their interests can converge.

The first few minutes of the victim-offender meeting set the stage for what followed. A positive approach was essential. Workers suggested that the offender shake hands with the victim; not only is it difficult to ignore an outstretched hand, but an outstretched hand is a symbol of peace. VORP staff also suggested an apology if the offender felt he had done something worthy of an apology. Following the introduction it was helpful for the third party to make a positive personal statement regarding the offender. A smile, used at the right moment, was an invaluable aid. It could be used during the introduction, as reassurance, as a go-ahead, for encouragement, or to relieve tension.

Eye contact was another component. Frequently, the victim or the offender would look at the third-party worker while speaking to the other person. Whenever this happened, it was pointed out. In at least one instance this situation boomeranged. When the VORP worker called to the offender's attention that he was not looking at the victim when he spoke to him, the offender said, "Sorry I didn't realize that," but the victim said, "Listen, lady, get off the kid's back. Don't you realize how difficult this is for the kid? It took a lot of guts for him to meet me and you should understand that."

Frequently "saying" was different from "doing." A victim might say that when he met the offender he was going to tell him something. When confronted with the offender, however, the victim seldom followed through, or, if he did, it was usually with a much weaker statement. Sometimes the offender reacted similarly. One case had to be returned to court because the victim was claiming a much larger amount of cash than originally reported to the police. The offender, waiting outside the court room, was nervous and apprehensive and said, "I'm not going to speak to that guy [the victim]. Don't you suggest that I shake hands with him because I won't." In a few minutes the victim appeared. He spoke and offered his hand. The offender responded to both gestures.

Each case was different and included its own problems. Presenting a typical case is difficult. However, one case illustrates a variety of the components encountered. The case involved Bob, aged 15, and Jim, aged 16. Bob, in juvenile court, and Jim, in adult court, were found guilty of 12 charges of breaking and entering and theft. There were a total of nine victims, some visited more than one time. Bob, Jim, and the VORP worker met with eight of the victims or their representatives (the ninth victim had moved away from the area). At each meeting Bob and Jim apologized to their victim and volunteered to rectify their wrongdoing. In most cases apologies were accepted, but one victim was extremely vindictive and another was uncooperative. After negotiations were completed, an agreement was signed by all concerned. The agreements and results were:

Victim 1: Restitution declined because of the youthfulness of the offenders. Apologies were accepted.

Victim 2: Reimbursed by an insurance company. Meetings held with both victim and the insurance agent. The insurance company had reimbursed the victim in the amount of $282, but the representative decided that a payment of $150 ($75 from each youth) would be satisfactory. This amount was paid in full.

Victim 3: The amount agreed upon was $36.50. The victim appeared hostile and vindictive toward both boys but particularly toward Jim. The victim's business was located close to Jim's home, and he claimed he was being harassed by Jim and his younger brother. The fathers of each boy were invited to a second meeting with the victim. Bob's father declined the invitation, but Jim's father came along. He made a sincere effort to rectify the situation. He told the victim that he had spoken to both of his sons about the alleged harassment. He gave the victim his phone number and asked that he be called if there were further problems. Jim and Bob paid the victim in cash. It is interesting that at the first meeting the victim treated me with as much hostility as he treated the offenders. When the victim received the cash payment he spoke pleasantly to me and thanked me, instead of the offenders. It appeared that in this case the meetings had little or no positive effect on the victim. The impact appeared to be the money.

Victim 4: In this case there was controversy regarding the amount of restitution. At first the victim said everything had been returned except two bottles of wine and a deck of cards. Police records verified this. Later the victim increased the amount, as he noted more articles were missing. After numerous meetings, during which a good deal of the victim's anger was directed at the worker, he agreed that Bob and Jim could shovel snow from his driveway as a form of restitution. According to reports of both offenders and their parents, the offenders shoveled the driveway around 9 PM one night. Later that night there was a heavy snowfall so that when the victim arrived at his office the next morning his driveway was filled with snow. The victim directed angry words at the worker and said that he "wanted to see them break their damn backs shoveling snow." In the end, the snow was shoveled during the day to the victim's satisfaction.

Victim 5: The amount agreed upon was $203.40 cash plus 25 hours of work each. The cash was paid but the victim did not follow through on the work agreement. Numerous reminders brought no results.

Victim 6: Restitution was declined. The representative of the victim (a club) was impressed with the offenders' presentation of themselves and their apologies. He praised the offenders for having the courage to meet with him. He acknowledged their "mistake" and he wished them both "the best of luck."

Victim 7: The agreement reached was restitution in the amount of $41. A work agreement was reached —10½ hours of work each. By the end of 6 months the victim had not followed through with any work assignment. Jim paid $21 in cash from money he earned picking strawberries. Bob had completed his term of probation and chose to forget the matter.

Victim 8: The amount agreed upon was $64.48, to be paid by 16 hours of work each. The victim did not follow through on any work assignment. Jim paid cash from money earned and Bob did nothing.

OFFENDER MOTIVATION

An important and controversial issue was motivation. Was a sincere desire on the part of the offender to right a wrong the only acceptable motivation? Could the experience be meaningful if an offender followed through on a victim-offender meeting and an agreement because of the threat of a remand date? An offender who had been difficult to deal with illustrates the issue. He acted bored, indifferent, and sometimes hostile and patronizing with his numerous victims and with the worker. He slouched and mumbled throughout each victim-offender meeting. His parents had conflicting attitudes; his mother appeared overly protective, whereas his father appeared disinterested. At a meeting with the parents, the father remained silent throughout the hour. Driving home from the final meeting and the completion of the restitution agreements, the worker was feeling depressed and discouraged because the experience appeared to have had no impact on the offender. This conversation ensued:

Worker: "How do you feel about this experience?"
Offender: "Mm. . . . I don't know. Mm. . . . How do you feel?"
Worker: "I have mixed feelings, some are good."
Offender: "What do you feel good about?"
Worker: "I feel good because you saw this through to the end. I'm not sure you did your best, but you did it and that is good."
Offender: "But my dad says I never do anything right and that I'm not good at anything."

Numerous times when the offender was motivated for what might appear the wrong reason, something intangible happened. For some offenders perhaps it was one of few positive experiences. One of the more gratifying cases was the "Vending Machine Wipeout." The offenders were Don and Ron, twins aged 20, and Bill, aged 19. The victim was Mr. Great, the owner of a small vending machine business. The offense occurred late at night, during the winter. One offender put money in the vending machine and received nothing. He became angry because "I was ripped off." There was a woody and marshy area across from the building, and the offenders decided to take the machine there, break the glass, and retrieve the goods. They could not lift the machine, however, because there were concrete blocks in its base to discourage its being moved. Not ones to give up easily, the offenders stole a nearby toboggan, pushed the machine to the door and onto the toboggan, and then pulled it across to the woods. They had only managed to smash the glass when police arrived. There was about 3 feet of snow in the woods. One offender ran and was caught immediately. Another lay down, sank into the snow, and after a lengthy search was caught because he sneezed as a policeman walked by. The third offender had jumped into some slushy, murky water; eventually he was discovered as well. They were held in custody for 22 days before they appeared before a judge and were remanded out of custody for 42 days to work with VORP. After court proceedings, the offenders met a VORP worker and were briefed about what was expected of them. They were cheerful, cooperative, and expressed a willingness to meet their victim and discuss restitution. All three were unemployed but appeared eager to find work.

Mr. Great, the victim, was contacted that evening. He was briefed on VORP and on what the program hoped to accomplish. He asked what was expected of him and was told to be open and honest in expressing his feelings. When asked to suggest a place for the meeting, he said, after some thought, it would be best to meet at the VORP Room.

The following day Mr. Great arrived early. This allowed further time to talk and answer his questions. The three offenders arrived and were introduced. The offenders shook hands and apologized to Mr. Great. Then all four looked quite uncomfortable and uneasy. A pregnant pause followed. The worker said, "Mr. Great knows the end result of your offense, but he doesn't know the details. Would you please fill him in." The offenders took turns telling the story and undoubtedly exaggerated a bit. Mr.

Great laughed, asked questions, and laughed again. Ron asked Mr. Great about his insurance. Mr. Great explained that he was unable to buy insurance because of the large amount of theft and vandalism in his business. The offenders were amazed—they thought everybody had insurance for everything. Don said, "You mean you just lost all that money yourself?" Mr. Great explained that it came out of that particular week's profit. This appeared to have an effect on the offenders.

Restitution was the next subject. The amount agreed upon was $120 ($40 each). Bill had found a job that morning, and he said he would pay this amount from his first pay. When asked if he had any urgent commitments, he confirmed that he had an overdue car payment. Mr. Great said, "I don't think you should cut yourself short; wait and pay me out of your second pay." Ron and Don promised to pay their $40 as soon as they found work. Mr. Great agreed to this. The offenders then asked if they could leave and were given permission. Mr. Great said that his driver would not be picking him up for another 10 minutes. The offenders looked at each other, and then one said, "Oh, well, we'll stay and keep you company." The conversation picked up speed, and Mr. Great forgot the time and ended up keeping his driver waiting 15 minutes. Later that month the offenders paid Mr. Great the amount agreed upon. Mr. Great thanked them and said that it was nice to receive money he hadn't expected. Ron said, "You know, Mr. Great is a real neat guy," and the other two agreed.

Perhaps the offenders were motivated at the onset because the meeting was court ordered and there was the possibility of their sentence being less severe if they followed through with a victim-offender meeting. By all appearances, however, something impalpable happened to the offenders along the way. Walton describes what happened as "an integration phase where the parties appreciate their similarities, acknowledge their common goals, own up to positive aspects of their ambivalence, express warmth and respect, and/or engage in other positive actions to manage their conflict."[4]

PROBLEM AREAS

Peacemaking between victims and offenders has few precedents in modern criminal justice. A number of unexpected problems were encountered and required careful attention. Two problem areas were peculiar to the juvenile offenders.

One issue to resolve was the role of parents of juvenile offenders. Experiences dealing with the parents of young offenders varied. VORP staff kept the parents informed of the process and suggested that they be supportive but allow the youth to carry out the process on his own. Parental involvement ranged from none to a desire to take over completely. On one occasion a father was invited to accompany his young son and the VORP worker to a particularly difficult meeting with a victim. The father said, "I'm not going. I didn't commit the crime and I'll have nothing to do with it." In another case both parents were kept informed and had been asked to allow their son to pay his victim. Arrangements were made; the offender and the VORP worker arrived at the victim's office and were told that the offender's mother had paid him earlier that day. It was difficult finding the right balance, but generally parental response was encouraging.

Another problem area was restitution for young offenders. Forms of restitution usually required creative thinking. Under certain circumstances, workers would suggest that the victim allow the offender to arrange a work assignment with him as a form of restitution. The safety factor in these cases was measured by common sense, sometimes mixed with a gut feeling. To date, all work agreements have been followed through without incident or any harm to a victim. In some cases, work assignments were not suggested in order to protect the offender (for example with a vindictive victim). The work done by young offenders for victims was usually of the nature of general cleanup, raking leaves, cleaning windows, and so forth. The prevailing minimum student wage rate was used to determine the value of the work.

One case involved two 15-year-old offenders who were students and were unable to find employment. After careful consideration it was decided that working for their victims could not be recommended. The VORP worker suggested a plan whereby each offender would work for his parents on contract. The contract was discussed and agreed upon by the offenders, their parents, and the worker. The youths were allowed freedom to refuse certain types of work. The worker suggested a time limit for each assignment, and again the youths and their parents had to agree. When all work assignments were completed, the youths were paid by their parents and in turn paid their victims.

An unexpected problem that was encountered was victims' attempting to victimize their offenders. The following three examples illustrate this factor. The first concerned the victim of an assault who submitted two bills, a dental bill for $191 and lost earnings of $363.60. Upon investigation it was discovered that only $44 of the dental bill was legitimate. The remainder of the bill was for the relining of upper and lower dentures. A check with the employer revealed that the victim had not lost any time from work. In another case, a victim attempted to increase the amount of restitution by $1400. The police records and the offender agreed upon one amount, but the victim stated that the police information was erroneous. VORP referred the case back to the court. The judge set down the original amount but informed the victim that this would not prevent him from taking the case to civil court. In still another case the victim received full restitution twice, once by the offender's payment and again by garnishment of the offender's wages.

A total of 75 offenders were involved in the various charges with the 61 offenders working with VORP. Frequently, two or more offenders involved in the same charge did not appear before the court at the same time or appeared before different judges. Consequently, one judge might refer an offender to VORP and another judge might not. This tended to create problems. Young offenders had difficulty understanding why the law allowed one offender to be held totally responsible for losses to the victim regardless of the number of offenders involved.

CONCLUSIONS

This type of project requires a considerable amount of time to carry through a victim-offender meeting and agreement. The mean amount of time spent in interviews with offenders was 2½ hours. This figure is not indicative of the amount of time spent working on each case and does not include time spent with victims, in court, conferring with judges, police, family, and lawyers. The project requires community and victim acceptance and cooperation; an unwilling victim can block the process.

Under some conditions, however, the objectives set out by the VORP Committee can be met. Victim-offender meetings, with the help of a third party, may be an alternative method for dealing with some crime in the community. Certain crimes may be dealt with as conflicts to be resolved. Victims and offenders can, in most cases, reach reconciliation regarding restitution and may reap other important intangible benefits. Clearly, more testing and research work need to be encouraged for this type of project.

REFERENCES

1. Stanford, Barbara. *Peacemaking: A Guide to Conflict Resolution for Individuals, Groups, and Nations* (New York: Bantam Books, Inc., 1976), p. 15.
2. Ibid., p. 18.
3. Walton, Richard. *Interpersonal Peacemaking: Confrontation and Third Party Consultation* (Reading, Mass.: Addison-Wesley Publishing Co., Inc., 1969), p. 98.
4. Ibid., p. 105.

Selected readings for Chapter 9

Galaway, Burt, and Joe Hudson, eds. *Offender Restitution in Theory and Action* (Lexington, Mass.: D. C. Heath and Co., 1977).

> This collection of papers was first presented at the Second National Symposium on Restitution, in 1977. Papers in this volume deal with the relationship of restitution programming to the multiple purposes of the justice system, the role of restitution within the field of victimology and victim service programs, the place of restitution within behavioral change theories, and available research about the use of restitution and the experience of pilot programming efforts.

Harland, Alan T. *Restitution to Victims of Personal and Household Crimes* (Albany, N.Y.: Criminal Justice Research Center, November 1978).

> National Crime Survey data are used to examine issues related to restitution programs. Among the issues dealt with are the amount of loss suffered by victims, recovery of losses, and the failure to report victimizations to the police.

Harland, Alan T., Marguerite Q. Warren, and Edward J. Brown. *A Guide to Restitution Programming* (Albany, N.Y.: Criminal Justice Research Center, January 1979).

> This report presents systematic information that can be used in the planning and administration of restitution programs. The report is written in a practical way, with the aim of facilitating the clear formulation of purposes and objectives of restitution programs and presenting alternative procedural approaches toward their achievement.

Schultz, LeRoy G. "The Pre-Sentence Investigation and Victimology," *University of Missouri at Kansas City Law Review* **35**:247-260, 1967.

> Suggests including material secured from victims and from a study of victim-offender interactions in presentence investigations and making this material available to courts for use at sentencing.

Vennard, Julie. "Compensation by the Offender: The Victim's Perspective," *Victimology* **3**:154-160, 1978.

> Reports on interviews conducted with 75 crime victims (45 victims of property offenses and 30 victims of assault) during 1974 in magistrates' courts in London. Most victims do not receive compensation outside the criminal justice system, and when compensation was ordered by the court, the offenders' interests were more likely to be considered than the victims'; suggests increased use of compensation (that is, restitution) within the courts as sanctions for offenders.

Chapter 10

VICTIM-SYSTEM INTERACTION

A □ *Making the criminal justice system accountable*
  MARVIN E. WOLFGANG

B □ *Victims' rights litigation: a wave of the future?*
  FRANK CARRINGTON

C □ *The role of the victim in the prosecution and disposition of a criminal case*
  DONALD J. HALL

A □ *Making the criminal justice system accountable*

MARVIN E. WOLFGANG

We speak of the criminal justice system as if it were an integrated, functionally flourishing operation. Yet it is a non-system, a failure. The reasons? There are many, but one is its unaccountability—except to itself. This so-called system is not a corporate entity. Its only allegiance is to itself. It has no moral conscience, no need to report to its immediate neighbors, let alone external agents. Thus it has become an index of our decadence, of our failure to treat each man as a part of humanity, of the pressure of numbers upon a bureaucracy that becomes bereft of emotion.

Reprinted, with permission of the National Council on Crime and Delinquency, from Marvin Wolfgang, "Making the Criminal Justice System Accountable," *Crime and Delinquency*, January 1972, pp. 15-22.

I intend to draw your attention to a few forms of accounting that I think deserve immediate response from the agents of control in this system.

Accountability means being responsible and making a public display or report of how well that responsibility is being met. To whom is the criminal justice system or any of its subparts responsible? What information should be reported? How should this information be distributed?

All parts of the criminal justice system should be accountable to the public at large, to the victim, and to the offender. Moreover, each subpart of the system should be accountable to the immediately preceding subpart.

ACCOUNTABILITY TO THE PUBLIC

It is part of the democratic process that public officials and organizations be on public display. Justice is not a private corporation. Even if it were it would have to reveal its assets and liabilities, certainly more than it now does as a public agency supported by taxes. Unfortunately, there is inadequate display of what in fact goes on in the police department, in the district attorney's office, and in the operation of the courts, probation, parole, and prisons. Annual police reports are often illustrated with increasingly sophisticated photographs of smiling father figures shaking hands with small children—Chamber-of-Commerce-style pamphlets that report more about repairs on cars than rapes of children. Police statistics kept on computer tapes are used mostly internally and are not part of the public domain.

As a citizen, I want to know more about how the police fared this past year. I want my police department to have more funds for research of its own, for regular surveys, for preparing documents that reveal its negative as well as its positive aspects to the public. The same holds true for the district attorney's office, the courts, the prisons.

This country is in the appalling state of having no national judicial statistics. We are one of the few countries in the western world in this condition. Our judicial system is so bogged down in its own intricacies, complexities, and chaos that it cannot—or does not—find the capacity to report the process of criminal justice. Some states are now developing bureaus of judicial statistics, and they are to be applauded. But the counting we get is not an accounting of how the system functions.

Prisons commonly have tables of commitments and discharges by crime type, age, race, sex, and a few other items. Can you tell from the data how a prison is run? Can you determine whether the captives are treated humanely? Can you predict a riot born from accumulated grievances by reading a prison annual report?

I could easily belabor these points but need not do so here. My main concern is that we, the public, are not getting the proper public display of crime control, crime adjudication, or criminal containment. What we are getting is, within each subsystem, excessive accounting to itself, to such an extent that its capacity to perform its basic and original functions is dissipated. I am referring to the enormous amount of paper-work now required in each agency—police, courts, probation, prison, parole—from the large cadre of workers who are expected to tabulate and describe their activities to their superiors in excruciating detail. The worst aspects of bureaucratization exist within each subpart of our criminal justice system, so that a kind of supervisory paranoia seems to have become institutionalized. That is, the lowest patrolman or field probation officer must type out—or have typed out—elaborate reports on his activities in order to satisfy a superior that he has been doing something supposedly related to his professional role. In fact, he often is doing little more than writing reports that no one really reads or cares about except when the man is eventually evaluated for a raise or promotion. I have seen twenty-two good and honest homicide detectives spend more than half of their salaried time typing, with two index fingers, elaborate reports on every hour's activity spent on their cases. And we all know the legacy from social work dogma that long ago invaded probation and parole so that tireless and often devoted officers spend abundantly more time writing glowing reports on cases than they ever spend talking with their probationers or parolees.

Give me a system which will allow a parole officer to spend an hour in a bar with a parolee, developing rapport and a true counselor relationship, and which will require the officer to record only a line or two about it. Give me a system which permits him to do what the principles of parole suggest and which requires merely a summary statement after a long relationship. Our officers are overloaded not so much with cases as with self-defeating unused reports to their own agency.

Our present accounting system promotes inefficiency, fabrication, and depersonalization of the consumers and the employees of the criminal justice system. Waste and ineffectiveness through bureaucratic techniques unrelated to the humanity of the offender or the officer are our present products.

I assert—but will never have the chance to test—that with half the probation officers and half the parole officers (hence at double their present salaries) and 80 per cent less time spent in writing reports, I could produce a probation and parole system that would be twice as successful.

"Successful" is the key word in the notion of accountability.

Imagine a business or industry in our competitive free-enterprise economic system that could long endure with the lack of success manifested by our criminal justice system. Think of the criminal justice system as a production, as Daniel Glaser once suggested. We have a production schedule, clients to be processed, a product (crime control, reduction of recidivism). What are the measures of our productivity? What index of production shall we use? Apprehension by the police? Crime complaints? Recidivism of probationers and parolees? What is our record? From one point of view it can be said that the criminal justice system—using ecological language—does the most recycling of almost any other social institution of our civilization. That is, we push people through the system and then return them to the initial phases more often than Coca-Cola does with its bottles. Recidivism is recycling, and it is promoted by the system itself more than by any other aspect of the social environment. The irony of it all is not that we fail to reform but that we *cause* the return to criminality by the way we treat, handle, and process individuals. Our successes (the non-recidivists) come out that way by chance; our failures are the direct result of our methods of processing. The criminal justice system is not responsible for new clients—that is, first-time offenders. But the system *is* responsible for second and multiple offenders.

As part of the public, I want this system and all its subparts to be accountable, to show me that production (crime control, nonrecidivism) is higher this year than last; that, compared

with complaints, more offenders have been arrested; that more are correctly prosecuted; that more are returned to society without further criminality. These are simple and conventional notions of successful operation.

In short, accountability requires evaluation. This is not a new notion, but I am suggesting that the public display of every police, court, probation, prison, and parole organization should be required and that these agencies should report how successful they have been and thereby take the responsibility for their failures.

The irony, from a cost-benefit point of view, is that a subsystem-announced increase in crime or criminals to be handled by the courts, or in prison, or on probation or parole is considered a good reason for increasing their budgets. I suggest that budgets and salaries be increased only when the subsystem shows a measure of *success*. Let us use the incentive motive of industry to promote successful functioning of the system.

On top of this efficiency-effectiveness mode of accountability, I also want some reporting on the humanity of the system. I want an almost anthropological report on how persons are treated from the moment of arrest to discharge from parole. Is there a sense of human dignity? Does the accused feel he is treated as a human being who is only under suspicion of having committed a given offense? Is the defendant something other than an object maneuvered by the formalities of the court? Does the probationer even *feel* he is viewed as a person rather than as a case? How dehumanized is the appearance of a man in prison? Can we devise new ways to react to these obviously human souls? And can we be accountable for these reactions? Perhaps we need a social-anthropological observer to report to the public on each of these layers of the criminal justice system and a new kind of index of these features.

ACCOUNTABILITY TO THE VICTIM

The whole criminal justice system—from police to parole—ignores the victim except as he contributes to the evidence against the offender. Only a few states have legislated victim compensation in principle; yet even these —New York, California, Massachusetts—have not provided funds to begin implementing the law. According to John Locke, we have a right to be protected from assault because of the social contract that each of us makes with society by investing some of our own will for the sake of the larger benefits from the collectivity. In the absence of total law enforcement, the state should therefore compensate the victim for its neglect and inefficiency, however inherent they may be in the structure of the state. Obviously we cannot have—and would not want—total efficiency in law enforcement. One of democracy's virtues is its inefficiency. Nevertheless, the individual victim should be compensated for loss. The state should settle its account with the victim.

The criminal justice system fails to communicate information to the victim, who deserves at least the satisfaction of knowing that efforts have been made by the police to detect and apprehend the offender. Most crimes against victims are not "cleared by arrest." As we know, 75-80 per cent of the FBI's index crimes do not result in apprehension. Criminals are probably more aware of these odds than are victims. But victims deserve a post-crime report. Some time after the crime at least a letter or a notice, if not a personal call, could be afforded the victim as a report of what was done on his case, stating that—as would be true in most cases—no further clues have been found to locate the offender or the property stolen, etc.

It might be argued that such a report would only increase still further the paper-work of the system and perhaps to some extent it would. But this is a way of accounting to that segment of the public that has been hurt by the failure of the entire social system and of its subsystem called the police. This is not paper-work *within* the police department.

There is yet another way in which accountability or responsibility to the victim needs to be improved. It has to do with courtesy. Said one recent victim: "By the time the police left I thought I was the criminal. I was questioned with discourtesy and abruptness. I was treated like a slob. And by the time the court

trial was completed I had missed seven days of work simply waiting in corridors and on hard benches for justice to begin. Neither the police nor the prosecutor's office treated me as if I were a victim of a serious crime. They were so busy with other things that I was almost totally ignored most of the time." Such is the fate of more than a few.

Rape is surely a complicated charge. We all know the problems of obtaining the evidence necessary for conviction. We know there are allegations of rape when none occurred. Yet there are legitimate complaints by real victims; if a woman reports a rape in which, they say, she submitted to avoid physical harm, the police discount her complaint on the assumption that she participated in the sexual act. One rape victim recently gave the following account of her experience with police attitudes: "I told the policeman what had happened. He was distant, seemed skeptical as he took notes, saying nothing to me that would indicate sympathy or concern. Perhaps it was the way I told my story . . . no tears . . . commenting on how skillful the intruder must have been to have climbed into my apartment in the first place. . . . The detective looked at me coolly and said, 'I still don't know exactly what he did do.' And then I realized that he hadn't believed a word."

When a woman is raped it is not only the phenomenon of rape itself that emotionally and physically affects her. The way her family and other supportive people and agencies respond are significant to her. There is little systematic information on how she is handled by the criminal justice system and the effects of this treatment. At Philadelphia General Hospital, Dr. Joseph Peters and his staff are in the process of starting a study of one thousand victims of rape to see, among other things, how the mental health of the victim is affected by the way she is dealt with by the criminal justice system.

Victims should be treated with dignity and courtesy, whoever they may be. They should be informed of the follow-up of their cases, whatever the outcome. They should be transported to the hearings and the trials. They should have the law and the importance of the rights of defendants explained to them. They should be compensated, at least for offenses against their person. In these minimal ways, our system of justice should account to them.

ACCOUNTABILITY TO THE OFFENDER

The rights of the criminal offender in connection with his arrest and the giving of evidence are probably as well protected in the United States as anywhere else in the world —at least in principle. The offender is also protected by the inefficiency of the system to which I referred earlier. It may be that the abuses and inefficiencies of the system cancel one another, and in this unplanned way the scales of justice held by the mythical figure may indeed be balanced.

Still, we are not fully accounting to the offender—that is, we are not properly exercising our responsibilities. Rights are not always well protected and we do not properly account for this deficiency. Excessive force by the police is not a myth; yet we have not set up a good independent system for recording and correcting these abuses. We invade privacy by electronic eavesdropping, for which we give no accounting; we jail when we should not; we fail to give treatment when we know what treatment might work: and we provide treatment without giving the offender the right to refuse it. We add a medical model of illness to violative behavior and label an offender with a term that gets stuck to his biography, as well as on his dossier, and is passed on as if he were little more than that label and no longer a person with a variety of possibilities. We then fail to tell him his status at reasonable intervals of time. We do not account for the psychiatric assertions we make about him. We present him with no right to rebut the claims made about him at a parole hearing. We do not give an adequate accounting for the psychological report or the chaplain's report or the social worker's report. Functioning with internal secrecy, we act as though these professionals have omniscience. Not that they claim it; but the system, which has grown with undaunted and unchallenged authority over inmates, has

placed the burden of responsibility for decisions on groups that have difficulty yielding power once given it.

Prison officials account only to prison boards chosen to support them. Prisoners who have grievances of even parochial form—regarding food, visits, mailing, etc.—still feel stymied in their efforts to be heard. In time, inmates will organize and form a union with former inmates, for the force of the stigma of being imprisoned has lost its thrust, and men who shared the hardships of deprivation will demand a direct accounting to them. Such a prisoner union is on its way and may promote more public display than we've had.

ACCOUNTABILITY TO OTHER PARTS OF THE SYSTEM

The criminal justice system begins with law enforcement, the police. They initiate or first respond to the initiation of criminal complaints and are the first feeders into the production line of the system. Thus they should receive information from each agency that comes after them. To measure their own operations, as well as to know the consequences of their investigative work, the police should want to have a follow-up of their cases. The district attorney, the courts, probation, correction, and parole should all account directly to the police on offenders processed through their systems. That simplified schedules or forms about each case should flow from police through parole is taken for granted as a necessary ingredient of a criminal information system. But what I am stressing here is the reverse flow for purposes of accounting.

I am not suggesting a hierarchical pyramid of accountability with linear hegemony that ends in the monolithic hands of the police. This is a line of production, a relay system, and I am only suggesting that when the stick is passed to the next runner, he has a responsibility to report back to his passer how well he ran and what happened to the stick. Were this now done in systematic style, better bookkeeping in each part of the system would be possible. What we have are aggregate reports with no individual case traceable unless something special is requested, which happens infrequently.

CONCLUSION

Professionals in the criminal justice field may feel that I can speak this way because I still stand outside as an observer, a critic with no constituency, or at least not the ones you have.

But I am not outside. I too have failed in some of my responsibilities, for in the value-free research in which most criminologists have been involved, there has been insufficient attention given to the meaning of dignity and freedom, inadequate notice of the importance of being aware and helping others be aware of their possibilities and capacities for choice.

In *The Coming Crisis of Western Sociology*, Alvin Gouldner complains about the objectification of man, or, as he puts it, the "autonomy of society" as a set of forces acting on individuals. One part of this argument is that when sociologists measure attributes of a person or his behavior, they somehow transform him into nothing more than the abstractions they have measured, thus robbing him of his humanity. Also, when they seek causal explanations of the properties they have measured, sociologists rob the individual of freedom by attributing his behavior to the explanatory variables rather than to his own decision.

This position is not entirely true. Nor is it entirely false. For I think most of us who have engaged in empirical criminological research—be it causal, predictive, or evaluative—have tended now and then to treat the subjects of our studies as objects denuded of all features of humanity save those we could adequately measure at the time of the research. We manipulate data that replace beings and the concept of being. In our search for dispassion and objectivity we divest ourselves of the sensuous—not sexual but sensuous—contact with the environment that can communicate other forms of information about crime, victims, offenders, law enforcement, and criminal justice.

I am exaggerating, of course, to give strength

to my argument. But its essence must be understood. Working in, for, and with the system has a tendency to promote in one a conservative ideology. I do not mean politically conservative. I mean conservation of the status quo, an ideology with vision tunneled by the boundaries of the system itself. Prophetic senses turn into a priesthood of defense for one's own niche. The bureaucracy turns vigor, enthusiasm, and imagination into rigidity, rationalization for faults, and intellectual banality. The demands of reform turn into requests for more of everything that preserves the system as it now is: more police, more cars, more probation officers, more courts and judges, more prison personnel. Innovations amount to additions rather than revisions.

And you too—prosecutors, police, judges, and others who use abstract rubrics to describe an offender and the causes of his behavior—turn him into a robot with a better chance to recidivate than to reform. You stereotype not only the criminal and the victim, by false classification and neglect, but also your peers outside your own subsystem. The police harbor a murky image of judges, parole boards of prisoners, prisoners of police, and so on, so that each person is robbed of his freedom to be what he should be, robbed of his dignity as a human being with many possibilities. He is locked into a label that he soon sews on the lapel of his own mind.

On top of this, the conservative ideology in criminal justice retains romantic illusions about both its own capacities and man's behavior. It readily fixes on some fantasy of reform like group therapy or halfway houses. "Get a man a job and he won't get in trouble—that's the most important thing of all" is a favorite romantic notion. Now I do not deny the value of employment on the path to reform of any previous offender. But so automatic and mechanistic has this rubric become that any form of wage-earning becomes a "job placement" and makes a man eligible for parole, no matter how phony or ephemeral the job. The system has become a hypocrite in an effort to show how obedient it is to its own rules. All of us have become conservers of it as we work in it and for it or study ways to make it, in its present form, simply more efficient in its hypocrisy.

We have focused long enough on the offender and his weaknesses. It is time we look to ourselves—to this chaotic, decaying, degrading system and indict it for its failures. Put it in the klieg lights of public display and think imaginatively of how to correct and revamp the system and the subpart to which you belong. All the intuitive, sensuous, sensitive skills and subjectivity you now employ to condemn criminals to the status of stereotyped objects should be shifted to viewing and reporting on the system under which you function. Making the criminal justice system accountable means making it more responsible and more humane.

B □ *Victims' rights litigation*

A wave of the future?

FRANK CARRINGTON

INTRODUCTION

American Jurisprudence 2d quite properly claims to be one of the most, if not *the* most, comprehensive legal encyclopedia in this country. Any attorney who has had the opportunity to peruse this work would be forced to agree. It is, therefore, an interesting and unfortunate commentary upon the state of law in our society that of the thousands of topics covered in this monumental compendium of knowledge, none deals with the victims of crime.

This is in no way a criticism of American Jurisprudence 2d. Rather, it is an indictment of a criminal justice system which has developed over the two hundred years of our nation's history, largely ignoring precisely those individuals and groups which should be its primary concern: the victims of crime. The problem has been summarized concisely by two noted authorities of American criminal justice. Donald E. Santarelli, while Administrator of the Law Enforcement Assistance Administration, stated the problem thus:

Reprinted by permission of the *University of Richmond Law Review* from vol. 11, No. 3, pp. 447-470, Spring 1977.

Put yourself in the shoes of a crime victim who finds himself to be a pawn on the criminal justice chessboard, who has to suffer all sorts of indignities, and then sees, as the final straw, the accused offender walking out free.[1]

Mr. Santarelli was echoed by Patrick V. Murphy, former Commissioner of the New York City Police Department, now the Executive Director of the Police Foundation:

The way crime victims are treated in many jurisdictions from their first contact with the police to their final hours in the courtroom is often insensitive. Rarely are their needs considered to any degree.[2]

The non-status of the victims of crime has been fostered to a large extent by certain groups and individuals who take the position that since the Constitution of the United States says noth-

---

1. Address by Donald Santarelli, National Conference of State Criminal Justice Planning Administrators, Williamsburg, Virginia, Jan. 14, 1974.
2. Murphy, *New and Continuing Projects Listed in Police Foundation's Grants*, CRIME CONTROL DIGEST, March 25, 1974, at 7.

ing about victims, they have no specific rights.[3] In terms of pure logic, this position is unassailable. The Constitution does not say anything about the rights of the law-abiding people who become crime victims. However, it might be difficult to get across to a young woman who has just been gang-raped that the document upon which our government is premised relegates her to the status of a mere "witness for the prosecution."

Additionally, our founding fathers, men of hard-headed common sense, were not so single-minded in their devotion to the rights of criminals and the criminally accused that they desired to exclude from consideration the rights of actual and potential victims. Conceding the fact that the rights of victims are nowhere spelled out in the Constitution or the Bill of Rights,[4] a realistic assessment of the attitudes of the framers of these documents warrants the conclusion that they simply took it for granted that one of the primary functions of government was to protect the innocent from the lawless. Thomas Jefferson, for example, whose enthusiasm influenced James Madison to steer the first ten amendments through the first Congress in New York in 1789, eleven years earlier had characterized the duty of the state to protect victims:

Whereas, it frequently happens that wicked and dissolute men, resigning themselves to the domination of inordinate passions, commit violations on the lives, liberties and property of others, *and, the secure*

enjoyment *of these having principally induced men to enter into society, government would be defective in its principal purpose, were it not to restrain such criminal acts* . . . .[5]

Constitutional debate aside, this article takes the position that the victims of crime *do* have rights, certainly not to the total exclusion of the rights of the accused, but with an eye to a balance in our criminal justice system. The article will, after a brief overview of what is currently being done to enhance victims' rights, focus on a developing field of law: the enforcement of victims' rights and efforts to prevent further victimization through litigation on behalf of actual and potential crime victims. This article is intended to alert the legal profession to the potential of victims' rights litigation, a practice of law in need of the dedication of a segment of the bar as has heretofore been done to protect the rights of the criminally accused.

CURRENT VICTIM SERVICES: FROM KINDNESS TO COMPENSATION

It is only within the past few years that certain elements of our society have specifically targeted crime victims as objects of their concern.[6] Victim services include direct services to victims at the intake stage by prosecutor's

---

3. In an interview with Barbara Palmer of the *Washington Star-News*, Mr. Alan Goldstein, legal staffer of the Maryland affiliate of the American Civil Liberties Union, espoused this view:
> Question: You have been outspoken in your opposition to the movement to strengthen rights of victims. You have said that 'victims don't have rights.' Could you explain this?
> Goldstein: Well, I don't mean that victims don't have rights in a general sense. But what they really are, in the criminal justice process, are witnesses for the prosecution and in that sense they do not have constitutional rights which are guaranteed to the defendant. . . .
Washington Star-News, July 18, 1975, at 1, col. 1.

4. The closest that the Constitution comes to addressing this subject is in the Preamble which speaks of a union formed to "establish justice [and] insure domestic tranquility. . . ."

5. The Writings of Thomas Jefferson 218 (The Thomas Jefferson Memorial Foundation 1905) (from the preamble to the Bill for Proportioning Crimes and Punishments in cases heretofore Capital) (emphasis added).

6. Pioneers in this area include: (1) The late Professor Stephen Schafer of Northwestern University and Professor Emilo Viano of The American University, who have developed concern for victims to a science in this country; (2) Donald Santarelli and Patrick V. Murphy who, as administrators of the Law Enforcement Assistance Administration (LEAA) and the Police Foundation respectively, funded innovative victim-oriented programs; (3) Dr. John P.J. Dussich who, while working in the office of the Governor of Florida, developed the concept of victim services as a practical and effective effort; (4) The National District Attorneys Association, which, with LEAA funding, set up the first system of victim-witness assistance offices in the country. This list is not exhaustive. Other individuals include Anna Forder and Anna Slaughter, Aid to Victims of Crime, St. Louis, Missouri; Rep. Eric Smith, Florida State Legislature; Probation Officer Jim Rowland, Fresno, California and Mrs. Kay Heyman, Illinois Law Enforcement Commission. Many others could have been included as "pioneers."

offices,[7] police departments[8] and private organizations.[9] Such services may be summed up concisely as treating the victim like a human being and not merely as a witness in some future criminal proceeding. The programs recognize the trauma associated with becoming the victim of a crime, and therefore make an effort to "smooth the way" for the victim who has become embroiled in the criminal justice process. Where these services are utilized, the police and prosecutors give the victim individualized attention and explain to him or her the complexities of the criminal justice process. Adequate notice of court hearings, assistance in finding a parking space near the courthouse and attractive waiting rooms are examples of the services provided. In short, an attempt is made to convince the victim (or witness) that the criminal justice system is working *for* him.

Additionally, efforts are made to assist the victim in such matters as intercession with employers and creditors if he should be injured by criminal action, replacement of needed items such as eyeglasses and locks on doors and general counselling services by sympathetic persons. All such humane and compassionate programs should be encouraged.[10]

Victim compensation legislation has been enacted in some twelve states, including Virginia, as of this writing.[11] Such legislation is premised upon the duty of the state to protect its citizens. The rationale is that if a citizen is victimized, the state has, by definition, failed in its duty, and thus should compensate the injured party. Although there are variations among the states, the statute in Illinois could be considered typical.[12] It provides for compensation by the state, through the Claims Division of the Illinois Attorney General's Office, to innocent victims of crimes who have cooperated with the police and the prosecution. Ten thousand dollars is the claim limit with a set-off for workmen's compensation, but not for social security. The victim is not eligible if the assailant was a relative. In Illinois,[13] need is not a factor in making the award.[14]

---

7. *See, e.g.,* NATIONAL DISTRICT ATTORNEYS ASSOCIATION, COMMISSION ON VICTIM WITNESS ASSISTANCE, SOCIAL SERVICE REFERRAL, AN IDEA TO HELP DISTRICT ATTORNEYS HELP CRIME VICTIMS (1976). *See also,* NATIONAL DISTRICT ATTORNEYS ASSOCIATION, COMMISSION ON VICTIM WITNESS ASSISTANCE, HELP FOR VICTIMS AND WITNESSES, AN ANNUAL REPORT (1976).

The Commonwealth's Attorney for Richmond, Virginia has recently begun a Victim/Witness Services Unit. The unit uses volunteers to help victims and witnesses better understand the procedures of the criminal justice system and cope with any problems that may arise as a result of their involvement. A similar program is getting under way in Portsmouth, Virginia. Richmond Times-Dispatch, Nov. 3, 1976, § A, at 14, col. 1.

8. For example, the police department of Fort Lauderdale, Florida has an on-going and extremely effective intake victim assistance program.

9. *E.g.,* Aid to Victims of Crime, Inc., Suite 1082, Arcade Building, 812 Olive Street, St. Louis, Missouri 63101; Victims Assistance Program of the Furance St. Mission, Box 444, Akron, Ohio 44309.

10. *See generally* Dussich, Victim Service Models and their Efficacy, July, 1975 (a paper presented to the International Advanced Study Institute on Victimology and the Needs of Contemporary Society, Bevogia, Italy)

11. The following states have passed some type of victim compensation statute: ALASKA STAT. § 18.67 (1974); CAL. GOV'T CODE §§ 13959-69 (West Cum. Supp. 1976); GA. CODE ANN. §§ 47-518 to 527 (1974); HAW. REV. STAT. § 351 (1968), *as amended* (Cum. Supp. 1975); ILL. ANN. STAT. ch. 70, §§

71-84 (Cum. Supp. 1976); LA. REV. STAT. ANN. §§ 46.1801 to .1821 (West Cum. Supp. 1976); MD. ANN. CODE art. 26A (Repl. Vol. 1973); MASS. ANN. LAWS ch. 258A (Cum. Supp. 1976); NEV. REV. STAT. §§ 217.010 to -.350 (Cum. Supp. 1975); N.J. STAT. ANN. § 52:4B (West Cum. Supp. 1976); N.Y. EXEC. LAWS §§ 620-35 (McKinney 1972), *as amended* (Cum. Supp. 1976); R.I. GEN. LAWS §§ 12-25-1 to -12 (Supp. 1975); VA. CODE ANN. § 19.2-368.1 *et seq.* (Supp. 1976); WASH. REV. CODE ANN. §§ 7168.010 to -.910 (Cum. Supp. 1975). For an analysis of the Virginia statute, see p. 679 *infra*.

12. ILL. ANN. STAT., ch. 70, § 71 *et seq.* (Smith-Hurd Cum. Supp. 1976). *See* Brooks, *How Well Are Criminal Injury Compensation Programs Performing?,* 21 CRIME & DELINQUENCY 50 (1975); Schafer, *The Proper Role of a Victim Compensation System,* 21 CRIME & DELINQUENCY 45 (1975); Rothstein, *How the Uniform Crime Victims Reparations Act Works,* 60 A.B.A.J. 1531 (1974); Schafer, *Compensation of Victims of Criminal Offenses,* 10 CRIM. L. BULL. 605 (1974).

13. ALASKA STAT. §§ 18.67.080 (1974); CAL. GOV'T CODE § 13964 (West Cum. Supp. 1976); MD. ANN. CODE art. 26A, § 12 (Repl. Vol. 1973); N.Y. EXEC. LAW § 631 (McKinney 1972). *Contra,* HAW. REV. STAT. §§ 351-31 to -33 (Cum. Supp. 1976); ILL. ANN. STAT. ch. 70 § 77 (Smith-Hurd Cum. Supp. 1976); MASS. GEN. LAWS ANN. ch. 258A, § 5 (West 1968). N.J. STAT. ANN. §§ 52:4B-12 (Cum. Supp. 1976); R.I. GEN. LAWS § 12-25-5 (Supp. 1975).

14. Through December 31, 1975, Illinois has awarded $898,901 to 287 crime victims whose claims have been substantiated. Wiedrich, *Crime Victim Aid Balancing Scales,* Chicago Tribune, Mar. 5, 1976, § 2, at 4, col. 1.

The Virginia compensation statute,[15] on the other hand, is based on a determination of financial need.[16] It establishes a Criminal Injuries Compensation Fund for reimbursing good Samaritans as well as victims.[17] Since the Fund is financed through a ten dollar fine imposed on persons convicted of certain crimes, it entails a restitution aspect while at the same time assuring qualifying victims compensation by deriving the money from an entire class of convicted criminals. It should be noted, however, that the statute has extensive limitations and exclusions.

Victim compensation is probably the wave of the future. Other states are considering legislation to this effect.[18] It is a logical and humane step, the single caveat (other than fiscal pressure) being that compensation to the victims should never be allowed to create a "third-party beneficiary" situation on the part of the perpetrator; that is, the fact that the state has compensated the victim should in no way mitigate the punishment of the offender.

A few states[19] have enacted legislation which permits offenders to make restitution to their victims as a condition of probation. Like compensation statutes, these laws are good in theory, but restitution laws have the drawback of turning our already overworked probation officers into collection agents.

The above treatment of current victim services, (*i.e.,* direct services, compensation and restitution) is admittedly cursory, but this is because the primary thrust of this article is the use of litigation to enforce victims' rights. Litigation on behalf of victims is a relatively new area of law, particularly at the appellate level. It differs also from the more conventional victim services in having the potential to prevent, by example, future victimization.

---

15. VA. CODE ANN. § 19.2-368.1 *et. seq.* (Supp. 1976).

16. *Id.* § 19.2-368.13.

17. *Id.* § 19.2-368.4.

18. For a history of compensation and restitution, see, S. SCHAFER, COMPENSATION AND RESTITUTION TO VICTIMS OF CRIME 1-144 (2d ed. 1970); Laster, *Criminal Restitution: A Survey of its Past History and an Analysis of its Present Usefulness,* 5 U. RICH. L. REV. 71 (1970).

19. *See* Jones, *More Judges Sentencing Criminals to Repay Their Victims Directly,* Christian Science Monitor, Dec. 8, at 1, col. 2.

VICTIMS' RIGHTS LITIGATION

The victim-plaintiff litigator in a civil court[20] is saying to his defendant: (1) you injured my client; or (2) by your willful or negligent conduct you were responsible for my client being injured by another and, therefore, you should respond in damages. Such litigation, if successful, vindicates the rights of the immediate victim, but, perhaps more importantly, if a body of victims' rights law develops, it will have the preventive aspect of putting would-be criminals and third parties who are responsible for victimization on notice that the law works to aid victims, in addition to punishing the wrongdoer.

Victim as defendant

The principal thrust of victims' rights litigation should be on the offensive; that is, the victim is the plaintiff. Before proceeding to this, however, it is worthwhile to digress briefly to consider a class of suit in which the victim is actually the defendant. Two cases are illustrative.

In 1972, a sixteen-year-old girl was robbed at gunpoint in a Chicago suburb. She was sufficiently alert to record the license number of the perpetrators' car and call it into the police. As a result, the robbers were arrested in the commission of another robbery. The girl identified the alleged robbers at a line-up. They then sued their victim in federal district court for conspiring with the police and prosecution officers to violate their civil rights under 42 U.S.C. § 1983 (1970).[21]

In 1974, Mrs. Nora Manis was robbed and beaten in her Winter Haven, Florida home. She positively identified Leamon Lee Miller as one of her assailants, and he was arrested. For reasons not stated in the record the charges against Miller were dismissed. Miller then sued Mrs. Manis for false imprisonment. The trial court found, as a fact, that Mrs. Manis' identification of Miller was "made in good faith, without malice and [was] in fact an honest mistake if not true."[22] The court also held that the arrest of

---

20. This article is not concerned with criminal prosecution by the state. The concern here is with the use of the civil court process to redress victims' rights.

21. Matthews v. Janega, Civil No. 74-C-70 (N.D. Ill., June 7, 1974).

22. Miller v. Manis, Case No. GC-G-74-1743, at 2 (Cir. Ct., 10th Cir., Fla., June 17, 1975).

Miller, based on Mrs. Manis' identification was lawful. Nevertheless, Mrs. Manis was found liable for $3,586.00 in compensatory damages to Miller for her good faith mistake.[23]

Cases such as these are of critical importance. If the victims of crimes were held liable in civil damages for a true, or mistaken, identification of the perpetrator, then it would not be an overstatement to say that the criminal justice system in this country would collapse. The path of the victim-witness throughout criminal proceedings is sufficiently difficult as it is. A recent survey by the Law Enforcement Assistance Administration (LEAA) indicates that perhaps half of the crimes in this country go unreported, in large measure because victims and witnesses have no faith in our criminal justice system.[24] If, in addition, victims and witnesses must identify the perpetrators of crime at their own financial peril, few would come forward.[25] Indeed, the appellate court, in reversing the Florida Circuit Court's holding in *Miller*, stated that it could find no authority for the proposition that a good faith, but mistaken, identification by the victim of the perpetrator of a crime would subject the victim to liability. There is ample authority to defend the victim who finds himself sued for such a good faith error.[26]

Thus, it would seem that the law is clearly on the side of the victims and witnesses, who make good faith, albeit mistaken, identifications of the perpetrators of crimes. This is as it should be; policy considerations dictate that victims be able to make their accusations to the police with relative impunity. In the words of the California Supreme Court, the victims of crime should not be held to the responsibility of guarantors of the accuracy of their identification.[27] Of course, a bad faith identification or accusation is still punishable under common law tort principles.[28]

Suits by victims against perpetrators

There is no legal reason why the victims of crime should not have a civil cause of action against their assailants (in cases of murder the survivor or personal representative of the decedent's estate would have the cause of action). Common law torts in assault, battery or wrongful death would lie. The reason that relatively few such lawsuits have been filed is that most criminals are judgment-proof because of indigence, and often in jail. As one commentator has noted, "Crimes of violence are not ordinarily committed by the rich."[29] This creates a real

---

23. *Id.*

24. U.S. Dep't of Justice, Law Enforcement Assistance Administration, Criminal Victimization Surveys in the Nation's Five Largest Cities (1975).

25. This author, who was involved in the defense of both cases, found very little case law on the subject of the victim as defendant. Fortunately, such case law as was found was favorable to the defendant's position. The victim in the Illinois case was dismissed. Matthews v. Janega, Civil No. 74-C-70 (N.D. Ill. June 7, 1974) at 3. The District Court of Appeal for the Second Judicial District in Florida found for Mrs. Manis, and reversed the trial court's award of damages. Manis v. Miller, 327 So. 2d 117 (Fla. 1976). *Manis* was considered to be of such importance that amicus curiae briefs in support of the victim-defendant were filed by the Attorney General of the State of Florida, the Florida Sheriffs Association, the Florida Prosecuting Attorneys Association and Americans for Effective Law Enforcement, Inc. The language of the Florida Appeals Court opinion is instructive. It held that:

> The question presented is whether, under Florida law, the court is required to award damages for a plaintiff against a defendant who has made a good faith, honest mistake as to the identity of a party in a criminal procedure, said mis-

take being one of the factors to the plaintiff's arrest and imprisonment.

> Clearly the question posed is one of substantial public interest and great concern. Prompt and effective law enforcement is directly dependent upon the willingness and cooperation of private persons to assist law enforcement officers in bringing those who violate our criminal laws to justice. Unfortunately, too often in the past witnesses and victims of criminal offenses have failed to report crimes to the proper law enforcement agencies. Private citizens should be encouraged to become interested and involved in bringing perpetrators of crime to justice and not discouraged under apprehension or fear of recrimination.

Id. at 117.

26. 327 So. 2d at 117-18. *See* Armstead v. Escobedo, 488 F.2d 509 (5th Cir. 1974); Turner v. Mellon, 41 Cal. 2d 45, 257 P.2d 15 (1953); Hughes v. Oreb, 36 Cal. 2d 854, 228 P.2d 550 (1951); Linnen v. Banfield, 114 Mich. 93, 72 N.W. 1 (1897); Shires v. Cobb, 534 P.2d 188 (Ore. 1975); White v. Pacific Tel. & Tel. Co., 162 Ore. 270, 90 P.2d 193 (1939).

27. Turner v. Mellon, 41 Cal. 2d 45, 257 P.2d 15, 17 (1953).

28. *See, e.g.,* W. Prosser, Law of Torts 834, 837 (4th ed. 1971).

29. Schultz, *The Violated: A Proposal to Compensate Victims of Violent Crime,* 10 St. Louis U.L.J. 238, 243 n.2 (1965).

problem for victims who go through the expense and often the trauma of re-living the crime only to get judgments that are, for all intents and purposes, worthless.

Nevertheless, newspaper accounts from across the country indicate that increasing numbers of such lawsuits are beginning to crop up. Apparently, in some instances, victims are able to convince attorneys, or vice versa, that actions for civil damages should be brought against the perpetrators of violent crimes. At least one jurist has called for such a development. Judge John B. Wilson, Jr. of the Marion County, Indiana, Criminal Court, in a speech before the Marion County Victim Advocate Program, suggested that victims of violent crimes should file civil lawsuits against those who have harmed them and that victim advocate groups should get state funds to finance such suits, just as many defendants receive free legal counsel. Judge Wilson said there is really very little deterrent to criminally inclined individuals in our legal system, and that the threat of civil action might provide some.[30]

The idea of state assistance in filing victims' rights lawsuits is certainly novel. Moreover, it would appear to stand up under analysis. We have seen the growth of any number of state-funded human rights and civil rights boards and commissions charged with the laudable task of enforcing the civil rights of our citizens. Why, then, should not the government get into the business of enforcing the rights of the victims of crime? The problem remains that even if there was state funding for the civil suits, thus taking the financial burden off victims, the result in most cases would be the same: an uncollectible judgment.

Some of the current crop of suits by victims against perpetrators have built into them a sort of catharsis for the victim. A recent case is of interest in this respect. In January of 1976, Mrs. Mary Knight of Montgomery County, Maryland received an award of $365,000 in civil damages against two men who had beaten and raped her in August of 1970. A jury assessed $40,000 in compensatory damages and $325,000 in punitive damages against William

D. Christianson and Edward E. David, both of whom had earlier pled guilty to rape and attempted rape charges.[31] According to Barry Helfand, an attorney for the victim, the case was the first of its kind in Maryland.[32] Mrs. Knight was outspoken about her ordeal and her motivation for filing the suit. She candidly told newspaper reporters that she did not believe that she would ever be able to collect the money, but she continued:

[T]he purpose of this trial wasn't to collect. The purpose of this trial was that it's high time somebody got off their tail and did something about "rape". . . .

I'm not a woman's libber . . . . I'm not one of these girls who thinks men are chauvinist pigs and gets insulted if a man opens the door for them. [But] so what if these guys are sitting in jail, big deal. What about my doctor bills? What about the hospital bills? What about the mental anguish?[33]

But of more importance to the victim than the potential monetary remuneration was the opportunity to express through the civil courts the outrage that she felt so strongly. This is made apparent when we consider the fact that Mrs. Knight knew before she filed the lawsuit that the civil jury would hear details of her sex life, and the fact that she had been a topless dancer. She persisted nevertheless, and the jury, by its verdict, vindicated her right not to be beaten and raped.[34]

---

30. Indianapolis Star, June 10, 1976, at 17, col. 3.

31. Washington Post, Feb. 1, 1976, § B, at 1, col. 6.
32. *Id.*
33. *Id. See also* National Observer, Feb. 14, 1976, at 7, col. 1.
34. Other examples of instances in which the victim has sued the perpetrator directly are: (1) The parents of a University of Virginia coed who had been stabbed to death in Charlottesville in 1972 were awarded $15,746 in a jury verdict against the killer. Washington Post, May 20, 1976, § C, at 16, col. 2; (2) The families of three prison guards at San Quentin killed in a bloody escape attempt in 1971 were awarded $2.1 million in a California Superior Court default judgment against the convicts accused of engineering and participating in the breakout attempt. San Francisco Chronicle, October 24, 1975, at 41, col. 4; (3) The wife of a Phoenix, Arizona man who was shot to death filed a $1.6 million suit against the convicted killer and his wife in Phoenix Superior Court. The case has bizzare overtones: the wife of the killer, desiring to make her husband jealous, lured him to a bar, then hugged and kissed the victim on the dance floor, whereupon the husband shot him. The allegation is that the killer and his wife negligently caused the victim's death. Arizona Republic, Aug. 2, 1975, § A, at 25, col. 5;
Footnote continued on p. 312.

Other similar lawsuits have been filed in other parts of the country.[35] The common thread running throughout all of the actions is that the plaintiff-victim (or personal representative) has elected to utilize the civil process to redress criminal injury. The problem common to all is the difficulty of collecting any judgments obtained. Most of the perpetrators are currently incarcerated and will be for quite some time, and none appear, from the reports of the cases, to be affluent.

The deterrent or preventive effect of such lawsuits is problematical. It is conceivable that if a sufficient number of civil suits was filed in a given jurisdiction over a period of time, a statistically valid sample could be tabulated from which it could be determined whether there is a measurable impact on crime rates. As it is, the paucity of lawsuits and their scattered nature provide insufficient data to resolve this question. This is not to say that such lawsuits should not be filed. Where recovery *is* possible, even in small amounts, the victim is surely entitled to be compensated by the criminal. Additionally, the mere fact that some attorneys are willing to file on behalf of victims indicates that there is a rising consciousness of victims' rights in the legal profession. Finally, and perhaps as important as anything else, is the cathartic effect illustrated by Mrs. Knight's successful suit against the men who raped and beat her. From her comments, it is apparent that if she never recovers a penny of the judgment award, at least she now believes that her right to go about her business without being molested has been vindicated in the civil courts.

Suits by victims against third parties

The theory behind this class of suits is that a criminal has injured a victim, and that one of the reasons that the criminal was in a position or at liberty to do so was that a third party negligently failed in some duty that he owed the victim, such as to provide proper security on the premises, to supervise the criminal or to confine the criminal safely.

Usually the third parties will not be judgment-proof as often as the criminals themselves, but there are practical and conceptual problems involved in third-party lawsuits. First, many defendants in such cases will be government entities—states and cities, parole boards, correctional administrations and so on. Consequently, an initial problem will be whether the defendant is absolutely immune from a civil suit under the doctrine of sovereign immunity.[36] Several states have waived tort immunity, in whole or in part,[37] and this obviates the problem in those that have.

A conceptual problem also arises of "second-guessing" the defendants' good faith decisions which led to the negligence complained of. For example, it would be unfair to hold a corrections administrator liable every time he released a convict on work release or on furlough, where that convict later victimized someone. The job of corrections officers and administrators is difficult enough as it is, without requiring them to act at their financial peril every time they make a disposition in a given case. It is for this reason that there is usually some additional factor involved when liability has been found against third parties: an unauthorized act or implementation.

A recent and important case, decided by the United States Court of Appeals for the Fourth Circuit, illustrates most of the principles involved in third-party victims' rights litigation. The case, *Semler v. Psychiatric Institute,*[38] involved a lawsuit by Mrs. Semler to recover damages for the death of her daughter, Natalie, who was killed by John Stephen Gilreath, a Virginia probationer who had been a patient

---

(4) An Edwardsville, Illinois dentist, whose office was burglarized five times in one year, filed suit against two of the convicted burglars in Madison County Circuit Court, seeking $50 in compensatory damages and $200,000 in punitive damages against them. St. Louis Post-Dispatch, June 2, 1976, § E, at 1, col. 1.

35. Washington Post, April 26, 1975, § B, at 2, col. 1; Phoenix Gazette, June 24, 1975, at 13, col. 5.

36. *See generally* 57 Am. Jur. 2d *Municipal, School, and State Tort Liability* § 1 *et seq.* (1971).

37. *See generally* Council of State Governments, Suggested Legislation (1973).

38. 538 F.2d 121 (4th Cir.), *cert. denied,* 97 S. Ct. 83 (1976).

at the defendant institute and who was released inadvertently. Gilreath's probation officer, Paul Folliard, was joined as a third-party defendant by the original defendants. The case was filed in the United States District Court for the Eastern District of Virginia based on diversity of citizenship. The trial court heard the case without a jury and awarded the plaintiff $25,000 jointly and severally against the psychiatric institute, Gilreath's psychiatrist (Dr. Wadeson) and probation officer Folliard.[39] The defendants appealed. The Fourth Circuit affirmed in a unanimous three-judge panel opinion.[40]

The facts were not really in dispute. Gilreath had been indicted in Fairfax County, Virginia for abducting a young girl in October of 1971. Pending his trial, and after he entered the defendant psychiatric institute for treatment, Dr. Wadeson wrote to Gilreath's attorney that, in his opinion, Gilreath would benefit from continued treatment, and that he did not "'consider him to be a danger to himself or others as long as he is in a supervised, structured way of life such as furnished here at Psychiatric Institute.'"[41] As a result of these representations, Judge William Plummer sentenced Gilreath on his guilty plea to twenty years imprisonment, but suspended the sentence, conditioned upon his continued treatment and confinement at the Institute. In the ensuing months, Judge Plummer, at the recommendation of Dr. Wadeson and at the request of the probation officer, allowed Gilreath to visit his family at Thanksgiving and Christmas, allowed additional three-day passes, allowed the probation officer to grant week-end passes at his discretion and then permitted Gilreath to be placed on day-care patient status. In August, Gilreath was discharged from the Institute on the assumption that Ohio probation authorities would accept him. When Gilreath was not accepted by the Ohio authorities he returned to Virginia, but Dr. Wadeson, with the consent of the probation officer, decided to enroll Gilreath in a therapy group that met two

nights a week, rather than return him to day-care status. This decision was made on September 19, 1973, without informing the court. On October 29, 1973, Gilreath killed the plaintiff's daughter.

The appeals court could find no Virginia case specifically on point, so it resorted to a general principle of Virginia tort law. The court found the applicable statement of law to be:

> To constitute actionable negligence there must be a duty, a violation thereof, and a consequent injury. An accident which is not reasonably to be foreseen by the exercise of reasonable care and prudence is not sufficient ground for a negligence action.[42]

The court then analyzed each of the elements of actionable negligence with regard to the facts of the specific case. It found the question of whether there was a duty owed to the general public, and to plaintiff's decedent in particular, to be a question of law,[43] and they found that there was such a duty.

In dictum that may bode well for the future of victims' rights litigation, the court next noted a general principle of law: "Confinement of criminals frequently is intended to protect the public, as well as punish and rehabilitate the wrongdoer."[44] However, the duty in this case could be premised, not on general principles, but on the state court judge's specific order which, in turn, was based on the judge's concern for the protection of the public.[45] The court of appeals found that a duty of "reasonable care"

---

39. *Id.* at 121.
40. 538 F.2d 121, 123 (4th Cir. 1976).
41. *Id.*

---

42. Trimyer v. Norfolk Tallow Co., 192 Va. 776, 780, 66 S.E. 2d 441, 443 (1951).
43. Chesapeake & Pot. Tel. Co. v. Bullock, 182 Va. 440, 29 S.E.2d 228, 230 (1944). The appeals court in *Semler* first analyzed and rejected defendants' contention that the state trial judge's order of confinement of Gilreath until release by the court was solely to rehabilitate Gilreath, and that their duty extended only to him. First, said the court, the nature of the defendants' duty depends in large measure upon the forseeability of harm to the public, or to Natalia Semler, if Gilreath were released in violation of the court's order.
44. 538 F.2d at 124.
45. It is apparent that the decision to release Gilreath was not to be simply a medical judgment based on the state of his mental health. The decision would also entail a judgment by the court as to whether his release would be in the best interest of the community. 538 F.2d at 125.

was owed.[46] "Reasonable care" in this case was delineated by the court's order to confine Gilreath until release by the court; the court order was violated, thus the standard of reasonable care was violated.

The court next determined that there was a breach of the duty owed. Defendants contended that the transfer of Gilreath from day-care to outpatient status was merely a normal progression of treatment, which required no prior judicial approval. The court of appeals, however, affirmed the federal trial court's finding that there was a significant difference between day-care and outpatient status, including the lack of supervision, lack of daily psychiatric treatment and failure to monitor essential medication for Gilreath. Failure to obtain the state trial judge's permission to transfer Gilreath to outpatient status was a breach of the duty owed.

The court then found that the death of Natalia Semler was proximately caused by defendants' negligence, upholding the civil trial court's finding, based on expert psychiatric testimony, that it was less likely that Gilreath would have killed her had he remained on day-care. In addition, the state court's order was based on the foreseeability of harm, thereby making the violation of that order, in itself, a demonstration of proximate cause.

Finally, the court found no error in the trial court's rejection of the defendant parole officer's contention that his actions were discretionary, and therefore immune. Under Virginia law, a state employee who exercises discretionary judgment within the scope of his employment is immune from liability for negligence, but not for the performance of ministerial acts.[47] While

a probation officer's policy decisions are discretionary, the manner in which such policy decisions are implemented is to be considered on a case-by-case basis in order to determine if they are ministerial.[48] In this case, the court found that the sentencing court's order, in effect, removed from the probation officer the discretion to release Gilreath. Since such an act had to be made in obedience to a mandate of the court, it was ministerial, and therefore not immune.[49]

Is *Semler* a watershed case in the area of victims' rights litigation, or is it merely a restatement of the law of negligence in light of the particular factual situation of the case? Earlier in this article it was postulated that in third-party victims' rights litigation, at least from the standpoint of not "second-guessing" the defendants' good-faith decisions, there must be "something extra" in the case if the plaintiff is to recover. In *Semler,* the something extra was, of course, the state court's order not to release Gilreath from confinement without its approval. Phrased another way, would the outcome have been the same if the order had been a mere administrative commitment of Gilreath to the Institute without further limitation on release? It seems likely that, absent the court order, the outcome would have been different for probation officer Folliard, at least insofar as the immunity question was concerned. This is so because the civil trial court premised its finding that Folliard's actions were ministerial, and hence not immune, precisely on the fact that he was operating under a mandate of the court, and simply had no discretion under which to act.

With regard to the defendants, Psychiatric Institute and Dr. Wadeson, it is more difficult to say whether they would have been liable, absent the violated court order. Certainly the court of appeals relied specifically on the state court's order to establish the duty which was found to have been breached; but, as noted, it also said that confinement of criminals is

---

46. The special relationship created by the probation order, therefore, imposed a duty on the appellants to protect the public from the reasonably foreseeable risk of harm at Gilreath's hands which the state judge had already recognized. 538 F.2d at 125. The court cited RESTATEMENT (SECOND) OF TORTS § 319 (1965), providing:

> One who takes charge of a third person whom he knows or should know to be likely to cause bodily harm to others if not controlled is under a duty to exercise reasonable care to control the third person to prevent him from doing such harm.

47. Lawhorne v. Harlan, 214 Va. 405, 200 S.E.2d 569 (1973).

---

48. Johnson v. State, 69 Cal. 2d 782, 447 P.2d 352, 73 Cal. Rptr. 240 (1968).

49. *Id.,* 447 P.2d at 362, 73 Cal. Rptr. at 250.

intended to protect the public, as well as to punish and rehabilitate the wrongdoer. While it is unclear what effect this language, standing alone, will have on prospective victims' rights litigation, the following cases may be illustrative.

A case involving an apparent breach, by a corrections officer, of a duty to protect the public arose under unusual circumstances in the State of Washington. In 1972, a convict, with the improbable name of Arthur St. Peter and a record of forty felonies and seventeen escape attempts, left the walls of the maximum security state penitentiary at Walla-Walla to have supper with a prison baker. He escaped through a bathroom window and, two weeks later, in the course of an armed robbery, shot and killed a fifty-four-year-old pawnbroker named Robert Taylor and wounded his wife, Lorraine.[50]

St. Peter had been free and unguarded when he made his escape under an ill-conceived "Take a Lifer to Dinner" program instituted by Warden Bobby J. Rhay. Mrs. Taylor sued Rhay and the State of Washington under the theory that the release of St. Peter was negligent, in that the program had never been authorized by the state legislature. The trial court instructed the jury that the warden did not have the authority to let prisoners outside the prison walls without specific authorization in the form of legislative programs. Mrs. Taylor

was awarded $186,000.00. The state elected not to appeal. Here again is a case of recovery by a victim against a third party for an obviously negligent action. Additionally, there is the "something extra" because Warden Rhay did not have the administrative authority to release the prisoner as he did.

Other cases have permitted recovery or denied a motion to dismiss in suits involving the general area of negligent release when the plaintiff was able to prove that the custodial facilities had a history of lax security, or that the escaped prisoner had a history of violent tendencies.[51]

It is difficult to generalize in this area. For one thing there is little appellate case law, and what there is is not uniform. It can perhaps be said that, absent absolute immunity or discretionary immunity,[52] cases on behalf of victims (or survivors) premised on a theory of negligent release or negligent failure to prevent escape can be won. While a showing of something extra, such as violation of a court order[53] or action in excess of administrative authority,[54] may not be essential to winning the case, it is certainly most helpful. The balance is delicate. On the one hand, it would not be fair to second-guess the already hard-pressed corrections and custodial officers when they make a mistake. On the other hand, if real negligence is demonstrated in the release or escape of a crim-

---

50. Taylor v. State, No. 211-130 (Super Ct., Pierce County, Wash., Sept. 10, 1973); see also Tacoma News Tribune, May 20, 1973, at 1.

51. Webb v. State, 91 So. 2d 156 (La. App. 1956) (negligence found based on faulty prison security and knowledge of violent record of prison escapee who shot plaintiff with a gun stolen from a prison guard). But cf. Green v. State, 91 So. 2d 153 (La. App. 1956). In Morgan v. County of Yuba, 230 Cal. App. 2d 938, 41 Cal. Rptr. 508 (1964) (the warden had promised plaintiff's decedent that he would warn him if a certain prisoner was released), although the warden was under no duty to give a warning in the first place, his failure to do so after his promise amounted to a breach of a duty upon which liability could be predicated. Contra. West Virginia v. Fidelity & Cas. Co., 263 F. Supp. 88 (S.D.W. Va. 1967) (no proximate cause); Ne Casek v. City of Los Angeles, 233 Cal. App. 2d 131, 43 Cal. Rptr. 294 (1965) (discretionary immunity); Hullinger v. Warrell, 83 Ill. 220 (1876) (no proximate cause); William v. State, 308 N.Y. 548, 127 N.E.2d 545 (1955) (No duty to particular victims of escapee).

52. See, e.g., Pate v. Alabama State Bd. of Pardons & Paroles, 409 F. Supp. 478 (D. Ala. 1976); Reiff v. Pennsylvania, 397 F. Supp. 345 (E.D. Pa. 1975), which held members of state probation and parole boards and state parole officers are immune from civil suit in the discretionary release of criminals who shot the plaintiff.

53. See, e.g., Semler v. Psychiatric Institute, 538 F.2d 121 (4th Cir. 1976). Of course, one way to ensure that an action will lie for violation of a court order would be through the enactment of state and federal legislation requiring that no person who has been convicted of a violent crime, and received probation conditioned upon psychiatric treatment, shall be granted any lesser degree of confinement, without prior approval by the committing court. This sort of legislation would have the advantage of placing questions of the safety of society within the criminal justice system, where they belong, rather than in the hands of psychiatrists.

54. See notes 46 & 47 supra and accompanying text.

inal who then victimizes another, it would seem that the victim should be entitled to recover. It may take years to resolve this conflict, but it is one which should engage the attention and energies of the legal profession.

Another type of victims' rights litigation against third parties arises in the form of suits alleging negligent failure to provide security which the defendant had a duty to provide the victim, which, if it had been provided, would have prevented the victimization. Provided there are no immunity problems, defendants can be government entities or private parties. The following cases are illustrative. In *Neering v. Illinois Central Railroad*,[55] the plaintiff, a regular commuter on the defendant's line, was assaulted, raped and robbed by a tramp lingering in the railroad station while the victim waited for her train. She and her sister had complained vigorously during an eight-month period preceding the attack that, with growing prevalence, bums and hobos were loitering in the station. The Illinois Supreme Court, finding that the defendant railroad company and its police were on notice of the dangerous condition, and that the attack was foreseeable, reversed a directed verdict for the defendants.

In *Bass v. City of New York*,[56] the plaintiff's decedent sued the New York Housing Authority which was the sole landlord for a low-cost housing unit in which the plaintiff lived. Although the housing unit covered sixteen acres and comprised ten fourteen-story buildings, there was only one housing authority policeman on duty at the time of the victim's death (and he was at lunch). The victim, a nine-year-old girl, was abducted while returning to school after lunch, carried to the roof of the project, beaten, raped and finally thrown off the roof. The trial judge awarded $100,000 to the victim's parents for pain and suffering, and $35,000 for her death, on the theory that the Housing Authority was negligent in failing to provide adequate protection for the residents after leading them to believe that this had been done.[57]

In *Rutledge v. Midwest Security Agency*,[58]

the plaintiff, a 52-year-old hospital cashier was attacked by two youths while she was entering her apartment, causing her to lose an eye. After settling with the building's landlord, the plaintiff sued the agency that provided the private security guards to the building. Her complaint alleged that the guards on duty did not patrol the area or disperse youths who regularly drank, smoked marijuana and abused tenants. On the night in question, certain guards were observed coming out of a lounge, and later sleeping in their cars. The plaintiff also argued that the guards were not adequately trained or screened. A jury awarded her $100,000.[59]

In November of 1974, a George Washington University coed reached a $6,000 settlement with the university in a suit alleging a failure to protect her from forcible sodomy and rape.[60] The young lady was sexually assaulted by a 17-year-old male. Her suit alleged that the campus police failed to arrest the rapist on a previous occasion when he sexually assaulted another student, that they failed to respond to the plaintiff's cries for help and that they assisted the defendant in the criminal case, out of a hope that his acquittal would prove favorable to the university in the civil action. The young lady's case against the university was strong, since statements made by her attacker prior to, and after, his criminal trial corroborated the victim's version of the incident. However, five days prior to trial, a settlement was reached, with the victim receiving $6,000, and the security officer, in a counterclaim of libel against the victim, receiving $1,000.[61]

---

55. 383 Ill. 366, 50 N.E.2d 497 (1943).
56. 61 Misc. 2d 465, 305 N.Y.S.2d 801 (Sup. Ct. 1969).
57. 305 N.Y.S.2d at 803.
58. No. 71L-16265 (Cir. Ct. Cook Co., Ill. July, 1965).

59. *Id.*
60. Goldenberg v. George Washington Univ., No. CA-416-72 (Super. Ct., D.C., Oct. 9, 1974).
61. *Id.* Recovery has been denied in a number of cases. In Cornpropst v. Sloan, 528 S.W.2d 188 (Tenn. 1975), the court found no liability on the part of the owners of a shopping center to customers assaulted in a parking lot when the premises did not attract a climate of crime or criminal elements, and there was no reason to know that acts posing a probability of harm were likely to occur. In Slater v. Alpha Beta Acme Markets, Inc., 44 Cal. App. 3d 274, 118 Cal. Rptr. 561 (1975), no recovery was allowed a customer against a supermarket. Two policemen and a plain clothes security officer were stationed in the store because of prior robberies. When another robbery took place the plaintiff was thrown to the floor by another customer, apparently as a security precaution.

The preventive aspect of these cases should not be ignored. Since we are all potential victims of crime, it should be of considerable interest to every citizen that, in addition to vindicating the rights of the actual victim in a given instance, such cases are likely to cause people and organizations responsible for protecting the public from criminals and would-be criminals to take greater care in the future. Thus, psychiatrists and probation officers who are made aware of the *Semler* case, and they all should be, will not be quite as ready to make similar dispositions of their other charges. Likewise, a third party who fails to provide adequate security, and is forced to pay in damages for this failure, will probably ensure that future security is adequate. Wardens tempted to initiate release programs of dubious value, and which do not adequately provide for public safety, will think twice if they learn of Mrs. Taylor's recovery against Warden Rhay. The importance of the preventive aspect of victims' rights litigation can be summed up succinctly: it is all very well to counsel and compensate a victim who has been hit on the head, but the chances are that he would rather not have been hit on the head in the first place.

Two recent cases have resulted in sensational amounts of damages in third party victims rights suits. In January, 1975, a Montgomery County, Maryland jury awarded $13,355,000 to a man whose wife was raped and murdered by an employee of a furniture leasing company in the El Dorado Towers apartments in White Oak, Maryland.[62] In July of 1976, a Brooklyn federal court jury awarded singer Connie Francis $2.5 million in damages against the Howard Johnson Motor Lodge in Westbury, New York. Ms. Francis had alleged that the motel was negligent in not providing adequate security and room door locks and, as a consequence, she was raped and traumatized to such an extent that she was unable to resume her singing career because she was afraid to stay alone in a motel room.[63]

The findings of *liability* in these two cases seem to square with the theories of third party victims' rights litigation discussed above: a duty to provide reasonable security of premises, a breach of that duty, reliance by the victims on an express or implied promise of security and proximate cause. However, the *size* of the awards causes this writer some problems, and, as usual, brings into sharp focus the inherent conflicts in most areas of victims' rights litigation. On the one hand, these cases are two examples of the most vicious sort of victimization, with a loss to the victims (or survivors) which cannot be measured in damages. On the other hand, the results of runaway jury verdicts, such as have occurred in medical malpractice cases, are all too clear. Excessive awards in medical malpractice cases have driven many insurance companies out of the field and increased the rates of those who will still write insurance astronomically, with the result that some physicians in high risk specialties are refusing to engage in their specialties. There is no easy solution to this problem. It can only be hoped that as victims' rights litigation de-

---

62. Yaeger, *$13 Million Damages in Rape-Murder,* Chicago Sun-Times, Jan. 24, 1975, at 1, col. 1. The $11,000,000 in punitive damages was awarded against the company which owned the apartment building, on the grounds that it had failed to provide the security that it had promised to its tenants. The $2,355,000 in compensatory damages was paid by the apartment owners and the furniture leasing company which had hired the decedent's murderer. The allegation against the employer was that it had failed to investigate the background of the employee, which would have shown that he had been convicted of armed robbery in the District of Columbia and that he was on parole at the time of the slaying. This case raises a particularly thorny problem with regard to an employer's liability for failure to investigate the background of an employee. Several states now have laws which prohibit or restrict employers

from requesting information about prospective employees' arrest record. See, e.g., ILL. REV. STAT. ch. 38, § 206-7 (1973). Other statutes require expungement of arrest records if no cinviction is obtained. See, e.g., CONN. GEN. STAT. ANN. § 54-90 (West Cum. Supp. 1976). S. 2008, 94th Cong., 1st Sess. (1975), would have gone even further. It was intended to prohibit law enforcement agencies from disseminating any criminal justice information, including records of arrests and convictions, to non-criminal justice agencies, including employers. Obviously, it would be grossly unfair to an employer to hold him liable for negligent failure to investigate the background of an employee if, under the law, the necessary information would not be available to him. If this could be proven, it should be an absolute defense to such a claim.
63. Des Moines Register, July 7, 1976, at 1, col. 5.

velops, a balance will be struck which will ensure that the victim is adequately compensated without creating the syndrome of runaway jury verdicts.

CONCLUSION

The victims of crime in the United States are long overdue their day in civil court. Our legal system has, for the most part, reached the point of providing a remedy whenever there is an injury. Yet, this aspect of civil litigation on behalf of crime victims has been largely ignored, as has its preventative aspect.

Victims' rights litigation can be classified basically into two areas—victim v. perpetrator; and victim v. third party. In the former class of cases, the practical aspect of uncollectable judgments may serve as a realistic bar to doing anything consistently successful for victims. In the latter class of cases, in many instances, collectibility is no bar; the defendants are not judgment-proof. Problems of immunity remain, although the trend seems to be away from ab-

solute sovereign tort immunity. In any event, if a person has been victimized through the negligence of a non-immune third party, and if the elements of negligence (duty, breach and proximate cause) can be alleged and proved, then the crime victim, as plaintiff, should have the same status in our legal system as other parties, injured by the negligence of others, have had for decades.

ADDENDUM

Since this law review article was written an important case in the area of victims rights litigation has been decided:

Grimm v. Arizona Board of Pardons & Paroles, S. Ct. Ariz., No. 12775-P.R. (April, 1977), in which the Arizona Supreme Court held that the state parole board was not immune from liability for the negligent release of a prisoner who, after his release, murdered plaintiff's decedent.

See also:

Valeu v. California, Cal. App., 2nd Appellate District, Division 3 (2nd Civ. No. 42554). In this non-published opinion, the Court held that the California Youth Authority was not immune from a lawsuit alleging that it negligently failed to supervise a releasee who subsequently assaulted the plaintiff. The case was subsequently settled for $265,000.

C ☐ *The role of the victim in the prosecution and disposition of a criminal case*

DONALD J. HALL

I. INTRODUCTION

A theoretical underpinning of the American system of criminal justice is the notion that a criminal misdeed is a wrong against the entire society.[1] Accordingly, the local, state and federal

governments, acting as the representatives of society, assume the duty and responsibility of prosecuting the individual wrongdoer. While the individual victim of a crime obviously is the party directly "wronged," society interjects and institutes the formal proceeding to ascertain criminal responsibility and determine the appropriate sanction to be imposed upon the accused. This constitutes a basic distinction between civil and criminal cases; the aggrieved individual is the named litigant in a civil case (the plaintiff); in a criminal case, the government prosecutes the defendant.[2]

Excerpted by permission of the *Vanderbilt Law Review* from vol. 28, no. 5, pp. 932-964, 980-985, October 1975.

1. W. LaFave & A. Scott, Handbook on Criminal Law 11 (1972). If society is deemed to be the "victim," the so-called "victimless" crime is a misnomer; *see* E. Schur, Crimes Without Victims (1965). It has been reported that ". . . the authorities do not agree among themselves as to which crimes are victimless." E. Schur & H. Bedau, Victimless Crimes: Two Sides of a Controversy 59 (1974).

2. W. La Fave & A. Scott, *supra* note 1, at 11, 14.

In recent years lawyers, legislators and commentators have evinced a growing interest in the person most directly affected by crime—the victim.[3] Perhaps the most widely studied topic in the field of victimology has been the compensation of victims of crime.[4] Other studies have suggested that in exercising their broad discretion police and prosecutors consider the desires of the victims.[5] No single research project, however, has undertaken carefully to assess the role that the victim plays in the prosecution and disposition of the criminal case. The purpose of this article is to describe and evaluate the ways in which a victim can influence the course of a criminal case, from investigation and arrest to parole release and clemency. Data concerning the roles that the victim may play in a criminal case have been gathered by the author through personal interviews with participants in the criminal justice system in Nashville, Tennessee. These participants include police officers, defense attorneys, prosecuting attorneys, judges, probation officers, parole board officials, and members of the Governor's staff.

Victims were not interviewed. Were it the purpose of this study to demonstrate the satisfaction or dissatisfaction of victims with the criminal justice system or to describe the victim's perception of his role, the views of victims certainly would have been solicited. The scope of this research is more limited, however, and the victim's perception of the system therefore is largely irrelevant. A victim of an armed robbery may believe that his "tough" attitude influenced the prosecutor to go to trial on the maximum chargeable offense. Similarly, the burglary victim may believe that his expression of leniency was responsible for the district attorney's decision to accept a plea of guilty to criminal trespass. Nevertheless, the individual best qualified to assess the *actual* role that the victim plays in these instances is the prosecutor.

Because of limitations on finances and research personnel, interviews were not conducted outside of the Nashville area. While it is not suggested that Nashville, Tennessee is necessarily representative of communities of its size,[6] it is suggested that the practices revealed herein are not significantly different from practices in other parts of the country. It is clearly desirable, of course, that similar studies be undertaken in other communities.

For purposes of this article, the victim of a criminal act is defined as a nonconsenting individual or group of individuals directly aggrieved by the defendant's conduct. Under this definition of "victim," concert-of-action crimes such as prostitution, gambling, and incest are excluded from consideration.[7] In a homicide case or in a case in which the victim is physically or mentally incapacitated, the survivor or representative, respectively, represents the individual victim's interest. Therefore, the term "victim" includes survivors or representatives of the individual personally harmed. While the victim's reporting of crimes is included as one facet of the victim's influence, his provocation of criminal attacks upon himself and fraudulent crime reporting by would-be victims are beyond the scope of this article.

This study focuses on a frequently observed situation: the police officer or the prosecutor,

---

3. One of the earliest studies is H. HENTIG, THE CRIMINAL AND HIS VICTIM (1948). Perhaps the most recent is by Greacen, *Arbitration: A Tool for Criminal Cases?*, 2 BARRISTER 10 (Winter 1975).
4. These studies focus on the desirability and feasibility of programs under which state or local governments compensate persons for physical injuries caused by criminal acts of others; *see, e.g.*, Annot., 32 A.L.R.3d 1446 (1970); Lamborn, *Toward a Victim Orientation in Criminal Theory*, 22 RUTGERS L. REV. 733 (1968); Schafer, *The Proper Role of a Victim-Compensation System*, 21 CRIME & DELIN. 45 (1975); Note, *But What About the Victim? The Forsaken Man in American Criminal Law*, 22 U. FLA. L. REV. 1 (1969).
5. W. LaFAVE, ARREST: THE DECISION TO TAKE THE SUSPECT INTO CUSTODY 110-11, 137-43 (1965) [hereinafter cited as LaFAVE]: F. MILLER, PROSECUTION: THE DECISION TO CHARGE A SUSPECT WITH A CRIME 173-78, 283-84 (1969) [hereinafter cited as MILLER].

6. As of January 1, 1975, Metropolitan Nashville had an estimated population of 469,000. RAND-McNALLY COMMERCIAL AND MARKETING GUIDE (1975).
7. Because there is no vocal victim in concert-of-action crimes, it is very difficult for law enforcement officials to apprehend and prosecute perpetrators of these crimes. Kaplan, *The Role of the Law in Drug Control*, 1971 DUKE L.J. 1065, 1075-80.

each of whom is given broad discretion in the exercise of his responsibilities,[8] has some evidence of possible criminal involvement but is unsure of how to proceed with the case, if at all. Given this situation, can the adamant victim of the crime persuade the policeman or prosecutor to pursue the arrest or prosecution? If the victim's wishes are taken into account, do any patterns of decision-making surface according to the crime involved or the stage at which the influence is exerted, or related to the victim's status, relationship to the accused, or the victim's age, sex, race, or other characteristic? In deciding how much weight to accord to victim's desires, what criteria are used? These questions also arise when the victim strongly advocates no arrest or prosecution. Similar issues are raised at other stages of the process when judges and correctional personnel are the decision-makers.

II. THE VICTIM'S ROLE AT VARIOUS STAGES
A. Reporting crimes

One of the simplest and most effective ways that a victim can prevent a wrongdoer from being arrested and prosecuted is to fail to report the crime to responsible officials. According to a recent study sponsored by the Law Enforcement Assistance Administration and the Census Bureau, the "real" crime rate for 1972 was five times higher than police figures in Philadelphia, almost three times as high as police figures in Chicago, Detroit, and Los Angeles, and slightly more than twice as high as official counts in New York City.[9] It should be emphasized that the crimes surveyed in the study were limited to serious offenses: rape, robbery, burglary and

assault. It is likely that the statistics would show even a greater disparity between police crime figures and actual crimes if all offenses, whether felony or misdemeanor, were included in the survey.[10] Interviews with Nashville prosecutorial officials disclose a *perceived* disparity similar to that disclosed by the L.E.A.A. statistics, but empirical data is not available.

Why is it that victims of criminal attacks do not report these incidents to the government officials? The Law Enforcement Assistance Administration study revealed that thirty-four percent of those who did not report personal crime said that their decision not to report was based upon lack of proof or their belief that "nothing could be done."[11] A slightly lesser percentage of persons did not consider the criminal episode significant enough to report and still fewer reported that they did not want to bother the police, that they were afraid of reprisal from the offender, or that taking action would cause too much personal inconvenience.[12] Another possibility, but a most difficult one to establish by empirical data, is that the offender has agreed to compensate the victim.[13]

Interviews with Nashville police officers and prosecutors revealed no reason to suspect that Nashville differs significantly from the cities surveyed by the L.E.A.A. in either the incidence of or the reasons for nonreporting. In addition to the reasons for nonreporting articulated by the L.E.A.A. study, however, local police officers frequently cited the "dirty-hand syndrome." This syndrome is illustrated by the victim who is assaulted by a prostitute and for obvious personal reasons decides not to report the incident to the police.[14] Similarly, an individual possessing property obtained

---

8. *See, e.g.,* United States v. Bell, 506 F.2d 207, 222 (D.C. Cir. 1974), in which prosecutorial discretion is described as "exceedingly broad." *See also* K. Davis, Discretionary Justice (1969).

9. The Tennessean (Nashville), Apr. 15, 1974, at 1, col. 4.

10. *See also* a more recent study by LEAA concluding that "only one-third of rapes, robberies, aggravated assaults and burglaries that actually occur" were reported during the first six months of 1973. The Tennessean (Nashville), Dec. 1. 1974, at 12, col. 3. In an earlier study, approximately one-half of the rapes, robberies, assaults, burglaries and larcenies in Dayton and San Jose for the year 1970 were

not reported; however, *more than half* of the unreported crimes involved alleged larcenies of *less than $50.* LEAA, Crime and Victims: A Report on the Dayton–San Jose Pilot Survey of Victimization 24 (1974).

11. *Supra* note 9.

12. *Id.*

13. See for example 15 Am. Jur. 2d *Compromise and Settlement* §§ 22.29 (1964) and Annot., 42 A.L.R. 3d 315 (1972), discussing the legality of such agreements and whether they effectively preclude criminal prosecution (they do *not*).

14. Interview with Sergeant Luther Summers, July 10, 1974 [hereinafter cited as Summers interview].

under questionable circumstances is reluctant to report the theft of that property to the police for fear of implicating himself in possible criminal wrongdoing.[15] In another case a person was criminally attacked but would not report the incident because to do so would have revealed his whereabouts at that time, with embarrassing consequences to that individual.[16]

Reinforcing the L.E.A.A. disclosures, the Davidson County District Attorney said that one reason for nonreporting is the "reputation of police inability to apprehend," and he suggested that only about five percent of the burglaries and one-tenth of one percent of car break-ins are solved.[17] Some police officers felt that many persons, especially those in the lower economic groups, do not report crimes because they distrust the "system."[18] Particularly in rape cases, the distrustful victim may actually fear the prospect of filing a criminal complaint.[19] Another instance of nonreporting, most applicable in less serious felonies, is the "family squabble." Often, the only way these offenses are made known to the police is that witnesses, usually neighbors, complain.[20] Perhaps the most troubling of all reasons for nonreporting is reflected by the statement of one officer that persons living in poor, predominately black sections of the city fail to report property crimes because "it is a part of their life."[21]

While the nonreporting of crime is an effective way to prevent the apprehension and prosecution of a suspect, it is not always determinative. Many criminal acts are committed in the presence of witnesses who will report the incident to police.[22] Secondly, knowledge of previously unreported criminal acts is gained through custodial interrogation carried out for the resolution of other crimes. Lastly, automobile license checks and similar screening devices sometimes reveal previously unreported criminal conduct.

B. Investigating crimes

Victims occasionally assist in the investigation of crimes in a more substantial way than by simply providing answers to officers' questions. While this role is not frequently observed, it can be a most useful, if not crucial, aid to the prosecutor. In one case, for example, the district attorney's office had been unable to locate a key witness to the crime, and the witness' testimony was deemed critical. Through the efforts of the victim, the witness was found, the testimony was adduced, and a conviction was obtained.[23]

C. Influencing the decision to arrest
(1) Arrest by victim

Under the statutes of most states, a private party may, acting in good faith, arrest another without a warrant, (1) for a misdemeanor constituting a "breach of the public peace" and committed in the citizen's presence, or (2) when a felony has been committed and the person making the arrest has reasonable cause to believe that the arrestee committed the felony.[24] Slight variations from these requirements are found in some states. For instance, in some jurisdictions a citizen may arrest another for a felony only if the felony is actually committed in his presence.[25]

Most cases involving the validity of citizen's arrests concern interpretations of the statutory

---

15. Interview with Officer Joe Blakely, Aug. 12, 1974 [hereinafter cited as Blakely interview].

16. Summers interview, *supra* note 14.

17. Interview with District Attorney Thomas Shriver, Aug. 9, 1974 [hereinafter cited as Shriver interview].

18. Summers interview, *supra* note 14.

19. Interview with Detective Dianne Vaughn, Aug. 28, 1974 [hereinafter cited as Vaughn interview]. Recent articles dealing with treatment accorded rape victims include Bohmer, *Judicial Attitudes Toward Rape Victims*, 57 JUDICATURE 303 (1974), and Note, *Rape and Rape Laws: Sexism in Society and Law*, 61 CALIF. L. REV. 919 (1973).

20. Blakely interview, *supra* nota 15.

21. *Id.*

22. In Dayton, Ohio, of 9,300 crimes reported to police in 1970, 2,370 (approximately 25%) were reported by someone other than the victim. A similar percentage (2,930 out of 11,190) was reported in San Jose, California. LEAA 1 CRIMES AND VICTIMS: A REPORT ON THE DAYTON–SAN JOSE PILOT SURVEY OF VICTIMIZATION 122 (1974).

23. Interview with Assistant District Attorney Ed Yarbrough, July 10, 1974 [hereinafter cited as Yarbrough interview].

24. *See, e.g.,* CAL. PENAL CODE § 837 (West 1970); TENN. CODE ANN. § 40-816 (1955).

25. 5 AM. JUR. 2d *Arrest* § 36 (1962).

"in presence" requirement.[26] Generally, courts have construed this standard strictly, resolving any ambiguity against the validity of the arrest.[27] Another significant body of case law in the area of private arrest treats the issue whether, to justify arrest by a private person, an offense must actually have been committed. The majority view seems to be that a reasonable belief alone is not sufficient to justify an arrest by a private person for an offense less than a felony.[28] When the crime allegedly committed is a felony, there is a split of authority whether the offense actually must have occurred or whether reasonable belief of the occurrence of the felony is sufficient.[29]

The private person who chooses to respond to a criminal wrong against him by arresting the alleged assailant assumes the risk of potential civil liability for false arrest, false imprisonment, or both.[30] The victim's or citizen's arrest is an extraordinary action that rarely occurs.[31] Because of the potential civil loss as well as personal risk involved in effectuating an arrest, it is unlikely that the citizen's arrest will or should become a mechanism to be utilized by the victim desiring to influence the arrest decision.

(2) Victim-police interactions

(a) INTRODUCTION. Statutes in some states make it a criminal offense for an officer to refuse or neglect to make an arrest once a warrant has been issued pursuant to a complaint by a victim. LaFave observes that it is an offense in a few states for an officer to "neglect making any arrest for an offense . . . committed in his presence."[32] The failure of an officer to arrest when no formal complaint or warrant has been issued is not a statutory criminal offense although some authority indicates that at common law an officer was bound by law to arrest for a felony committed in his presence.[33] Many states prohibit an officer from making a warrantless arrest for misdemeanors not committed in his presence.[34] Thus, a police officer frequently relies upon a victim's complaint in proceeding against an offender when the offense is less than a felony and is not committed in the officer's presence. The victim's willingness to file a formal complaint is cited frequently as a major determinant of whether a police officer will abide by the victim's wishes at the arrest stage. Three distinct attitudes may be displayed by a victim at the arrest stage: (1) the victim may aggressively press an officer for the arrest of a suspect; (2) the victim may take affirmative action to persuade the officer not to arrest a suspect of the reported crime; or (3) the victim may be ambivalent. How police react to these attitudes depends largely on characteristics of the victim and the crime.

(b) VICTIM'S "DIRTY HANDS." As a general rule, police will not arrest a suspect if the complaining party is an individual who is involved in conduct of questionable legality. This principle

---

26. *See, e.g.,* People v. Martin, 225 Cal. App. 2d 91, 36 Cal. Rptr. 924 (Dist. Ct. App. 1964).

27. *See* 5 AM. JUR. 2d *Arrest* §§ 35, 36 (1962). A private citizen cannot, for example, make an arrest for a misdemeanor committed earlier. In Protective Life Ins. Co. v. Spears, 231 So. 2d 510 (Miss. 1970), the "victim" of what he believed to be an attempted automobile homicide arrested his attacker some hours after the incident. The crime allegedly committed by the attacker was reckless driving, a misdemeanor, and the court held that an attempted arrest after the incident had transpired was not legal. In People v. Martin, 225 Cal. App. 2d 91, 36 Cal. Rptr. 924 (Dist. Ct. App. 1964), police officers outside their jurisdiction and thus acting as private citizens arrested a man on the belief that he was violating the state's drug laws. Concluding that no offense was then being committed, the court stated that a citizen's arrest for a misdemeanor may not be made when the offense was "neither committed nor attempted in the citizen's presence." *Id.* at 94, 36 Cal. Rptr. at 926.

28. *See* People v. Martin, 225 Cal. App. 2d 91, 36 Cal. Rptr. 924 (Dist. Ct. App. 1964), 6A C.J.S. *Arrest* § 14 (1975).

29. 5 AM. JUR. 2d *Arrest* § 36 & n.19 (1962).

30. *See, e.g.,* FOOTE, *Tort Remedies for Police Violations of Individual Rights,* 39 MINN. L. REV. 493 (1955).

31. Nashville officers recalled very few cases of citizens' arrests, either attempted or accomplished.

32. LAFAVE, *supra* note 5, at 78-79. Most courts have rejected claims that an officer is civilly liable for failure to arrest. *See* Annot., 41 A.L.R. 3d 700; Comment, *Crime Victim Recovery for Police Inaction and Underprotection,* 1970 LAW & SOC. ORDER 279, 286-87. When protection is extended to an individual, however, negligent police performance is actionable. *See, e.g.,* Schuster v. City of New York, 5 N.Y.2d 75, 154 N.E.2d 534, 180 N.Y.S.2d (1958).

33. 5 AM. JUR. 2d *Arrest* § 24 (1962).

34. *Id.* § 30.

is invoked in the case of a victim who complains to police that he has been robbed by a prostitute.[35] Professor LaFave, referring to the example of a man whose car was stolen by a prostitute, suggested that the police might seek to find the stolen car but are unlikely to attempt to find or prosecute the prostitute-thief.[36] The apparent, though unarticulated, rationale is that the victim's misconduct precludes police action despite his lawful right[37] to complain about the crime and seek police assistance in apprehending the offender. Similarly, if a "wrongdoing" victim desires not to prosecute, police invariably honor his request.[38]

(c) "RELATIONSHIP" BETWEEN VICTIM AND OFFENDER. It is widely recognized that if the victim and his alleged offenders are related by friendship, marriage, family or contract, the relationship is a particularly important element in determining the outcome of police-victim interaction. If, for example, the victim and offender are related contractually as landlord and tenant, the police are not likely to intervene to make an arrest in a dispute involving that relationship unless the victim vigorously asserts his desire for an arrest and indicates his willingness to cooperate. LaFave believes that the reason for this disinclination of the police to abide by the victim's desires is that the victim often has the alternative remedies of dissolving the legal relationship, or seeking civil relief, or both.[39] The relationship between the victim and the alleged offender may have an impact even when the alleged crime is rape. One writer found that when the alleged rapist was the victim's date, Philadelphia police acting at the arrest stage deemed unfounded forty-three percent of the rape complaints. On the other hand, when the victim and offender were stran-

gers, only eighteen percent of the rape reports were so deemed.[40]

Perhaps the continuing relationship between victim and offender that most significantly affects the interaction between police and victim is the family dispute.[41] One commentator who has studied extensively this problem maintains:

The general pattern of police treatment of domestic disputes evidences recognition . . . that such situations are socially distinguishable from criminal activity in general.

Police respond but they generally do not arrest . . . . District Attorneys listen to complaints but generally do not charge. If an arrest is made and charges are filed, the prosecutor or judge often receives a request from the victim, who has since reconciled with the offender, that the charges be dismissed. Compliance is generally summary.[42]

The above commentator further observes that police in Detroit will not even respond to a call for assistance made by a spouse who claims an assault arising from a marital dispute unless the spouse indicates a willingness to file a complaint and prosecute. Except in the most extreme cases the Detroit police department refers intrafamily violence victims to social services groups prior to any preliminary police investigation.[43] Commentators note that in the absence of serious injury, possession of a weapon, insistence by one of the disputants upon signing a complaint, or repeated calls, police officers are unlikely to heed the victim's request for an arrest in an intrafamily dispute case.[44]

The Nashville study buttresses these observations and conclusions. When the police officer is called to the scene of an intrafamily dispute, the officer perceives that his role changes from law enforcer to peacemaker. One reason for this perception is the officer's belief that the com-

---

35. Summers interview, *supra* note 14.

36. LaFave, *supra* note 5, at 142, 143 & n.66.

37. W. LaFave & A. Scott, *supra* note 1, at 409.

38. Blakely interview, *supra* note 15; Summers interview, *supra* note 14.

39. LaFave, *supra* note 5, at 119.

40. Comment, *Police Discretion and the Judgment that a Crime Has Been Committed—Rape in Philadelphia,* 117 U. Pa. L. Rev. 277, 291 (1968). *See also Rape and Rape Laws, supra* note 19, at 928 (citing the Philadelphia study).

41. As the term connotes, it sometimes is very difficult to allocate blame to any one family member; thus the labels "victim" and "offender" are somewhat arbitrarily assigned to the participants.

42. Parnas, *Police Discretion and Diversion of Incidents of Intra-Family Violence,* 36 Law & Contemp. Prob. 539, 543 (1971).

43. *Id.* at 547.

44. LaFave, *supra* note 5, at 122; Parnas, *The Police Response to the Domestic Disturbance,* 1967 Wis. L. Rev. 914, 937-40.

plaining spouse will not seek criminal prosecution after passions have cooled. For example, a patrolman reported that when he has any doubts that a spouse will "follow through," he requires the spouse to swear out an arrest warrant before he will make the arrest.[45] Presumably, the appearance before the magistrate affirms or crystallizes the complainant's desire to prosecute. As the degree of serious physical injury increases, however, "victim control" lessens, regardless of the relationship between the parties. For example, when police learned of an attempted murder, and the victim declared that he had no desire to cooperate with the police or to prosecute the suspected assailant, who was believed to be the victim's wife, the police declared their intention to proceed with the arrest over the victim's protestations.[46]

(d) VICTIM'S RACE. The decision to arrest may, to some extent, depend upon the race of the complaining victim. In the case of simple assault, for instance, some policemen have expressed the view that assault is an "acceptable means" of settling disputes between Negroes. When both victim and offender are black, LaFave notes that police are not likely to invoke the criminal process through an arrest:

Such offenses as bigamy and open and notorious cohabitation are overlooked by law enforcement officials, and arrests often are not made for carrying knives or for robbery of other Negroes. However, the practice is most strikingly illustrated by the repeated failure of the police to arrest Negroes for a felonious assault upon a spouse or acquaintance unless the victim actually insists upon prosecution.[47]

LaFave maintains that in crimes perpetrated against Negroes by Negroes the victim's control of the arrest decision does not decrease as the seriousness of the offense increases.[48] One reason cited for the disinclination to proceed with

an arrest unless the black victim of a black offender adamantly insists upon it is the probability that the victim will not proceed with formal prosecution of his assailant. In one study, for example, it was found that in thirty-eight of forty-three felonious assaults reported in one precinct during a one-month period the victims refused to prosecute.[49] The Philadelphia rape study supports the view that race influences the decision to arrest. It was found that the police are more likely to believe that a rape allegation is unfounded when both victim and assailant are black than when both are white or when one is white and the other black.[50]

Interviews with Nashville police failed to disclose tangible evidence of discrimination in handling victim-police interactions. One black detective, however, pointed to the apathy of lower economic groups toward the criminal justice system, and he attributed this attitude to the individual's belief that his needs go unheeded by police.[51] Officers did not agree, however, with LaFave's statement that, as a matter of practice, Negroes' claims of felonious assault are handled differently from those of white victims. More detailed and systematic research techniques are required to establish reliably that racial discrimination is nonexistent in victim-police dealings.

(e) VICTIM'S STATUS. One of the most frequently mentioned variables in the field of police-victim interaction—and the most difficult to quantify—is the victim's real or perceived status in the community. Rarely, however, will an official responsible for making an arrest decision expressly acknowledge the influence of this variable. The comment usually made by police is, "I'm sure it goes on, but I don't do it." One judge who admitted considering the victim's status in deciding whether to issue arrest warrants justified his practice on the ground that

45. Blakely interview, *supra* note 15.
46. The Tennessean (Nashville), Feb. 8, 1974, at 21, col. 8. This theme is further developed in § e.
47. LaFave, *supra* note 5, at 111. *See also*, Goldstein, *Police Discretion Not to Invoke the Criminal Process: Low-Visibility Decisions in the Administration of Justice*, 69 Yale L.J. 543, 575 (1960).
48. LaFave 112.

49. According to the author, most of the original calls to the police were for ambulance service rather than to request arrest of the assailant. Goldstein, *supra* note 47, at 574 & n.64.
50. *Police Discretion, supra* note 40, at 302.
51. Summers interview, *supra* note 14.

"the victim's status is relevant in deciding the credibility of the report."[52] Additional reasons for considering a victim's status may include officials' fear of publicity and concern that a dissatisfied victim will complain to superior officers or governmental officials.

(f) VICTIM'S MOTIVES. Another variable in victim-police interactions is the victim's motive for seeking an arrest. Many times, arrest is sought as a means of pressuring the arrestee to make restitution for the harm done to the victim. A common example is the merchant who calls upon the police officer to arrest an individual for passing a worthless check.[53] Generally, when restitution is made and the victim does not thereafter seek arrest or prosecution, the police will not proceed further. When restitution appears to be the sole motive behind the complaint, the police, to insure the victim's continued cooperation, frequently demand that the victim file a formal complaint.[54]

While restitution is the dominant motive behind some victims' complaints to police, other self-serving reasons for "feigned" arrests have been cited. In intrafamily encounters, for example, a victim's plea for the arrest of a spouse may be motivated by a desire for revenge or a desire to "cloud" the spouse's record so as to affect pending property or custody controversies.[55] It has been suggested, too, that a purported rape victim will sometimes seek an arrest to force marriage or attain personal revenge.[56] When police believe that the victim is seeking an arrest for restitution, revenge, or other ulterior purposes, officers tend to discount the victim's pleas. Victims' motives are of relatively little importance to most arrest decisions, however, because few situations arise in which the victim's subjective intent is discoverable.

(g) SEVERITY OF THE CRIME. As a general proposition, the policeman's view of the seriousness of a particular crime (or the way in which crime is committed) will determine the extent to which the policeman's arrest decision is influenced by the victim's desires.[57] For example, a victim's expressed desire for or against arrest may be decisive in a worthless check case; in the case of a forged instrument, however, the officer's decision to arrest will be influenced to a much lesser degree by the victim's attitude.[58] In minor property crimes in which no force or violence is involved, the determination by the police not to arrest will usually be decisive unless a victim indicates a clear willingness to cooperate with the police. Thus, the refusal of the victim to sign a complaint under such circumstances will almost assuredly terminate further police investigation.[59]

In juvenile cases when the offenses are minor, police frequently decide not to investigate because the cases are not considered important enough to warrant the expenditure of substantial amounts of law enforcement resources.[60] A prevailing police attitude is that juveniles often commit minor offenses because of "immature judgment" or "youthful exuberance" and therefore pose no major threat to society. Because of this attitude the police are likely to ignore the desires of a person victimized by a juvenile offender. Rather than arrest juvenile offenders, police are inclined to give them warnings to "throw a scare" into them.[61]

(h) OTHER CONSIDERATIONS. A recent study of rape cases in Philadelphia revealed that the police officers' perception of the credibility of a rape allegation is influenced by the age of the complainant. Thus, Philadelphia police are more likely to conclude that a rape complaint is legitimate when the complaining party is an adult rather than a juvenile.[62] The same study disclosed that the police considered when and to whom the victim made her report in determin-

---

52. Interview with the Honorable Leslie Mondelli, Davidson County General Sessions Judge, Oct. 2, 1974 [hereinafter cited as Mondelli interview].

53. LaFave, *supra* note 5, at 51.

54. *Id.* at 118, 119.

55. Blakely interview, *supra* note 15.

56. Note, *The Corroboration Rule and Crimes Accompanying a Rape,* 118 U. Pa. L. Rev. 458, 460 (1970).

57. LaFave 117: Blakely, Summers and Vaughn interviews; interview with Detective Russ Hackett, July 10, 1974 [hereinafter cited as Hackett interview].

58. LaFave 117; Hackett interview.

59. *See* LaFave 21 n.16.

60. *Id.* at 106.

61. *Id.* at 106, 107.

62. *Police Discretion, supra* note 40, at 302.

ing whether to proceed with a rape case.[63] Another variable is the disgruntled victim's ability to pressure lackadaisical police through publicity.[64] Recently a victim dissatisfied with police inaction complained to the news media that criminal wrongdoing was going unpunished. The story appeared in a local newspaper,[65] and within a few days police action was initiated.

The identity of the alleged offender also influences the decision whether to arrest. The victim's wish that no arrest be made may be disregarded even when the crime is minor—if, (1) the offense is committed by someone known to the police as a "bad actor," or (2) police have expended significant resources for the apprehension of the suspect on previous charges. In both cases, the decision to arrest is based primarily on considerations unrelated to the victim. One author maintains that even in a minor case, when the offender is a known criminal, police will, if necessary, subpoena a recalcitrant victim as a witness.[66]

D. Influencing the bail decision

The theoretical basis for the release of an accused on bail pending trial is that bail is a means of assuring the court that the accused will be available for the trial.[67] The major considerations taken into account in determining the amount of bail are the defendant's assets and liabilities, his family ties, and any other information relevant to the question of whether he is likely to flee the court's jurisdiction prior to trial.[68] Any amount that exceeds the mythical figure needed to guarantee the defendant's presence is excessive and constitutionally proscribed.[69]

In Nashville, the typical bail hearing is an informal proceeding usually involving only the judge, defendant, and arresting officer; seldom does the victim appear. In some cases, however,

the victim does express his views on the pretrial release of the accused. The victim's opinion becomes known either through the victim's presence when bail is set, or by the transmittal through the police officer or, less often, through the district attorney's office. The author's field research revealed conflicting opinions about the effect a victim's attitude can have on the bail decision. One criminal court judge stated that the amount of bail depends only upon the offense and the offender.[70] Two other judges echoed this statement, but added that some weight is placed on the district attorney's recommendation (which, presumably, could be based upon the victim's attitude).[71] On the other hand, two judges were of the opinion that the victim definitely *does* have an impact at the bail hearing;[72] and one observed that the victim's attitude is crucial when release on recognizance is contemplated.[73]

Prosecutors also were divided over the victim's role in the bail decision. The Davidson County District Attorney noted that the amount of bail may be determined by a victim's statement that threats had been made by the defendant.[74] Another prosecutor observed that even if the judge announces his unwillingness to consider the victim's feelings, the victim can influence the setting of bail simply by appearing before the judge and evoking sympathy for himself and disdain for the accused.[75]

In summary, the victim in most cases has no effect on the bail decision because he usually is not present during the hearing. Moreover,

---

63. *Id.* at 286.
64. *See* Goldstein, *supra* note 47, at 552 n.15.
65. Nashville Banner, July 13, 1974, at 3, col. 3.
66. *See* LaFave 49; Goldstein, *supra* note 47, at 574.
67. Gusick v. Boies, 72 Ariz. 233, 233 P.2d 446 (1951).
68. *See* ABA Project on Standards for Criminal Justice, Pretrial Release § 5.1 (Tent. Draft 1968).
69. Stack v. Boyle, 342 U.S. 1 (1951).

---

70. Interview with the Honorable Allen R. Cornelius, Davidson County Metropolitan Criminal Judge, Sept. 4, 1974. [hereinafter cited as Cornelius interview].
71. Interview with the Honorable Raymond Leathers, Davidson County Metropolitan Criminal Judge, Sept. 9, 1974. [hereinafter cited as Leathers interview]. Interview with the Honorable Gale Robinson, Davidson County General Sessions Judge, Sept. 3, 1974 [hereinafter cited as Robinson interview].
72. Mondelli interview, *supra* note 52; interview with the Honorable Donald Washburn, Davidson County General Sessions Judge, Sept. 24, 1974 [hereinafter cited as Washburn interview].
73. Mondelli interview.
74. Shriver interview, *supra* note 17.
75. Yarbrough interview, *supra* note 23.

even when the victim's views are made known, judges and prosecutors disagree on whether his views influence the judge's determination. Thus, the victim's impact on this phase of the criminal proceeding is seemingly minimal.

E. Influencing the decision to prosecute

The victim's role in the arrest decision overlaps another distinct stage of the criminal justice process: the initiation of formal prosecution by the state's attorney. The public prosecutor often becomes involved in a criminal action even before an arrest is made. Some states, for example, require the concurrence of both judge and prosecuting attorney for the issuance of a warrant.[76] An obvious effect of this statutory requirement is to involve the victim in the case long before the formal decision to prosecute is made. Many victims of crime, especially crimes involving real or threatened personal injury, seek aggressive prosecution of the wrongdoer. Some victims, however, are ambivalent about formal prosecution, and some actually seek to discourage the prosecutor from pursuing criminal charges.

It has been observed that victim-prosecutor interaction may be affected significantly by the manner in which the arrest stage blends into the formal prosecution stage. A victim's influence over the decision to prosecute is lessened when the alleged criminal conduct is reported to the prosecutor by police rather than by the victim. If the victim does file a complaint directly with the prosecutor, personal contact between the district attorney and the victim facilitates greater victim control over the exercise of prosecutorial discretion.[77]

The prosecuting attorney has great discretion in determining whether to prosecute, what precise offense to charge, and whether to negotiate the charge.[78] The duties of prosecuting attorneys are usually prescribed in vaguely worded statutes that broadly outline their re-

sponsibilities. For example, Tennessee requires that the district attorney "prosecute on behalf of the state in every case in which the state is a party, or in any wise interested."[79] In some jurisdictions explicit exceptions to this general prosecutorial duty have been promulgated. Wisconsin declares that district attorneys are under no duty to prosecute "common assault and battery" charges,[80] and a United States attorney "may forego his prosecution" and surrender an offender to state authorities when the offender is a juvenile arrested for "an offense punishable in any court of the United States."[81] Few state legislatures have attempted to control the exercise of prosecutorial discretion or to delegate control to courts, victims, or other persons. Regardless of victim participation, only in rare cases will courts review or direct when or how a prosecution is to be conducted.[82]

(1) Victim bypassing prosecutor

In some states, a victim can obtain the issuance of a warrant initiating prosecution without first obtaining the district attorney's consent.[83] In Michigan, for example, warrants may be issued without the prosecutor's approval if the complainant deposits "security for costs" with the court.[84] While provisions like the Michigan statute permit victims unilaterally to institute criminal proceedings, these provisions do not address the question whether the accused can be tried without the district attorney's cooperation.

Nevertheless, some attempts have been made by aggrieved victims in criminal cases to bypass

---

76. *See, e.g.,* MICH. STAT. ANN. §28.1195 (1972); MILLER, supra note 5, at 5.

77. MILLER 16.

78. *See* MILLER 158; note 8 *supra* and accompanying text.

79. TENN. CODE ANN. § 8-703(1) (1973).

80. WIS. STAT. ANN. § 59.47 (1958); *see* Note, *Statutory Discretion of the District Attorney in Wisconsin,* 1953 WIS. L. REV. 170.

81. 18 U.S.C. § 5001 (1970); *see* Schwartz, *Federal Criminal Jurisdiction and Prosecutors' Discretion,* 13 LAW & CONTEMP. PROB. 64, 85 (1948).

82. Ferguson, *Formulation of Enforcement Policy: An Anatomy of the Prosecutor's Discretion Prior to Accusation,* 11 RUTGERS L. REV. 507, 509, 511 (1957).

83. According to Miller, this occurs prior to a bindover order by magistrates, ". . . and so the criminal prosecution may be begun without the prosecutor's knowledge or against his wishes." MILLER, *supra* note 5, at 309, citing KAN. STAT. ANN. §§ 62-601, 62-602, 63-201 (1964) and WIS. STAT. ANN. §§ 954.01-.02 (1958).

84. MICH STAT. ANN. § 28.1195 (1972); *see* MILLER, 309.

completely the prosecutor. Case law dealing with a victim's circumvention of the district attorney is scarce. In one interesting case a citizen who had been involved in an affray with an alleged reckless driver retained an attorney who requested the district attorney to file criminal charges against the driver. After the district attorney refused to bring charges, private counsel successfully petitioned a local judge to disqualify the district attorney. The prosecutor sought a writ of prohibition to bar the lawyer from prosecuting. Characterizing the issue as whether an individual can institute a criminal proceeding "without conference, approval or authority of the district attorney," the court granted the writ and held that "the decision of when and against whom criminal proceedings are to be instituted is one to be made by . . . the district attorney."[85] California law thus requires that criminal complaints "be approved, authorized or concurred in by the district attorney before they are effective in instituting criminal proceedings."[86] Similarly, in *Keenan v. McGrath*,[87] a prisoner filed a "criminal" complaint in a federal district court, charging correctional officers with conspiracy to deny him his constitutional rights. The court dismissed the complaint after determining that the action was an effort by the prisoner to prosecute criminally prison guards. The First Circuit affirmed, observing:

Not only are we unaware of any authority for permitting a private individual to initiate a criminal prosecution in his own name in a United States District Court, but . . . to sanction such a procedure would be to provide a means to circumvent the legal safeguards provided for persons accused of crime . . . .[88]

Judges, prosecutors, and defense attorneys interviewed by the author could recall no case in which a victim or complainant attempted to institute criminal proceedings without the cooperation of the prosecutor. A variation of this theme

—private prosecution—has been employed in Tennessee and other states, however.[89]

(2) Victim participation in the decision to charge

(a) THE ADAMANT VICTIM. Nashville prosecutors agree that adamant victims are observed most frequently in cases involving serious felonies—homicide, aggravated assault, rape, and armed robbery. The prevailing prosecutorial view is that the victim who most vigorously seeks full enforcement of the criminal law is the survivor of the deceased in a homicide case. Local prosecuting officials concede that "great weight" is given to the victim's desires in serious felony cases, especially homicides.[90] This could mean that if the district attorney determines that the facts and circumstances of a case do not clearly warrant prosecution for an unlawful homicide, the adamant victim could overcome the prosecutor's reluctance to charge. For example, the Nashville district attorney submitted a homicide case to the grand jury after three previous "no true bills"; but for the survivor's attitude, the case probably would not have been pursued.[91]

Although the victims' desires are important in serious felony cases, the weight given these desires varies according to the facts and circumstances of the particular case as well as the attitude of the individual prosecuting attorney. One assistant district attorney stated his policy as follows:

If I were faced with a case in which I believed that the facts reasonably supported a murder of first degree charge, I would proceed with this charge irrespective of the desires of the victim. On the other hand, if I felt that the facts reasonably supported a voluntary manslaughter offense but perhaps would not justify the

---

85. People v. Municipal Court, 27 Cal. App. 3d 193, 199, 204, 103 Cal. Rptr. 645, 649, 653 (1972).
86. *Id.* at 206, 103 Cal. Rptr. at 655.
87. 328 F.2d 610 (1st Cir. 1964).
88. *Id.* at 611.

89. This topic will be discussed in § III(D) *infra.*
90. Interview with Assistant District Attorney Robert Schwartz, July 5, 1974 [hereinafter cited as Schwartz interview]; Shriver interview, *supra* note 17; Yarbrough interview, *supra* note 23.
91. Shriver interview. When the case was submitted the fourth time, explained the District Attorney, "[S]omehow we got a true bill. But the judge promptly dismissed it for lack of speedy trial, and I think he was correct in doing so, and we could have never won the case . . . I feel these people [family of deceased] had a right to be heard."

more serious murder first degree category, the victim's desires might be strong enough to convince me to increase the charge to murder first degree. In a case of serious felony, then, I will sometimes pay heed to the victim's intent to "over-charge" but not to "undercharge."[92]

Another assistant district attorney referred to this practice as "passing the buck."[93] While the prosecutor's judgment may be confirmed later by his inability to obtain an indictment or a conviction, the victim's immediate desires are met and the determination of no criminal responsibility is delayed until a judge or jury takes action. Another assistant district attorney,[94] while expressing concern for the victim's feelings, stated that he does not honor a victim's request to prosecute vigorously in either serious or petty cases because he considers it his duty to exercise independent professional judgment on the merits of each case. He recalled two or three cases in which victims who were dissatisfied with his decisions asked the district attorney to review the decisions. In each case, the assistant district attorney's determination remained unaltered.

Unlike the adamant victim of a serious crime, the adamant victim of a nonserious crime has relatively little influence over the prosecutor's charging decision. Thus, if the prosecuting attorney believes that the facts do not justify charging a nonserious crime, the prosecutor will probably dismiss the action irrespective of the presence of an adamant victim. One commentator has noted, for example, that in family disputes the prosecutor's office will impose a waiting period to give the persistent victim "cooling-off" time before initiating prosecution. If the district attorney then decides to honor the victim's insistence upon prosecution, the victim is "forcefully warned that [he or she] must follow through and cannot drop out at the last minute." This threat has been implemented in some prosecutors' offices by requiring the victim with a change of heart to pay court costs.[95]

A recurring example of prosecutors' disregard for the adamant victim's desire to prosecute is the case in which the victim is pressing for prosecution solely as a means to bring about financial restitution from the offender.[96] One Nashville prosecutor objected vociferously to the merchants' attempts to use the district attorney's office as a "collection agency" in bad check cases.[97]

(b) THE RELUCTANT VICTIM. Although the victim who desires no criminal prosecution of his offender usually can preclude it by failing to report the offense,[98] the crime sometimes comes to the attention of police or prosecutors by means other than the victim's report.[99] Moreover, occasions arise when the victim reports the offense but subsequently decides not to seek

---

92. Schwartz interview.

93. Yarbrough interview.

94. Interview with Assistant District Attorney Aaron Wyckoff, Aug. 16, 1974 [hereinafter cited as Wyckoff interview].

95. Parnas, *Prosecutorial and Judicial Handling of Family Violence,* 9 Crim. L. Bull. 733, 739 (1973).

96. Note, *Prosecutor's Discretion,* 103 U. Pa. L. Rev. 1057, 1069 (1955). Miller suggests that if the victim presses for prosecution for a minor property crime, the victim may be required to agree to pay court costs for failing to cooperate. Miller, *supra* note 5, at 181.

97. Schwartz interview, *supra* note 90. *Compare* Miller 271, *with* Newman, *infra* note 118, at 164. Miller says:

Victims of minor property crimes, such as recipients of bad checks normally are interested only in restitution for the loss suffered by them, and they seek the aid of the prosecutor solely to achieve that end. Although they are usually willing to threaten prosecution, seldom are they willing to actually assist in prosecution, even if restitution is not made. Indeed, that situation is seldom presented because offenders readily make restitution if given the opportunity as an alternative to charging. Prosecutors, for the most part, are willing to allow the criminal processes to be used to gain that objective, although they often express some dissatisfaction with their status as "collection agencies."

Newman's view is as follows:

Occasionally bad check, minor theft, and property damage cases are dismissed when restitution is made and when the offender is a person whose reputation or that of his family would be excessively harmed by formal conviction and sentencing. Often these cases are handled at the prosecution stage, where the prosecuting attorney will drop the charge when restitution is made. Some prosecutors, however, argue that their office is not a "collection agency" and persist in prosecution even though the defendant has made monetary amends.

98. Section II(A) *supra.*

99. *See* note 22 *supra* and accompanying text.

prosecution of the alleged offender. To what extent can a reluctant victim so influence a prosecutor as to prevent or stall prosecution? A public prosecutor must, of course, "be sure that the complaining witness will assist the state when the case comes up before trial."[100] A reluctant victim can be compelled by legal process to participate in the trial, but "in practice this is not done."[101] In almost all nonserious cases, therefore, a reluctant victim's desire not to prosecute is honored by the prosecutor.[102]

Occasionally, a victim is hesitant to cooperate with the prosecutor's office in the prosecution of a serious felony. While hesitant victims only occasionally are found in homicide or attempted homicide cases, they frequently are encountered in cases of rape. Regardless of the reasons for the victim's reluctance,[103] the vast majority of rape cases in which the victim opposes prosecution are dismissed. Because of the peculiar importance of the victim's testimony in this crime,[104] the state's case is almost totally undermined when the victim is unwilling to participate in a trial.[105] Each prosecutor interviewed in the Nashville field study said that a rape case would not proceed to trial if the victim did not desire prosecution of the accused.[106] Thus, the deference accorded the wishes of rape victims contrasts with that accorded victims of other serious felonies; the uncooperative victim of an armed robbery or attempted murder will not be accorded so great a degree of "control" over prosecutorial discretion.[107] When the crime charged is a nonserious felony or misdemeanor, it is common for the prosecutor to abide by the request of a reluctant victim.[108] Nashville prosecutors agree that in "less serious criminal cases," the victim's desire to dismiss the criminal charge against the accused usually is honored.[109] While the "less serious crime" standard is imprecise, prosecutors generally exclude from this category crimes in which real or threatened physical force is used. In domestic squabbles, however, even when force is used against one spouse, the complainant's request to dismiss the charge frequently is honored by the district attorney's office.[110] The Davidson County Public Defender provided an illustration of how local prosecutors balance a victim's reluctance against the seriousness of the crime: if restitution is made by the offender in a "bad check" case, a dismissal request is honored; on the other hand, if the crime is forgery, the victim's desire to dismiss is not honored.[111]

The reaction of Davidson County judges to the reluctant victim is very similar to that of prosecutors and public defenders. If the offense is not serious and if the district attorney, acting at the victim's request, recommends dismissal, the judge will dismiss the case.[112] One judge indicated that a victim's desire to dismiss a charge growing out of a family dispute would be honored even without the district attorney's recommendation; otherwise, the prosecutor's recommendation would be necessary.[113]

In summary, if the crime charged is a misdemeanor or nonserious felony, chances are good that the case will be dismissed if the victim so desires unless specific circumstances other

---

100. Baker, *The Prosecutor—Initiation of Prosecution,* 23 J. CRIM. L.C. & P.S. 770, 782 (1933).
101. MILLER, *supra* note 5, at 29.
102. *Id.* at 173. *See* Kaplan, *The Prosecutorial Discretion— A Comment,* 60 NW. U.L. REV. 174, 184 (1965); Klein, *District Attorney's Discretion Not to Prosecute,* 32 L.A.B. BULL. 323, 327 (1957).
103. *See* note 56 *supra* and accompanying text.
104. *Id.* A rape allegation, for example, may be supported by nothing more than the victim's uncorroborated claim that the crime occurred.
105. Miller reports that in statutory rape cases, prosecutors "usually allow their charging decision to be controlled by the [victim's] attitude . . . when . . . opposed to charging." MILLER 177.
106. Shriver, Schwartz and Yarbrough interviews.
107. *Id.*

---

108. MILLER 174, 261-62; Note, *supra* note 96, at 1060, 1069.
109. Shriver, Schwartz, Wyckoff and Yarbrough interviews.
110. Interview with Assistant Public Defender Robert McGowan, Aug. 9, 1974 [hereinafter cited as McGowan interview]. It is interesting to note that this defender has contacted victims personally regarding the "dropping of charges."
111. Interview with Public Defender James Havron, July 9, 1974 [hereinafter cited as Havron interview].
112. Cornelius interview, *supra* note 70; Leathers interview, *supra* note 71; Mondelli interview, *supra* note 52; Washburn interview, *supra* note 72.
113. Robinson interview, *supra* note 71.

than the victim's desires predominate. With the exception of the crime of rape, however, the reluctant victim's desires will not be heeded by the prosecutor in a serious felony case.

(3) Selection of charge

The selection of the particular charge, like the decision to prosecute, is an executive decision within the prosecutor's discretion and hence is not controlled by the judiciary.[114] Professor Miller has observed:

Although it has been suggested that . . . a trial court must be able to control charge selection to prevent limitation on its sentencing discretion, the law in general has not taken this position, and judicial opinions instead reflect the view that one of the essential functions of the prosecutorial office is the selection of the charge which the prosecutor deems most appropriate.[115]

The choice of criminal charge often is intricately influenced by the general considerations that a prosecutor takes into account in making the initial decision to prosecute. The impression that a victim makes on a prosecuting attorney may affect the prosecutor's appraisal of the strength of his case. This strengthened belief may lead the prosecuting attorney to charge a more serious crime to obtain a better bargaining position for the plea negotiation process.

The Nashville field study disclosed varying opinions about the victim's influence on the charge. One view is that in a serious felony case the victim's request for either a greater or lesser charge is not accorded great weight by the prosecutor.[116] On the other hand, two prosecutors suggested that the victim's attitude does influence the prosecutor's charging decision.[117] Commentators have reported that some prosecutors subscribe to the practice of "down-grading the charge when victim, complainants, or

witnesses are disreputable. . . ."[118] One general prosecutorial attitude is common to both the "prosecuting" and "charging" processes: the prosecutor will listen attentively to the victim who desires to "over-charge" in a serious felony case but not to the victim who desires to "over-charge" in a misdemeanor or nonserious felony case; conversely, the victim desirous of "under-charging" will experience greater success with misdemeanors or nonserious felonies than with serious crimes.

(4) Involvement in plea bargaining

The bargaining between defense counsel and the prosecuting attorney, a much-discussed topic,[119] is another phase of the criminal justice process in which significant, low-visibility decisions are made. The result of the negotiation process is made known, but the means by which the outcome is reached go unnoticed. Bargaining assumes, of course, that a formal charge has been or is about to be placed against the accused and that the defendant seeks an exchange whereby a guilty plea to the offense charged or to a lesser offense will be offered for a concession from the prosecutor's office, usually a recommended sentence. In this context, does the victim have any influence over the decision by the government to accept or reject a tendered agreement?

The literature on the plea bargaining process is characterized by its almost total disregard for the role of the victim. Typically, matters to be evaluated by a prosecutor in bargaining include the nature of the offense, the condition of the defendant at the time the offense was committed and at the time of trial, the strength of the state's case, and the strains of the prosecutor's case load. Only one article purporting to catalog such considerations lists the victim's de-

---

114. Newman v. United States, 382 F.2d 479 (D.C. Cir. 1967). People *ex rel.* Leonard v. Papp, 386 Mich. 672, 683, 194 N.W.2d 693, 699 (1972).

115. MILLER, *supra* note 5, at 169.

116. Havron interview, *supra* note 111; Wyckoff interview, *supra* note 94.

117. Schwartz interview, *supra* note 90; Yarbrough interview, *supra* note 23. Schwartz stated that he might "over-charge" in a serious felony because of an adamant victim, but would not "under-charge."

118. *See, e.g.,* D. NEWMAN, CONVICTION: THE DETERMINATION OF GUILT OR INNOCENCE WITHOUT TRIAL 120 (1966). The author states that ". . . the disrepute of the victim mitigates the criminal conduct of the defendant."

119. *See, e.g., id.;* PRESIDENT'S COMM'N ON LAW ENFORCEMENT AND ADMINISTRATION OF JUSTICE, TASK FORCE REPORT: THE COURTS, 9-13 (1967); Note, *The Unconstitutionality of Plea Bargaining*, 83 HARV. L. REV. 1387 (1970); Note, *Guilty Plea Bargaining: Compromises by Prosecutors to Secure Guilty Pleas*, 112 U. PA. L. REV. 865 (1964).

sires as a variable that should be considered by the district attorney.[120] The American Bar Association's standards relating to pleas of guilty ignore altogether the victim's role in plea bargaining.[121] Similarly, standards relating to the prosecution and defense functions identify no role for the victim in discussions about pleas.[122] The major works by Professors Miller and Newman make general references to the victim's role in plea bargaining. While recognizing that the victim's attitude must be considered by the prosecutor,[123] Miller does not suggest that a victim has or should have a direct role in the negotiations. Similarly, Newman describes a somewhat passive and indirect role for the victim in the bargaining process.[124]

Contrary to the views of Miller and Newman is the view shared by members of the Davidson County District Attorney's office that the victim is indeed directly and personally involved at the plea bargaining stage of the criminal justice process. The prosecuting attorney communicates with the victim in an attempt to explain the nature of the bargaining process and to articulate precise reasons for his belief that the tendered plea is or is not desirable.[125] If the prosecutor fails to sway the victim to his viewpoint, the victim's opposition to the negotiated plea can influence the prosecutor to reject the offer.[126] This especially is true in serious felony cases, particularly unlawful homicide and rape. When the crime is less serious, the victim's opposition is not as likely to deter the prosecuting attorney from accepting the plea. One assistant district attorney said that he personally contacts the victim of any crime before submitting to defense counsel an offer to charge a lesser offense. The victim will not necessarily be contacted, however, if the prosecutor simply expresses his willingness to accept a guilty plea to the offense charged and make a recommendation that the minimum sentence be imposed.[127]

It was learned from the Davidson County Public Defender's office that a relative or friend of a defendant has on occasion contacted the victim, who has then called the public defender's office to express a desire that the defendant be treated leniently. The public defender's office in this instance would inform the district attorney's office of the victim's call to encourage dismissal or favorable plea negotiations.[128] One assistant public defender recalled an occasion when he contacted a victim, the sister of the accused, to suggest that she seek a dismissal of the charge. The defender believes that the victim did communicate with the prosecutor's office because the case was dismissed.[129]

Judges confirm that the victim is involved in the plea bargaining process. One trial judge urges the district attorney to contact the victim and inform him of the bargaining process so that he will fully understand the disposition of the case.[130] Another judge, however, while admitting that the victim plays a role in plea bar-

---

120. Alschuler, *The Prosecutor's Role in Plea Bargaining,* 36 U. Chi. L. Rev. 50, 53 (1968). He indicates this is an "extraneous" factor.

121. ABA Project on Standards for Criminal Justice, Pleas of Guilty (Tent. Draft 1967). The standards are couched in terms of interaction between prosecutor, defendant, defense counsel and the court.

122. ABA Project on Standards for Criminal Justice, Pleas of Guilty (Tent. Draft 1967), ABA Project on Standards for Criminal Justice, The Defense Function & The Prosecution Function (Tent. Draft 1970). One oblique reference to the victim's role is made in relation to Pleas of Guilty § 1.8(a) (iv):

> In some case there may be good reasons for avoiding a public trial. This is particularly true in rape and indecent liberties cases where the victim would have to appear in court and repeat the details of what transpired. Testifying in public in these kinds of criminal cases is not only humiliating but may be a severely traumatic experience for the victim, especially for a child . . . [I]n cases of this kind it would seem most appropriate to grant charge or sentence concessions to the defendant who by his plea protects the interest of the victim. This is currently the practice of many courts.

123. "[A] prosecutor is likely to accept a plea to a considerably reduced charge . . . because of . . . a reluctant complainant and . . . a belief that prosecution is undesirable . . . when the victim does not feel sufficiently agreeable to prosecute." Miller, *supra* note 5, at 105.

124. Newman, *supra* note 118, at 68-69.

125. Shriver, Schwartz, Wyckoff and Yarbrough interviews.

126. Shriver interview.

127. Yarbrough interview.

128. Havron interview.

129. McGowan interview, *supra* note 110. Of course, he was unable to say that this was the *only* reason for dismissal.

130. Leathers interview, *supra* note 71.

gaining, voiced his opposition to the victim's involvement. This judge supported his position by alluding to a case in which a man and wife had a domestic quarrel that ended with the fatal shooting of the wife. The husband's counsel and the prosecuting attorney negotiated an agreement whereby the accused would plead guilty to voluntary manslaughter and the state would recommend punishment of not more than ten years in the penitentiary. Immediately before this agreement was submitted to the court the prosecutor contacted the victim's family—a brother residing in another state. The brother refused to approve a voluntary manslaughter plea and insisted that the case be tried on the original charge of first degree murder. By the time the prosecution and defense were ready to try the case, however, the brother had lost interest, and a plea of voluntary manslaughter was accepted pursuant to the original agreement. In that case, according to the judge, the victim's family should have had no say in the bargaining process: the prosecutor had no duty to "satisfy" the brother of the deceased; on the contrary, the district attorney's duty was to see that "justice was done to the accused."[131]

The Nashville field study establishes that in general the victim plays a very significant role in the plea bargaining process. While the weight attached to the victim's desires may vary from one prosecutor to another, it is clear that the victim's desires are considered by the district attorney's office in deciding whether to submit an offer to defense counsel and whether to accept a tendered plea from the defendant.

F. Influencing post-conviction decisions

(1) Sentence

All jurisdictions provide a framework within which matters to be considered in sentencing are heard and evaluated. Within this framework the victim's views may be made known in three ways. First, testimony in aggravation or mitigation of the sentence to be imposed may be adduced in person or by affidavit.[132] Secondly, the victim's desires may be conveyed, expressly or impliedly, by the prosecutor.[133] Thirdly, the victim's attitude may be set forth in the presentence report compiled by the probation officer.[134] Research data concerning the victim's role in the sentencing process is scant and unsatisfactory. Professor Dawson's book contains two brief references to the role of the victim in the sentencing and probation processes,[135] but little attempt is made to clarify or measure the impact that a victim has on the sentencing decision.

Some courts have expressly recognized that concern for the victim is a legitimate consideration in sentencing. For example, in *Petition of Keefe*[136] the defendant sought a writ of prohibition to stop the trial judge from sentencing him after he pleaded guilty to careless operation of an automobile. Apparently, the defendant was asked whether he would bind himself to make restitution to the victim, and it was implied that his willingness to make restitution would be taken into consideration in imposing the sentence. The defendant asserted that the concern for the victim expressed by the judge was improper. In denying the petition, the Vermont Su-

---

131. Cornelius interview, *supra* note 70.

132. Annot., 77 A.L.R. 1211 (1932). This annotation recognizes the majority rule to be that "it is correct practice to hear evidence by affidavit or otherwise, in aggravation or mitigation . . . ."

133. Teitelbaum, *The Prosecutor's Role in the Sentencing Process: A National Survey*, 1 AM J. CRIM. L. 75, 81 (1972). Next to the law enforcement viewpoint, the most important contribution that a prosecutor should make to the court is "the victim's viewpoint regarding the appropriate sentence."

134. Dressler says:

The court will want to consider the complainant's attitude, particularly in instances where he has been physically injured or has lost a considerable amount of property to the offender. The judge will not necessarily act accord-

ing to the wishes of the injured person, yet he will want to have that individual's attitude defined in the report.

D. DRESSLER, PRACTICE AND THEORY OF PROBATION AND PAROLE, 109-10 (2d ed. 1969).

Articles dealing with pre-sentence investigations ignore altogether the victim's attitude as a component of the report. *See, e.g.*, Judicial Conference of the U.S., *Pilot Institute on Sentencing*, 26 F.R.D. 231 (1961); Hardman, *The Function of the Probation Officer*, 24 FED. PROB. 3 (Sept. 1960); Treger, *The Pre-Sentence Investigation*, 17 CRIME AND DELIN. 316 (1971).

135. R. DAWSON, SENTENCING: THE DECISION AS TO TYPE, LENGTH AND CONDITIONS OF SENTENCE, 17 n.8, 33 (1969).

136. 115 Vt. 289, 57 A.2d 657 (1948).

preme Court declared that it was "proper for the court in determining the severity of the sentence to be imposed to be able, in its discretion, to consider whether arrangements for restitution have or have not been made."[137] Similarly, the Arizona Supreme Court rejected an inmate's challenge to the use of a probation officer's report that contained statements made by victims of related crimes.[138]

The Tennessee sentencing procedure, unlike that of many other jurisdictions,[139] allocates to the jury the dual function of finding guilt or innocence and setting the appropriate sentence in one trial.[140] The victim's role at the sentencing stage in Tennessee is not as influential as it is at other stages in a criminal proceeding. In states that use other sentencing procedures, the victim may have a more direct effect on the sentence.

Because the jury serves as fact-finder and sentencer, most Nashville prosecutors believe that the most dramatic and effective way for a victim to influence the sentence is to make a favorable impression as a witness. Although one assistant district attorney expressed the opinion that the sentencing stage is one facet of the criminal process over which the victim has very little control,[141] another prosecutor remarked that victims have influenced his sentencing recommendations to the jury in the presentation of the state's closing arguments.[142] Nashville trial court judges agree with most of the prosecutors that the victim influences the sentence and that this influence usually is transmitted to the jury when the victim testifies against the accused.[143]

(2) Probation

Victims may be involved in a probation release decision in one of two ways. First, a bargained plea might, with the victim's knowledge or approval, incorporate a recommendation of probation.[144] Secondly, if the defendant moves for suspended sentence and release on probation, the victim may participate directly in the judicial resolution of this request. Normally, a probation decision is based upon the probation officer's report and the prosecutor's statement of support or nonsupport for the conditional release. Nashville probation officers sporadically contact victims in the course of their investigations, though their inquiry is not necessarily for the purpose of gauging the victims' receptivity to probation.[145] The victim's attitude toward probation, if known, is included in the officer's report for consideration by the sentencing judge.

The Davidson County District Attorney related that victims' wishes and desires influence his decision to recommend or oppose probation.[146] An assistant prosecutor described his practice of consulting victims in advance of probation hearings to learn of their attitudes. If he believes that probation should be granted, he advises the victim of his right to appear at the probation release hearing and express his views to the trial judge. Probation was granted in three cases in which victims opposed the prosecutor's recommendation of probation.[147]

The victim's role in the probation release decision ultimately is determined by the individual judge. One judge reported that the considerations bearing on his probation decision include

---

137. *Id.* at 291, 57 A.2d at 658.

138. State v. Nelson, 104 Ariz. 52, 448 P.2d 402 (1968). No error was found when the witnesses gave statements to the probation officer describing how similar rapes occurred in another state.

139. *See* PRESIDENT'S COMM'N ON LAW ENFORCEMENT AND ADMINISTRATION OF JUSTICE, TASK FORCE REPORT: THE COURTS 26 (1967).

140. TENN. CODE ANN. §§ 40-2704, -2706, -2707, (1956). Efforts are now underway, however, to substantially modify this procedure. *See* TENN. CRIM. CODE & CODE OF CRIM. PROC. § 40-2301, *et seq.* (Proposed Final Draft 1973).

141. Schwartz interview, *supra* note 90.

142. Wyckoff interview, *supra* note 94.

143. Cornelius, Leathers, and Mondelli interviews. Judge Cornelius, while conceding this fact, disapproved of this practice—especially in cases in which a "special prosecutor" represents the victim's interest. *See,* § III(D) *infra.*

144. *See* § II(E) (4) *supra.*

145. Interview with Tom Stephens and Ed Fowlkes, Tennessee probation officers, June 24, 1974. Fowlkes explained that one reason for victim contact is to assess the psychological needs of the defendant.

146. Shriver interview.

147. Wyckoff interview.

the crime committed, the defendant's personal background, and the defendant's need for rehabilitation, but do not include the victim's feelings.[148] A contrary view was offered by another criminal court judge who employs the following unusual probation procedure:

When a motion for suspended sentence has been set for hearing, the probation department prepares a presentence investigation report. The reporting officer does *not* recommend or oppose probation; I decide it in a "neutral" setting. The victim of the crime is *subpoenaed* to appear at the probation hearing. The serving officer is instructed to inform the victim of his *right* to appear and testify; if the victim desires not to attend, he is not forced to do so.

Approximately ninety-eight percent of victims subpoenaed do appear in court, many of whom testify as to the release of defendant on probation. In the cases in which the victim adamantly opposes probation, this has influenced a decision denying the probation request. Correspondingly, if the victim does not appear or offer testimony, or if he testifies "favorably," this influences a grant of probation.[149]

A more visible and tangible form of victim participation is observed when the defendant is released on probation on the condition that he make restitution to the victim. Power to grant probation conditioned on restitution is expressly given by statute in some states[150] and elsewhere is implied in a statutory grant of broad discretion to the sentencing judge.[151] The Federal Probation Act provides that "while on probation . . . the defendant . . . may be required to make restitution or reparation to aggrieved parties for actual damages or loss caused by the offense for which conviction was had. . . ."[152] Commentators have recognized that probation releases are increasingly conditioned upon restitution to the victim.[153] The President's Commission on Law Enforcement and Administration of Justice reported:

Financial reimbursement to victims is another condition used quite frequently in probation. It is not uncommon for a large probation agency to supervise the collection of millions of dollars in restitution for crime victims each year. Restitution can serve a very constructive purpose and of course it represents practical help for the victim. The central problem is to make certain that the rate of such payments is related to the ability of the offender to pay . . . perhaps the best approach is for the probation officer to include in his presentence report an analysis of the financial situation of the defendant, an estimate of a full amount of restitution for the victim, and a recommended plan for payment.[154]

Generally, the defendant is given the opportunity to make restitution when the loss involves damage to property rather than personal injury.[155] One author concludes that restitutionary probation is most often granted in bad check cases and larceny cases in which the stolen property has not been recovered.[156] The Nashville field survey buttresses this conclusion: reparation as a condition of probation release depends upon the nature of the offense and the agreement of the victim.[157] One example of probation conditioned upon restitution was recited by a criminal court judge who disapproves of the victim's having a role in probationary decisions:

The case involved a defendant accused of stealing an automobile. Defense counsel . . . negotiated a plea . . . [in return for the prosecutor's recommendation of] release on probation on the condition that restitution be made to the victim. I late discovered that the defendant had agreed to pay the victim on a monthly installment basis for the value of the automobile taken. Upon learning from the probation officer that there was a dispute as to the restitution agreement, I refused to release the defendant on probation under

---

148. Cornelius interview.

149. Leathers interview.

150. *See, e.g.,* MICH. STAT. ANN. § 28.1133 (1954).

151. DAWSON, *supra* note 135, at 102.

152. 18 U.S.C. § 3651 (1970).

153. ABA PROJECT ON STANDARDS FOR CRIMINAL JUSTICE, PROBATION § 3.2 (1970); C. NEWMAN, SOURCEBOOK ON PROBATION, PAROLE AND PARDONS 116 (2d ed. 1964).

154. PRESIDENT'S COMM'N ON LAW ENFORCEMENT & ADMINISTRATION OF JUSTICE, TASK FORCE REPORT: CORRECTIONS 35 (1967).

155. Jacob, *Reparation or Restitution by the Criminal Offender to His Victim,* 61 J. CRIM. L.C. & P.S. 152, 155 (1970); Best & Birzon, *Conditions of Probation: An Analysis,* 51 GEO. L.J. 809, 826 (1963).

156. DAWSON, *supra* note 135, at 106.

157. Interview with Malcolm McCune, Assistant Public Defender, Aug. 9, 1974 [hereinafter cited as McCune interview]; Mondelli interview, *supra* note 52.

these circumstances. Therefore, I think that probation should be decided upon grounds other than the feelings of the victim.[158]

Although most restitutionary probation releases may follow convictions for crimes against property, recently publicized cases show that these releases sometimes are granted even in cases of serious felonies against the person. For example, it was reported that a man who pleaded guilty to a charge of manslaughter was released on probation for a period of ten years on the condition that he pay $150 a month to the three surviving sons of the victim.[159] Similarly, a man convicted of vehicular manslaughter was ordered to pay for the college education of his victim's two small children at the rate of $1,500 per year for five consecutive years; the victim's widow reportedly was "satisfied" with this disposition.[160] Persons interviewed in Nashville, however, did not disclose any case in which the defendant had physically harmed another person and was granted probation on the condition of his making restitution.

Typical of cases recognizing the propriety of restitutionary probation is *United States v. Berger,*[161] in which the defendant was convicted of violating the Fair Labor Standards Act for, *inter alia,* paying wages below the minimum standard. The defendant was placed on probation on the condition that he compensate the workers who had been victimized by his practices. Responding to the defendant's challenge to this condition, the Second Circuit stated, "Clearly the court could make reparation for losses caused by the offense for which conviction was had a condition of probation provided there were such losses."[162] In a similar case,[163]

the defendant pleaded guilty to theft and was placed on probation conditioned upon his making restitution to the victim. The Alabama Criminal Appellate Court found that no constitutional rights of the defendant were impaired by the conditional release.[164] The involvement of victims in the probation release decision, however, is not universally approved. In *Conyers v. People*[165] the defendant was guilty of unlawfully killing another person's animals. Sentenced to a term of two to three years in the state penitentiary, the defendant asked the Colorado Supreme Court to disqualify the district attorney who had prosecuted him and had recommended that he not be released on probation. Accompanying the defendant's application were affidavits indicating that the prosecutor had promised a local livestock association that he would not recommend probation in cases such as the one in which the defendant was involved. The livestock association had written the district attorney requesting that he not recommend probation for the defendant, and the prosecutor thereafter advised the defendant's attorney that he would oppose probation. The Colorado Supreme Court directed the trial court to consider the defendant's motion for probation on its merits and not to consider any recommendation from the district attorney.[166]

(3) Parole release and clemency

Unlike inmates in many other jurisdictions, an inmate in Tennessee is not eligible for release on parole under a determinate sentence until he has served a minimum of one-half of his sentence or thirty years, whichever is less.[167] Because of the inordinately long time that inmates must serve before reaching parole eli-

---

158. Cornelius interview, *supra* note 70.

159. The Tennessean (Nashville), July 1, 1974, at 4, col. 3.

160. The Tennessean (Nashville), June 5, 1974, at 14, cols. 5-6.

161. 145 F.2d 888 (2d Cir. 1944), *cert. denied,* 324 U.S. 848 (1945).

162. *Id.* at 891.

163. Warner v. State, 52 Ala. App. 361, 292 So. 2d 480 (Crim. App. 1974). *See also* Karrell v. United States, 181 F.2d 981 (9th Cir. 1950) (actual damages caused by false certificates and papers concerning claims for home loan guaranty benefits); State v. Foltz, 14 Ore. App. 582, 513 P.2d 1208 (1973)

(restitution to welfare department for money improperly paid); State v. Morgan, 8 Wash. App. 189, 504 P.2d 1195 (1973) (restitution to assault victim for medical expenses, lost wages, and "pain and suffering"); People v. Miller, 256 Cal. App. 2d 348, 64 Cal. Rptr. 20 (1967) (restitution for injuries caused by grand theft).

164. Warner v. State, 52 Ala. App. 361, 292 So. 2d 480, 484 (Crim. App. 1974).

165. 155 P.2d 988 (Colo. 1945).

166. *Id.* at 990.

167. TENN. CODE ANN. §§ 40-3612, -3613.

gibility,[168] it is very likely that the victim's interest in the offender's release on parole wanes. This attenuation of interest would account for the paucity of contact between the Parole Board and the victim at a parole release hearing. The Tennessee Board of Pardons and Paroles serves the dual function of making parole release decisions and screening clemency petitions before they are submitted to the Governor's office.[169] Prior to deciding whether to release an inmate on parole, the Board distributes to state judges, district attorneys, and local news media a "docket" on which appear the names of eligible inmates. When a petition for clemency is to be considered, the board sends an explanatory letter to state judges, district attorneys, and news media announcing the inmate's petition.[170] According to almost every prosecuting attorney interviewed, only in the most unusual case does the prosecutor respond either affirmatively or negatively to these communications from the Parole Board. The prevailing opinion among the prosecutors and judges is that the parole release question, which is essentially whether the convict is rehabilitated and ready to be returned to society, should be answered by the Parole Board in deliberations uninfluenced by judges' or prosecutors' views.[171] In some

cases, victims have contacted prosecutors and judges concerning forthcoming parole release decisions; in these instances, the victims were advised to communicate directly with the Tennessee Board of Pardons and Paroles.[172]

A victim may appear personally before the Board to express his opinion concerning a parole release or clemency decision. According to the Board, however, there have been very few cases in which victims have made their views known to the board either directly or through their influence upon the opinions of judges or district attorneys. It appears that victims' views, when expressed, are taken into account but are given relatively little weight. The most influential factors are the inmate's prison record and evidence of rehabilitation. The chairman of the Parole Board stated that no victim had appeared personally during his tenure, but another member observed that victims have been present at hearings in past years.[173]

A parole release hearing observed by the author suggests the way in which victims' views are transmitted to and considered by the Board. An inmate with a background of poverty and "general lawlessness," who was incarcerated for the offenses of second degree burglary and arson, was being considered for parole release. A

---

168. While in many jurisdictions certain offenders are not eligible for parole, most states provide for parole eligibility in terms of a minimum sentence served or a part of a maximum sentence. *See* DAWSON, *supra* note 135, at 222. Under Wisconsin law, for example, an inmate must have served one-half of the minimum term or 20 years of a life term. WIS. STAT. ANN § 57.06(1) (a) (Supp. 1975).

169. TENN. CODE ANN. §§ 40-3603, -3612, -3613, -3623 (Supp. 1974).

170. Interview with Tennessee Board of Pardons & Paroles, Charles Traughber, Chairman, and Joe Mitchell, Board Member, July 27, 1974 [hereinafter cited as Parole Board interview]. The third member of the Board, Dorothy Greer, was unavailable.

171. For a case in which responses were made, the trial judge responded in part:

While it is my usual policy not to interefere with the action of the Pardon and Parole Board, this is one man that I believe should not receive executive clemency at this time. He was convicted of a heinous, atrocious, vicious crime and fled the jurisdiction of Tennessee and was caught in a foreign jurisdiction, brought back to Nashville and found guilty and sentenced to a long number of years in the penitentiary. . . .

. . . In my judgment, he should continue to serve his time.

The district attorney also opposed parole:

[W]hile I have no personal knowledge of how he conducted himself at the State Penitentiary, or what justification you see for affording him executive clemency, I do feel it important to point out that he was convicted by a duly impaneled jury of kidnapping for robbery and . . . the jury provided that his sentence would be without possibility of parole. Kidnapping for robbery is an extremely serious crime and it seems to me that it would do substantial violence to the legislative intent of that statute to propose executive clemency in order to get around the expressed judgment of the jury who heard the evidence in this case. While I am sure the persons who have worked with [the inmate] at the penitentiary are convinced that [the inmate] is seriously rehabilitated, his previous criminal record does not suggest that this man should be treated as an innocent first offender. I am enclosing herewith a copy of his record for your perusal.

172. Leathers interview, *supra* note 71; Shriver interview, *supra* note 17; Wyckoff interview, *supra* note 94.

173. Parole Board interview.

"field report" read by one of the Board members included a lengthy description of the victim, the owner of a house that was burned to the ground. The report described the victim's status in the community, his work habits, and his living habits. The inmate was then brought before the Board and the circumstances surrounding the crime were recounted. The Board, after further deliberation, decided to grant parole. The Board chairman later explained that he had been contacted by the victim prior to the parole release hearing, and the victim had "expressed concern" that the inmate might be released. Because the chairman believed that this was an unusual circumstance, he directed that a field study be conducted to gather information on the crime, the victim, and the views of the community from which the inmate came. This data was thought to be relevant for at least three purposes: (1) to establish the credibility of the victim should he appear at the hearing; (2) to uncover any mitigating circumstances surrounding the crime; and (3) to gather information about the attitudes of the community to which the inmate intended to return.[174] The victim did not appear at the hearing, but the information was presented to the Board nevertheless.

Victims also are involved in the parole release decision through restitutionary plans similar to probationary release conditioned on restitution.[175] While restitutionary parole is much less common than restitutionary probation,[176] one program of parole release and restitution that is receiving much attention is the "Rehabilitation Through Restitution" program in Minneapolis, Minnesota. Under this experimental project convicts sentenced for nonviolent property crimes enter into written agreements with their victims by which they agree to make restitution for property taken or damaged. If the victim refuses to cooperate, a symbolic contract with the state establishes a specific number of hours of unpaid volunteer work to "make good the crime." The agreement then is presented to the

parole board, and the prisoner is released to a half-way house where he must reside while he is employed in an outside job to fulfill the agreement. The inmate must remain in the program until he is fully released from parole restrictions. Started in 1972, the program as of June 3, 1974, had enrolled fifty-eight inmates. Only a "modest success" is claimed for the program as eighteen of the fifty-eight participants have disappeared, committed new crimes, or violated the terms of the agreement to the extent that full incarceration was required.[177] To date this program has not been employed in Tennessee.[178]

When the Parole Board recommends that the Governor grant clemency, the Board's report to the chief executive includes all of the information that it has gathered, which may in some cases include statements from victims. The Governor's office, however, follows a policy of not contacting or communicating with victims concerning clemency decisions.[179]

It is impossible to ascertain the precise weight, if any, that the Governor places on the desires of victims when those desires are known to him. For example, one aide noted that the Governor approved a commutation on the express condition that the offender not be returned to his home county. It cannot be determined whether this condition was based upon a recommendation of the judge or prosecuting attorney,[180] the Governor's perception of "community sentiment," or the victim's actual or perceived attitude.

· · ·

---

174. Id.

175. See Dressler, Practice and Theory of Probation and Parole 241 (2d ed. 1969).

176. See Dawson, supra note 135, at 311.

177. Time, June 3, 1974, at 48.

178. The Board attempted such a release in one case, but was rebuffed by the attorney general on the ground that it would be discriminatory unless made available in all cases of parole release.

179. Parole Board interview, supra note 170. Interviews with H. R. McDonald, Jr. and Robert J. Kabel, members of Governor Winfield Dunn's staff, June 27, 1974. According to these interviewees, approximately 60-75% of the clemency petitions approved by the Board are ratified by the Governor.

180. Under the Board's "letter policy." See text accompanying note 166 supra.

V. SUMMARY AND RECOMMENDATIONS*

This study confirms that the victim plays a significant informal role in the prosecution and disposition of a criminal case.[263] The extent to which a vocal victim influences the criminal proceeding depends upon a number of variables, some of which are difficult to quantify. General patterns, however, can be identified. First, the victim exercises greater control over preliminary stages of the process, such as arrest, than later phases, such as sentencing and paroles. Secondly, the victim of a misdemeanor or nonserious felony is better able to effect the dismissal of charges than the victim of a serious felony. Thirdly, the desires of a victim seeking rigorous prosecutions of a serious-crime offender are given greater consideration than the desires of reluctant victims of the same offenses. Fourthly, the wishes of reluctant victims of nonserious crimes are more likely to be honored than are the desires of aggressive victims of such crimes. Lastly, and perhaps most importantly, the victim's influence over the criminal case depends upon the receptivity and malleability of the individual with whom the victim interacts (police officer, prosecutor, or judge). The common denominator in all cases is the exercise of discretion—by police, prosecutors, judges, and correctional officials.

Although the victim sometimes exercises considerable informal influence through the day-to-day workings of criminal justice, the victim's formally recognized role is limited. Mandamus and removal actions by disgruntled victims are ineffective tools for controlling critical discretionary decisions. Compromise statutes, while expressly affording the victim an identifiable role in the decision to dismiss a case, are applicable only to a narrow class of criminal offenses. Private prosecution of the offender is available only to victims who can afford the services of privately retained prosecutorial assistance.

The general conclusions set forth above raise important questions. Should the victim have any influence over a criminal case? If so, over what kinds of cases should he have influence? What stages in the criminal process and what decisions should the victim affect? What should be the considerations in deferring to his wishes? How much weight should be accorded his desires?

To answer these questions attention should first be focused upon those basic objectives of the criminal justice system that relate to the victim's place in the system. It is submitted that the following objectives are desirable:

1. Crimes should be reported to responsible officials as promptly and accurately as possible.
2. Victims of crimes should be treated with respect and fairness.
3. Victims should have confidence in the criminal justice process and experience a sense of satisfaction with its outcome.[264]
4. Criminal offenders should be made to appreciate the consequences of their criminal acts, and they should be deterred from repeating their crimes.
5. A criminal offender should be accorded treatment by enforcement, prosecutorial, and judicial officials roughly equivalent to that accorded similarly situated criminal offenders.
6. Police, prosecutors, and judges should make decisions based upon relevant and material information.

It is highly desirable that officials at almost all stages of the criminal case know and consider the attitudes of victims. Attention to the feelings of the victim should encourage the reporting of crimes and engender confidence in

---

*Editors' note: Sections III and IV, along with footnotes 181-262 have been omitted here.

263. Beyond doubt, the Nashville field study refutes the very recent comment that "the victim plays virtually no role in the criminal case." The same commentator also boldly stated:

The victim's view is never sought or considered. He is not consulted about the original charge, any reduction of charge, or the sentence to be imposed. He is not part of the decision-making process, nor is he privy to the reasoning of the judge who imposes the sentence.

Greacen, *supra* note 3, at 11-12.

---

264. "Satisfaction" encompasses (1) the victim's belief that revenge has been carried out against the offender, and (2) the victim's personal, monetary satisfaction.

our criminal justice system. Moreover, consideration for the victim's plight usually demonstrates respect for him. It might appear inconsistent to recommend greater attention to the wishes of victims while simultaneously urging equal treatment for offenders. Equal treatment of offenders is impossible if the dispositions of similar petty larceny cases, for example, differ because in one case the victim desires the return of property without criminal prosecution while in another case the shopkeeper seeks vigorous enforcement of the larceny law. Therefore, the proposition that victims be accorded significant consideration must be applied in conjunction with another recommendation of even greater importance: the exercise of official discretion must be limited and confined to assure consistency and fairness. Thus, a decision to arrest or prosecute—or any other decision in the criminal process—should be influenced by the complainant's attitudes only within guidelines promulgated to assure fairness to the victim, society, and the alleged offender. The American Bar Association,[265] the National Advisory Commission on Criminal Justice Standards and Goals,[266] and numerous commentators[267] support the standardization and minimization of unbridled discretion.

The guidelines for official discretion should reflect the idea that society's interest in dealing with the offender grows as the criminal act becomes more serious. Hence the victim's role should decrease in importance as the gravity of the crime increases. Prosecutors should follow written procedures for communicating with victims prior to or during plea negotiations. Written standards should identify points that prosecutors may properly consider in weighing victims' attitudes (*e.g.,* the crime, the relation-

265. ABA Project on Standards For Criminal Justice, The Urban Police Function § 4.2 (1973); ABA Project on Standards For Criminal Justice, The Prosecution Function & The Defense Function §§ 3.4(b) .9(b) (c) (1971).
266. *See* Standards 1.1, 2.1 and 3.3, as reported in 14 Crim L. Rep. 2097 (Oct. 31, 1973).
267. See Davis, *supra* note 8. *See also* Amsterdam, *Perspectives on the Fourth Amendment,* 58 Minn. L. Rev. 349 (1974), in which a similar proposal to ameliorate discretion associated with warrantless searches is articulated.

ship of the offender to the victim, the defendant's prior record). Police officers, too, should be given explicit guidance for handling arrest decisions. Once discretion-governing standards are operative, deviation from the standards should be subject to review by either a judge or an administrative appellate tribunal.[268]

Whether or not governmental officials agree to specific requests of victims, it is essential that they communicate effectively with citizens aggrieved by criminal wrongs. The simple task of explaining to victims the nature of the criminal justice system, how it operates, and how the victim will be involved in it is relatively easy and is not very time-consuming. Even if the victim's attitudes should be given no significant weight, as in bail decisions, for example, the benefits of the simple dissemination of information seem enormous.

Any reform of the victim's role in the criminal process must take account of restitution, which may be made prior to the reporting of the crime, during the preliminary stages of the criminal prosecution in return for the dismissal of the case, as a component of probation release, or in some jurisdictions, as a condition of parole release. Private restitutionary arrangements made prior to the reporting of crimes should not be condoned because society has an interest in maintaining a structure within which police and public prosecutors make "screening" decisions about criminal conduct. Once a criminal wrong is reported to responsible officials, however, reparation plans should be viable options for victims and defendants. First, the prospect of obtaining compensation should encourage victims to report crime and cooperate with prosecutorial officials. Secondly, the knowledge that the offender has paid for the injuries inflicted by his criminal act may satisfy the victim's need for retribution and vindication. Thirdly, compensatory plans may be rehabilitative in that the offender may more clearly understand his personal responsibility for oc-

268. This writer cannot anticipate the myriad fact situations which should be encompassed by such rules. For a more detailed analysis of this suggestion and ways of implementing it, see Davis, *supra* note 8, at 80-96, 126-33, 188-212 (1969).

casioning harm.[269] Lastly, restitutionary programs may deter future criminal behavior.[270] The same benefits should accrue from statutory victim compensation plans[271] that require offenders to reimburse the state for its payments to victims.[272]

Certain practices disclosed by this research should be discontinued. The policy of according weight to a victim's feelings depending on the victim's status, wealth, race, sex, or age does not forward any worthy objective and clearly conflicts with the goals of treating victims fairly and developing their confidence in the criminal justice system. Also, to the extent that judges accord any weight to the victim's desires in setting bail, they are influenced by immaterial data. Similarly, the victim's attitude is immaterial to the question whether to release an inmate on parole.

Should the practice of employing private prosecutors be encouraged or discouraged?[273] Private prosecution, although permitted in some parts of Tennessee, is no longer allowed in Davidson County, principally because privately retained attorneys have a financial interest in the outcome of the litigation. According to local offi-

cials,[274] private prosecutors lack the impartiality that is demanded of a public prosecutor. If district attorneys are not active in pursuing prosecutions, as one proponent of private prosecution asserts, perhaps the appropriate remedy is the employment of special assistants at public expense[275] or, if necessary, the ouster of the prosecutor. To inject into the system a private attorney employed by the victim—a victim who necessarily has adequate financial resources—contradicts the American notion of evenhanded justice. Moreover, if recommendations like those made herein are adopted and applied fairly, victims should not find it necessary to employ private counsel to prosecute offenders.[276]

The last recommendation, although difficult to implement, is the cornerstone of all the previous recommendations: police officers, prosecutors, and judges should be selected cautiously. Because of the many vital discretionary functions performed by these persons, it is essential that they exercise good judgment. Regardless of the degree to which discretion can be restricted by written rules, these persons must weigh circumstances and exigencies in individual cases to reach results beneficial to the

---

269. Ron Johnson, supervisor of the Minneapolis "Rehabilitation through Restitution" program, *supra* note 177, stated:
 It's one thing to break into a garage. It's another to have to look the owner in the eye afterwards. We are building a sense of responsibility.
Another writer characterizes this concept as "punitive restitution;" this approach seeks to establish "the functional responsibility of the Offender to the Victim." Poole, *Criminal Justice; A Systems Analysis Approach,* 1 LAW & LIBERTY 5, 7 (1975).
270. SCHAFER, RESTITUTION TO VICTIMS OF CRIME, (1960), reports:
 The institution of restitution is able . . . to make good the . . . loss of the victim . . . [and] . . . help the task of punishment.
Id. at 125.
 [It may] . . . be reformative as well.
Id. at 126.
271. *See* note 4, *supra.*
272. One writer commented:
 The offender should understand that he injured not only the state and law and order but also the victim—primarily the victim. . . . The institutions of compensation and restitution can not only make good the injury or loss of the victim but also, at the same time, help the task of punishment. This is where victim compensation should fit into the criminal justice system.

Schafer, *The Proper Role of a Victim-Compensation System,* 1 CRIME & DELIN. 45, 46 (1975). *See also* ABA PROJECT ON STANDARDS FOR CRIMINAL JUSTICE, SENTENCING ALTERNATIVES & PROCEDURES, § 2.7(c) (iii) (1968) (recommending that the amount of a fine should take into account the defendant's ability to make restitution to the victim); ABA PROJECT ON STANDARDS FOR CRIMINAL JUSTICE PROBATION, § 3.2(c) (viii) (1970) (listing restitution to the victim as an appropriate condition of probation).
273. Arguments for and against this practice are presented in Note, *Private Prosecution, supra* note 234 and 50 N.C.L. REV. 1171, 1175 (1972).
274. Cornelius interview, *supra* note 70; Shriver interview, *supra* note 17.
275. *See e.g.* TENN. CODE ANN. § 8-606 (Supp. 1973) (authorizing employment of additional counsel by the Governor and state attorney general "where the interest of the state requires"); TENN. CODE ANN. § 8-706 (Supp. 1973) (giving the circuit or criminal court the power to appoint a district attorney general pro tem if the district attorney "fails to attend any term . . . or is disqualified. . . .").
276. Effective review procedures as outlined by DAVIS *supra* note 8, should minimize the incidence of disenchanted victims.

victim, society, and to a lesser extent the accused. Those responsible for selecting these
persons, whether the electorate, officials having
appointive powers, or directors of personnel,
should give greater attention to the kind of decision-makers they are selecting.

Selected readings for Chapter 10

Carrington, Frank. *The Victims* (New Rochelle, N.Y.: Arlington House, Inc., 1977).

> The criminal justice system does not protect or serve victims largely because of the le-
> niency with which offenders are handled. Suggests the need for legal representation for
> victims to be sure their interests are protected.

Denno, Deborah, and James A. Kramer. "The Effects of Victim Characteristics on Judicial Decision
Making," in McDonald, William F., ed. *Criminal Justice and the Victim* (Beverly Hills, Calif.: Sage
Publications, Inc., 1976), pp. 215-226.

> This paper presents the results of a study dealing with the effects of the judge's reaction
> to victim characteristics as it affects the sentencing decision. In addition, attention is
> given to physical and situational characteristics of the victim that may influence the over-
> all reaction of the judge.

Schneider, Elizabeth M., and Susan B. Jordan. *Representation of Women Who Defend Themselves
in Response To Physical or Sexual Assault* (New York: Center for Constitutional Rights, no date).

> This volume was developed to be of assistance to defense attorneys representing women
> who commit homicide after they have been physically or sexually assaulted or after their
> children have been molested or abused. Extensive case law citations are provided, and the
> issues and implications involved in choosing a defense and the strategic problems in-
> volved in implementing the defense in the courtroom are presented.

Williams, Kristen N. "The Effects of Victim Characteristics on the Disposition of Violent Crimes,"
in McDonald, William F., ed. *Criminal Justice and the Victim,* (Beverly Hills, Calif.: Sage Publications, Inc., 1976), pp. 177-214.

> This article presents an empirical analysis of the effects of victim characteristics on de-
> cisions made by prosecutors, judges, and juries concerning cases against defendants
> charged with violent crimes in the District of Columbia.

Ziegenhagen, Eduard A. *Victims, Crime and Social Control* (New York: Praeger Publishers, Inc.,
1977).

> A consistent theme in this book is the social role of the crime victim. The victim is seen
> as an integral component in social control. Attention is given to exploring the attributes
> of the victim's role in other cultures in an attempt to answer such questions as why some
> persons are recognized as victims and others are not, how victim surrogates act on behalf
> of the victim, the types of remedies selected, and their implementation and results.

SECTION FOUR

Services for crime victims

The four chapters in this final section of the book deal with alternative types of victim service programs. Chapter 11 deals with crime prevention programs based on environmental design considerations; Chapter 12 contains two papers introducing the variety of program types; Chapter 13 moves to a presentation of three case illustrations of different types of victim assistance programs; and Chapter 14 addresses developments in the idea and practice of compensation to crime victims.

In recent years there has been growing interest in the use of the physical environment as a means of reducing certain types of criminal activities. Physical design is seen as having both a direct and indirect impact on crime. Examples of direct impact include the use of such "target hardening" devices as dead bolt locks, burglar alarms, and unbreakable glass. However, it is obvious that these devices alone cannot prevent crime. A more indirect way in which physical design affects crime is by discouraging criminal behavior and facilitating legitimate behavior. Various physical elements of a city can be used to encourage activity that limits the opportunity for crime. Included here would be street lights, design of alleyways, building design, street layout, and so on. For example, street lights can discourage certain types of criminal behavior and at the same time encourage pedestrian traffic and citizen surveillance. Chapter 11 is a report first published in *Nation's Cities* that describes the major ideas and practical applications of crime prevention through environmental design. It is important to keep in mind the relationship between the ideas expressed in this article to those discussed in Chapter 5, which dealt with the differential vulnerability of certain categories of people to being victimized.

Chapter 12 contains two articles providing an overview of victim assistance programs and the variety of issues confronting them. More detailed illustrations of specific types of programs are then provided in Chapter 13.

The first paper in Chapter 12, by political scientists Anne Schneider and Peter Schneider, identifies the major types of service components in victim assistance programs and critically considers some of the major issues confronting these programs. Though most types of victim programs aim at providing a variety of services, the Schneiders suggest that programs can usually be identified in relation to the emphasis placed on either social services, advocacy services, prevention services, or services designed to reduce the hardships experienced by victims in the justice system. Each type of service must deal with such issues as organizational auspices, target audience, purpose, effectiveness, and funding arrangements. Of these, perhaps the most significant issue confronting victim programs is that of funding. This is aggravated by the fact that time-limited federal funds used to start most victim programs are running out at a time when state and local governments are reducing spending for all types of human services. Local victim service programs need to develop alternative and perhaps more unconventional types of funding arrangements or face the prospect of being consolidated into existing social welfare and criminal justice agencies and, in the process, losing much of their distinctive focus on crime victims. There are a number of funding possibilities. One suggestion involves levying a financial penalty on convicted criminals, the proceeds to be used for the operation of victim services. The state of California, for example, has incorporated this type of provision in compensation statutes, and legislation has been introduced in Minnesota that would disburse the proceeds of such a "user's tax" to all types of victim programs.

The second paper in Chapter 12, by political scientists Edward Ziegenhagen and John Benyi, presents a somewhat different way of conceptualizing victim service programs. Six categories of victim-oriented programs are identified and examined according to such considerations as the type of problem condition addressed, program goals, and intervention approaches. Ziegenhagen and Benyi note that programs vary in relation to how they operationally define victims as service recipients, and these definitions follow from the type of organization delivering the services. Attention is then placed on assessing the extent to which victims in alternative types of programs perform social control functions.

Chapter 13 moves to a consideration of four specific types of victim programs —programs for battered women, rape victims, victims as witnesses, and a multipurpose victim crisis center. All of these programs have been discussed in general terms in the preceding chapter, and here the reader is presented with case illustrations.

The first paper, by Shirley Oberg and Ellen Pence, both of whom administer programs for battered women in Minnesota, describes the development, implementation, and operation of programs and services for battered women in that state. Minnesota offers the interesting example of a state that has allocated a relatively substantial amount of public money for the development of battered women programs to be administered by a state corrections agency. As noted by Oberg and Pence, local involvement in establishing and operating programs has been stimulated by the use of service contracts with the state agency, as well as through an advisory task force involved in implementing all aspects of the legislative mandate. One indication of the success of this grassroots effort has been the passage of new legislation in Minnesota increasing state funding for 1980-1981 to 3 million dollars. This legislative appropriation reflects the institutionalization of programs and services for battered women in Minnesota and, as a consequence, raises issues about the extent to which program staff will become part of the very institutions to which they were, in large part, a response.

Jayne Thomas Rich, a retired police lieutenant who is active in prevention efforts and services for rape victims, elaborates further the notion of community-based, community-controlled program development. She describes several programs for rape victims and analyzes what is necessary for the programs to reach goals involving victim support, institutional reform, community education, and law reform. Problems encountered by the programs include funding, staffing, credibility with criminal justice agencies, failure to attract minority women, and jurisdictional issues with more established and traditional agencies.

Steven Chesney and Carole Schneider describe the development and operation of crime victim crisis centers in the third paper in this chapter. Chesney has been responsible for the evaluation and Schneider for the planning and administration of this program. The programs themselves have been implemented and operated by a private agency on contract from the Minnesota Department of Corrections for the purpose of delivering a variety of services to crime victims in designated areas of Minneapolis and St. Paul. Services provided include crisis intervention with victims immediately following the criminal incident, public education, crime prevention, and referral and brokerage services with established social welfare and criminal justice agencies.

As Chesney and Schneider point out, this type of program needs to coordinate its efforts closely with law enforcement agencies to receive referrals. If victim referrals are not forthcoming, for whatever reason, program staff must either redefine their functions or undertake more aggressive outreach activities. This, then, begs questions addressed in the preceding chapter about the appropriate location for victim assistance programs and the kinds of services actually needed by crime victims. To what extent should such services, when required, be provided by existing social service agencies as compared with specialized victim assistance programs?

David Lowenberg's paper also addresses this issue of program location. Lowenberg is a practitioner with a national reputation in the victim service field, and his paper describes the integrated victim-witness program in Pima County, Arizona. The program presented here has a number of interesting dimensions. First, it contains a diversity of service components, including crisis intervention teams linked with law enforcement officers, a social service referral component working closely with established community agencies, a dispute settlement program that acts as an alternative to the criminal justice system, and a victim-witness assistance component to assist victims as witnesses in the prosecution of the criminal case. The program is administered by the office of the county attorney, and this location may have had something to do with gaining initial credibility with established criminal justice and social welfare agencies in the community. However, Lowenberg notes difficulties similar to those faced by the Minnesota Crisis Centers in getting police referrals, especially during the early period following program implementation.

Alan Harland and LeRoy Lamborn, authors of the two papers in Chapter 14, have backgrounds in both law and social science. This training is reflected in their analysis of the legal issues and program applications of state compensation to crime victims.

Although often used interchangeably, the ideas of restitution and compensation refer to very different types of programs. As noted in Chapters 8 and 9, restitution refers to payments made by the criminal offender or defendant in the form of money or services to either the direct crime victim or the community. Compensation, on the other hand, refers to payments made by the state to crime victims. As Harland makes clear, compensation payments are civil in character and reflect a social responsibility for helping to spread the losses that result from specific categories of crime.

Harland's paper covers the major developments and issues in this program area, explains common program practices, identifies primary types of eligibility criteria, and suggests some likely future program directions. Lamborn focuses his paper much more on the limits of compensation awards, which, as he sees it, make compensation programs a relatively ineffective remedy for most crime victims. Running through these papers on compensation by Harland and Lamborn are issues addressed in earlier chapters, including those of victim culpability, intrafamily victimization, and the economic, social, and psychological costs associated with criminal victimization.

Chapter 11

CREATING SAFE ENVIRONMENTS

A □ *Crime prevention through environmental design*

A □ *Crime prevention through environmental design*

THE CPTED CONCEPT

EDWARD J. PESCE

Crime prevention through environmental design, or CPTED (pronounced sep-ted), is a relatively new idea in fighting crime and the fear of crime. While designing changes in the physical environment to reduce crime is not a new notion in itself, CPTED adds to this notion a combination of changes in the physical environment with changes in people's reaction to their environment—in other words, a combination of effective *design* and *use* of the environment. CPTED incorporates physical, social, law enforcement, and management techniques to achieve its goal of reducing crime and the fear of crime. It is a concept that can work not only in housing, but in businesses, parks, public buildings, transportation systems, industries, and schools as well.

The goal of CPTED is to reduce opportunities for crime that are often inherent in the structure of buildings and the layout of neighborhoods and streets—in blind alleys, unlighted streets, and dense shrubbery, for example. It involves the close cooperation of agencies, organizations, and individuals at all levels, from the federal government to the local resident who de-

velops an interest and sense of responsibility in doing his or her part to protect the neighborhood from crime. In fact, it is only with the conscious and active support of the residents of a neighborhood in maintaining the physical changes in their neighborhood and in detecting and reporting crimes that crime prevention through environmental design can work. A key part of CPTED is the change in attitude among residents made possible by changes in the physical environment; reducing the opportunity for crime allows people the freedom to move about their community without fear of being harmed.

Several projects have been set up across the country to examine the relationship between the environment (used here to mean both physical structures and the attitudes of citizens) and crime, including projects in Broward County (Ft. Lauderdale), Florida; Denver; San Jose; Chicago; Jacksonville; Minneapolis; San Antonio; Portland, Oregon; Atlanta; and Hartford. Many of the projects have been funded by the federal government in conjunction with state and local agencies. This report centers around demonstration projects in a commercial setting in Portland, Oregon, residential settings in Minneapolis and Hartford, and an educational setting in Broward County, Florida. The National Institute of Law Enforcement and Criminal Justice (NILECJ) funded the research and evalu-

Reprinted with permission from *Nation's Cities* magazine, a publication of the National League of Cities, December 1977, pp. 16-28 (excluding photographs).

ation effort for the Minneapolis, Portland, and Broward County projects under contract with the Westinghouse National Issues Center while the Hartford project was funded directly by NILECJ. Both the Westinghouse and Hartford efforts were part of an experimental project, testing CPTED concepts and strategies, which will be completed by July 1, 1978.

The purpose of all these projects is to adapt the idea of crime prevention through environmental design to different communities so that it can be used in other cities. These CPTED projects are aimed principally at crimes such as homicide, rape, robbery, assault, burglary, larceny, autho theft, arson, and vandalism. Generally excluded from this list are white collar crimes such as fraud and embezzlement, crimes against the government, organized racketeering, morals offenses, family offenses, and disorderly conduct.

CPTED strategies include three kinds of crime prevention: punitive, mechanical, and corrective. Punitive prevention means creating an environment in which it is apparent that a potential criminal is likely to be detected, apprehended, and punished. Mechanical prevention involves placing physical obstacles in the way of the potential offender to make it more difficult for him to commit a crime. Locks and window bars are part of mechanical prevention, but equally important are the layout of streets and buildings, the location of community facilities, and other design principles. Corrective prevention is perhaps the most fundamental of the three because it involves eliminating criminal motives.

These means of crime prevention through environmental design are achieved in four ways: access control, surveillance, activity support, and motivation reinforcement. The key to access control is setting up barriers to prevent unauthorized people from entering an area, primarily through making a building or area less vulnerable to unauthorized entry. The primary aim of surveillance is to keep intruders under observation by means of police patrols, electronic devices, or organized programs among residents and users of an area. Surveillance can be aided by improving street lighting and eliminating visual barriers such as fences, shrubs, and walls. Activity support involves increasing human use of an area by making it more attractive. It might be as complex as building a recreation center or as simple as placing benches in a shopping mall. Activity support enhances surveillance because it increases the number of people in an environment. Activity support does not consist of physical changes alone but can also include activities that foster a spirit of community among residents, such as a flea market or a clean-up day. Motivation reinforcement has two goals: to encourage residents and users of an area to have and enact positive attitudes about their living and working environment and to discourage potential offenders by increasing the risk of apprehension and by reducing the payoff of crime. Altering the scale of a large, impersonal environment to create one that is smaller and more personalized, for example, can give residents more sense of community and security. Improving the quality and attractiveness of houses, schools, and subway cars; organizing occupants; or changing management policy are some other examples. Projecting a positive community image to others is a significant deterrent to criminal behavior.

It should be emphasized again that crime prevention through environmental design involves more than physical changes in a community; the changes must be backed by citizens, citizens' organizations, public service groups, law enforcement agencies, and local, state, and, in some cases, federal governments. It is precisely the combination of strategies, rather than individual strategies applied randomly or in isolation, that makes CPTED a most promising crime prevention tool for our cities.

CPTED IN A COMMERCIAL SETTING
JOHN W. McKAY

The opening of a small donut shop is, in most areas of the country, an unheralded event. But on Union Avenue in Portland, Oregon, the new Winchell's Donut Shop is looked upon as a symbol of the revitalization of a commercial strip.

Portland businessman Reuben Roth also believes in the future of the strip. In November, 1976, he announced the first major new investment on Union Avenue in more than two years —a $225,000 BMW auto dealership on the site of his used car lot.

These events contrast sharply with the area's recent history. The Union Avenue corridor is a commercial strip 50 blocks long and 4 blocks wide running through northeast Portland. Surrounding Union Avenue are predominantly single-family residences. The corridor faced deterioration, increasing crime, and a general decline in conditions during the late 1960s and early 1970s. Violent crimes had become disproportionately high, based on the area's share of the city's population. In a 1973 survey, Union Avenue business people perceived the crime level, more than any other factor, to be the largest impediment to the successful operation of their businesses. In fact, almost one-fourth of them reported a desire to move in the next year or two.

Economic vitality is often very directly related to crime and the crime rate. Abandoned, boarded-up stores provide hideouts for offenders. Unattractive commercial areas decrease the likelihood that new business will come in. They also warn away potential customers. As businesses close, there are fewer "eyes on the street" that would give customers and nearby residents a sense of safety. As unemployment rises, so does the number of street corner loiterers. Fear of crime increases accordingly.

Until recently, Union Avenue was typical of many declining inner-city commercial areas throughout urban America. A major revitalization effort by the city of Portland that includes crime prevention through environmental design has begun to turn the area around.

In October, 1974, the corridor was selected by the Westinghouse National Issues Center to be the site of the commercial demonstration. At that time, although the Union Avenue corridor had already been a proposed redevelopment site (a Model Cities redevelopment program had been drafted some five years earlier), little action had been taken to redevelop the area. Most improvements in the northeast section of Portland had approached the boundaries of this 200-block corridor but stopped short of the corridor itself.

The prevalent corridor crimes are assault, robbery, purse-snatching, and burglary (both commercial and residential). To guide the demonstration project development, the staff identified a number of crime prevention objectives:

- Reduce opportunities for crime and reduce fear of crime by making streets and open areas more easily observable and by increasing activity in the neighborhood
- Provide ways in which neighborhood residents, business people, and police can work together more effectively to reduce opportunities and incentives for crime
- Increase neighborhood identity, investor confidence, and social cohesion
- Provide building security surveys and public information programs to help business people and residents protect themselves from crime
- Make the area more accessible by improving transportation services
- Remove crime incentives by providing alternatives to carrying cash on the streets
- Improve the effectiveness and efficiency of police patrol operations
- Encourage citizens to report crimes

A number of these steps to solve the corridor's crime problems have already begun. A Safe Streets for People project is providing outdoor lighting, dial-free emergency telephones, and sidewalk and landscaping improvements. Also part of Safe Streets are a block watch program and a program setting up certain homes as safe havens. Residents and frequenters of the corridor have participated in neighborhood clean-ups and Sunday markets. A public awareness campaign is under way to discourage people from carrying cash on the streets. One of the alternatives suggested is carrying travelers checks, which are available at low rates, can be cashed only by the owner, and do not require check book balancing. And some banks are offering bill-paying services through which the bank will pay a customer's bills upon deposit of a Social Security or regular check.

The Union Avenue Redevelopment Plan, adopted by the Development Commission in mid-1975, provided $4.5 million for street improvements. These funds will help construct a center strip, four-lane avenue with off-street parking. Landscaping will lend a softening touch along the roadway. The design for the avenue is nearing completion, and construction is expected to begin in 1978.

The Tri-Met system, Portland's bus authority, built specially designed bus shelters on the avenue to aid the effort. The shelters incorporate a number of crime prevention features including high visibility and adequate lighting. These, and a $400,000 street lighting project funded by LEAA, combined to bring more people out on the street and into commercial establishments. Another transportation improvement is a bus program for the elderly and handicapped.

Dennis Wilde, the director of Portland's Bureau of Planning, notes that the CPTED program has had a positive impact on the community. He believes that strong citizen support is necessary to ensure success of the plan. "The crime reduction and prevention component of the Union Avenue Redevelopment Plan is one available ingredient but not the whole pie."

In the spring of 1977, interviews with corridor business people found that more than half had increased sales in the last two years and that 90 percent of them had no intention of relocating in the near future. In part, this turnaround could be attributed to police security surveys. A total of 210 surveys (including 176 businesses) were conducted along the corridor. Follow-up work showed that by March of 1977, roughly 55 percent of the businesses were in complete or partial compliance with the survey recommendations. In the first 10 months of 1976, there was a 29 percent reduction in commercial burglaries on Union Avenue, compared to a 9 percent reduction for the city as a whole. This reduction carried over into the first quarter of 1977, at which time a sharp decline, 61 percent, was registered. (Caution should be used in crediting this reduction solely to the building surveys or in assuming such a decrease will continue, because of the limited time period on which these findings were based.)

If renovation of existing businesses and the opening of new ones are indications of a reverse

in the decline of the avenue, then the Salvation Army, which is spending $250,000 to renovate its facility, is giving additional hope to a revitalized strip. The Salvation Army has been joined by approximately 20 new businesses in the last year.

While Portland's Union Avenue might not be characterized as a glowing success story, the neighborhood is recuperating, if not yet fully recovered. The vital signs are good, and the prognosis is very promising. Crime prevention through environmental design is being used in surrounding residential areas in Portland, as well. For example, the Portland Crime Prevention Bureau used Department of Housing and Urban Development funds to buy locks that were installed by local veterans working with a Comprehensive Employment and Training Act grant from the Department of Labor. The Crime Prevention Bureau emphasized that locks were only one part of any successful burglary prevention program, neighborhood cooperation being another and perhaps a more important element.

While the Portland residential program has not been in operation long enough to be declared a success, Seattle's community crime prevention program has and is. Relying on neighborhood cooperation, block watches, property identification, and security inspection, Seattle reports a 48 to 61 percent reduction in household burglaries for participants. In fact, the program has been so successful that LEAA's National Institute for Law Enforcement and Criminal Justice has recently selected it as an exemplary project.

Other cities, too, recognize the need to control crime to improve the health of urban businesses. Jacksonville, Florida, for example, has under construction in its downtown plan a street improvement program that uses crime prevention through environmental design, which the city hopes will promote greater downtown activity and public and private investment. Improvements include high-intensity lighting, a uniquely designed traffic control system, landscaping, and pedestrian crossing improvements. The street improvement program is designed to allow buses to circulate more freely and to allow riders to transfer between these more easily; it includes a fringe and peripheral parking system for cars.

San Antonio, Texas, the picturesque Spanish town with the San Antonio River flowing through the downtown area called the Paseo del Rio, presents a unique illustration of crime prevention techniques. The Park Rangers were established in 1968 to patrol the river's mixture of commercial establishments and residences. They wear distinctive uniforms and must qualify under the state statutes as peace officers and, as such, receive regular training from the police academy. They patrol on foot and in light boats along the river. Their patrol has been made more effective by the upgraded lighting along the Paseo del Rio. They carry portable radios to maintain complete communications with the police department.

The positive impact of crime prevention on the economic health of cities is a good sign. The fact that cities such as Portland can reverse the deterioration of commercial areas and increase business through a combination of strategies gives rise to hope that the social, economic, and physical decline of our cities can be reversed. Crime prevention through environmental design is one important element in the formula for better health.

CPTED IN A RESIDENTIAL SETTING
LYNN OLSON

Crime prevention brings to mind images of police officers on every corner, but the cities of Minneapolis and Hartford have found that these images aren't always necessarily true. Crime prevention programs begin with people—people familiar with crime prevention, people active in their community. Changes in people's behavior, changes in the environment (installing street lights or locks, for example) and cooperation among city services (public works, economic development, building inspection, housing and redevelopment authority) add up to comprehensive crime prevention programs. Two crime prevention experiments in Minneapolis and Hartford might well be called experiments in urban conservation.

In 1975, Minneapolis Mayor Al Hofstede and City Council President Lou DeMars asked the state of Minnesota to use part of an LEAA technical assistance grant to develop a crime prevention plan for Minneapolis. Both were concerned with the need to revitalize inner-city neighborhoods and improve an atmosphere that fostered crime and the fear of crime. Crime was seriously affecting not only tangibles, such as property values, but also citizen attitudes and behavior.

At the same time, the Westinghouse National Issues Center, under contract with the National Institute for Law Enforcement and Criminal Justice of LEAA, had selected the Willard-Homewood neighborhood in Minneapolis as a residential demonstration site for the NILECJ-sponsored crime prevention through environmental design program. A close working partnership was formed among Westinghouse, the Governor's Crime Control Planning Board staff, city officials, and citizens. Support and leadership from the city and contributions by individual citizens and citizens' organizations were major catalysts in launching a dramatic experiment in crime prevention.

The major criteria used to choose the Willard-Homewood neighborhood included: the severity of the crime problem, the types of crimes most often committed in the neighborhood, the presence of active community organizations, and the presence of ongoing city activities to which projects could be tied. Because the project generated a great deal of enthusiasm and showed potential in preventing crime in the neighborhood, the Governor's Crime Control Board expanded the demonstration to include two other neighborhoods in Minneapolis, Lowry Hill East and Hawthorne. Planning in the Willard-Homewood area was funded by NILECJ, while the Minneapolis Governor's Crime Control Planning Board funded planning for the other two neighborhoods. LEAA funds were provided to implement all three demonstrations. Willard-Homewood is composed mainly of single-family homes. Thirty-five percent of its residents are members of a minority. It is the only neighborhood of the three with a significant minority population. Lowry Hill East is mainly young, single, and transient. The area is one of the most densely settled in the city, with a population of just under 8,000, 36 percent of whom are between the ages of 18 and 24. Lowry Hill East is characterized by large, older houses and new and old apartment houses; 80 percent of the property is rental. In Hawthorne, 57 percent of the homes—mostly one- and two-family—are owner-occupied. The neighborhood is made up of many families with children, 23 percent of which are on AFDC [aid to families with dependent children]. Twenty-two percent of the residents are 62 years or older.

The residents of Willard-Homewood demonstrated a disproportionate level of fear of crime compared to residents of other neighborhoods. Both Westinghouse and the Governor's Community Crime Prevention staff tried to pinpoint the characteristics of fear of crime, crime patterns, offender-victim behavior and attitudes, and environmental factors that affect crime. Some of the items they looked at were housing values, street and alley layout, pedestrian uses, location of bars, and lighting. They conducted victimization and fear surveys. To promote citizen involvement and interaction, a major element of the CPTED program, they held more than 85 local meetings in Willard-Homewood to inform citizens and elicit their ideas about how to deal with residential burglary, robbery, assault, theft, and vandalism. Residents sometimes found these studies and meetings frustrating. Willard-Homewood Neighborhood Coordinator Van White, a longtime local activist, explained, "Over the years our neighborhood has been studied to death. We want action now." But citizen interaction does pay off. The foundation of the crime prevention strategies in these neighborhoods is built on existing citizen support groups: several strong community organizations in Willard-Homewood, the existing block-club structure in Hawthorne, and the Lowry Hill East neighborhood association. Neighborhood crime prevention coordinators have been hired to keep the neighborhoods in touch with the city.

While the police were not ignored in the Willard-Homewood project, they no longer have sole responsibility for crime prevention. The city designed a strategy that included citizen participation, agency interaction, and the support of the police department. Police surveillance and patrol supplement activities by individual citizens, such as voluntarily adding locks and alarms to residences and businesses; providing surveillance for houses that are empty because residents are at work all day or out of town; watching over the neighborhood and reporting suspicious events or people; and helping to keep youth productively occupied. Residents and business people were encouraged to take a more active role in their neighborhoods. Physical improvements planned for Willard-Homewood include housing rehabilitation, better lighting, altered traffic circulation, and amenities such as gateways and street signs that promote neighborhood identity and positive community image. These same strategies, with some local variations, were also used in the other two Minneapolis neighborhoods.

Dorothy James, the neighborhood coordinator in Hawthorne, says that her biggest job is to convince people that this time something really will be done about crime, and she thinks she's succeeding. Because Hawthorne is a Housing and Redevelopment Authority emphasis area, many programs already under way can aid in community crime prevention. Close coordination with HRA will be provided by the neighborhood coordinator and its Crime Prevention Task Force.

Lowry Hill East presents an interesting contrast to Willard-Homewood and Hawthorne. The emphasis there is almost exclusively on organization. Lucy Gerold is beginning the arduous task of establishing block clubs in a neighborhood that had no strong community organization. Gerold's work already has paid off. On a Sunday in August when police came into the neighborhood searching for a suspect, it was a new block captain who told police where to find the suspect.

No less important than citizen involvement is city hall involvement. In an interview, Minneapolis CPTED Project Director Sheldon Strom and former Project Director Bob Viking, stressed the importance of locating the program management right in city hall. According to Strom, "the neighborhood residents now have a spokesperson in the city. We can get things done for them that they had a hard time calling attention to before. And it gives the program real political visibility." Adds Viking, "If we can prove the cost-effectiveness of some of the things that we are going to do with federal funds, such as installing traffic diverters [and] constructing alley modifications, then we can get [CPTED] built into the normal city processes and programs. Crime prevention will be brought into our planning on a routine basis, something that's just not done now."

The three Minneapolis projects were funded in May, 1977 with $476,000 in LEAA money from the Governor's Crime Control Planning Board to improve the quality of life; reduce crime and the fear of crime; test and evaluate these crime prevention strategies; develop a model process for comprehensive community crime prevention; and increase residents' involvement in the project. Council President DeMars is sure that if the projects are successful, the city will expand and support these concepts when federal funding expires. "We're committed to finding new ways of preventing and reducing crime in Minneapolis. We've relied for too long solely on our police department. The city is going to make other departments accountable, too. This project shows us that the building inspection department, the public works department, the social services department, and others all must consider crime prevention when they initiate their activities."

Recommendations based on the three Minneapolis projects were included in a publication of the Governor's Crime Control Planning Board staff.

Among the report's recommendations are:
- Adoption of a security ordinance requiring residences and business to meet minimum security standards
- Police participation in review of commercial and housing developments to ensure that adequate crime prevention measures are built into them
- Programs to inform residents and businessmen of steps they can take to make their homes and buildings more secure
- Redesigning streets to make them less accessible and vulnerable to burglars
- An experimental lighting program in residential areas

The workplan for each demonstration neighborhood shows the variety of approaches each undertakes. Common features among the three neighborhoods are the home and business security surveys conducted by police and a neighborhood coordinator with one or two aides to staff the programs. One of the most significant features of the Minneapolis program is the system for coordinating city and neighborhood proposed by Westinghouse in its Willard-Homewood demonstration plan and the attempt to build upon what already exists in each neighborhood.

In Hartford, a similar program began several years earlier when NILECJ asked the Hartford Institute of Criminal and Social Justice to develop a program to investigate how social and physical environment changes, coupled with a different response by police, could result in a reduction in crime and the fear of crime. The project was to be aimed at specific crimes—robbery, burglary, and purse-snatching—all crimes that involve a confrontation between people, often strangers, and that tend to enhance the level of fear in a community. The city of Hartford would work with NILECJ and the Hartford Institute, but it was understood from the beginning that the city would provide funds only if the residents of the area approved the plans. A key figure in coordinating all groups and obtaining support was City Council Majority Leader Nicholas Carbone. As in Minneapolis, a close working partnership and the support of local government were essential to setting up the crime prevention project.

Planners in Hartford chose the North Asylum Hill area as the site of their demonstration project. This is an area in transition, a residential area characterized by apartment houses, multifamily homes, and an increase in minority population; one that is beginning to see some deterioration in the form of abandoned buildings. The area has a range of income levels and a high crime rate, although not the highest in the city. While there is no new development in North Asylum Hill, the neighborhood is located close to the center of the city and is ringed by commercial and other urban development. The area is also a major commuters' route.

The CPTED project in Hartford has three major goals: (1) restructuring the physical environment in order to reduce crime and the fear of crime (the principal crimes there are burglary, robbery, and purse-snatching); (2) involving area residents and merchants in individual and group activities to help reduce crime; and (3) encouraging more responsive and effective police activity in the area.

The CPTED project was unique in Hartford because it was the first such project tried on a neighborhood scale rather than just in a building or on a single block. A team of urban designers, criminologists, and community organizers arranged for site surveys, crime analyses, interviews with offenders, physical design analyses, traffic and pedestrian counts, household surveys, and observers on the street watching the movements of people in the area. The surveys yielded several important findings. First, burglary, robbery, and purse-snatching were occurring mainly on residential side streets, rather than on the major thoroughfares. Second, there was a tremendous degree of anonymity in the area, and residents were extremely reluctant to use public ways. Third, the level of fear was disproportionately high for the rate of crime (a similar finding was made in the Willard-Homewood neighborhood). Fourth, residential side streets had become major thoroughfares for commuters, dividing and disturbing the neighborhood. Fifth, most offenders in the area did not live there but traveled from adjacent areas. And finally, the police had done all they could on the crime problem; a new approach was needed.

To help restore the residential character of the neighborhood and give residents more control over and pride in their area, the team focused on changing traffic patterns by closing some streets, narrowing entrances to others, and converting some to one-way. The role of the residents was enhanced by the creation of two new community organizations and the strengthening of a third, existing group. The citizens' groups and a Police Advisory Committee (which included representatives from the citizens' organizations and police) also helped greatly in establishing communication among the project directors, the police, the city, and the citizens. The Hartford Police Department was "extremely cooperative," reports a project team member, in agreeing to assign permanent police teams to an area to foster a cooperative attitude between police and residents and to enable the police to understand better the needs and concerns of the residents.

Citizen support was the key to all these plans since, without it, there would have been no local program funding. The actual changes made, after discussions with residents, were quite different from those designated by planners, but they represented a workable compromise which was completely carried out in summer, 1976. The city council voted to fund the project through CETA and community development funds. Evaluation of the project is now under way.

The Hartford experience pointed out several important points which should be considered in any area planning a CPTED approach to crime prevention. First, it is important to develop among residents an understanding of what the problems are and what solutions are proposed. Second, it also is important to involve the police in the planning process and to have the support of the local government. Finally, the lesson learned in both Minneapolis and Hartford is that each area is unique, and solutions must be addressed to a given community.

Residential crime prevention through environment design is catching on in other cities as well. Inglewood, California, has just begun a program to include security planning in all new commercial, residential, and recreational buildings. Cincinnati has incorporated security improvements and renovations into a public housing project. Boston has a similar project in public housing with the added objective of increasing tenant involvement and concern about crime control. Coordination of city services and involvement of neighborhood residents may not be panacea. But our frustrated attempts to control crime through law enforcement and our inability to prevent crime through the improvement of social and economic conditions may lead to the conclusion that CPTED is the best way for city government to decrease the crime rate.

CPTED IN SCHOOLS
PAULA CHIN WEGENER

"Far too often, youngsters arriving at our public schools today are faced with an environment dominated by fear, destruction, and chaos. . . . The primary concern in many modern American schools is no longer education but preservation." Thus concluded Senator Birch Bayh, former chairman of the Subcommittee to Investigate Juvenile Delinquency, in reviewing the results of his subcommittee's investigation of the juvenile delinquency problem. Included in that investigation were a nationwide survey and a series of public hearings on school violence and vandalism. Statistics collected by the subcommittee highlight the extent of the problem. Between 1970 and 1973:

School-related homicides increased 18.5 percent.

Robberies increased 36.7 percent.

Rapes and attempted rapes increased 40.1 percent.

Assaults on students increased 85.3 percent.

Assaults on teachers increased 77.4 percent.

Burglaries of buildings increased 11.8 percent.

Drug and alcohol offenses on school property increased 37.5 percent.

Most disturbing is the increase in the number of dangerous and deadly weapons on campus. Cleveland City Council Member John Barnes estimated on the basis of a random sampling that there could be as many as 350 Saturday night specials in just five of his city's high schools on any given day.

Testimony during the subcommittee hearings from teachers and administrators dispelled the popular notion that school violence and vandalism are found only in large metropolitan and inner-city schools. Affluent and rural communities reported that they, too, experience escalating problems with drugs, weapons, violence, and vandalism. While not every school suffers from serious violence and vandalism problems, no school can afford to think that "it can't happen here."

The effects of such incidents—increased fear among students and teachers and the consequent decline on morale and the quality of education—are debilitating. A Philadelphia study found that 54 percent of all boys thought the streets to and from school were dangerous; 44 percent rated school yards as dangerous; 21 percent thought school rooms were dangerous. A significant portion of the soaring absentee rates (for example, on any given day 200,000 of New York City's 1.1 million students, or 18 percent, are absent) can be attributed to fear of violence.

Estimated nationwide losses for school thefts, vandalism, burglary, and arson are enormous—$590 million in fiscal 1975 alone, more than was spent on textbooks. "My system suffered $3.5 million in property losses alone in 1974," said Dr. Manford Byrd, deputy superintendent of schools in Chicago, "to which can be added $3.2 million for our security programs and $3 million for watchman services. This $10 million must be taken from funds that would otherwise be available for education programs at a time when funds for education are severely limited."

Vandalism has its hidden costs as well. One is the increasing price a school district is forced to pay for insurance coverage with larger deductibles. Other hidden costs are reflected in the inventories of paint, glass, and other repair tools and materials that must be kept on hand. Perhaps the worst cost is the interference with the teaching program caused by the destruction of equipment and supplies.

The need to restore personal security and a safer environment in our schools is obvious. A most encouraging sign is the number of crime prevention programs being put in place by schools across the country. Many of these schools are incorporating CPTED strategies.

The CPTED demonstration program, developed by the Westinghouse National Issues Center for NILECJ in four Broward County, Florida, high schools, addresses four distinct concerns: property protection, personal defense, educational policy, and restoring confidence. Within these broad concerns, each strategy is designed to treat crimes and fears specific to each school's environment: breaking and entering in parking lots, assaults in restrooms, and vandalism in corridors, for example.

To protect property, the CPTED program has tried to increase surveillance of school grounds, equipment areas, student lockers, and other areas. Surveillance devices, such as audio burglar alarms, are used during nonschool hours, and the use of some parts of buildings is limited because of high crime rates. For example, locker rooms are kept locked except at the beginning and end of each class period, some parking lots are locked throughout the school day, and vulnerable areas such as bicycle compounds are located in easily observed areas.

To improve personal security, the program is increasing "natural surveillance" by putting windows in corridors and classroom doors, promoting self-policing programs, reducing or eliminating causes of congestion in crowded areas, controlling access to various areas, and trying to foster a sense of belonging to and responsibility for the school environment.

The educational policy component of the CPTED program involves instilling a sense of responsibility in teachers, students, and administrators, primarily with respect to security problems but also with respect to identifying and helping students who may be having problems adapting to the school environment. School security staff members are also being used to prevent, report, and investigate behavior problems, and students and teachers are helping in providing active surveillance of school property. Scheduling activities in otherwise little-used areas increases natural surveillance, thereby lessening the fear of using those areas.

To restore confidence, the program is encouraging activities within schools that increase community involvement and support for CPTED educational priorities, enhance school pride, and improve and humanize the physical quality and image of the school buildings. These strategies are designed to provide uses of school facilities that attract public involvement; promote public awareness of school, faculty, and student achievements; develop extracurricular activities that encourage social interaction by all segments of the student population; and allow for informal social activities away from unsafe and unsupervised areas.

By itself, each change in the school's environmental design or use can have only a limited impact. Taken together, however, they can have far-reaching changes, one of which is a change in attitude.

Broward County students and teachers were surveyed to determine the incidence of crime and the fear it generated. This information serves as baseline data for future comparisons. According to the survey, the most crime-prone areas in the schools were parking lots, classrooms, locker areas, restrooms, and corridors. The major crimes: theft, assault, rape, breaking and entering, vandalism, and extortion. With these survey results in mind, the schools set about making some changes. An empty, unused courtyard is being transformed into a miniplaza to attract informal social activities away from unsafe and unsupervised areas. An LEAA grant is paying for this transformation. Aesthetically pleasing hedges and wood pole gates were installed around parking lots to define boundaries, control access by cars, and improve parking lot surveillance. Buses were rerouted to reduce the congestion, which often led to incidents of crime. Fear-producing areas such as restrooms, stairwells, and unused corridors, were redesigned to make surveillance easier. Portable two-way radios were given to school staff to enable rapid response to problems and improve communications.

A continuing evaluation of Broward County's CPTED program has implications for school districts throughout the nation. There are encouraging signs that other school districts are ready to use the lessons.

Since most vandalism takes place when the schools are unoccupied, one way to reduce opportunities for crime is by increasing the use of school buildings in evenings and on weekends. Adult education classes, parent effectiveness classes, recreation programs, and student hobby programs are some ways to expand usage.

Financially strapped schools may want to consider the unusual approach taken by San Antonio. During closed hours, all the lights of the school are turned off. According to Sam Wolf, director of safety and security services, "A lighted school is to kids what a lighted candle is to moths—it attracts them." He decided to test this idea as a way to reduce the city's annual burglary and vandalism toll ($157,435 in 1972). Despite some initial confusion that resulted in helpful citizens calling him during the night to suggest that burglars were turning out all the lights or that there must be a power failure at the school, the experiment resulted in a 31 percent decrease in the costs of repairing vandalism, with a savings of $45,000 after three months. An additional $90,000 in utility costs was saved during the same period. In five years this blackout policy has reduced vandalism and burglary by 66 to 80 percent.

Modern technology eased at least three problems in Washington, D.C., where the number of broken window panes dropped from 47,000 in 1973 to 24,000 in 1976 following the replacement of glass panes with plastic. Nonporous epoxy paints that are resistant to most writing materials and relatively easy to clean provided a partial solution to the recurring problem of graffiti on walls. Computerized serial numbers placed on school equipment helped police uncover fencing operations and recover $30,000 worth of materials.

CPTED calls for school policies to encourage student involvement and participation. If students develop a proprietary interest in their schools, they are more likely to want to preserve and defend them. In a successful program in San Francisco, students are told that any money not spent to repair damages during the year may be spent by them for anything they want, within reason, at year's end.

The charge of our educational system, we must remember, is to establish an atmosphere in which education can best take place. Accelerating crime and vandalism have crippled this mission, but so have outmoded education policies and practices. A proper learning environment is designed to facilitate involvement and not to frustrate it.

School property and structures are much safer these days, thanks in part to the surveillance of human and electronic eyes and ears. The key to preventing crime involves a combination of physical design, community organization, citizen action, and law enforcement. Programs having elements of participation and interaction succeed because they develop a proprietary interest in the school and a concern about what happens to it.

CPTED AND STREET LIGHTS
LISA WELKE

Street lighting is one of the major physical strategies in many CPTED programs for both residential and commercial areas. Preliminary results of a NILECJ-sponsored national evaluation in 15 projects across the country indicate that increasing street lighting reduces the fear of crime. There is also some indication that, all other things being equal, people feel safer at night in streets with more uniform lighting levels; however, the actual effects of lighting on the rate of crime are as yet undetermined. The 15 projects yielded some other interesting results. Harrisburg, Pennsylvania, found that the new street lighting improved the reaction time of police, as well as their ability to "cover" fellow officers and to identify suspects. Milwaukee police also reported that new lighting made their patrol more effective. An LEAA-funded street lighting project in the Capitol Hill section of Denver has proven particularly successful. Although this district included only 2 percent of Denver's land area and only 8 percent of the city's residents, the area was the site of 25 percent of the city's rapes, 21 percent of the robberies, 13 percent of the burglaries, and 12 percent of the aggravated assaults.

The characteristics of Denver's Capitol Hill made it an ideal site for the project. Earlier, the area was lighted only minimally by street lights located at the corners of 600-foot-long blocks although it was an area heavily used by pedestrians at night. This lighting was rendered even less useful by tall trees lining the sidewalks. The area is active at night, with many businesses located along a major thoroughfare in the center of the district. The population is made up largely of young and mobile residents, but contains a large concentration of older citizens.

Thirty-foot lights, placed mid-block and on the corners, made a substantial difference in the attitudes of residents of the area. A survey of citizens showed that most felt safer in the area following the installation of the street lights;

some even said they now went out more at night because of the lights. Another immediate result was a reduction in violent crime. A less tangible benefit is the fact that the lights made other crime prevention methods possible: for example, a new motorcycle police patrol is more visible and, therefore, more effective.

CPTED AND MASS TRANSIT
LISA WELKE

Critics did not hesitate to express skepticism about safety in the newly opened Metro, Washington, D.C.'s subway system. They speculated that the crime rate would result in low ridership and questioned the possibility of establishing a safe, crime-free environment in the subway. These critics have been proved remarkably wrong. During the first year of operation, just ended, Metro experienced only 46 incidents of crime involving minor offenses.

Metro's success represents a perfect illustration of the CPTED concept in operation. After visiting the world's major mass transit systems to compile workable ideas, Metro architects determined that one of their concerns in planning and designing the transit system would be to achieve a sense of well-being in the environment. As a result, Metro was designed to instill a sense of security in its riders as well as to minimize opportunities for crime.

Metro architects hoped to diminish people's fear of going underground by creating a spacious environment in which passengers would be able to see everything. A minimum of columns and centrally located attendants' booths help this wide-open design to offer the rider almost complete visibility throughout the station. In addition, there are no long passageways; instead, the route between surface and station is relatively short so that riders do not lose their orientation once they are underground. The absence of long passages also discourages people from lingering after trains have departed.

Metro stations are virtually free of hiding places where criminals might conceal themselves. The installation of indirect, soft lighting provides ample illumination of stations and, at the same time, reduces glare and elimi-

nates shadows. Finally, because of the criminal activity public bathrooms tend to foster in subways (across the nation they have been closed) Metro opens public bathrooms only on request.

In areas where the system is in full operation, how does Metro plan to protect its stations and facilities? Metro Security Director Angus B. McLean says that "there is no substitute for manpower." During the first phase of the Metro security program, uniformed transit police heavily staffed all trains. "Our objective," McLean continues, "is to prevent crime from occurring. We have to demonstrate to potential offenders that they have little chance of getting away should they decide to commit a crime." According to the study *Improvement of Mass Transit Security in Chicago,* "potential offenders do in fact try to estimate the risks of criminal activity and are deterred if they perceive an increased threat of apprehension. . . ." This is precisely what Metro security officials plan to do—increase the risk to criminals.

Metro has also developed a sophisticated communications system that connects its station attendants and police to the operations control center. The control center, in turn, can communicate directly with all local police, fire, and rescue teams in case of an emergency. Closed-circuit television cameras placed in blind spots can be monitored from the attendants' booths. These are only two examples of crime prevention design concepts that have been successfully demonstrated in the Metro system. Metro's overall success in preventing crime is substantial proof that with sufficient, effective manpower and planned architectural design, environments can be made safe.

CPTED AND PUBLIC WORKS DEPARTMENTS
LEWIS F. HANES

The public works department must be a partner in the development of an urban or suburban CPTED program. This department has the responsibility for the planning, construction, and maintenance of many of the physical strategies included in a CPTED effort. In addition, building inspection is often part of public works and should include a review of crime prevention barriers as part of the normal inspection of renovated or rehabilitated premises. Public works personnel provide a practical point of view in CPTED program planning and implementation. They may be able to identify potential impacts of CPTED strategies on municipal services; street closings, for example, may require rerouting of refuse pick-up trucks. Public works' involvement during design and engineering of a CPTED physical strategy may help reduce the ultimate costs of strategies since crime prevention can be introduced at the outset of a public works project at no additional or modest cost. But perhaps the most conspicuous opportunity for public works in crime prevention through environmental design is through the building inspection program. Many cities are developing security checklists to aid building inspectors. At present, compliance with security improvement suggestions is usually voluntary. In the future, it is likely that a trend will develop requiring building owners to comply with minimum security standards. Meanwhile, the building inspection program provides a mechanism for public works departments to suggest security-related modifications that can reduce crime within a community.

CPTED AND LAW ENFORCEMENT ACTIVITIES
IMRE R. KOHN

Law enforcement agencies can support community-based prevention efforts from the CPTED point of view by improving the efficiency and effectiveness of police actions in deterring crimes and in responding to calls for assistance; involving citizens in cooperative efforts to prevent crime; and promoting sound resident security practices. Law enforcement activities can be very helpful in providing residents with a means of controlling their environment; however, the effectiveness of any policing action depends on the cooperation of residents. The police can encourage citizens to safeguard their homes by developing brochures telling homeowners, renters, and business people how to improve security; carrying out se-

curity inspections and follow-ups; sponsoring property identification programs; and providing personnel to advise builders, architects, and urban planners. Police crime analysis and patrol practices can also be effective. For example, in Minneapolis residents complained about the danger of being victimized behind their rows of houses in alleyways that provided an undetected approach and escape route for burglars and muggers. Extra police units, both bicycles and cars, were assigned. The early results show a reduction in burglaries and a generally reduced feeling of fear among residents. The police also found that less frequent patrols conducted at irregular intervals worked as well as continuous patrols in discouraging offenders and enhancing the residents' sense of security.

CPTED AND CITY PLANNING AGENCIES
JANET FROHMAN

Crimes against property increased drastically in the past decade and victimized a huge number of Americans. In 1974 there were an estimated 16,863,020 attempted or completed household offenses, including burglary, larceny, and vehicle theft. In other words, approximately one out of thirteen U.S. residents fell prey to these crimes. The rates for businesses were much higher—approximately one out of four businesses were victimized.

City planning agencies can play an effective role in preventing such crimes by establishing zoning ordinances that prevent land use that is incompatible with the security interests of the community and by setting public management policies to avoid placing public facilities in locations with crime problems. City planning agencies also can review the crime-related implications of proposed public developments. Urban planners should consider new developments from the standpoint of potential impacts upon victim and offender populations, that is, whom will they attract and how will they be used. Planners can also determine what special security measures might be required for a particular location in terms of crime statistics for that area.

City planning agencies also can play an important part in preventing the construction of buildings that pose crime hazards to occupants. Such building performance specifications should center around the ability of a building or facility to withstand break-in. Security can be increased by installing various kinds of hardware devices on building doors and windows. For instance, many recent building security codes require the installation of deadbolt locks on exterior doors. These added security measures make it harder for a criminal to enter a building, thereby increasing the risk of being discovered.

Cities' attempts to adopt building security ordinances have produced positive results in many localities. But security codes differ from one community to the next, making the responsibility to develop and distribute security products difficult for the manufacturers and suppliers. Generally speaking, suppliers and manufacturers are very interested in providing equipment which will meet the city's minimum security regulations. But their problems, and the cost to the taxpayer, increase if unique designs are required for every jurisdiction.

One solution at the local level might be for communities to agree on a compromise between their various security ordinances in order to stabilize these costs and, at the same time, develop mutually effective performance specifications for security codes. Even better would be the acceptance of a model code detailing the most effective security products and procedures that could be adopted by individual cities. One such code has been prepared by the Model Ordinance Service of the International Association of Chiefs of Police. Another has been drafted by the International Conference of Building Officials, an organization that sets the pattern for code development in all parts of the country. According to the February 1977 edition of *Hotline,* the National Crime Prevention Institute's newsletter, the ICBO code, which has been "thoroughly researched . . ., meets the requirements of law enforcement agencies, equipment manufacturers, and the construction industry . . . [and] can be adopted quickly by communities across the country."

POLICY IMPLICATIONS
JOHN W. McKAY

"The idea that people will respond to their environments is nothing new. Using the idea to reduce crime is new, and has exciting possibilities." So says B. M. Grey, director of the National Crime Prevention Institute at the University of Louisville.

Crime prevention through environmental design is one of the only crime control policies presently being advocated that would reduce the pressure for expansion of the criminal justice system. It should decrease the number of offenses, and consequently the number of arrests, trials, and people jailed. If this is the case, should other criminal justice programs that are successful in the detection, apprehension, prosecution, and incarceration of offenders be given a lower priority? Definitely not. Criminal justice is not an either/or proposition. It is an extremely complex process established to handle complicated human difficulties.

Five key questions should be considered before any CPTED principle or program is adopted:

1. Appropriateness of CPTED—Is the CPTED concept appropriate for the perceived problems and required solutions?
2. Scope of Coverage—What should be the scope and emphasis of the policies?
3. Authority and Responsibility—What mix of skills is desired and who should be responsible for seeing the policies become part of everyday actions by various departments and agencies?
4. Community Participation—To what extent should community participation be included?
5. Strategy Priorities—What CPTED strategies are preferred or applicable, and in what areas of the city?

Once these questions have been answered, it is important to define the areas in which CPTED can be applied. These might include efforts to beautify neighborhoods, develop recreation facilities, improve transportation services, and take on other quality-of-life projects that relate, however indirectly, to crime prevention. CPTED principles can also be used in the design of new communities or locales where crime may occur in the future.

Many programs have priorities that are not consciously oriented to crime prevention, but, when viewed from a CPTED perspective, they may have important crime-related implications. For example, public transportation programs can be planned in ways that will improve the security of passengers in waiting areas and reduce exposure of riders to street crimes. Changes in street traffic patterns can be made to increase the number of "eyes on the streets" (motorists and pedestrians) or to reduce tendencies for outsiders to pass through private neighborhoods. Insurance and business or home loan programs can provide incentives for clients to improve the security of their premises. Banks can provide special programs that encourage residents not to carry cash on the streets.

Policy decisions must be made in terms of the size of the target area and the diversity of the crime prevention program activities. If the idea of CPTED is applied on a limited scale to a geographically cohesive community, should a local planning team concern itself with what happens outside of that community? If yes, then to what extent? A key decision has to be made about the extent to which individuals and groups outside of the planning area should become involved in the planning process.

In most communities, there is a variety of programs, either planned or under way, in which CPTED concepts can be used. If crime prevention through environmental design can be incorporated into existing programs, personal security and the quality of life can be improved that much more cost-effectively.

But many communities will not have what it takes (receptive political climate, management capacity, etc.) to integrate CPTED into existing city operations. In such communities, it is important to assign responsibility for the planning and incorporation of CPTED principles. This responsibility might be vested in existing agencies and departments, a new division of an agency or department, or a new and separate agency. Obviously the group that will be assigned responsibility will be determined by a number of factors, which should include these: legislative constraints and charter requirements, ability to interact with different groups and agencies, access to key decision makers, available resources and qualifications of personnel, workloads and commitments, and interest in the problem.

The successful use of CPTED ideas will require the assistance, support, and cooperation of many agencies, organizations, and individuals within the community. It is important to identify potential participants and what form their participation might take. If CPTED has support from the key elected and appointed city officials and a strong coalition of citizen groups, it is highly probable that other types of support will follow.

People can make a difference. Former Attorney General Edward Levi once remarked that he was amazed that people tolerated a crime rate as high as this country's. Citizen attitudes and tolerance levels are tied directly to the probable success of a crime prevention program. A citizen must be able to see that his or her involvement and support contribute to the success of a program that benefits him or her.

Throughout the accompanying articles, the role of the citizen is stressed. Not only does crime prevention through environmental design affect the physical design of the community, ideally it also affects the interaction of the citizens. Criminals will respond to the environment, and the citizen has a major role to play in creating an environment which will bring a noncriminal behavior response.

Citizen participation can be passive (monthly reports or newsletters to the local civic group) or active (residents assuming roles in the planning and implementation process). Experience in the CPTED projects thus far suggests encouraging active participation in the design and development of CPTED activities. Participants need specific roles and functions—field surveys, data collection advisory boards, educational meetings, and monitoring changes in the physical and social setting of the target site are a few possible ones. Active participation not only provides an additional resource base for city planners and officials, but also permits continuous education about the effective design and use of the environment.

There are endless choices to be made in crime prevention through environmental design. For example, if a planning decision calls for physical improvements in a neighborhood, choices must be made among installing better street lighting, converting through streets to cul-de-sacs, changing the color and texture of streets and sidewalks, creating parks and playgrounds out of empty lots, and so forth. And each type of change involves varying degrees. Street lighting, for example, can be improved on every street, every third street, or on only the most heavily used streets. Furthermore, types of street lamps differ in cost. It is important, then, to set priorities.

Priorities for implementation should be developed after:

- Discussion of alternatives with community leaders
- Review of existing (funded), planned, and potential physical and social programs
- Review and analysis of crime patterns (when? where? how?) with attention to possible changes in the physical environment to prevent these crimes
- Consensus among the decision makers, planners, and implementers on whether the program should emphasize territorial defense, personal defense, law enforcement, confidence restoration, or a combination of these

It should be said again here that crime prevention through environmental design does work in reducing and preventing crime. It works because people can do something about crime, people do respond to their environment, and people do take responsibility for their own safety.

The criminal justice system cannot be viewed as solely responsible for preventing crime. Crime is too complex a human activity and affects too many of us. Municipalities need to draw on all their resources to attack the problem of crime.

CPTED is one element municipal personnel should keep in mind in all aspects of city government. Even without massive implementation funds, individual CPTED strategies can be incorporated into such everyday municipal activities as zoning, planning, construction, and public works. Municipalities can use their own initiative in involving CPTED strategies in routine agency operation and funding at the local, regional, and state level. The lesson to be learned from CPTED is an important one: crime is not an isolated phenomenon. It is built into all elements of our everyday lives, but it can be minimized through a concerted and imaginative planning effort.

Crime prevention through environmental design is not *the* solution to the crime problem in our cities. It is one element, one piece of a rather obscured and fuzzy puzzle, which, in combination with other solutions, will forge a new atmosphere and vitality in our urban areas.

Selected readings for Chapter 11

Brantingham, Paul J., and Frederic L. Faust. "A Conceptual Model of Crime Prevention," *Crime and Delinquency* **22**:284-296, 1976.
> The public health model of primary, secondary, and tertiary preventions is suggested as a way of organizing the wide array of activities considered crime prevention.

Cirel, Paul, Patricia Evans, Daniel McGillis, and Debra Whitcomb. *An Exemplary Project: Community Crime Prevention* (Washington D.C.: U.S. Government Printing Office, 1977).
> A detailed report of one of the Law Enforcement Assistance Administration's exemplary projects; it describes a community-wide program in Seattle, Washington, designed to reduce the incidence of household burglary. Results and costs are presented, as well as suggestions for replication of the program.

"Crime Resistance: A Report," *FBI Law Enforcement Bulletin* **46**(3):3-11, 1977.
> Describes programs of four police departments to engage in community organization efforts to assist citizens in low-cost, self-help, crime prevention activities.

Dingemans, Dennis F. "Evaluating Housing Environments for Crime Prevention," *Crime Prevention Review* **5**(4):7-14, 1978.
> Six townhouse developments were rated regarding defensible space (based on Newman's territoriality and surveillance standards) and compared on burglary rates. Townhouses with the best defensible space designs had higher burglary rates than those with good defensible space designs. Perhaps residents with highest defensible space designs felt more secure and, thus, were more vulnerable.

Jeffery, Clarence Ray. *Crime Prevention Through Environmental Design* (Beverly Hills, Calif.: Sage Publications, Inc. 1971).
> An interdisciplinary approach to the problem of crime control; traces the origins of crime control measures, analyzes their effectiveness, and argues for a new and different approach to crime.

Morris, Norval, and Gordon Hawkins. *Letter to the President on Crime Control* (Chicago: University of Chicago Press, 1977).
> Offers a series of suggestions regarding the operation of the criminal justice system to reduce crime.

Newman, Oscar. *Defensible Space: Crime Prevention Through Urban Design* (New York: Macmillan Publishing Co., Inc., 1972).
> Describes how architectural design of public housing projects contributes significantly to the high levels of crime, and discusses ways design might be used to reduce crime through increasing sense of territoriality and surveillance.

Stanley, Paul R. A. *Crime Prevention Through Environmental Design* (Toronto: Solicitor General of Canada, May 1976).
> This report presents the origins and basic assumptions of the environmental design approach, provides an overview of current work in this area, and suggests some guidelines for applying design techniques in crime prevention work.

Washnis, George J. *Citizen Involvement in Crime Prevention* (Lexington, Mass.: D. C. Heath & Co., 1975).
> A review of 37 projects in 17 American cities that involve citizens working with police in activities such as block clubs, neighborhood watch programs, anticrime crusades, police-community councils, and neighborhood patrols.

Chapter 12

VICTIM SERVICE PROGRAM MODELS

A □ *Victim assistance programs: an overview*
ANNE LARASON SCHNEIDER and PETER R. SCHNEIDER

B □ *Victim interests, victim services, and social control*
EDUARD A. ZIEGENHAGEN and JOHN BENYI

A □ *Victim assistance programs*

An overview

ANNE LARASON SCHNEIDER and PETER R. SCHNEIDER

The major impetus for what one writer has called the "reinvention of the victim" began in the late 1960s.[1] The movement was supported initially by an interesting coalition of liberals and "law and order" conservatives. Conservatives, distressed over what many considered an excessive concern for the rights of criminals, viewed victim-oriented programs as a welcome shift in the attention of the criminal justice system, whereas support from liberals was prompted primarily by the realization that criminal victimization is a major problem for the disadvantaged segments of society.

Scholars who have traced the declining importance of the victim in criminal proceedings note that in ancient times, when political systems were far less complex than they are today, crime victims were instrumental in determining the sanctions that would be imposed on the offender.[2] As political systems developed, however, offenses against individuals came to be viewed as crimes against society rather than against any specific victims, and the provision of safety, justice, and punishment increasingly became the responsibility of the state rather than the responsibility of individuals or private groups.

Proponents of victim assistance programs point out that in American criminal proceedings today, victims have no legal standing to act as advocates of their own interests. The prosecutor in criminal proceedings is not responsible for acting in the interests of the victim, but is responsible for protecting the public interest. As DuBow and Becker state, "There exists for the victim no institutionalized way of controlling decisions regarding the prosecution or disposition of a case."[3] Offenders have lawyers to protect their interests, but even in the pretrial phases of criminal cases, victims will not have anyone other than themselves to speak for or represent their interests. In cases that involve violent confrontations between two individuals (such as rape or assault) there may be concerted efforts to show that the victim was at fault or in some way provoked the incident, thereby exonerating the offender. Given the comparatively powerless position of a victim in the criminal justice system, it is not surprising to find a social and political movement organized around charges that the system is insensitive to the needs, rights, and interests of crime victims.

One of the problems inherent in the system, from the victim's perspective, is the lack of attention to victim preferences concerning the disposition of a case. Another problem identified by victim advocates is that there is no guarantee, in most jurisdictions, that any attention will be given to the inconveniences or losses produced by the crime or its immediate aftermath. Although there are a large number of publicly provided social, welfare, and health services in most communities, crime victims generally have no particular claim on any of these in their specialized role as victims.

In a similar way, crime victims have no special claim on the protection and prevention activities carried out by law enforcement agencies. Even though victims may fear that the same persons will commit subsequent offenses against them, they may be even more fearful of an escalation in the nature of the offense if they report the crime and attempt to prosecute the offenders.

Victims who report crimes and become witnesses often encounter additional costs and inconveniences associated with their experiences within the criminal justice system because of the delay and insensitivity that accompany the proceedings.[4]

The key problems identified by those who have studied the topic or who are advocates of victim assistance can be summarized as:

1. Lack of officially recognized representation for the victim during the legal proceedings
2. Lack of any special claim by victims on the social, health, and welfare services that could provide for the emergency or longer-term needs of victims or victims' families

3. Difficulty in recovering the direct monetary losses suffered during the crime
4. Additional losses (monetary and nonmonetary) attributable to the victim-witness experiences during the legal processing of the case
5. Lack of any special claim on future protection from the system to prevent similar types of offenses against the victim

Victim assistance programs have been implemented in many jurisdictions around the country in recognition of the problems named above. Between 1970 and 1975, the Law Enforcement Assistance Administration (LEAA) spent $22.4 million for victim assistance programs; by 1977, the amount had risen to $49.3 million, with more than 100 federally funded programs. Even after 7 years of experience with victim assistance, most of the fundamental issues have not been resolved. There is no established operational model for these programs. The approaches differ from one another in relation to the target audience, the types of services provided, program organization, the purposes of the program, and the underlying rationale for the services being provided.[5] It is not an overstatement to say that there is a lack of consensus about what the government *should* do for crime victims and very little scientifically reliable information concerning the social consequences of various approaches to victim assistance.

Four major types of program components tend to dominate the assistance efforts:

1. Counseling, emergency services, and social services for victims
2. In-system services designed to assist victims and witnesses in dealing with the inconveniences of the criminal justice system
3. In-system advocacy on behalf of the victim's rights and interests during the legal processing of the case
4. Prevention programs targeted specifically at prior crime victims

Many, perhaps most, of the victim programs are multipurpose and focus on several components simultaneously. Some limit their target audience to certain subsets of victims or witnesses. There are programs designed specifically for rape victims, several that focus on elderly victims, an increasing number of programs for victims of juvenile crimes, and scattered examples of programs exclusively for battered wives.

In the subsequent sections of this paper we review the major components of the programs and discuss some of the issues that are most relevant for each.

ADVOCACY PROGRAMS

There are three broad types of in-system advocacy programs:

1. Programs to increase the victim's control or influence over the disposition of the case, especially during plea bargaining or sentencing
2. Restitution programs in which the prosecutors urge the judge to require that the offender pay restitution to the victim
3. Compensation policies that provide for public payments to the victim for some or all of the losses attributable to the crime

One of the more notable characteristics of existing programs is the relative absence of successful efforts to increase the victim's role during legal processing of the case. Two practical problems have contributed to this. Programs organized and funded outside of the traditional criminal justice system agencies have difficulties in gaining the confidence of law enforcement and prosecutor offices. Programs that are a part of the criminal justice system either have not attempted to increase the victim's role in the legal process or have had difficulty in implementing reforms.

For example, the Multnomah County (Portland), Oregon, program originally proposed to increase the role of the victim during plea bargaining, but this aspect of the program was never implemented successfully.[6] McDonald, in his excellent historical review of the role of the victim, names several programs that had the intent of increasing the victim's influence in the legal proceedings, but there is no information at this time on whether the programs were successful in their efforts.[7] DuBow and Becker provide accounts of two civilian groups that attempted to increase their power in relation to

the court.[8] One hired a lawyer to represent its interests, but the victims' lawyer found his task very difficult because he had no officially recognized status with the court.

Some rape relief programs have provided advocacy-type services for rape victims, but there is only scanty information available on the results of these efforts. A Tacoma, Washington, program provides an advocate to accompany victims to the medical examination and to the initial interview by law enforcement officials. The evaluation of this program notes that the quality of evidence from the medical examinations was better when the victim was accompanied by the advocate.[9] The report also shows that the prosecutor's office accepted for prosecution a much lower proportion of cases from among the program clients than from among rape victims who contacted the police directly. Although one could argue that program clients had weaker cases, evidence in the study showed the conviction rate for program cases accepted for prosecution to be twice as great as for the police cases. Thus, the evidence indicates that the prosecutor required a stronger case from the independent rape program than from the police before accepting the case for prosecution.

Perhaps the most successful types of advocacy programs (successful in the sense of being implemented and accepted within the criminal justice system) are those that emphasize and encourage the court to order the offender to pay restitution to the victim. In fact, the use of restitution in juvenile court proceedings apparently is a fairly common practice for property offenders at the disposition phase of the proceedings. The results of a survey of 200 randomly selected juvenile courts show that 86% of the courts require restitution for at least some types of juveniles who have committed certain types of offenses.[10] The survey also shows, however, that only 7% of the programs were clearly designed to serve the victims of crimes. The others either reported that their major objective was to rehabilitate the offender or that both rehabilitation and victim assistance were equally important goals.

Historically, restitution was intended to benefit the offender more so than the victim, and most of the current evidence indicates that the same is true today.[11] Recent initiatives by LEAA and by the Office of Juvenile Justice and Delinquency Prevention are designed to fund restitution programs that place major emphasis on offender rehabilitation and secondary emphasis on victims. Burt Galaway made the point very clear when he wrote, "Promoting restitution as a program to help crime victims is popular but questionable." He went on to say:

The vast majority of crimes go unsolved, many of those that are solved through arrest of an offender do not result in conviction, and for many offenders for whom convictions are secured, restitution may not be considered an appropriate sanction. . . . If the primary social objective is protecting the welfare of crime victims, then other programs—such as . . . victim compensation—are likely to become more effective than offender restitution.[12]

Even though compensation approaches in which the state pays the victim could be superior as a means of returning to the victim some or all of the monetary loss, the current state-level compensation programs fall far short of their potential for redressing victim losses.[13] Compensation programs tend to be very limited in scope and level of payments provided to the victim, and they currently exist in less than half of the states.

Although it might appear that restitution, compensation, and efforts to increase the victim's role during legal processing of the case are similar approaches to victim assistance, the underlying justifications for each of the three are markedly different. Perhaps the only common element is that each involves an effort to improve victim attitudes toward and cooperation with the criminal justice system.

Compensation approaches are based on the philosophy that the provision of safety and punishment are public goods but that failure to provide safety results in both public and private damages. The victim, therefore, should be compensated by the public for private damages but has no private right to influence the punishment. Thus, it is the interest of the public that must be represented in criminal proceedings that determine the punishment or rehabilitation plan for the offender.

Restitution programs, however, cannot be justified by this argument. Restitution implies that the *offender* (not the state) owes something to the victim, and it implies that the victim is more entitled to repayment from the offender than is the state. The restitution approach gives higher priority to the private nature of criminal acts than to their public consequences if one analyzes it from the victim's perspective. But when restitution is conceptualized as part of the punishment, as a therapeutic (rehabilitative) act by the offender, or as a "just" outcome in the absence of compensation programs, then the problem of public versus private justice does not arise. Perhaps the popularity of restitution results partially from the fact that it meets, in a limited way, the desire for "private" justice without altering the current philosophy of the criminal justice system.

Proponents of an increased role for victims in plea bargaining and other aspects of the legal processing of a case have not made it clear whether the justification for this change is a shift in the system toward a "private justice" perspective or whether the purpose is to reverse the trend toward lenient treatment of offenders. If the latter provides the motivation for advocating in-system victim participation, then the victim's increased influence could be justified or rationalized by arguing that the victim is not acting on behalf of personal interests or revenge but is, in fact, a better representative of the public interest than is the prosecutor.

In general, it appears that each of the three major types of victim advocacy programs is beset with difficulties. Restitution is hard to justify as an approach to victim assistance, although it clearly has a role in terms of offender rehabilitation or punishment. Compensation programs are easier to justify from the victim's perspective, but the expense of this approach has limited the number of programs and the extent of their coverage. The rationale for advocacy in plea bargaining and sentencing is not clear, and, if it is based on a return to a more private system of criminal justice, it is not likely to find much support from the criminal justice system.

The rationale for these approaches could be

stated in empirical rather than normative terms. Victim assistance programs could improve victim and community support for the criminal justice system. It is a well-recognized principle that citizen support is a crucial ingredient to the effectiveness of the criminal justice system. At this time, however, these has been so little research about the impact of victim advocacy on victim or community attitudes that one cannot justify these types of assistance programs on the basis of scientific evidence that they improve support for the system. Conversely, there is no scientific evidence to show that these programs do not have a positive impact on community support.

SOCIAL SERVICE COMPONENTS

Most victim programs have implemented a social service component. The services provided include such things as transportation from the scene of the crime, counseling to relieve fears and emotional trauma, emergency facilities, referrals to other community agencies that can provide short-term or longer-term social welfare services, child care services for witnesses, and so on. Some programs, such as one in Ft. Lauderdale, Florida, have a 24-hour hotline service for victims to call and mobile victim-assistance vans that can be dispatched by the police department to the scene of a crime. Others have a victim "advocate" whose role in advocacy is in relation to social-service agencies in the community rather than advocacy within the legal system itself.

Social service components are justified on the grounds that victims need the services, but at least some of the programs have found that the need is not as great as expected, particularly if rape victims are handled by another program and if the crime has to have been reported to authorities for the individual to be eligible for the program. The experiences of the Multnomah County program are instructive in this regard.[6] Program personnel found that requests for social services initially were very high, primarily because of victims' mistaken impression that the program could compensate them for losses suffered as a result of the crime. After the initial misconceptions were corrected, the

requests for emergency shelter, transportation, baby-sitting, referrals to community agencies, and so on constituted about 10% of all victim requests for assistance. The social service advocate in Multnomah County also found that victims generally were not eligible for longer-term social services or, if they were eligible, were already receiving the services. Similar types of experiences have been encountered by other programs. Data from the eight victim-witness programs funded through an LEAA grant to the National District Attorneys Association indicate that less than 4% of the victims required social service referrals.[14]

The implication is not that the victims have no need for social services, for many of them do. The point, however, is that the need can easily be overestimated.

There are two major issues involved in the organization and delivery of social services to crime victims. One of these is whether there should be a single program for all victims or whether there should be specialized programs for rape victims, battered wives, the elderly, or other identifiable types of victims.

The argument has been made that since victims tend to have very similar needs, there should be one program, administered through the criminal justice system, for all of them.[4] Although this argument may be reasonable from a treatment perspective, it overlooks the fact that victims of crimes of an especially sensitive nature often do not report their victimization to the authorities and may be quite unwilling to participate in a program that is identified with the criminal justice system or any government agency. Thus, programs for rape victims normally are operated by independent organizations. They accept clients who have not reported the crime and who, from a legal perspective, are not bonafide victims. Battered women have not been (and are not) a target audience for the broad-based victim programs. The system may not recognize these women as victims, even if the crime is reported, and many instances of intrafamily violence are never reported to authorities. Recognition that battered women need special programs and that the eligibility requirements of multiservice vic-

tim centers located within criminal justice agencies generally exclude them is evidenced by recent initiatives from both the National Institute for Mental Health and LEAA to begin special programming efforts for this target population.

The second organizational issue is whether counseling and other social service–oriented components of a program should be funded and operated within a criminal justice system agency or whether this type of programming belongs in a social service agency. One argument that has been used to support programs in the criminal justice system is that this system has the major responsibility of protecting citizens from crime. Thus, when it fails to do so, it is responsible for the losses that result. The more practical justification is that the criminal justice system suffers from a lack of public confidence and support because of high crime rates and can recoup some support through "public relation" efforts such as victim service programs. On the other hand, if one views the social and health agencies as specialists in the delivery of these types of services, then the victim programs that focus on social service delivery have a difficult task in justifying their receipt of funds from criminal justice agencies.

LEAA has always required, as a condition of funding, that the victim programs identify purposes that will have an impact on crime or result in "system improvement." Thus one finds numerous examples of rape relief programs whose stated goals are to increase reporting of rape, increase arrests, increase convictions, and bring about a reduction in the frequency of rapes when, in fact, the major or only true purpose of the program is to provide social services to rape victims.

Another approach taken by at least some programs is to postulate that the provision of an integrated-service approach from within the criminal justice system will increase victim satisfaction with the system, reduce victim alienation, and through these changes bring about an increase in victim reporting of crimes and victim willingness to prosecute. There is some evidence from research studies that victim alienation (or lack of it) from the system is strongly associated with the victim's experiences during the most recent victimization and is not primarily a product of long-term social learning experiences.[4,6]

Intensive analysis of a very small number of clients from the Multnomah County program indicates that victims' intentions to cooperate with the system if they are again victimized are related to their level of alienation, which, in turn, is related to their experiences with the system. Thus, the authors concluded that it would be theoretically possible for victim assistance programs to increase cooperation with the criminal justice system.[6] Even if additional research substantiates these results, it is likely that programs whose claims to crime reduction and system improvement rest on theoretically possible linkages to *intentions* about future cooperation will experience difficulties in obtaining continued funding from criminal justice sources. Although victim assistance is a politically popular idea, local jurisdictions may be unwilling to reallocate funds from the more traditional criminal justice functions when the federal funds for victim assistance dry up.

It is philosophically difficult to justify the funding of social services to victims of criminal acts as a part of the criminal justice system. As before, the problem is that crimes are committed against society. If the victim of a criminal act wishes to receive private damages, he or she is expected to seek these through civil proceedings. It is far simpler to develop a rationale for providing social services to victims as part of the overall social, health, and welfare systems. Crime victims could be given special priority for receiving social or health services if there were sufficient public support for this. The social, welfare, and health systems have as their major purpose the provision of services to persons who need them, and, in contrast with criminal justice system provision, there is no conflict with the underlying rationale or purpose of the system.

IN-SYSTEM SERVICES

Another approach to victim programming is to provide services to crime victims and witnesses during the time their cases are being pro-

cessed through the criminal justice system. The underlying motives for these services are that there is considerable loss of time and income for victim-witnesses during court processing, cases often are dismissed because of uncooperative victims or witnesses, and the unpleasantness of the experience can result in future nonreporting of crimes as well as other types of future uncooperative behavior. In addition, the waste of time and income loss are unnecessary and indicate an inefficiency in the system.

The best-known programs of this type include the eight victim-witness programs funded by an LEAA grant through the National District Attorneys Association Commission on Victim Witness Assistance[14] and the Vera Institute program in Brooklyn, New York. Program components include the following:

1. Explanations and information about the criminal justice system and the parts of the system with which the victim or witness will become involved
2. Telephone or mail contact to advise victim-witnesses of the need to appear in court or of the progress of their cases
3. A "telephone alert" system in which the witness is called to court only *after* it is definitely determined that his or her testimony will be needed on that day
4. "Convenience services," including such things as escorts from the courthouse entrance, a comfortable reception area, cafeteria services, parking facilities, maps of the courthouse, and so on.

These programs also offer to contact the witness's employer, if necessary, to request time off with pay for court appearances, and they assist victims or witnesses in property return. Most of the programs established to provide services during the court processing also offer social services but, as noted earlier, the need for these is not as great as the need for assistance with court processing of the case.

In contrast with advocacy and the social service components, the in-system approach to victim programming addresses a variety of system improvement objectives that are not in conflict with the basic rationale of the criminal justice system. There is evidence from at least some of the programs that the approach is effective. An evaluation of the police-witness alert system by the Vera Institute indicates that this program component saved more than 6,500 appearances by police officers during an 8-month time period and could save the police department more than $2 million per year.[15] Other evidence from the Vera report suggests that improved attendance by civilian witnesses increases guilty pleas and results in a decline in dismissal rates. In the program examined by the Vera report, attendance by witnesses increased, but the no-show rate of civilian witnesses was still alarmingly high (45%).

A question that still remains to be answered is whether in-system assistance programs increase victim-witness cooperation. An LEAA-sponsored study by Frank Cannavale suggests that communication problems between witnesses and prosecution account for much of the presumed "uncooperative" behavior by witnesses.[16] He notes that prosecutor-perceived "noncooperation" was not primarily produced by system-level difficulties that discouraged witnesses from cooperating, but was attributable to system-level factors that led the prosecutor to misinterpret the true intentions of witnesses. He goes on to say:

This finding does not rule out the possibility that system-related difficulties, such as trial delay, also influenced witnesses not to cooperate and, therefore, helped account for the prosecutor's noncooperative label. To the extent that additional factors explaining the witness' motivation not to cooperate were, in fact, present, they simply "paled" in this sample of witnesses . . . since so much "noncooperation" apparently resulted from prosecutors' perceptions based on considerations other than witness behavior.[17]

The in-system approach to victim-witness assistance is not without its critics. DuBow and Becker point out that these programs co-opt the victims and reduce the possibility of stronger, advocacy-style reform.[18]

VICTIM RECIDIVISM PROGRAMS

Considerably less emphasis has been given to program components that focus on breaking a cycle of victimization for persons who are par-

ticularly prone to being victimized. Perhaps part of the reason for this lesser emphasis is lack of substantial evidence that an individual who is victimized once is more likely than other persons to be victimized again. If this is true, then prevention efforts would be more cost-effective if they were targeted primarily at prior victims. If victimization incidents, on the other hand, are unrelated to subsequent incidents, then crime prevention programs have no particular reason to focus on prior victims rather than on high-risk populations or on the general population.

At this time, there has been very little research that would indicate the comparative effectiveness of crime prevention programs targeted at prior victims compared with programs that select high-risk persons or areas regardless of whether they have been victimized. A study in Portland, Oregon, based on victimization survey data, shows that persons who were burglary victims in 1974 and who began participating in a crime prevention program at that time had relatively normal burglary victimization rates in 1977. A group of persons who were victims in 1974 but who, as of 1977, still were not participating in the prevention program had burglary rates almost three times greater than normal.[19] This indicates that prior victims would be a good source of clients for prevention programs. Another type of crime in which there is clear evidence of victim recidivism is intrafamily assault, including wife battering and child abuse.

For crimes in which there is evidence of victim recidivism, assistance programs that focus on prevention activities are more likely than any other type of victim-oriented approach to have an impact on crime reduction. Thus, it would not be surprising to find an increasing emphasis on this approach as programs near the end of federal funding and begin searching for alternative program components that make it easier to obtain local or state funds from criminal justice system sources.

SUMMARY AND CONCLUSIONS

Four major types of victim program components have been developed in response to the recognition that victims are the "forgotten persons" in the criminal justice system. These components are:

1. Counseling, social services, and emergency services for victims
2. In-system services to reduce inconveniences experienced by victims and witnesses during their dealings with the criminal justice system
3. In-system advocacy on behalf of the victim's rights and interests, including restitution, compensation, and efforts to increase the victim's role in determining the disposition of the case
4. Prevention efforts targeted specifically at prior crime victims

Although these components are conceptually distinct, most victim programs are multipurpose organizations and attempt to provide most if not all of the services mentioned above.

Advocates justify some of the program components by arguing that victims *should* have certain rights or receive certain services. These arguments require further justification in legal or political theory, and in many instances, the existing programmatic efforts cannot be justified on this basis. Others argue that the provision of certain rights or services will have desirable consequences for the criminal justice system and society as a whole—an argument that requires the support of more scientific evidence than is currently available.

Increasing the victim's role in plea bargaining or sentencing of criminal defendants clearly is inconsistent with the prevailing philosophy that the purpose of criminal proceedings is to provide public (not private) services, including deterrence, rehabilitation, punishment, or "justice." Restitution from offender to victim as a part of the criminal proceedings is an inefficient mechanism for victim recovery of losses since only a small minority of victims will ever receive restitution. Compensation efforts are still very limited in scope and coverage, at least partly because of their expense.

Social services for crime victims are fairly easy to support as a part of the social, health, and welfare system, but there are difficulties when these are located within a criminal justice agency. Two groups of victims—rape victims

and battered wives—tend to have more need for emergency and social services but, because rape and intrafamily violence frequently go unreported, victims are excluded from eligibility when the program is located within a criminal justice agency.

In-system services may have a longer future within criminal justice agencies if they are able to demonstrate cost-effective consequences for the system.

One of the more disheartening characteristics of the last 7 years' experience with victim assistance programming is the lack of research or evaluation. Such studies could provide a stronger justification for victim assistance programming by examining its impact on victim and community support for the criminal justice system or by showing that the better protective measures taken by victims could reduce crime through a reduction in victim recidivism. Although a few studies have been conducted, there has been no broad-based comparative evaluation of victim-assistance programs, and there has been an insufficient amount of research that could be used to guide (or justify) program efforts.

Although victim programming is still in its infancy, it already is confronting a crisis. Funding for most of these programs came from the federal government, and there was never any intention on the part of the federal agencies to fund such programs on a continuing basis. LEAA funds are designed to prompt innovative approaches in local communities, and, after 3 years, local jurisdictions are expected to provide funds for continuation if they believe the programs are worthwhile. Given the problems discussed previously in clearly identifying program goals and rationale, and given the general lack of evaluation results, these programs may have difficulty in generating the type of support needed to be continued as a part of the local budgetary process. As noted throughout this chapter, there is still considerable confusion and disagreement about the underlying philosophy of these programs and the type of theory that would justify government support for victim assistance. At this time, victim programming as a multiservice approach located within criminal justice agencies needs a better-developed normative theory and considerably more evaluation and research.

These comments should not be viewed as criticisms of victim assistance programs or as an overly pessimistic appraisal of the future prospects for victim assistance. Many innovative social programs begin without consensus about why or whether the government should provide the services. And some exist for many years before the research community identifies the social or individual consequences of the innovations. On the other hand, innovative programs that develop from temporary ideological shifts in public sentiment are prone to disappear if they cannot develop either a normative or empirical justification.

NOTES

1. McAnany, Patrick D. "Restitution as Idea and Practice: The Retributive Prospect" (Paper presented at the Second Symposium on Restitution, St. Paul, Minn., November 14-15, 1977), p. 1.
2. An excellent historical review of the role of the victim is contained in McDonald, William F. "Two Hundred Years: A Mixed Blessing for Victims of Crime" (Speech prepared for delivery at the Law Enforcement Assistance Administration Region VIII Supervisory Board Conference, 1977). The gradual alienation of the victim from the legal process is discussed in DuBow, Fredrick L., and Theodore M. Becker. "Patterns of Victim Advocacy," in McDonald, William F., ed. *Criminal Justice and the Victim* (Beverly Hills, Calif.: Sage Publications, Inc., 1976), pp. 144-164.
3. DuBow and Becker, p. 147.
4. Knudten, Richard D., Anthony C. Meade, William G. Doerner, and Mary S. Knudten. *Victims and Witnesses: Their Experiences with Crime and the Criminal Justice System,* Executive Summary (Washington, D.C.: National Institute of Law Enforcement and Criminal Justice, 1977).
5. Relatively detailed descriptions of five victim services programs are contained in Baluss, Mary E. *Integrated Services for Victims of Crime: A County-based Approach* (Washington, D.C.: National Association of Counties Research Foundation, 1975). Other descriptions may be found in McDonald, (see note 2) and unpublished documents prepared by the programs themselves.
6. For a description and evaluation of this program, see Schneider, Anne L., and Paul D. Reiter, *The Victim and the Criminal Justice System: An Evaluation of the Multnomah County Victim Assistance Program* (Portland: Oregon Research Institute, 1976).
7. McDonald (see note 2).
8. DuBow and Becker (see note 2).

9. Barlow, Steve, and Mary Layman. *Rage Relief Evaluation*. (Tacoma, Wash.: Law and Justice Planning Office, 1977).

10. See Schneider, Peter R., and Anne L. Schneider. "Restitution Requirements for Juvenile Offenders: A Survey of the Practices in American Juvenile Courts," *Juvenile Justice* (in press).

11. An excellent overview of the concept of restitution, including its historical development and current application, is Laster, Richard E. "Criminal Restitution: A Survey of Its Past History and an Analysis of Its Present Usefulness," *University of Richmond Law Review*, vol. 5, no. 71, pp. 71-98, 1970. For descriptions of existing programs, see Edelhertz, Herbert. *Restitutive Justice: A General Survey and Analysis* (Seattle, Wash.: Law and Justice Study Center, Battelle Human Affairs Research Centers, 1975); and Hudson, Joe, Burt Galaway, and Steven L. Chesney, "When Criminals Repay Their Victims: A Survey of Restitution Programs," *Judicature*, vol. 60, no. 7, February 1977, pp. 313-321.

12. Galaway, Burt. "Issues in the Use of Restitution as a Sanction for Crime" (Presented at the National Institute on Crime and Delinquency, Minneapolis, June 1975).

13. The writings on victim compensation are far too numerous to be listed here, but special mention should be given to Geis, Gilbert "Crime Victims and Victim Compensation Programs," in McDonald (see note 2); Edelhertz, Herbert, and Gilbert Geis. *Public Compensation for Victims of Crime* (New York: Praeger Publishers, 1974); and two bibliographies: Marcus, Marvin, Robert J. Trudel, and Robert J. Wheaton. *Victim Compensation and Offender Restitution* (annotated) (Washington, D.C.: National Criminal Justice Reference Service, 1975); and Harland, Alan, and Bruce B. Way. *Restitution and Compensation to Crime Victims* (Washington, D.C.: National Criminal Justice Research Center, 1977).

14. McKenna, Robert. "The National District Attorneys Association Commission on Victim Witness Assistance," *Victimology*, vol. 1, no. 2, pp. 321-326, 1976.

15. *Alert Task Force Report*, (New York: Vera Institute of Justice, Victim/Witness Assistance Project, April 8, 1976).

16. Cannavale, Frank, Jr., and William D. Falcon, eds. *Witness Cooperation* (Lexington, Mass.: D. C. Heath & Co., 1976).

17. Ibid. p. 97.

18. DuBow and Becker, p. 159.

19. This finding is contained in Schneider, Anne L., and L. A. Wilson II. "The Efficacy and Equity of Public Initiatives in the Provision of Private Safety," (Paper prepared for presentation at the Western Political Science Association meeting, Los Angeles, March 16-18, 1977).

B □ *Victim interests, victim services, and social control*

EDUARD A. ZIEGENHAGEN and JOHN BENYI

It seems advisable to begin a consideration of victim services with exploration of the term *victim* and its bureaucratic implications. In the most general sense, the term is one of moral approbation suggesting undeserved suffering.[1] Although it is sufficiently common and is seemingly well understood in respect to diffuse expressions of public sentiment, severe difficulties are encountered when it becomes necessary for state and private bureaucracies to identify victims as clients. Client status implies that such individuals have a legitimate claim to the services and resources of organizations. Therefore, it becomes necessary for bureaucratic organizations to differentiate between individuals and groups that have appropriate status and those who do not. In order to accomplish this objective, particular criteria must be instituted.

Some determination must be made as to whether prospective clients are in fact victims, and if they are victims, it must be ascertained whether they are clients. This seemingly simple differentiation requires operational definitions of both victims and clients and is a task addressed by all victim service programs.

However, it is rarely addressed in a manner that is mutually satisfying to prospective clients and organizations charged with providing services. For example, are program services to be confined solely to those who are victims of crimes? If this is the case, are victims of some crimes to be given different treatment or higher priority for treatment than persons who are victims of other crimes? How is it to be verified that an individual is in fact a victim of crime, and what individual or group is to provide such verification? Are persons legitimately victims if they suffer injury or losses as a result of behavior that they have provoked, or are persons legitimate victims only if there is no evidence of provocation? How is evidence of provocation to be established, and what persons or organizations are to provide such information? Can persons legitimately claim services if they have attained victim status by victimizing themselves, or must second or even third parties be involved? As can be expected, victim and client status conferred upon claimants varies greatly among programs and, in many instances, within programs, although some basic implications of the term *victim* can be identified tentatively for victim service purposes.

The term *victim* clearly lacks descriptive precision, and its meaning often varies directly with its social function. For example, to the police, prosecutors, and judges, victims serve as a source of information concerning the occurrence of a crime and are used in proceedings against the accused. For professional criminals, victims are merely sources of opportunity for exploitation and, therefore, in criminal terminology become suckers, chumps, or marks. Even in programs that are designed to provide services for persons identified as victims, there is a tendency to conceive of victims in a manner that is peculiar to the social function of the organization providing the services. Victims who apply for state awards to balance the losses or injuries they have sustained become claimants, and in the case of initiating civil action in a court of law, victims are, of course, plaintiffs. Bureaucratic responses to victimization tend to emphasize those characteristics of the victim that best correspond to the character of the bureaucratic organization providing such services.

Victim service programs tend to vary greatly in terms of the characteristics of the victim-client population that are considered most relevant to the program's orientation, the goals of the program, and the actions deemed necessary to meet those goals. The nature of the problem, the goals to be pursued, and the action to be taken are vastly different if viewed from the perspective of the criminal and the police, but they are also different in the eyes of the police, the

courts, corrections officials, and the individual victim.

VICTIM SERVICE TYPOLOGIES AND PROGRAM PERFORMANCE

A systematic comparison can be made to identify the major attributes of programs in respect to various aspects of victimization. Programs can be compared on the basis of three major attributes: (1) the identification of the major problem—the aspect of victimization that serves as the rationale for initiating the program; (2) the goals of the program, which specify the desired outcomes to be attained in response to the perception of the problem; and (3) the type of intervention that is characteristic of the program and that specifies the means by which program goals are to be attained. Table 1 provides a display of the six program categories and the goals, types of intervention, and perceived problems related to each category.

Victim compensation

Compensation by the state to the victim of violent crime is perhaps the most highly visible service program as well as the one that has received the greatest amount of analysis.[2] Victims of violent crime receive monetary awards from the state to compensate for losses sustained as a result of criminal action. The client population is composed of innocent victims of crime, based on the presumption that awards should be denied to persons responsible for provoking criminal acts. Emphasis is placed on restoring the financial condition of the victim by matching, within particular limits, financial losses sustained after other sources of funds have been exhausted. Insurance funding must be drawn upon before awards are provided by the state. Many programs also have provisions that require applicants to report each incident to the police and to have the incident verified as a crime by the police.

Many of these programs contain a variety of provisions that exclude a large portion of the victimized population. Exclusions are most often based on tests that are employed to determine the level of financial hardship endured

Table 1. Victim service typologies and program attributes

Program attributes	Program category					
	Victim compensation	Offender restitution	Victim-witness	Crisis intervention	Victim advocacy	Neighborhood justice
Problem	Default	Losses Crime	Presumed guilt of offender	Injury	Debt Presumed guilt of offender	Disagreement
Goal	Compensation	Recompense Rehabilitation	Conviction	Amelioration	Recompense Retribution	Reconciliation
Intervention	Award	Collection Supervision	Testimony of victim	Relief Counseling	Prosecution Litigation	Mediation

by the victim, the degree to which victims themselves may be responsible for the impact of criminal behavior, and the degree to which victims have been cooperative with law enforcement authorities.

Compensation programs devised and administered by the state are most often based on the unofficial recognition of default on the part of the state in its supposed ability to protect its citizens from unlawful behavior. The state requires a monopoly on the legitimate use of force and, therefore, denies such action to its citizens. Accordingly, the state assumes an obligation to protect its citizens if they are to be denied reliance upon force. Although the state may be in default when its citizens suffer from criminal behavior, few states are willing to admit negligence and, thereby, open themselves to a wide variety of legal claims from crime victims.[3] Compensation becomes the goal to be pursued in response to the problem of default, which in a sense allows the state to be immune from the volume and expense of negligence claims. Intervention in these instances takes the form of an award by the state to the victim, in accord with the state's assessment of the severity of the victim's losses or injuries balanced against the possible role that the victim may have had in precipitating such losses and injuries. Awards not only represent a clearly delineated point at which the victim must terminate claims for action, but the process by which awards are made reduces the victim's

role as a claimant against the state. No particular interest of the victim in the disposition of the offender's case is recognized.

Some observers maintain that victim compensation by the state represents an effort to lessen the degree of victim dissatisfaction when the state fails to impose retribution. Compensation programs viewed from this perspective are merely attempts by the state to protect itself from the victim's demands for retribution.[4]

Offender restitution

Offender restitution programs represent a comparatively unusual concordance of victim interests with those of criminal justice system professionals.[5] Recompense of the victim for injuries or losses sustained as a result of criminal action is combined with the interests of the state in rehabilitation of the offender. Many offender restitution programs are based on the assumption that both objectives can be attained through confrontations between the victim and the offender with a view toward arriving at the means by which the offender will restore the losses claimed by the victim. The process by which the victim's needs are met is expected to contribute to the offender's discovery and appreciation of the injustice suffered by the victim and the need to refrain from criminal behavior in the future. The success of such an effort is based on the willingness of both offender and victim to participate in this process and to agree upon the extent and nature of the victim's losses and a specification of the acts to be undertaken by the offender to redress such losses.

From the viewpoint of the state, the problem is the occurrence of crime, but from the individual victim's perspective, the problem is essentially debt. Criminal behavior troubles the state, but losses sustained as a result of criminal action trouble the individual. The goal of offender restitution may also be expected to differ from that of compensation programs, since recompense for the victim from the offender is expected to be the goal pursued in response to the problem of losses. However, rehabilitation of the offender is the goal that is of most interest to the state. Restitution, very much unlike compensation, is based on the capability to act directly on the offender's behavior. Successful intervention is closely related to the capability to supervise the offender's behavior in order to prevent further criminal acts. Concurrently, the offender is expected to behave in a manner that will eventually lead to the collection of whatever is owed the victim to balance out the losses sustained.

Generally, offender restitution does not involve instances of violent crime, both because victims of such crimes fear encounters with offenders and because it is often difficult to ascertain the extent of loss suffered. It is also difficult to identify the nature of restitution that is within the capability of the offender. In practice it would appear that the greater share of offender restitution programs are based on instances in which the victim is an organization and the offenses involve losses of property. Organizations appear to be less vulnerable than individuals, and supervision of offenders is of a less personal nature. Conversely, the impersonal nature of such relationships may not have the anticipated impact on rehabilitation of the offender as is assumed to be the case of interaction between individual victims and the offender.

Victim-witness programs

Victim-witness programs entail the efficient use of information from the victim for the purpose of initiating proceedings against the offender and concluding such proceedings with the conviction of the offender.[6] Such programs can be viewed as an effort on the part of the criminal justice system to provide some accommodation of the victim's interests in proceedings against the accused, while concurrently narrowing the scope of the victim's participation to that of a witness.

Victim-witness services reflect a comparatively narrow set of problems, goals, and types of intervention. In a sense, victim-witness programs are designed to address what is perceived as a management problem suffered by criminal justice professionals in proceedings against the accused. The problem is the possible weakness of the prosecutor's case against the accused without the testimony of the victim. The objective is to prosecute those who are expected to be guilty of crime and to secure conviction. These goals have been selected through the establishment of prosecutor's offices, for whom conviction is the immediate objective rather than punishment, rehabilitation, or even deterrence. In this case, intervention is the testimony of the crime victim as a witness in a manner that will provide for the conviction of the accused. There may well be a tendency for such programs to be concerned with victims only insofar as they can be used to secure organizational priorities and without reference to whatever objectives individual victims may have.

In most programs, victim services are directly provided only to the extent that they encourage victims to conform to a witness role. Most victim-witness programs stress services that entail verification of witnesses' phone numbers and addresses, provide for witnesses to be notified about their desired appearance during proceedings, and, in some instances, lessen opportunities for intimidation of the witness by the accused or the associates of the accused. No need is seen to enlarge the decision-making role of the victim in proceedings. In most instances, victims are actively discouraged from pursuing prosecution of the accused if the crime is not perceived as serious by criminal justice professionals or if the case against the offender is perceived as too weak or defective to permit a successful prosecution.

Crisis intervention

Crisis intervention programs probably vary more in terms of victim clientele and the variety of services offered to cope with difficulties sustained by victims than any other single program type.[7] As their name implies, crisis intervention programs are designed to provide services that are addressed to the most immediate and pressing needs of victims who have suffered as a result of crime or antisocial behavior. Such programs are designed to match the variety of difficulties sustained by the victim with a variety of services that can be put at the immediate disposal of the victim. Most programs respond to immediate psychological and physical needs. These needs are often addressed by attempts to provide an appreciative perception or understanding of the victim's plight, while concurrently providing food, clothing, and shelter if required.

In practice, crisis intervention usually is directed to the needs of female victims of violent crime, which often occurs within a family context. This emphasis reflects the strong ideological preferences of many program sponsors for addressing needs that are believed to exist as a result of the destructive aspects of social structure and its coordinate individual relationships. Crisis intervention, in this context, is seen as a response to deprivations suffered by women through no fault of their own. Programs tend to emphasize particular problem areas, such as battered wives or victims of rape.

Crisis intervention may also be employed in addressing the problems of victims when injuries or losses are self-inflicted, as in cases of drug abuse. In some instances, programs may stress services for both victims and offenders, as in the case of family and parent centers when children are the focus of harmful behavior.

Particular emphasis is on empathy, supplemented by attention to physical needs. Sometimes these efforts may be complemented by recommendations for legal recourse. Battered wives may be encouraged to institute legal proceedings against husbands, or victims of rape may be convinced to testify against offenders, although such action is rarely considered to be of first priority.

Victim advocacy

Victim advocacy programs can be as diverse in terms of problems, goals, and intervention as crisis centers. This program category includes virtually any acts or procedures that address the full range of what may be troubling from the victim's viewpoint. However, victim advocacy is most often concerned with the problem of debt and presumed guilt, and it focuses primarily on victim-offender interactions in a legal context.[8] The problem is that the offender has engaged in behavior proscribed by law and such behavior has resulted in losses sustained by the victim. The goal in such instances would take the form of recompense with respect to the problem of debt and retribution with respect to the problem of the offender's presumed guilt. Intervention appropriate to such goals is provided by the state in the form of prosecution to address the question of presumed guilt and civil litigation to address the issue of debt. Whether either of these two types of intervention is in fact available to the individual victim is based on the assumption that the offender is known, has been arrested, and is available for such proceedings. Additionally, the reluctance of the state to prosecute in a wide variety of instances when the goals of criminal justice professionals conflict with those of the victim is well known.[9] Civil litigation against the offender remains an option open to the victim if the costs of litigation are less than those of the injuries or losses sustained and if such costs are within the victim's financial capacity. Criminal justice professionals tend to resist giving the victim a role beyond that of witness in proceedings against the accused.

The development of a victim advocate role provides opportunities for victims and their representatives to play a part in the decision-making process. An attorney acting in representation of the victim is essentially the victim's advocate and may appear in some jurisdictions in support of the prosecutor in proceedings against the offender; in other instances, although they are few in number, the victim's advocate may be solely responsible for prosecuting cases. Such efforts are initiated in response to the generally low priority given victim interests by judges and prosecutors in proceedings against the offender. As might be anticipated, criminal justice professionals generally do not welcome the intrusion of victim advocates. Victims and their advocates are generally seen as contributing to demands on time and resources that are in short supply. Additionally, many prosecutors and judges view victim interests as only private expressions of preference, which must give way when in conflict with the overriding priorities of the criminal justice system. Therefore, the intrusion of victim advocates in proceedings such as plea bargaining often is similarly rejected by criminal justice professionals as unwarranted; if their expression is allowed, victims' interests are assigned lower priority than those of the prosecution or the defense of the accused.

Neighborhood justice

Although the term *victim* is rarely employed, the neighborhood justice centers can be conceived of as victim service programs in the sense that they provide the means by which losses can be addressed by those individuals who believe they have sustained such losses as a result of criminal behavior.[10] Neighborhood justice centers offer the opportunity for disputants to arrive at a settlement that is acceptable to both parties and that avoids criminal proceedings. In such programs, the services of mediators are made available for the purpose of responding to disputes between persons within particular communities. As a rule most victims' claims of losses entail crimes that are of a less serious nature but that are sufficiently serious to be perceived as the basis for the initiation of action.

Unlike offender restitution programs, the desired outcome of mediation proceedings is a settlement reached before it becomes necessary to initiate criminal proceedings, although in the event of failure to arrive at a settlement agreeable to both parties, criminal proceedings can be employed. Neighborhood justice centers have objectives similar to those of offender restitution programs, without necessarily identifying the parties to the dispute as victims or offenders. Emphasis is placed on the disputants' recognizing that losses have been sustained on the part

of one or both the parties and that some appropriate response must be forthcoming to remedy the situation. The interests of the state, although present in the form of a general preference for minimizing destructive behavior (which is often a product of disputes), are subordinated to the interests of the disputants so long as resolution takes a form that is not contrary to the law and that is acceptable to both parties. The goal in such programs becomes one of reconciliation between the parties involved, and mediation by third parties constitutes the appropriate intervention. Such services are often linked with a possible recourse to criminal prosecution or civil litigation as an alternative in the event that those against whom claims are being made are not inclined to participate in meaningful discussions.

The value of the neighborhood justice center approach to victimization lies in its grounding in the traditional role of dispute settlement without invoking the direct intervention of the state, with its substantially lessened capacity to deal with disputes other than through threat of penal sanctions.

PROGRAM PERFORMANCE AND SOCIAL CONTROL

Noting that victim service programs differ in terms of the problems they address, the goals they seek to attain, and the interventions they employ may be useful in identifying the range of victimization phenomena now being addressed. More important, however, such information is useful in an assessment of the degree to which such programs address propositions central to victimization. It has been hypothesized elsewhere that these phenomena are closely related to the performance of social control functions within a society.[11] Specifically, victims are responsible for the maintenance of societies within particular limits of normative variation in that: (1) victims are the primary detectors of variation from the norm of social behavior; (2) victims play a part in determining the nature of losses or injuries in respect to prevailing social norms; (3) victims participate in identifying normatively valid responses to losses and injuries; and (4) victims participate

Table 2. Victim service programs and performance of social control functions

Social control function	Program category					
	Victim compensation	Offender restitution	Victim-witness	Crisis intervention	Victim advocate	Neighborhood justice
Normative detection	Yes	No	No	Yes	Yes	Yes
Normative definition	No	No	No	Yes	Yes	Yes
Response designation	No	Yes	No	Yes	Yes	Yes
Response execution	No	Yes	No	No	Yes	Yes

in executing responses to variation from the norm of social behavior.

Societies vary greatly in the degree to which victims participate actively in the performance of social control functions, and generally the ability of victims to act as agents of social control is directly related to the degree that societies control antisocial behavior and crime successfully. If the centrality of the victim's role in the process of social control is acknowledged, then the degree to which victimization programs contribute to the victim's role as an agent of social control should be considered. The information in Table 2 represents an effort to assess the degree to which each of the six categories of victim service programs functions in support of each aspect of the victim's role as an agent of social control. This assessment is made in respect to generalized attributes of programs within each category rather than in respect to the attributes of any single program.

Normative detection

Normative detection refers to victim behavior that focuses public attention on antisocial or criminal acts. Victims may report crimes to the police in some societies or may announce the occurrence of antisocial behavior to other members of a community. In both cases victims' detection is a prerequisite for social action that modifies or corrects deviation from social norms or law. Victim service programs may either support or discourage the victim's role as detector.

Most victim compensation programs, for example, are designed to encourage this role by linking monetary awards with the reporting of the crime. Generally, financial reimbursement from the state is available only if the victim is prepared to notify the police.

Victim advocacy programs operate in a similar manner with regard to detection. The state will not provide a victim with counsel if a crime has not been reported. Nor can a private prosecutor employ criminal proceedings in a case in which law enforcement agencies have not been notified of the crime's commission. Under advocacy programs, the only recourse available to the victim who does not report a crime is a civil suit.

Although crisis intervention programs do not normally require that a crime be reported as a prerequisite for their services, they generally do encourage the victim to do so, although this may be a secondary or even tertiary objective. Since crisis centers deal with specific classes of victims (rape victims, for example), the notification of law enforcement agencies has several anticipated effects: (1) the full weight of the criminal justice system is brought to bear on the offender, thus at least temporarily preventing an immediate recurrence of the criminal activity; (2) the victim is safeguarded from further deprivations by a particular offender; and (3) the incident is recorded by the criminal justice system and added to local, state, and federal aggregate data; this encourages the enactment of stronger laws to deal with the crime in question and provides greater legal safeguards for the entire class of victims.

Like crisis intervention programs, neighborhood justice programs do not generally require that a crime be reported before action is taken. However, the threat of criminal proceedings is often employed as an inducement for a civil (and out-of-court) settlement of disputes. In some of these programs, the crime must be reported, and the prosecutor's office refers the matter to a citizen dispute center, again, using the threat of criminal legal action to motivate a civil settlement. Thus four of the six program types directly or indirectly encourage the victim's role as a detector of criminal activity.

Offender restitution and victim-witness programs, on the other hand, tend to place very little emphasis on this role. Offender restitution is closely linked with the processing of the offender by the criminal justice system. These programs address issues respecting the disposition of the offender after a determination of guilt is made. It is not until that point in the proceedings that the victim's role emerges.

Victim-witness programs function primarily in support of priorities established by criminal justice professionals. As most of these programs are designed and administered by the prosecutor's office, relatively little emphasis is placed on the victim's role as a detector of crime, which is considered to be a responsibility of the police. Therefore, victim-witness programs do not attempt to provide incentives for crime reporting.

Normative definition

Normative definition refers to the classification of behavior as criminal, antisocial, or within acceptable variation. Crime is a legal concept, and no crime exists where law defining the activity as such does not also exist. If the victims of a particular type of antisocial behavior (wife beating, for example) do not represent such behavior as meriting intervention by the state, it is unlikely that the behavior will be classified as crime and its precipitators subjected to legal sanctions. Thus the victim can play a central role in the definition of variation from the norm.

Crisis intervention programs are not necessarily limited to providing services for victims of crime. Victims of antisocial behavior may seek their services and be accepted as clients, thereby actively participating in the definition of particular behavior in terms of social norms. As a result of the reformist inclinations on which many crisis intervention programs have been established, documentation of instances of antisocial behavior is considered an important function of the organization. The active participation of victims in reporting incidents and describing the impact of antisocial behavior is considered to be a high priority concern. Program personnel are also active advocates of the criminalization of antisocial behavior; this encourages the victim role of normative definition to a high degree.

Under victim advocate programs, victims generally provide their own definition of which criminal or antisocial acts are salient to their interests. Civil and criminal courts are viewed as resources upon which victims can draw to satisfy particular interests after having defined the acts in question as either criminal or merely antisocial. In this sense, civil courts are used to represent both the identification of harmful behavior from the perspective of the individual victim and the opportunity to identify such behavior as variation from the social norm. In the event that the criminal justice system is called upon, the system is used to meet individual interests rather than preferences internal to the system itself. For example, it may serve the individual's interests to threaten the offender with the prospect of criminal prosecution as an inducement to redress whatever wrongs have been suffered, regardless of whether criminal justice professionals feel prosecution is warranted.

Neighborhood justice centers by definition are committed to addressing a wide range of behavior that may be of interest to the victim. Although generally designed to deal with criminal behavior, such centers also appear to consider dispute situations that contain the potential for serious losses or injuries. Therefore citizen dispute centers are particularly sensitive to victims as detectors and definers of variation from the social norm. Since the disagreement under consideration is treated as a dispute rather than a question of law, victims have an important role in specifying the nature of losses or injuries with respect to prevailing social norms. In each of the above program types, the identification of variation from social norms and the specification of losses or injuries that result from such deviation provide opprotunities for socializing both offenders and victims to a set of norms appropriate to the society of which they are a part. However, compensation, offender restitution, and victim-witness programs provide no such opportunities.

Compensation programs allow no part for victims in the determination of the relationship of their losses or injuries in respect to prevailing social norms. Consideration of victim losses is confined to specific behavior that is of high priority interest to the state, that is, crime, not antisocial behavior. Since the victim's role in offender restitution programs is allowed to emerge only after a determination of guilt has been made following criminal proceedings, these programs display no concern with victims who suffer losses as a result of antisocial behavior. The victim must accept the state's definition of the social significance of the offender's acts that led to the victim's losses or injuries.

Similarly, victim-witness programs subordinate the victim's definitional role to the interests of the state. The determination of whether a crime has, in fact, occurred is generally considered to be a police function. Following this, the prosecutor's office must decide whether a reported crime merits prosecution. Only after this decision has been reached is the victim's perspective of the event considered. The prosecutor may draw upon the information provided by the victim concerning the extent of injuries or losses, but such information is employed to establish the severity of the charges and to enhance the prospects for conviction. At no stage in the proceedings does the victim's central role of definition of variation from social norms emerge.

Response designation

Response designation refers to the victim's role in defining the type and degree of responses appropriate to variations from the norm. Victim participation in the development of responses to

normative deviation emphasizes the costs of deviation in respect to the injuries or losses suffered by the victim. A balance between costs to the offender and losses to the victim is secured to deter future criminal or antisocial behavior as well as remedy undeserved losses or suffering.

Offender restitution programs provide victims with a clearly recognized role in the identification of normatively valid responses to individual losses. Such a determination follows the offender's conviction and is usually made in the process of deliberation with a representative of the criminal justice system as well as with the offender. This procedure provides representation for the interests of the victim and the state, along with an acknowledgment of the offender's obligations to the victim. However, under restitution programs, victim response designation occurs only in the postconviction disposition of the offender, and then only for certain classes of crimes (generally those involving property loss); this severely limits the victim's role in response designation.

Crisis intervention programs allow for a wide range of response designation in an inverse manner from offender restitution. Under these programs the victim's role in response designation occurs before the involvement of the criminal justice system instead of after. Since the victim services of crisis centers are provided whether or not a crime is reported, the victim is free to choose the degree and type of response. However, crisis centers are generally active in encouraging the victim to use the system.

Although these programs generally have *not* developed a set of internal priorities exclusive of the interests of individual victims, preconceived priorities of staff members may conflict with the victim's interests. For example, a staff member may draw upon feminist ideological tenets in perceiving and analyzing conflicts within families (particularly those between husbands and wives), whereas the victim may not. Therefore, victim preferences in respect to normatively valid responses to losses or injuries may or may not be congruent with the orientations of crisis intervention centers.

Like the crisis center, victim advocacy programs tend to operate in a manner that is most consistent with the victim's interests. The victim is provided with legal counsel to aid in the response decision as well as other decisions.

Similarly, neighborhood justice programs provide victims with a wide range of response designations. Although the interests of the state are not always represented in deliberations at citizen dispute centers, the communication of information in an informal atmosphere and the use of language easily understood by the disputants stand in stark contrast to criminal or civil proceedings in which the victim and offender (or plaintiff and defendant) play no major part and must contend with proceedings beyond their understanding.

Under victim-witness programs, normatively valid responses to criminal behavior are determined solely by law enforcement agencies. The victim plays no part other than that of providing information. Victim compensation limits responses to victimization to a monetary award by the state. Both these program types are based on the presumption that the state is an entirely competent mechanism not only for compensating victims and determining normatively valid responses to victimization but also for preventing (to some degree) further instances of victimization without considering the victim's role. This presumption seems questionable, particularly in light of the state's reluctance to make awards to victims who are believed to have precipitated crimes. If victims can and do precipitate crimes, then the victim is an important actor in the genesis of crime, the victim's role has implications for both the determination of the normatively valid response to the victimization and the prevention of further instances of victimization, and that role must be considered.

Response execution

The final aspect of the victim's role, response execution, involves the victim's participation in imposing responses to injuries and losses and monitoring the offender's performance. As with response designation, victim participation in response execution emphasizes costs of social deviation to the offender. Here, however, it is on a more personal level. The offender is allowed to perceive directly the extent of the harm he has inflicted. He is also placed in a position where the type and severity of his punishment are determined by the one he has wronged. This type of personalized deterrent may be much more effective than the impersonal processing of the criminal justice system, and may provide greater motivation for rehabilitation. Thus, in ideal circumstances, victims should be deeply involved both in the specification of responses to crime and the supervision of the execution of whatever response is deemed appropriate.

Offender restitution, neighborhood justice, and some victim advocate programs offer the most clear-cut victim role in respect to response execution. With offender restitution, it is often the victim who monitors the degree to which the offender conforms to the agreement. Monitoring can take the form of simple reporting procedures concerning the receipt of monetary restitution or, in some instances, it may entail supervision of the offender in the event that particular services must be provided. In citizen dispute programs, it is the victim-disputant who must be convinced of the accuracy and viability of the restitution. A resolution of the dispute, however, can occur only if the offender-disputant acts in accordance with whatever settlement is agreed upon during the proceedings and the victim-disputant acknowledges the offender's compliance.

Under victim advocacy, some criminal justice jurisdictions have developed decision-making roles for victims in an effort to provide a systematic review of individual victim priorities during proceedings against the offender. Therefore, victims have some part to play in the decisions of criminal justice professionals regarding prosecution, the disposition of the accused during trial, and the ultimate disposition of the offender during sentencing. Although most victim advocacy programs do not provide opportunities for the victim to act with respect to the full range of social control functions, there appears to be no good reason why advocacy programs could not do so.

In contrast, victim compensation and victim-witness programs provide no opportunities for the victim to participate in execution of the response. The disposition of the criminal in both instances is not considered a legitimate issue for victim involvement, although some witness programs do inform the victim of the sentence imposed. With both of these program types, the execution of the response to the victimization is unrelated to any interest the victim may have, aside from the receipt of the award in compensation programs.

In crisis intervention programs, victim participation in the execution of responses varies greatly, depending on the abilities of the victim and the resources placed at the victim's disposal. In particularly serious circumstances it is not surprising that the state is often called upon to intervene to prevent further injuries to the victim. Pursuit of such a solution, however, results in a loss of decision-making control by the individual victim, both in respect to identification of responses to losses or injuries as well as in respect to execution of whatever response is selected.

It can be readily seen that social control functions of victims are more likely to be performed if victim service programs act in close conformity with the interests of individual victims. Although most programs entail sponsorship or direction by the state, the degree of involvement by the state seems to be inversely related to the degree that victims perform social control functions. This relationship would suggest the need for reassessment of the ultimate purpose of service programs for victims, as well as the need for systematic monitoring and assessment of their operations.

NOTES

1. Ziegenhagen, Eduard A. *Victims, Crime, and Social Control.* (New York: Praeger Publishers, Inc., 1977), p. 1.
2. For the most comprehensive description see Edelhertz, Herbert, and Gilbert Geis. *Public Compensation to Victims of Crime.* (New York: Praeger Publishers, Inc., 1974).
3. The instances of liability may be broadening if a recent New York State decision is upheld. A supreme court judge ruled that New York City's immunity to suits by crime victims does not exist for crimes committed on common carriers, in this case, the subway.
4. Miers, David. *Responses to Victimisation: A Comparative Study of Compensation for Criminal Violence in Great Britain and Ontario.* (Milton Trading Estate, Abington, Oxon: Professional Books Ltd., 1978).
5. See Galaway, Burt, and Joe Hudson. *Offender Restitution in Theory and Action.* (Lexington, Mass.: D. K. Heath & Co., 1978) for a good selection of program variations.
6. See Cannavele, Frank J. *Witness Cooperation with a Handbook of Witness Management* (Lexington, Mass.: D. C. Heath & Co., 1975), and Ash, M. "On Witnesses: A Radical Critique of Criminal Court Procedures. *Notre Dame Lawyer* **48**:386-425, 1972.
7. For example, see *Child Abuse and Neglect: The Problem and its Management,* vol. 3, *The Community Team, An Approach to Case Management and Prevention* (Washington, D.C., U.S. Department of Health, Education and Welfare, 1976), and O'Sullivan, Elizabeth Ann. "What has Happened to Rape Crisis Centers?: A Look at Their Structures, Members and Funding," *Victimology* **3**:45-62, 1978.
8. See McDonald, William F. "Notes on the Victim's Role in the Prosecutional Stages of the American Criminal Justice Process" (Paper presented at the Second International Symposium on Victimology, Boston, 1976) and Barlow, Hugh. "Crime Victims and the Sentencing Process" (Paper presented at the Second International Symposium on Victimology, Boston, 1976).
9. For example, see Reiss, A. J. "Discretionary Justice in the United States," *International Journal of Criminology and Penology* **2**:181-205, 1974.
10. McGillis, Daniel, and Joan Mullen provide a description of neighborhood justice center program variations in *Neighborhood Justice Centers: An Analysis of Potential Models* (Washington, D.C.: U.S. Government Printing Office, 1977).
11. Ziegenhagen, pp. 17-18.

Selected readings for Chapter 12

Baluss, Mary. *Integrated Services for Victims of Crime* (Washington D.C.: National Association of Counties, 1975).

> This monograph discusses who victims are, what their needs might be, and how some communities have responded to meeting these needs. Models and alternatives for integrated victim service programs are described, and significant issues associated with such programming efforts are assessed.

Bard, Morton, and Don Sangery. *The Crime Victim's Book* (New York: Basic Books, Inc., Publishers, 1979).

> Victimization creates a crisis in the lives of victims. The reasons for this crisis, typical victim reactions, and the stages of crisis and crisis resolution are described. Orientation is provided regarding likely victim experiences with the criminal justice system.

Barkas, J. L. *Victims* (New York: Charles Scribner's Sons, 1978).

> Based on extensive personal interviews, the book describes the experiences of crime victims and reviews some of the variety of programs and services being established to help ease and prevent the pains of victimization.

Gordon, James S. "Alternative Human Services in Crisis Intervention," *Victimology* **2**:22-30, 1977.

> A variety of services have developed in the last 10 years as alternatives to established mental health facilities and social service agencies. The assumptions, attitudes, and practices that make these services useful and responsive to the people they serve are discussed.

Ziegenhagen, Eduard A. *Victims, Crime, and Social Control* (New York: Praeger Publishers, 1977).

> Chapter 6 in this volume discusses the components of selected victim service programs as well as the rationales on which they have been justified.

Chapter 13

ALTERNATIVE VICTIM SERVICES

A □ *Responding to battered women*
SHIRLEY OBERG and ELLEN PENCE

B □ *Background notes on community-based services for rape victims*
JAYNE THOMAS RICH

C □ *Crime victim crisis centers: the Minnesota experience*
STEVE CHESNEY and CAROLE S. SCHNEIDER

D □ *An integrated victim services model*
DAVID A. LOWENBERG

A □ *Responding to battered women*

SHIRLEY OBERG and ELLEN PENCE

During the first few years of the feminist movement of the late 1960s and early 1970s, women's energy in organizing was geared primarily toward public confrontation of the social and political system that exploited them. Demonstrations and legal action were geared toward broad political change that would bring relief from an oppressive condition to large numbers of women. Frustrated by the seemingly endless barriers to overcome and faced with the increasing needs of individual women for immediate help, many feminist organizations began providing alternative services to women in crisis situations. Hotlines, rape crisis centers, abortion clinics, and shelters for battered women became the bases from which many feminist women operated.

Providing direct services to women instead of organizing exclusively for changes in the existing systems (such as the welfare, judicial, medical, law enforcement, and social service systems) has had multifaceted implications for the women's movement. On one hand, by providing needed services for women, the movement has in a very real way changed the lives of thousands of women who would have otherwise been untouched by the feminist movement. Provision of services has made women who use those services aware of how sexism in this society affects their lives and has enabled them to see that their problems are not individual problems caused by their own personal failure as women but are a reality shared on some level by all women. It is this awareness that radicalizes women and leads them to take both individual and group action to change their condition and, consequently, the reality of all women.

On the other hand, the move to direct service provision has brought with it the need to constantly fight a natural tendency toward co-optation. Most of the millions of dollars it takes to operate these alternative services must come from the very systems the movement is confronting. To receive and retain this financial backing and to assure full use of services, it is necessary to establish a broad base of support and legitimacy in local communities and to allow women who do not share feminist philosophy to comfortably seek and use the services offered. This necessitates a move toward a philosophical base that can be accepted by a large segment of the population.

A service-oriented women's movement must interact with society to effectively provide services to individual women. It is difficult when dependent on society to also attempt to radically change it. Attacking an institution that serves to maintain the status quo is like punching a giant marshmallow. It may temporarily change its shape, but it remains the same marshmallow and eventually returns to its original shape. These institutions (for example, welfare, educational, social service, and judicial institutions) have an amazing ability to adapt to the demands of people excluded from fully participating in the social and economic mainstream without changing the status quo in any meaningful way.

This ability to adapt to demands without addressing the fundamental issues that created them marks these institutions' current response to the demands of the battered women's movement. Though mental health centers, welfare agencies, counseling centers, police training academies, and researchers are all responding on some level to the needs of battered women, the responses for the most part are not based on

the philosophical principles of those who were pioneers in challenging the "right" of men to beat their partners—the basis on which grassroots service providers in battered women programs operate today.

The philosophical principles of grassroots service providers—that is, people outside the established institutional system who have organized to respond to an issue directly affecting them—have at their core a realization of the complexities of how women are trapped for years and even lifetimes in abusive relationships. Many women who were initial organizers in the battered women's movement had personally experienced violence in their own relationships and consequently responded to battered women as neither sick nor masochistic.

These grassroots services understand that in this society there is an imbalance of power between men and women. Men are in control of the economic and political structure of this country, and that control extends into the family. Men and women are socialized to conform to the broader structure of society. The violence used toward women in the media, the exclusion of women from fully participating in the economy, and the socialization of women to be passive, caregiving, and emotionally dependent provide the sanctions for men to maintain that same control in their intimate relationships with women. Women who work in shelters fully realize that one fourth of the men in this country use violence against their partners to establish their control. With some men, it is to establish control in the relationship. With others, violence toward their partners is a twisted form of feeling in control of other parts of their lives.

Grassroots organizations that were being initiated and growing rapidly throughout the country in the early 1970s served to bring the crime of wife beating out from "behind closed doors" and to give women who were in abusive relationships the permission to talk about it. Focussing attention on the abuse of women forced the recognition that this is perhaps the dominant form of violent crime in this country and brought about the institutional response we see today.

The Law Enforcement Assistance Administration spent $3.6 million in 1977 and 1978 to fund family violence programs. Millions of dollars have been spent to fund professional researchers who have conducted studies on battering that only verified what shelters had been saying through their experience in working with thousands of battered women. State legislatures are funding shelters across the country. With the institutional response comes a very basic change in philosophy. The institutions do not see sexism as the cause of battering. Rather, battering is seen as a symptom of dysfunctional families. With this change in understanding concerning the cause of battering has come a change in the institutions' understanding of women who seek services. Women who are battered are commonly viewed as enablers of the batterer, as part of the family system that breeds violence, as women who have learned to become victims and who merely need to become more assertive. Men who batter are seen as victims of dysfunctional families, as socially sick, as chemically dependent, as somehow not a part of a broader systematic oppression of women. These types of responses often imply a participation by women in their own victimization. Women are often required by service and judicial systems to seek counseling with their abusers, on the premise that he cannot change his violent behavior unless she somehow changes her behavior. Agencies forming new shelters often require mental health screening tests of women housed there.

Today, most of the shelters organized directly under established social service or mental health agencies, or under their guidance, are not staffed by battered women or by women who understand their commonality with battered women, but by a new breed of professionals who give lip service to feminist ideology and who place themselves in a position of power and abused women in the position of clients. Although many of the original people in the battered women's movement may lament its changing directions, they must also take credit for knowing that thousands of women will seek and find safe housing, that some men will find treatment and stop battering, and that many women and children will find a new life free of violence.

BATTERED WOMEN'S MOVEMENT IN MINNESOTA
History

The grassroots organizers of battered women's programs in Minnesota have been fortunate in that they have been able, to a large extent, to maintain control of the funds provided by foundations, government, and private individuals and, as a result, have also been able to maintain much of the original philosophy of their pioneer programs. In fact, staff from the two shelters that existed in the state in 1976, along with a group of professionals concerned with improving society's response to battered women, drafted the first piece of Minnesota legislation to specifically deal with battering. The purposes of this legislation were to:

1. Secure ongoing funding for both the existing shelters and the new shelters
2. Develop a statewide educational program on battering for professionals and the public
3. Document incidents of battering in the state

The intent was to build into the law assurances that the funding would go to grassroots organizations and that information on the incidence of battering would be used primarily to document the need for programming and not for research as an end in itself. Finally, it was intended that people working on the issue, including women who have been battered, be involved in the implementation of the legislation.

The legislation passed in 1977 provided $475,000 to fund four or more pilot shelters for battered women, $50,000 for an educational program, and $75,000 for administration. The legislation also mandated that all medical, law enforcement, and social service professionals in the state report incidents of battering to the administering state agency, and $25,000 was appropriated to establish a data collection system. The overall program was to be administered by the Minnesota Department of Corrections with a nine-member advisory board made up of direct service providers.

The legislation was implemented largely in the form intended by the women who originally drafted it. Three reasons contributed to the successful implementation of the legislation: first, the original group of concerned women found a powerful legislative sponsor in the Minnesota senate who understood the issue. Second, the department of corrections, the administrating agency, consistently implemented the recommendations of the advisory task force and encouraged their participation in every aspect of decision making. Third, the state of Minnesota has historically supported populist, grassroots, and cooperative movements. The effort to provide services to battered women through grassroots organizations rather than through established institutions was valued by state leaders. Both governors who have held office since the passage of the legislation have been supportive of a grassroots approach.

Shelters

In addition to funding the two existing urban shelters, the legislative funds were used to open four new shelters in small cities and rural areas in the state. Women's Advocates Shelter in St. Paul served as a model for the new shelters in the state. Basically, each shelter provides protective residence, advocacy for women, advocacy for children, transportation, food and clothing, support groups, public education, professional assistance, follow-up, and an emotionally supportive environment.

It is difficult to describe the functioning of a shelter. Much of what happens to a woman living in a shelter has little to do with programming but is the result of a process whereby different women and children living together find a common strength in a place where it is safe for them to be themselves. Monica Erler, a staff person at Women's Advocates Shelter wrote an article in that shelter's monthly newsletter to tell in a beautiful way what shelters are all about. Women's Advocates is an old three-story house. The upstairs has two offices and a large meeting room; the middle floor, bedrooms; and the downstairs, a kitchen, living room, small office, and playroom. Ms. Erler writes:

This newsletter is *Upstairs* and the writer is an upstairs person who worked downstairs for four years. Downstairs is the house. It's the five bedrooms on second floor and still more it's the kitchen, the playroom, the living room and the little office on first floor. It's the women and the children who live on Grand Avenue. Downstairs is alive all the time. It may rest a little between 3:00 AM and 6:00 AM. Downstairs is 12 or more folks gathered around the counter in the kitchen sharing their lives, heartaches and laughs. It's children bouncing in and out to talk with mothers, to share play discoveries, to cry about a hurt.

Downstairs is running to the petty cash box for dimes for the pay phone and quarters for the washer and dryer in the basement. It is loads and loads and loads of laundry. It is dishes for 20 people, 3 times a day. It is the endless search for space to hang winter wraps. It is snow and sand on the bare wood floors and countless little fingerprints on the large grey windows. Downstairs is TV in one room and stereo in another. It is cigarette smoke and popsicles. Comic books and frayed magazines. It is chaos and it is security. It is strangers of all races, creeds and colors thrown together for a time by circumstances in their lives, becoming friends sometimes.

Downstairs is a dishwasher that doesn't wash dishes. It's patches of new plaster here and there where old plaster is falling off the walls. Downstairs is torn linoleum nailed to a floor that is walked over every half minute all day long. Downstairs is countless worn out rugs and sofas. Downstairs is home to over 2000 people in 4½ years.

Downstairs is women and children beginning a process of change that is beyond any dream of the best of dreamers. Downstairs is Women's Advocates Shelter and Program.

Daily operations of Minnesota shelters are similar. Shelters are designed to first provide safety but, beyond that, to provide support for women who are in abusive relationships to take whatever control of their life they can, given the nature of their partners' violent behavior. Supporting women involves helping to break through the isolation they are experiencing by providing a communal living environment with other women in the same situation. A woman coming into a shelter invariably feels guilty; she often feels that the abuse happened because she somehow failed in the relationship with her partner. Living with other women in the same situation forces her to see that her problem is shared by many women. Listening to their experiences and witnessing their fear validates her own experience. If she continues to blame herself or deny her own fear, she must also blame the other residents of the shelter and deny the reality of their dangerous living situations. When women come to shelters from situations of total isolation, they find a community that welcomes them and gives them permission and support to change their lives. This involves hours of talking and listening. Shelter staff understand that all relationships involve conflict but only those involving a violent person will result in physical abuse. As residents are given permission to share their feelings of guilt, they are also confronted by each other's acceptance of the responsibility for being abused. As feelings of shame, guilt, fear, and isolation are openly discussed, women find themselves in a much stronger position to take control over their lives.

As women turn to the welfare, legal, and social service systems for assistance in carrying out their decisions, their feelings of powerlessness increase when they find that these systems are poorly designed to provide the necessary resources. Each shelter in Minnesota provides individual advocacy for women. Shelter staff provide women with information on available resources, and in many cases staff accompany women as they approach the system for services. Shelter staff continually work on changing the policies and attitudes of institutions to make them effective resources for battered women. Every shelter faces the task of balancing its energies between advocacy for individual residents and the long, arduous task of changing institutional policies and procedures. In its annual report to the department of corrections, the staff of Harriet Tubman Shelter addressed that issue:

The Shelter staff is consistently overwhelmed in its attempt to meet the need for shelter and advocacy. As long as women requesting shelter are turned away the pressure for individual advocacy services will not diminish. But community education, professional training, building networks and changing policies and procedures of other service networks does create a counterweight to the heavy load of individual

women in crisis. In contrast to the daily demand for individual advocacy, where crisis is as real and ever-present as a phone ringing, systems advocacy seems less tangible. The major priority is to help women, to provide non-stop service. Because funding barely supports this crisis-intervention service of shelters, systems advocacy activities must be fit in more or less around the edges and between the cracks. We continue to strive, however, for some kind of link between changing the system that battered women face and working with women who are battered. The satisfaction of seeing system responses compels us to work toward enlarging and deepening that response. To recognize the inter-relationship between systems and individual advocacy is in itself a balancing act maintained through the tension created by the multiple demands of each sector.

In June 1980, eight new shelters opened, financed primarily through state funds. These have brought the number of shelters currently operating in Minnesota to fifteen. Five shelters are located in the seven-county area surrounding Minneapolis and St. Paul, and ten more are located in nonmetropolitan areas of the state.

Although providing safe shelter for women is the highest priority in terms of state funding, people working on the issue recognize the limits of shelters. Over 1300 women and children were housed in six shelters during 1978, yet 79% of the women seeking shelter were turned away because of lack of space. Even after the number of shelters in the state doubles, it is anticipated that a high percentage of women will be turned away because of lack of space.

Education

Many women who must remain with their partners because of lack of shelter space are faced with few legal or physical protections from continued assaults. There is no equivalent system of programming for the violent partners of battered women. Social attitudes that wife beating is a family matter and not a public matter still prevail. In response to these issues and problems, Minnesota finances a statewide educational program. Besides serving as a vehicle for educating professionals and community people in an attempt to change attitudes, the educational program has generated a broad base of legislative support. This support resulted in the 1979 legislature's passing the most comprehensive state-financed battered women program in the country by increasing the 1977 two-year appropriation from $625,000 to $3 million in 1980–1981. As noted earlier, the community education component of the program was allocated $50,000 for 1977-1978 activities. A portion of these funds was used to develop several tools to be made available to locally based education groups statewide. These tools consisted of:

1. Two slide-and-tape presentations; one geared toward understanding the effects of battering on the family and the circumstances that may trap women in abusive relationships, the other geared toward assisting in workshops designed to reexamine professionals' responses to battered women (including law enforcement, medical and social service professionals)
2. A training program for professionals and a training team available to local organizations wishing to sponsor workshops on responding effectively to victims of battering
3. A state manual on developing an awareness of the problems, needs, and concerns of victims of battering as well as a consideration of effective responses within professions to women who are abused
4. A 30-second television public service announcement encouraging viewers to participate in local efforts to deal with battering
5. A library of books, films, articles, and research papers related to battering, for use by community education groups statewide

Grants were made to twelve community groups, one in each of the state's eleven economic development regions and one group organized to work in the rural and urban Indian community for the purpose of conducting educational programs for the public and facilitating training for professionals. The $2,800 grants made to each group were intended to cover the mailing, printing, transportation, and out-of-pocket expenses of volunteer speakers' bureaus.

The recommendation by the advisory task force to the administering agency to equally distribute the limited education funds by region was debated for many hours. On the one hand, issuing small grants was seen as helping to continue the expectation that women committed to this issue have to work without pay. Yet at the same time it was recognized that available funds should be stretched to assist the growing number of local organizations forming to work on the issue. Financially supporting these groups would ensure a power base during the next legislative session.

Although grants were made to only one organization in each region, most organizations involve several groups. For example, a grant was made to a shelter to conduct a community education program in the region, but the funds and responsibilities were equally distributed among five organizations within the region, with the shelter acting only as the fiscal administrator.

Since the inception of the statewide education program, over 30 organizations have been formed throughout the state to address the issues surrounding battering. In addition to functioning as a catalyst for the organization of local groups, the education program is serving to sensitize many professionals to the problems and needs of battered women. As professionals have begun to examine their own interaction with abused women, they have also joined with grassroots organizations to effect changes within the systems from which battered women seek help. This includes the medical, judicial, and law enforcement systems. Emergency rooms are beginning to adopt special protocols for dealing with abused women, some police officers are carrying referral cards for shelters, and the courts are slowly beginning to use their power to provide added protection for battered women. Although these changes often seem insufficient to advocates and women who face seemingly insurmountable odds in seeking help from a system poorly designed to provide physical protection and economic assistance, they represent a real movement toward more meaningful change.

Finally, the educational effort, including speaking engagements, television and radio appearances, newspaper articles, posters, and mailings, has reached thousands of men and women in violent relationships, giving them permission to seek help for what was once considered just a "family matter." It is expected that these efforts will result in a dramatic increase in the number of women and men who will turn to the system for assistance.

A hotline for men in violent relationships and several voluntary therapy groups have recently been formed to meet the increasing demand for services for the batterer. The missing link in working on this issue has always been the reluctance of the batterer to seek assistance. As voluntary groups form, the development of a growing awareness of the need to work with the violent partner on a meaningful level is anticipated, whether or not he voluntarily seeks help.

Data collection

The financial provision of the 1977 legislation required all medical, law enforcement, and social service agencies to report incidents of battering to the administering state agency. There were two significant results of that data collection effort. First, it provided essential data to demonstrate the need for services and education in all parts of the state. Second, it opened the door to many agencies for educational and training workshops. After the law was passed, many agencies, hospitals, and police departments requested speakers to explain the law and the reporting system.

CONCLUSION

Those who drafted the original legislation establishing a state program for battered women in Minnesota have found that by employing a statewide task force and involving grassroots organizations, their intent has been fully realized. Though no one has the illusion that battering is subsiding in Minnesota, most of those working on the issue recognize that tremendous changes have occurred. With success has come the responsibility of maintaining a philosophical perspective that serves to empower women and eliminate the roots of violence toward them rather than merely caring for them as victims.

B □ *Background notes on community-based services for rape victims*

JAYNE THOMAS RICH

Before the early 1970s, public discussion of rape was generally taboo. The women's movement at the beginning of the 1970s, however, focused attention on rape as the ultimate invasion of one's person. Women's groups examined the treatment of the rape victim by the male-dominated institutions with whom she came into contact, and found these institutions to be sexist and insensitive—in effect, "re-raping" the victim.

Adapted by permission of University Research Corporation, Washington, D.C., from *Rape and Its Victims: Participants Handbook,* 1977.

In response to these perceptions, rape crisis centers were developed to deal with the victim not only in regard to the systematic re-raping, but also with regard to the ongoing trauma experienced by a substantial number of rape victims.[1] The thrust of these centers was to provide support and counsel to victims and non-victims alike and to develop political strategies for obtaining public and private support needed to secure more sensitive and effective services for rape victims from hospitals and the criminal justice system. Gradually, their efforts have been rewarded, as more traditional organizations have become involved in rape-related projects. "At each level of government, both legislators and administrators are now involved in the effort to control rape and to make the criminal justice system more responsive to the needs of the victim."[2]

Corinne Whitlatch, Director of the Polk County Rape/Sexual Assault Care Center in Des Moines, Iowa,[3] characterizes community groups that have been "instrumental in the anti-rape movement" as follows:

1. Rape centers.
2. Government and community task forces—temporary and quasi-official bodies whose primary purpose is to investigate the ways that rape cases and victims are handled and make recommendations for improvement. Often study the law on rape. Typically composed of representatives of police, sheriff's office, hospitals, medical and mental health agencies and related community service organizations.
3. Social action within other organizations
   a. For services—traditional service organizations such as YWCA and Planned Parenthood develop programs, usually counseling, in response to the needs of rape victims.
   b. For the purpose of reform—two very different types of organizations: (1) those associated with national women's rights organizations, most especially N.O.W. [the National Organization For Women] and the National Women's Political Caucus and (2) crime prevention and criminal justice support organizations.

Examples of various kinds of organizational structures, funding sources, and services follow. No attempt is made here to evaluate their impact on increasing rape convictions.

In Alexandria, Virginia, the Alexandria Rape Victim Companion Program has been in full operation since August 1, 1975, and offers a variety of services to victims and their families: (1) to provide trained companions to victims of sexual assault throughout the formal post-rape process; (2) to offer crisis intervention counseling to victims of rape; (3) to provide information and referrals to victims and their families; (4) to educate the public about rape; and (5) to provide a liaison between the victim and the police, hospitals, and court personnel and to work toward reforms in these institutions concerning the treatment of rape victims.

This program was conceived by a concerned citizen who volunteered her time for a year to develop and establish the program in conjunction with the Alexandria Commission on the Status of Women. The year preceding the full operation of the program was spent in research, planning, and establishing working relationships with the police, hospitals, and the prosecutor's office, and developing and training volunteers.

The Alexandria Commission on the Status of Women provides office space, supplies, and nominal funds to the program. For the fiscal year 1976 the city has provided $4,500 to be used as salary for the program coordinator. A telephone coverage for the program has greatly enhanced the effectiveness of the service. In addition, the program has two "bell boy" remote signal devices which allow the on-call volunteers a certain amount of freedom of movement without decreasing the level of service. The program is recruiting VISTA [Volunteers in Service to America] volunteers to help coordinate services.

There are 28 adult female volunteers, five adult male volunteers, and one youth volunteer. In addition, there are Spanish-speaking volunteers and those with knowledge of sign language. All of the volunteers have undergone an intensive eighteen-hour training program and receive three hours of in-service training per month. The training program, designed by a psychologist, includes various crisis intervention and effective listening techniques and enables volunteers to assess the victim's emotional state. Presently the program is trying to strengthen the mental health referral programs in the area with the hope of establishing special rape victim counselors.

In addition to the telephone referral and companion services, the program is attempting to establish a formal speakers bureau to handle the increasing demand for speaking engagements. The program has working relationships with the Alexandria Police, the hospitals, and the Virginia Commonwealth Attorney's Office and, through regular meetings, has worked to revise their procedures.

The Women's Medical Center (WMC) in Washington, D.C., provides a range of services to women, including medical treatment, gynecological care, counseling, and workshops in a variety of subjects of interest to women. Due to an increasing demand, the WMC has instituted a formal set of policies and programs for victims of sexual assault which include: (1) gynecological and medical care, particularly follow-up treatment; (2) crisis intervention and general support counseling; (3) informational and liaison services between victims and the police and courts; (4) workshops and courses in self-defense; and (5) a speakers program aimed at rape prevention. Organizationally, the WMC consists of a board of trustees, a staff of counselors, administrators, and on-call consulting physicians. The Center is private and operates on a fee basis adjusted on a sliding scale relative to the client's income.

The Washington, D.C., Department of Human Resources Sexual Assault Program consists of both emergency medical care at D.C. General Hospital, a follow-up program designed to meet a variety of the health and emotional needs of rape victims, and a 24 hour crisis intervention hotline with a special number for rape victims.

The Rape Hotline, staffed by telephone counselors with training on the handling of rape victims, will assist victims at various post-rape stages. The follow-up unit, in operation since 1965, is designed to contact and assist all victims of sexual assault in D.C. and provide services based on the individual needs of victims. The follow-up unit is staffed with two public health nurses experienced in working with victims of sexual assault.

The essential follow-up procedure includes obtaining victim information from the police and the hospitals in D.C. and making an initial telephone contact with the victim and a home visit if necessary. The primary purposes of the follow-up unit are: (1) to contact the victim either by phone, personal interview, or both, assess how she is coping with the situation, and, accordingly, offer short-term emotional support and counseling or make longer-term mental health referrals; (2) to provide information to the victim concerning the results of the medical tests done during the emergency treatment, particularly those tests for venereal disease and

pregnancy; (3) to provide a liaison between the Sexual Assault Squad of the police department and the Department of Human Resources; and (4) to assist the victim with any personal arrangement she must make as a result of the assault. In addition, the follow-up unit operates an outreach program with the victim six weeks after the assault, if a continuing relationship was not maintained, in order to check back with her as to her general welfare and to aid in arranging for the necessary medical follow-up at that time.

There are seven identifiable rape crisis and support programs in the Washington, D.C., metropolitan area. In addition, all jurisdictions have access to general hotlines in times of crisis. However, these hotlines normally advise and help rape victims contact the nearest rape crisis program. Both the University of Maryland and the American University in D.C. have general mental health and crisis-oriented services available to the student population providing other approaches to rape.[4]

An exemplary project identified by LEAA [the Law Enforcement Assistance Administration] is the Polk County Rape/Sexual Assault Care Center (R/SACC) in Des Moines, Iowa, which offers medical and social support services to rape victims, aids law enforcement and criminal justice personnel in the investigation and prosecution of sexual assault offenders, and provides the community of greater Des Moines with public and professional rape education programs.

The hard costs of the program, according to LEAA's report, consist almost entirely of salaries: for the coordinator, the contact worker, and clerical support staff. Office space is supplied without charge by a participating hospital, and a special prosecutor's time is funded as a normal function of the District Attorney's office. Volunteer workers have provided almost all other services. Total annual cost for a program serving over 100 victims a year in a community of about 300,000 is less than $35,000.

The Seattle Rape Reduction Project combines and coordinates two rape-oriented community service programs—the Rape Relief Project and the Sexual Assault Center. Together, these projects provide hotline and follow-up crisis counseling to meet initial and long-term victim needs, medical care and treatment intended both to serve the victim's immediate needs and preserve the necessary evidence for successful prosecution, community and professional education and training programs, and a liaison with Seattle's law enforcement and prosecutorial agencies.

The connecting thread for the two service components is the Rape Reduction Project Office which is responsible for:

1. Maintaining project publicity, a crucial aspect of the program, intended to encourage victims who do not report to the police to seek either medical treatment at the Sexual Assault Center or information through the Rape Relief Office.
2. Coordinating staff meetings between Rape Relief and Sexual Assault Center on a weekly basis.
3. Coordinating meetings with the County Prosecutor's Office and the Morals Unit of the Police Detective Bureau on a monthly basis.
4. Project fiscal coordination and production of necessary reports and correspondence.

In its first year of operation the project focused on institutional procedures for rape treatment, investigation, and prosecution. The police effort was two-pronged: making changes at the bureau level and providing training at the academy. At the bureau level, the morals unit investigators were informed about the existence and role of victim advocate/counselors. They were also encouraged to work closely with the prosecutor's office in preparing the case for trial. At the training academy, the Rape Relief training materials became part of the curriculum, and a member of the Rape Relief staff trained academy instructors in presenting the new techniques in rape investigation and interrogation through films, text, and most important, role-playing activities. In both instances, the importance of preserving medical evidence was stressed. In addition to these efforts, personnel changes were recommended and adopted by the Morals Unit. The six-person bureau is now made up of two women and four men; the sergeant in charge is a woman.

During the ensuing two years, a great deal of mutual respect and cooperation developed—to the extent that it is not uncommon for police investigators to suggest that the victim contact one or the other of the service agencies if she has not already. The bureau sergeant explained that such a practice is as much intended to aid in the investigation of the case as it is to provide services for the victim. She was adamant in suggesting that the Rape Relief and Sexual Assault Center were responsible for many cases' continuing through prosecution—not only due to training provided the police but also the support provided the victim. Since this, of course, relates also to cases where the police were contacted after the Rape Reduction staff were involved, the process is truly a two-way operation.

The Prosecutor's Office has also changed its protocol. In the first instance the office becomes immediately involved in the investigation. This not only provides a continuity of evidence gathering but also is instrumental in limiting the number of times the victim is forced to tell her story. The investigation is further aided by the assignment of a single assistant D.A. to each rape case during the preparatory stage. Due to the existence of a separate trial bureau, the case is, however, turned over to another D.A. when the time comes to go to court. Although there is no specific prosecuting trial attorney for rape cases, the case assignment procedure has resulted in the informal designation of certain attorneys for these cases. Given the new priority on rape cases (partly dictated by the improved evidence and new law), those attorneys have been drawn from the pool of prosecutors designated to handle the more serious and difficult cases.

Regardless of the structure providing the service, goals of rape crisis centers and other community-based groups include victim support services, reform of institutional responses to rape victims, community public education, and law reform. Focus is often narrowed to one or two of these goals because of limited personnel, physical plants, and/or financial resources.

The primary focus of most groups is to provide supportive services to the victim. The nature of these services varies from counseling at the time of the initial report to follow-up contact and counseling over an extended period. These steps are representative:

A. Reporting and recording
1. Operate 24 hour hotline phone service
2. Provide crisis counseling
3. Provide information and reassurance on victim's concerns about law enforcement and medical procedures
4. Contact and counsel with family/friends
5. Encourage reporting by giving accurate information and providing support to victim
6. Ease confusion when jurisdictional transfer is necessary
7. Provide transportation for victim to police and/or hospital
8. Arrange for babysitting, temporary housing needs
9. Provide alternative help to victim if a personal problem results in an unfounded reporting of rape
10. Protect confidentiality and provide counseling and medical referral for nonreporting victims
11. Provide for the special needs of minority victims

B. At the hospital
1. Stay with the victim before the examination and insure her privacy
2. Do crisis counseling
3. Explain and emotionally prepare victim for pelvic examination
4. Prepare victim to verbalize the details of the sexual acts
5. Personalize the examination so victim doesn't feel treated as an object
6. Insure victim's understanding of consent forms and her rights
7. Provide clothing to victim and provide transportation home
8. Counsel victim on decisions related to possible pregnancy
9. Insure medical follow-up for VD tests
10. Assess need (and refer for) long-term counseling

11. Be of assistance in developing options when fee payment is a problem

C. During the investigation
1. Facilitate the victim's contact with the investigator—notify, transport, and accompany
2. Counsel with victim regarding concerns not relevant to criminal case
3. Inform victim of and protect her rights
4. Counsel with victim to encourage her cooperation with investigation and lessen negative reactions
5. Counsel with family and friends to encourage cooperation with and positive response to victim

D. During the prosecution
1. Provide counseling and support to lessen victim's negative reactions and encourage cooperation with prosecutor and procedures
2. Facilitate victim's contact with prosecutor/court by notifying, transporting, accompanying, and assisting with school and employment absences, etc.
3. Inform and assist victim with civil suits and victim compensation when relevant
4. Inform victim of and protect her rights.

While the advocate is supporting and counseling the victim, she is also noting points in the process where reform is indicated. Her strategies for reform may be those of persuasion or of direct or indirect pressure. Organizations such as NOW have been leaders in the movement for law reform. The Prescriptive Package published by LEAA described many reforms in the delivery of service by hospitals, police, and prosecutors, many of which were effected in response to the demands and requests of community-based service delivery groups.[5] In order for these groups to be effective, they must be cognizant of the state of the art and be aware of current research findings, both for their own purposes and to conduct a meaningful public education program.

One product of community-based agency research and educational efforts should be the identification and reform of rape laws which discriminate against the victim. Changes in the historical perspective of rape from a jurisprudential point of view are critical. Citizen groups have identified as major points of discrimination the requirement that a victim's allegation of rape be cooroborated and the introduction of the victim's prior sexual history as "evidence" that intercourse was consensual.

PROBLEMS

Major problems for community-based service delivery are funding, staffing, credibility and acceptance by criminal justice institutions, failure to attract minority women, and jurisdictional problems.

The traditional role of women has precluded their having adequate access to the skills, training, and knowledge of resource development required for the organization, planning, and management requirements of obtaining funding and allocating resources. A recognition of this lack has led to a proliferation of seminars, workshops, and other training programs to help women overcome this handicap. While government grants have been obtained by community-based groups, the search for matching funds has been a problem area, as is the search for operating funds when the expiration of government grants approaches. Those crisis centers which have existed on the largesse of private donors, the enthusiasm of volunteers, and fees from speaking engagements also are seeking to obtain more stable funding. Thus, these agencies are entering the competition for funds along with more traditional organizations.

Significant trade-offs can occur between community-based agencies and traditional agencies in the provision of rape-related services through coordination at the decision-making level. Policy-makers for these agencies, through a joint assessment of the needs of their organizations, clientele, and the community and an examination of resources available within and outside their organizations, can plan for a pooling of resources at their points of interaction, resulting in a reduction of money and personnel allocations within each organization. Interaction with courts, hospitals, and police as facilitators of the criminal justice process evokes acceptance and validation of the services offered by community-based centers.

A change of priorities for service or of organizational goals could be a highly desirable strategy for rape crisis centers which would benefit from crisis intervention skills employed by rape counselors in wife abuse and child abuse units. An expansion of the services of rape crisis centers to the victims of these offenses would benefit the center as well as the victim. Victim/witness units also require counseling, advocacy, and support skills such as those employed by rape crisis counselors. The inclusion of such non-rape-related concerns not only helps the centers obtain funds, but also provides increased benefits to the community and the criminal justice system. Crisis centers assure an additional benefit of increased acceptability by police prosecutors and hospitals as a vital link in the victim's movement through the process.

Staffing, largely a volunteer effort for rape crisis centers, has been a problem for several reasons, including the normal waning of enthusiasm among volunteers, faulty initial perception by volunteers as to their roles as counselors with subsequent drop-out, emergencies diverting volunteers who are scheduled for duty, changes in schedules of volunteers, particularly when college students staff the centers, and desire of volunteers for paid employment.

As women's groups become more knowledgeable about funding sources they rely less on volunteers at the management levels. They tend also to abandon the collectivist form for more conventional organizational structure.

The overriding problem for these groups, who *can* provide support to the victim with little money and small staffs, is how to gain acceptance by the institutions dealing with rape victims. A part of this institutional resistance emanates from the perception (by police and prosecutors especially) of these groups as composed of strident, militant females.[6] Professional social workers, too, often reject the efforts of volunteer counselors. Many centers overcome this resistance by establishing a formal or informal "sharing" of service delivery, in which a division and definition of tasks are made for each organization. The example in this country of disparate groups sitting down together to solve problems of labor-management relations, intercultural or ethnic differences, and so forth, points the way to community-based groups, police, prosecutors, and hospitals to establish communication in order to understand and appreciate each other's concerns. To overcome resistance, institutional administrators must be shown how the goals of community-based services impact on each other and how everyone benefits from the coordination. Community-based service delivery can be an effective catalyst which leads to higher clearance rates and conviction rates at little or no additional cost in terms of money and personnel to governmental agencies dealing with rape victims.

In areas where there is a substantial minority population, rape crisis centers fail to attract, as clients or as workers, a representative number of minority women. Minorities, accustomed to getting what they perceive to be separate and insensitive treatment by white, middle-class institutions, choose not to be involved. Many poor black women, it is theorized, fail to report rape even to crisis centers because of their perception of the treatment of black males by the criminal justice system as brutal and inhumane.

An extensive community education campaign (through media, especially ethnic-oriented media, churches, schools, etc.) will have some effect. The plan of Women Organized Against Rape (WOAR) in Philadelphia is, however, a more direct approach to the problem. WOAR intends to establish satellite rape crisis centers in each of the ethnic areas of Philadelphia, involving residents of the community in the activities of their own neighborhood centers as workers. Evaluation of this program should show increased use of the center, not only by poor minority women, but also by other women, because of the convenience.

Jurisdictional problems may include some of the issues previously discussed, but may also include items such as:

1. Who pays the hospital for treatment of the victim and evidence collection?
2. Who staffs victim/witness service units in various organizations?
3. Who provides follow-up services to the victim (a) after the examination, (b) after the trial?

4. Should the victim be compensated for her injuries/trauma? Who will pay for this?

The use of volunteers can answer many, if not all, of these questions. In addition to providing direct support to the victim, volunteer community-based groups can:

1. Relieve hospital personnel of non-medical and/or time consuming duties.
2. Act as liaison with the victim, the police, and the medical staff.
3. Act as resource person to the doctor regarding evidence-gathering and recording.
4. Insure that consent forms are signed.
5. Communicate with victim's family.
6. Prepare victim to describe the details of the sexual acts.
7. Inform doctor of status of criminal case.
8. Counsel with doctor and provide information to facilitate doctor's testimony.
9. Assist hospital in developing medically and legally complete exam procedure.
10. Help develop and facilitate medical records release procedures.
11. Help develop procedures to insure protection of chain of evidence.
12. Serve as communication liaison between hospital/police and hospital/prosecutor.
13. Impact on insurance company regulations, criminal code definitions, etc., that affect payment for examination.

Services to the law enforcement agencies may be any of these:

1. Calm victim.
2. Alleviate victim's fears about talking to police.
3. Urge victim to be truthful.
4. Get victim out of criminal justice system if report is inappropriate.
5. Provide "third party reports" on assaults not reported.
6. Maintain victim's cooperation when jurisdictional transfer is necessary.
7. Insure prompt medical examination.
8. Maintain evidence by informing victim not to bathe, etc.
9. Contact, communicate with, and "control" family.
10. Provide community education that im-

proves image of criminal justice system's handling of rape cases.

11. Provide community education that encourages and emphasizes importance of prompt reporting.
12. Provide community education that informs of necessity of preservation of evidence.
13. Provide community education about general and sex crime prevention.
14. Help agencies deliver rape prevention speeches.
15. Keep track of victim and facilitate investigator/victim appointments.
16. Be a resource to investigator on unrecorded details of medical examination and reporting.
17. Optimize victim cooperation by support and explanation of procedures.
18. Insure that post-examination development of bruises be reported and documented.
19. Communicate with and encourage cooperation of family and friends.
20. Relieve investigator of dealing with noncriminal case concerns of victim/family.
21. Provide in-service training in working with rape victims.
22. Serve as liaison with hospital emergency, laboratory, and medical records departments.
23. Help with research, data compilation, etc., on sex crimes.
24. Provide agencies with in-service training in working with rape victim, crisis intervention skills, etc.
25. Keep agencies updated on current research findings.
26. Keep agencies informed of educational opportunities and relevant tools.
27. Encourage responsible practices by the media regarding their news reporting of sex crimes.
28. Be a resource to the prosecutor about unrecorded details of police and medical contact.

Activities in the community which will assist various components of the criminal justice system are:

1. Enhance the law enforcement agency's ability to investigate, identify, and apprehend those justly accused of sex crimes.
2. Identify and advocate humane modifications in investigatory procedures.
3. Encourage and provide education that addresses criminogenic perceptions of male-female relationships.
4. Provide an educational program that encourages reporting of sex crimes.
5. Be an educational resource that provides speakers, films, and printed materials, and a resource for media and schools/teachers.
6. Research and make recommendations for school curriculum, library, and AV purchases.
7. Research and organize lobbying efforts for law reform.
8. Encourage sensitive, responsible media reporting of sex crimes that doesn't hinder effective reporting.
9. Provide an educational program that is consistent with current research findings about rape, rape prevention, victims, and offenders.
10. Provide for the special needs of minority victims and encourage equality in the response by agencies.
11. Increase the ability of the criminal justice system to convict those guilty of sex offenses.
12. Advocate acceptable priority handling of rape cases.

Areas in which community-based groups may assist prosecutors and courts are:

1. Inform prosecutor of previously undisclosed information relevant to or having potential impact on the prosecution.
2. Provide potential jurors with education that is consistent with current research findings about rape, victims, offenders.
3. Improve image of criminal justice system's handling of rape cases.
4. Lobby for reforms in laws and jury instructions.
5. Encourage responsible reporting by the media.

6. Serve as liaison with police and hospitals in development of procedures.
7. Keep track of and be able to contact victim.
8. Inform victim of court appearances, postponements, etc.
9. Provide transportation and guide victim to and between prosecutors and procedures.
10. Provide the support and counseling to victim necessary to maintain her cooperation.
11. Relieve prosecutor of dealing with non-criminal case concerns of victim/family.
12. Insure collection of complete medical evidence.
13. Be a resource to prosecutor in interpreting medical and laboratory reports.
14. Keep track of doctor and maintain doctor's cooperation by facilitating court appearances.
15. Inform and explain rationale to victim when case is dismissed or pled out.
16. Identify and advocate humane modifications of the court process.
17. Insure and educate the public regarding the necessity of protecting the rights of due process.
18. Educate potential jurors with accurate information about rape.
19. Provide the community with information regarding the judicial handling of rape cases.

FOOTNOTES

[1] Ann W. Burgess and Linda Lytle Holmstrom, *Rape, Victim of Crisis* (Bowie, Maryland: Robert J. Brady, Company, 1974).
[2] Lisa Brodyaga, et al., *Rape and Its Victims: A Report for Citizens, Health Facilities, and Criminal Justice Agencies* (Washington: U.S. Government Printing Office, 1975).
[3] Gerald Bryant and Paul Cirel, *A Community Response to Rape: Polk County Rape/Sexual Assault Care Center* (Washington: U.S. Government Printing Office, 1977).
[4] The Treatment of Rape Victims in the Metropolitan Washington Area (Washington: Metropolitan Washington Council of Governments, 1976).
[5] Lisa Brodyaga, et al., *op. cit.*
[6] Bryant and Cirel, *op. cit.*

C □ *Crime victim crisis centers*

The Minnesota experience

STEVE CHESNEY and CAROLE S. SCHNEIDER

The movement promoting services for crime victims has come about with the growing perception of the criminal justice system's lack of justice for the victim. We expect the victim's input in the apprehension and conviction of the offender, but for the most part the victim is a forgotten individual. At worst, the individual is victimized again by the criminal justice system's neglect, resulting from its struggle to operate an offender-oriented approach.

Historically, crime victims have not viewed themselves as a group of individuals with a right or a need for service. The frequent failure to report crime bespeaks an attitude of frustration and impotence. Further, the victim is often blamed for the crime either because of carelessness or because "he or she asked for it."

As interest in providing services to crime victims develops, policy decisions must be made concerning at least three alternative ways to define target groups:

1. Victims of a specific crime within a large area can be selected as the focus of services. Examples of this are rape centers that are concerned only with rape victims and serve an entire county

2. Certain populations can be chosen for services, such as victim services for the elderly
3. A geographic area can be defined, such as certain precincts or a community within a city, and services can be provided to all victims within the assigned area.

Many victim services have developed from an orientation to help a particular type of victim or victims at a particular stage of the criminal justice system. Thus, there are specialized services for rape victims, battered women, witnesses of crime, the elderly, and assault victims. Each of these services has sought to meet the needs of its particular clientele at one particular point in the system. Often these services have developed as a response to specific incidents of victimization.

Two major problems have resulted from the development of specialized victim service models. First, large groups of victims (including most males and victims of burglary, robbery, and intimidation) are usually not eligible for help. Second, these service models have tended to intervene only at specific points in the victimization process. For example, rape crisis centers intercede immediately after victimization, whereas victim-witness programs step in at the time of offender prosecution. Large numbers of victims with very real service needs are ignored either because of the nature of the crime or because of the organizational needs of the service program.

THE PLANNING PROCESS

Legislation was passed by the 1977 Minnesota Legislature directing the Commissioner of Corrections to establish at least three centers to provide direct crisis intervention, emergency transportation, referral, and other services to victims of crime. The centers were also directed by legislation to coordinate and encourage the development of crime victim services in other social service agencies, to educate the public as to the programs' availability and the needs of crime victims, and to encourage the development of educational programs to reduce victimization.[1]

The Victim Services Division of the Department of Corrections solicited proposals from public and private nonprofit agencies for establishing such centers. Two proposals were selected for funding; one by a private agency to establish centers in Minneapolis and St. Paul, the other by a rural Minnesota county. More data are available from the two urban programs which are the focus of this discussion.

The model of service delivery planned for the urban centers involved assisting victims at all postvictimization stages. The services were meant to be integrated so as to provide a continuum of services from immediately after the crime through the prosecution process. Clearly, the centers were meant to provide a wide range of services to different types of victims from many different social classes and racial groups.

Two features of the service model deserve special attention, because they proved to be less important in the actual operation of the centers than was anticipated. The types of services delivered were expected to be characterized by crisis intervention—service delivery immediately after the victimization designed to stabilize the victim's emotional state, reduce the trauma of victimization, and initiate contact for later staff follow-up. This approach relied on police patrolmen's calling crisis center workers to the scene as quickly as possible. Further, it was assumed that workers would have to be on call 24 hours a day, 7 days a week, and be willing to go out to the victims, rather than wait for the victims to present themselves to the agency office.

Second, the two centers were planned to be *community-based* rather than citywide or countywide. One was located in a storefront, the other in a multiagency community service center to facilitate walk-in victim contact as well as community visibility. The area of primary publicity and police contact was limited in each city to an identifiable neighborhood and one or two police precincts. Since the service model was the first implemented, there was little guidance as to how large an area such an agency could comfortably handle. The decision was made to err in the direction of caution rather than ambition so as to maximize the chances for successful operation.

Community-sized programs were also selected to facilitate publicity, organize blocks for crime prevention, and establish the major types of referral relationships necessary. Additionally, the programs were expected to have strong volunteer staff components drawn largely from the communities they served.

Those involved in the planning process also determined a need for temporary home repairs immediately after a burglary or break-in. Because many victims are unskilled or elderly and unable to make temporary repairs, such as boarding a window or replacing a door lock, program budgets included monies for plywood, nails, locks, and tools.

Planners also recognized that trying to provide all the services a victim might need would be unfeasible; referral to outside agencies was anticipated to be an important component of victim service. Long-term counseling was to be done outside the centers, thus freeing center staff for more short-term service.

In implementing the centers, much of the staff's time and effort initially were expended in securing police cooperation by trying to sensitize and educate individual police officers about victims' needs. The police are usually the first to deal with a person after the criminal incident, and sensitive treatment of the victim by the police can do much to lessen the trauma of victimization and encourage that person to seek further help with any problems. Second, the planners saw the police as the critical referral source for clients because of their unique postvictimization role. Should the police be unenthusiastic about the crime victim crisis centers, victims might receive no services or be contacted much later, when help might be more difficult to give. For these reasons, the police departments were involved in the planning stages of the centers. The police chiefs of Minneapolis and St. Paul sat on the centers' executive advisory boards (as they still do), and police officers were invited to visit the centers. Police were involved in identifying the services that victims needed and that the centers were prepared to deliver, and police officers were given brochures to distribute to noncrisis victims. Beginning with the planning stages, staff

members also spoke before community groups and churches, publicized the centers through local mass media, and made contact with other social service agencies in the communities.

PROGRAM OPERATION

The Minneapolis Crime Victim Crisis Center opened in October 1977 and the Saint Paul center in December 1977. During the first year of program operation, each center provided services to about 1,000 crime victims. The most common types of victimization were burglary (45% of all cases) and assaults (21%). A wide variety of crimes made up the remainder. A small proportion of cases in each center were persons who sought help for problems other than criminal victimization.

During the first year, the centers served primarily white women, 21 to 30 years of age, although minority persons were served in greater proportion than would be expected from their representation in the community. Persons over 64 represented 20% of the center's clientele.

Crisis intervention was originally predicted to form the basis of service delivery. This service model was changed substantially because of a relatively small number of crisis-oriented cases being referred to the centers. Only 12% of the clients received emergency-type services in the first year of operation. Counseling, referral, and informational activities were the major services provided. Outreach attempts were made to victims of crime by reviewing police daily logs and contacting each victim of felony-type crimes. This was done because of the assumption that the small number of clients resulted from a lack of police cooperation in making referrals. In fact, subsequent research by the Minnesota Department of Corrections found that the need for such services was less than originally estimated in the neighborhoods involved. Original program estimates indicated that half the reported victims of crime were potential crisis intervention clients; preliminary findings estimate the actual figure to be from 15% to 20%. About 10% of property crime victims and about one third of the victims of violent crime may be in need of crisis intervention services. The existence of need was confirmed, but its magnitude was initially overestimated. In response to the research and experience, each center has moved moved to expand well beyond its immediate neighborhood.

As a result of the initial low volume of referrals, outreach attempts accounted for the majority of cases during the first year of program operation. This caused concern among the funding bodies because of relatively high program costs in relation to the small amount of actual service delivery to clients. Outreach clients were usually contacted only once and typically received service of an advice or referral nature.

Costs per client were computed by summing costs attributed to service delivery (excluding community education and program evaluation functions) and dividing by the number of victims served. The average cost per victim was about $70.00. Because of the proportion of time spent with such clients, crisis-oriented cases were estimated to cost more, averaging nearly $233.00, whereas outreach and cases involving only short interviews averaged less than $33.00 each. Preliminary information on the second year of program operation shows that the number of victims referred to the centers has risen considerably and fewer outreach attempts are now being made. The result should be greater staff concentration on serious problems as well as lower costs per crisis case because of more complete use of staff time and reduction of time-consuming outreach activities.

The extremely wide range of cases seen by the centers can best be illustrated by a few examples.

• The call on this case came in at 11 PM. I met the police officer at the victim's house. She lived alone and was badly shaken. Her apartment had been ransacked and burglarized while she was out to dinner with friends. Appropriately, the police officer felt he could not leave her alone, as she was close to hysteria and had no close friends she could call at that hour. I stayed with her until 2:30 AM, at which time she and I both felt she was in control of herself. During my stay with her, she was able to discharge all her emotions. We went through her ransacked bedroom, listed items that were missing, and made a list of things to be done the following day. The follow-up involved more phone contacts, which were to help with filing insurance claims and putting pressure on the landlord to install a very necessary outside light and to secure the locks. Her reaction to our services was overwhelmingly appreciative.

• We received a request from the City Attorney's office to perform an immediate witness assistance and counseling service. The victim was a young mother of three who was a victim of battering. Her husband had a drug problem and a previous record. On the day of the trial she was prepared to drop the charges because of intimidation by the offender. Our task was to try to counsel her and provide the appropriate support and information so that she would follow through with the original charges. After 4 hours of counseling, and with the help of a member of Alcoholics Anonymous, she decided to carry out the charges. The trial was held the following day, at which time a staff person was with her for the entire time to provide additional support. The offender was found guilty. The victim felt good about her decision and has been referred on to other support groups.

• Identified from the police daily reports, a middle-aged man whose family's house had been burglarized the night before was contacted by telephone. The man noted that the loss was covered by his insurance but expressed some concern over the possibility of a repeat burglary. Staff members described to him various crime prevention services available. He reported that he would contact the police and ask for a premise survey. The entire contact lasted less than 10 minutes.

Clients are routinely mailed a questionnaire that allows them to rate service quality. Less than 1% of the evaluations are more negative than positive. Those persons victimized by violent crimes or burglaries tended to be more positive in their evaluations than victims of impersonal crimes such as thefts. Apparently the intensity of the victim's problem, not the extent of service delivery, is related to positive client evaluations of service delivery.

PROBLEMS IN PLANNING AND IMPLEMENTATION

Potential problems of cooperation from the communities, police departments, and other agencies were foreseeable and were dealt with early. An executive advisory board was established during the planning stages and comprised the police chiefs, county attorneys, state commissioner of corrections, and state director of public safety. In addition, each center established community advisory committees. Both groups are involved in designing and evaluating the programs. The advisory groups give the power structure and the communities the sense of ownership necessary for real interest and cooperation. Although this approach has been successful, the process can limit the timeliness and quality of input and guidance received from the groups. Some difficulties have been encountered in resolving differences among the advisory bodies and the governing board of the parent agency.

Recruiting minority staff was difficult but was particularly important in view of the alienation toward police among some minority groups. The very nature of victim services implies working relationships with the criminal justice system that are in conflict with the value system of many potential staff members. Minority leaders in the communities assisted in recruiting minority staff to further the centers' commitment to hire staff representative of the communities served by the program. This enhanced community involvement. Staff from the minority communities have been particularly helpful in bringing minority clients to the centers, and the use of volunteer staff recruited directly from the communities has helped keep personnel sensitive to the needs of the neighborhoods.

Developing and maintaining good relationships with police patrol officers are continuing processes. Despite the cooperation of police administrators, convincing individual officers to refer victims to the centers is an issue of direct personal communication between center staff and the police officers. The staff reached police through attendance at police precinct roll calls, ride-alongs in police patrol cars, and open houses with free food at the centers. Although the continued existence and success of the centers has given the program credibility in the eyes of most policemen, there remains some resistance among a few officers. Resistance is especially high in one precinct, which has had a history of bad experiences with inner-city social service programs. Working relationships

with the police can be easily lost. During the first months of operation, a change in city administration caused the transfer of half the police personnel in one precinct, leaving program staff to reeducate a new complement of law enforcement officers.

Since the centers act as a referral source for traditional social service and income assistance programs, relationships with them have been generally good, although careful monitoring was needed to weed out programs not willing or able to help center clients. Potential exists for territorial battles between specialized victim programs and a multipurpose victim service agency. This problem occurred in one of the cities when police began referring victims of sexual assault to the Crime Victim Crisis Center rather than to a older program for victims of sexual assault with which the police were dissatisfied. Some formal mechanism may be needed to avoid fighting over clientele, especially when helping resources are scarce.

Defining a new occupational role was challenging. The first few weeks were particularly difficult because of the anxiety of the unknown, for example, what kinds of requests would come, what the element of physical danger involved was, and so forth. Along with this were problems resulting from the sporadic nature of requests for victim assistance. The police requested that someone be in the office until midnight on weekends even though they call infrequently during these hours. Requests for service quite often come at times when volunteers are not in the office, requiring the staff person to go out alone. When calls were infrequent, staff often thought they could be just as careful by locking the office, going home, and responding to calls via the answering service.

Program flexibility created another dilemma. Looseness of approach and lack of written policy allowed the program to take action quickly as unforeseeable problems developed. The fact that no person seeking help was turned down because of established rules was helpful in developing enthusiasm and self-confidence in the staff and trust and credibility with both police officers and the community. However, flexibility may also result in a lack of focus or direction to the program and may cause floundering until the program is well established. Nevertheless, no good alternative exists, and skillful administration is necessary to the success of any innovative program that needs to avoid becoming overly structured during the early stage of operation.

A particular set of advantages and disadvantages resulted from the centers' multiple funding sources. The centers were able to avoid total dependence on only one source of money. However, the burden of accountability to six different reporting requirements and different budgeting cycles made coordination among agencies a burden.

During program planning, the most time-consuming problems concerned the acquisition of appropriate physical facilities. Obtaining leases, remodeling, and arranging for reliable 24-hour telephone answering service took far more time and energy than arranging for initial publicity, hiring and training staff, and securing community and police involvement in planning the centers.

The Minneapolis and St. Paul Crime Victim Crisis Centers show that services to crime victims that are not restricted by type of victimization or socioeconomic group are needed and can be successful. Continued efforts should be made to replicate this program in other cities and in rural areas to make the nation's criminal justice system truly responsive to the needs of crime victims.

REFERENCE

1. Minnesota Statutes §§ 241.55-241.58 (1977).

D □ *An integrated victim services model*

DAVID A. LOWENBERG

Although one might tend to assume a priori that the victim has legal rights, he does not.
Honorable Herbert Brownell [1]

For 200 years, the United States criminal justice system has expended an exorbitant amount of tax revenue to ensure the legal rights and social welfare of most crime perpetrators. Concurrently, the criminal justice system has virtually ignored the legal rights and social welfare of most crime victims and witnesses. From apprehension to conviction, the legal rights of the criminal offender are protected; after conviction, the counseling and social service needs of the criminal offender are met by correctional treatment programs.

The public is becoming outraged by the gradual realization that tax dollars are primarily being used to expand services for the perpetrators of crime and not for the innocent victims of crime. Consequently, the law-abiding citizen-

ry is becoming more fearful that the scales of justice are weighted to benefit the criminal population, not the victims and witnesses of crime.

In 1967, the President's Commission on Law Enforcement and Administration of Justice was the first national government body to propose that the victims of crime be consulted to learn more about the problem of crime.[2] Six years later, the National Advisory Commission on Criminal Justice Standards and Goals specifically proposed that victimization surveys should be conducted to provide more accurate data on reported crime statistics.[3] The National Crime Panel of the Law Enforcement Assistance Administration (LEAA), created in the early 1970s, is one of the most significant and promising efforts to employ sophisticated survey techniques to collect information on the experiences of individuals, households, and businesses as victims of crime.[4]

One salient finding reported by the National Crime Panel is that a substantial number of crime victims do not report crimes that they know have occurred.[5] Another survey, conducted in the District of Columbia, found that of the 2,964 cases involving lay witnesses that were rejected, not pressed, or dismissed, 1,246 (42%) failed because of lack of witness cooperation.[6] Research studies, such as the two cited above, have made criminal justice administrators more aware that citizen cooperation is essential to halt the proliferation of crime. Thus, the critical problem is to determine why a significant number of citizens are reluctant to cooperate with law enforcement and the courts.

This problem is addressed in part by other research. Examining how the victims of crime are processed through the criminal justice system, Professors Linda Holmstrom and Ann Burgess, of Boston College, found that our government neglects victims and that victims feel no one cares about their welfare. They also found that when victims of crime participate in the prosecutorial process, the legal proceeding aggravates their suffering by not assisting them in their transportation and parking problems, loss of time and income, and child care.[7]

In Milwaukee County, a federally funded research study of a witness service program entitled Project Turnaround found that many of the victims and witnesses interviewed indicated that they will be less cooperative in the future. The survey respondents stated they will be less cooperative because of the time delay in a trial and the routine and disrespectful way in which they were handled by criminal justice agencies.[8] Michael Ash, who was involved in Project Turnaround as the first assistant district attorney liaison, declares that for some victims and witnesses each subpoena and appearance in court is accompanied by tension and terror prompted by fear of the unknown. In short, Mr. Ash contends that the court experience is dreary, time-wasting, depressing, exhausting, confusing, frustrating, numbing, and endless.[9]

Once the victim and witness population enter the criminal justice system, they are bombarded with legal, psychological, and sociologi-

cal terminology that, in most cases, is foreign to them. To add to the unpleasantness, victims and witnesses have to repeat several times to different persons how they were victimized or what they observed. Furthermore, they receive no explanation of how the judicial system operates or how legal decisions are reached.

As stated earlier, law enforcement cannot satisfactorily deal with crime and offenders without also dealing with victims and witnesses. This contention is buttressed by a Rand Corporation research report that focused on the practices followed by 156 city and county law enforcement agencies in criminal investigations. The report states that the single most important determinant of whether a case will be solved is the information the victim supplies to the patrol officer.[10] Even though the importance of the crime victim and witness population is widely known, most criminal justice agencies still regard this population as secondary to the offenders.

Other sociological research indicates that victims of crime are also treated as a second-level priority by the social service system. Victims are least able to cope with the personal and social problems that crime presents, least able to manipulate existing services on their behalf, and less likely to challenge procedures or individuals unresponsive to their problems.[11] In summation, there are few legal or social incentives for a victim or witness to voluntarily cooperate with law enforcement or the court.

PROGRAM OBJECTIVES

These findings prompted a growing national awareness of, and concern about, the plight of victims and witnesses of crime. In light of this awareness and concern, the Pima County (Arizona) Attorney's Office initiated a dialogue with the Tucson Police Department in early 1975 to discuss how the two agencies could better serve victims and witnesses in the community. This dialogue led to an exhaustive review of the state of the art with reference to the impact of victim and witness assistance on the criminal justice system. Thereafter, the county attorney's office conducted an informal survey of law enforcement and judicial personnel to ascertain their viewpoints about the priority needs of victims and witnesses in both the legal and social environments.

In mid-1975, the county attorney's office submitted a 10-page concept paper to LEAA, proposing to establish a comprehensive service delivery system for victims and witnesses. In response, LEAA invited the county attorney's office to prepare a grant application. Without hesitation, the county attorney's office began to expand the concept paper, with the Tucson Police Department and the sheriff's department providing technical assistance for the program proposal.

The authors of the proposal designed the program to attain three principal objectives:

1. To enhance the quality of justice by satisfying the emotional, social, and informational needs of victims and witnesses
2. To increase the willingness of victims and witnesses to cooperate with police and prosecutors after they have reported a crime
3. To save the county attorney's and the law enforcement personnel's time by reducing their involvement in social work functions

To achieve these ambitious objectives, the program would have to help victims and witnesses recover from the trauma of crime and would have to alleviate the major difficulties associated with participating in the judicial process. Therefore, the architects of the proposal set up the program to provide a myriad of immediate and secondary supportive services to victims and witnesses 24 hours a day, 7 days a week.

In November 1975, LEAA notified the county attorney's office that its 1-year grant proposal for $152,941 to operate a victim-witness program had been approved. For the next 4 months, an interdisciplinary team of professionals, consisting of prosecutors, police, and counselors, screened job applications for the eight victim witness staff positions. Then the county attorney, police chief, and sheriff decided to assign supervisory and line staff to become liaisons with the victim witness staff for the purpose of developing a sound interagency relationship. Together, the agency liaisons and the victim-witness staff engaged in an extensive education campaign to enlighten the prosecutors and the police about how to maximize usage of program resources.

EMERGENCY SERVICES

On a 24-hour basis, the program staff is on call to law enforcement personnel to administer crisis intervention services to victims (or their families) of crime, domestic violence, and catastrophic death. When a commissioned officer determines that a victim requires emergency supportive services, the officer instructs the communications dispatcher to summon the program staff, by means of a paging system, to the scene. During the transition period, the officer stays with the victim to provide protection and comfort until the staff arrives to assume the case.

The staff provides each victim an average of 5 hours of crisis intervention and follow-up assistance. The staff always gives the referring officer feedback about the status of the victim within a couple of days. The most frequent crisis intervention services rendered by the program are: short-term counseling, companionship for support and protection, alternative temporary housing, and food.

The staff realized from the inception of the program that they would have to rely on community volunteers to help handle the crisis victim case load. To recruit volunteers, the staff prepared public service announcements for the electronic media, encouraged newspaper reporters to write about the program, and presented the program to university classes and civic organizations. After the recruitment stage, volunteers attend a 20-hour crisis management session to learn how to deal with the emotional and social needs of victims in crisis. Following their classroom training, the volunteers accompany a patrol officer for an 8-hour shift to learn more about the role of law enforcement personnel.

After completing the training, the volunteers are supervised in the field by staff or by seasoned volunteers. The volunteers always respond to victim crisis referrals in teams of two for self-protection and to learn from one another. There are a total of 40 active volunteers, and each contributes about 20 hours of work to the program every month. In addition, the volunteers receive in-service training once a month, during which a specialized topic is addressed by the staff or by outside experts.

For the crisis intervention referral process to be successful, patrol officers must have the skills to evaluate the emotional and social state of a victim and must know how to make use of the program's services. During the same period that the volunteers were being trained, the staff and the law enforcement liaisons combined efforts to develop an experimental training course in crisis identification and management for seasoned officers. The officer feedback about the training showed that they were pleased with the content and the format and that they had begun to use the program's services more frequently. As a result, the police trainers invited the staff trainers to teach academy recruits how to make a diagnosis of and contain a crisis situation.

For the first 18 months of operation, most uniformed officers were hesitant to employ the emergency services of the program until the staff established a track record of being reliable, helpful, and cooperative. As soon as the program began to be accepted as a legitimate and essential resource, the officer referral rate of victim crisis cases increased substantially. Moreover, the patrol officers encouraged the staff to expand the definition of victims who are eligible to receive emergency services to cover victims of all crisis situations (such as attempted suicide, car accidents with injuries, and residential fires).

In accordance with the demand for more services, the victim-witness staff met with the law enforcement liaisons to revamp the crisis intervention operation to enable the program to handle the escalating referral rate. To fulfill this need, the law enforcement agencies agreed to take turns furnishing the program with an unmarked car. A staff member and volunteer drive the unit as a team every evening between 6 PM and 3 AM. Outside these hours, the staff and volunteers still respond to law enforcement referrals through the paging system.

The law enforcement communication dispatchers refer to the program unit on the air as CRISIS One. CRISIS is an acronym for Community Response Into Situations Involving Stress. The majority of the 90 emergency service referrals received by the program per month are initiated by law enforcement personnel during the time CRISIS One is operational.

SOCIAL SERVICES

As delineated in the grant proposal, one of the paramount missions of the program is to develop a strong link between the criminal justice system and the social service system. The staff realized from the onset that a comprehensive supportive service network consists of integrated crisis intervention services and follow-up social services. If either crisis intervention or follow-up service is not part of the supportive service network, then many victims and witnesses will not receive the help necessary to satisfy both short-term and long-term needs.

Each staff member selected key community service agencies to approach with the intent of developing interagency relations. The staff made contact with the administrators of the agencies to educate them about the plight and needs of victims and witnesses and to learn about their eligibility guidelines and operation. This exchange of information lead to victims' and witnesses' receiving priority status with reference to obtaining services promptly from several of the community agencies. In turn, the program staff offers community agency caseworkers training in crisis intervention.

Almost all of the 50 social service cases handled by the program on a monthly basis are referred by police, prosecutors, and social workers during office hours. When a police officer encounters a victim or witness who requires social service assistance during the evening or the weekend, the official telephones the program office and leaves the pertinent information on a message recorder to be retrieved by the staff the next morning. The social services most often needed by victims and witnesses are: medical care, housing, food, employment, legal aid, and mental health counseling.

Some community service agencies have even awarded the program small grants to augment services in special areas. The Pima Council on Aging gave the program a 1-year grant to improve services for elderly persons. The following year, the Pima County Human Resource Department gave the program a 1-year grant to provide more follow-up services to victims. Furthermore, the Information and Referral Service Program helps answer telephone inquiries to the program that require immediate attention after office hours.

An in-house social service increasingly requested by victims of domestic violence and neighborhood feuds is conflict resolution through mediation. In mid-1978, some of the deputy county and city attorneys began to converse with the program staff about the well-known fact that the courtroom is not the proper setting and that the adversary system is not the proper mode for settling a complex, deep-rooted interpersonal conflict. As an outcome of these conversations, the staff was directed by the county attorney's administration to create an alternative procedure to traditional court handling of peace bond cases and criminal misdemeanor cases involving a continued interpersonal relationship.

Within a month, the county and city prosecuting attorneys started diverting interpersonal conflict cases from the criminal courts to the program for mediation. The program staff strives to attain three goals with each case referred for mediation: (1) avoid court intervention, (2) avoid law enforcement intervention, and (3) resolve the conflict in a peaceful manner. If a mediation agreement is not reached in 3 weeks, the staff refers the case back to the attorney for further prosecution proceedings.

Immediately following the receipt of each of the 20 cases referred per month, a staff member contacts both parties by telephone to understand their viewpoint about the conflict and to gain their respect and trust. If both parties verbalize a commitment to work on solving the problem, the mediator usually schedules a face-to-face session to discuss their desires and their concessions. At the end of the session the mediator presents the parties with a formal contract

to sign, which details their agreement. Subsequently, the mediator stays in contact with both parties for about 2 months to make sure they are complying with the conditions of the agreement.

COURT SERVICES

The dissemination of court-related information to witnesses involved in the judicial system was the first service offered by the program. On a daily basis, the staff receives from the file room clerks of the county attorney's office a list of witnesses in cases that are being processed through superior court (felonies) or juvenile court. The staff routinely sends every witness a form letter to explain the purpose of the program, the stages of the prosecution proceedings, and the current status of the case.

As a case progresses, the staff sends each witness a second form letter to present trial information, and then a third form letter to present the final court disposition. Frequently, witnesses contact the staff to request additional information related to their case or to request supportive service assistance. Finally, the staff encourages the witnesses, through correspondence, to allow the program to work with them to verbalize their points of view through judicial channels about the condition of release, restitution, and sentence.

In addition to the case information service, the program also renders a number of social services to witnesses participating in the prosecutorial process. Witnesses most often request the following four program services: transportation to and from court, escort to court, child care supervision, and individual counseling. The staff relies on office volunteers to help the witnesses secure court services and community agency services.

The deputy county attorneys are the primary source of referrals to the program of witnesses who need supportive services. At first, the program staff relied on the county attorney's administration to persuade the trial attorneys to refer their witnesses to the program for services. To make the staff more readily available to the prosecutors, the county attorney relocated the program office to quarters adjacent to those of the criminal division. This relocation greatly enhanced the witness referral rate by attorneys to the program.

After 1½ years of using the program resources, the senior trial attorneys began to ask the staff to work with the most serious cases. Accordingly, the staff works intensely with the victim and family in child abuse and molestation cases and with the families of homicide victims to meet their emotional and social needs. In addition, the staff offers witnesses in protective custody emotional support around the clock. Likewise, the staff collaborates with the prosecutors and the police to conceal from noncourt personnel the whereabouts of a witness who is in danger of being harmed.

A priority witness service that continues to be developed by the program is a court alert system. The staff received technical assistance from professional staff in other jurisdictions about how to set up a court information system to benefit witnesses. By working closely with the trial attorneys and the court, the staff is able to alert both civilian and law enforcement witnesses about the time they will be called to testify and about when they will not have to testify because of a continuance, plea, or dismissal. An estimated 500 witnesses a month receive case information, supportive services, or alert notification from the program.

RESEARCH AND EVALUATION

To comply with the grant guidelines, the county attorney's office was obligated to retain an outside research firm to evaluate the program. Through a competitive bidding process, the county attorney's office selected Stanford Research Institute to conduct the evaluation. The program also employed a full-time researcher to assist Stanford Research Institute with day-to-day statistical activities. This research team has prepared an extensive evaluation plan to undertake program studies in efficiency, impact, and cost.

The first-year evaluation focused on the degree of achievement in getting the program under way and on the outcomes of the program's activities. The staff and volunteers did a superb job of assessing and meeting the needs of victims and witnesses served by the program. Furthermore, the staff did a very good job of gaining the support of and referrals from law enforcement and trial attorneys. Finally, the staff was extremely active in public education and excited a great deal of media coverage in their activities.[12]

At the end of the evaluation report, Stanford Research Institute presented recommendations relating to increased efficiency and effectiveness of the program. The three major recommendations involved greater use of volunteers, increased services to witnesses, and increased follow-up on social service referrals.[13] In response, the staff worked assiduously during the second year to implement those recommendations to the greatest extent possible.

The second-year evaluation focused on the costs and benefits of the program. The crisis intervention and follow-up assistance saved law enforcement about $5,000 annually. The witness alert system saved law enforcement $97,000 annually in court time. In addition, direct social services saved the victims and witnesses $25,000 annually. Overall, the program produced $127,222 in annual measurable social benefits compared with an annual operation cost of $121,560.[14]

One of the main purposes behind the two-year evaluation scheme was to furnish Pima County policymakers with specific information to help them decide whether to continue funding the program after the depletion of grant funds. Stanford Research Institute determined that the program sufficiently satisfied the objectives to satisfy victim and witness needs, to increase victim and witness cooperation, and to save time for police and prosecutors. Thus, Stanford Research Institute informed local policymakers that the evaluation findings show that the program deserves to continue operating at its present level of funding.

On July 1, 1978, the Pima County Board of Supervisors and the mayor and city council of Tucson voted to absorb the total operating cost of the program into the local government budget. Before the vote, the elected officials received numerous telephone calls and letters from volunteer advocates, civic organizations, and community leaders expressing support for the program. Moreover, the electronic and written media used the evaluation findings as a basis to back the program. This favorable input by the community plus the personal philosophy of the elected officials led to the institutionalization of the program.

REFERENCES

1. Brownell, Herbert. "The Forgotten Victims of Crime" (Speech delivered to the Association of the Bar of the City of New York, March 1976).
2. President's Commission on Law Enforcement and Administration of Justice. *Task Force Report: Crime and Its Impact* (Washington, D.C.: U.S. Government Printing Office, 1967), p. 2.
3. National Advisory Commission on Criminal Justice Standards and Goals. *A National Strategy to Reduce Crime* (Washington, D.C.: U.S. Government Printing Office, 1973), p. 32.
4. Kalish, Carol B., and others. *Crimes and Victims* (Washington, D.C.: United States Department of Justice, 1974), p. 1.
5. "Victims of Crime Silent" (*Arizona Evening Tribune,* November 28, 1974), p. 70.
6. Institute for Law and Social Research. "Witness Coopera-

tion Study," mimeographed (Washington, D.C.: The Vera Institute, 1974), p. 1.
7. Holmstrom, Linda, and Ann Burgess. "Victimization by Government: Failure to Help the Victims of Violent Crime" (Paper delivered at the Annual Meeting of the American Society of Criminology, Chicago, November 2, 1974).
8. Knudten, Mary, Richard Knudten, and Anthony Meade. "Crime Victims and Witnesses as Victims of the Administration of Justice," mimeographed (Milwaukee, Wisc.: Marquette University, 1974), pp. 3-12.
9. Ash, Michael. "On Witnesses: A Radical Critique of Criminal Court Procedures," *Notre Dame Lawyer* **48:**388-389, 1972.
10. "Detectives Rarely Solve Mysteries Study Shows" (*Arizona Daily Star,* February 14, 1976).
11. Baluss, Mary. "Integrated Services for Victims of Crime: A County-Based Approach," draft only (Washington, D.C.: The National Association of Counties Research Foundation, September 27, 1974), p. 1.
12. Stanford Research Institute, *An Evaluation of the Victim-Witness Program of Pima County* (Menlo Park, Calif., 1977), pp. 16-57.
13. Ibid., pp. 71-74.
14. Stanford Research Institute. *An Evaluation of the Victim-Witness Program of Pima County,* (Menlo Park, Calif., 1978), pp. 8-19.

Selected readings for Chapter 13

Bard, Morton. "The Rape Victim: Challenge to the Helping Systems," *Victimology* **1:**263-271, 1976.
    Examines relevant research and suggests changes that must be made if victims of sexual assault are to be effectively served by helping systems. Fragmentation impedes service delivery; integration and humanization are necessary to serve the victim, criminal justice system, and society as a whole.
Blackmore, John. "Focusing on the Victim: Aid Programs Offer Everything From New Looks to New Identities," *Police Magazine* **2:**24-33, 1979.
    Reviews the variety of victim aid programs resulting from the Law Enforcement Assistance Administration (LEAA) crime victim initiative launched in 1974.
Bryant, Gerald, and Paul Cirel. *An Exemplary Project: A Community Response to Rape* (Washington, D.C.: U.S. Government Printing Office, 1977).
    An LEAA exemplary project report describing in detail the operations, results, and costs of the Polk County Rape/Sexual Assault Care Center in Des Moines, Iowa.
Burgess, Ann Wolbert, A. Nicholas Groth, Linda Lytle Holmstrom, and Suzanne M. Sgroi, eds. *Sexual Assault of Children and Adolescents* (Lexington, Mass.: D. C. Heath & Co., 1978).
    A collection of papers dealing with ways of intervening with sexually assaulted young people. Particularly useful for officials in the justice system in terms of showing them how to deal most appropriately with such crime victims.

Cannavale, F. and W. Falcon. *Improving Witness Cooperation* (Washington, D.C.: U.S. Government Printing Office, 1976).

> This is a summary report of a survey of 1,000 witnesses in the District of Columbia. The central objective of this study was to probe why individuals who had been identified as witnesses at crime scenes were later labeled by prosecutors an noncooperators.

Doerner, William, Richard Knudten, Anthony Meade, and Mary Knudten. "Correspondence Between Crime Victim Needs and Available Public Services," *Social Service Review* **50**:482-490, 1976.

> A Milwaukee survey identifying the needs of crime victims and available services. Assistance with crime-related expenses was the major need, but social agencies placed little emphasis on financial assistance.

Micholson, George, Thomas W. Condit, and Stuart Greenbaum. *Forgotten Victims: An Advocates Anthology* (Sacramento: California District Attorney's Association, n.d.).

> A collection of materials prepared for California's Forgotten Victims Week, 1977. Identifies needs of several victim categories and suggest a variety of possible services.

Mills, Patrick, ed. *Rape Intervention Resource Manual* (Springfield, Ill.: Charles C Thomas, Publisher, 1977).

> Information was obtained from 54 rape crises centers around the country; provides practical material to people who deal with rape crises on a daily basis.

O'Sullivan, Elizabeth Ann. "What Has Happened to Rape Crisis Centers? A Look at Their Structures, Members, and Funding," *Victimology* **3**:45-62, 1978.

> Analysis of data received from a mail survey of 90 rape crisis centers that had opened before 1976, were autonomous from any public agency, and that provided direct services to victims. The centers were similar to other grassroots organizations providing services; thus the observations may be helpful to other groups.

Pizzey, Erin. *Scream Quietly or the Neighbors will Hear* (London: Penguin Books, Ltd. 1974).

> The volume describes the nature of the problem of battered women and the way battered women's refuges came into being in Great Britain, particularly in relation to the battle to get such programs established and the struggles encountered with the institutional agencies of the court, social services, and the medical profession.

Schuchter, Arnold. *Prescriptive Package: Child Abuse Intervention* (Washington, D.C.: U.S. Government Printing Office, 1976).

> An LEAA prescriptive package report analyzing the problem of child abuse and conceptualizing a model intervention system.

U.S. Department of Health Education and Welfare, National Center on Child Abuse and Neglect, *Planning and Implementing Child Abuse and Neglect Service Programs: The Experience of Eleven Demonstration Projects* (Washington, D.C.: U.S. Government Printing Office, 1977).

> Identifies essential elements for good program development, and is designed to assist communities seeking new and improved programs to help protect children and help troubled parents.

U.S. Department of Justice, Law Enforcement Assistance Administration, *Forcible Rape: The Criminal Justice System Response,* 11 vols. (Washington, D.C.: U.S. Government Printing Office, 1978).

> Results of a 2-year study by the National Institute on Law Enforcement and Criminal Justice. Includes guidelines for criminal justice officials' responses to rape victims, medical and legal information, analysis of legal issues, and a literature review.

Chapter 14

VICTIM COMPENSATION

A □ *Victim compensation: programs and issues*
ALAN T. HARLAND

B □ *Victim compensation programs: an overview*
LeROY L. LAMBORN

A □ *Victim compensation*

Programs and issues

ALAN T. HARLAND

EXISTING AND CONTEMPLATED PROVISIONS FOR COMPENSATION
Legislation

In July 1977, the state of Oregon joined the growing number of jurisdictions in the United States in which certain limited classes of crime victims can be compensated from public funds for losses stemming from their injuries. This addition to the rolls of victim compensation law (H.B. 2278, May 18, 1977, effective July 1, 1977) followed a pattern that has been set by approximately one half of the states in this country,[1] by an increasing array of foreign jurisdictions,[2] and in several "model" compensation pronouncements.[3]

The earliest compensation programs in modern times[4] were established in New Zealand (1963) and Great Britain (1964). Before the decade was out, legislation followed in California, New York, Hawaii, Georgia, Maryland, and Massachusetts. In 1971, New Jersey added its legislative contribution, and the number of

states enacting compensation laws has increased every year since. In 1976 alone, compensation bills were approved in Kentucky, Pennsylvania, Tennessee, Virginia, and Wisconsin.

Not all of this legislation has led to active compensation programs. In one state the implementation of such a program has been delayed because of a constitutional challenge to the law,[5] and in Rhode Island the enabling legislation passed in 1972 will not become effective until the passage of supporting federal law. In the federal jurisdiction itself, compensation acts have been before Congress since the introduction by Senator Ralph W. Yarborough of S.2155, the Criminal Injuries Compensation Act, in 1965.[6] Despite repeated consideration of similar proposals in the intervening years, and after hearings for which the reports run to almost 1,500 pages,[7] no final action has been taken. If enacted, federal legislation would provide compensation for victims of federal offenses, and, more important, it would provide extensive financial support for state programs.

Program structure

For students of public administration and political science, as well as those in the field of criminal justice, the organizational variety among compensation schemes offers a wealth of material for investigation. In a majority of jurisdictions, compensation is the responsibility of relatively autonomous administrative boards. Usually composed of three to five members, such boards may be created solely for the purpose of administering victim compensation, as is the case in New York and Maryland. In such cases, the parent agency is frequently the state department of public safety, the state department of law, or the state department of justice. In California, original control by the Department of Social Welfare was shifted in 1967 to the State Board of Control; in Hawaii, the Compensation Commission operates under the auspices of the Department of Social Services and Housing.

A common alternative approach has been to frame compensation legislation within an existing structure such as workmen's compensation. This is the route taken in the recent Oregon legislation, and it follows precedent set in states such as Washington and North Dakota. In this context, programs are usually housed within the state department of labor or the state department of industry, and compensation awards are closely tied to workmen's compensation schedules.

Victim compensation boards are frequently appointed by the governor, usually for periods of 5 to 7 years. In addition, some boards are aided by investigative staff, whereas others, such as the five-member board in Delaware, investigate claims themselves. Relatively few of the board members are required to serve full time, although exceptions to this exist in states such as New York, Pennsylvania, and New Jersey. In New Jersey, board members are expressly barred from outside employment, but are paid at the same level of compensation as judges.

A third major administrative option for victim compensation programs has been to proceed through the court system. Although Delaware offers a board only housed within the administrative office of the court, in other states the programs themselves are actually run by the courts. In Massachusetts, for example, compensation is assessed by the district court judge, whereas Illinois operates through the court of claims. In Tennessee, the circuit court is the deciding body, although the payments themselves are made through the board of claims.

Investigative responsibilities in such programs, and for some administrative boards, as in North Dakota, rest with the attorney general, or with the district attorney, as in Tennessee. If the moribund legislation in Rhode Island is ever revived, it calls for administration of compensation through a special session of the superior court.

One further organizational category of interest is that of funding for compensation programs. Very few states—for example, Delaware and Kentucky—allocate specific funding amounts in the legislation creating compensation programs. In addition to general appropriations, however, it is common to establish special victim indemnity funds that may be used by the programs or to give access to general or emergency funding accounts of the state.

In each case, more and more jurisdictions have introduced the use of additional, compensatory fines upon conviction of appropriate offenders. Such penalties, and, in at least one case, court fees, are assessed in a variety of ways. They include fixed amounts, such as a five, ten, and twenty-one dollar fine in Maryland, Pennsylvania, and Tennessee respectively; California adopts a more flexible approach, under which violent offenders may be required to pay fines to the state treasury fund on a scale in proportion to the offense committed.

Program practice

Compensation awards are made following procedures that are fairly standardized across programs, most of which involve screening to exclude ineligible cases from recovery. The procedure is usually initiated by the injured victim, through a formal application to the board or court, setting out the nature of the claim and certain personal items of information from which eligibility is determined. After review for eligibility, the case may be investigated through contacts with law enforcement agencies and witnesses; if necessary, a formal hearing will be held. Such hearings are commonly subject to the appropriate rules of evidence and appellate procedures; counsel may be present, and subpoena power may be exercised. Hearings are frequently held by a single board member, with full board review if requested by the applicant or the state. Payment of awards can be made in a lump sum or over protracted schedules. Emergency awards can be made in most jurisdictions pending a final award decision in cases in which special hardship is shown.

Eligibility criteria

Although programs vary in the degree to which eligibility criteria are present, there is a broad consensus as to the types of restrictions employed. The most important limitations on qualifying for an award may be discussed in terms of: (1) compensable claimants, (2) compensable offenses, (3) compensable losses, and (4) miscellaneous restrictions.

Compensable claimants in a majority of jurisdictions include not only the actual victim who suffers injury, but also the victim's dependents in the case of injury resulting in death. In addition, similar awards may be made for persons injured while attempting to aid crime victims (good samaritans), and in each instance payments can be made to third parties who assume responsibility for burial expenses or medical costs.

A few of the earlier statutes in states such as California, Maryland, and New York require that the claimant be in financial need or demonstrate undue financial hardship. In addition, the claimant must not have recovered losses from collateral sources, such as insurance, civil suit, restitution from the offender, or other forms of compensation. If such recovery occurs after the compensation is made, the board or court is entitled to seek the return of the corresponding part of its award in subrogation proceedings.

Further restrictions on possible claimants include exclusion of victims closely related to, living with, or having a sexual relationship with the offender. In a small number of states, such as Washington, inmates committed to state institutions or prisons are not eligible for compensation. Victims who are not residents of the state are excluded in a few statutes, and Pennsylvania has a rather interesting reciprocity requirement, under which out-of-state visitors injured in Pennsylvania may be compensated only if their own state would return the service under similar circumstances. Finally, awards may be withheld or reduced according to the extent to which the victim was responsible for or involved in the criminal activity resulting in injury.

Compensable offenses are restricted almost entirely to violent crimes, although there is no requirement that the offender be convicted or even apprehended. Approximately one third of the compensation states work within specifically defined offense categories, usually including murder, rape, kidnapping, and manslaughter. Other states simply compensate for any criminal behavior resulting in death or injury. In general, persons who have suffered physical injury as a result of criminal victimization will rarely be excluded because of the specific offense listing. However, motor vehicle offenses are precluded unless the vehicle is used as a weapon.

Compensable losses are almost exclusively limited to unreimbursed medical costs, loss of past and future earnings due to physical injury, funeral and burial expenses for the victim, and consequent loss of support by dependents. Property losses are virtually never compensable, except in a limited number of states, such as Hawaii, where good samaritans may so recover and in states, such as Tennessee, where damage to spectacles, prosthetic devices, and other personal items may be covered.

A growing number of states, such as Hawaii, Louisiana, Minnesota, New Jersey, and Wisconsin, provide compensation for pain and suffering or nervous shock. Still other states, no doubt mindful of the rape victim who may suffer relatively low medical costs, allow compensation for extreme mental suffering (Delaware) and pain and suffering as a result of a sex offense (Tennessee). Most jurisdictions, however, do not cover pain and suffering, and a minority of states, such as Illinois and Pennsylvania, explicitly forbid such payments.

Most states that make provision for pain and suffering awards also pay compensation for pregnancies growing out of sexual offenses. Similarly, Nevada allows for counseling for rape victims, and Delaware pays for psychiatric care for victims in extreme mental suffering. A final, related loss category in a handful of states includes nonmedical remedial care and job or vocational training after injury.

On a quantitative rather than qualitative level of loss, two further restrictions on eligibility for compensation are the minimum and maximum loss criteria. More than one half of all the existing U.S. programs cut off payments at $10,000. Some of these allow further expenses in cases of death; Pennsylvania, for example, allows $15,000 under such circumstances, whereas Wisconsin permits a separate award of $2,000 to cover burial and funeral expenses. Although foreign programs like Great Britain's operate without upper limits on recovery (the awards being coextensive with damages recoverable at common law), the most generous limits in America are $50,000 in Louisiana and $45,000 in Maryland. It should be remembered, however, that programs in foreign jurisdictions such as Canada,[8] Australia,[9] Great Britain,[10] and Sweden[11] operate within widespread social welfare networks that reduce the costs of compensation. This is especially true, for example, when one compares the compensable costs of medical care and hospitalization in the United States with the virtually free system in Great Britain.

In addition to the typical $10,000 ceiling on payments, the vast majority of programs also require that the claimant have lost not less than $100 or 2 weeks' salary. The minimum loss is most often justified as an administrative expedient to avoid the time and expense of processing minor claims. What is considered minor ranges from zero in Hawaii, to $25 in Delaware, to $100 in more than half of the programs, up to $200 in Illinois and Wisconsin.

Miscellaneous restrictions on victim compensation cover a broad range of concerns. Claimants are required by most states, for example, to have reported the crime to the police within a specified period of time, usually 2 or 3 days. In addition, the victim is required to cooperate fully with law enforcement agencies in their handling of the case. Similarly, the victim may be required by the board or court to submit to a medical examination, provide documentation of losses, and, in a few cases, evidence a financial need for compensation.

Claims for compensation must be filed before deadlines that range from 6 months to 2 years. This requirement can usually be waived if the claimant can show good cause. At the time of filing a claim, a few programs require a small application fee.

RATIONALE FOR COMPENSATING VICTIMS

Webster's dictionary defines a victim as "someone injured, destroyed, or sacrificed under any of various conditions." A question is frequently raised, therefore, about the justification for focusing on those suffering from a criminal victimization as opposed, for example, to persons who are the victims of a natural disaster, such as lightning or flood. The logical first question, of course, asks why either type of victim should be compensated by the state.

Very briefly, victim compensation has most commonly been advanced either as a right to which the victim is entitled or as a natural extension of welfare principles. For example, compensation is often seen as a right that existed in ancient laws, but that was gradually removed by sovereign interference into what were formerly private disputes. Under this view, as the State's role in arbitrating these disputes grew, compensation previously due the victim was appropriated by the State in the form of fines and judgment fees.[12] Rather than paying a debt to the victim, the offender now pays his "debt to society." The next appropriate step, it is argued, must be to follow the universalization of the debt by giving the victim the right to collect from society as a whole.

An alternative approach used to justify compensation as a right of the victim has been to suggest that the State has failed to protect the victim, from whom it takes taxes for law enforcement and corrections. Under this version of the "rights" argument, propounded by the noted criminologist Enrico Ferri[13] and former Supreme Court Justice Arthur Goldberg,[14] the victim has been denied the protection due him, and society must assume the responsibility for restoring the status quo.

When justified as simply another welfare measure, victim compensation is counted among other moral obligations of society to help all persons, such as the poor and the ill, who suffer through little fault of their own. In this context, the most forthright statement has been made by the eminent Oxford lawyer, Rupert Cross:

I am content to do without theoretical justifications. . . . After all, these are questions of public welfare and they should be determined by public opinion. Human needs account for the most of the Welfare State, and its evolution has nothing to do with tortuous reasoning. . . . If there is a widely recognized hardship, and if that hardship can be cheaply remedied by state compensation, I should have thought that the case for such a remedy was made out, provided the practical difficulties are not too great. The hardship in these cases is undoubtedly widely recognized.[15]

Whether approached as a question of right or as one of welfare, the prevailing view among most commentators seems to be that victims simply deserve to be compensated. However, fearing the fiscal implications of granting this at the level of a right, most legislation avoids the issue or deals with it vaguely only in statutory preambles.[16]

SALIENT ISSUES FOR VICTIM COMPENSATION PROGRAMS
Theory vs. practice

One of the more frustrating exercises for the student of victim compensation is to endeavor to match either of its popular rationales with many of the restrictions placed on eligibility. How does the exclusion of members of the offender's family or the requirement of financial hardship correspond to the notion that compensation is a right of the victim? Similarly, if the rationale is truly one of welfare or hardship, should the victim's contributory negligence or

culpability be relevant to the compensation decision? And, most important, how does the exclusion of property loss accord with either theory? Might not the results of an extensive burglary for an uninsured family be more devastating than minor injuries, even to the head of the household?

In contemplating these and similar questions of theory-fitting, one should not lose sight of the political realities that often temper and frequently override other concerns. On the issue of financial need, for example, Edelhertz and Geis point out that:

Such tests of financial need cannot be justified on either philosophical or practical grounds. There is no denying, however, that they are politically attractive and in some instances are considered a concession that must be made to secure passage of victim compensation legislation.[17]

Easily the most pressing political reality, and perhaps the most frequently raised issue in compensation debates, is the question of expense. Legislators may be swayed by theoretical arguments or, more often, by dramatic examples of victim injury,[18] but ultimately the deciding question for many elected officials will be: How much does it cost?

The cost of compensating victims

Speculation about the impact of victim compensation on public expenditures, above all else, undoubtedly shaped the early programs during the 1960s. Few answers were available at that time to the crucial questions that would indicate potential financial outlay: How many crimes occur each year in which the victim is injured? How extensive are such injuries? What is the cost to victims, as opposed to medical or other insurance agencies?

Early programs, therefore, were introduced with the restrictive eligibility and loss requirements discussed above. Moreover, the fears of those early programs continued into even the most recent enactment and have translated into the same kinds of restrictions. Legislators have been subjected to outrageously speculative cost estimates ranging from relatively small amounts to patently absurd exaggerations.

In May 1977, the governor of Indiana vetoed compensation legislation, based in part on his attorney general's estimate that the annual cost to the state treasury might be higher than $1,392,620,000.[19] This kind of fear has led to a very restricted view of the scope of compensation programs, not only in political but in more liberal academic circles. Recommendations continue to be made, for example, that minimum qualification amounts should be included in compensation legislation to "avert budgetary crises."[20]

The effects of such limitations on eligibility are shown dramatically in a recent work by Sutton and Garofalo,[21] in which the authors project costs for a national compensation program. Relying on data available from nationwide surveys in which respondents were asked about their experiences as crime victims,[22] the authors project costs for a national compensation program under a variety of assumptions. In 1974, of approximately 6 million personal victimizations that involved contact between victim and offender, only 1.5 million (25%) resulted in physical injury to the victim. In slightly more than 1 million of these (64%) there was no need for medical attention. Most dramatic, however, is the finding that in the half million victimizations for which medical attention was required, 97% suffered losses below $100. The result is that these 97% would not qualify for compensation for medical losses in most states today because of the minimum loss requirement.

Based on very liberal, national estimates, for 1974, of the cost of medical reimbursements, earnings reimbursements, and claims from survivors of homicide victims, Sutton and Garofalo project total costs for a national program of $144 million, under existing restrictions, to $261 million with no minimum loss requirement.[23] The discrepancy between such estimates for a national program and the projection of more than $1 billion for Indiana alone is indicative of the uncertainty facing legislators in this area.

THE FUTURE OF COMPENSATION

The future of victim compensation programs and the shape they will take are linked inextricably with at least three major possible developments. The first of these is the future crime rate, which seems inevitably to be rising. The second factor concerns the future of the welfare state itself. In the United States, for example, if attempts to implement a national medical care program succeed in the future, the areas of need for compensation will shift dramatically. The ultimate step in this direction might be to follow the New Zealand precedent by integrating victim compensation into a sort of universal, no-fault insurance program for almost all victims of injurious events.[24]

Finally, in the United States the third and most immediate determinant of future activity for compensation programs will be the role taken by the federal government. If presently contemplated legislation is passed, the federal government would cover all the costs of compensation for federal offenses, and half the costs for offenses designated as compensable by the individual states. Such an incentive seems likely to stir many of the states with no programs to begin to compensate their victims of violent crimes.

Hopes have been high for passage of a federal victims of crime act for several years now, and prediction under such circumstances becomes unwise. However, the pressure to take some action must be mounting after more than 10 years in which compensation bills have been proposed. The Oregon legislation mentioned at the outset of this discussion was the culmination of almost an identical history. Crime victims must hope that the parallel will be maintained.

NOTES

1. National Association of District Attorneys' Commission on Victim Witness Assistance. *State Victim Compensation Statutes* (Washington, D.C.: National Association of District Attorneys, 1977).

2. For a comprehensive bibliography of literature dealing with domestic and foreign compensation programs, see Harland, Alan, and Bruce Way. *Restitution and Compensation to Crime Victims: A Bibliography* (Albany, N.Y.: Criminal Justice Research Center, 1977).

3. Rothstein, Paul F. "How the Uniform Crime Victims Reparation Act Works," *American Bar Association Journal* **58:**1531-1535, 1974.

4. For an extensive review of the ancient and nineteenth century history of victim compensation, see Bernstein, Jesse. *A Study of the Evaluation of the Concept of Restitution and Recently Enacted Victim Compensa-*

tion Laws in New York and Other Jurisdictions (Ann Arbor, Mich.: Xerox University Microfilms, 1972).

5. Meade, Anthony C., Mary S. Knudten, William Doerner, and Richard D. Knudten. "Discovery of a Forgotten Party: Trends in Crime Victim Compensation Legislation in the United States," *Victimology* **1**:421-432, 1976.

6. Yarborough, Ralph W. "S.2155 of the 89th Congress: The Criminal Injuries Compensation Act," *Minnesota Law Review* **50**:255-269, 1965.

7. United States House of Representatives Committee on Judiciary, Subcommittee on Criminal Justice, 96th Congress. *Crime Victim Compensation: Hearings* (Washington, D.C.: U.S. Government Printing Office, 1976).

8. Burns, P., and A. M. Ross. "Comparative Study of Victims of Crime Indemnification in Canada: British Columbia Microcosm," *University of British Columbia Law Review* **8**:105-135, 1973.

9. Chappell, Duncan. "Providing for the Victims of Crime: Political Placebos or Progressive Programs?" *Adelaide Law Review* **4**:294-306, 1972.

10. Samuels, Alec. "Criminal Injuries Compensation Board," *Criminal Law Review*, pp. 418-431, 1973.

11. Edelhertz, Herbert, and Gilbert Geis. *Public Compensation to Victims of Crime*, (New York: Praeger Publishers, 1974).

12. Jacob, Bruce R. "Reparation or Restitution by the Criminal Offender to His Victim: Applicability of An Ancient Concept in the Modern Correctionsl Process," *Journal of Criminal Law, Criminology and Police Science* **61**:152-167, 1970.

13. Ferri, Enrico. *Criminal Sociology* (New York: Agathon Press, Inc., 1967).

14. Goldberg, Arthur J. "Equality and Government Action," *New York University Law Review* **39**:224, 1964.

15. Cross, Rupert. "Compensating Victims of Violence," *The Listener* **49**:816, May 16, 1963.

16. Such preambles, or clauses at the beginning of a statute, explain the reasons for its enactment, but neither enlarge existing powers nor create new ones.

17. Edelhertz and Geis, p. 271.

18. In New York, compensation legislation was accelerated after the stabbing death of a good samaritan in a New York City subway. In Washington, the state's legislation was passed after testimony by the quadriplegic victim of a brutal robbery-assault. And before the Oregon legislation was passed, approximately 80 victims of violent crimes appeared in a sort of victim rally at the State Capitol in Salem.

19. Governor's Message to the Senate, May 1977.

20. Meade and others, p. 431.

21. Sutton, L. Paul, and James Garofalo. *Potential Costs and Coverage of a National Program to Compensate Victims of Violent Crimes*, Analytic Report SD-VAD-5, Law Enforcement Assistance Administration, National Institute of Law Enforcement and Criminal Justice (Washington, D.C.: U.S. Government Printing Office, 1977).

22. Hindelang, Michael J. *Criminal Victimization in Eight American Cities: A Descriptive Analysis of Common Theft and Assault* (Cambridge, Mass.: Ballinger Publishing Co., 1976).

23. Sutton and Garofalo, pp. 44-46.

24. Palmer, G. W. R. "Compensation for Personal Injury: A Requiem for the Common Law in New Zealand," *American Journal of Comparative Law* **21**:1-24, 1973.

B ☐ *Victim compensation programs*

An overview

LeROY L. LAMBORN

Specialized government programs for the relief of victims of crime have become increasingly popular in recent years. New Zealand established the first of the contemporary crime victim compensation programs in 1963, and similar plans have since been adopted in many common law jurisdictions, including Great Britain, Hong Kong, Ireland, Northern Ireland, all of the states of Australia, two territories and eight of the ten provinces of Canada, and half of the states of the United States. Civil law countries having compensation programs include Austria, Denmark, Finland, France, the Federal Republic of Germany, the Netherlands, Norway, and Sweden. Despite their common concerns and similar backgrounds, the programs vary considerably both in pretentions toward and effectiveness in meeting the victims' needs. This paper examines the variations in the scope of benefits and the limitations on awards that affect the adequacy of crime victim compensation programs.

The typical crime victim compensation program serves only as a remedy of last resort to provide reimbursement of certain direct financial costs to certain victims of certain crimes. In the typical program, the person directly injured as a result of a crime of violence is entitled to reimbursement for reasonable hospital and medical expenses and a limited award for income lost because of injuries sustained. If he dies from his injuries, his dependents are entitled to limited awards for funeral and burial expenses and for lost support. With very minor exceptions, the victim receives no award for loss of or damage to property, for injuries received through violations of traffic laws, or for pain and suffering. Nor does he receive full compensation for his injuries, in that most programs place upper and lower limits on awards, and some jurisdictions provide that applicants must demonstrate serious financial hardship as a prerequisite to benefits. Further, the victim deemed partially responsible for the crime receives at most a reduced award, and the victim injured by a close relative usually receives nothing. As a result of all of these limitations on benefits the vast majority of crime victims are not covered by the programs.

PROPERTY DAMAGE

The person whose property is lost or destroyed through larceny or arson is as much a "victim of crime" as the person who suffers personal injury or death through rape or murder. Moreover, the expense of repair or replacement of criminally damaged or stolen property amounts to billions of dollars annually, much more than the expense of criminally caused personal injuries. Yet the vast majority of crime victim compensation programs allow awards for personal injuries only. The primary justification for this restriction is the necessity of limiting program expenditures. The cost of compensating victims of property damage would be substantial, especially if fraud were not controlled and if property owners became careless because of the promise of reimbursement of losses. A second justification—that insurance

renders compensation unnecessary—is not persuasive, because many people cannot afford the premiums and because insurance companies not infrequently decline to issue policies in selected areas and cancel the policies of those who file claims. A third justification—that property damage is not as serious as personal injury—is not persuasive, because the destruction of one's home or business, or even the theft of a social security check, may have consequences far more serious than, for example, a minor personal injury received in a mugging.

Recognition of the importance in at least some circumstances of reimbursement of property loss has caused a variety of exceptions to the general rule of no compensation. For example, Northern Ireland has long provided awards for malicious damage to agricultural property and for damage to other property maliciously caused by rioters or members of illegal associations. Several jurisdictions have statutes, independent of any crime victim compensation act, that impose civil liability for property damage on the municipality that fails to prevent a riot. A few states also provide limited reimbursement for property damaged by escaped prisoners or for property damaged in an applicant's attempt to prevent the commission of a crime or to apprehend a criminal. The most common exception to the general rule of no compensation for property loss is that victims of personal injuries are reimbursed for the expenses of repairing or replacing damaged or stolen eyeglasses, dentures, hearing aids, and other prosthetic devices.

VIOLATIONS OF TRAFFIC LAWS

The rubric of *crime victim* includes the person injured through a violation of a traffic law. Although in some jurisdictions most traffic law violations are characterized as civil, the more serious remain criminal, and in many states traffic law violations are misdemeanors or even felonies. The collisions resulting from traffic law violations involve annual losses of millions of dollars for hospital and medical expenses and lost income. Thus a legislature intent on limiting the cost of its crime victim compensation program and aware that a large part of the costs of automobile collisions are reimbursed through insurance would exclude from coverage those losses caused by violations of traffic laws. No crime victim compensation program provides comprehensive benefits for victims of traffic law violations. Some explicitly bar awards for victims of traffic offenses; others accomplish the same end by not including traffic law violations in the list of crimes for which awards will be made. In either case the deliberate use of an automobile as an instrument of assault is usually treated as an exceptional situation that justifies compensation. A few jurisdictions also provide benefits for victims of reckless driving or for persons injured by an automobile being used in the commission of another crime.

PAIN AND SUFFERING

"Pain and suffering," as the phrase is used in the civil courts, encompasses a variety of bases of monetary recovery beyond the victim's expenditures for medical and hospital care and past and future loss of income. The phrase includes the physical and psychological discomfort of the criminal experience and its aftermath, disfigurement, loss of faculties, and loss of enjoyment of life, all of which are viewed as very real hardships to the victim. Often amounts far in excess of the victim's out-of-pocket losses are awarded for pain and suffering, primarily because the criminal and others are thought to be deterred from committing future crimes by the threat of this extensive civil liability.

Most crime victim compensation programs do not provide awards for the victim's pain and suffering. The primary reason for this exclusion from coverage is the substantial expense involved. A second reason is that determination of the amount of such an award is often difficult. A third reason is that the state is not the wrongdoer and, therefore, should not be subject to expenses justified primarily by the hope of preventing wrongs. A few jurisdictions, however, do provide awards for pain and suffering, on the theory that the victim should be made whole on a basis as close as possible to the civil model. Barring awards for pain and suffering also would mean that many victims of sexual offenses would receive nothing. An additional possible rationale for granting recovery is that the state, by virtue of its failure to prevent the crime, can be viewed in at least some circumstances as a wrongdoer. Requiring that it pay for the victim's pain and suffering might encourage increased government efforts to prevent future crimes.

The common ban on awards for the victim's pain and suffering is express in some jurisdictions. In others the same end is achieved by a low upper limit on benefits that bars meaningful awards for pain and suffering. Some jurisdictions provide awards for pain and suffering but impose special reduced upper limits on those awards, and some states allow awards for pain and suffering only for victims of sexual offenses. A more generous attitude is displayed in a jurisdiction, such as Washington, that adopts the schedule of benefits used in its worker's compensation program. Although the benefits do not approach those available in a civil action against the wrongdoer, they assure some compensation for pain and suffering. A few jurisdictions explicitly grant awards for pain and suffering. Hawaii, for example, commonly expends about 40% of its awards budget for such payments, the only limit being its general upper limit of $10,000. Great Britain attempts to pay to the victim of crime the amount for pain and suffering that he would receive in a civil action.

UPPER LIMITS ON AWARDS

Because of a legislative fear of uncontrolled expenditures, the compensation available to any one victim of crime is limited. The limitations of the early programs were established before the extensive and intensive surveys of crime victims and before any substantial operational experience. Even the more recent programs appear to have been influenced more by statutory precedent than by operational experience or the results of the victim surveys. The latter sources indicate that the physical injuries received by the vast majority of crime victims are minor, involving no more than outpatient medical treatment and 1 or 2 days' absence from work. In contrast, a very small percentage of crime victims suffer very serious injuries, which might be termed catastrophic in view of their effect on the person's life. A low upper limit operates to deny those victims adequate medical treatment and to provide them and their dependents with adequate support for only a limited period. Thus, most compensation programs, by imposing low upper limits on awards, exclude from meaningful recovery those with the most serious injuries while saving the state only relatively small amounts.

The upper limits on awards take a variety of forms, the most common being a ban on benefits for a victim in excess of a specified amount. Upper limits of this sort have ranged from $1,000 in South Australia, to $15,000 for lump-sum payments and $175,000 for periodic payments at a maximum rate of $500 per month in Ontario. The most common upper limit in the United States is $10,000. Such upper limits usually apply not only to the person directly injured by crime, regardless of the number of dependents, but also to the death benefits available to his dependents, regardless of number. Some jurisdictions, apparently concerned about the potential expenses of large-scale terrorist activities, also limit the amounts available to all of the victims of any one criminal transaction. Ontario, for example, restricts lump-sum payments to $100,000 and periodic payments to $175,000. Some jurisdictions have different upper limits for different purposes. For example, the Alberta statute places a special upper limit of $10,000 on awards for pain and suffering; and several states limit funeral and medical expenses to "reasonable" amounts. Other jurisdictions, though restricting awards for lost income and support, do not limit awards for hospital and medical expenses.

The most generous approach appears to be that of Great Britain, which attempts to provide benefits on the basis of the damages available in a civil action. Thus the victim receives a lump-sum award for hospital and medical expenses, for pain and suffering, and for lost earnings for the estimated period of need, which may be lifelong. The only restriction is that his award for lost income cannot exceed twice the average of industrial earnings.

LOWER LIMITS ON AWARDS

The out-of-pocket cost of medical treatment and lost income for the vast majority of crime victims is minor. Most of them can, without great hardship, absorb the unreimbursed expenses of outpatient hospital treatment or loss of income for 1 or 2 days. Yet those costs, if multiplied by the millions of occurrences, could not be absorbed easily by the government. Moreover, the cost of processing small claims in all cases would be substantial, in many cases exceeding the awards to the victims. For these reasons most jurisdictions impose lower limits on benefits, that is, minimum amounts below which awards will not be made.

For some victims, of course, an $80 hospital bill or loss of income for 3 days results in substantial deprivation—either forgoing medical treatment or living on a subsistence diet until the loss is made up. Responding to such needy victims has not caused exorbitant expense to the programs that impose no lower limits on awards, presumably because the inconvenience of applying for compensation deters most who can absorb the loss easily from seeking reimbursement. Moreover, the full-scale investigation required for determination of the substantial claim is unnecessary where the amount requested is small.

The lower limits vary from $25 to $250, the most common amount in the United States being $100 or loss of income for 2 weeks. Massachusetts requires a deduction from all awards, thereby requiring that all victims absorb the first portion of the expense of the crime. The result of the typical lower limit on awards is that most victims of crimes of violence against the person are excluded from benefits.

MEANS TESTS

To ensure that limited government funds are available only to the persons most in need of them, some legislatures deny benefits to victims of crime who have not suffered serious financial hardship. A provision of this sort is, in effect, a floating lower limit tied to the resources and losses of the individual victim. The statutory requirements vary, with some states denying benefits if the board finds that "the claimant will not suffer serious financial hardship," some requiring that the victim show "need for such indemnification," and some merely directing the board to consider the need of the applicant in its determination of awards.

The means tests are unpopular with commentators and with the administrators of the programs. The tests require burdensome paperwork for all involved and force the boards to make difficult and unpopular decisions. Victims who are deterred from applying for benefits by what they view as an invasion of privacy and victims one step above "serious financial hardship," whose tax payments have for years supported the compensation program for others, uniformly consider the means test to be unfair. Administrators estimate that elimination of the means test would, because of insurance coverage of many losses and because of lower administrative costs, increase expenditures by only a small percentage.

Efforts to reduce the impact of the means tests include administrative regulations that allow certain assets of a victim to be disregarded in the assessment of the effect of his loss on his life. Thus, in New York, such things as the victim's home, automobile, and savings equal to 1 year's net income are exempted from consideration. In addition, a victim not presently suffering serious financial hardship is permitted to reopen his claim if his assets become depleted.

THE VICTIM-CRIMINAL RELATIONSHIP

Crime victim compensation programs typically exclude from benefits persons injured by close relatives, by other persons living in the same household, or by those with whom they have a sexual relationship. Although such an exclusion has the incidental effect of reducing expenditures, its primary purposes are removal of a possible incentive for victimization and prevention of fraud. The theory is that, without the exclusion, a person might deliberately injure a member of his family for the purpose of appropriating or sharing the benefits intended for the victim. Factual investigations might also prove difficult when family members are suspected of acting in collusion.

Although total exclusion has the advantage of certainty that crime is not encouraged and that fraud is reduced, the result is an automatic bar of awards for such totally innocent victims as most abused children and battered spouses. One wonders at the justification for denying support for the minor children of the murder victim merely because she was killed by her husband rather than by a stranger.

Total exclusion ignores the possibility that less radical measures might be equally as effective at achieving the goals of discouraging crime and reducing fraud. Such measures include requirements that the victim actively cooperate in the prosecution of the criminal, that he stop living with the criminal, that payments for expenses be made directly to the physician and hospital, that awards for pain and suffering be denied, that payments for minors be placed in trust, and that the responsibility of the victim for the crime be more closely investigated in such cases. The jurisdictions that do not bar awards to victims injured by relatives or that allow benefits when denial would cause a serious injustice have not found that their policies are inappropriate.

VICTIM RESPONSIBILITY

Crime victim compensation programs commonly require that benefits be reduced or denied if the victim is deemed responsible for the commission of the crime. Such provisions are based on a feeling that it is inappropriate that victims be rewarded for receiving injuries attributable to them. The greatest extensions of this concept are found in Great Britain and Northern Ireland. The British scheme requires consideration of the victim's conduct, character, and way of life not only before the crime but also after the injury was inflicted. Northern Ireland allows the denial of benefits to members of illegal organizations, even if their victimization was unrelated to the illegal membership and their membership had ceased years earlier.

A denial of benefits on the basis of victim responsibility would seem appropriate if property damage were compensable, because the owner's knowledge that he alone would bear the loss for property damage attributable to him would probably lead him to exercise greater care than if he expected to receive compensation for all losses. Presumably, however, few persons would deliberately engage in conduct leading to personal injuries for the purpose of receiving limited reimbursement of medical expenses and lost income. Most victims who are subject to reduced awards did not seek injury; they were merely negligent. If their fear of injury did not deter them from risky conduct, it is unlikely that reduction of benefits would. They are thus victims of crime who, because of their carelessness, receive reduced awards for medical expenses. Unfairness is especially apparent when the dependents of a victim receive reduced awards for lost support because their parent was partially responsible for his own death.

Administrators of the programs commonly note the difficulty of ascertaining the existence of victim responsibility and assessing its extent. And commentators rather uniformly criticize the opportunity for arbitrary, subjective assessments of behavior that is involved in such judgments.

NOTES

This paper provides only a brief overview of crime victim compensation programs. More detailed information and citations to primary sources are found in Carrow, D. *Crime Victim Compensation: Program Model* (Washington, D.C.: U.S. Department of Justice, 1980); Edelhertz, H. and G. Geis. *Public Compensation to Victims of Crime* (New York: Praeger Publishers, 1974); Harland, A. "Compensating the Victims of Crime," *Crim. L. Bull.* **14**:203, 1978; Garofalo, J., and L. Sutton. *Compensating Victims of Violent Crime: Potential Costs and Coverage of a National Program* (Washington, D.C.: U.S. Government Printing Office, 1977); Lamborn, L. "The Propriety of Government Compensation of Victims of Crime," *G. Wash. L. Rev.* **41**:446, 1973; Lamborn, L. "The Scope of Programs for Governmental Compensation of Victims of Crime," *Ill. L. F.* **1973**:21, 1973; Lamborn, L. "The Methods of Governmental Compensation of Victims of Crime," *Ill. L. F.* **1971**:655, 1971; Lamborn, L. "Crime Victim Compensation: Theory and Practice in the Second Decade," *Victimology* **1**:503, 1976; Meiners, R. *Victim Compensation: Economic, Legal, and Political Aspects* (Lexington, Mass.: D. C. Heath & Co., 1978); and Miers, D. *Responses to Victimisation: A Comparative Study of Compensation for Criminal Violence in Great Britain and Ontario* (Milton Trading Estate, Abington, Oxon: Professional Books Ltd., 1978).

Selected readings for Chapter 14

Brooks, James. "Crime Compensation Programs: An Opinion Survey of Program Administrations," *Criminology* **11**:258-274, 1973.

> Uses a mail survey of administrators of victim compensation programs to secure their views regarding board membership, procedures used by the boards, applicant requirements, compensable crimes, nature of payments to victims, and exclusions from awards.

Doerner, William G. "State of Victim Compensation Programs in Action," *Victimology* **2**:106-108, 1977.

> Uses official reports to analyze programs in terms of volume of claims, board decisions, and public awareness. Finds several problems in the administration of the programs, including inadequate staffing, inordinate time taken to decide on an application, and lack of victim awareness of the program.

Edelhertz, Herbert, and Gilbert Geis. *Public Compensation to Victims of Crime* (New York: Praeger Publishers, 1974).

> This volume provides detailed information on the development, implementation, and operation of compensation programs, with a specific focus on operation of the New York program.

Garofalo, James, and L. Paul Sutton. *Compensating Victims of Violent Crime: Potential Costs and Coverage of a National Program* (Washington, D.C.: U.S. Government Printing Office, 1977).

>The purpose of this report is to estimate the cost of a national program to compensate victims of violent crime. Although the report recognizes that many assumptions are necessary to produce cost estimates, it concludes with three such estimates of the total cost for a national program of victim compensation.

Harland, Alan T., and Bruce Way. *Restitution and Compensation To Crime Victims: A Bibliography* (Albany, N.Y.: Criminal Justice Research Center, 1977).

>This is a comprehensive bibliography on literature dealing with domestic and froeign victim compensation programs.

Hudson, Joe, and Burt Galaway, eds. *Considering the Victim: Readings in Restitution and Victim Compensation* (Springfield, Ill.: Charles C Thomas, Publisher, 1975).

>The articles contained in this book deal with the historical development and the philosophical, social, psychological, and comparative applications of victim compensation.

Lamborn, LeRoy L. "Reparations for Victims of Crime: Developments and Directions," *Victimology* **4**:214-228, 1979.

>Reviews the development of victim compensation programs, analyzes present problems with programs, and suggests future directions—the programs will expand to other jurisdictions and restrictions on benefits will be reduced.

Lamborn, LeRoy L. "Compensation for the Child Conceived in Rape," *Victimology* **1**:84-97, 1976.

>Examines victim compensation statutes and administration; finds the programs very inadequate for the child conceived as the result of a rape.

Meiners, Roger E. *Victim Compensation: Economic, Legal, and Political Aspects* (Lexington, Mass.: D. C. Heath & Co., 1978).

>Includes legal background, recent legislation, and cost estimates. Analyzes victim compensation views of the victim, criminal, and state. Does not favor development of government-supported victim compensation schemes.

INDEX